Management of Retail Enterprises

Robert F. Lusch
University of Oklahoma

MANAGEMENT OF RETAIL ENTERPRISES

KENT PUBLISHING COMPANY
Boston, Massachusetts
A Division of Wadsworth, Inc.

To: Katharina, for what we might have been
Virginia, for what we might be

Senior Editor: *David S. McEttrick*
Production Editor/Designer: *Dale Anderson*
Cover Designer: *Catherine Dorin*
Production Coordinator: *Linda Card*

 Kent Publishing Company
A Division of Wadsworth, Inc.

Printed in the United States of America
1 2 3 4 5 6 7 8 9—86 85 84 83 82

Library of Congress Cataloging in Publication Data
Lusch, Robert F.
      Management of retail enterprises

      Includes index.
      1. Retail trade—Management. I. Title.
HF5429.L78   658.87   81-17201
ISBN 0-534-01072-5   AACR2

Preface

Orientation

This textbook was written to describe and explain the process of retail management. Many prior and existing retail texts do a good job of describing retail management, but few adequately explain the retail management process. I hope this book accomplishes both purposes.

This book has a comprehensive orientation, which focuses on all levels of retail planning and management—strategic, administrative, and operations. Throughout the book we also stress the need to apply creative and analytical thought processes to these three types of planning. Furthermore, emphasis is placed on a solid understanding of the financial and performance dimensions of retail enterprises. We basically argue that strategic, administrative, and operations planning should be directed at achieving high levels of financial performance. Many real life examples, both contemporary and classic, are used to illustrate this important link and other important points.

Additionally, we include end-of-chapter questions and problems and exercises, both of which allow the student to assess his or her understanding of the text material. Finally, twelve cases of moderate length, each of which focuses on actual retail problems, are presented to help the student apply abstract concepts to the solution of common retail problems.

Acknowledgments

Many individuals have been helpful to me in formulating my thoughts about retailing. But most important in this regard have been my colleagues in the Distribution Research Program at the University of Oklahoma, especially Bert C. McCammon, Jr.

I would also like to thank the individuals who contributed cases to this text. These include J. Robert Foster, University of Texas at El Paso; Virginia Newell, Norman, Oklahoma; James M. Kenderdine, University of Oklahoma; Jack J. Kasulis, University of Oklahoma; David Karp, Loyola Law School (Los Angeles, California); Donald J. Bowersox, Michigan State University; M. Bixby Cooper, Michigan State University; Douglas M. Lambert, Michigan State University; Donald A. Taylor, Michigan State University; William A. Staples, University of Houston at Clear Lake City; Robert A. Swerdlow, Lamar University; and Jack A. Lesser, Miami University.

I would also like to thank the many individuals who reviewed various parts of this manuscript. These include: Roger Kerin, Southern Methodist University; William Lundstrom, Old Dominion University; Elizabeth Hirschman, New York University; Jac Goldstucker, Georgia State University; William A. Staples, University of Houston at Clear Lake City; Richard Lutz, University of California at Los Angeles; and James M. Kenderdine, University of Oklahoma.

Special thanks are due to Debbie Coykendal for her proficient typing of all parts of the manuscript. The critical comments on all parts of the manuscript by Ray Serpkenci and Virginia Lusch were also invaluable. Dave McEttrick and Dale Anderson at Kent Publishing Company were most helpful and always made excellent suggestions for improving the manuscript and its production.

Robert F. Lusch
Norman, Oklahoma

Short Contents

Contents

PART II　　STRATEGIC PLANNING AND MANAGEMENT　　　　　　*71*

4　　Understanding Channel Behavior　　　　　　*73*

7 | Understanding the Socioeconomic and Technological Environments

8

Understanding the Legal Environment

12 | **Location Planning and Management**   *335*

18

Retail Promotion: Personal Selling   *544*

19   Customer Service Planning and Management   *563*

I

RETAIL PLANNING AND MANAGEMENT: AN OVERVIEW

1

Overview *It is the purpose of this chapter to acquaint you with the nature and scope of retailing. We will also look at some of the commonly held beliefs about retail careers and will delineate the prerequisites for success in retail management. This introductory chapter will also familiarize you with the approach we will use throughout this text to study and learn about the management of retail enterprises.*

Perspectives on Retailing

THROUGHOUT RECORDED HISTORY the societies that progressed most rapidly have had strong economic and retail sectors. Because rapidly progressing societies need a strong retail sector, the focus of this text will be on how to manage and plan retail enterprises to achieve high levels of performance. To do this, we will be using a micro rather than a macro lens. That is, we will concentrate on how individual retail enterprises manage and plan. We will not delve into the very worthwhile topic of how the retail sector of the economy, in aggregate, should be structured or managed and planned through government policies.[1]

Although rapidly progressing societies have had strong retail sectors, the retail trades have not always been admired by philosophers and other members of society. Often, persons employed in retailing were considered low in status. Consider the ranking of occupations that Aristotle developed:

> Now in the course of nature, the art of agriculture is prior, and next comes those arts which extract the products of the earth, mining and the like. Agriculture ranks first because of its justice: for it does not take anything away from men, either with their consent, as does retail trade and mercenary arts, or against their will, as do the warlike arts. Further, agriculture is natural, for by nature all derive their sustenance from the earth.[2]

Despite the wisdom of philosophers such as Aristotle, thousands of years of commerce have made retailers acceptable members of society, and in many cases, the most valued members. Witness the excitement in a small town when a K-mart or McDonald's decides to locate there.

WHAT IS RETAILING?

Retailing is the final move in the progression of merchandise from producer to consumer. Quite simply, any firm that sells merchandise to the final consumer is performing the retailing function. Regardless of whether the firm sells to the consumer in a store, through the mail, over the telephone, door to door, or through a vending machine, it is involved in retailing.

Although retailing can be thought of as the final move in the progression of merchandise from producer to consumer, it is not a static or homogeneous business function. Retailing is continuously changing in many exciting ways. Consider, for example, some of the obvious new developments in retailing that occurred during the last two centuries. Department stores were unheard of in the early 1800s; in the early 1900s, supermarkets were nonexistent; fast food chains and discount stores were not common in the early 1950s; home improve-

1. Some examples of the macro approach to retailing are Elizabeth C. Hirschman, "A Descriptive Theory of Retail Market Structure," *Journal of Retailing* 54(Winter 1978): 29–48; Louis P. Bucklin, *Competition and Evolution in the Distributive Trades* (Englewood Cliffs, N.J.: Prentice-Hall, 1972); and Margaret Hall, John Knapp, and Christopher Winsten, *Distribution in Great Britain and North America* (London: Oxford University Press, 1961).
2. E. E. Foster (translator), "The Works of Aristotle," *The Oeconomica Oxford* 10(1920): 1343a–43b.

ment centers were unthought of in the early 1960s; and catalog showrooms were just beginning to emerge in the early 1970s. It is quite apparent, therefore, that retailing has changed considerably since its origins and can be expected to continue to change in the future.[3]

WHY RETAILING CHANGES

Why has retailing changed in the past, and how will it change in the future? The answer lies in the disquieting fact that retailing does not operate in a closed or controlled environment. Rather, the retail sector and the individual retailer are continuously influenced by external forces. These will be discussed in considerable detail in Chapters 4 through 8, but for now, let us recognize the following: the behavior of consumers, the behavior of competitors, the behavior of channel members, the legal system, the state of technology, and the socioeconomic nature of society. Exhibit 1.1 depicts these external forces (see page 6).

There are few principles or truths of retailing—things we know for certain. However, one truth is that new forms of retailing will emerge as a response to changing environmental factors. Supermarkets were a response to the economic depression of the 1930s and the need for consumers to purchase groceries at the lowest possible prices. Shopping centers were a response to the suburban exodus and the increased mobility brought about by the automobile. Fast food restaurants grew up as more family members entered the work force and time became a scarce commodity. The list could continue, but our point should be clear: as the environment changes, retailing must change to survive and prosper. Retailing, then, is similar to a biological species that evolves in response to its environment.

THE MAGNITUDE OF RETAILING

The magnitude of retailing can be, in part, assessed by reference to the most recently published *Census of Retail Trade.*[4] The U.S. Department of Commerce conducts the census of retailing every five years, in the years ending in 2 and 7 (and releases the data about two years later). Thus, the most recently available census is for 1977. In 1977 there were 1.8 million retail establishments in the United States, or 25 retail establishments for every thousand households. These establishments were not, on average, "mom and pop" operated stores. This fact is evidenced by their average annual sales volume of $390,000 in 1977.

3. For a further discussion of changes that have occurred in retailing, see William R. Davidson, Albert Bates, and Stephen Bass, "The Retail Life Cycle," *Harvard Business Review* 54(November–December 1976): 89–96; Delbert J. Duncan, "Responses of Selected Retail Institutions to Their Changing Environment," in Peter Bennett (ed.), *Marketing and Economic Development* (Chicago: American Marketing Association, 1965), pp. 583–602; and William J. Regan, "The Stages of Retail Development," in Reavis Cox, Wroe Alderson, and Stanley Shapiro (eds.), *Theory in Marketing* (Homewood, Ill.: Richard D. Irwin, 1964), pp. 139–53.

4. U.S. Bureau of the Census, *1977 Census of Retail Trade* (Washington, D.C.: U.S. Government Printing Office, 1977).

EXHIBIT 1.1
**External Forces
Confronting
Retail
Enterprises**

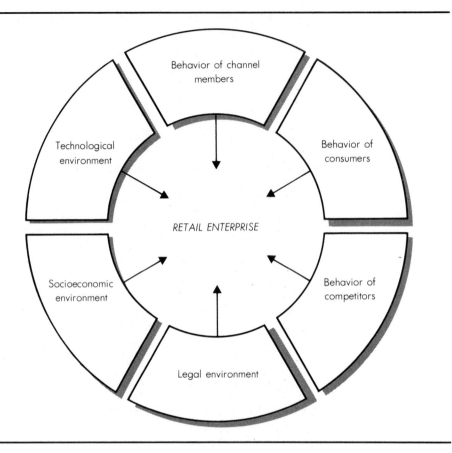

Historical Size Trends　As we mentioned previously, retailing is not static; therefore, one might expect the preceding statistics to have changed over time. Exhibit 1.2 provides the historical data to paint this portrait of change, showing that retailing has grown larger over the last half century. In 1929 the average retail establishment had an annual sales volume of $33,000, but by 1977 the average annual sales volume had risen to $390,000. Obviously, most of this dramatic rise was due to inflation, but even after adjusting for inflation we see that the typical retail establishment in 1977 had sales of $110,000 in 1929 dollars. Therefore, the typical retail establishment in the United States has more than tripled in sales volume over the last half century.[5] Stores have become larger. This trend will also be revealed if you compare the number of stores per thousand households in 1929 against the number in 1977, as shown in Exhibit 1.2. In 1929 there were fifty, but by 1977 the number had dropped to twenty-five. Thus, each store on average was serving twice as many households in 1977 as in 1929.

5. For a discussion of the growth of large-scale retailing in the United States, see Walter Gross, "The Development of Large-Scale Retailing in the American Economy," *Georgia Business* 26(March 1967): 1–5.

EXHIBIT 1.2
Number and Size of Retail Establishments (1929–1977)

YEAR	NUMBER OF ESTABLISHMENTS (thousands)	TOTAL SALES (millions)	AVERAGE SALES PER STORE	AVERAGE SALES PER STORE INFLATION ADJUSTED[a]	STORES PER THOUSAND HOUSEHOLDS
1929	1,476	$ 48,330	$ 33,000	$ 33,000	50
1933	1,526	25,037	16,000	22,000	N/A
1939	1,770	42,042	24,000	29,000	51
1948	1,770	130,521	74,000	52,000	45
1954	1,722	169,968	98,000	63,000	36
1958	1,788	199,646	112,000	66,000	35
1963	1,708	244,202	143,000	80,000	31
1967	1,703	310,214	176,000	90,000	30
1972	1,912	459,000	240,000	98,000	28
1977	1,855	723,100	390,000	110,000	25

[a] In 1929 dollars

Source: U.S. Bureau of the Census, *Statistical Abstract of the United States; Historical Statistics of the United States: Colonial Times to 1970* (Washington, D.C.: U.S. Government Printing Office, 1975).

Size by Line of Trade Although these statistics are insightful, they are somewhat misleading since they average together all forms of retailing. To get a clearer perspective, let us look more closely at three familiar forms of retailing—grocery stores, department stores, and gasoline service stations. In 1977 there were 178,835 grocery stores in the United States, or 2.4 for every thousand households. These stores had average annual sales of $826,000. On the other hand, there were only 8,807 department stores in the United States in 1977, which translates to 0.1 store for every thousand households. As you might expect, these stores were large; they had an average annual sales volume of $8.7 million. Finally, we note that there were 176,465 gas stations in 1977, or 2.4 per thousand households. Gas stations had an average annual sales volume of $320,000 in 1977. Exhibit 1.3 (see page 8) provides similar statistics for other lines of retail trade. A careful study of this exhibit shows that retailing in the United States is a significant economic sector. Furthermore, we see that stores are, on average, large. It is not surprising, therefore, that the problems of managing a retail enterprise are significant.

The $5 Billion Club In 1979 there were eleven retail chains in the United States with annual sales in excess of $5 billion (today there are several more). As shown in Exhibit 1.4 (page 9) Sears, Roebuck led the pack in 1979 with sales of $17.5 billion and profits of $810 million. Sears operated 3,680 stores with a labor force of 424,000 employees. The average store had a sales volume in excess of $4 million and over a hundred employees. Thus, the manager of the typical Sears store is managing a large and complex business. And the chief executive officer of Sears, Roebuck has even more problems and obstacles to overcome in trying

EXHIBIT 1.3
Number and Size of Retailers by Line of Trade (1977)

LINE OF TRADE	NUMBER OF ESTABLISHMENTS	TOTAL SALES (millions)	AVERAGE SALES PER STORE	STORES PER THOUSAND HOUSEHOLDS
Retail trade total	1,885,068	$723,134	$ 390,000	25.0
Building materials, hardware, garden supply, mobile home dealers	90,357	38,860	430,000	1.2
Department stores	8,807	76,909	8,733,000	0.1
Variety stores	17,376	7,095	408,000	0.2
General merchandise (not dept. or variety stores)	22,728	9,944	438,000	0.3
Grocery stores	178,835	147,759	826,000	2.4
Other food stores[a]	73,136	10,182	139,000	1.0
Automotive dealers[b]	139,006	149,952	1,079,000	1.9
Gasoline service stations	176,465	56,468	320,000	2.4
Apparel and accessory stores	140,126	35,564	254,000	1.9
Furniture, home furnishing and equipment stores	138,579	33,176	239,000	1.9
Drug and proprietary stores	49,570	23,196	468,000	0.7
Eating and drinking places	368,066	63,276	172,000	5.0
Miscellaneous retail trade[c]	419,199	56,313	134,000	5.7
Nonstore retailers[d]	32,818	14,440	440,000	0.4

[a] Includes meat and fish markets; fruit and vegetable markets; candy, nut, and confectionery stores; retail bakeries; and dairy products stores.

[b] Includes auto and home supply stores and boat, motorcycle, and recreational vehicle dealers.

[c] Includes liquor stores, used merchandise stores, sporting goods stores, bicycle shops, book stores, stationery stores, hobby stores, camera shops, gift stores, luggage and leather goods stores, sewing and piece goods stores, fuel and ice dealers, florists, cigar stores, newsstands, pet shops, typewriter stores, and optical goods stores.

[d] Includes mail-order houses, automatic merchandising machine operators, and direct selling establishments.

Source: U.S. Bureau of the Census, *1977 Census of Retail Trade* (Washington, D.C.: U.S. Government Printing Office, 1977); U.S. Bureau of the Census, *Statistical Abstract of the United States* (Washington, D.C.: U.S. Government Printing Office, 1979); and author's calculations.

to direct the entire organization, with its 3,680 stores, along a continued growth path.[6]

Entry Barriers   Together, the statistics on aggregate retailing activity in the United States and on the largest retail chains suggest that retailing is large and complex. In addition, retail management decision making is becoming increasingly sophisticated. Once it was considered an easy entry industry, but now substantial barriers are rising. Competition is intense for high traffic locations, and costs of construction and lease payments have accelerated drastically over the last decade. Consider the data in Exhibit 1.5, which shows the capital expenditures required in 1979 to construct a variety of new stores (see page 10).

The average supermarket constructed in 1979 was almost 32,000 square feet, and construction costs were almost $1.4 million. This excluded the cost of land, which was probably $200,000 to $300,000, and inventory to stock the store, which was probably another $250,000 to $300,000. Thus, to enter the supermarket business with a single new store in a good location, with adequate inventory, approximately $2 million in investment capital would be required.

RETAILING FROM TWO PERSPECTIVES

All economic systems are comprised of **supply** and **demand** components. The **supply** component is typically comprised of private and public enterprises pro-

EXHIBIT 1.4 **The $5 Billion Retailing Club (1979)**	*MOST RECENTLY COMPLETED FISCAL YEAR*			
RETAIL CHAIN	*Sales (millions)*	*Earnings (millions)*	*NUMBER OF RETAIL UNITS*	*NUMBER OF EMPLOYEES*
Sears, Roebuck	$17,514	$810.1	3,680	424,000
Safeway Stores	13,718	143.3	2,481	148,876
K-mart	12,731	358.0	1,894	243,000
J. C. Penney	11,274	244.0	2,154	206,000
Kroger	9,029	85.7	1,738	118,400
F. W. Woolworth	6,785	180.0	6,040	204,000
A & P	6,684	(3.8)	1,542	63,000
American Stores	6,121	62.8	1,063	63,700
Federated Department Stores	5,806	203.2	349	112,500
Lucky Stores	5,736	98.1	1,283	63,000
Montgomery Ward	5,251	73.4	944	110,000

Source: "$100 Million Club,"© *Chain Store Age Executive*, August 1980, Lebhar-Friedman, Inc., 425 Park Ave., NY, NY 10022, p. 25. Used by permission.

6. In the 1970s Sears, Roebuck experienced substantial growth and profit problems. See "A CSA Special Report," *Chain Store Age: General Merchandise Edition*, January 1980, pp. 81–116; and "Strategy Error Has Sears Watching Profit Edge," *Advertising Age* 49(April 3, 1978): 2.

EXHIBIT 1.5
Capital Expenditures for Constructing New Stores (1979)

LINE OF TRADE	AVERAGE NEW STORE SIZE (square feet)	CAPITAL EXPENDITURES PER SQUARE FOOT	CAPITAL EXPENDITURES PER NEW STORE
Supermarkets	31,914	$42.41	$1,353,000
Department stores	81,978	65.14	5,340,000
General merchandise stores	67,801	50.81	3,445,000
Drugstores	15,490	43.98	681,000
Discount department stores	73,876	45.31	3,347,000
Home improvement centers	36,955	42.39	1,567,000
Apparel stores	3,146	45.21	142,000
Shoe stores	2,810	45.10	127,000

Source: "Industry Profiles"© *Chain Store Age Executive,* August 1980, Lebhar-Friedman, Inc., 425 Park Ave., NY, NY 10022, pp. 53–94, and author's computations. Used by permission.

ducing and marketing goods and services to the demand side of the economy. The **demand** side is composed of households or private and public enterprises that have the buying power to purchase goods and services. It is the interaction between supply (sellers) and demand (buyers) that determines prices, competitive intensity, and profit levels.

Those statements are obviously oversimplified, but the point is that the student and retail manager should study an economic sector (such as retailing) from both demand and supply perspectives in order to properly understand it.[7] The retail executive cannot maximize store profits by focusing only on supply factors such as labor, merchandise, and store layout. He or she must also pay attention to demand factors such as household income, household transportation costs, households per square mile, and consumer lifestyles.

Imagine yourself as a retail entrepreneur who recently designed and built a 6,000–square foot drugstore. You are working long hours and are doing an excellent job managing your employees and merchandise. You built your drugstore in a small town where the land and building costs were relatively low but in which there was already an abundance of drug retailers. The town is characterized by a stagnant economy in which average household incomes have remained stable for several years and in which many younger households are moving to a larger city thirty miles to the north to find better employment opportunities. It doesn't take long for your financial statements to reveal the disheartening news that profits are not what you expected. Why? You did not properly balance supply and demand factors in your decision-making process.

The major problems in managing a retail enterprise, which we alluded to earlier, are related to either the supply or demand side of retailing or both. In short, the major problem is to interrelate supply and demand factors effectively in order to produce profit that is sufficient for the survival and growth of the retail enterprise. Therefore, whatever is learned about retailing must be related

7. A retail text with a strong economic orientation is Douglas J. Dalrymple and Donald L. Thompson, *Retailing: An Economic View* (New York: Free Press, 1969).

to dollars and cents. It is the bottom-line objective that cannot be ignored—in the short, intermediate, or the long run.

A RETAIL CAREER

Managing demand and supply factors in order to achieve profit sufficient for survival and future growth sounds like a job for a(n)

Economist	yes _____	no _____
Accountant	yes _____	no _____
Financial analyst	yes _____	no _____
Personnel manager	yes _____	no _____
Marketer	yes _____	no _____

The answer is yes to all of the above! A retail store manager needs to be capable in all these areas. In this section, we will demonstrate the validity of this statement.

Common Beliefs   Students may have certain perceptions of retailing that tend to turn them away from pursuing it as a career. Sometimes this is good, since not all individuals are suited for retailing. However, it can be unfortunate when inaccurate perceptions turn a student from a potentially rewarding retail career to another career that may only appear to be more promising. By examining some common beliefs, we will see a more accurate picture of retailing.[8]

College Education   Is college a prerequisite to a career in retailing? It depends. For a retail career that would not progress beyond assistant buyer or department manager, the answer is probably no. A college degree would be helpful, but not required. However, for career advancement with a fast-track progressive retailer, or a career in top management (store manager, vice president, chief executive officer), college training is increasingly becoming a prerequisite. Some retail firms are even recruiting MBAs to fill entry-level management positions.

Salary   Is retailing competitive in terms of compensation? A recent graduate with a bachelor's degree who is seeking a first position can probably get a higher salary in fields other than retailing. In general, retailers offer 10 to 15 percent below what college graduates can earn from manufacturers, insurance companies, and many other campus recruiters. That, however, is only the short-run perspective. In the long run, the retail manager or buyer is most often directly rewarded on performance. An entry-level retail manager or buyer who does exceptionally well can double or triple his or her income in three to five years.

8. Two articles that also may be helpful in this regard are "Retailers Upgrade Recruitment and Training," *Chain Store Age Executive*, March 1979, pp. 56, 61, 62; and "The New Breed That Runs the Big Stores," *Business Week*, June 26, 1971, pp. 54–58.

EXHIBIT 1.6 **Top Executive Salaries in Retailing (1979)**[a]	RETAILER	CHAIRMAN OF THE BOARD	PRESIDENT
	Winn-Dixie Stores, Inc.	$395,000	$316,000
	Safeway Stores, Inc.	374,000	259,000
	Southland Corporation	364,000	359,000
	F. W. Woolworth Company	375,000	281,000
	J. C. Penney Company	398,000	270,000
	Sears, Roebuck & Company	596,000	394,000

[a] Represents salary and bonus

Source: Based on data from *Business Week* (May 12, 1980), p. 83.

Although entry-level salaries can be low, they are misleading since higher-level retail managers receive salaries comparable to their counterparts in other industries. Consider, for example, the data in Exhibit 1.6, which shows the total annual compensation of a variety of chief executive officers (CEOs) in retailing.

Career Progression   Can one advance one's career rapidly in retailing? The answer, a definite yes, obviously depends on both the retail organization and the individual. A person capable of handling more responsibility than he or she is given can move up quickly; if that person works for a retail firm too small or growing too slowly to promote, he or she can easily receive a deserved career advancement by joining another retail organization.

There is no standard career progression chart, but a typical example may be useful. A college graduate starting a career with a department store chain might start as either a buyer trainee or store management trainee and progress as shown and discussed in Exhibits 1.7 and 1.8 (on page 14). The material in these exhibits was developed by Foley's, a leading department store in the Southwest and part of the Federated Department Stores, Inc., empire.

Geographic Mobility   Does retailing allow one to live in the area of the country where one desires? Yes and no. Retailing exists in all geographic areas in the United States where there is sufficient population density to support it. In the largest 200 to 300 cities in the United States, there will generally be sufficient employment and advancement opportunities in retailing. However, opportunities may not be enough for some individuals. In order to progress rapidly, a person must often be willing and able to make several geographic moves, all of which may not be attractive in terms of life style. Rapidly growing chain stores almost axiomatically find it necessary to transfer individuals in order to have the capacity to open stores in new geographic areas. Fortunately, these transfers are generally coupled with promotions and salary adjustments. Finally, a person may stay in one geographic area if he or she wants to. However, this may cost that person opportunities for advancement.

Women in Retailing   In the past, retailing has been viewed as a good career for women. But the role of women in retailing was most often restricted to the

EXHIBIT 1.7
**Management
Training
Program
for Buying**

CORPORATE BUYING ORGANIZATION

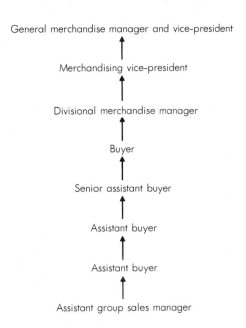

General merchandise manager and vice-president

↑

Merchandising vice-president

↑

Divisional merchandise manager

↑

Buyer

↑

Senior assistant buyer

↑

Assistant buyer

↑

Assistant buyer

↑

Assistant group sales manager

HOW DO YOU MAKE THINGS HAPPEN?

Assistant Group Sales Manager You'll work closely with a [group sales manager] in managing a volume responsibility of one to two million dollars. You will build skills in staff supervision, floor merchandising, inventory control, and business communications.

Assistant Buyer You'll be an understudy to a Buyer and assist with the buying, planning, pricing, distributing, and promoting of merchandise.

Senior Assistant Buyer You'll be responsible for several classifications of merchandise. You'll make trips to market and be groomed for your next promotion as a Buyer.

Buyer You'll run your own department making the decisions for buying, planning, pricing, distributing, and promoting your merchandise. It's like having your own business with the capital and advice of Foley's to help you. You are responsible for your department's profits, volume, share of the market, image, and more.

Divisional Merchandise Manager You will manage a major segment of Foley's corporate buying organization. You would have 5 to 9 buyers and their staffs reporting to you. Your objective will be the development of your segment of the business through effective management of the merchandising executives reporting to you.

Source: Reprinted with permission of Foley's, Inc.

EXHIBIT 1.8
**Management
Training
Program
for Store
Management**

WHAT ARE SOME OF THESE RESPONSIBILITIES?

Assistant Group Sales Manager   You'll learn the ins and outs of the Group Sales Manager job as you assist a GSM in day to day business functions.

Group Sales Manager   You'll put your management skills to work as you coordinate the personnel, merchandising and operations aspects of five to ten selling departments. Your success in this job will depend on your effectiveness as a manager of 30–40 people and your ability to control a dollar volume averaging one million dollars.

Divisional Sales Manager   You will manage a major segment of the retail operation of one of Foley's branch stores. You would report to the Assistant Store Manager-Merchandising and you would have 4 to 8 Group Sales Managers reporting to you. Your sales volume responsibility could range from 5 to 20 million dollars. Your objective will be the development of the managers reporting to you so they can better manage, control, and direct the efforts of their areas to maximize profitable retail sales volume.

Store Manager   You will have responsibility for the total operation of a Foley's location with a multi-million dollar sales volume. You'll make decisions in both merchandising and support areas that will have impact on your store and on the entire Foley's organization.

Source: Reprinted with permission of Foley's, Inc.

sales floor, the buying office, or middle management. Women typically found the door shut when it was time to move into the top executive suite.

In the late 1970s equal opportunity for women in retailing became more of a reality. For example, during this period about 125 women were vice presidents of major department stores. Breakthroughs into the presidential ranks included Pamela Grout, president of Associated Dry Goods, Powers Dry Goods division; Joanna Bradshaw, president of Workbench Inc., an independent chain of "life style" furniture stores; Judy Stewart, president of August Max, a ten-store specialty chain that is a division of U.S. Shoe; and Eve Levinson, president of Contempo Casuals, a specialty retail division of Carter Hawley Hale.[9]

Societal Perspective Societies throughout recorded history have never viewed merchants with great favor. Professional merchants, however, are respected and desirable members of their communities, their state and nation. Leading retail executives are well-rounded individuals with a high social consciousness. Many of them serve on the boards of nonprofit arts organizations, as regents or trustees of universities, on local chambers of commerce, on school boards, and in other service-related activities.

Not only outside their retailing career, but also within it, retailers serve society. Take a moment to envision a world without merchants or retailers. How could any advanced industrial society survive in their absence? It couldn't! It is the unscrupulous, deceiving merchant that society can do without, not the professional merchant. This happens to be true in all professions. There are unscrupulous lawyers, doctors, and ministers who give those professions a negative image at times. On the other hand, there are professional and ethical lawyers, doctors, and ministers, who are good for their professions and society as a whole. It is not the profession that dictates one's contribution to society, but the soundness of one's ethical principles. Early in your career (preferably as a student) you need to develop a firm set of ethical principles to help guide you throughout your managerial career.

Prerequisites for Success What is required for success as a retail executive? Many people respond to this question with this simple answer: "hard work." The work is hard; the hours almost always exceed forty per week, and a six-day week is not unusual for a retail executive. However, work is not the only prerequisite. Let us look at some others.

1. **Analytical skills.** To be successful, the retail executive must be able to solve problems through numerical analysis of facts and data in order to plan, manage, and control. The retail executive is a problem solver on a day-to-day basis. An understanding of the past and present performance of the store, merchandise lines, and departments, is necessary. It is the analysis of this performance data that forms the basis of future actions in the retailing environment.

9. "Equal Opportunity for Women Comes Slowly in the Executive Suite," *Chain Store Age Executive*, June 1980, pp. 27–29.

2. **Creativity.** The ability to generate and recognize novel ideas and solutions is known as creativity. A retail executive cannot operate the store totally by a set of preprogrammed equations and formulas; there is no standard recipe for retailing. Therefore, retail executives need to be idea people as well as analysts. Success in retailing is the result of sensitive, perceptive decisions that require imaginative and innovative techniques.

3. **Decisiveness.** Decisiveness is the ability to make rapid decisions and to render judgments, take action, and commit oneself to a course of action until completion is achieved. A retail executive must be an action person. Better decisions could probably be made if more time were taken to make them. However, more time is frequently unavailable because variables such as fashion trends and consumer desires change quickly. Thus, an executive must make decisions on these matters quickly, confidently, and correctly in order to be successful.

4. **Flexibility.** Flexibility is the ability to adjust to the ever-changing needs of the situation. The retail executive must have the willingness and enthusiasm to do whatever is necessary (although not planned) to get the job completed. One major principle of retailing is that surprises never cease. Because plans must be altered quickly to accommodate changes in trends, styles, and attitudes, successful retail executives must be flexible.

5. **Initiative.** Retail executives are doers. They must have the ability to originate action rather than wait to be told what to do. This ability is called initiative. To be a success, the retail executive must monitor the numbers of the business (sales volumes, profits, inventory levels), and seize opportunities for action.

6. **Leadership.** Leadership is the ability to inspire others to trust and respect your judgment and the ability to delegate and to guide and persuade these others. Retail executives must be managers. Successfully conducting a retail operation means depending on others to get the work done, for in any large-scale retailing enterprise, one person cannot do it all.

7. **Organization.** Another important quality is the ability to establish priorities and courses of action for yourself and others and the ability to plan and follow up to achieve results. This prerequisite is organization. Retail executives are manipulators and jugglers of many things—a variety of issues, functions, and projects. To achieve goals, the successful retailer must set priorities and organize personnel and resources.

8. **Risk taking.** Retail executives are gamblers. They should be willing to take calculated risks based on thorough analysis and sound judgment; they should also be willing to accept responsibility for the results. Success in retailing often comes from taking calculated risks and having the confidence to try something new before someone else does.

9. **Stress tolerance.** Retail executives must be able to perform consistently under pressure and to thrive on constant change and challenge. They must be resilient. As the other prerequisites to success in retailing suggest, retailing is fast paced and demanding.

These nine prerequisites to success in retailing are not intended to scare you off. In fact, if you are a student or a young retail executive, you probably do not yet possess all nine. The important thing for a person beginning a retail career is the desire to acquire them. If you do desire these abilities, this book will help you move toward that goal. And, if you acquire and develop these abilities, your career in retailing will progress more rapidly. In Exhibit 1.9 we present some case studies of rapid career progression in retailing.

THE STUDY AND PRACTICE OF RETAILING

As we have seen, the first two prerequisites to success as a retail executive are analytical skills and creativity. These attributes also represent two methods for the study and practice of retailing.

Analytical Method   The analytical retail executive is a finder and investigator of facts, reducing, synthesizing, and dissecting them in order to make decisions systematically. To make these decisions, the executive uses models and theories of retail phenomena that enable him to structure all dimensions of retailing.[10] An analytical perspective can result in a standardized set of procedures, success formulas, and guidelines.

Consider, for example, a manager operating a McDonald's restaurant, where everything is preprogrammed, including the menu, decor, location,

EXHIBIT 1.9
**Career
Advancement
in Retailing**

- Starting at an annual salary of $14,000 in the assistant buyer's program at a large department store chain, a young woman in her early twenties soon became acting manager of the women's sportswear department in a branch store. But the parent company, seeking potential superstars, transferred her to a buyer's position in another store division. After only two years in the field, she is earning $25,000 a year.
- Born in 1951, a sales-promotion vice president of a major department store found his marketing major important in his career, working for only two companies. At twenty-nine, he earns about $50,000 a year.
- After graduating in 1961 from college with a degree in business administration, a retailing recruit began as an executive trainee in one store and moved three times to other retail companies, advancing in grade each time. A few years ago he was appointed vice president for merchandising of one store and in 1978, in a climax to his seventeen-year career, was elected president of a major specialty store at the age of forty. Today he earns $175,000 a year in that post.
- Now thirty-one years old, the personnel head of a large retail chain made it to that post in only eight years, having graduated from college in 1971. He, too, moved around, with three jobs in his career. But the last one has earned him a salary of $90,000 a year, which should be rather satisfying at his still early age.

Source: Based on data from Kenneth B. Noble, "Fields of the Future: The Bosses Predict the Needs," *The New York Times,* October 14, 1979, p. 22.

10. The analytical approach to retailing has been espoused for over fifty years. See Walter Hoving, "More Science in Merchandising," *Journal of Retailing* 5(October 1929): 3–9; and Paul H. Nystrom, *The Economics of Retailing* (New York: Ronald Press, 1915).

hours of operation, cleanliness standards, customer service policies, and advertising. The manager needs only to gather and analyze facts to determine if the preestablished guidelines are being met and to take appropriate corrective actions if necessary.

Creative Method   Conversely, the creative retail executive is a producer or inventor of ideas. This executive tends to be a conceptualizer and has a very imaginative and fertile mind. He uses insight and intuition more often than facts, and the result is usually a novel way to look at or solve a retail problem. It is possible to operate a retail establishment, in most part, with creativity. However, in the long run, using only creativity will not be adequate; analytical decision making must be used so an executive can profitably respond to unforeseen events in the environment.

An example is Kaleidoscope, Inc., a retail mail-order firm. In 1974 Susan Edmondson invested $5,000 and began operating her business out of the carriage house in her backyard. Her buying technique was creative and nonanalytical. She bought what her insight and intuition suggested — jewelry, home furnishings, gourmet foods and cookware, children's toys, and some clothing. All were items that basically appealed to her. As a result her target market was a composite Susan Edmondson, an affluent woman between thirty and fifty years old. In spite of these purely intuitive methods, Kaleidoscope prospered. In fact, by 1978 the firm's sales had reached $16 million.

The story doesn't end there, however. Susan and her husband had made no analytical assessment of the company's financial future and the capital requirements necessary to enlarge the business. Soon they found that order processing couldn't keep up with the incoming mail and inadequate computers bled the firm of money. Lawsuits followed. Susan and her husband were divorced, which stopped the line of communication between the management team. Soon employees with no formal knowledge of business or finance were making spur-of-the-moment decisions without any regard for the future. In February of 1979, only a few months after reporting a $16 million sales year, Kaleidoscope, Inc., filed for bankruptcy.[11]

A Two-Pronged Approach   As shown through the McDonald's example and the Kaleidoscope sketch, retailing can indeed be practiced from both extremes. However, the retailer who employs both approaches is most successful in the long run. It is obvious what happened to Kaleidoscope, but isn't McDonald's very successful using only the analytical method? No. The McDonald's franchisee can operate analytically quite successfully. However, behind the franchisee is a franchisor who is creative as well as analytical. On the creative dimension was the development of McDonald's characters, such as Ronald McDonald, the Grimace, and the Hamburglar, and selected menu items such as the Egg McMuffin and Big Mac. On the analytical dimension was the development of standardized lay-

11. John R. Halbrooks, "A High Fashion Sales Whiz Who Was," *INC,* May 1979, pp. 80–82.

outs, fixtures, equipment, and employee training. It is the combination of the creative with the analytical that has made McDonald's what it is today.

In all fields of retailing, the synthesis of creativity and analysis is necessary. Roger Dickinson, a former retail executive and now professor of marketing, has stated that "many successful merchandisers are fast duplicators rather than originators."[12] To decide who or what to duplicate requires not only creativity, but an analysis of the strategies that retailers are pursuing. This is an exercise in weighing potential returns against risks. Dickinson further states that "creativity in retailing is for the sake of increasing the sales and profits of the firm."[13] If creativity is tied to sales and profits, then one cannot avoid analysis, for profit and sales statistics require analysis.

Retailers in the 1980s cannot do without either creativity or analytical skills. In this book we will attempt to develop your skills in both of these areas. At the outset, however, you should note that the analytical and creative methods for studying retailing are not that disparate. Whether you use creativity or analytical skills, they will be directed at solving problems. The similarities between the creative process and the analytical or scientific method of solving problems are presented in Exhibit 1.10.

A PROPOSED ORIENTATION

The approach to the study and practice of retailing that is espoused in this book is an outgrowth of the previous discussion. This approach has four major orientations: (1) environmental, (2) planning, (3) profit, and (4) decision making.

Retailers should have an environmental orientation, which will allow them to adapt continuously to external forces in the environment. Retailing is not static. With the social, legal, technological, economic, and other external forces

EXHIBIT 1.10 **Problem Solving from Two Perspectives**	*CREATIVE PROCESS*	*ANALYTICAL OR SCIENTIFIC PROCESS*
	1. Problem is sensed.	1. Problem is defined.
	2. Relevant data are gathered.	2. Existing knowledge is assessed.
	3. Logical thinking employed to try to solve problem, but the problem is not solved.	3. Formation of concept and specification of hypothesis.
	4. Period of frustration and tantalization.	4. Acquisition of meaningful new data.
	5. Flash of insight.	5. New data are organized and assessed in relevant ways.
	6. Process of verification.	6. Evaluation and conclusion.

Sources: Lewis E. Walkup, "Creativity in Science Through Visualization," *Journal of Creative Behavior,* 1(Summer 1967), pp. 283–84; and Gerald Zaltman, Christian R. A. Pinson, and Reinhard Angelmar, *Mothatheory and Consumer Research* (New York: Holt, Rinehart and Winston, 1973), pp. 13–15.

12. Roger Dickinson, "Creativity in Retailing," *Journal of Retailing* 45(Winter 1969–1970): 4.
13. Dickinson, "Creativity in Retailing."

always in flux, the retailer finds it necessary both to assess these changes in an analytical perspective and to respond with creative actions.

Retailers should have a planning orientation, which will help them to adapt systematically to a changing environment. Planning is deciding today what to do tomorrow. A retailer who wants to have the competitive edge must plan for the future now. Special emphasis will be placed in this text on the development of creative retail strategies.

Retailers should have a profit orientation, since all retail decisions will have an immediate effect on either the income statement or the balance sheet or both. The profit orientation will therefore focus on fundamental management of the balance sheet and income statement. Analytical tools that show how to evaluate the profit impact of retail decisions will be discussed.

Retailers should have a decision-making orientation, which will allow them to focus efforts on the need to collect and analyze data for making intelligent retail decisions. To aid in this process, a retail information system is needed to help retail executives program their operations for desired results.

THE OUTLINE

This book is composed of nineteen chapters and twelve retail case studies. The conceptual and theoretical material in the text and the case studies are intended to reinforce each other. The cases provide a pedagogical way to bring the real world into your studies, by launching you into the kind of situation you might face some years later as a retail manager. Through careful analysis of the cases and discussion with fellow students you will discover retailing concepts that can be vividly retained because of the concrete context. Furthermore, the cases will require you to think of yourself as a retail decision maker who must make decisions with less than perfect information.

Retail Planning and Management: An Overview   The book is divided into four parts. The first part, "Retail Planning and Management: An Overview," consists of the first three chapters. Chapter 2, "The Retail Planning Process," will give an overview of the concepts of strategic, administrative, and operations planning and management in retailing. Chapter 3, "The Retail Information System," will help you develop a framework for collecting and gathering information that you need for optimal retail planning, management, and decision making.

Strategic Planning and Management   In Part II of the book the focus is on external factors confronting the retail enterprise and how to respond to them. Five chapters specifically examine in detail these external forces:

- Chapter 4, "Understanding Channel Behavior"
- Chapter 5, "Understanding Consumer Behavior"
- Chapter 6, "Understanding Competitor Behavior"
- Chapter 7, "Understanding the Socioeconomic and Technological Environments"
- Chapter 8, "Understanding the Legal Environment"

The second part of the book concludes with Chapter 9, "Development of Strategic Plans." This chapter illustrates how the retailer must develop a strategy to respond to the external forces that were reviewed.

Administrative Planning and Management   In Part III we discuss administrative planning and management. Our concern here is with the structuring and designing of a retailer's resources in order to maximize its performance potential. Three chapters comprise this part, each dealing with a major resource in retailing:

- Chapter 10, "Financial Planning and Management"
- Chapter 11, "Human Resource Planning and Management"
- Chapter 12, "Location Planning and Management"

Operations Planning and Management   In the fourth and final part of the book we discuss operations planning and management. Our concern is with how to maximize the efficiency of the retailer's resource conversion process, or in other words, to maximize the profit of current operations. Operating decisions are day-to-day decisions and involve the bulk of the retailer's activity and energy. The seven chapters in this part are:

- Chapter 13, "Merchandise Planning and Management"
- Chapter 14, "Credit and Cash Planning and Management"
- Chapter 15, "Building and Fixture Planning and Management"
- Chapter 16, "Price Planning and Management"
- Chapter 17, "Retail Promotion: Advertising, Sales Promotions, and Publicity"
- Chapter 18, "Retail Promotion: Personal Selling"
- Chapter 19, "Customer Service Planning and Management"

A Management Framework   The division of major parts of this text into the strategic, administrative, and operations dimensions of planning and management provides a logical framework for the management of retail enterprises. Retailers must first analyze their mission and objectives in regard to trends in the external environments in order to identify opportunities and develop strategy. In this regard, the retail information system is very important. Strategies, however simple or complex, require resources—financial, human, and locational. Administrative planning and management deals with the acquisition and management of this trio of resources. Finally, resource acquisition necessitates resource utilization, and this requires operations planning and management, discussed in the last part of this text. Operations planning and management includes the management of buildings and fixtures, cash and credit, and merchandise as well as the management of price, promotion, and customer service.

SUMMARY

What is retailing? Retailing is the final move in the progression of merchandise from the producer to the consumer. It is effectively combining creative and analytical skills to make a profit in an ever-changing environment.

What possibilities does a retailing career offer to the retailing student? In the long run, a retail career can offer salary comparable to other careers, definite career progression, and geographic mobility.

What are the prerequisites for success as a retailing executive? Besides hard work, the nine prerequisites for success are analytical skills, creativity, decisiveness, flexibility, initiative, leadership, organization, risk-taking, and stress tolerance. These are all important, but it is especially important for the retail executive to work at developing an attitude of openness to new ideas and a willingness to learn.

From what perspective should retailing be studied? Since retailing represents an economic sector, it should be studied from both a supply and demand perspective. It is the interaction between supply (sellers) and demand (buyers) that establishes price levels, competitive intensity, and profit levels. Demand and supply factors should be studied by using both analytical and creative processes.

In this book we utilize four orientations to the study and practice of retailing, an environmental orientation, a planning orientation, a profit orientation, and a decision-making orientation. These four orientations are related to strategic, administrative, and operations planning and management in retail enterprises.

QUESTIONS

1. It has been argued that when retailers surpass $100 million in annual sales volume they become less flexible. How can large retailers remain flexible as they grow?

2. What changes do you foresee in the business environment over the next five years? How do you think retailing will change as a result of the changing business environment you foresee?

3. No specific mention was made of marketing in this first chapter. What do you see as the relationship between retail management and marketing management?

4. What concepts and techniques from economics and finance do you believe would be most helpful in retail decision making? Why?

5. Why do you think the average retail store has more than tripled in size over the last fifty years?

6. In today's economic environment the retailer should be more concerned with supply factors than demand factors. Agree or disagree and defend your position.

7. A retail manager who is both creative and analytical will definitely succeed. Agree or disagree and defend your position.

8. Is managing a large retail store with one hundred employees any different than managing your own store with only two employees? Why?

9. Regardless of the line of retail trade, the major problems of managing a retail enterprise are identical. Agree or disagree and defend your position.

10. If you were on the board of directors of one of the largest retail chains in the United States and had to head a committee to select a new president for the retail chain, what criteria would you use to evaluate the potential candidates? Why?

2

Overview *In this chapter we will define and discuss planning. To facilitate this discussion we will introduce a retail planning and management model, which will serve as a frame of reference for the remainder of this text. In short, this simple model illustrates the importance of three types of planning and management in retailing: (1) strategic, (2) administrative, and (3) operations. These three types of planning, if properly conducted, will lead synergistically to high performance financial results for the retail enterprise.*

The Retail Planning and Management Process

IN MOST ENDEAVORS, a well-defined plan of action can mean the difference between success and failure. For example, a responsible military officer would not attack the enemy without a well-defined plan. The quarterback of a football team outlines a plan for the squad to follow before each offensive play. Candidates for political office increasingly rely upon precise strategy in order to win elections. Similarly, a clearly defined plan of action is an essential ingredient of retail management.[1]

THE NEED FOR PLANNING

Why is planning so important? Superior strategy can offset numerous advantages of the competitor, just as David's simple but well-defined strategy allowed him to conquer the giant, Goliath. Using carefully conceived and strategically superior marketing programs, many small companies have taken significant shares of the market from their larger competitors.

A pair of examples of well-recognized retailers in the United States will help to illustrate the importance planning can have in determining a retailer's future. The two examples deal with S. S. Kresge and Montgomery Ward.

S. S. Kresge

S. S. Kresge was a declining old-line variety store chain that was muddling through the post–World War II era. With astute planning, however, it became the fastest growing retailer in the 1960–1980 period.[2] Let us examine how it accomplished this.

In 1957 Harry B. Cunningham, then a general vice president of the firm, was assigned to travel the country to study, first-hand, retail trends. Cunningham traveled for two years and finally confirmed that variety stores—like the earlier five-and-dime stores—had somehow drifted away from their original formula for success: low margins and high turnover. Instead of pricing merchandise to stimulate sales, they were pricing it on the basis of current costs and sales. In the 1950s the variety stores were extremely vulnerable, as supermarkets, discount houses, and other new mass merchandisers began beating them at their own game.

In 1959 Cunningham was named president and chief executive officer and ordered another two-year study to focus exclusively on discounting. When the results were in, Cunningham gave discounting the final go-ahead. He was de-

---

1. The need for retailers to spend more time on planning is emphasized in Arnold Becker, "Development of Retail Store Strategies," speech delivered at a meeting of the Retail Research Society, New York, June 29, 1977.

2. For a more detailed discussion of Kresge and K-mart, see "How Kresge Became the Top Discounter," *Business Week*, October 24, 1970, pp. 62–63ff.; "Retailing: K is for Krunch," *Sales Management*, November 29, 1971, p. 3; "K-mart: The Tail That Wags the Kresge Dog," *Merchandising Week*, July 9, 1973, pp. 8ff.; and "What Woolworth Didn't Know Apparently Kresge Did," *Financial World*, May 22, 1974, pp. 18–19.

termined, however, to avoid the merchandising mistakes of the discounters flooding the market. The result was K-mart, a conveniently located, one-stop shopping unit, where customers could buy "quality" merchandise at discount prices. In March 1962 Kresge opened its first K-mart in Garden City, Michigan, and by the late 1960s Kresge was the unquestioned leader in the discount arena. In fact, by 1979 Kresge had become the third largest retailer in the United States, with annual sales in excess of $12 billion.

Montgomery Ward   The second example is not one of a successful plan, but of an inaccurate assessment of the environment coupled with a failure to recognize or admit that the assessment was inaccurate. In this situation the retailer continued to pursue a strategy designed for an improper environment.

After World War II, Sewell Avery, chairman of the board of Montgomery Ward, believed that a depression was imminent.[3] Avery believed that after the war the economy would not be able to maintain its pace, because of the halt in war production and the large number of servicemen who would be trying to find employment. At the time, Montgomery Ward had the managerial and financial resources to expand, but it decided on a no-growth strategy based on Avery's prediction of a depression. Had a depression occurred, Avery would have been a hero; as it was, he was far from a hero.

Unfortunately after it was clear that no depression was on the horizon, Avery still insisted on a no-growth policy. At the same time, Sears was moving aggressively by adding new stores and remodeling existing ones. As a result, sales at Sears accelerated from $1.9 billion in 1948 to $2.9 billion in 1954. In comparison, sales at Wards slipped from $1.1 billion in 1948 to $0.9 billion in 1954.

Planning Defined   Both of the preceding examples show that flexibility in planning is a key ingredient in determining the future of a retail enterprise. But, what is planning?

In principle, planning is a simple concept. **Planning,** of whatever type, is deciding in the present what to do in the future. Future can be any upcoming time: tomorrow, next month, next year, or even five, ten, or one hundred years from today. Such a definition is short, but adequate.

THE RETAIL PLANNING AND MANAGEMENT MODEL

At the conclusion of Chapter 1 we mentioned that this book would have a planning orientation, an environmental orientation, a profit orientation, and a decision-making orientation. These four orientations will be explained throughout this text with the aid of a retail planning and management model, pre-

3. For an insightful discussion of Montgomery Ward during this time, see Robert F. Hartley, *Marketing Mistakes* (Columbus, Ohio: Grid, 1976), pp. 7–17.

sented in Exhibit 2.1.[4] At this point you should take several moments to reflect on this model, which should be viewed from top to bottom.

The retail planning and management model suggests that a retailer must engage in three types of planning and management: (1) strategic, (2) administrative, and (3) operations. Each is undertaken in order to achieve high performance results. For the present time, you should think of high performance results as a financial result substantially superior to the industry average. Later we will give you a more precise definition.

Strategic Planning and Management   Strategic planning and management is concerned with how the retailer responds to external forces, in order to establish the general direction the retailer will follow. In principle, this involves determining which strategy best reflects the line(s) of trade in which the retailer will operate; which market(s) will be pursued, and in what fashion they will be pursued. Part II of this text is devoted to an in-depth discussion of strategic planning and management in retail enterprises.

The initial step in the strategic planning and management process is to state the firm's mission and objectives clearly and concisely. Notice the retailer's mission and objectives at the top of the model in Exhibit 2.1. The statement of mission and objectives involves more than proclaiming the desire to achieve high performance results. For example, consider the statement of objectives in Exhibit 2.2 of a leading Canadian chain of home improvement centers. These objectives involve not only statements regarding financial performance ("to increase earnings per share and achieve an acceptable return on shareholder's equity") but also statements regarding employee satisfaction, markets to be served, and community affairs (see page 28).

The second step in strategic planning and management is assessing external forces. Remember that a retailer develops strategy by identifying opportunities that arise from external forces. Strategic opportunities do not exist internally within the firm; they are derived from the firm's environment. Strategic opportunities arise from a company's ability to exploit environmental opportunity.

Major external forces that should be assessed are also profiled in the top part of the retail planning and management model. They are:

1. **Channel behavior.** The behavior of members of the retailer's marketing channel can have a significant impact on the retailer's future. For example, are certain channel members, such as manufacturers and wholesalers, establishing their own retail outlets? Or, are wholesalers requiring larger minimum orders and less attractive credit terms? Behaviors such as these could have implications for the retailer's strategy.

2. **Consumer behavior.** The behavior of consumers will obviously have a significant impact on the retailer's future. Specifically, the retailer will need to understand the determinants of shopping behavior so that likely changes in that behavior can be identified and appropriate strategies developed.

---

4. This model is an adaptation and reflection of major concepts presented in H. Igor Ansoff, *Corporate Strategy* (New York: McGraw-Hill, 1965).

EXHIBIT 2.1   **The Retail Planning and Management Model**

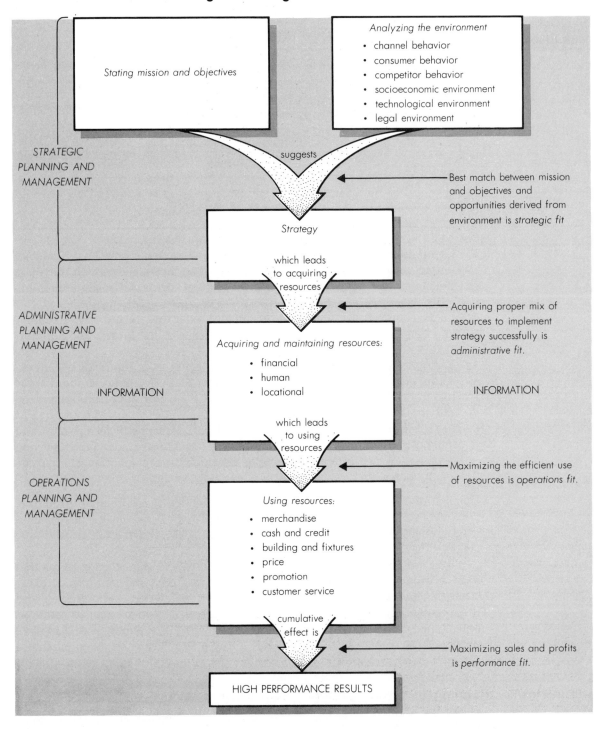

EXHIBIT 2.2
**Objectives of
Revelstoke
Companies, Ltd.**

· To serve and satisfy an increasing number of customers.
· To provide the men and women in our Company with the opportunity for advancement and increased personal satisfaction.
· To demonstrate entrepreneurship, leadership and high standards throughout the economy.
· To participate in markets which experience above average growth.
· To maintain closely competitive market conditions.
· To keep our manner of doing business simple and economical.
· To strive for excellence as opposed to imitating others and accepting how things were done in the past without question.
· To increase earnings per share and achieve an acceptable return on shareholders' equity.
· To support community affairs where we are located on a basis consistent with the size of our Company.
· To have fun.

Source: Revelstoke Companies, Ltd., *Annual Report* (1975).

3. **Competitor behavior.** How competing retailers behave will have a major impact on the most appropriate strategy that the retailer should develop. Retailers must develop a competitive strategy that is not easily imitated in a highly competitive arena.
4. **Socioeconomic environment.** The retailer must understand how economic and demographic variables will influence sales in the future, and adapt its strategy according to these changes.
5. **Technological environment.** The technical frontiers of the retail system encompass potentially new and better ways of performing standard retail functions. The retailer must always be cognizant of opportunities for improving operating efficiency.
6. **Legal environment.** The retailer should be familiar with local, state, and federal regulation of the retail system. It must also understand evolving legal patterns in order to be able to design future retail strategies that are legally defensible.

Detailed discussions of these forces will be provided in Chapters 4 through 8. For now, you should realize that the external forces are uncontrollable by a single retailer, but that threats emanating from these external forces are translated by a successful retailer into opportunities.

By examining both its mission and objectives and the external forces that it is confronted with, the retailer should arrive at several possible or likely strategies. By obtaining the best match between its mission and objectives and the opportunities derived from external forces, it should be able to settle on one as the best strategy. When this is accomplished, the retailer is said to have obtained a **strategic fit** (see Exhibit 2.1). Once a strategic fit has been obtained, the retailer can move on to administrative planning and management.

Administrative Planning and Management   Administrative planning and management involves the acquisition and maintenance of resources that are necessary to carry out the retailer's strategy. It involves the structuring and designing of resources in order to maximize the retailer's performance potential. As shown in the retail planning and management model (see Exhibit 2.1), the retailer must be concerned with acquiring three categories of resources: financial, human, and locational.

Most retailers will not have all of the resources necessary to implement a strategy. Therefore, external resource bases may need to be tapped. For instance, the retailer without the necessary middle management and retail clerks to carry out its strategy might have to hire employees away from other companies. At the same time, it may lack sufficient financial capital to implement the strategy, and may have to obtain additional debt capital or sell stock to increase equity capital. Finally, it may have to acquire the needed locational resources. The retailer may need certain locations for stores over which it presently does not have control.

Part III of this book will be devoted to administrative planning and management, with a separate chapter devoted to each type of resource. At this juncture, the essential point to remember is that a retailer can develop a well-conceived and thought-out strategy, but, if it does not know how to obtain and organize the necessary resources to put that strategy into practice, then all is wasted.

When the retailer acquires the proper mix and quantity of resources to implement and carry out its strategy and thus maximize its performance potential, then it is said to have achieved an **administrative fit.** Refer to the retail planning and management model (Exhibit 2.1) to observe where the administrative fit occurs.

Operations Planning and Management   Operations planning and management is concerned with maximizing the efficiency of the retailer's use of resources. It is conducted to convert resources into sales and profits. In other words, its aim is to maximize the performance of current operations.

Most of the retailer's time and energy is devoted to operations planning and management, since such planning is essentially a day-to-day activity. Reference to the retail planning and management model shows that operations planning and management involves planning and managing buildings and fixtures, credit and cash, merchandise, price, promotion, and customer service. These are decision areas that need day-to-day attention. For example, sales clerks need to be scheduled, inventory maintained, credit granted, customers served, advertisements placed, and so on. In other words, someone has to run the store.

A good strategic fit and administrative fit will mean little if a retailer fails to be concerned about the "nuts and bolts"—the day-to-day activities—in the operation of the store. This is precisely what retail analysts suggest happened to Kentucky Fried Chicken. Too much attention was paid to long-range strategic planning, "and not enough time to running the store."[5]

5. "Kentucky Fried Chicken Bone in Heublein's Throat?" *Advertising Age,* March 7, 1977, pp. 3, 56.

In Part IV we will focus on operations planning and management, the real guts of retailing. In your first several years in a retail career your concern will be almost exclusively with operations planning and management. The grand strategies (strategic planning) and acquisition of resources (administrative planning) will be handled by people higher up in the retail organization.

When the retailer is able to do a good job at operations planning and management, that is, when it effectively uses the resources at its disposal, then it can be said to have achieved an **operations fit.** Refer to Exhibit 2.1 to see where the operations fit occurs.

High Performance Results   The last portion of the retail planning and management model suggests that the cumulative effect (the payoff) of well-designed and executed strategic, administrative, and operations plans will be high performance results. Failure in any of these areas will severely hamper the retailer's performance and prevent it from achieving high performance distinction.

Finally, you should note that the retail planning and management model is enveloped in a web of information. The intent here is to illustrate the need for information in all phases of retail planning and management. In Chapter 3 we will discuss in detail the role of the retail information system in the retail enterprise.

THE HIGH PERFORMANCE IMPERATIVE

The need to strive for high performance results is tied to the extremely competitive nature of retailing. Entry barriers are relatively low, and thus new retail entrepreneuers are continually entering the marketplace. As a consequence, profit levels naturally deteriorate. A retailer should aim for high performance results so that if planned results are not achieved, at least it still has a chance of achieving average operating results. The retailer that aims only for average results will often find itself having to confront a sobering income statement and balance sheet.

McCammon has outlined a set of planning premises for the 1980s that reinforce the need to plan the business so as to be an industry leader. We will briefly review these premises.[6]

Planning Premises for the Eighties

Continuing Inflationary Pressures   The consensus among economists is that inflation in the 1980s is extremely unlikely to fall below 6 percent and probably will be in the 8 to 12 percent range. By historical standards in the United States, especially using the 1950s and 1960s as a benchmark, these figures are high. This expected rate of inflation will affect retailers in at least two major areas.

---

6. Another good review of planning premises and the business environment in the 1980s can be found in Carter F. Bales, Donald J. Gogel, and James S. Henry, ''The Environment for Business in the 1980s,'' *The McKinsey Quarterly,* Winter 1980, pp. 2–21.

First, the cost of replacing inventory and fixed assets will be considerably higher than historical costs. Second, consumer purchasing power will be sharply curtailed, which will immediately affect retail sales and thus profitability.

High Interest Rates　As prices rise rapidly, so will the cost of money. Interest rates are unlikely to fall below 8 percent, and occasional prime rates in excess of 12 percent can be expected. By historical standards, this rate of interest is high, and it has two implications for retailers. First, the cost of financing inventory will increase significantly, thus putting pressures on increased inventory productivity. Second, the cost of providing consumer credit will increase, so a potential sales tool will be weakened.

Recurring Capital Crises　The retail industry will experience a significant shortfall in terms of the capital infusion it needs to remain competitive and growing in the 1980s. As the government uses more and more deficit financing, capital is siphoned off from industry uses. In addition, high interest rates and relatively low price/earnings ratios make additional debt financing or equity sales less attractive than historically. The net result will be more pressure on generating capital internally versus externally and more pressure from suppliers to get retailers to finance more of the inventory in the marketing channel.

Erratic Growth Rates　The economy will probably be more cyclical and will not be characterized by the linear growth curves we experienced in the 1950s and 1960s. This "roller coaster" type of economy will increase the need by retailers to recognize the turning points. When will a period of prosperity reverse itself and when will a period of recession reverse? Miscalculation of these turning points can have a drastic negative effect on performance.

Intensified Competition　Because of the preceding factors, real economic growth in the United States, especially in retailing, will be limited. As a result, the only way to increase the business at an above average rate will be to take market share from one's competitors. Competitors will not willingly let market share be taken, and therefore intensified competition will ensue. Retailers will need to develop major strategic thrusts to help insulate them from intensified levels of competition and to achieve inroads into another's market share.

Unrivaled Market Opportunities　There is an inverse relationship between the obstacles that confront a retailer and market opportunities. All of the preceding issues can be turned into opportunities by the creative retailer, but it is not easy to do this, and many retailers will not grasp the opportunity. However, those that stand up to the challenge can lead the industry in performance.

Comment　　These planning premises offer evidence that retailers will face a major performance imperative throughout the 1980s. The need to strive to be an industry leader should be paramount. Industry leaders do not randomly surface, rather they are created and engineered over time by astute management combining the principles of creative and analytical retail management to develop top-flight strategic, administrative, and operations plans. The retail planning and management model is a useful frame of reference in this regard.

PERFORMANCE MEASURES

What are the high performance measures in retailing? As in manufacturing or wholesaling, the ultimate measures are financial. Societal goals are also important; however, in the long run, social and profit goals are consistent. Retailing is extremely competitive and therefore, if a retailer continues to earn an attractive financial return, the firm must be doing what society wants. When consumers stop patronizing a retail store, there is an indication that the retailer is not doing as good a job as it once was at providing wanted goods and services at prices customers are willing to pay. Therefore, in a competitive retail environment, there is a direct correlation between societal and financial returns.

The standard financial performance criteria in retailing can be partitioned into three groups: (1) profitability, (2) liquidity, and (3) growth. Each of these will be discussed briefly in this chapter and in Chapter 9.

Profitability

A retailer's profit performance can be clearly specified using the **strategic profit model,** displayed in Exhibit 2.3.[7] This model multiplies a retailer's profit margin by its rate of asset turnover to arrive at its return on assets (the formulas for profit margin and rate of asset turnover are in the exhibit). Thus, if a retailer has a profit margin of 2 percent and a rate of asset turnover of 3.0 times, then it automatically will have a return on assets of 6 percent ($2\% \times 3.0 = 6\%$). The retailer's return on assets depicts the profit return the retailer achieved on all assets invested in the enterprise regardless of whether the assets were financed by debtors or the owners of the firm.

The return on asset figure is multiplied by the firm's financial leverage to yield return on net worth. In the preceding example, if the firm had financial leverage of 2.0 times (see the formula in the exhibit), and this was multiplied by the return on assets of 6 percent, the results would be a return on net worth of 12 percent ($6\% \times 2.0 = 12\%$). The retailer's **return on net worth** depicts the profit the owners of the retail enterprise achieved on the dollars they had invested in the firm.

As is readily evident, the strategic profit model focuses on three important financial ratios: (1) profit margin, (2) asset turnover, and (3) financial leverage. Following is an examination of each.

Profit Margin   The **profit margin** is the ratio of net profit (after taxes) to net sales and shows how much profit a retailer makes on each dollar of sales after all expenses and taxes have been met. For example, if a retailer is operating on a profit margin of 2 percent, it is making two cents on each dollar of sales. In

7. Bert C. McCammon, Jr., and William L. Hammer, "A Frame of Reference for Improving Productivity in Distribution," *Atlanta Economic Review* 59(September–October 1974): 9–13.

EXHIBIT 2.3 **The Strategic Profit Model**

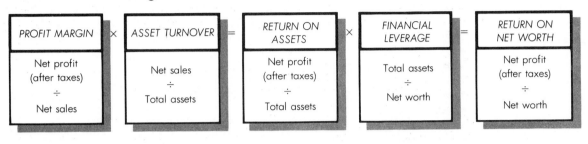

general, retailers operate on lower profit margins than manufacturers. The profit margin ratio is derived exclusively from income or operating statement data and does not include any measures from the retailer's balance sheet. Thus, it does not show how effectively a retailer is using the capital at its disposal.

Asset Turnover The **rate of asset turnover** is computed by taking the retailer's net sales and dividing by total assets. This ratio tells the retail analyst how productively the firm's assets are being utilized. Put another way, it shows how many dollars of sales a retailer can generate on an annual basis with each dollar invested in assets. Thus, if a retailer has a rate of asset turnover of 3.0 times, it is generating three dollars in sales for each dollar in assets. In general, retailers experience higher rates of asset turnover than do manufacturers. It is important to note that the asset turnover ratio incorporates key measures from the income statement (sales) and the balance sheet (assets), and as such shows how well the retailer is utilizing its capital to generate sales.

Financial Leverage One popular measure of **financial leverage** is total assets divided by net worth. This ratio helps to depict the extent to which the retailer is utilizing debt in its total capital structure. The low end of this ratio is 1.0 times and depicts a situation in which the retailer is using no debt in its capital structure. As the ratio moves beyond 1.0, the firm is using a heavier mix of debt versus equity. For example, when the ratio is 2.0 times, the firm has two dollars in assets for every dollar in net worth or equity. Therefore, one dollar of assets was externally financed. In that case, the firm has 50 percent debt and 50 percent equity.

Higher rates of leverage can increase the return on net worth to a retailer. However, higher rates also increase the retailer's risk because as the proportion of debt increases the retailer is faced with higher fixed interest payments. These interest payments must be met every operating period regardless of the retailer's cash flow. This makes highly leveraged retailers very vulnerable to downturns in the economy, increasing the risk they must bear. Exhibit 2.4 helps to demonstrate this point by profiling eleven publicly held retailers that have filed for bankruptcy, and their corresponding excessive use of financial leverage. Most financial analysts agree that for almost all industries (manufacturing,

EXHIBIT 2.4 **Death by Excessive Leverage**	*RETAIL FIRM*	*YEAR FILING FOR BANKRUPTCY*	*PREVIOUS YEAR'S FINANCIAL LEVERAGE*
	Abercrombie & Fitch	1976	4.3
	Arlans	1973	5.5
	Daylin	1975	5.3
	W. T. Grant	1975	9.5
	Interstate Stores	1974	4.3
	Mangel Stores	1974	14.0
	National Bella Hess	1974	5.3
	Neisner Brothers	1977	18.3
	Parkview-Gem	1973	3.1
	Unishops	1973	3.5
	Kennedy and Cohen	1975	6.5

Source: Albert D. Bates, "The Internalization of Retail Strategy" paper presented at symposium on Distribution Strategies for the 1980s, Norman, Oklahoma (January 1979). Reprinted with permission of the author.

wholesaling, and retailing), financial leverage ratios above 2.5 are too risky. In general, a leverage ratio in the vicinity of 2.0 is considered comfortable for a retail firm.

Targets The proper programming of the preceding set of three ratios allows the retailer to achieve its desired (target) rates of return on assets and net worth. To determine what the target should be, however, one needs to examine how retailers in general have fared historically in the economic environment. An examination of Exhibit 2.5 reveals that over time retailers in the United States have increased their financial performance by increasing their profit margins and their asset turnover and by leveraging their operations more highly. The net result has been a significant increase in the rates of return on assets and on net worth. However, most, if not all, of the increase in performance has been offset by the higher rates of inflation in recent years.[8]

The most crucial revelation from the data in Exhibit 2.5 is that the standards of performance change over time. For example, in 1960 the average retailer in the United States had a return on assets of 2.3 percent. Therefore, in order to have been termed "high performance," a retailer would have had to achieve a return of around 4 to 5 percent. In 1970 the average retailer had achieved a return on assets of 4.2 percent, but this was no longer a high performance achievement. Rather, a return on assets of 6 to 7 percent was required. By 1980 retailers in the United States were, on average, achieving a return on assets of 4.0 percent, but once again, this return was not high performance because the standards had changed so that a return of 8 to 10 percent

8. An insightful analysis of how retailers fared from 1965 to 1974 in terms of the strategic profit model is provided in Albert D. Bates, "The Troubled Future of Retailing," *Business Horizons* 19(August 1976): 22–28.

EXHIBIT 2.5 **The Strategic Profit Model (1960–80)**

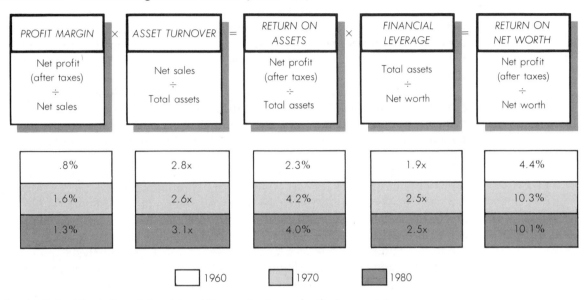

PROFIT MARGIN	×	ASSET TURNOVER	=	RETURN ON ASSETS	×	FINANCIAL LEVERAGE	=	RETURN ON NET WORTH
Net profit (after taxes) ÷ Net sales		Net sales ÷ Total assets		Net profit (after taxes) ÷ Total assets		Total assets ÷ Net worth		Net profit (after taxes) ÷ Net worth
.8%		2.8x		2.3%		1.9x		4.4%
1.6%		2.6x		4.2%		2.5x		10.3%
1.3%		3.1x		4.0%		2.5x		10.1%

☐ 1960   ☐ 1970   ■ 1980

Sources: Federal Trade Commission, Internal Revenue Service, and author's computations.

was needed to be in this category. Because high performance results vary over time, the profitability goals of retailers should not be static. Whatever the current rates, however, retailers need to aim for a return on assets and net worth that will place them in the upper quartile of firms in their industry.

Liquidity

Profitability portrays only part of the retailer's financial performance. An equally important dimension is liquidity. **Liquidity** represents the firm's ability to meet its current payment obligations. It has been said that financial analysts look at profitability, but credit analysts look at liquidity. Liquidity is crucial to the retailer for two reasons. First, if a retailer has too much liquidity, then working capital is not being fully utilized. If this is the case, attractive options for using this working capital are probably being ignored or discarded in order to minimize the risks of being insolvent. However, having too much liquidity over time can be just as risky as not having enough. Second, not enough liquidity can mean that a retailer may not be able to take advantage of opportunities to purchase merchandise at attractive prices when suppliers need to move inventory rapidly.

In general then, liquidity is important to the retailer because it protects the company from economic downturns and potential insolvency and also provides the needed flexibility to capitalize on unexpected merchandising opportunities.

Financial analysts generally use three financial ratios to evaluate liquidity. The most popular is the ratio of current assets to current liabilities, which is often called the **current ratio**. This ratio is the basic measurement of a retailer's solvency. The conventional wisdom of finance suggests that retailers should maintain a current ratio of approximately 2.0 times.

A second ratio is called the **quick ratio** and is computed as current assets less inventory divided by current liabilities. The quick ratio is a more stringent measure of a firm's ability to repay its current debt. Again, the conventional wisdom of finance suggests that retailers should maintain a quick ratio of 1.0 times.

The third, and final, liquidity ratio is the **acid-test ratio** and is computed as cash (and equivalents) divided by current liabilities. This ratio received considerable attention during the 1969–70 and 1974–75 credit crises. Analysts contend that a retailer's cash should be equal to 15.0 to 20.0 percent of its current liabilities.

An examination of how retailers in the United States have performed in terms of liquidity over the last twenty years is provided in Exhibit 2.6. As you can see, retailers have experienced a drastic deterioration of liquidity. For example, in 1960 retailers had a current ratio of 2.6 times, but by 1980 this ratio had dropped to 1.7 times. During this period, retailers went from a position of too much liquidity to one of a lack of liquidity. Most retail analysts agree that any further deterioration of liquidity could have serious consequences on the long-run competitive viability of retailers in the United States.

EXHIBIT 2.6 **Desirable Retail Liquidity Ratios (1960–1980)**	*LIQUIDITY RATIO*	*1960*	*1970*	*1980*
	Current (current assets to current liabilities)	2.6x	1.9x	1.7x
	Quick (current assets less inventory to current liabilities)	1.5x	1.2x	0.7x
	Acid-test (cash to current liabilities)	30.1%	12.9%	10.6%

Sources: Federal Trade Commission, Internal Revenue Service, and author's computations.

Growth   A high performance retailer cannot be one that experiences average or below average growth. Rather, growth must be significantly greater than the industry average in order to position the retailer apart from other retailers. To achieve this position, one must increase sales by at least 1.5 times the industry rate of growth. Thus, if the industry over the last year grew at 10 percent, then a high performance retailer would need to achieve a growth in sales of at least 15 percent.

Performance Standards   From our preceding discussion, we can formulate a set of standards for gauging high performance results. These standards will need to be adjusted according to general trends, but at the time of this writing, it was clear that a return on assets (after taxes) of 8 to 10 percent and a return on net worth (after taxes) of 15 to 20 percent was necessary to be rated high performance. These returns should be achieved without exceeding a leverage ratio of 2.2 times. Also, a current ratio of 2.0 times, a quick ratio of 1.0 times, and an acid test ratio of 15 to 20 percent would be essential to pass the liquidity tests of a high performance retailer. Finally, the ability to increase sales at 1.5 times the industry rate of growth would be essential.

PROFILES OF HIGH PERFORMANCE RETAILERS

Now let us look at some actual cases to illustrate the preceding discussion. As we saw in Exhibits 2.5 and 2.6, most retailers in the United States in the 1970s were achieving a return on net worth in the 10 to 15 percent range, had excessive leverage (typically above 2.4 times), and generally had a current ratio (current assets divided by current liabilities) of less than 2.0 times. Was it possible, through good planning, to achieve a return on net worth significantly greater than 15 percent, without excessive leverage, while maintaining adequate liquidity and enlarging the business at a rapid pace? The answer is yes, and the following examples confirm this answer.

Toys 'R' Us

Toys 'R' Us was a pioneer in the super–toy store movement of the early 1970s and consequently has consistently achieved high performance results. The strategy developed and fine tuned by Toys 'R' Us involves the application of **supermarket retailing** principles to toy stores.

The supermarket concept involves five basic principles directed at improving retail productivity and reducing the cost of distribution. As itemized by Bates and McCammon, these principles are:[9]

1. Self-service and self-selection displays
2. Centralization of customer services, usually at the checkout counter
3. Large-scale, low-cost physical facilities
4. A strong price emphasis
5. A broad assortment and wide variety of merchandise to facilitate multiple-item purchases

Toys 'R' Us has effectively applied these principles; a typical Toys 'R' Us outlet contains over 35,000 square feet of selling space, generates annual sales of over $4 million, and operates on a gross margin of 30 percent. Therefore, Toys 'R' Us relies on a competitive pricing policy and economies of scale to generate high performance results.

A financial profile of Toys 'R' Us is provided in Exhibit 2.7. The company operated on a profit margin of 5.6 percent and had an asset turnover of 2.1 times, which yielded a return on assets of 11.6 percent. When coupling this with modest financial leverage of 1.9 times, Toys 'R' Us was able to achieve a 22.1 percent return on net worth. Toys 'R' Us was also growing in sales and profits at over 20 percent compounded annually.

9. Albert D. Bates and Bert C. McCammon, Jr., ''Reseller Strategies and the Financial Performance of the Firm,'' paper presented at the Structure, Strategy and Performance Conference, Graduate School of Business, Indiana University (1975), p. 14.

EXHIBIT 2.7   **Financial Profile of Five High Performance Retailers**

COMPANY	STRATEGIC THRUST	STRATEGIC PROFIT MODEL RATIOS (1979)					LIQUIDITY	COMPOUND ANNUAL GROWTH RATES (75/76 to 79/80)	
		Net Profits to Net Sales	Net Sales to Total Assets	Net Profits to Total Assets	Total Assets to Net Worth	Net Profits to Net Worth	Current Assets to Current Liabilities	Net Sales	Net Profits
Toys 'R' Us	Supermarket retailing	5.6%	2.1×	11.6%	1.9×	22.1%	2.0×	21.7%	29.7%
Avon Products, Inc.	Nonstore retailing	10.5	1.7	17.8	1.6	29.2	2.1	15.5	13.0
Scotty's, Inc.	Market intensification	4.3	2.6	11.0	1.8	19.9	2.4	30.6	53.6
Brooks Fashion Stores, Inc.	Store positioning	8.7	2.1	18.3	1.4	26.1	2.6	26.4	29.1
Melville Corporation	Retail diversification	5.0	2.6	13.1	1.8	24.0	2.6	22.2	23.0

Source: Corporate annual reports.

Avon Products, Inc.   Avon is the premiere **nonstore retailer** in the world. Nonstore retailing is not a new strategy; Avon has been engaged in it since 1886, and both Sears and Ward's have pursued nonstore retailing through their catalog operations for decades. Nonetheless, in the 1970s nonstore retailing began to reemerge as a major competitive force in American retailing. As consumers become more pressed for time and disenchanted with shopping itself, nonstore retailing or direct marketing can be expected to become more prevalent.

Avon primarily markets 700 beauty products to 80 million customers through an extensive network of 1.2 million independent representatives in thirty countries. The independent representatives sell the products door-to-door with the aid of a catalog and samples. Avon also owns two nonstore retailing subsidiaries. Avon Fashions sells apparel by mail order and Geni markets tableware and sewing ware by the party-plan method.

The preceding brief discussion suggests that Avon is increasingly becoming a major competitive force in the nonstore arena. This is evidenced by glancing at their strategic profit model ratios in Exhibit 2.7. Avon has a healthy 10.5 percent profit margin and an asset turnover of 1.7 times, which combine to create a 17.8 percent return on assets. The use of debt by Avon is minimal, as evidenced by their financial leverage of 1.6 times. The profit margin, rate of asset turnover, and financial leverage when multiplied together yield a 29.2 percent return on net worth for Avon. In addition, Avon maintains a sound liquidity position, illustrated by their current ratio of 2.1 times.

Scotty's, Inc.   Scotty's, a home improvement chain operating almost exclusively in Florida, has as its major thrust **market intensification**. Specifically, Scotty's restricts its expansion efforts to a limited number of core markets rather than expanding erratically into geographically distant markets. Almost without exception, market concentration retailers have performed better than their national counterparts.

Some very important advantages accrue to firms following a policy of contained expansion. These include advertising economies arising from having multiple outlets in a single market, maximum utilization of a small number of distribution centers, high levels of customer awareness, and fast access to top management to prevent or resolve operating problems at the store level. For instance, "[Scotty's] underlying strategy . . . is to locate new retail stores where they can immediately take advantage of an established reputation, a comprehensive advertising 'umbrella' coverage, and the already efficient product supply support from the company's central warehouse and distribution center."[10]

Market intensification results in strategic, administrative, and operating advantages that can dramatically affect profitability. The financial profile of Scotty's that is provided in Exhibit 2.7 demonstrates this. Scotty's has achieved a return on net worth of almost 20 percent, has maintained excellent liquidity, and has increased sales and profits at over 30 percent per year.

Brooks Fashion Stores, Inc.   Brooks Fashion pursues a strong **store positioning** strategy. In store positioning one identifies a well-defined market segment according to demo-

10. Scotty's, Inc., *1980 Annual Report*, p.4.

By concentrating its outlets in a given market, Scotty's is able to utilize its distribution centers profitably. (Photo courtesy of Scotty's, Inc.)

graphic or lifestyle variables and subsequently appeals to this segment with a clearly differentiated approach. For example, Brooks Fashion has as its target market segment the fashion-conscious female in the eighteen-to-thirty age group who purchases apparel in the medium price range. Thus, their position is clearly in between stores offering high-fashion items at higher prices and stores concentrating on the less fashionable, lower-priced items. Brooks locates in shopping malls and uses a "forward fashion" look to attract customers into its stores with current styles and appealing merchandise that is attractively displayed.

In a highly competitive and overstored market, store positioning offers an avenue for achieving high performance results. The financial profile of Brooks Fashion Stores, Inc., in Exhibit 2.7 helps to reinforce this point. Brooks achieves a return on net worth in excess of 25 percent with only a modest use of debt. At the same time Brooks has excellent liquidity and has experienced compound average growth rates in sales and profits in the 26 to 29 percent range.

Melville Corporation   The strategy that the Melville Corporation pursues is **retail diversification.** In the late 1970s, this $2 billion retailer operated:

- 1,585 promotional footwear departments in all United States K-marts, supplying value-conscious consumers with complete assortments of footwear for the entire family
- 1,210 popular priced Thom McAn specialty shoe stores, selling men's, women's, and children's footwear (Melville also distributes the Thom McAn brand through 2,200 dealers)
- 69 Marshall's promotional stores, selling quality brand name apparel for men, women, and children consisting of postseason items, overruns, and close-outs
- 384 CVS health and beauty aid stores conveniently located, selling a wide range of health care and personal products
- 455 Foxmoor young women's apparel stores, specializing in meeting the needs of students, young marrieds, and career women for fashionable, casual merchandise at moderate prices
- 381 Chess King young men's apparel stores, focusing on the fourteen- to twenty-two-year-old, offering basic and fashion merchandise in depth and variety at moderate prices
- 52 Vanguard men's stores, offering better-grade branded footwear with special appeal to eighteen- to thirty-year-olds
- 7 Open Country stores, providing high-grade branded footwear appealing to the outdoor action–oriented consumer of all ages
- 14 Melville Footwear Manufacturing plants, producing popular priced men's, women's, and children's footwear, principally for Melville retail divisions
- Metro Pants, manufacturing and marketing popular priced men's and young men's pants and jeans sold to major department stores and specialty chain stores

The problems of managing multiple retail businesses are complex, although as consumer markets become more diverse, a growing number of retailers will probably diversify their operations, despite the managerial problems and risks involved. The performance of the Melville Corporation indicates that retailers can be successful with a well-executed retail diversification strategy. For example, Melville has achieved a profit margin of 5 percent and an asset turnover of 2.6 times, which resulted in a return on assets of 13.1 percent. Melville has limited its use of debt, as indicated by its financial leverage of 1.8 times, and has achieved a return on net worth of 24 percent. Melville has substantial liquidity and has experienced increases in sales and profits of 22 to 23 percent per year (see Exhibit 2.7).

RETAIL PLANNING PERSONALITIES

A retailer's **planning personality** is the way it views future time and the need to plan for it. In retailing there tend to be four rather distinct planning personalities: (1) the discounter, (2) the extrapolator, (3) the goal setter, and (4) the cyberneticist.

A small retail operation may only have one person responsible for planning (i.e., the store owner) and thus one planning personality will project itself. A large retail chain, however, may have an entire staff of corporate planners. It is possible, therefore, that all four planning personalities would be projected in the planning process. This, however, may not be as likely as you would expect, because firms tend to hire planners that fit the personality mold they are most comfortable with. As we review these four planning personalities, try to identify the one that best describes your orientation toward the future.

The Discounter   The **discounter** has little faith in planning. He or she believes that the future is terribly uncertain and, therefore, that attempts to plan beyond the foreseeable future are futile. The concern is with the immediate, the seeable. Planning is for next week's promotions or, at the extreme, for merchandise that needs to be purchased next season. In no way does this individual plan for two, five, or ten years into the future. The more distant events are in the future, the more this planner discounts them in the present. Essentially, the philosophy espoused is: "Why worry about the long-run if we can't make it through the short-run?"

Why does the discounter pay relatively little attention to the distant future? Quite frequently it is because previous attempts at gauging the market have failed. Perhaps, even in planning for next season, this individual may have often misgauged the market and, therefore, feels strongly that assessing the retail environment five years hence would be next to impossible. Or, perhaps, once an attempt was made to assess the retail environment over the long run and events did not occur as envisioned.

The discounter has rationalized that uncertainty rules out planning. However, nothing could be further removed from the truth. If there were certainty, planning would not be needed. That is, if the retailer knew everything that was going to happen, then its course of action would be obvious; it would logically fit into a world of certainty. But with uncertainty, the retailer must plot its own course of action and consequently planning becomes more of a necessity. The more the uncertainty, the greater the need for planning, not vice versa. An uncertain future does not justify the discounting of it.

A retailer will not be able to achieve high performance results over the long run if it continually discounts the future. The retailer must create its own future.

The Extrapolator

The **extrapolator** is the manager who views the future as an extrapolation of the past. This retail planner has an engineering orientation and feels that the systematic analysis of historical data will allow the retailer to plan successfully. In the 1950s and 1960s extrapolators were quite successful in planning. The reason was that retail sales and the economy in general were moving on a fairly predictable growth curve. But in the 1970s, this approach to planning produced disquieting results. The basic historical relationships had changed: inflation rose dramatically, consumer life styles changed, energy prices exploded, and peacetime federal budgets had record-setting deficits. Whenever basic historical relationships change, the extrapolation approach to planning meets with failure. Retail planners need to take into account historical patterns, but they should not become mere extrapolators of historical patterns and trends.

The Goal Setter

The **goal setter** is a visionary. This person establishes a goal in the distant future and devotes all of his energy to achieving that goal. Often the goals set by goal setters are unrealistic. The goal setter, in most part, ignores the reality of the past or present. Strengths and weaknesses do not matter. What matters is the desire to achieve the goal. Many notable historical figures were goal setters, such as Henry Ford, John D. Rockefeller, Richard D. Nixon, and Vince Lombardi. Any of these individuals, if they had sat down and systematically analyzed their past and present and the future, would not have tried to accomplish what they ended up accomplishing. But they did not systematically analyze the past, present, and future; rather, they focused efforts totally on their visionary goal(s).

Retailers that are pure goal setters tend to be extremely successful or to fail. There is a tendency to recognize only the goal setters that succeed, but most goal setters fail. They often fail because they ignore the downside risks of what they are attempting to accomplish. The probability of success is so slim and that of failure so great that a strict goal-setting philosophy toward retail planning is not wise.

The Cyberneticist

The type of planning orientation that is most appropriate for retailers is the cyberneticist orientation. A **cyberneticist** is a systems thinker. This individual is oriented not only to all departments and functions within the firm but also to all external forces the retailer faces. Furthermore, this person can see the linkage between occurrences external to the firm and internal affairs.

In essence, the cyberneticist is a composite of the three preceding planning personalities. He or she recognizes (1) the uncertainty of the future (as does the discounter), (2) the historical path the retail enterprise has taken (as does the extrapolator), and (3) the goals it would like to achieve in the future (as does the goal setter). Also, the cyberneticist carefully analyzes the retailer's strengths and weaknesses and those of its competitors. In addition, he or she systematically assesses how the future might be different than the past. The cyberneticist combines all of this information to establish goals and develop plans for accomplishing them. As such, the retail plans, if successfully carried through, can be expected to yield an acceptable or attractive payoff on risks taken. The great majority of high performance retailers adopt a cyberneticist planning orientation.

Comment   Although four planning personalities have been delineated, do not feel that you must nicely categorize yourself into one of them. The categories are not rigid abstractions. Depending on the situation in which you find yourself, you might move from one personality type to another. Pure extrapolation may work for short-term labor scheduling, but for planning long-term store strategies, the cyberneticist orientation would be more appropriate. The key is to be flexible and adaptive to the task of planning.

SUMMARY

Planning and the financial performance of the retailer are intertwined. High performance results do not just happen; they are engineered through careful strategic, administrative, and operations planning: deciding in the present what to do in the future. Not all retailers can achieve high performance results, but the ones that do will be the ones that did best job at planning. The future of a retail enterprise, in large part, is determined by the quality of its planning.

In retailing, three types of planning are necessary. Strategic planning consists of matching the retailer's mission and goals with available opportunities. Administrative planning involves planning for the acquisition of resources that will be necessary to carry out the retailer's strategy successfully. And operations planning consists of planning the efficient use of available resources in order to manage the day-to-day operations of the firm successfully. When the retailer succeeds at these three types of planning, it will achieve high performance results.

High performance retailers can be distinguished by their profit, liquidity, and growth records. Rather than simply looking at a retailer's profits, a more accurate view of a retailer's success is derived by multiplying the retailer's profit margin by its asset turnover to arrive at return on assets. This number is then multiplied by the retailer's financial leverage to arrive at return on net worth. Liquidity represents the firm's ability to meet its current payment obligations. Three liquidity ratios should be monitored in retailing: the current ratio, the quick ratio, and the acid-test ratio. Finally, there are growth requirements in retailing. A high performance retailer should be capable of increasing its sales at 1.5 times the industry average.

Retailers tend to have one of four planning personalities. Discounters believe that the future is too uncertain to warrant planning; extrapolators believe the future can be planned by extrapolating from historical trends; goal setters focus exclusively on desired goals and ignore the reality of their strengths and weaknesses in the present. Last are the cyberneticists, who are the systems thinkers and are both internally and externally oriented. Cyberneticists consider past trends, present strengths and weaknesses, the uncertainty inherent in planning for the future, and desired goals. In short, they are a composite of the three preceding planning personalities.

QUESTIONS

1. Identify measures of financial performance, in addition to those mentioned in this chapter, that could be used to gauge a retailer's financial performance.

2. Return on assets is a better measure than return on net worth for assessing a retailer's financial performance. Agree or disagree and explain why.

3. Rank the four planning personalities in terms of the most desirable to least desirable. Defend your ranking.

4. Is planning in a high inflation environment more or less difficult for a retailer than planning in a low inflation environment? Why?

5. In today's economic and competitive environment what standards are necessary to achieve the distinction of being a high performance retailer.

6. Define the concept of planning. Would planning by a manufacturer differ from planning by a retailer?

7. What is strategic fit? How does a retailer know when a strategic fit has occurred?

8. Do you agree with the planning premises for the 1980s outlined in this chapter? Explain your answer.

9. Which financial performance criteria in retailing are most important: (a) profitability, (b) liquidity, or (c) growth? Why?

10. What types of planning would you expect each of the following to be involved in: (a) the president of a $100 million retail chain, (b) an assistant store manager, (c) the director of personnel for a local chain of four supermarkets? Defend your answer.

PROBLEMS AND EXERCISES

1. Obtain data on the most recent financial performance of the retailers identified in this chapter as high performance retailers. Are they still high performance retailers? If not, why have they lost this distinction?

2. A major retail chain is undergoing an executive search to find a director of corporate planning. Write a job description for this position.

3. For the following hypothetical retailer, compute these financial ratios: current ratio, asset turnover, return on assets, profit margin, return on net worth, financial leverage, and acid-test ratio.

Annual Net Sales	$614,321
Total Assets	203,340
Net Profits (after taxes)	21,398
Net Worth	77,601
Cash	3,442
Current Liabilities	75,345
Current Assets	115,419

4. Compare the financial performance of the following two retailers, which are in the same line of retail trade. Which is the better performer? Why?

Measure	Retailer-1	Retailer-2
Annual Net Sales	$748,000	$1,031,000
Cash on Hand	$ 4,500	$ 15,200
Net Profit (after taxes)	$ 15,000	$ 31,000
Current Ratio	1.8×	2.1×
Financial Leverage	2.4×	1.8×
Return on Assets (after taxes)	7.0%	9.0%
5-year compound annual growth in net sales	18.4%	7.3%
5-year compound annual growth in net profit (after taxes)	15.0%	8.1%
Earnings per share	$ .92	$1.18
Dividends per share	$ .24	$ .80

5. Interview the manager of a local supermarket or apparel store to determine his or her philosophy on planning. Would you categorize the manager as a discounter, extrapolator, goal setter, or cyberneticist? Be sure to have a good idea of the questions you will ask during the interview before you make your visit.

3

Overview   *The purpose of this chapter is to illustrate the role of information in planning and management. Information will be shown to play a role in all types of retail planning and management. In fact, we will see that information is a pervasive force in retail decision making.*

The Retail Information System

A DOMINANT THEME of this book is retail decision making to achieve high performance results. Throughout the book we will show that the best formula for achieving high performance results contains two components—(a) analytical decision frameworks and skills, and (b) methods of creative problem solving. Unless, however, the retail decision maker has relevant information, his or her bag of analytical frameworks and skills and creative problem-solving orientations will be worthless. Thus it is appropriate, at this point, to focus our attention on the retail information system (RIS).

INTRODUCING THE RIS

An RIS could consist of a store owner's regularly reading a retail trade association magazine, talking to customers to determine how satisfied they are with the merchandise and services of the retailer, and regularly studying the store's quarterly income statement and balance sheet. We, however, do not wish to define an RIS in terms of what it *might be* in a typical retail enterprise, but in terms of what it *should be* in a model retail enterprise; that is, we want to give a normative definition. Thus, the **retail information system** (RIS) will be defined as a blueprint for the continual and periodic systematic collection, analysis, and reporting of relevant data about any past, present, or future developments that could or already have influenced the retailer's performance.

Several prominent features of the RIS, as defined, should be highlighted:

1. Both *continual* and *periodic* collection of relevant data should occur. Data should be continually collected on those activities that are always in a state of flux such as the retailer's financial performance or competitor behavior. Data should be periodically collected when a nonrecurring problem arises, such as a capital budgeting or inventory productivity problem.
2. The data collection activities should be *systematic*. The world is drowning in data. Retailers must decide what information they need and collect only that information in an orderly fashion.
3. *Analysis* and *reporting* of data are important parts of the RIS. The data cannot merely be dumped on the executive's desk. To be useful, they must be analyzed and put in a reportable format. You cannot give a retail executive a computer tape with 300,000 bits of data and tell her that here is the information requested. It is not information until it is analyzed and placed in a reportable format that the executive can understand.
4. The data can be about the *past*, *present*, and *future*, all of which can be relevant for retail decision making. Most accounting information is historical: it tells where the retailer has been. However, point of sale (POS) terminals provide data on what is happening now (present), and six-month monetary projections by the Federal Reserve System tell what will likely happen to interest rates in the future.

You should observe that this definition of the RIS is an ideal, but it is worth striving for.

In this chapter we elaborate on what an ideal RIS should look like. We will not, however, discuss the many procedures for the systematic collection and analysis of data. These topics are best covered in many of the fine books on marketing research.[1]

The Need for Information   Chapters that follow this one will explicitly and implicitly demonstrate that the need for information in the management of a retail enterprise is pervasive. This fact can also be made clear by referring to our retail planning and management model in Exhibit 3.1. In this model you should note that a web of information envelops strategic, administrative, and operations planning and management.

Assume you are the general manager of a local chain of three women's apparel stores. You need to develop a new strategy. Could you develop it without information? Perhaps, but you could develop a better strategy by obtaining information on your competitors, consumers in your trade areas, the local economic climate, recent technological developments in retailing, and so on. Now place yourself in other decision-making roles—needing to adjust prices, reevaluate your consumer credit policy, or borrow additional capital. Making any of these decisions without information would be unwise. In short, whatever retail decisions need to be made, they can be better made with information.

The Amount of Information   Decision making in retailing can be improved with more information. Unfortunately, however, retail executives cannot make decisions with complete information. Complete or perfect information would be extremely expensive or even impossible to obtain. The expense would not only be in terms of direct dollar outlay for the information but also in the time needed to gather and analyze it. This extended period of time can represent an opportunity cost of postponing a decision. For example, if you own and operate a restaurant and you want to open a second restaurant in the same city, you may decide to gather data on the best location. The longer you take to gather the information on the best possible site, the longer you will put off opening a potentially profitable restaurant. If you wait too long, your competition may open another restaurant or restaurants, which could saturate the market and lower the likelihood that your new restaurant will be profitable.

The Scope of the RIS   A retail information system should have a broad scope. Exhibit 3.2 (see page 50) shows a model RIS. You can see that an RIS should have two major operating components or subsystems. One subsystem should be directed at the identification of problems or potential problems confronting the retail enterprise. This subsystem should be designed to compile information continuously on constantly changing events affecting the retail enterprise. The other subsystem should be dedicated to the solution of problems that the retailer faces. Generally, this subsystem would be used to compile information to help solve both recurring and nonrecurring problems.

1. See, for example, Gilbert A. Churchill, Jr., *Marketing Research: Methodological Foundations* (Hinsdale, Ill: Dryden Press, 1979); or Keith K. Cox and Ben M. Enis, *The Marketing Research Process* (Pacific Palisades, Calif.: Goodyear, 1972).

EXHIBIT 3.1   **The Retail Planning and Management Model**

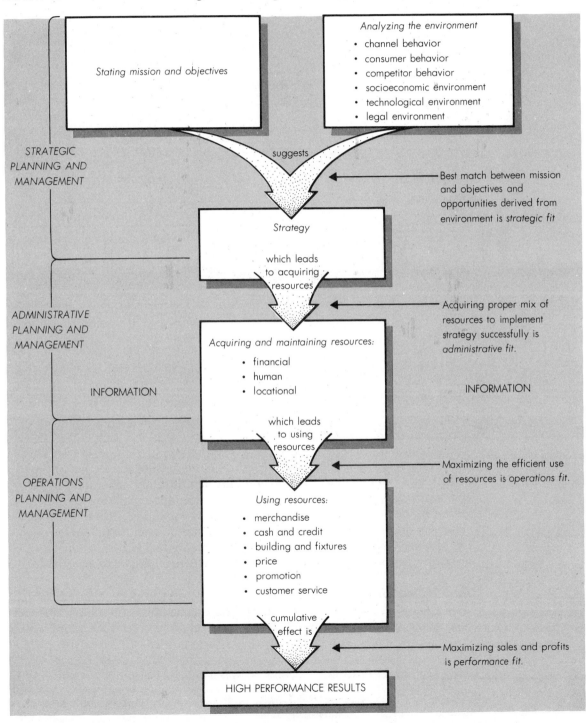

EXHIBIT 3.2   **The Retail Information System**

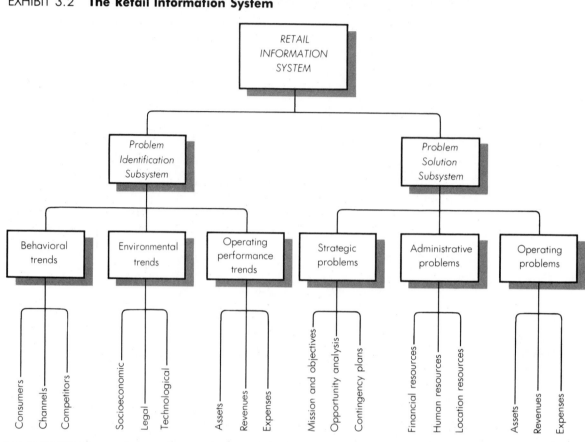

The Problem Identification Subsystem   A more detailed inspection of the RIS in Exhibit 3.2 will show that the **problem identification subsystem** monitors and scans trends in behavioral, environmental, and operating performance areas.[2] In the behavioral area, three patterns are monitored: that of consumers, channels, and competitors. In the environmental domain, three environments are scanned: legal, socioeconomic, and technological. Finally, in the area of operating performance, asset, revenue, and expense trends are monitored.

The Problem Solution Subsystem   A more careful inspection of Exhibit 3.2 shows that the **problem-solving subsystem** can be utilized to obtain information[3] on several areas, all of which represent either recurring or nonrecurring

2. For a useful introduction for some of the material to follow, see M. S. Moyer, "Market Intelligence for Modern Retailers," *California Managment Review* 14(Summer 1972): 63–69.

3. Most frequently this information is obtained via research. See Doreen Mangar, "Marketing Research New Retail Sales Tool," *Stores* May 1979, pp. 37–40; or Frank Moyons, "Research in Retailing," *Retail Control,* May 1966, pp. 33–44.

problems in the retail enterprise. The major problem areas coincide with the areas of strategic, administrative, and operations management and planning. Strategic problems relate to mission, goals, and objectives; opportunity analysis; or contingency planning. Administrative problems involve capital structure and generation, organization structure and human resources, or location analysis. Operating problems will either be related to assets or involve revenue or expense management.

In this chapter we will discuss each component of the model RIS, allowing you to obtain a fairly broad and general understanding of the information requirements of retail decision makers.

THE PROBLEM IDENTIFICATION SUBSYSTEM

We begin our discussion of the model retail information system by focusing on the problem identification subsystem. The central goal of this subsystem is to highlight for the retail executive, on a continuing basis, the major problems that the retailer is about to encounter or is presently encountering.

Monitoring Consumers Most retailers will scan the behavior of their customers in a casual manner. The smallest retailers may simply listen to customer complaints or

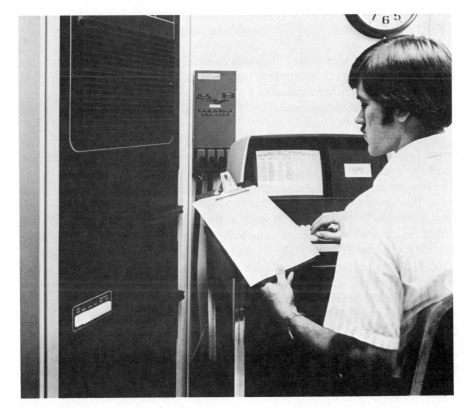

Computerized retail information systems are becoming increasingly popular among large-scale retailers. (Photo courtesy of Fed Mart.)

casually converse with regular customers about their needs, wants, and level of satisfaction. This can be quite cost-effective for the small, single-outlet retailer. More formal methods of collecting information on customer behavior, though they may provide a better monitor, may not be worth the cost.[4]

The larger the retail enterprise, the more likely it is to benefit from a formal and continuous monitoring of consumer behavior trends. This is because as the retail enterprise grows, the retail decision makers become increasingly removed from regular face-to-face contact with the consumer. Thus, the decision maker cannot obtain a casual or subjective appreciation for changes the consumer is experiencing.

If the retailer decides that a continual monitoring of consumer behavior patterns would be valuable—and this author believes it would be for most large-scale retail enterprises—then regular data collection is needed on three crucial consumer behavior variables: purchase probabilities, attitudes, and customer satisfaction.

Purchase Probabilities   Information on **purchase probabilities** (how likely a consumer is to purchase a particular product within the next six months) will allow the retailer to keep appraised of the products it should stock and promote. For instance, a home improvement center may discover by collecting purchase probability information that there has been a significant increase in the number of households planning to add a patio deck. Armed with this information, the retail executive can develop special promotions and merchandising programs to attract these households to his store.

Consumer Attitudes   Consumer attitudes toward the retailer's store and operation can be a significant determinant of patronage behavior. Changing attitudes can help forewarn the retailer of problems on the horizon. In Chapter 5, we will discuss an attitude model that retailers can use to monitor their performance.

Customer Satisfaction   Information on customer satisfaction with both the retailer and the merchandise it sells will indicate whether the customer's visit to the store was rewarding (a good experience) or unsatisfying (a bad experience). If there is dissatisfaction with both the retailer and its merchandise then the customer is less likely to choose that store in the future, decreasing sales. Many restaurants and motels ask their patrons to fill out a brief questionnaire on how satisfied they were with their visit or meal. Also, many auto dealers and furniture retailers send recent customers a letter encouraging them to call or write if they are dissatisfied with their recent purchase. In both situations, the respective retailers are able to obtain information on customer satisfaction at a relatively low cost and take corrective actions if dissatisfaction is seen to be rising.

4. A low cost method for obtaining information on consumer trends is to actively read articles in retail trade related publications, such as Stanley J. Winkelman, "Understanding Today's Consumer." in R. Patrick Cash (ed.), *The Buyer's Manual* (New York: National Retail Merchants Association, 1979), pp. 483–94.

Additional Information In principle, there would be nothing, except for cost, preventing the retailer from collecting information on other aspects of consumer behavior. However, top priority should be given to continual collection of data on the three variables discussed. Chapter 5 will help you identify other areas that may be worth investigating.

Monitoring the Marketing Channel

The retailer is part of a larger marketing channel system, which few can totally control. Most retailers must adapt to the behavior of other organizations in the channel. Therefore, the behavior of channel members should be monitored.

In Chapter 4 we will illustrate some of the intricacies of adapting to the marketing channel. Here, let us focus on obtaining information on alternative merchandise supply sources, alternative facilitating agencies, financial performance of channel partners, and channel conflicts.

Merchandise Supply Sources If a retailer becomes too dependent on a few sources of merchandise then its ability to bargain and negotiate with the suppliers will be hampered. The suppliers may even try to dictate how the retailer should conduct business. The best way to avoid this unfortunate circumstance is to be continually aware of alternative supply sources. Even if a retailer has found that Supplier X always has the best merchandise for the lowest price, it should not become complacent and stop looking for a better deal.

High priority should be placed on designing an ongoing system of information collection to alert the retailer to the best deals. For instance, many supermarkets constantly evaluate their present wholesale sources of supply against alternative sources. This helps them assess the terms of their present suppliers. Also, present suppliers will be more cooperative if they know the retailer is always keeping abreast of the terms being offered by their competitors.

Facilitating Agencies Most retailers rely on a number of facilitating agencies (banks, ad agencies, brokers, insurance firms, etc.) to assist them. Just as the retailer should monitor alternative merchandise supply sources, it should also monitor the availability and strengths and weaknesses of alternative facilitating agencies. Are there public warehouses or advertising agencies that can do a better job at a more competitive price? The retailer should have access to information that can help answer such basic questions.

Financial Performance of Channel Partners As much information as possible should be obtained about the financial performance of channel partners. What is happening to their profit margins, inventory turnover, credit policy, cash flow, labor productivity, sales growth? Whenever any member of a marketing channel begins to have financial problems, it will start to squeeze its channel partners (for instance, attempting to cut credit terms, increase minimum order quantity size, or raise prices) to increase its performance at the expense of the retailer. By monitoring channel member performance, the retailer can have counter-moves developed to minimize any unfair pressure the poorly performing supplier may try to exert. This is not to suggest that a retailer should not help a supplier in need, but that a retailer should not allow a supplier to take unfair advantage of it.

Retailers may be able to obtain more information about suppliers than they may realize. Most large suppliers are publicly held corporations, and therefore any stockholder of record can receive annual and quarterly financial statements. Also, any publicly held corporation must file detailed financial statements with the Securities and Exchange Commission in the form of a 10-K report, which is public record and available, through the SEC or directly from the reporting company, to any stockholder. The 10-K has a wealth of financial information that is typically not provided in the standard annual report to stockholders. A retailer that is not a stockholder in the supplier can get this information too. Disclosure, Inc., is a company based in Dallas that will provide, at a modest cost, a copy of any corporation's 10-K or annual report. Investors Management Service, based in Denver, can provide similar data, on computer tape, on over 5,000 publicly held companies in the United States.

Channel Conflict   A final area of channel behavior that should be monitored is the level of conflict. For every significant channel interface, the retailer should identify any sources of conflict. Specifically, it must be able regularly to answer such questions as: To what extent do the channel partners have goals that are not compatible with mine? To what extent does each channel partner try to unduly control various aspects of my business? To what extent do channel partners perceive significant events in the economic, social, legal, and technological environments differently than I do? It is better to know of potential conflict than to learn after the conflict has become manifest and more difficult to resolve.

Monitoring Competitors

Almost any retailer will tell you that it is more interested in what its competitors are doing than in how channel partners or consumers are behaving, but all three behaviors are equally important.

All retailers, small or large, have some means of monitoring competitors' activities. At the simplest level, this may consist of reading or listening to competitors' ads and shopping their stores personally to inspect merchandise, prices, displays, and store decor. More sophisticated monitoring may involve systematic collection and analysis of data on all relevant aspects of competitor behavior, including market saturation, pricing, merchandise mixes, promotion, market shares, and trade areas.

Market Saturation   The extent to which a particular market area, typically a town or city, is overpopulated with retailers in a particular line of trade is **market saturation.** The best measure of market saturation, because data are readily available, is square feet of store space (F) in a particular line of retail trade for a particular market area, divided by the population (POP) of the market area. When F/POP is high, the market is saturated with retail space and competitors compete more aggressively for consumer expenditures. When

F/POP is relatively low, just the opposite is true. Not surprisingly, therefore, *F/POP* is a good predictor of potential profits in a particular market area. The lower *F/POP* is, the greater the profit potential. On the other hand, high *F/POP* forewarns of profit problems.

Pricing The retailer should determine a bundle of goods on which it desires to be most competitive. For example, a grocery store may identify 135 items out of the 4,200 it stocks that it wants to be visibly price competitive on. Once the bundle has been established, the retailer should compute price indices that show its price for each item compared to the price each of its major competitors is charging. These indices should be constructed regularly—probably weekly or monthly. When analyzed on a longitudinal basis, trends in these price indices will vividly demonstrate the extent to which the retailer is continuing to be price competitive.

Merchandise Mixes How strong is the retailer's assortment of merchandise in relation to key competitors? Is it deeper, wider, and of a lower or higher quality? How has this changed over time? In short, is the retailer's assortment of merchandise competitive? Only ongoing data collection can provide a meaningful answer to this important question. Therefore, the retailer must systematically and regularly send out employees to shop competing retailers to provde he needed answers.

Promotion There are two fundamental questions the retailer will want its information system to answer regarding competitor's promotional efforts. First, how much are competitors spending on promotion in relation to it? Second, what is the quality of competitors' promotional activities?

Neither question is easily or cheaply answered. A detailed analysis would be needed of competitors' advertising, sales promotion activities, publicity efforts, and personal selling. Because such a task would be a burden, most retailers may decide to collect data on a regular basis on only competitor's advertising, and in some cases, on their sales promotion activities. For example, many apparel retailers will develop an ongoing file of competitors' newspaper advertising. Everyday ads of competitors are clipped and placed in this file and then once a month the intensity and quality of competitors' advertising will be analyzed. This simple process will allow the retailer to spot any significant deterioration in its advertising in relation to competitors.

Market Share What are the respective market shares of the retailer and its competitors, and how are these changing? The best indicator of future profit performance is market share. In most lines of retail trade, the firm with the dominant market share tends to be the dominant profit producer. If a retailer observes its market share slipping then it should be forewarned of profitability problems.

Retailers that sell a wide range of merchandise will ideally want to obtain market share data by merchandise line. Rather than only comparing competitors' market shares as a whole, a department store manager may find it most useful to have market share data on particular departments: household furnishings, menswear, women's apparel, children's clothes, sporting goods, jewelry, toys, and lawn and garden equipment. However, the collection of such information may be extremely expensive and therefore may not be worth the cost.

Trade Area   Is the trading area of the retailer (i.e., the geographic area from which its patrons come) stable, shrinking, or expanding? A shrinking trade area is a bad omen; an expanding one is good. Many of the previously discussed items—market saturation, competitive pricing, competitive merchandise assortments, and competitive promotional strength—will affect trade area size. The less competitive the retailer's pricing, merchandise assortment, and promotion, the more its trade area will shrink. Again, the more saturated the market, the more the trade area will shrink.

It is relatively easy to obtain information on trade area. If one has the addresses of the store patrons, one can easily construct a trade area map. One owner-manager of a record store continually held contests in which patrons of the store would fill out entry blanks with their names and addresses to qualify for a weekly drawing of a free album. Each month the color of the entry blanks would change. Therefore, at the end of each month, the owner could go back and plot on a map where patrons came from, enabling him to observe quickly any change in the size or nature of his trading area by comparing one month's map to the previous month's.

Monitoring the Socioeconomic Environment   Events in the socioeconomic environment that should be monitored can be categorized into demographic, psychographic, and economic trends. These trends will be discussed in detail in Chapter 7.

Major demographic trends that may be particularly useful to monitor are changing household size, educational levels, age distribution of household members, population growth, and geographic migration. Psychographic trends that may be particularly insightful are changes in leisure-time activities, work habits, and religious, family and cultural values. Economic trends that should be followed are changes in disposable personal income, in household expenditure patterns, in discretionary income, and in the use of credit.

If the retailer desires highly personalized continuing data on demographic, psychographic, and economic trends in its trade area, the price will not be cheap. National data tells the retailer little about the socioeconomic dynamics of its trade area, but some secondary data on its area may be available. Many local newspapers in large cities conduct regular surveys of the geographic area of their readership, and this geographic area may closely approximate the retailer's trade area, especially if the retailer sells shopping goods. These surveys collect data on a large number of demographic, economic, and in some cases psychographic variables. If the retailer advertises in the newspaper conducting the survey, much of the data can be obtained free or at modest cost.

The U.S. Census Bureau can also provide a wealth of deomographic data on census tracks. However, this data is collected only every ten years and therefore becomes quickly dated. Occasionally, local governments will conduct special surveys to obtain current demographic data.

Monitoring the Legal Environment In Chapter 8 we will study the legal environment of retailing. Although a disquieting fact to most retailers, the legal environment is always in a state of flux. To avoid costly legal errors, the retailer should design its RIS to keep it alerted of changes in that environment. In fact, the larger the retail enterprise, the higher priority this area should receive.

No retail manager or store owner can be expected to monitor all the relevant changes in the legal environment. Fortunately, all the major retail trade publications devote a fair amount of space to the retail implications of pending legislation. Many large retail enterprises may even have a legal staff to keep top management aware of changes in the legal environment. Sears, J. C. Penney, and McDonald's all have sizeable legal staffs.

Probably the legal area of most immediate practical concern to the retailer is tax law. Changes in tax laws will generally have a significant effect on most major retail decisions. For example, a favorable change in the investment tax credit can make store remodeling or expansion an attractive plan. Or a change in an energy tax credit for buildings with energy saving equipment can influence how a retailer may construct a new store building. Tax laws can influence other decisions such as inventory valuation methods, executive compensation plans, or recording of credit sales. As a result, retailers need to monitor tax legislation continually.

Retail corporations that are publicly held should also stay informed of the regulations of the Securities and Exchange Commission (SEC) and the accounting standards established by the Financial Accounting Standards Board (FASB). All publicly held retailers must abide by the SEC guidelines in reporting to stockholders. The FASB develops generally accepted accounting principles (GAAP), which are not legal requirements. However, a retailer that wants its financial statements to receive an unqualified opinion by a certified external auditor will follow the GAAP.

Monitoring the Technological Environment Technology, as we will see in Chapter 7, is the application of science in order to develop new methods of doing things. It is always at work slowly but continually to change the nature and scope of retailing.

The retailer can monitor the technological environment at two stages: the basic science stage or the applied science stage. In either case, the retailer will want to monitor technology as related to four areas of innovation: management techniques, merchandising techniques, equipment and fixtures, and construction and building.

A retailer desiring to monitor any of the four areas at the basic science stage could read the academic journals in the underlying disciplines. For example, to monitor management and merchandising at the basic science level, the retailer might read such journals as the *Journal of Finance, Journal of Retailing, Journal of Marketing,* or *Administrative Science Quarterly.* Unfortunately, most topics and concepts discussed in the academic, business related journals take a long time to get to the applied science stage, because many practical problems of implementation remain to be worked out. Many never get there. For example, the techniques of quantitative capital budgeting and inventory control were discussed in the *Journal of Finance* in the 1950s but are just now beginning to become popular in the actual practice of retail management. Similarly, the use of experimental designs to test the effectiveness of promotional displays was illustrated in the *Journal of Marketing Research* in the 1960s but still has not received widespread acceptance by retailers.

Utilizing a similar approach, the retail manager could read the academically oriented publications in engineering, computer science, and architecture to obtain a glimpse of future technology in equipment and buildings. But again, the lead time between the basic science stage and the application would probably be too great to be of any practical value.

Generally, it will be more beneficial for the retail executive to monitor technology at the applied level. To do this most effectively, executives should regularly attend industry trade shows and read trade-related journals such as *Stores, Chain Store Age, Progressive Grocer, Advertising Age,* and *Business Week.* All of these publications report on innovations that can be or are being applied to retailing.

Monitoring Assets   The accounting system should be designed to be part of the RIS, since it can be an important vehicle for portraying financial operating performance trends.[5] As such, it can assist the retailer in identifying operating performance problems.

An RIS should have the capability to monitor the retailer's assets continually. At the most basic level the retailer may design the RIS to construct a balance sheet at the end of each operating period (typically a month or a quarter) for assessing the magnitude and composition of its assets. By comparing the current balance sheet to prior ones, the retailer can examine the growth of its asset base and the extent of changes in the composition of its assets. More detailed analysis of period-to-period balance sheets and the general ledgers used to construct them will provide information on the sources and uses of capital. Thus, we see that the balance sheet is a very useful piece of information.

To see the kind of information that can be obtained from year-to-year balance sheets, look at Exhibit 3.3. It shows that John's Western Wear Store increased its total assets from 1980 to 1981 by $11,000. Most of the increase came in current assets—specifically inventory. The balance sheets also show that this asset growth was largely financed by increases in accounts payable, notes payable, and owner's equity.

Performance Standards   Using basic balance sheet data, the retail analyst can compute financial ratios to evaluate the retailer's performance. For example, three such ratios are the liquidity ratios that were introduced in Chapter 2: the current ratio (current assets ÷ current liabilities); the quick ratio (current assets

5. Robert Stevens, "Using Accounting Data to Make Decisions." *Journal of Retailing* 51(Fall 1975): pp. 23–28.

EXHIBIT 3.3   **John's Western Wear Store 1980 and 1981 Balance Sheets**

ASSETS	1980	1981	CHANGE	LIABILITIES AND OWNERS' EQUITY	1980	1981	CHANGE
Cash	$ 5,000	$ 5,000	—	Accounts payable	$ 20,000	$ 25,000	$ 5,000
Accounts receivable	20,000	23,000	$ 3,000	Notes payable	15,000	18,000	3,000
Inventory	40,000	50,000	10,000	Total current liabilities	$ 35,000	$ 43,000	$ 8,000
Total current assets	$ 65,000	$ 78,000	$13,000	Long term liabilities	$ 15,000	$ 13,000	$ (2,000)
Fixed assets	35,000	33,000	(2,000)	Owner's equity	$ 50,000	$ 55,000	$ 5,000
Total assets	$100,000	$111,000	$11,000	Total liabilities and equity	$100,000	$111,000	$11,000

less inventory ÷ current liabilities); and the acid-test ratio (cash ÷ current liabilities). First, the retailer must have some target level for each of these ratios. That is, it must have a goal or desired level of liquidity, which could be based on industry norms. Generally, the goal is not point specific, but reflects a desired range for the financial ratio; for instance, the target current ratio may be between 1.9 and 2.1. Second, the retail analyst must compare actual performance to targeted performance and note any significant deviation from the target. Third, significant deviations from targeted performance should be investigated. This third step takes us into the problem solution subsystem of the RIS.

For a more concrete illustration, see Exhibit 3.4 (page 60), which gives a control chart for the current ratio for Sid's Appliance Center. The dashed lines show that management wants the current ratio to fall between 1.9 and 2.1. Between 1975 and 1979 it falls within this range but in 1980 it falls below 1.9. Thus, in 1980 management needs to investigate the cause of this significant drop in liquidity. A careful investigation of the possible causes might reveal that credit customers have significantly slowed their rate of payment on past installment sales.

The retailer can also use data from the balance sheet, in conjunction with other data it has access to, to construct measures that reflect how well it is utilizing its assets. A handful of these more popular measures are as follows:

1. **Sales per dollar invested in inventory** (total dollar sales ÷ average inventory investment). This is a measure of inventory turnover that shows how productive the retailer's investment in inventory has been. A high rate of turnover is better than a low one if everything else is held constant.
2. **Sales per square feet of selling space** (total dollar sales ÷ square feet of selling space). This is a measure of space productivity. The higher its value, the more productively the retailer is using its selling space.
3. **Sales per dollar invested in assets** (total dollar sales ÷ total dollars invested in assets). This is a basic measure of asset productivity. It shows for each dollar invested how much the retailer has generated in sales. It is a key

EXHIBIT 3.4
**Control Chart
for
Current Ratio
for Sid's**

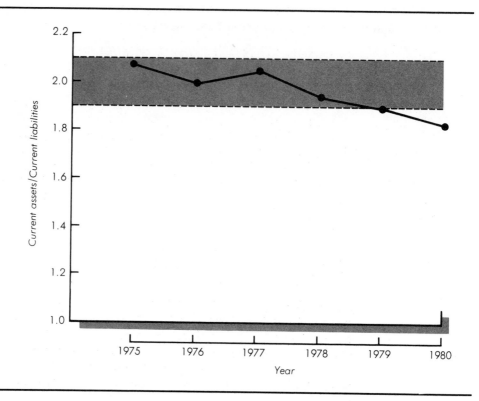

component of the strategic profit model that was introduced earlier in the book.

4. **Credit sales per dollar invested in accounts receivable** (total dollar credit sales ÷ average accounts receivable). This measure shows how quickly retailers are collecting from their customers that purchase on credit. The larger the measure, the better.

For each of the preceding measures, and probably many others, the retailer should develop standards of performance.

Auditing Assets   Imagine yourself as a retail executive making decisions based on accounting information. One thing you would want to be assured of is that you have *valid* information. This would be especially true if you were a top executive for a large chain, since you would not be able to visit each store regularly. Thus you would have to rely totally on accounting data to keep you informed of what was happening at each store. If the numbers on the balance sheet tell you that there is $4 million in inventory on hand, how do you know that this is in fact the case? Unless you chose to go count the inventory yourself you probably don't know.

For these reasons, the retailer should regularly have an independent audit done of its accounting records and system to ensure their validity. In fact, if the retailer is a publicly held corporation, the SEC requires an independent audit of its annual financial statements to its stockholders.

Retailers would also be well advised to implement an ongoing internal audit, to ensure continual protection of its assets. The internal audit department would regularly want to be able to answer questions such as these:

- Are merchandise shipments made only on the basis of approved instructions?
- Are stringent physical controls and paperwork procedures exercised over in-store transfers?
- Are departmental inventory records maintained in total as well as on an individual store basis?
- Are merchandise units that show erratic or unusually high shrinkage results policed on an interim basis?
- Are customer refunds properly approved and controlled?
- Are sales drawers locked and no one afforded access to them while a cashier is on break?
- Does electronic surveillance equipment receive a daily check?
- Are physical inventories of stores' fixtures and equipment taken periodically with differences reported to management?[6]

Naturally, these are only a few of the questions that the internal audit department should be regularly answering. Whatever the case, the internal audit department will have as its job the protection of the retailer's assets so that the accounting records and information derived do indeed reflect reality.

Monitoring Revenues and Expenses By monitoring revenues and expenses, the retailer is able readily to identify any significant gaps in planned profit levels and thus to develop appropriate remedial actions.

Income Statement All of the data that the retailer needs to be kept informed, at a basic level, about revenues and expenses in the retail enterprise can be presented in a detailed income statement. Thus, at the most fundamental level of analysis, the retailer will want to design its RIS to generate regularly a detailed income statement.

Since the magnitude of dollars on a retailer's income statement can change from period to period, it is best to have the income statement constructed in both dollars and percentiles (in which sales are equated to 100 percent). The percentile income statement facilitates the comparison of operating periods over time. Thus, a retail executive can quickly read if advertising, utilities, wages, or any other expense is behaving differently in relation to sales than it has historically.

The percentile income statement will also allow us to apply the standards of performance concept we discussed earlier. A standard income statement can be developed in which each expense is programmed to be a standard percent-

6. These questions are only a few of hundreds of such questions suggested in *A Retailer's Guide to Accounting Controls* (New York: Price Waterhouse, 1979).

age of sales. Percentages on the actual income statement can then be compared to the standard in order to gauge performance and identify any significant problem areas.

Many retail trade associations conduct annual studies of operating results, which show the average operating performance of the retailers that belong to the trade association. These studies can help the retailer develop standards. In Exhibit 3.5, we present a retail trade association's composite operating or income statement.

It is important that the retailer give careful consideration to the frequency with which its RIS generates income statement data. The income statement should be prepared often enough to allow management to take corrective action if an expense is out of control or if revenues are below standard. An annual income statement will not suffice; monthly or bimonthly statements would be much better. If you were a retail manager, you would not want to find out about a problem eight months after it occurred; at that point it may be too late.

EXHIBIT 3.5 **Composite Operating Statement for Floorcovering Retailers**	Net sales (including installation)	100.00%
	Cost of sales (including installation)	68.74
	Gross margin	31.26
	Operating expenses	
	Payroll (including payroll taxes and employee benefits) 15.20%	
	Advertising (less coop) 3.59	
	Samples 0.18	
	Utilities and telephone 1.15	
	Rent or occupancy 3.04	
	Depreciation (trucks, fixtures, and equipment) 0.58	
	Bad debt losses 0.48	
	Interest paid (excluding mortgage interest) 0.36	
	All other 4.69	
	Total operating expenses	29.27
	Operating profits	1.99
	Other income and expenses	
	Other income 0.94	
	Other expenses 0.31	
	Net other income	0.63
	Net profits (before taxes)	2.62
	Net profits (after taxes)	1.74%

Source: Bert C. McCammon, Jr., and Robert F. Lusch, *1977 Operating Results Study, Floorcovering Retailers* (Norman, Okla.: Distribution Research Program, University of Oklahoma, 1978), p. 20. Reprinted with permission of the authors.

Segmental Reporting   In most cases, it will be advantageous for the retailer to develop individual income statements for separate segments of the enterprise. For example, if the retail enterprise consists of a chain of forty-eight drugstores, it would be beneficial to prepare a separate income statement for each drugstore and a composite income statement for all forty-eight. This allows performance problems to be pinpointed more easily.

Segmental reporting can also be implemented at the store level. A chain of home improvement centers may wish to analyze separately the profit performance of its lumber products, lawn and garden products, small tools and appliances, and home decorating and fixtures. Therefore it may construct an income statement for each category, assigning expenses to each.

In the Sears 1981 business plan, the company for the first time in its ninety-four-year history developed precise sales, expense, and profit goals for every sales level right down to each individual store.[7] Many other large chain retailers are also beginning to include segmental reporting and planning as part of their RIS.

Inflation   Because of the rapid inflation of the 1970s and early 1980s, the dollars reported in income statements lost much of their meaning. For example, suppose that as a retailer you notice that your heating bill rose in one year from $79,381 to $90,687. What caused this increase? Were you consuming more energy, or could the increase be due to higher energy costs? A similar argument can be presented for wages, rents, phone service, advertising, and so on. To exercise better control, the manager needs to know not only total dollar expense but also the expense per unit and number of units utilized. When these are multiplied together, total dollar expense for a particular expense category is obtained.

THE PROBLEM SOLUTION SUBSYSTEM

Once the problem identification RIS subsystem has been used to spotlight key problems, the problems must be solved. Frequently, this problem solving requires additional information, and it is the role of the problem solution subsystem to gather that information. There are three broad categories of problems, which parallel the three types of retail planning and management portrayed in the model in Exhibit 3.2—strategic, administrative, and operations. Let us look at some of the major problems that can occur in each of these areas and briefly discuss the types of information needed to solve them.

Strategic Problems   Three strategic problems that can occur are (1) obsolescence of mission or objectives, (2) faltering strategy, and (3) inadequate contingency plans. The retailer can use the RIS to help solve each type of problem.

7. "New Sears Retail Plan Sets Precise Goals for Sales, Costs, Profits at Every Store," *Wall Street Journal*, December 3, 1980, p. 25.

Mission and Objectives   A retailer may have serious strategic problems if its mission and objectives are obsolete. This will usually occur when the retailer's environment and competition changes significantly. For example, most drugstores between 1910 and 1950 could have had a mission of providing their immediate neighborhood (a ten- to twelve-block radius) with their medicinal needs. But such a mission today would be questionable given the advent of the super drugstore with over 20,000 square feet of space capable of merchandising a wide variety of nondrug products.

Alternatively, a retailer's mission may still be appropriate but the objectives may be out of touch with reality. In the 1960s a 10 percent return on equity objective was reasonable. But in the 1980s, with rates of inflation sometimes approaching 20 percent, this goal would be foolish.

The preceding examples suggest that retailers may occasionally need to conduct research on the appropriateness of their mission and objectives. Otherwise, a change in the retailer's mission and objectives might be based only on intuition. The entire planning process begins with the statement of mission and objectives; if they are not appropriate then the entire planning process will suffer. It is, therefore, in the retailer's best interest to spend money and time to collect relevant information before restating its mission and objectives.

Faltering Strategy   The retailer may be comfortable with its mission and objectives but uncomfortable with the ability of its present strategy to fulfill them.[8] Therefore, a detailed search for new strategic opportunities and the analysis of them may be warranted.

By capitalizing on data from the RIS on significant behavioral and environmental trends, the retailer may be able readily to identify several significant opportunities. Once opportunities have been identified, the retailer will need to collect additional information on each to allow each to be thoroughly analyzed and evaluated. Finally, the best of them will be selected for strategic development and implementation.

In Chapter 9, we will discuss a variety of research techniques that are useful for generating and developing retail strategies.

Inadequate Contingency Plans   Perhaps the retailer is satisfied with its mission and objectives and with its current strategy. However, upon analysis of data from the problem identification subsystem of its RIS, it notes considerable turbulence in the social, economic, and legal environments. It begins to question how well it is positioned against negative developments in these environments. In short, this retailer sees that although it is currently very successful, it does not have any contingency plans. The retailer must conduct special research to help formulate such plans.

Administrative Problems   Administrative problems arise in relation to the acquisition and management of the resources the retailer needs to carry out its strategy. In this

---

8. J. L. Schlacter and J. E. Withers. "Analysis of a Retail Firm's Marketing Strategy Through the Use of a 'Return on Investment Model,'" *Retail Control*, December 1973, pp. 2–32.

regard, three types of resources are especially important: financial, human, and locational.

Financial Resources   The problem identification subsystem of the RIS can help the retailer identify financial resource problems that the problem solution subsystem of the RIS can help it to solve. For example, monitoring of economic trends using the problem identification subsystem may alert the retailer to the fact that interest rates are rapidly rising and are expected to remain high for at least a year. At the same time, monitoring of the balance sheet may alert the retailer to the fact that a $10 million bond issue is maturing in six months. This pair of events should trigger problem recognition. The problem, which must be solved with the help of the problem solution subsystem, is how to generate $10 million in capital to retire the bond issue and subsequently restructure the balance sheet. Obviously, additional information will need to be collected to solve this perplexing problem.

Of course, the retailer might identify other capital-related problems that will require a special research effort. Some examples are evaluation of how to finance the construction of a new warehouse, analysis of the economics of factoring accounts receivable, exploration of new technology for increasing the productivity of capital invested in inventory, and evaluation of a new cash management system.

Human Resources   The problem solution subsystem should also be used to help solve the retailer's human resource problems. Once again, the problem identification subsystem may have been instrumental in calling to the retail executive's attention the presence of a human resource problem—such as low or deteriorating sales per employee. But it is the problem solution subsystem that must obtain the necessary information to solve the problem.

Human resource problems can have many forms, including morale problems, motivation problems, productivity problems, turnover problems, conflict problems, and organizational design problems.

Often, human resource problems can best be solved by using the talents of external consulting organizations, which provide an independent analysis and opinion of the cause. People in the retail organization are often personally too close to the human element to be objective researchers. Nonetheless, the practice of having outside consultants conduct the research should still fall within the domain of the RIS. Basically, the retail manager is freely admitting that information is needed, but it can obtain the most valid information by contracting with an independent consulting agency to conduct the research and analyze the results.

Location Resources   A retailer's store location is one of the most valuable resources in its arsenal. But this resource can change in value as the retailer's trade area changes. When this happens, the retailer may discover that its location is no longer optimal.

To solve a location problem, the retailer needs information to help it evaluate alternatives. Reasonable alternatives may be to close the store, modify its merchandise mix, modify the store image, or keep the store operating as is but seek a new location. In Chapter 12 we will discuss several research approaches for solving location problems.

Operations Problems   Operations problems are those which are related to operations planning and management as illustrated in the retail planning and management model in Exhibit 3.1. The solution of common operating problems will be the focus of Chapters 13 through 19.

Operating problems involve day-to-day management activities. Most can be quickly and effectively solved by an experienced and talented retail manager. However, for the occasional unique problem, special information is needed. Most operating problems are related to assets, revenues, or expenses. Let us briefly examine these problem areas.

Assets   Operating problems may relate to any of the individual assets the retailer must manage on a day-to-day basis. Consider the following problems:

- Inventory is disappearing from the stockroom daily.
- There has been a significant slowdown in customers paying their bills.
- The store roof has developed a leak.
- The air conditioning system repeatedly breaks down.

To solve these problems properly, the manager may require information that is not readily available; he or she will thus need to use the RIS.

Let us illustrate a typical problem in more detail. Assume you are a store manager and the air conditioner regularly breaks down. Would you conclude that all that needs to be done is to replace the old air conditioner with a new unit? We hope not. Careful analysis of the technological environment will reveal that there is a wealth of new air conditioning technology, which can have a significant effect on operating costs. At the same time, these lower operating costs must be compared to the higher initial cost of a technologically superior air conditioning system. Also, there may be other, less tangible costs and benefits. What will be the effect of a new air conditioning system on employee morale and customer loyalty? Therefore, the apparently simple problem of whether to replace an air conditioner cannot be properly solved in the absence of substantial information.

Revenues and Expenses   Other operating problems that arise can be related to various revenue and expense items. And, the ability to solve these problems may require more information than the manager has at his or her disposal.[9] What might be some of these problems? Consider the following:

- Sales of a previously popular merchandise line drop 38 percent.

9. For example, advertising problems may be researched with the aid of experimental designs. See Ian Fenwick, "Advertising Experiments by Retailers." *Journal of Advertising Research* 18(August 1978): 35–36.

- Employee overtime hours rise by 21 percent in a single month.
- There is a significant rise in merchandise returns and allowances.

The retail manager would probably have only a few good hunches of the causal factors unless the preceding situations had been closely studied. However, even if the manager had a few hunches, additional information would be required to help determine which hunch was correct.

When we earlier discussed monitoring operating performance trends in the problem identification subsystem, we provided a framework for comparing standard with actual performance. This framework can be a good source for identifying significant revenue and expense problems. The problem solution subsystem can then be used, if needed, to gather additional information to solve these problems.

ORGANIZING THE RIS

How should the RIS be organized in the retail enterprise? The answer depends on the scope of the RIS. If the RIS is nothing more than a beefed-up accounting system then the retail controller is probably the best person to manage it, but if it is the comprehensive system that has been proposed, one consisting of both problem identification and problem solution subsystems, then the controller may not be the appropriate person. He or she would not have the time to manage such a comprehensive system.

We propose an RIS manager who would manage both RIS subsystems. This manager would need inputs from the controller, the legal counsel, the store or department managers, the buyers, and anyone else in the enterprise who would be either a potential user or potential provider of information to the RIS. The RIS manager would have to be a very special and talented individual. In order to interact with a wide range of people on a broad array of topics, over which he or she had little authority, the manager would have to be persuasive and diplomatic; also, he or she would need to be knowledgeable in all aspects of the retail enterprise. The RIS manager must be just as comfortable conversing with a store manager, warehouse manager, buyer, or corporate lawyer.

Don't be misled into believing that an RIS manager is a necessity. The manager's contribution to the organization must justify the cost. If the RIS manager—or even the RIS itself—won't help decision makers make more profitable decisions, then the position is an unnecessary luxury.

Obviously, the retailer with only several employees cannot justify a comprehensive RIS and an RIS manager. Nonetheless, the small retailer should embrace the notion that it should remain cognizant of changes in consumer, competitor, and channel behavior; of changes in the socioeconomic, legal, and technological environments; and of changes in asset, revenue, and expense performance. Further, when significant problems occur, even a small retailer should try to get the best data available within its established cost constraints to solve the problem.

SUMMARY

In this chapter we delineated the nature and scope of a retail information system (RIS). An RIS was defined as a blueprint for the continual and periodic systematic collection, analysis, and reporting of relevant data about any past, present, or future developments that could influence or have influenced the retailer's performance.

An RIS should have two major operating subsystems. The problem identification subsystem should provide constant feedback on behavioral, environmental, and operating performance trends in order to identify current or potential problems. Behavioral monitoring should involve scanning the behavior of consumers, competitors, and channel members. Environmental monitoring should involve scanning the socioeconomic, legal, and technological environments. Monitoring operating performance should involve regular analysis of the retailer's assets, revenues, and expenses.

The problem solution RIS subsystem should be designed to generate information to help solve special management problems in strategic, administrative, and operating areas. For each, special research may be necessary for effective problem solving.

The types of strategic problems for which the problem solution RIS may need to generate information are those related to reformulation of the retailer's mission and objectives, those related to identification and analysis of strategic opportunities, and those involving developing contingency plans. Administrative problems that may involve special data collection may be categorized as capital, human resources, and location problems. Finally, operations problems can be those which are primarily asset related or primarily revenue and expense related, but which in either case require special data collection for proper solution.

QUESTIONS

1. A well-known French philosopher, Paul Valéry, has stated, "Once destiny was an honest game of cards which followed certain conventions with a limited number of cards and values. Now the player realizes in amazement that the hand of his future contains cards never seen before and the rules of the game are modified by each play." Comment on the relevance of this statement in regard to the need for and design of retail information systems.

2. How might the retail information system be used to assess the appropriateness of the retailer's target return on equity?

3. How is the problem identification subsystem different from the problem solution subsystem?

4. How much information should retail decision makers have at hand when making decisions? Does your answer vary depending on the type of decision being made?

5. Should accountants be the managers of retail information systems? Defend your answer.

6. What is the role of the computer in the retail information system?

7. Is it more crucial to monitor the consumer or the marketing channel?

8. If you were the owner-manager of a local furniture store, how would you obtain information on your competitors?

9. Explain how operating performance standards can be used to help identify key management problems in retailing.

PROBLEMS AND EXERCISES

1. Assume you are the owner-manager of a local hardware store in a city of 140,000 people. You wish to design a basic, low-cost retail information system. What should be the major subcomponents of this system? Prioritize your information needs (that is, what is the most important information you desire, the second most important, and so on).

2. You plan to obtain a staff research position with a chain store retailer on graduation. Identify from your college catalog the five most useful business courses to prepare you for this job. What courses in nonbusiness disciplines would be helpful? (Hint: look at course offerings outside the business college.)

3. Get copies of your local evening newspaper for the last several weeks. Clip all the advertisements placed by supermarkets. Analyze the ads for content and write a 500-word statement on the competitive behavior of several of the supermarkets in your city.

4. Go to the library and get a copy of the most recent Census of Retailing for a SMSA with which you are familiar. What information is available on the structure of retailing in this SMSA? Is this information useful?

5. Obtain copies of the last twelve issues of *Chain Store Age Executive* and *Stores*. What information can you obtain on technology in retailing, legal developments, and the socioeconomic environment?

SUGGESTED READINGS

Goldberg, Joel. "Understanding the Computer as a Merchandising Aid," in R. Patrick Cash (ed.) *The Buyer's Manual* (New York: National Retail Merchants Association, 1979), pp. 203–44.

Mason, J. Barry and Morris L. Mayer. "Retail Merchandise Informa-Systems for the 1980s." *Journal of Retailing* 56 (Spring 1980): 56–76.

"Research Offers Multifaceted Benefits to Retailers," *Marketing News*, May 18, 1979, p. 20

Rothman, Marion Burk. "MIS Understood." *Stores* 62 (June 1980): 44–46.

Silver, Alvin M. "Effective Management Systems." *Stores* (June 1971), pp. 29–31.

II

STRATEGIC PLANNING AND MANAGEMENT

4

Overview *The purpose of this chapter is to illustrate the retailer's need to analyze and understand the behavior and responsibilities of the members of the marketing channel or channels to which it belongs. To accomplish this goal, we will first discuss how all the activities in the marketing system must be performed by the retailer or other members of the marketing channel. We will follow this discussion with a review of the different types of marketing channels to which a retailer can belong. Finally, we will make practical suggestions on how to better manage marketing channel relations.*

Understanding Channel Behavior

The System Is the Solution

The Marketing System
The Marketing Functions
Pervasiveness of the Functions
Marketing Institutions

Conventional Marketing Channels

Vertical Marketing Systems
Corporate Systems

Contractual Systems
Administered Systems

Managing Marketing Channel Relations
Dependency
Power
Conflict

Summary

AT THE OUTSET of this text, we stated that retailing is the final movement in the progression of merchandise from producer to consumer. Many other movements occur over time and geographical space, all of which need to be executed properly for the retailer to achieve optimum performance. In this chapter we will discuss how these moves and retailing fit into the larger marketing system.

THE SYSTEM IS THE SOLUTION

Let us consider an example. Suppose the final move occurred on July 17 at 10:47 A.M. when the customer of a department store in downtown Chicago purchased a new coat. At some prior time (probably six months to a year earlier) that coat was manufactured. Later, it was warehoused and still later, put on display in the department store. The final move occurred in Chicago, but it was preceded by moves at other geographic locations. Manufacturing may have occurred in South Carolina and warehousing in New York. Thus, before the final retail transaction, many moves need to occur involving many players other than the retailer; the retailer cannot properly perform its job without these others. The retailer is only part of a complex marketing system—obviously an important component, but not the only one.

When you view the retailer as part of a larger marketing system, you should see it as a member of one, or even several, marketing channels. A **marketing channel** is a set of institutions that are necessary and incidental in moving goods from points of production to points of consumption. As such, marketing channels are comprised of all the institutions and all the marketing activities (spread over time and geographical space) in the marketing process. The marketing channel that collectively does the best job at performing marketing activities will be able to achieve dramatically higher levels of performance. Thus, you should realize that whole marketing channels compete with each other; competition does not take place on the level of the single retailer. Firestone tire dealers don't compete with Goodyear tire dealers; rather, the marketing channel for Firestone tires competes with the marketing channel for Goodyear tires. Similarly, K-mart doesn't compete with Woolco; rather the marketing channels that K-mart utilizes are in competition with the marketing channels that Woolco has structured. We will discuss this competitive frame of reference in more detail in Chapter 6.

Why should the retailer view itself as part of a larger marketing system? Why can't it simply seek out the best assortment of goods for its customers, sell them the goods, make a profit, go to the bank, and forget about the system? The answer is straightforward. The retailer can forget about the system, and make a short-run profit, but in the long run, the system will forget about the retailer. If that happens, then profits sufficient for survival and growth will be difficult if not impossible to achieve. Thus, the system is the solution because it can help the retailer improve long-run, bottom-line performance.

THE MARKETING SYSTEM

The marketing system can be defined in a variety of ways. For instructional purposes, we will define the **marketing system** as that set of institutions performing marketing functions (activities), and the relationships between these institutions and functions, that are necessary to create exchange transactions with target populations. Thus, we will view the marketing system as largely synonymous with the marketing channel.

Exhibit 4.1 is a graphical representation of the marketing system. Study it closely. You will notice that this exhibit portrays many of the links between institutions and functions that are necessary to bring about final exchange with some target population. Also, you should note that the marketing system is affected by five external forces: consumer behavior, competitor behavior, the socioeconomic environment, the technological environment, and the legal environment. These external forces are uncontrollable by the retailer or any other institution in the marketing system but need to be taken into account when retailers make decisions. Remember that the retail management and planning model (Exhibit 2.1) also dramatizes the importance of considering these external forces in retail decision making.

EXHIBIT 4.1 **The Marketing System**

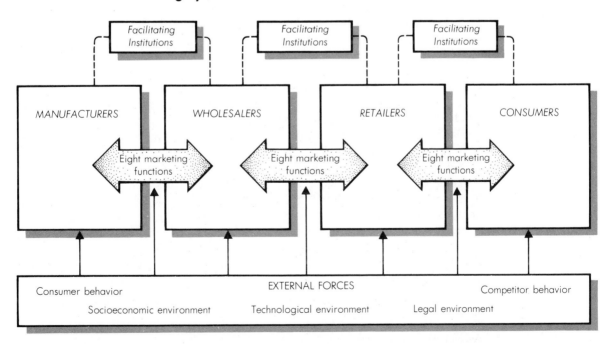

The Marketing Functions   What marketing functions need to be performed in the marketing system? Eight functions are necessary: buying, selling, storing, transporting, sorting, financing, information, and risk taking.[1] Each will be briefly discussed.

Buying   Before much selling can be done in the marketing system, considerable buying needs to occur. The manufacturer who sells a finished product needs first to procure many items (raw materials, subcomponents, supplies, etc.) that enter the production process. Before the wholesaler can sell, it needs to buy; and before the retailer can sell it also needs to buy. In short, buying is as important a function in marketing as selling.

Selling   Selling is the function that is most typically associated with marketing, and it obviously is important. It involves all activities that are necessary and incidental to contacting and persuading customers to purchase. Selling activities involve advertising, personal selling, and sales promotions.

Storage   Storage becomes necessary when there is a discrepancy between the time at which supplies are created and the time at which demand occurs. For example, corn comes into harvest within a relatively short time; however, people desire to consume corn throughout the year. For another example, an apparel manufacturer may have a production run of 1,000 size 7 blue dresses within two days, but the demand for those dresses will not occur simultaneously, and thus storage becomes necessary.

Transporting   Transportation becomes necessary when the place of supply is removed from the place of demand. Production occurs in geographical pockets, such as apparel in the North and Southeast, and autos in the Midwest. But demand occurs throughout the United States in rough proportion to income and population density. As a result, merchandise needs to be transported. The only alternative would be to produce all products in all locations where people reside—which would obviously be extremely expensive. Imagine an auto plant and an apparel factory in every city and town in the United States.

Sorting   Sorting needs to occur because both demands and supplies are heterogeneous.[2] Matching these heterogeneous demands and supplies involves four sorting processes. **Sorting out** refers to the breaking down of heterogeneous supplies into more homogeneous groups. For example, the grading of corn into different quality groups is a sorting out process. **Accumulation** refers to the building up of larger homogeneous supplies. For example, the bringing together of grade 2 corn from thousands of farms across the country is a matter

1. For a more detailed discussion of marketing functions consult Franklin W. Ryan, "Functional Elements of Market Distribution," *Harvard Business Review* 13(January 1935): 205–21; and Edmund D. McGary, "Some Functions of Marketing Reconsidered," in Reavis Cox and Wroe Alderson (eds.), *Theory in Marketing* (Homewood, Ill.: Richard D. Irwin, 1950), pp. 263–79.

2. Alderson was one of the first to discuss in detail the sorting function. See Wroe Alderson, *Marketing Behavior and Executive Action* (Homewood, Ill.: Richard D. Irwin, 1957).

of accumulation. **Allocation** is the breaking down of homogeneous supplies into smaller lots. For example, the grain elevator that has accumulated large supplies of grade 2 corn can in turn sell it off in smaller quantities. Finally **assorting** is the building up of assortments of products for use in association with each other. Consumers typically seek an assortment of goods, and retailers serve the consumer by building these assortments. For example, the consumer goes to the supermarket for more than corn; he or she also seeks a good selection of other vegetables, as well as meat, dry groceries, and so on.

Financing If it is recognized that there are discrepancies between the time that demand occurs and the time supplies are created and also between points of production (supply) and points of consumption (demand), then it becomes clear that someone needs to finance these discrepancies. Inventories, warehouses, and trucks or other transportation modes become necessary, and they also require financing.

Information Sellers know what their supplies are and buyers know what their demands are, but without information the seller doesn't know what the buyer wants and the buyer doesn't know what the seller has available. Information becomes essential, therefore, to match supplies properly with demands.

Risk Taking Marketing puts the firm out on a limb. It is obvious that demands cannot be forecast precisely. Therefore products will be produced or purchased for resale and a demand for them will not materialize. And then the firm can incur a loss.

Pervasiveness of the Functions Regardless of the economic system—capitalistic, socialistic, or communistic—these eight marketing functions will exist. They are pervasive and cannot be eliminated. They can, however, be shifted or divided among the insitutions and consumers in the marketing system.

All new forms of retailing were created by rearranging the marketing functions among institutions and consumers. For example, department stores capitalized on the opportunity to perform more of the sorting process. Department stores were created specifically to build a larger and better assortment of goods. No longer was it necessary to travel to one store for a shirt, another for slacks, and yet another for shoes; the necessary assortment could be procured in a single store. As another example, supermarkets increased the workload on the consumer by shifting more of the information, buying, and transporting function to them. Before there were supermarkets, the consumer could have the corner grocer hand-select the items and deliver them to his or her house. But with the supermarket came self-service. It was now up to consumers to locate the goods desired within the store, select them from an array of products, and transport them home. For performing more of the marketing functions, the consumer was compensated with lower prices.

A marketing function does not have to be totally shifted to another institution in the marketing system or to the consumer but can be divided among several entities. For example, the manufacturer who does not want to perform the entire selling function could have the retailer perform part of the job through in-store promotions and local advertising. At the same time, the manufacturer could assume some of the task through national advertising.

The retailer, however, will not want, or be likely to have, the financial capital to exclusively perform all eight marketing functions. For this reason the retailer must view itself as being dependent on others in the marketing system.

Marketing Institutions   What institutions are involved in performing the eight marketing functions? There are many more than you might initially envision. These institutions can be meaningfully broken into two categories: the **primary marketing institutions,** or those which take title to the goods, and the **facilitating institutions,** or those which do not actually take title but facilitate the marketing process by specializing in the performance of certain functions. Exhibit 4.2 is a classification of the major institutions participating in the marketing system.

Primary Marketing Institutions   There are three primary marketing institutions: manufacturers, wholesalers, and retailers. Each takes legal title to the goods as they flow through the marketing channel. Students of business often do not think of manufacturers as marketing institutions, since they produce goods. But manufacturers cannot exist by only producing goods; they must also market the goods produced. In marketing, they often need the assistance other institutions can provide in performing the eight marketing functions. In 1977 there were 358,502 manufacturers in the United States.

EXHIBIT 4.2
Institutions Participating in the Marketing System

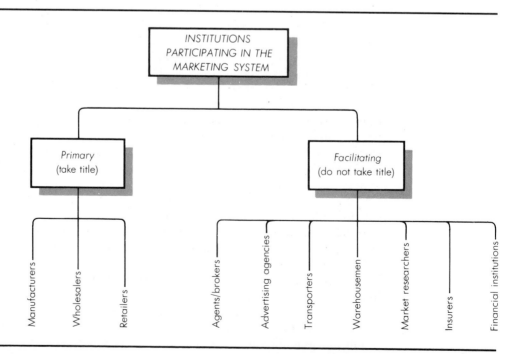

A second primary marketing institution is the wholesaler. Wholesalers buy and resell merchandise to retailers and other merchants and to industrial institutions and commercial users. In 1977 there were 382,837 wholesalers in the United States, each performing some aspect of the eight marketing functions.

The third primary institution is the retailer. In the United States in 1977 there were 1,885,068 retailers. Retailers can also perform portions of all the eight marketing functions. Since the focus of this text is on retailing, let us examine how a typical retailer can contribute to the performance of these eight functions.

Buying is a side of retailing that the consumer rarely notices. Think for a moment, however, when you walk into a department store, how much effort had to be devoted to buying in order to bring together the assortment of merchandise you see. In all probability, the merchandise presented comes from the four corners of the world. Many top retail executives started their careers as assistant buyers, just as you probably will.

Consumers most frequently identify selling with retailing. Retailers need to sell, not just have merchandise available. To do this, they must advertise, use sales promotions, and frequently use personal selling to ensure that merchandise is moved in adequate quantities.

The storage function in retailing is best thought of in terms of the inventory and floor space necessary to have the merchandise available at the time and place it is demanded.

Retailers also help perform the transportation function. Often retailers will have to transport the goods from the point of purchase (manufacture or wholesale) to the retail store. At other times the retailer needs to deliver merchandise to the customer's residence. Retailers may therefore need to be concerned with both inbound and outbound transportation. Thus, the location of the retailer is important.

Retailers do a considerable amount of sorting, especially assorting. Retailers can be viewed as basically building assortments of merchandise that match consumer demand patterns.

The retailer cannot operate consistently on a profitable basis without information on consumer wants and needs, changing economic conditions, competitive trends, etc. A lack of such information will most likely cause error in the retail planning and management process. In a complex environment the retailer needs timely and relevant information to aid in making intelligent decisions.

The retailer cannot avoid risk taking since nothing is certain. The consumer may reject the merchandise the retailer selected. There may be a recession, or households may leave the retailer's trading area and new households may not move in. The merchandise may not arrive on time, it may arrive damaged, or it may not be what was ordered. The store may burn down, or customers may injure themselves in the store. The management of these risks is becoming an increasingly important function in retailing.[3]

Finally, the retailer will perform part of the financing function. The retailer

3. "The Perils and Premiums of Retailing," *Chain Store Age Executive*, July 1980, pp. 34–51.

will need to finance all the preceding functions with either debt or equity capital.

Facilitating Institutions   A variety of institutions facilitate the performance of the marketing functions. Most of these institutions specialize in one or two functions; none of them takes title to the goods.

Institutions that facilitate buying and selling in the marketing system are agents and brokers that include the freelance broker, the manufacturer's agent, the sales agent, and the purchasing agent. These agents and brokers are independent businessmen who receive a commission when they are able to bring buyer and seller together to negotiate a transaction. Seldom do agents or brokers take physical possession of the merchandise. The purchasing agent aids in buying and the others assist in the selling. C. Glenn Walters provides a concise description of these agents and brokers:[4]

> 1. **The free lance broker** has no permanent ties with any principal, and he may negotiate sales for a large number of principals over time. There is no limitation on the territory in which sales occur but the agent is strictly bound by his principal for prices, terms, and conditions of sale.
>
> 2. **The manufacturer's agent,** like the free lance broker, negotiates for the sale of products for his principal. The manufacturer's agent has a rather loose arrangement with his principal that is seldom permanent beyond a year. This arrangement is usually renewed but can also be terminated on notice. The agent is strictly bound by his principal for the territory, prices, terms, and conditions of sale. Manufacturer's agents normally negotiate sales for several principals, but they have jurisdiction over only a part of the manufacturer's total output. A merchant using a manufacturer's agent does not need a sales force, but must have a sales department with a head to coordinate the activities of the agents and to establish policy.
>
> 3. **The sales agent** has long-term arrangements with from one to a very restricted number of principals. This agent sells the entire output for his principal and has no limitation on the territory in which he operates or on prices, terms, or conditions of sale. The sales agent also frequently finances his principals. When a merchant uses a sales agent there is no need for any sales department because the agent handles all sales functions.
>
> 4. **Purchasing agents,** sometimes known as resident buyers, specialize in seeking out sources of supply for some merchant principal. They operate on a contractual basis for a limited number of customers and receive a commission just as sales agents do. Purchasing agents usually operate in the central market headquarters for a particular type of product. They are specialists on sources, prices, quality, shipping, fashion, and other considerations surrounding the purchase of merchandise. Chain stores make considerable use of resident buyers; so occasionally do department stores.

Advertising agencies also facilitate the selling process by designing effective advertisements and advising management on where and when to place these advertisements.

---

4. The following four definitions are taken from C. Glenn Walters, *Marketing Channels* (Santa Monica, Calif.: Goodyear, 1977), p. 136. Reprinted with permission of Goodyear Publishing Co., Inc.

Institutions that facilitate the transportation function are motor, rail, and air carriers, and pipeline and ship companies. These firms offer differing advantages in terms of delivery, service, and cost; generally, the quicker the delivery, the more costly it will be. Transporters can have a significant effect on how efficiently goods move through the marketing system and can be a major source of conflict when they fail to perform their jobs properly.

Imagine you are the lawn and garden department manager for a local discount store. You are waiting on a shipment of 300 fifty-pound bags of lawn food for a special national promotion. You placed your order in plenty of time and should have received the product two days ago. On calling the manufacturer, you discover that the product was sent out last week by truck for delivery to you two days ago. You then try to trace the shipment through the trucking company only to find that nobody seems to know where your shipment is, or when (or if) it is expected to arrive. This type of incident is often a cause for considerable conflict between the retailer and transporter, the manufacturer and the transporter, the retailer and the manufacturer, and even the retailer and the customer—when the goods don't arrive on schedule after they have been advertised, the customers become irritated with the retailer.

The major facilitating institution involved in storage is the public warehouse. A **public warehouse** will store goods for safekeeping in return for a fee. Space charges or fees are typically based on cubic feet used per month, but some warehouses are now charging daily fees. Frequently, retailers may take advantage of special buys but have no space in their store or warehouse and will thus find it necessary to use a public warehouse.

A variety of facilitating institutions assist in providing information in the marketing system. For example, at the very heart of the business communications system in the United States are the postal and telephone systems. The role of the mail and phone in transmitting information is pervasive. In addition, computer and computer service firms are playing an increasing role in information transmission. In fact, many retailers can now order many types of merchandise by using on-line computer ordering techniques. An order is typed into a computer console at the retail firm and is directly fed into the wholesaler's or manufacturer's computer, which will then print out a purchase order and warehouse routing slip to show what items to pull from the warehouse and ship to the retailer. Also assisting in the information function are market research firms, which can provide problem-solving information in specialized areas.

There are also facilitating institutions that aid in financing, such as commercial banks, savings and loan associations, and stock exchanges. These institutions can provide or help the retailer obtain funds to aid in financing marketing functions. Retailers frequently need short-term loans for working capital requirements (that is, to handle increased inventory and accounts receivables) and long-term loans for continued growth and expansion (adding new stores or remodeling).

Finally, insurance firms can facilitate by assuming some of the risk-taking function in the marketing system. Insurance firms can insure inventories, buildings, trucks, equipment and fixtures, and other assets that are instrumental to the retailer and other primary marketing institutions in performing their jobs. They can also insure against employee and customer injuries.

After reviewing the functions and institutions in the marketing system, we can now examine how the primary marketing institutions can be arranged into a marketing channel.

CONVENTIONAL MARKETING CHANNELS

A large part of the marketing system consists of the marketing functions and the primary marketing institutions that perform them—but how might these functions and institutions be arranged into a marketing channel? Bert McCammon has elaborated on two basic channel patterns: the conventional marketing channel and the vertical marketing system. Exhibit 4.3 provides a classification of these major channel patterns.

A **conventional marketing channel** is one in which each member of the channel is loosely aligned with the others. Predictably, the major orientation is toward the next institution in the channel. Thus, the manufacturer interacts with and focuses efforts on the wholesaler, the wholesaler focuses efforts on

EXHIBIT 4.3   **Marketing Channel Patterns**

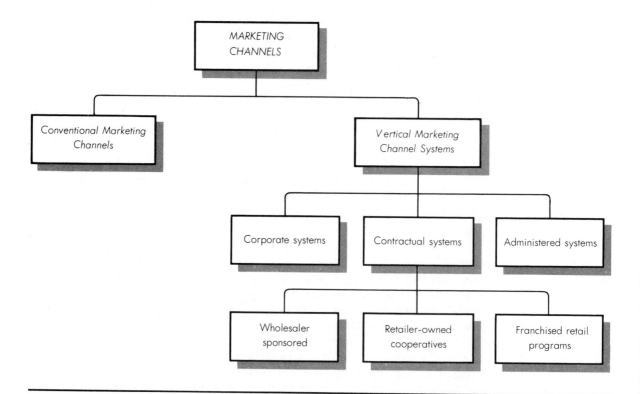

the retailer, and in turn the retailer focuses efforts on the final consumer. In short, the marketing channel consists of a series of dyads in which the members recognize each other but not those outside.

The conventional marketing channel pattern, although historically predominant in the United States, is a sloppy and inefficient method of conducting business. It fosters intense negotiations in each dyad in the channel, but the channel members do not see the possibility of shifting or dividing the marketing functions among *all* channel participants. Therefore, it is an unproductive mode for marketing goods. Thus, it is not surprising that it has been on the decline in the United States since the early 1950s.

VERTICAL MARKETING SYSTEMS

McCammon has defined **vertical marketing systems** as "professionally managed and centrally programmed networks that are preengineered to achieve significant operating economies and maximum market impact. Stated alternatively, vertical marketing systems are rationalized and capital intensive networks that are programmed to realize technological, managerial, and promotional economies."[5] There are three types of vertical marketing systems—corporate, contractual, and administered—each of which has grown explosively since the early 1950s.[6]

Corporate Systems   The **corporate system** typically consists of either a manufacturer who has vertically integrated forward into the channel to reach the consumer or a retailer who has vertically integrated backward into the channel to create a self-supply network. The first type includes manufacturers such as Singer (sewing machines), Sherwin Williams (paint), Hart, Schaffner and Marx (men's apparel), Famolare (shoes), and Xerox (office equipment), which have created their own warehousing and retail outlets. The second type includes retailers such as Sears, which obtains over 50 percent of its merchandise from manufacturers in which it has an equity interest. For example, Sears obtains over 50 percent of its appliances from Whirlpool, over 50 percent of its apparel items from Kellwood, over 40 percent of its tires and tubes from Armstrong Rubber, and over 30 percent of its hand tools from EASCO, in each of which it has substantial equity.[7] In Exhibit 4.4, we present a case study of Revco Drug. Revco is aggressively pursuing a strategy to create for itself a corporate marketing channel.

5. Bert C. McCammon, Jr., "The Emergence and Growth of Contractually Integrated Channels in the American Economy" in Peter D. Bennett (ed.), *Marketing and Economic Development* (Chicago: American Marketing Association, 1965), pp. 496–515.

6. Bert C. McCammon, Jr., Alton F. Doody, and William R. Davidson, "Emerging Patterns of Distribution" a paper presented at the 1969 Annual Meeting of the National Association of Wholesalers, Las Vegas, Nevada, January 15, 1969. Reprinted in Bruce J. Walker and Joel B. Haynes (eds.), *Marketing Channels and Institutions: Selected Readings*, 2nd ed. (Columbus, Ohio: Grid, 1978), p. 195.

7. Carol J. Loomis, "The Leaning Tower of Sears," *Fortune*, July 2, 1979, pp. 78–85.

EXHIBIT 4.4
Backward Integration into Manufacturing

Revco D.S., Inc. is aggressively pursuing a strategy of backward integration into manufacturing in order to create for itself a self-supply network. As a drug retailer, Revco has experienced phenomenal growth. Starting in 1947 with a single store in Detroit, it grew to over 1,100 stores by the late 1970s. By that time, it had become the largest discount drugstore chain in the United States.

Revco is attempting to further bolster its growth record by investing substantial capital in drug manufacturing. Drug manufacturing acquisitions by Revco have included:

- Private Formulations Inc., a maker of vitamins and food supplements
- a 12 percent interest in a new pain killer and anti-inflamatory drug called Prinar
- Winning Laboratories Inc., a maker of vitamins and food supplements
- Barre-National Inc., a producer of cough syrup, medicated shampoos, and liquid antibiotics
- Carter-Golgau Laboratories Inc., a manufacturer of liquid vitamin B-12

The manufacturing ventures are already paying off, for their after-tax profit margins are higher than those of the retail drug division. In addition, Revco is fulfilling its goal of creating a self-supply network. Roughly one third of the 400 private-label items stocked in a Revco drugstore are now manufactured in company facilities.

Source: Based on data from Revco D.S., Inc., *Annual Reports,* and "Revco: A Discount Drug Retailer Expands into Manufacturing," *Business Week,* November 12, 1979, pp. 122, 124.

In corporate systems it becomes much easier to program the channel for target productivity and profit goals, since a well-established authority structure exists there, allowing a well-defined individual or group to lead the channel. Thus, independent retailers that have aligned themselves in a conventional marketing channel are at a significant disadvantage when competing against a corporate vertical marketing system.

Contractual Systems   **Contractual** vertical marketing systems include wholesaler-sponsored voluntary groups, retailer-owned cooperatives, and franchised retail programs. Each of these channel types allows for a more coordinated and system-wide perspective than do conventional marketing channels; however, they are more difficult to manage than corporate vertical marketing systems because the authority and power structures are not as well defined. What is principally required is that channel members give up some autonomy to gain system economies and greater market impact.

Wholesaler-Sponsored Voluntary Groups   These groups are created when a wholesaler brings together a group of independently owned retailers, grocers for example, and offers them a coordinated merchandising and buying program that will provide them with economies such as their chain-store rivals are able to obtain. The independent grocers in return agree to concentrate their purchases with that wholesaler. It is a voluntary relationship; that is, there are no membership or franchise fees. The independent grocers may terminate this relationship whenever they desire, so it is to the wholesaler's advantage to build competitive merchandise assortments and offer other services that will keep the voluntary group satisfied.

It is not uncommon for the voluntary group wholesaler to offer the retailer the following services: store design and layout, store site and location analysis, inventory management systems, accounting and bookkeeping systems, insurance services, pension plans, trade area studies, advertising and promotion assistance, and employee training programs. Accordingly, the better the services and merchandising programs put together by the wholesaler, the more loyal the retailer will become. Given such a situation, the wholesaler can become the channel leader and more readily program the channel for high performance results.

In Exhibit 4.5 we profile some of the retail support services that McLain Grocery Company (a voluntary group wholesaler) provides to its Independent

EXHIBIT 4.5 **Support Services McLain Offers to IGA Retailers**	SUPPORT SERVICE	DESCRIPTION
	Financial counsel	Qualified McLain personnel answer IGA retailers' financial questions. Upon request, an IGA retailer may receive advice on financing store expansion, cash-flow problems, loans, and other related financial concerns.
	Engineering	The store engineering and store development department offers retailers designs for new stores, additions, and remodelings. Expert advice on equipment and its procurement is offered. Market analysis services are provided, which prove invaluable to a retailer planning a new store or moving to a new location. Professional consumer research is offered to help retailers appraise customer acceptance. Energy saving advice is given directly, and tips are published in a weekly merchandiser.
	Computer service	McLain data processing facilities provide case labels as a pricing aid to retailers; electronic ordering for speed, accuracy, and backroom space saving; commodity purchase analysis reports on a scheduled basis; and many other benefits.
	Advertising	The emphasis of the advertising program is built around "IGA," and by continuous use of IGA banners and themes gives the impression of a large chain-like advertising campaign rather than a small one-store effort. In addition to placing newspaper, handbills, radio, and TV ads, the department lends assistance in planning special sales, promotions, anniversary sales, and grand openings.
	Retail accounting	The accounting department handles bookkeeping, tax preparation, bill-out service, computerized payrolls, and many other accounting-oriented functions. Assistance is communicated by standardized forms, computer printouts, telephone and visits by McLain's accountants for special problems.
	Retail training	The training department provides IGA retailers with a comprehensive training program for management and employees which includes all facets of merchandising, marketing, in-store security, and other appropriate functions. The Meat Management Institute, unique in the industry, conducts classes using programmed workbooks, lectures, and video demonstrations.
	Printing	The printing department continually provides printed material including letterheads, cash register refund forms, bag stuffers, envelopes, store directories, etc.

Source: From McLain Grocery Company, *Annual Report for Year Ending April 1979*, pp. 8–9; adapted by permission of McLain Grocery Company.

Grocers' Alliance (IGA) retailers. You should carefully examine the description of these services to get a flavor for how voluntary group wholesalers can assist independent retailers.

Wholesaler-sponsored voluntary groups have represented a major strategic thrust in marketing channels since the mid 1960s. They are now prevalent in many lines of trade. Consider for example, Independent Grocers' Alliance (IGA) in the grocery field, Ace in the hardware field, Western Auto in the automotive accessories field, Ben Franklin in the notions and general merchandise field, and Economost in the drug field. Exhibit 4.6 dramatizes the pervasiveness of voluntary group programs in the hardware field.

Retailer-Owned Cooperatives Another common form of contractual vertical marketing systems are retailer-owned cooperatives. These systems are organized and owned by retailers, and are most common in the grocery field (for example, Associated Grocers and Certified Grocers). They offer scale economies and service to member retailers, which allow them to compete with larger chain-buying organizations.

Retailer-sponsored cooperatives differ from wholesaler-sponsored voluntary groups in channel leadership patterns and competitive intensity.

Generally, wholesaler-sponsored voluntary groups have been more effective competitors than retailer-sponsored cooperatives, primarily because of the difference in channel organization between the two. In the former, a wholesaler can provide strong leadership because he represents the locus of power within the voluntary system. In a retailer-sponsored cooperative, power is diffused throughout the re-

EXHIBIT 4.6
Voluntary Group Chains in Hardware Retailing (1980)

NAME	VOLUME (millions)	TOTAL STORES
Cotter & Company	$1,250	6,800
Ace Hardware Corporation	660	4,000
Hardware Wholesalers, Inc.	455	2,500
American Hardware Supply	380	3,700
Coast to Coast Stores, Inc.	300	1,200
Gamble's, Division of Gamble-Skogmo, Inc.	175[a]	893
Our Own Hardware Company	118	950
United Hardware Company	79	700
Handy Wholesale Hardware Co.	27	325
General Mercantile, Inc.	11	250
Bay Cities Wholesale Hardware Co.	10	200
KVD, Inc.	10	140
Connecticut Hardware Supply Co.	5.5	50
Master Distributors	1.3	72

[a]Estimate

Source: "Hardware Retailing," 1980–81 Hardware-Home Center Market Media Fact File (Indianapolis, Indiana: National Retail Hardware Association, 1980). Reprinted by permission.

tail membership, and therefore role specification and concomitant allocation of resources are more difficult to accomplish. In voluntary groups, the retail members have relinquished some of their autonomy by making themselves highly dependent on specific wholesalers for expertise. In retailer cooperatives, individual members tend to retain more autonomy and thus tend to depend much less strongly on the supply unit for assistance and direction.[8]

Franchises The third type of contractual vertical marketing system is the **franchise,** which can be defined as:

> licensing of an entire business format where one firm (the franchisor) licenses a number of outlets (franchisees) to market a product or service and engage in a business developed by the franchisor using the latter's trade names, trademarks, service marks, know-how, and methods of doing business.[9]

Franchisors can come from many positions in the marketing channel. The franchisor could be a manufacturer, such as Chevrolet or Midas Mufflers; a service specialist, such as Kelly Girl or Manpower; or a retailer franchising other retailers, such as McDonald's or Kentucky Fried Chicken.

Franchise systems are not a recent phenomenon; major oil companies and auto manufacturers have used franchised retail outlets for over a half century. However, franchising in other lines of trade has experienced spectacular growth since the mid-1960s. Exhibit 4.7 provides statistics on the magnitude of franchising in the United States (see page 88). As you can see, franchise retail sales represent over 30 percent of all retail sales in the United States.

Franchising has become highly popular because it offers significant advantages to both the franchisor and franchisee. To the franchisor it offers these advantages:

1. Capital advantages will be gained since franchisees are typically charged a franchise fee. The franchisor can use these fees as a major source of working capital, allowing it to grow at a much more rapid pace without diluting its equity in the business.
2. Reduction in fixed overhead expenses will accrue to the franchisor since the high cost of maintaining company-owned outlets will be eliminated.
3. More motivated managers will be obtained because the franchisees, as independent businessmen, will be more committed to developing markets than would salaried employees.[10]

The franchisee receives the following significant advantages:

1. Uncertainty is reduced, since the approach to doing business has been proven successful by the franchisor.
2. A consumer franchise will accrue to the franchisee, since in many cases a well-known trademarked product or service is offered.

8. Louis W. Stern and Adel I. El-Ansary, *Marketing Channels* (Englewood Cliffs, N.J.: Prentice-Hall, 1977), p. 405.
9. Stern and El-Ansary, *Marketing Channels*, pp. 406–7.
10. Bert Rosenbloom, *Marketing Channels* (Hinsdale, Ill.: Dryden Press, 1978), pp. 305–9.

EXHIBIT 4.7   **Franchising in the United States (1977)**

KINDS OF FRANCHISED BUSINESS	ESTABLISHMENTS (number)			SALES (millions)	
	Total	Company-Owned	Franchisee-Owned	Company-Owned	Franchisee-Owned
Total—all franchising	450,800	85,941	364,859	$38,139	$215,236
Automobile and truck dealers	31,680	300	31,380	7,628	124,413
Automotive products and services	48,718	4,634	44,084	2,200	4,316
Business aids and services	32,227	5,529	26,698	563	2,826
Accounting, credit, collection agencies, and general business systems	3,749	57	3,692	8	132
Employment services	3,410	904	2,506	349	547
Printing and copying services	1,927	130	1,797	13	169
Tax preparation services	8,438	4,192	4,246	114	98
Real estate	11,449	114	11,335	37	1,692
Miscellaneous business services	3,254	132	3,122	42	188
Construction, home improvement, maintenance, and cleaning services	13,093	373	12,720	83	1,007
Convenience stores	14,144	9,395	4,749	2,458	1,862
Educational products and services	1,878	323	1,555	45	189
Fast food restaurants (all types)	51,972	14,527	37,445	5,653	12,527
Gasoline service stations	176,450	35,290	141,160	11,308	45,230
Hotels and motels	5,186	995	4,191	1,578	3,571
Campgrounds	1,057	19	1,038	6	103
Laundry and drycleaning services	2,769	67	2,702	11	218
Recreation, entertainment, and travel	4,242	73	4,169	26	214
Rental services (auto-truck)	6,888	1,843	5,045	1,260	846
Rental services (equipment)	1,421	156	1,265	63	129
Retailing (nonfood)	41,760	11,142	30,618	3,511	6,819
Retailing (food other than convenience stores)	13,299	904	12,395	1,350	1,881
Soft drink bottlers	2,146	70	2,076	308	8,738
Miscellaneous	1,870	301	1,569	88	347

Source: U.S. Department of Commerce, *Franchising in the Economy: 1977–1979,* January 1979, p. 32.

3. Managerial advice and assistance are offered the franchisee, helping to ensure his success.

4. Lower capital outlays are frequently involved than if he were to develop the business totally on his own initiative.

5. Higher financial returns are often gained than a totally independent businessman would realize.[11]

Although franchise systems offer significant advantages to both franchisor and franchisee, conflict is common. Franchisor-franchisee conflict frequently occurs over the following issues:

11. Rosenbloom, *Marketing Channels.*

1. How should the direct channel profits be divided? The establishment of fees and margins, specification of investment requirements, and location of expense incurring activities are involved.
2. When should franchisee investment in new or upgraded facilities be required, and who should participate in this decision?
3. How far should the franchisor go in saturating a single market area with franchise outlets?[12]

The most important determinant in avoiding conflict in a franchise system is the contract. Basically, the contract should not be inherently one-sided in favor of the franchisor. Several principles to guide franchise contract development have been suggested:

1. The contract should be frank, completely disclosing the relationship between franchisor and franchisee. The objective is to make explicit all mutual rights and obligations with performance standards to ensure that neither party may reasonably claim that he was deceived by the other.
2. The provisions should be fair so that neither party may claim unreasonable dominance by the other.
3. The contract should be tailored to the specific situation, recognizing the uniqueness of individual franchise systems and the difficulty of designing a generalized franchise contract.
4. Contract provisions should be enforceable so that no one party can use economic strength for cavalier violation of agreed-on covenants.[13]

A plea for intelligent contract design so as to avoid ambiguity (a major source of conflict) has been made. It has been suggested that ambiguity can be removed by:

1. Specifying the unique roles of the contracting parties.
2. Making operating procedures as specific as possible within the confines of antitrust regulations and local market differences.
3. Specifying in substantial detail the performance obligations of both parties.
4. Specifying how performance standards will be established and revised.
5. Specifying criteria for new outlet penetration of given markets.
6. Specifying reasonable causes leading to termination.[14]

The franchise contract gives the franchisor legitimate power to control the marketing channel. In addition, the franchisor obtains power by providing the franchisee with services and assistances that increase franchisee dependence, and thus franchisor power.[15] These assistances are provided when the franchisor helps the franchisee establish his or her initial business, and include: market survey and site selection, facility design and layout, lease negotiation advice,

12. R. Ronald Stephenson and Robert G. House, "A Perspective on Franchising," *Business Horizons* 14(August 1971): 35–42.

13. Jerold G. Van Cise, "A Franchise Contract," *Antitrust Bulletin* 14(April 1969): 325–46.

14. Stephenson and House, "Perspective on Franchising," p. 38.

15. Shelby D. Hunt and John R. Nevin, "Power in a Channel of Distribution: Sources and Consequences," *Journal of Marketing Research* 11(May 1974): 186–93.

financing advice, operating manuals, management training, and employee training programs. After the franchisee is established and in business, continuing assistance is provided by the franchisor to help ensure that the franchisee continues to do a good job. This ongoing assistance typically includes: field supervision, merchandising and promotional materials, management and employee training, quality inspection, national advertising, centralized purchasing, market data and guidance, auditing and record keeping, management reports, and group insurance plans. Although the franchisor can obtain control through the contract and providing the above services and assistances, there arise many legal problems in controlling a franchise system. These legal problems are discussed in considerable detail in Chapter 8.

Administered Systems   The final type of vertical marketing system is the administered system. **Administered vertical marketing systems** are, in principle, similar to conventional marketing channels, but here one of the channel members takes the initiative to lead the channel by applying the principles of effective interorganizational management. Administered systems, although not new in concept, have grown substantially since the 1960s.

Frequently, administered systems are initiated by manufacturers. As McCammon has observed,

> Manufacturing organizations . . . have historically relied on administrative expertise to coordinate reseller marketing efforts. Suppliers with dominant brands have predictably experienced the least difficulty in securing strong trade support, but many manufacturers with "fringe" items have been able to elicit reseller cooperation through the use of liberal distribution policies that take the form of attractive discounts (or discount substitutes), financial assistance, and various types of concessions that protect resellers from one or more of the risks of doing business.[16]

Exhibit 4.8 provides a listing of some common concessions that manufacturers might use to get retailers to support their marketing programs.

Manufacturers can also develop an administered system through **programmed merchandising agreements.** McCammon has defined these agreements as "a 'joint venture' in which a specific retail account and a supplier develop a comprehensive merchandising plan to market the supplier's product line. These plans normally cover a six month period but some use a longer duration."[17] Exhibit 4.9 (page 92) profiles the activities covered in programmed merchandising agreements. Manufacturers that have used programmed merchandising agreements include General Electric (on major and traffic appliances), Baumitter (on its Ethan Allen furniture line in nonfranchised outlets), Sealy (on its Posturepedic line of mattresses), Villager (on its dresses and sportswear lines), Scott (on its lawn care products), Norwalk (on its upholstered furniture), Keepsake (on diamonds), and Stanley (on hand tools).

16. Bert C. McCammon, Jr., "Perspectives for Distribution Programming," in Louis P. Bucklin (ed.), *Vertical Marketing Systems* (Glenview, Ill.: Scott, Foresman, 1970), p. 45.
17. McCammon, "Perspectives," p. 48.

EXHIBIT 4.8
**Common
Concessions
Manufacturers
Offer to Gain
Retailer
Support**

"PRICE" CONCESSIONS

Discount Structure
Trade (functional) discounts
Quantity discounts
Cash discounts
Anticipation allowances
Free goods
Prepaid freight
New product, display, and advertising allowances (without performance requirements)
Seasonal discounts
Mixed carload privilege
Drop shipping privilege
Trade deals

Discount Substitutes
Display materials
Premarked merchandise
Inventory control programs
Catalogs and sales promotion literature
Training programs
Shelf-stocking programs
Advertising matrices
Management consulting services
Merchandising programs
Sales "spiffs"
Technical assistance
Payment of sales personnel and demonstrator salaries
Promotional and advertising allowances (with performance requirements)

FINANCIAL ASSISTANCE

Conventional Lending Arrangements
Term loans
Inventory floor plans
Notes payable financing
Accounts payable financing
Installment financing of fixtures and equipment
Lease and note guarantee programs
Accounts receivable financing

Extended Dating
E.O.M. dating
Seasonal dating
R.O.G. dating
"Extra" dating
Post dating

PROTECTIVE PROVISIONS

Price Protection
Premarked merchandise
"Franchise" pricing
Agency agreements

Inventory Protection
Consignment selling
Memorandum selling
Liberal returns allowances
Rebate programs

Inventory Protection (cont.)
Reorder guarantees
Guaranteed support of sales events
Maintenance of "spot" stocks and fast delivery

Territorial Protection
Selective distribution
Exclusive distribution

Source: Bert C. McCammon, Jr., "Perspectives for Distribution Programming," in Louis P. Bucklin (ed.), *Vertical Marketing Systems* (Glenview, Ill.: Scott, Foresman and Company, 1970), pp.36–37. Reprinted with permission.

EXHIBIT 4.9
Plans and Activities Covered in Programmed Merchandising Agreements

MERCHANDISING GOALS

1. Planned sales
2. Planned initial markup percentage
3. Planned reductions, including planned markdowns, shortages, and discounts
4. Planned gross margin
5. Planned expense ratio (optional)
6. Planned profit margin (optional)

INVENTORY PLAN

1. Planned rate of inventory turnover
2. Planned merchandise assortments, including basic or model stock plans
3. Formalized "never out" lists
4. Desired mix of promotional versus regular merchandise

MERCHANDISE PRESENTATION PLAN

1. Recommended store fixtures
2. Space allocation plan
3. Visual merchandising plan
4. Needed promotional materials, including point-of-purchase displays, consumer literature, and price signs

PERSONAL SELLING PLAN

1. Recommended sales presentations
2. Sales training plan
3. Special incentive arrangements, including "spiffs," salesmen's contests, and related activities

ADVERTISING AND SALES PROMOTION PLAN

1. Advertising and sales promotion budget
2. Media schedule
3. Copy themes for major campaigns and promotions
4. Special sales events

RESPONSIBILITIES AND DUE DATES

1. Supplier's responsibilities in connection with the plan
2. Retailer's responsibilities in connection with the plan

Source: Bert C. McCammon, Jr., "Perspectives for Distribution Programming," in Louis P. Bucklin (ed.), *Vertical Marketing Systems* (Glenview, Ill.: Scott, Foresman and Company, 1970), pp.48–49. Reprinted with permission.

MANAGING MARKETING CHANNEL RELATIONS

Retailers who are not part of a contractual system or corporate channel will probably be participants in several marketing channels, since they will need to acquire merchandise from many suppliers (wholesaler or manufacturer). Predictably, these marketing channels will either be conventional or administered. If the retailer desires to improve its performance in these channels then it must understand the principle concepts of interorganizational management.

Interorganizational management is the management of relationships between organizational entities. In a marketing channel, it involves one member, such as a retailer, managing its relations with other organizations in the channel, such as wholesalers and manufacturers. The retailer operating in a conventional marketing channel could apply the concepts of interorganizational management in order to move the channel toward becoming an administered channel. Alternatively, if the retailer is a party to an administered channel then an understanding of the basic concepts of interorganizational management will help the retailer to appreciate the need for one channel member to lead and organize the channel and for all channel members to work in unison so that they can compete effectively with other marketing channel systems for scarce consumer dollars.

What then are the basic concepts of interorganizational management that you as a retail executive need to understand? They are dependency, power, and conflict.

Dependency

As we mentioned earlier in this chapter, all marketing systems need to perform eight marketing functions. These functions are performed by a multitude of institutions in the marketing channel. Each of the respective institutions, however, cannot isolate itself; it depends on other institutions in order to do an effective job.

Retailer *A* is dependent on Suppliers *X*, *Y*, and *Z* to get the goods delivered safely, on time, and in the right quantities. On the other hand, each supplier depends on the retailer to put a strong selling effort behind the goods, displaying the merchandise and helping to finance consumer purchases. If Retailer *A* does a poor job, each supplier can be adversely affected; conversely, if even one supplier does a poor job, Retailer *A* can be adversely affected. Therefore, in all channel alignments, each party depends on the others to do a good job.

When each party is dependent on the others, we can say that they are **interdependent.** Interdependency is the basic root of conflict in marketing channels.[18] When conflict arises someone needs to exercise power. However, before we explore the concepts of power and conflict, let us examine the concept of dependency in more detail.

18. Louis W. Stern and Ronald H. Gorman, "Conflict in Distribution Channels: An Exploration," in Louis W. Stern (ed.), *Distribution Channels: Behavioral Dimensions* (Boston: Houghton Mifflin, 1969), p. 156.

Generally, the retailer's dependency on the supplier is a function of (1) the retailer's motivational investment in goals that the supplier can mediate, and (2) the retailer's alternatives for mediating its goals.[19] This relationship can be better understood through a hypothetical example. Assume that the management of Lifestyles (a hypothetical catalog showroom) is highly committed to achieving a 20 percent return-on-investment goal. Lifestyles purchases the majority of its merchandise from a single supplier, who provides a merchandise line that will yield a very attractive profit margin. It is clear that this attractive margin will significantly help the showroom attain its goal. Further assume that Lifestyles is not able to locate any other suppliers that can supply merchandise lines with such attractive profit margins. Obviously, then, the retailer is very dependent on the supplier. To see if you can comprehend the concept of dependency, create a situation in which the retailer would not be very dependent on the supplier.

Power

We can use the concept of dependency to explain power, but first, we must define power: the **power** of the supplier over the retailer is the ability of the supplier to control the decision variables of the retailer.[20] The more dependent the retailer is on the supplier, the more power the supplier has over the retailer. For example, a powerful beer supplier could get a dependent package store to give its products prime shelf space and special promotional emphasis. A fact of life in the marketing channel, therefore, is that the more a retailer allows itself to become dependent on a supplier, the more the supplier will be able to influence the retailer's actions.

A second explanation of power is that the more **bases of power** that A has over B, the more power A has over B.[21] There are five bases of power:

1. **Reward power** is based on the ability of A to mediate rewards for B.
2. **Expertise power** is based on B's perception that A has some special knowledge.
3. **Referent power** is based on the identification of B with A. B wants to be associated or identified with A.
4. **Coercive power** is based on B's belief that A has the capacity to punish or harm if he doesn't conform to A's desire.
5. **Legitimate power** is based on A's right to influence B, or alternatively B's belief that he should accept A's influence.

In this preceding framework A (the power holder) could be either the supplier or the retailer.

The retailer can use the concepts of dependency and bases of power to

19. Richard M. Emerson, "Power-Dependence Relations," *American Sociological Review* 27(February 1962): 31–41.

20. This definition of power is similar to most power definitions in the behavioral literature. See Herbert Simon, "Notes on the Observation and Measurement of Power," *Journal of Politics* 15(November 1953): 503; and Herbert Goldhammer and R. Shils, "Types of Power and Status," *American Journal of Sociology* 45(1939): 171.

21. J. R. P. French and Bertram Raven, "The Bases of Social Power," in Darwin Cartwright and Alvin Zonder (eds.), *Group Dynamics: Research and Theory* (New York: Harper and Row, 1968).

develop strategies to equalize its power with the supplier or possibly even to become more powerful than the supplier. Here are some realistic examples of what the retailer might do in this regard:

1. The retailer could develop expert power by obtaining information on consumer's needs and providing this information to suppliers.
2. The retailer could maintain multiple sources of supply in order to avoid the coercive power of any single supplier.
3. The retailer could use scarce shelf space as a reward to key suppliers.
4. The retailer could establish referent power by building a strong consumer franchise so that the consumer becomes more loyal to its store than to a brand.
5. The retailer could develop a strong store brand program to avoid the coercive power of national brand producers.
6. The retailer could band together with other retailers in order to purchase in larger quantities and employ reward power with suppliers.

This is not an exhaustive list. Why not take a moment to see if you can add three more examples.

Conflict

Conflict between retailers and their suppliers is inevitable since retailers and suppliers are interdependent. Interdependency has been identified as the root of all conflict in marketing channels; however, there is more to understanding conflict than its direct tie to interdependency. Exhibit 4.10 provides a model of the conflict process to serve as a frame of reference for the discussion.

Interdependency and Conflict Potential As can be seen in Exhibit 4.10, conflict involves several stages.[22] First, as we have said, interdependency needs to exist among the retailer and supplier. Without interdependency there will exist no potential for conflict. Also, the greater the interdependency between supplier and retailer the greater the potential for conflict. However, more than just a potential for conflict needs to exist for a retailer and supplier to engage in conflict. Latent sources of conflict are also necessary.

Latent Conflict **Latent conflict** is any underlying situation that if left unattended, could eventually result in conflictful behavior. In the retailer-supplier dyad, there are three major sources of latent conflict: perceptual incongruity, goal incompatibility, and domain dissensus.

  Perceptual incongruity occurs when the retailer's or supplier's perception of reality is different from the other's.[23] To illustrate, a retailer may perceive

22. This process model of conflict relies heavily on Louis R. Pondy, "Organizational Conflict: Concepts and Models," *Administrative Science Quarterly* 12(September 1967): 328–41.

23. Perceptual incongruity is identified as a source of conflict in Morton Deutsch, *The Resolution of Conflict* (New Haven: Yale University Press, 1973), p. 16; Joseph A. Litterer, "Conflict in Organizations: A Re-Examination," *Academy of Management Journal* 9(September 1960): 183; and Louis W. Stern and James L. Heskett, "Conflict Management in Interorganizational Relations: A Conceptual Framework," in Louis W. Stern (ed.), *Distribution Channels: Behavioral Dimensions* (Boston: Houghton Mifflin, 1969), p. 294.

EXHIBIT 4.10
**Conflict in the
Marketing
Channel**

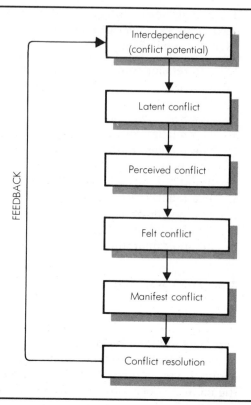

that the economy is entering a recession and therefore inventory investments should be slashed, while the supplier may perceive that the economy will remain strong and therefore inventory investments should be maintained or possibly increased. In the marketing channel, perceptual incongruity is a major source of conflict. For example, consider the following areas which the retailer and supplier would perceive differently: the quality of the supplier's merchandise, the potential demand for the supplier's merchandise, the consumer appeal of the supplier's advertising, the best shelf position for the supplier's merchandise. See if you can identify other areas of potential perceptual incongruity.

A second source of latent conflict is **goal incompatibility.**[24] In this situation the goals of the supplier or retailer (if pursued) would hamper the goal attainment of the other. For instance, consider a womenswear supplier with a sportswear line that it wants the consumer to perceive as having a high quality and status image. A high retail price would be consistent with this goal. However, the retailer might believe that its return-on-investment goals could be better

24. Goal incompatibility is identified as a source of conflict in Stuart M. Schmidt and Thomas A. Kochon, "Conflict: Toward Conceptual Clarity," *Administrative Science Quarterly* 17(September 1972): 359–70; Bertram H. Raven and H. T. Eachus, "Cooperation and Competition in Means-Interdependent Triads," *Journal of Abnormal and Social Psychology* 67(1963): 307–16; and Stern and Heskett, "Conflict Management in Interorganization Relations," p. 294.

achieved if the sportswear were heavily discounted and higher volume could be sold. Clearly, the retailer's profit goals are not compatible with the supplier's image goals.

The problem is not necessarily one of comparing profit goals to image goals. Even if the retailer and supplier both have a return-on-investment (ROI) goal, they can still have incompatible goals, because what is good for the retailer's ROI may not be good for the supplier's ROI. Consider the price element in the transaction between the supplier and retailer. If the supplier obtains a higher price, its ROI will be better but the ROI of the retailer will be lower. Similarly, other key elements in the transaction between the retailer and supplier—such as advertising allowances, cash discounts, order quantity, and freight charges—can result in conflict.

Because suppliers have different goals than the retailers they serve, they often engage in behavior that is in conflict with the retailer.[25] For instance, when retailers place orders with suppliers they often give a cancellation date. This date tells the supplier that if the merchandise can't be shipped by that date then the order should be cancelled. But many suppliers will ignore the cancellation dates and ship the merchandise late. What can a gift store do with a shipment of valentines that arrive on February 15? Another common practice is the substitution of merchandise when the supplier is out of the ordered items. The supplier may substitute colors and styles that the retailer does not want. A fabric store in a college town may place an order for midnight blue and gold, the team colors, for the homecoming celebration. In the past, there has been a sellout of all material in these colors, and this year the celebration is expected to be even bigger. Imagine the retailer's dismay on unpacking the order to find that the supplier has substituted royal blue for the darker shade. Finally, retailers will often receive invoices requesting immediate payment before they receive the merchandise.

The case study presented in Exhibit 4.11 deals with conflict between manufacturers and retailers over trade promotions. Much of this conflict is due to incompatible goals.

A third source of latent conflict is **domain dissensus.**[26] Domain refers to the decision variables that each member of the marketing channel feels it should be able to control. When the members of the marketing channel agree on who should make which decisions, domain consensus exists. Where there is disagreement on who should make decisions then domain dissensus exists.

Consider the case of an automobile manufacturer and an automobile dealer. The dealer believes it should be able to make decisions regarding employees, local advertising, retail pricing, hours of operation, and remodeling and expansion. However, the manufacturer believes that it should be consulted on hours of operation and remodeling and expansion. As a consequence there exists some domain dissensus in the auto manufacturer–auto dealer dyad.

25. For a discussion of conflict areas, see "Vendors! We Need Better Communication!" *The Discount Merchandiser,* January 1980, pp. 114–115.

26. Domain dissensus is identified as a source of conflict in Louis W. Stern and Ronald H. Gorman, "Conflict in Distribution Channels: An Exploration," in Stern (ed.), *Distribution Channels,* pp. 156–75.

EXHIBIT 4.11
Conflict Between Manufacturers and Retailers

Manufacturers will often offer trade promotions to retailers (such as free goods, price off, pay them to handle coupons). The intent is that these trade promotions will encourage the retailer to promote the items to build traffic and increase sales.

Manufacturers and retailers frequently come into conflict over the form and amount of trade promotions. Retailers sometimes view promotional efforts initiated by manufacturers as encouraging profitless brand switching rather than increasing sales and profits. Manufacturers, on the other hand, complain that retailer-initiated promotions sometimes damage brand franchises which have been carefully and expensively nurtured over years. Worse yet, manufacturers complain that retailers frequently take advantage of them by "absorbing" trade promotions without passing their benefits along to consumers. In this case, although manufacturers may gain the good will of retailers, they clearly benefit less than they would if the trade promotion achieved its intended purpose of inducing retailers to advertise, display, price reduce or otherwise promote their products to consumers.

Source: Reprinted with permission from "Retail Promotions as a Function of Trade Promotions: A Descriptive Analysis," by Michel Chevalier and Ronald C. Curhan, *Sloan Management Review* (Fall 1976), p. 20, by permission of the publisher. Copyright ©1976 by Sloan Management Review Association. All rights reserved.

Perceived Conflict   **Perceived conflict** is a cognitive stage. It represents the point at which either the supplier or retailer becomes aware of one or more of the three preceding sources of latent conflict. For instance, in our example of the womenswear supplier that was pursuing a high-priced, quality image for its sportswear line and the retailer that was heavily discounting the brand to achieve a higher return-on-investment goal, perceived conflict would not occur until the supplier became aware of the retailer's pricing strategy. Note that none of the three sources of latent conflict will necessarily ever be perceived. If they are not perceived, conflict will not progress beyond the latent stage.

Felt Conflict   **Felt conflict** consists of stress, tension, or hostility resulting from perceiving a conflict. It is thus the affective dimension of conflict. Not all suppliers and retailers that perceive a source of latent conflict will experience felt conflict; some may have a high tolerance for perceived conflicts. They may realize that there is a basic source of conflict, but may feel that it isn't worthwhile getting upset. Alternatively, they may simply be too busy with other matters to waste time worrying and getting frustrated over the source of conflict.

Manifest Conflict   **Manifest conflict** is the behavioral or action stage of conflict. This stage is often characterized by verbal or written threats or other actions by the supplier or retailer to block the other from what it is doing. Manifest conflict will not always follow felt conflict for a variety of reasons. Possibly the supplier or retailer experiences felt conflict but determines that it might not be worth the effort (i.e., there is little to gain) by engaging in manifest conflict. Or, the retailer may experience felt conflict but also realize that the supplier has considerably more power rendering any engagement in manifest conflict futile.

Conflict Resolution Manifest conflict offers the most potential harm to the retailer-supplier dyad and thus needs to be resolved as soon as possible. If properly resolved, the manifest conflict could actually be functional—for example, if the retailer and supplier could more efficiently or effectively perform their respective jobs.

There are two major conflict resolution mechanisms—**withdrawal** and **procedural resolution.**[27] In a retailer-supplier conflict, withdrawal should be viewed only as a last resort. However, if the retailer and supplier fail through all reasonable means to resolve their conflict, then their relationship may be dissolved, in which case, each will need to seek a new channel partner.

Procedural resolution is more common than withdrawal. If the retailer and supplier are each dependent on the other and interested in a continuing relationship then most conflicts can be resolved. There are three means of procedural resolution: reconciliation, compromise, and award.

Reconciliation is a situation in which "the value systems of . . . the parties so change that they now have common preferences in the joint field: they both want the same state of affairs or position in the joint field and so conflict is eliminated."[28] For example, in the situation of perceptual incongruity previously outlined, the retailer perceived that a recession was on the horizon whereas the supplier perceived continued prosperity. As a result, the retailer desired to reduce inventories, but the supplier wanted it to maintain or even increase inventory. Ultimately, the supplier and retailer got into a rather heated argument. Finally, the supplier was able to present some overwhelming evidence (based on some economic forecasting models a consulting firm had developed) that caused the retailer to revise its perceptions and come to hold the same view as the supplier.

A second form of procedural resolution is **compromise.** Compromise is the result of a situation "in which the value systems are not identical and the parties have different optimum positions in the joint field; however, each party is willing to settle for something less than his ideal position rather than continue the conflict."[29] To continue our preceding example, the supplier and retailer, after heated debate, may decide to compromise on their original positions. The retailer may decide not to cut inventory as much as it had initially planned if in turn the supplier will finance more of the retailer's inventory investment by providing forty five-day instead of thirty-day payment terms. In a conflict that is resolved by compromise, each party relinquishes part of their initial position. In marketing channels, compromise is the most common form of conflict resolution.

Award is the result of a settlement that is reached "because both parties have agreed to accept the verdict of an outside person or agency rather than continue the conflict."[30] An award is typically the result of a legal trial or arbi-

---

27. Kenneth E. Boulding, *Conflict and Defense* (New York: Harper and Brothers, 1962).
28. Boulding, *Conflict and Defense*, p. 310.
29. Boulding, *Conflict and Defense*, p. 310.
30. Boulding, *Conflict and Defense*, p. 310.

tration. The courts have settled many conflicts in marketing channels, specifically between retailers and suppliers.

In addition, state and federal legislatures have passed legislation to equalize the balance of power between retailers and their suppliers and thus reduce or resolve conflict. For example, when automobile dealers and manufacturers clashed over automobile distribution and marketing policies, state and federal legislation was passed in an attempt to equalize the balance of power between them.[31] Similar legislation resulted in regulating franchisors in the 1970s.[32]

When **arbitration** is used to resolve a conflict, parties voluntarily submit their dispute to a third party whose decision will be considered final and binding.[33] Many franchise channels and administered vertical marketing systems have established formal arbitration boards.[34] These boards consist of industry representatives and are chaired by an independent arbitrator—perhaps a retired judge. This approach can be highly pragmatic since it "provides for a third party to enter and resolve a dispute before it becomes too difficult to settle in a reasonably friendly fashion."[35] Using arbitration to resolve channel conflicts offers five advantages:

1. Arbitration is fast. The parties to a dispute can be quickly informed that a quarrel exists and told the time of a hearing; the evidence can then be heard by a panel and the decision rendered all within a few weeks.
2. Arbitration preserves secrecy. Outside parties can be banned from the hearings. Decisions that are not matters of public record can be kept secret.
3. Arbitration is less expensive than litigation. There is an element of cutting corners that takes place, reducing the cost of a tolerable decision.
4. Arbitration confronts problems in their incipient stage when they are easier to solve. The attitude can become, "We have a potential problem here; let us solve it before positions and options get too fixed."
5. Arbitration often takes place before industry experts. In many instances, the arbitrator or the arbitration panel is composed of those who know an industry and its practices. Some argue that this produces a fairer decision.[36]

Feedback   If you refer back to Exhibit 4.10 you will notice that conflict doesn't end with resolution. After the conflict is resolved, there will be feedback. In other words, the outcome of the conflict will affect future conflict. How satis-

31. Stewart Macaulay, *Law and the Balance of Power* (New York: Russell Sage Foundation, 1966).

32. Shelby D. Hunt and John R. Nevin, "Tying Agreements in Franchising" *Journal of Marketing* 39(July 1975): 24–25; Shelby D. Hunt and John R. Nevin, "Full Disclosure Laws in Franchising," *Journal of Marketing* 40(April 1976): 53–62; and James T. Haverson, "What's in Store at the Federal Trade Commission," *Franchising and Antitrust* (Washington, D.C.; International Franchise Association, 1975), pp. 20–29.

33. Stern and El-Ansary, *Marketing Channels*, p. 305.

34. Robert F. Weigand and Hilda C. Wasson, "Arbitration in the Marketing Channel," *Business Horizons* 17(October 1974): 39–47.

35. Weigand and Wasson, "Arbitration," p. 39.

36. Robert F. Weigand and Hilda C. Wasson, "Arbitration in the Marketing Channel," *Business Horizons* 17(October 1974): 39. Reprinted with permission.

factory the resolution was to the parties and what they learned about each other during the entire conflict process will influence their future behavior toward each other. Also, a retailer's conflict with one supplier may provide useful information on how to handle similar conflicts with other suppliers.

SUMMARY

The system must be viewed as the solution. If the retailer ignores the marketing system in order to maximize short-run profits then in the long run, the system will forget about the retailer. And if the system forgets the retailer then profits sufficient for survival and growth will vanish.

In learning to work within the marketing system, the retailer needs to recognize that eight marketing functions are necessary in all marketing systems: buying, selling, storage, transporting, sorting, financing, information, and risk taking. The retailer can seldom perform all of these functions exclusively and therefore must rely on other primary and facilitating institutions in the marketing system. Although the marketing functions are pervasive they can be shifted or divided among the institutions in the marketing system.

The institutions in the marketing system can be arranged into two primary marketing channel patterns—conventional and vertical. A conventional marketing channel is one in which each member of the channel is loosely aligned with the others, each member recognizing those it directly interacts with but ignoring all others. Conventional marketing channels are on the decline in the United States, while vertical marketing systems are becoming dominant. In the vertical marketing system all parties to the channel recognize each other and one party programs the channel to achieve technological, managerial, and promotional economies. Three types of vertical marketing systems are corporate, contractual, and administered.

The retailer, in order to operate efficiently and effectively in any marketing channel, needs to understand the basics of interorganizational behavior. Key concepts that need to be understood are dependency, power, and conflict. By understanding these concepts, the retailer can learn to interact productively with other marketing channel members.

QUESTIONS

1. In this chapter we stated that K-mart's marketing channels are in competition with Woolco's. Would this totally be the case if both K-mart and Woolco buy from some of the same suppliers? For example, assume they both buy calculators from Texas Instruments.

2. Facilitating marketing institutions are powerless in the marketing channel. Agree or disagree and explain your reasoning.

3. How might a small local chain of five grocery stores increase its power in the marketing channel?

4. Can a retailer lead the marketing channel?

5. During economic recession, conflict in the marketing channel is likely to increase. Agree or disagree and explain why.

6. Using the strategic profit model as a frame of reference, show how certain components of the model might help to explain conflict between retailers and their suppliers.

7. What are the marketing functions performed in a marketing channel?

8. What is a resident buyer?

9. How do wholesaler sponsored voluntary groups benefit independent retailers?

10. What are the advantages of the franchised form of distribution/marketing to the franchisor and franchisee?

11. What are the advantages of using arbitration to resolve conflict in the marketing channel?

PROBLEMS AND EXERCISES

1. Attempt to design a marketing system for food products in which you can eliminate any one of the eight marketing functions.

2. Interview the owner or manager of a local fast-food franchise to determine the extent to which the franchisor attempts to control the franchisee's business decisions. Also try to find out the extent of any franchisor-franchisee conflicts that have recently occurred.

3. Assume that you are the owner-manager of a shoe store chain that, in the past, has emphasized high-quality shoes at discount prices. Recently, however, your customers have been complaining that one of the lines you carry looks shoddy and doesn't hold up well. This line comes from your biggest supplier and has always been a favorite of your customers. You therefore become uneasy, for although you have other suppliers your buyer has always been able to deal more effectively with this, your major one. After looking at this same line of shoes in competing stores you begin to suspect that you are receiving second- or third-quality merchandise from this supplier, although you have been paying for first quality. Is there a conflict in this situation? If so, between whom? Could your buyer be involved? How can this conflict be resolved? Using the means of resolution of conflict outlined in this chapter, try to resolve this conflict.

4. Visit a department store and interview one of the buyers. Try to determine the amount of negotiation that typically occurs between a buyer and supplier of a merchandise line. What types of things are negotiated? How important is the timing of delivery of the merchandise? Have delivery delays resulted in conflict in the past?

SUGGESTED READINGS

Lusch, Robert F. "Channel Conflict: Its Impact on Retailer Operating Performance." *Journal of Retailing* 52(Summer 1976): 3–12.

Mallen, Bruce. "Functional Spin-off: A Key to Anticipating Change in Distribution Structure." *Journal of Marketing* 37(July 1973): 18–25.

"Mr. Retailer, You're a Manufacturer for a Day!" *Merchandising* (November 1976): 19–24.

Robicheaux, Robert A, and Adel I. El-Ansary. "A General Model for Understanding Channel Member Behavior." *Journal of Retailing* 52(Winter 1976–77): 13–30, 93–94.

Rosenberg, Larry J, and Louis W. Stern. "Toward the Analysis of Conflict in Distribution Channels: A Descriptive Model." *Journal of Marketing* 34(October 1970): 40–46.

Rosenbloom, Bert. "Conflict and Channel Efficiency: Some Conceptual Models for the Decision Maker." *Journal of Marketing* 37(July 1973): 26–30.

Shuptrine, F. Kelly, and J. Robert Foster. "Monitoring Channel Conflict With Evaluations from the Retail Level." *Journal of Retailing* 52(Spring 1976): 55–74.

Stern, Louis W., and C. S. Craig. "Interorganizational Data Systems: The Computer and Distribution." *Journal of Retailing* 47(Summer 1971): 73–86, 91.

5

Overview *This chapter will focus on the behavior of consumers in a retail setting. As a mechanism for focusing our attention, we will develop a retail patronage model to help us describe and explain how consumers make retail patronage decisions.*

Understanding Consumer Behavior

IN CHAPTER 4, the role of retailing in the marketing system was discussed, with special emphasis on the role of the retailer in the marketing channel. In this chapter we will show that the performance of the retailer within the marketing channel is heavily influenced by the behavior of consumers. This is true whether the retailer is conventional or uses nonstore methods (direct mail or door-to-door). In either case, the retailer consummates transactions with consumers. In one case, the transaction is within the store and in the other case, it is within the consumer's home, but in both cases the behavior patterns of the consumer cannot be ignored. Let us now explore the behavior of consumers in a retail setting through the lens of a retail patronage model.

A RETAIL PATRONAGE MODEL

Before we present the retail patronage model, we should first recognize several relevant points. First, any model, by its very nature, is an abstraction (that is, the model is not the real thing; it is only a representation of reality). However, it should be (and we believe this model is) relatively representative of reality. Second, in the consumer behavior literature there has been no concentrated effort to construct a comprehensive model of retail patronage behavior.[1] As a result, our model has been created by piecing together what is known about consumer behavior in general and the specific research studies done on retail patronage behavior. Third, the model is intended more as a teaching aid than as a framework for serious empirical testing. Fourth, the retail patronage model in its full form depicts patronage behavior for a store (thus the nonstore retailing situation is not fully incorporated). After we develop the model in detail, we will discuss how the model would change for a nonstore retailing transaction.

Now let us examine the patronage model in Exhibit 5.1 (page 106). On first examining the model you will note that it is a process model moving from left to right. The process begins when the consumer recognizes a need to shop—to buy, to obtain information, to socialize, or for other personal reasons. The consumer then evaluates shopping alternatives and selects a store or stores to visit. Each store as it is visited continues to be evaluated so the consumer can decide whether to stay in the store and shop or to leave. The consumer will obtain closure if the offerings in the store are favorably evaluated. Finally, we move to the outcome stage in which the consumer either purchases, postpones purchase, or does additional searching. Since the consumer is a learning animal, information is continually being stored for future use in shopping situations and, therefore, the model has a feedback loop which goes through the consumer's learning processes. In addition, each stage of the model, from problem recognition through outcome, is affected by the information sources that continually bombard the consumer.

---

1. Currently, Professor Bill Darden at the University of Arkansas is working on constructing and refining such a model.

EXHIBIT 5.1   **A Retail Patronage Model**

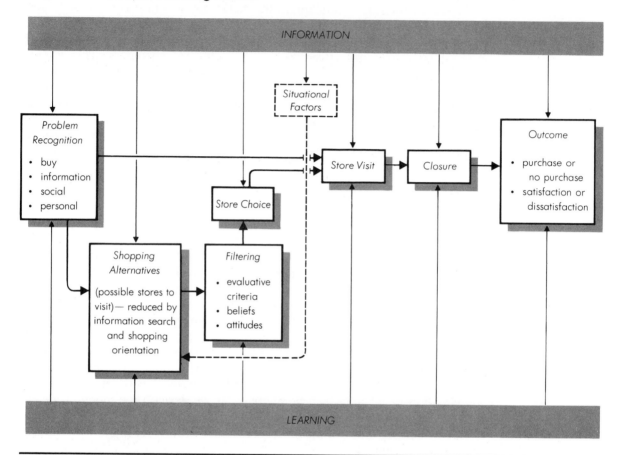

PROBLEM RECOGNITION

The first step in the retail patronage model is problem recognition. **Problem recognition** occurs when the consumer's ideal state of affairs departs sufficiently from the actual state of affairs so as to place the consumer in a state of unrest. In short, the consumer is disturbed enough by the difference between the actual and ideal state, that he or she begins thinking of ways to resolve the difference. In Exhibit 5.2, a separate illustration of the problem recognition stage in the retail patronage model is presented.

Arousing Problem Recognition   In the store patronage model, we see that problem recognition can be aroused by either information sources or learning processes. Information sources may alert or remind the consumer of a discrepancy between the actual

EXHIBIT 5.2
**The Problem
Recognition
Stage**

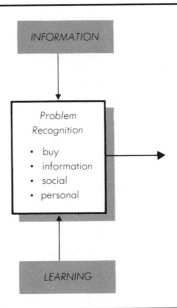

and ideal state. For example, the consumer may see an advertisement for a sleeper sofa that is on sale at a local department store. While seeing the advertisement, the consumer recalls that relatives will be visiting in the near future to spend a week. Almost instantly this person recognizes the problem of not having a place for the relatives to sleep.

Alternatively, problem recognition may be the direct outgrowth of learning processes. For example, the consumer may have to learn (through experience) that approximately every other day the household will run out of milk and bread. Thus, every other day (even without checking the bread box or milk bottle) the consumer recognizes the need to replenish these staples.

We urge you, as you progress with us through this model, to place yourself within the model's framework. The last time you went shopping, how did you recognize the need to shop? Did an information source cause you to recognize the problem or did the problem recognition result from a psychological process such as learning?

Ideal State   Retailers must recognize that the **ideal state** is consumer or household-specific. What may be the ideal for one consumer is not the ideal for another. Also, the retailer must not use its ideal to gauge the consumer's ideal. For example, the TV-appliance retailer may believe that the ideal state of affairs is a TV in each room of the house and that any house with less than this number has a problem that the retailer can help solve. This is clearly not realistic. The ideal is determined by a host of factors such as income, social class, reference group, age, educational level, and occupation, most of which the retailer has little or no control over.

Actual State   The retailer cannot measure the consumer's actual state by casual observation. The consumer's **actual state** depends on how the consumer perceives it. An outsider may look at a family of eight in a small house and conclude that the actual state is undesirable. The household itself, however, may perceive the actual state quite differently. Retailers generally have little control over a household's actual state.

Retailer-Induced Problem Recognition   Should the retailer try to stimulate problem recognition? To do so, it would have to be able to alter the consumer's actual or ideal state. However, as we have previously indicated, the retailer has little control over these two states. Therefore, the retailer would, in most part, be wasting dollars by attempting to induce problem recognition.

The consumer is bombarded by thousands of messages daily and therefore must screen out most of them. The stimuli (information) that will be perceived are those which relate to problems he or she has already recognized. Consequently, the retailer can better spend its dollars by focusing efforts on consumers who have already recognized a need to shop.

Information on Problem Recognition   The consensus among consumer behavior analysts is that problem recognition can be measured by collecting information on intention to purchase. Purchase intentions can be measured by a variety of techniques,[2] but the method that is most valid is the probability-of-purchase scale.[3] "The purchase-probability technique requests that consumers estimate the probability that they will purchase a particular product or brand within a designated time period on the following type of scale."[4] The scale is shown in Exhibit 5.3. The technique has been successfully used for such diverse product categories as automobiles,[5] household appliances,[6] low-price convenience items,[7] and several grocery-product categories.[8]

Although marketing managers in manufacturing concerns have frequently used purchase-probability scales in developing marketing strategies, retail managers have not capitalized on their use. This is unfortunate since such scales

2. F. T. Juster, *Consumer Buying Intentions and Purchase Probability* (New York: National Bureau of Economic Research, 1966).

3. D. H. Granbois and J. O. Summers, "On the Predictive Accuracy of Subjective Purchase Probabilities," in *Proceedings of the Third Annual Conference on the Association for Consumer Research* (Chicago: American Marketing Association, 1972), pp. 502–11.

4. Carl E. Block and Kenneth J. Roering, *Essentials of Consumer Behavior: Concepts and Applications*, 2nd ed. (Hinsdale, Ill.: Dryden Press, 1979), p. 386.

5. Granbois and Summers, "Predictive Accuracy of Subjective Purchase Probabilities," p. 506.

6. R. W. Pratt, Jr., "Understanding the Decision Process for Consumer Durables: An Example of the Longitudinal Approach," in P. D. Bennett (ed.), *Marketing and Economic Development* (Chicago: American Marketing Association, 1965), pp. 244–60.

7. A. Gruber, "Purchase Intention and Purchase Probability," *Journal of Advertising Research* 10(February 1970): 23–27.

8. S. Banks, "The Relationship Between Preference and Purchase of Brands," *Journal of Marketing* 15(October 1950): 145–57.

EXHIBIT 5.3 **The Probability-of-Purchase Scale**

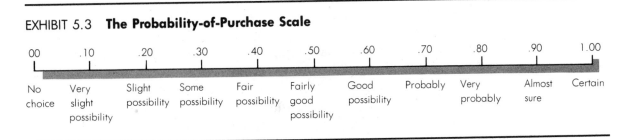

00	.10	.20	.30	.40	.50	.60	.70	.80	.90	1.00
No choice	Very slight possibility	Slight possibility	Some possibility	Fair possibility	Fairly good possibility	Good possibility	Probably	Very probably	Almost sure	Certain

can provide the retailer with information that could be quite useful in the design of promotion and merchandising. Let us construct a hypothetical, although not unrealistic, example.

The Great American Furniture store is a locally and independently owned single-outlet retailer located in a rapidly growing city of 138,000 (45,000 households). Due to the geographical compactness of the city, Great American Furniture is able to attract patrons across the entire city. It offers a full line of furniture in several price ranges from low to moderately high in several styles. The owner of the store, Lou Johnson, has obtained the services of a marketing research firm to conduct a survey of 900 households randomly selected from the city's 45,000. The head of the household will be asked to provide certain demographic characteristics (income, number of children, education, etc.) and to respond to the probability-of-purchase questions in Exhibit 5.4.

Using the data collected, Lou Johnson was able to estimate the equivalent number of households that would be in the market within the next six months for various pieces of furniture. He was able to do this with the following equation:

$$N_i = \overline{P}_i H$$

EXHIBIT 5.4 **Probability-of-Purchase Questions for Great American Furniture Survey**

In regard to each of the following items, please indicate, as best you can, the likelihood that your family would purchase each of the items within the next six months.

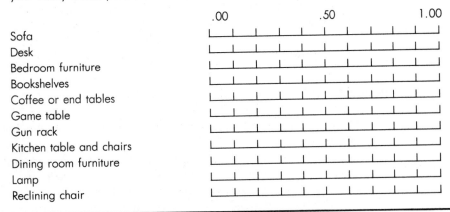

Sofa
Desk
Bedroom furniture
Bookshelves
Coffee or end tables
Game table
Gun rack
Kitchen table and chairs
Dining room furniture
Lamp
Reclining chair

where:

N_i = expected number of households that will be in the market for item i within the next six months

$\overline{P_i}$ = average probability of a household purchasing item i within the next six months

H = total number of households in the retailer's market area.

For example, if Great American Furniture found out that the average probability of a household purchasing a sofa in the next six months was 17 percent, then the expected number of households that would buy sofas would be .17(45,000) or 7,650 households. Using this technique, Lou Johnson arrived at the following estimates of the number of households that would be purchasing various furniture items in the next six months:

Sofa	.170(45,000) = 7,650 households
Desk	.024(45,000) = 1,080 households
Bedroom furniture	.130(45,000) = 5,850 households
Bookshelves	.143(45,000) = 6,435 households
Coffee or end tables	.070(45,000) = 3,150 households
Game table	.089(45,000) = 4,005 households
Gun rack	.040(45,000) = 1,800 households
Kitchen table and chairs	.120(45,000) = 5,400 households
Dining room furniture	.051(45,000) = 2,295 households
Lamp	.075(45,000) = 3,375 households
Reclining chair	.214(45,000) = 9,630 households

Using the preceding results, Lou Johnson could readily determine on which furniture items to place more advertising and promotional effort: those items with the highest purchase probability, which are those items for which the problem recognition stage has been reached. Also, note that since data on demographics were collected, Great American Furniture could statistically assess whether households of a certain demographic profile were more likely to be planning to purchase certain furniture items than other households. For example, although overall the average probability of a household purchasing a gun rack within the next six months was only 4 percent, it might be found (from proper statistical analysis) that the average probability is 14 percent among households with incomes less than $19,000 and with the husband in a blue-collar job. Since this is the case, advertising of gun racks directed at this group would be more likely to catch them in a problem recognition stage.

Types of Problem Recognition   Up until this point, we have implicitly assumed that the consumer shops because he or she recognizes the need to buy a particular item. However, shopping behavior may be triggered by the recognition of needs other than buying. As shown in Exhibit 5.2, shopping behavior can be the outgrowth of four types of problem recognition: (1) recognition of the need to buy; (2) recognition of the need to gather information; (3) recognition of the need to socialize, and (4) recognition of other personal needs. The first two needs are quite obvious and are the ones that most frequently come to mind when one thinks of shopping. That is, consumers frequently shop simply to buy the things for which they recognize a need. They may also shop to gather information. They may want information on which product is superior, or they may know all the characteristics of the goods they are interested in but shop to obtain information on which retailer has the best price.

The second pair of needs (social and personal) have been elaborated upon by Edward Tauber.[9] These motives are only tangentially related to purchasing behavior. Rather, they are related to using the shopping experience to satisfy other needs that have been recognized by the consumer in the problem recognition stage.

According to Edward Tauber, **social motives for shopping** include the following:[10]

1. Social experiences outside the home. The marketplace has traditionally been a center of social activity . . . many parts of the United States still have "market days," "county fairs," and "town squares" that offer a time and place for social interaction. In urban environments contemporary equivalents exist in sidewalk sales, auctions, and swap meets. . . .

2. Communication with others having a similar interest. Many hobbies center around products or services, such as boating, collecting stamps, car customizing, and home decorating. Stores that offer hobby-related goods serve as a focal point for people with similar interests to interact. People like to talk with others about their interests, and sales personnel are frequently sought to provide special information concerning the activity.

3. Peer group attraction. The patronage of a store sometimes reflects a desire to be with one's peer group or a reference group to which one aspires to belong. For instance, record stores are common "hangouts" for teen-agers. This "shopping" attraction is not necessarily related to the motive of common interest since the gathering spot tends to change over time; in many cases the shopper may have limited interest in the product category and little intention to make a purchase. . . .

4. Status and authority. Many shopping experiences provide the opportunity for an individual to command attention and respect. In few other activities can a person expect to be "waited on" without having to pay for this service. A person can attain a feeling of status and power in this limited "master-servant" relationship. . . .

5. Pleasure of bargaining. For many shoppers, bargaining is a degrading activity; haggling implies that one is "cheap." Others, however, appear to enjoy the process believing that with bargaining goods can be reduced to a more reasonable price . . . an individual prides himself in his ability to make wise purchases or to obtain bargains.

Some of these social motives can be combined with the previously mentioned buying and information motives. Shopping does not necessarily arise from any single motive.

9. Edward M. Tauber, "Marketing Notes and Communications—Why Do People Shop?" *Journal of Marketing* 36(October 1972): 47–48.

10. Reprinted with permission from Edward M. Tauber, "Marketing Notes and Communications—Why Do People Shop?" *Journal of Marketing* 36(October 1972): 48, published by the American Marketing Association.

Tauber has also identified and described a set of **personal motives for shopping.** These include:[11]

1. Role playing. Many activities are learned behaviors, traditionally expected or accepted as part of a certain position or role in society—mother, housewife, husband or student. . . .

2. Diversion. Shopping can offer an opportunity for diversion from the routine of daily life and thus represents a form of recreation. . . .

3. Self-gratification. Different emotional states or moods may be relevant for explaining why (and when) someone goes shopping. For example, a person may go to a store in search of diversion when he is bored or go in search of social contact when he feels lonely. Likewise, he may go to a store to buy "something nice" for himself when he is depressed. . . .

4. Learning about new trends. Products are intimately entwined in one's daily activities and often serve as symbols reflecting attitudes and life styles. An individual learns about trends and movements and the symbols that support them when he visits a store. . . .

5. Physical activity. An urban environment characterized by mass transportation and freeway driving provides little opportunity for individuals to exercise at a leisurely pace. Shopping can provide people with a considerable amount of exercise. . . .

6. Sensory stimulation. Retail institutions provide many potential sensory benefits for shoppers. Customers browse through a store looking at the merchandise and at each other; they enjoy handling the merchandise, and are either trying it on or trying it out. Sound can also be important, since a "noisy" environment creates a different image than one which is characterized by silence or soft background music. Even scent may be relevant; for instance, stores may possess a distinctive odor of perfume or of prepared food. . . ."

STORE CHOICE

Once the consumer has established a need to shop, he or she will next proceed to an evaluation of the shopping alternatives, which will yield a set of store choices. These store choices will strongly influence the actual store visit. The store choice process portion of the model is presented in Exhibit 5.5.

Shopping Alternatives   After recognizing the need to shop, the consumer may consider shopping alternatives before deciding which store to visit. We are careful to state that the consumer may consider alternatives, because it is possible that the store choice will be based on habitual behavior. This is one reason that in the store choice process model, learning processes are shown as influencing shopping alternatives. For example, if the consumer has learned from prior experience that when the household depletes its supply of milk, soda pop, bread or other convenience goods, the best way to acquire these goods is to take a short trip to the local Circle K, 7-11, Stop and Go, or other convenience food store, then effectively no shopping alternatives are considered. The consumer driven by habit patronizes the most conveniently located store that is open.

11. Reprinted with permission from Edward M. Tauber, "Marketing Notes and Communications—Why Do People Shop?" *Journal of Marketing* 36(October 1972): 47, published by the American Marketing Association.

EXHIBIT 5.5
**The
Store Choice
Process**

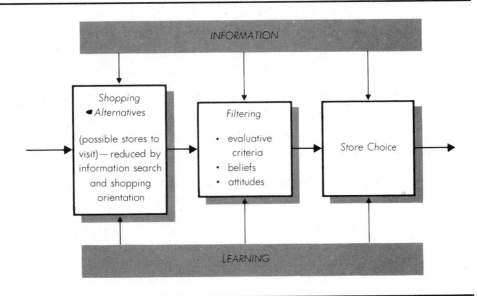

Four Situations If we consider that the consumer is primarily shopping to buy or obtain information, rather than to socialize or satisfy personal needs, then we can identify four basic situations that can confront the consumer at the shopping alternative stage of the model.

1. The consumer knows the exact product wanted and at which store to purchase the item. This can occur because the consumer is a learning animal. Using past experience, the consumer may have arrived at an adequate solution for many shopping problems. Items of relatively low value that are frequently purchased tend to belong in this category (toothpaste, milk, bread, soda pop). However, goods of higher value can also fall in this category. Some people when they recognize a need to buy a new car, can be both brand and store loyal. When confronted with a need to buy a new car, they may go directly to the local Lincoln-Mercury dealer and purchase a new Lincoln because they have learned in the past that this is an acceptable and satisfying method of problem solving.

2. The consumer recognizes a shopping problem and using prior learning knows which store to visit but does not know the specific product or brand that is desired. This situation may occur more often than you might expect. For example, a household has recognized a need to purchase a used automobile for their teenage daughter. They have come to trust a local used car dealer and thus they decide to not consider any other dealers. However, they have not decided on the exact make of car to purchase and plan to follow the dealer's advice, since he has always treated them fairly.

3. The consumer may not have a store choice in mind but may have decided on the product and brand to purchase. Since the product and brand have been determined, the customer has in a sense restricted the evaluative process to those stores that carry the item. The consumer, however, may not

have knowledge of all of the stores that carry the item and thus some searching may be required. To illustrate—a household has had the picture tube fail on their television and they decide that rather than repair it that they will purchase a new set. Their old set was an RCA and it operated perfectly for twelve years until the recent failure. They have noticed several ads on TV for RCA sets and they decide to buy a new RCA color, twenty-five-inch console. The dealer they bought their old set from twelve years ago is no longer in business. Therefore, they start to watch the newspaper for appliance, furniture, and department stores that advertise RCA sets. They also check the yellow pages for local RCA dealers.

4. The consumer recognizes a shopping problem but has not decided on either the store or the product and brand. This situation requires the largest amount of information search and decision making. For example, a woman has just received a promotion at the bank at which she works and a 25 percent salary increase. She and her husband, over the last year, have put off purchasing several major durable goods that needed replacing, but they feel they need a new car, living room furniture, and a washer and dryer. Even with the 25 percent raise they cannot afford all of these items. More importantly, since they are young, they have little prior information and experience regarding the various retailers in the city. Therefore, this household is coming up with a set of shopping alternatives, and must engage in extensive search for both products and retail outlets.

Information Search   The preceding discussion suggests that shopping alternatives are influenced by learning processes and information sources. This basic relationship is illustrated in the store choice process model in Exhibit 5.5. Learning processes and information sources are both related to the consumer's information search. This point can be clarified by recognizing that the consumer can search for information either internally or externally. **Internal search** is the mental recall or review of what the consumer has learned from prior shopping behavior or prior processing of information (i.e., friends' comments about stores or advertisements for selected retailers). **External search** is the seeking of information from any source outside the individual. External search could include going to the yellow pages, calling a friend for advice on where to shop, or looking through the morning newspaper for store advertisements.

The retailer can influence the shopping alternatives in the consumer's choice set in several ways. Through past actions and interactions with the consumer, the retailer will in part influence what the consumer has learned. If the retailer has satisfied the consumer in the past, then the consumer will remember; conversely, if the retailer dissatisfied the consumer in the past, the consumer will similarly remember. If the retailer has a high level of advertising, the consumer is more likely to recall the retailer in internal search activity. Naturally, there are other examples of how prior retailer actions will influence the consumer's internal search. Try to develop some examples on your own. Likewise, the retailer can affect the set of shopping alternatives considered by manipulating retailer-controlled information sources. This simply translates into the careful design of the retailer's current promotion activities.

Shopping Orientations   Once the consumer has decided on a set of shopping alternatives, the need will arise to evaluate each store in the set in order to decide which to visit first. Before discussing this evaluation process, it is important to note that consumers possess different shopping orientations, and that these orientations can have a profound effect on the evaluative process.[12]

In a now classic study, Gregory Stone identified **four major shopping orientations:** (1) economic, (2) personalizing, (3) ethical, and (4) apathetic. There was also a residual category of unique or indeterminate individuals. Quoting directly from Stone's research, each type can be profiled:[13]

1. The economic consumer. Here was the closest approximation to the "economic man" of the classical economist. This type of shopper expressed a sense of responsibility for her household purchasing duties: she was extremely sensitive to price, quality, and assortment of merchandise, all of which entered into the calculus of her behavior in the market. She was interested in shopping. Clerical personnel and the store were, for her, merely the instruments of her purchase of goods. Thus, efficiency or inefficiency of sales personnel, as well as the relative commensurateness of prices, quality, or the selection of merchandise, were decisive in leaving her with a pleasant or unpleasant impression of the store. The quality she demanded of a "good" clerk was efficiency.

2. The personalized consumer. This type of consumer shopped "where they know my name." It was important that she shop at her store rather than "public" stores. Strong personal attachments were formed with store personnel, and this personal relationship, often approaching intimacy, was crucial to her patronage of a store. She was highly sensitized to her experiences in the market, obviously they were an important part of her life. It followed that she was responsive to both pleasant and unpleasant experiences in store. Her conception of a "good" clerk was one who treated her in a personal, relatively intimate manner.

3. The ethical consumer. This type of shopper shopped where she "ought" to. She was willing to sacrifice lower prices or a wider selection of goods "to help the little guy out" or because "the chain store has no heart or soul." Consequently, strong attachments were sometimes formed with personnel and store owners or with "stores" in the abstract. These mediated the impressions she had of stores, left pleasant impressions in her memory, and forced unpleasant impressions out. Since store personnel did not enter in primarily as instrumentalities but rather with reference to other, more ultimate ends, she had no clear conception of a "good" clerk.

4. The apathetic consumer. This type of consumer shopped because she "had" to. Shopping for her was an onerous task. She shopped "to get it over with." Ideally, the criterion of convenient location was crucial to her selection of a store, as opposed to price, quality of goods, relationships with store personnel, or others. She was not interested in shopping and minimized her expenditure of effort in purchasing goods. Experiences in stores were not sufficiently important

12. For an empirical study which demonstrates that consumers with different shopping orientations exhibit different preferences for sources of information, see George P. Moschis, "Shopping Orientations and Consumer Uses of Information," *Journal of Retailing* 52(Summer 1976): 61–70, 93.

13. Reprinted from "City Shoppers and Urban Identification: Observations on the Social Psychology of City Life," *American Journal of Sociology* 60(1954): 36–45 by Gregory P. Stone by permission of the University of Chicago Press.

to leave any lasting impression on her. She knew few of the personnel and had no notion of a "good" clerk.

In regard to these shopping orientations, you should realize that they do not necessarily describe any individual but are a composite. Similarly, an individual can possess features that are characteristic of more than one orientation. The predominant orientation would depend on the situation. In shopping for some items, the consumer could be an economic shopper whereas for other goods or on other occasions the shopper may be apathetic.

Empirical tests by William Darden and Fred Reynolds support the Stone typology of shopper orientations.[14] Darden and Reynolds, however, found that the personalizing dimension should be divided into small store personalizing and a more general chain store depersonalizing factor. In Exhibit 5.6, a list of the statements they used to measure shopping orientations is provided. Each respondent was asked to choose one of five levels of agreement with each statement: (1) strongly agree, (2) agree, (3) neither agree nor disagree, (4) disagree, or (5) strongly disagree.

Evaluative Criteria   The shopping alternatives will be assessed by the consumer on a set of evaluative criteria. **Evaluative criteria** are typically "expressed in the form of the attributes or specifications used to compare various alternatives."[15] Since our focus is on store patronage, the evaluative criteria we are concerned with are **store attributes.**

Three things should be recognized about evaluative criteria. First, the attributes of a store are both objective and subjective. Take, for example, the physical attributes of a store. The size of the store can be objectively measured, whereas the effect of the store layout (also a physical attribute) on how comfortable the consumer feels while shopping in the store rests solely in the mind of the consumer and thus is subjective. Second, the number of evaluative criteria that most individuals can mentally handle when evaluating alternatives is from six to nine.[16] Third, an individual's evaluative criteria are shaped by shopping orientations and learning processes.

Several studies have been conducted on the attributes that consumers use to evaluate stores.[17] Eight of the more frequently used attributes are:

14. William R. Darden and Fred D. Reynolds, "Shopping Orientations and Product Usage Rates," *Journal of Marketing Research,* 8(November 1971): 505–8.

15. James F. Engel, Roger D. Blackwell, and David T. Kollat, *Consumer Behavior,* 3rd ed. (Hinsdale, Ill.: Dryden Press, 1978), p. 388.

16. Engel, Blackwell, and Kollat, *Consumer Behavior,* p. 369, suggest six or fewer criteria are used. However, Fishbein suggests that as many as nine are used. Martin Fishbein, "Attitude, Attitude Change, and Behavior: A Theoretical Overview," in Philip Levine (ed.), *Attitude Research Bridges the Atlantic* (Chicago: American Marketing Association, 1975), pp. 3–16.

17. Many of these studies fall under the guise of store image studies. A review of over twenty of these studies is provided in Douglas J. Lincoln and A. Coskun Samli, "Definitions, Dimensions, and Measurement of Store Image: A Literature Summary and Synthesis," in Robert S. Franz et al. (eds.), *Proceedings, Southern Marketing Association,* (Southern Marketing Association, 1979), pp. 430–433.

1. Price
2. Merchandise (including quality, style and fashion, assortment, national versus private labels)
3. Physical characteristics (including decor, layout, and floor space)
4. Sales promotions
5. Advertising
6. Convenience (including hours, location, ease of finding items, parking)
7. Services (including credit, delivery, returns, and guarantees)
8. Store personnel (including helpfulness, friendliness, and courteousness)

EXHIBIT 5.6
**Shopper
Orientation
Scales**

ECONOMIC BUYER

1. Large department stores give better service
2. Department stores have more reasonable prices
3. Department stores have a wider selection of goods
4. Big chains offer better bargains
5. Shopping is too expensive in small stores
6. Prices are higher at smaller stores

DEPERSONALIZATION IN BIG STORES

1. Because people have to wait on themselves, chain stores are run like a factory
2. The big stores have no heart
3. Local merchants give better service
4. Chain stores are impersonal
5. Chain stores do not try very hard to please you
6. I feel at home in a small store

SHOPPING APATHY

1. Shopping is really a bother in any store

SUPPORT FOR LOCAL MERCHANTS

1. It would be better if all stores were owned by local merchants
2. Chain stores put people out of work
3. You have to give the independent merchant a chance to earn a living

SMALL STORE PERSONALIZING

1. Sales people get to know you and your needs better at local stores
2. Local merchants make an effort to please you
3. Local merchants take more interest in you
4. People are friendly at local stores

Source: Reprinted with permission from William R. Darden and Fred D. Reynolds, "Shopping Orientations and Product Usage Rates," *Journal of Marketing Research* 8(November 1971): 506, published by the American Marketing Association.

This list of attributes is not intended to be exhaustive and not all components of all attributes apply to all store types. For example, when evaluating grocery stores, the style or fashion of merchandise is not relevant.

Attitude Formation   A deeper understanding of the store-choice process can be obtained by referring back to Exhibit 5.5. The model there shows that the process of developing store choices is heavily influenced by the attitude formation process.

An attitude is a mental and neural state of readiness to respond, which is organized through experience and exerts a directive or dynamic influence on behavior.[18] Attitudes have traditionally been viewed as being comprised of three dimensions: cognitive, affective, and behavioral. The **cognitive dimension** refers to the understanding or perception of an attitude object. The **affective dimension** concerns the feelings of like or dislike toward an object. The **behavioral dimension** refers to the action tendencies toward the attitude object. Consequently, in terms of store-related behavior, we can speak of a person's understanding or perception of a store, a person's like or dislike of a store, and a person's predisposition or tendency to shop at a store. Furthermore, communication theory suggests that people move through cognitive, affective, and behavioral stages in the purchase process.[19] However, there is disagreement regarding the order in which the stages occur.[20]

Recent attempts at analyzing attitudes have been more analytical and are more useful for studying and understanding store patronage behavior. The basis of contemporary attitude models is as follows:

$$BI \simeq A = f(E, B)$$

where:

BI = behavioral intention toward an object
A = attitude toward an object
E = importance of evaluative criteria on which an object is evaluated
B = belief about the object based on various attributes or evaluative criteria

In the preceding model, *one can think of the object as the store*. We see in this model that behavioral intentions are separated from the attitude itself and that a favorable attitude does not necessarily lead to behavior, only to a behavioral intention. Precise definitions of the major items in the preceding attitude model follow:

1. **Evaluative criteria:** Desired outcomes from choice or use of alternatives, expressed in the form of the attributes or specifications used to compare various alternatives.

18. G. Allport, "Attitudes," in C. Murchison, (ed.), *Handbook of Social Psychology* (Worcester, Mass.: Clark University Press, 1935), pp. 798–884.

19. Philip Kotler, *Marketing Management: Analysis, Planning and Control*, 4th ed. (Englewood Cliffs, N.J.: Prentice-Hall, 1980), pp. 474–75.

20. Michael L. Ray, *Marketing Communication and the Hierarchy-of-Effects* (Cambridge, Mass.: Marketing Science Institute, November 1973).

2. **Beliefs:** Information that links a given alternative to a specified evaluative criterion, specifying the extent to which the alternative possesses the desired attribute.
3. **Attitude:** A learned predisposition to respond consistently in a favorable manner with respect to a given alternative (referred to earlier as the affective dimension).
4. **Intention:** The subjective probability that beliefs and attitudes will be acted on.[21]

In Exhibit 5.5, notice that the four components (evaluative criteria, beliefs, attitude, and store choice) lead up to the actual store visit. Fishbein and Rosenberg have both developed models for relating some or all of these components.[22] Market researchers, however, have not strictly used either the Fishbein or Rosenberg model. Rather, they have developed their own attitude models, frequently referred to as multiattribute models. For our purposes a useful multiattribute model is the one developed by Talarzyk and Moinpour.[23] We will formulate their model in terms of an attitude toward a retail outlet.

$$A_b = \sum_{i=1}^{n} W_i B_{ib}$$

where:

A_b = attitude toward retail outlet b
W_i = weight or importance of store attribute i
B_{ib} = evaluative aspect or belief with respect to utility of alternative outlet b to satisfy attribute i
n = number of attributes important in selection of a retail outlet

This is a **compensatory model** because the strength in one attribute can offset a weakness in another.[24]

An Example

A consumer is evaluating three retail outlets to decide which one to visit. This consumer believes that for the type of shopping being undertaken, six evaluative criteria (store attributes) are relevant: (1) competitive prices, (2) convenient location, (3) helpful store personnel, (4) wide merchandise assortments, (5) attractive store decor, and (6) informative advertising. The weights (W_i) the consumer attached to each of these attributes on a scale of one to five are

21. Engel, Blackwell, and Kollat, *Consumer Behavior,* p. 388.
22. Martin Fishbein, "The Relationship Between Beliefs, Attitudes and Behavior," in Shel Feldman (ed.), *Cognitive Consistency* (New York: Academic Press, 1966), pp. 199–223; Milton J. Rosenberg, "Cognitive Structure and Attitudinal Effect," *Journal of Abnormal and Social Psychology* 53(1956): 367–72.
23. W. W. Talarzyk and Reza Moinpour, "Comparison of an Attitude Model and Coombsion Unfolding Analysis for the Prediction of Individual Brand Preference," paper presented at the Workshop on Attitude Research and Consumer Behavior, University of Illinois (December 1970).
24. A **noncompensatory model** is one in which a weakness on a given attribute cannot be offset by strength on another—if an attribute is rated too weakly the retail outlet is eliminated from the choice set. Compensating models have received more attention in the literature and thus we will limit discussion to them.

EXHIBIT 5.7
A Consumer's Multiattribute Evaluation of Three Retail Outlets

ATTRIBUTE	IMPORTANCE (W_i)[a]	RATING (B_{ib})[b]		
		Outlet A	Outlet B	Outlet C
Competitive prices	4	2	3	5
Convenient location	3	5	4	2
Helpful store personnel	4	3	3	4
Wide merchandise assortment	5	2	4	5
Attractive store decor	2	1	2	4
Informative advertising	2	4	3	4

[a]Scale values: (1) very low importance, (2) low importance, (3) average importance, (4) high importance, (5) very high importance

[b]Scale values: (1) strongly disagree, (2) disagree, (3) neutral, (4) agree, (5) strongly agree

presented in Exhibit 5.7. This consumer has evaluated three retail outlets and has formed beliefs about how each store performs on each of the respective attributes. The rating each store received on each attribute by this consumer is also provided in Exhibit 5.7.

Using the formal multiattribute model that we presented and the data presented in Exhibit 5.7, we can compute the attitude score (A_b) for this particular consumer for each of the three retail outlets. The appropriate computations are as follows:

$$\text{Outlet } A = (4 \cdot 2) + (3 \cdot 5) + (4 \cdot 3) + (5 \cdot 2) + (2 \cdot 1) + (2 \cdot 4)$$
$$= 55$$
$$\text{Outlet } B = (4 \cdot 3) + (3 \cdot 4) + (4 \cdot 3) + (5 \cdot 4) + (2 \cdot 2) + (2 \cdot 3)$$
$$= 66$$
$$\text{Outlet } C = (4 \cdot 5) + (3 \cdot 2) + (4 \cdot 4) + (5 \cdot 5) + (2 \cdot 4) + (2 \cdot 4)$$
$$= 83$$

These computations lead us to expect that the consumer will most likely patronize retail Outlet C. The highest attitude score for Outlet C suggests that this outlet performs best (in the mind of the consumer) on the attributes the consumer believes to be of highest importance. A careful examination of the data in Exhibit 5.7 will validate this suggestion. Outlet C is thus the consumer's store choice.

Situational Factors   Unfortunately, there will not be a perfect correlation between store choice, which resulted from attitude formation, and store patronage. Situational factors will inevitably intervene between the time intentions are formed and when traveling to the store begins. Situational factors are of three broad types: economic, social, and informational.

The consumer's economic status may change, which could trigger a change in problem recognition or evaluative criteria. Assume, for example, that the consumer is laid off from work. What was previously a problem (need to buy a new stereo) may no longer be perceived as a problem, or it may still be viewed as a problem but price may become a much more important criterion.

The consumer may also experience a change in the social environment. Most important in this regard is a change in reference-group orientation. Reference groups are of three major types: membership, aspirational, and dissociative. A **membership group** is one in which a person is a recognized member. An **aspirational group** is one to which a person does not currently belong but to which one aspires to be a member. **Dissociative groups** are those with which the individual does not want to be identified.

Reference groups provide a frame of reference for how individuals behave. Let us illustrate the concept in terms of our store patronage model. A college freshman, arriving on campus, decides that she needs to buy some new clothes. Her parents gave her a Penney's charge card to use while she is away at college. She therefore intends to take the bus to the Penney's store downtown. That evening she goes to her first sorority rush. The next morning she runs across a few of the sorority girls she met the evening before and they are excited about the prospects of her becoming a sorority sister. They invite her to spend the afternoon with them doing some shopping at a few campus dress and sportswear shops. Since she needs some new clothes, she decides to purchase them that afternoon at one of the campus shops that the girls think is a fabulous place to shop.

A final situational factor may be the receipt of new information. The new information could change the degree to which a problem is recognized or one's attitude toward various stores. For example, the consumer is in his car driving to the hardware store but hears an advertisement over the radio that Sears is having their semiannual sale on all carpentry tools and home decorating items. He then drives past the hardware store and travels the additional four miles to the local Sears store. Another example: The consumer decides to buy a new stereo and has decided to spend Saturday afternoon visiting several local stereo dealers. On Friday afternoon, while sitting in the doctor's office, she reads an article in *Popular Science* that states that within the next year there will be major improvements in stereo technology. The consumer decides to put off buying the stereo and keeps her money in the bank.

Retailer Implications   The discussion of the store choice section (see Exhibit 5.5) of the more complete retail patronage model (see Exhibit 5.1) is of value beyond just deepening our understanding of consumer behavior. It also has several managerial implications.

The attitude scores that were developed from the multiattribute attitude model can be used to predict retail sales or market share. For this to be possible, the retailer would need to develop an ongoing research program to gather data regularly on consumer attitudes toward its store and competing stores.

The retail analyst who conducts a continuing attitude survey will want to examine at least two phenomena. He or she will want to examine how the importance that consumers attach to various store attributes change over time. This will reveal the extent to which consumers are seeking different benefits over time or if the benefits sought are longitudinally stable. Next, the analyst will want to examine consumer beliefs regarding how each retailer performs on each of the attributes over time.

To illustrate this point, let us consider the data presented in Exhibit 5.8. These data show the attitude toward two retail outlets over three years in terms of components of the multiattribute attitude model. We see that consumers are increasingly seeking retail outlets that have more competitive prices and more convenient locations. The importance of helpful store personnel, wide merchandise assortments, attractive store decor, and informative advertising have remained relatively constant over the three-year period. However, we see that consumers believe that Retailer *A*'s prices have become less competitive and that store personnnel are not as helpful as previously. On the favorable side, consumers perceive an increase in the informativeness of Retailer *A*'s advertising. Turning to Retailer *B*, we can see that consumers believe that its prices have become more competitive and its personnel more helpful. On all other store attributes the consumer perceives Retailer *B* as doing as well or slightly better than three years ago. In the eyes of the consumer, then, Retailer *B* is doing a better job in increasing its performance than Retailer *A*.

If one were to compute the composite attitude score for Retailer *A* and Retailer *B* over the three-year period (using the equation on page 119) it would be seen that consumers overall still have a more favorable attitude toward Retailer *A*. However, this situation is quickly changing. Exhibit 5.9 dramatically reveals that Retailer *A* is quickly losing its favorable position. This is good news for Retailer *B*, but disheartening for Retailer *A*. Since a change in attitude is a lead indicator of a change in sales or market share, we would predict that the market share of Retailer *B* will increase in the forthcoming year unless Retailer *A* is effective in reversing its decline in relative performance.

Another use of attitude data is for fine tuning retail strategy. This can be illustrated by referring to the preceding example. It is clear that Retailer *A* needs to do something—but what? The retailer should do something that is important to the consumer and that will give it a unique competitive advantage. Retailer *B* stands out in terms of having competitive prices, and consumers are increasingly placing heavier emphasis on prices in their attitude formation; thus Retailer *B* is benefiting. But if Retailer *A* decided to offer more competitive

---

EXHIBIT 5.8   Multiattribute Ratings of Two Retail Outlets over Three Years

ATTRIBUTE	IMPORTANCE (W_i)[a]			RETAILER A RATING (B_{ia})[b]			RETAILER B RATING (B_{ib})[b]		
	1977	1978	1979	1977	1978	1979	1977	1978	1979
Competitive prices	3.9	4.0	4.3	2.2	2.2	2.0	3.4	3.6	3.9
Convenient location	3.1	3.4	3.6	3.2	3.2	3.1	3.6	3.6	3.7
Helpful store personnel	4.0	4.0	4.0	4.2	4.2	4.0	2.9	3.0	3.3
Wide merchandise assortment	2.7	2.7	2.8	3.9	3.8	4.0	3.1	3.1	3.2
Attractive store decor	3.4	3.3	3.4	4.4	4.5	4.5	1.9	1.9	2.0
Informative advertising	3.7	3.6	3.8	2.7	2.9	3.1	2.4	2.4	2.5

[a]Scale values: (1) very low importance, (2) low importance, (3) average importance, (4) high importance, (5) very high importance
[b]Scale values: (1) strongly disagree, (2) disagree, (3) neutral, (4) agree, (5) strongly agree

EXHIBIT 5.9
Ratio of Two Retailers' Composite Scores over Three Years

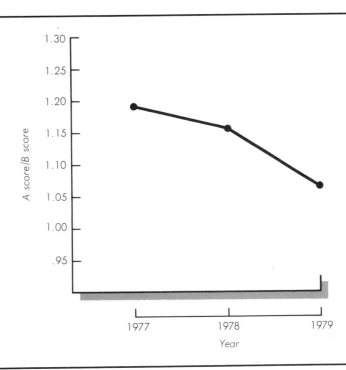

prices, it would be competing head-on with Retailer *B* and also it would create no differential competitive advantage. Consequently, Retailer *A* would be better off trying to develop a stronger nonprice strategy, perhaps on the store personnel or advertising attributes. Take a moment to see if you could develop a nonprice strategy for Retailer *A*.

Finally, the retail analyst can use the multiattribute data to perform a benefit segmentation. **Segmentation** is a procedure for breaking a heterogeneous market into more homogeneous groups. It will be discussed in more depth in Chapter 9. For now, all you need to recognize is that not all shoppers look for the same benefits from stores. In terms of the multiattribute model, some consumers attach a very high weight to competitive prices whereas other consumers attach low weight to it. In this regard, Exhibit 5.10 (page 124) continues our hypothetical example. Here Retailers *A* and *B* can see that there are five unique segments in terms of benefits being sought. In this case, the segments have the following profiles:

1. **Economic segment.** This segment comprises 34 percent of the market and attaches highest importance to competitive prices, helpful store personnel, and informative advertising. These benefits help this shopper to make economically good purchase decisions.
2. **Elegant segment.** This segment comprises 16 percent of the market and attaches highest importance to attractive store decor and helpful store personnel. These benefits help make this shopper feel elegant and important while shopping.

3.   **Convenience segment.** Comprising a substantial 26 percent of the market, this segment is more interested in convenient location and informative advertising. Both of these attributes help this consumer do his or her shopping chores quickly.

4.   **Naive segment.** This segment comprises 14 percent of the market. This segment is "naive" because they expect everything from a store. They want competitive prices, convenient location, helpful personnel, relatively wide assortments, attractive store decor, and informative advertising. Thus, it is always complaining about stores, because no store performs well on all attributes.

5.   **Other segment.** Comprising 10 percent of the market, this segment includes people that could not be categorized in any of the preceding segments. It is hard to figure out what motivates this segment.

With this additional information, which was derived from the multiattribute data, Retailer *A* could better fine tune its retail strategy. In short, it could decide which segment(s) of the market it should attempt to attract. Where do you believe Retailer *A* should place its emphasis? What additional information might it need to make this decision?

THE STORE VISIT PROCESS

We are at the point in our overall store patronage model where the consumer has arrived at the store. The consumer has progressed through problem recognition, the evaluation of shopping alternatives, the shopping intentions, and is now at the store. Remember, however, that the store the consumer is now at may not be the one that he or she intended to visit because of the possible intervention of situational factors. In Exhibit 5.11 we provide the store visit process model, which is a component of the overall store patronage model presented in Exhibit 5.1.

Evaluative Criteria   Perhaps one of the most important things to recognize is that although the evaluative criteria were mentioned in the store choice model, they are still (covertly) operating. Specifically, a consumer who enters a store and immediately

EXHIBIT 5.10
Ratings of Store Attributes by Shopper Segments

ATTRIBUTE	RATINGS BY SEGMENT					
	Economic (34%)	Elegant (16%)	Convenience (26%)	Naive (14%)	Other (10%)	Total (100%)
Competitive prices	4.9	3.7	3.5	4.7	4.4	4.3
Convenient location	3.7	2.9	4.5	4.0	2.3	3.6
Helpful store personnel	4.1	4.7	3.5	4.2	3.3	4.0
Wide merchandise assortments	3.0	2.3	3.2	3.0	2.0	2.8
Attractive store decor	2.9	4.3	3.3	3.9	3.2	3.4
Informative advertising	4.1	3.1	3.8	4.0	3.7	3.8

EXHIBIT 5.11
**The Store
Visit Process**

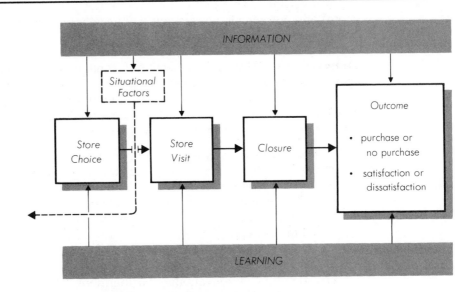

realizes it is not the type of store he or she expected, may directly turn around and leave the store. For example, the consumer may have expected the store to have friendly and helpful employees but on entering cannot find any sales assistance. What the consumer believes about the store must be reinforced during the store visit or else he or she will change that attitude or behavior.

In-Store Effects Every consumer who enters the store is by definition a better prospect than the consumer who does not enter. However, the extent to which this prospect is converted to a customer will depend on in-store effects. In this regard, in-store effects are of four major types.

Point-of-Purchase Advertising Any communication vehicle, typically in print form, within the store is called **point-of-purchase advertising,** including signs, banners, special merchandise displays, counter signs, price cards, window signs, posters, elevator cards, flags, and similar devices that inform the consumer about the product or store offering. These promotion vehicles provide the consumer with information that can be used in deciding whether the product fits his or her needs. They can alert consumers about products they had not thought about purchasing on entering the store. Since many purchases are **unplanned** (the consumer does not decide to purchase until in the store), point-of-purchase advertising can trigger, in the consumer's mind, what is needed.

Store Personnel Personnel, especially sales personnel, are a second major in-store influence. Sales personnel can assist the consumer to find merchandise and can answer questions about various products. Increasingly, retailers in the United States have become self-service and, therefore, the role of sales personnel has declined. This trend, however, is not pervasive. For example, jewelry stores and automobile dealers still rely heavily on sales personnel to influence the in-store customer.

Atmospherics   Atmospherics are the "conscious designing of space and its various dimensions to evoke certain effects in buyers."[25] They concern how the consumer perceives the in-store environment and whether he or she is comfortable in it. Philip Kotler identifies four situations in which atmosphere will be an especially important in-store influence:[26]

1. *"Atmospherics is a relevant marketing technique primarily in situations where the product is purchased or consumed and where the seller has design options."* For example, atmospherics are more likely to be important to a restaurant with sit-down facilities than to one that only has a carry-out service. Also, manufacturers of consumer goods are less likely to be able to use atmospherics than are retailers.

2. *"Atmospherics becomes an important marketing tool as the number of competitive outlets increases."* This becomes another means by which one business can be differentiated from another. Furthermore, this kind of competitive action is more difficult for competitors to counter than are price changes or even assortment carried.

3. *"Atmospherics is a more relevant marketing tool in industries where product and/ or price differences are small."* Savings and loan associations often seek differentiation through the use of atmospherics because regulatory requirements necessarily result in considerable similarity among them. Their efforts typically take shape through the skillful use of interior decor and related promotional strategy.

4. *"Atmospherics is a more relevant marketing tool when product entries are aimed at distinct social classes or life style buyer groups."* The May Company basement, with its unique merchandising strategy, is likely to appeal to the working class. Consequently, its atmosphere must be consistent with bargain-basement retailing. This environment is in considerable contrast to other departments in the very same store that cater to an upper-middle-class clientele.

Merchandise Inspection   The final in-store influence is merchandise inspection. The consumer inspecting merchandise will be either favorably or unfavorably impressed. Much of this the retailer will have relatively little influence over—the package, label, information on label, etc. However, the retailer can control the extent to which the consumer is allowed to handle the merchandise. Although it is necessary to keep some items, like diamonds, under lock and key, extensive security measures can discourage customers. Furniture stores with signs reading "do not sit on the furniture" or glassware shops that warn

25. Philip Kotler, "Atmospherics as a Marketing Tool," *Journal of Retailing* 49(Winter 1973–74): 50.

26. Philip Kotler, "Atmospherics as a Marketing Tool," *Journal of Retailing* 49(Winter 1973–74): 52–53. Reprinted with permission.

you not to touch can cost more in lost sales than they save the retailer in merchandise. An appliance store needs floor samples that customers can see at work; everything cannot be on a shelf in a box. The ability to inspect merchandise is a very important in-store influencer. Recognizing this importance, Target Stores will have a display model for each item in their housewares department that will be keyed to boxes of the goods on the shelf.

Closure

During the store visit the consumer should be able to obtain closure. **Closure** refers to the process of bringing consumers to the point where the evidence before them conclusively suggests that the product or service being offered should be bought.[27] Closure needs to be differentiated from outcome: closure is deciding to buy; the actual buying (which sometimes may not follow closure) is outcome. Instrumental in obtaining closure is positive reinforcement from each of the in-store influences that we have delineated.

Closure should not be forced on the consumer. If the retailer is concerned about long-run goodwill then the customer should not be pressured or persuaded to purchase a product or service that is not in his or her best interest. This is simply good retail ethics and practice. It is also a consumer orientation on which high performance retailing must rest.

One of the most frequent causes of not obtaining closure is that the retailer is out of stock on the item the consumer is seeking to purchase.[28] However, even if the item is out of stock, closure may still occur, and the effect on the retailer may still be favorable. How could this happen?

There are three sets of effects that can accrue to the retailer as a result of a stockout: favorable, unfavorable, and questionable. Favorable effects are brand switching, switching attributes within brands, and product-class substitution. Assume the consumer goes to the store to buy a six-pack of twelve-ounce Schlitz canned beer and finds out that this item is not in stock. The consumer could switch to another brand, perhaps Miller or Budweiser. Or, he could switch attributes; for example, he could switch to twelve-ounce Schlitz in bottles rather than cans. Or, he could switch to another product class and decide to buy some Gallo wine. In the short run, all of these effects are good for the retailer, because the consumer is finally able to reach closure in the store. However, in the long run, if the retailer repeatedly is out of stock on items, then the consumer will begin to patronize that store less often.

In the short run, the effect on item stockout could be immediately unfavorable to the retailer. This could happen for two reasons. The consumer may, on finding the item out of stock, simply decide to shop at another store. Or, the consumer may terminate shopping altogether. She may become frustrated and decide that it is no longer worth the time and effort to search for the item.

The effect on the retailer could be called questionable if only in the longer run will we know whether the consequence was favorable or unfavorable. There are two questionable effects: when the consumer takes a "raincheck"

27. Block and Roering, *Essentials of Consumer Behavior*, p. 494.

28. A model of consumer stock-out behavior can be found in: Philip B. Schary and Martin Christopher, "The Anatomy of a Stock-Out," *Journal of Retailing* 55(Summer 1979): 59–70.

and when he postpones shopping. If the consumer finally uses the raincheck to purchase the item or if he resumes the shopping at the initial store, at some later date, then the consequence was acceptable to the retailer. However, if the raincheck is not used or the customer resumes shopping at a different store, then the consequence is definitely not in the initial retailer's favor.

Outcome

The final step in the store-patronage process is called outcome. There are two basic outcomes: a purchase occurs or a purchase does not occur. Let us examine the latter category first.

If the consumer decided not to purchase, then the consumer was disappointed with either the retail outlet or the merchandise available at the outlet or both. All of us have either heard stories or have experienced firsthand the situation of going to purchase something and being treated so poorly that we left the store in disgust. Sometimes, however, we may be treated well but simply not be satisfied with the merchandise that is available. For example, it may not look as good as it did in the advertisements we watched on television. There are, of course, the unfortunate circumstances where the consumer is upset with both the retailer and the merchandise available. For example, the merchandise isn't what you want but the retail salesperson continues to pressure you to purchase the item. You leave in disgust and are not likely to forget this distasteful experience. This brings to light a key point about the outcome of the store trip. Consumers have memories and base future behavior on whether their shopping trips have been rewarding or punishing. If the visit to the retail outlet was rewarding, then the probability of a future visit is enhanced. If the visit was punishing, then future visits to that retail outlet will be less probable. In addition, the retailer needs to recognize that many consumers are very vocal about their pleasures and displeasures with retailers. They will not hesitate to tell their friends, acquaintances, and even strangers about their experiences, creating either favorable or unfavorable word-of-mouth advertising for the retailer. The retailer's success could be influenced by this word-of-mouth advertising.

The logical alternative to the nonpurchase outcome is to enter into and complete a transaction with the retailer. It is hard for a consumer to know, before making a purchase, whether he or she will be totally satisfied with that purchase after the transaction has taken place. The four possible states are presented in Exhibit 5.12.

In Exhibit 5.12, we see that one possible state of affairs is where the patron is satisfied with the product purchased and the retail outlet that was patronized. This consequence is quite good for the retailer and manufacturer of the product since the consumer's behavior is strongly reinforced and future loyalty to the brand and retailer will be enhanced.

All of the other states involve some degree of dissonance in regard to the product or retail outlet or both. **Dissonance** is doubt that occurs when the consumer becomes aware that unchosen items have desirable attributes.[29]

29. Block and Roering, *Essentials of Consumer Behavior*, p. 517.

EXHIBIT 5.12
**Possible
States of
Postpurchase
Satisfaction**

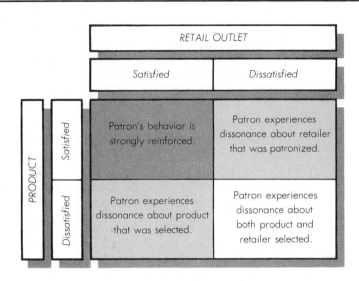

		RETAIL OUTLET	
		Satisfied	Dissatisfied
PRODUCT	Satisfied	Patron's behavior is strongly reinforced.	Patron experiences dissonance about retailer that was patronized.
	Dissatisfied	Patron experiences dissonance about product that was selected.	Patron experiences dissonance about both product and retailer selected.

A consumer, upon purchasing a new Ford, may be very satisfied with its performance, handling characteristics, and gasoline consumption. But after owning the car for a week, she sees the same automobile (similarly equipped) advertised by another local dealer for $300 less. The consumer, therefore, experiences dissonance because of not having shopped both Ford dealers.

How do consumers reduce dissonance? There are two basic ways: the consumer can reassess the attractiveness of unchosen alternatives, or the consumer can search for information to validate the choice made. For example, the consumer who bought the Ford may ask friends about the reputation of the dealer that she did not patronize. She may find that this dealer offers very poor service and tends to not stand behind the factory warranty. Hence, she rationalizes that the added $300 paid was probably worth it in the long run since the patronized dealer is reputed to offer excellent service.

Using the same example, we may find a situation where the consumer is satisfied with the Ford dealer but is dissatisfied with the car itself. Shortly after the customer took delivery on the car a leak developed in the transmission. The dealer was very cooperative and immediately repaired the leaky transmission. One hundred miles later a rattle developed in the dashboard. Again the dealer was cooperative and found the source of the problem. The consumer, at this point, is experiencing a high level of dissonance regarding the purchase of the Ford, although very satisfied with the dealer's service and attitude. If you were this consumer, how might you reduce this dissonance?

Another situation could occur. Perhaps this customer discovers that the automobile could have been purchased at a lower price from another dealer that has a better reputation for service and fair treatment of the customer than the dealer who was patronized. How might this dissonance be reduced?

This discussion on postpurchase satisfaction suggests that the retailer's job is not finished just because a transaction has been completed. The consumer will naturally engage in postpurchase evaluation. If the result is satisfaction with the retailer, then the retailer will occupy a favorable position in the consumer's mind. If the result is dissonance about the retailer and the dissonance cannot be adequately resolved, then the retailer will occupy an unfavorable position in the consumer's mind. Since the consumer may attempt to reduce dissonance by gathering additional information, the retailer might find it useful to direct some of its promotional activity at those who already have purchased, attempting to assure them that they patronized the right retailer. This is especially true for retailers who sell major durable goods. For example, dissonance can be reduced substantially by the mere receipt of a letter from the salesperson who sold you your car urging you to not hesitate to stop by or call if you experience any problems or have any questions on how to care for your new car.

THE NONSTORE RETAIL PATRON

The preceding discussion of the retail patronage model focused exclusively on store retailers. However, the model is equally applicable to nonstore retail situations. Let us briefly examine several aspects of the model in a nonstore retailing light.

Problem Recognition   Nonstore retailers can play an important role in arousing problem recognition. For instance, the direct mail, door-to-door, or party plan retailer can get better exposure in the home than the store retailer and therefore may have a better chance of creating problem recognition.

Nonstore retailers can also be an important source of information in the buying process. For example, consumers may consult their Sears or Penney's catalog to obtain knowledge of price ranges and competitive offerings. Perhaps in the near future consumers may use in-home computer consoles to scan the offerings of local retailers.

Shopping Alternatives   When the consumer evaluates shopping alternatives he or she may be favorably predisposed toward certain nonstore retailers because of their performance on certain attributes. For example, many nonstore retailers offer competitive prices, wide merchandise assortments, and the convenience of in-home shopping.

Also, the nonstore patron may have different shopping orientations than the patron of a store. The nonstore patron may be apathetic when it comes to shopping, viewing it as an onerous task that is to be done as fast as possible. Thus the consumer may prefer the nonstore alternative.

Store Visit   The nonstore patron may not be able to visit stores. Possibly the patron is an invalid or aged. Alternatively, the patron may live at too great a distance from the stores that carry the type of merchandise desired. Such an individual would favor a nonstore retailer.

Comment   The retail patronage model is general enough to explain both store and non-store patronage behavior. You should take a moment to place yourself in a non-store retailing situation and to trace your anticipated behavior in terms of the retail patronage model.

SUMMARY

The purpose of this chapter was to develop a model that would be helpful in explaining and describing the behavior of retail patrons. The retail patronage model developed was a process model that moved the consumer through problem recognition to evaluating shopping alternatives and then to the development of store choice intentions. Intentions in turn lead to a store visit. However, situational factors may intervene to prevent the consumer from behaving according to initial intentions. During the store visit the consumer continues to evaluate the store and product offerings. The consumer is influenced while in the store by point-of-purchase advertising, store personnel, atmospherics, and the merchandise. While in the store, the consumer should obtain closure (that is, the evidence will conclusively suggest that the product or service being offered should be purchased). Finally, if the consumer makes a purchase, he or she may eventually be satisfied or dissatisfied. In fact, the consumer could develop satisfaction or dissatisfaction for the retail outlet or merchandise acquired, or both. Dissonance can be the cause of this dissatisfaction, and therefore the retailer should conscientiously attempt to reduce post-purchase dissonance.

QUESTIONS

1. Do consumers shop in a rational manner?

2. How do consumers typically go about shopping for a new car in contrast to a new item of clothing such as a shirt or blouse?

3. How much control does the retailer have over patronage behavior?

4. Can a purchase be made without problem recognition?

5. Discuss the concept of postpurchase dissonance. How can the retailer overcome it?

6. What are the problems in using the retail patronage model to develop retail strategy?

7. What are evaluative criteria? What evaluative criteria did you use the last time you purchased a pair of shoes? Would you have used different criteria if you were purchasing a stereo?

8. Develop a list of things an apparel retailer could do to increase the probability that once consumers entered the store they would not leave without making a purchase.

9. How important do you believe situational factors are in determining retail patronage behavior? Think about some of your recent store visits.

10. Of the concepts identified in the retail patronage model, which do you believe a retailer should design its information system to collect data on? How frequently would you recommend the data be collected?

PROBLEMS AND EXERCISES

1. Assume you are a retail consultant who has been hired by a national supermarket chain to conduct some research on attributes consumers use to evaluate stores. How would you go about developing a list of store attributes upon which to base your research?

2. A home improvement retailer has just completed a research study of households in its trade area to assess the likelihood of the household engaging in home improvement projects over the next six months. The trade area consists of 12,000 households, and 500 were randomly sampled to participate in the research study. The following results were obtained:

Home Improvement Project	Average Likelihood
Room addition	.08
Enclosed patio	.13
Outdoor decking	.09
New carpeting or tile	.18
Outdoor painting	.29
Indoor painting	.36
Add fireplace or wood stove	.09
Storm windows	.11
Insulation of attic	.13
Swimming pool	.03
Kitchen remodeling	.07
Air conditioning	.08

How do you suggest the retailer use this data? What other data should have been collected?

3. Using some recent research, a supermarket retailer has found that consumers evaluate supermarkets on five dimensions: (1) convenient location, (2) competitive prices, (3) attractive and clean store decor, (4) quickness of check-out lines, and (5) wide merchandise assortment.

This retailer also had research conducted on the components of the consumer's multiattribute model. The research assessed not only the supermarket's performance in terms of the multiattribute model, but also its major competitor's performance. The results were as follows:

Attribute	Importance Weight[a]	Supermarket Rating[b]	Competition Rating[b]
Convenient location	8.3	9.1	7.8
Competitive prices	8.9	6.3	9.1
Attractive and clean store decor	6.2	7.1	6.8
Quick checkout lines	6.4	8.4	8.3
Wide merchandise assortment	5.9	6.3	8.1

[a] Scale values range from 1 to 10 with 1 depicting low importance and 10 depicting high importance.
[b] Scale values range from 1 to 10 with 1 representing strongly disagree and 10 representing strongly agree.

Interpret these results. Can you make any suggestions to the retailer conducting the research? Can you recommend any additional data that should have been collected?

4. A locally owned menswear store has experienced two consecutive years of declining sales. The management of this store has called you in as a consultant to identify the cause of the declining sales. Using the retail patronage model as a frame of reference, develop as many hypotheses as you can regarding the cause of the decline in sales. After you have developed the hypotheses, design a questionnaire to collect the data to test them.

5. Visit a gift shop, ice cream store, or jewelry store and assess the atmospherics of the store. Relate your feelings and thoughts on the store's atmosphere in 250 words or less.

SUGGESTED READINGS

Dash, Joseph F., Leon G. Schiffman, and Conrad Berenson. "Risk- and Personality-Related Dimensions of Store Choice." *Journal of Marketing* 40(January 1976): 32–39.

Gentry, James W. and Alvin C. Burns. "How 'Important' Are Evaluative Criteria in Shopping Center Patronage?" *Journal of Retailing* 53(Winter 1977–78): 73–86.

Gillett, Peter L. "In-Home Shoppers—An Overview." *Journal of Marketing* 40(October 1976): 81–87.

Hansen, Robert A. and Terry Deutscher. "An Empirical Investigation of Attribute Importance in Retail Store Selection." *Journal of Retailing* 53(Winter 1977–78): 59–72, 95.

Harrell, Gilbert D., Michael D. Hutt, and James C. Anderson. "Path Analysis of Buyer Behavior Under Conditions of Crowding." *Journal of Marketing Research* 17(February 1980): 45–51.

James, Don L., Richard M. Durand, and Robert A. Dreves. "The Use of a Multi-Attribute Model in a Store Image Study." *Journal of Retailing* 52(Summer 1976): 23–32.

Monroe, Kent B. and Joseph P. Guiltiman. "A Path-Analytic Exploration of Retail Patronage Influences." *Journal of Consumer Research* 2(June 1975): 19–28.

Wheatley, John J. and John S. Y. Chiu. "The Effects of Price, Store Image, and Product and Respondent Characteristics on Perceptions of Quality." *Journal of Marketing Research* 14(May 1977): 181–86.

6

Overview *The behavior of competitors is an important component in the retail planning and management model, because effective planning and management in a retail enterprise cannot be accomplished without the proper analysis of competitors. After reviewing the ways of categorizing retailers, therefore, we will develop a detailed model of retail competition. We will then elaborate on a host of concepts that help to explain retail competition. Later in the chapter, we will discuss the evolution of retail competition and conclude with a discussion of competition from nonstore retailers.*

Understanding Competitor Behavior

Categorizing Retailers
Census Bureau
Number of Outlets
Margins Versus Turnover
Location
Size

A Model of Retail Competition
The Competitive Marketplace
Market Structure
The Demand Side of Retailing
The Supply Side of Retailing
The Profit-Maximizing Price
Nonprice Decisions
Competitive Actions

Types of Competition
Intra- and Intertype Competition
Divertive Competition

Competition for Market Share
Developing a Protected Niche

Retail Competition and Military Principles

Evolution of Retail Competition
The Wheel of Retailing
The Retail Accordion
Natural Selection
The Dialectic Process
The Retail Life Cycle

Competition from Nonstore Retailers
Nature and Scope
Nonstore Growth

Summary

RETAILERS that strive to achieve high performance results must be effective competitors. They must be on the offensive and set the trend for others to follow. If they compromise and resort to being on the defensive, their performance will surely lag behind that of the industry leaders.

No retailer, however clever, can design a strategy that will totally insulate it from competitive actions. No retailer can get a patent for an innovative merchandising strategy. Furthermore, the low entry barriers in retailing mean that the retailer can count on being copied by others if it unearths a profitable strategy. Note for instance the growth of fast-food chains, discount department stores, and home improvement centers in the 1970s.

Thus, if you plan to become a retail executive, you must develop the talent for designing and implementing innovative competitive strategies. Furthermore, you need to recognize that in retailing, competition in the marketplace is a fact of life.

CATEGORIZING RETAILERS

A categorization of retailers can help you understand competition in retailing. However, there is no single acceptable method of classifying retail competitors, although many classification schemata have been proposed. We will review the five most popular (see Exhibit 6.1).

EXHIBIT 6.1
Categorizing Retailers

CENSUS BUREAU	NUMBER OF OUTLETS	MARGIN/ TURNOVER	LOCATION	SIZE
2-digit SIC code	Single unit	Low margin/ low turns	Central business district	By sales volume
3-digit SIC code	2–10 units		Neighborhood shopping center	By number of employees
4-digit SIC code	11–99 units	Low margin/ high turns		
	100+ units	High margin/ low turns	Community shopping center	
		High margin/ high turns	Regional shopping center	
			Super-regional shopping center	
			Free-standing	

Census Bureau   The U.S. Bureau of the Census, for purposes of conducting the census of retail trade, classifies all retailers into eight two-digit standard industrial classification (SIC) codes, shown on page 136.

1. Building materials, hardware, garden supply, and mobile home dealers (SIC 52)
2. General merchandise group stores (SIC 53)
3. Food stores (SIC 54)
4. Automotive dealers and gasoline service stations (SIC 55)
5. Apparel and accessory stores (SIC 56)
6. Furniture, home furnishings, and equipment stores (SIC 57)
7. Eating and drinking places (SIC 58)
8. Miscellaneous retail stores (SIC 59)

Generally, these two-digit SIC codes are too broad to be of much use by the retail analyst.

The more than forty, three-digit SIC codes provide much more information on the structure of retail competition. Let us examine the summary statistics on these codes in Exhibit 6.2. At one extreme we see the average department store (SIC 531) has a sales volume of $8.7 million, whereas the typical used merchandise store (SIC 593) has annual sales of $57,000. At the same time we can notice considerable variability in the number of retail establishments per thousand households. Overall there are twenty-five, but there are only 0.12 department stores (SIC 531), and only 2.38 gas stations (SIC 554) per thousand households.

In almost all instances, the SIC code reflects the type of merchandise the retailer sells. The major portion of a retailer's competition arises from other retailers in its SIC category. General merchandise stores (SIC 53) are the outstanding exception to this general rule, especially department stores (SIC 531). General merchandise stores, due to the breadth of merchandise carried, compete with retailers in most other SIC categories. Likewise, most retailers must compete to a considerable extent with general merchandise stores, because those larger stores will probably be handling many of the same types of merchandise the smaller, more limited line retailer is selling. Of course, in a very broad sense, all retailers will compete with each other since they are all vying for the same limited consumer dollars.

Number of Outlets   One method of classifying retailers, which aids in understanding their competitive strength, is by the number of outlets each operates. Generally, retailers with several units are a stronger competitive threat because they can spread many fixed costs, such as advertising and top management salaries, over a larger volume of sales and can also frequently achieve economies in purchasing. However, single-unit retailers do have their advantages. They are generally owner- and family-operated and thus tend to have harder working, more motivated employees. Also, they can focus all their efforts on one trade area and therefore better tailor their merchandise to that area.

Exhibit 6.3 (page 138) profiles the changing role of single-unit retailers from 1963 to 1977. From these statistics it can be seen that the proportion of sales attributable to 100 or more unit retailers has grown dramatically. At the same time, it can be seen that the share accounted for by retailers with 2 to 99 units has remained relatively constant.

EXHIBIT 6.2 Scope of Retail Trade by Type of Store

SIC CODE	LINE OF TRADE	NUMBER OF ESTABLISHMENTS	SALES (millions)	SALES PER ESTABLISHMENT	ESTABLISHMENTS PER 1,000 HOUSEHOLDS
	Total for all retail trade	1,855,068	$723,134	$ 389,815	25.02
521	Lumber and other building materials dealers	28,932	24,726	854,616	.39
523	Paint, glass, and wallpaper stores	11,655	2,401	206,046	.16
525	Hardware stores	26,451	6,087	230,119	.36
526	Retail nurseries, lawn, and garden supply stores	15,487	1,789	115,499	.21
527	Mobile home dealers	7,832	3,857	492,469	.11
531	Department stores	8,807	76,909	8,732,764	.12
533	Variety stores	17,376	7,095	408,295	.23
539	Miscellaneous general merchandise stores	22,728	9,944	437,513	.31
541	Grocery stores	178,835	147,759	824,553	2.41
542	Meat and fish (seafood) markets, including freezer provisioners	16,852	3,780	224,305	.23
543	Fruit stores and vegetable markets	7,853	1,088	138,559	.11
544	Candy, nut, and confectionery stores	8,973	643	71,612	.12
546	Retail bakeries	19,906	2,300	115,548	.27
545	Dairy products stores	8,289	1,258	151,744	.11
549	Miscellaneous food stores	11,263	1,113	98,850	.15
551	Motor vehicle dealers—new and used cars	30,793	121,883	3,958,140	.42
552	Motor vehicle dealers—used cars only	37,016	6,945	187,626	.50
553	Auto and home supply stores	46,957	12,861	273,890	.64
555	Boat dealers	6,556	2,600	396,642	.09
556	Recreational and utility trailer dealers	5,232	2,894	553,053	.07
557	Motorcycle dealers	6,386	1,980	309,998	.09
559	Automotive dealers, n.e.c.	6,066	789	130,123	.08
554	Gasoline service stations	176,465	56,468	319,996	2.38
561	Men's and boy's clothing and furnishings stores	22,683	6,943	306,098	.31
562,3,8	Women's clothing and specialty stores and furriers	53,572	13,458	251,204	.72
565	Family clothing stores	21,556	8,055	373,666	.29
566	Shoe stores	27,891	5,650	202,583	.38
564,9	Other apparel and accessory stores	14,424	1,459	101,132	.19
571	Furniture and home furnishings stores	82,591	20,316	245,979	1.11
572	Household appliance stores	17,554	4,734	269,698	.24
573	Radio, television, and music stores	38,434	8,126	211,437	.52
58	Eating and drinking places	368,066	63,276	171,914	4.96
591	Drug and proprietary stores	49,570	23,196	467,952	.67
592	Liquor stores	44,354	12,967	292,363	.60
593	Used merchandise stores	49,834	2,850	57,189	.67
594	Miscellaneous shopping goods stores	164,635	20,882	126,839	2.22
596	Nonstore retailers	32,818	14,440	440,009	.44
598	Fuel and ice dealers	20,246	10,171	502,376	.27
5992	Florists	29,375	2,400	81,704	.40
5993	Cigar stores and stands	3,629	460	126,793	.05
5994	News dealers and newsstands	7,763	533	68.624	.11
5999	Miscellaneous retail stores, n.e.c.	99,363	6,049	60,879	1.34

Source: U.S. Bureau of the Census, *1977 Census of Retail Trade* (Washington, D.C.: U.S. Government Printing Office, 1977).

EXHIBIT 6.3 **The Decline of Single Unit Retailing**	NUMBER OF UNITS	SALES AS A PERCENTAGE OF TOTAL			
		1963	*1967*	*1972*	*1977*
	Single unit	63.4%	60.2%	54.9%	52.0%
	2–10 units	11.1	10.5	10.5	11.2
	11–99 units	9.8	10.6	9.4	9.9
	100+ units	15.8	18.6	25.2	26.9

Source: U.S. Bureau of the Census, *Census of Retail Trade* (Washington, D.C.: U.S. Government Printing Office, 1963, 1967, 1972, 1977).

The August 1980 issue of *Chain Store Age Executive* listed more than 150 retailers in the United States with over 100 outlets. Retailers with over 100 units are therefore becoming a major competitive force in the retail industry.

The Department of Commerce in conjunction with the Bureau of the Census classifies any retailer with eleven or more units as a **chain-store retailer.** Exhibit 6.4 shows, using this eleven-unit criterion, how many retailers are chain stores for total retail trade and several more popular lines of retail trade. The statistics in this table reveal that chain-store retailing is significant and that more than half of the retail sales of department stores, variety stores, and grocery stores are accounted for by chain stores.

EXHIBIT 6.4 **Multiple-Unit Retailing by Selected Lines of Trade (1977)**	LINE OF TRADE	SALES AS A PERCENTAGE OF TOTAL		
		Single unit	2–10	11+
	Total retail trade	52.0%	11.2%	36.8%
	Department stores	1.4	5.9	92.7
	Variety stores	16.4	4.3	79.3
	Grocery stores	28.6	11.7	59.7
	Women's ready-to-wear stores	35.9	20.8	43.3
	Furniture stores	63.3	23.4	13.3
	Drugstores	41.6	10.3	48.1
	Liquor stores	69.1	9.9	21.0

Source: U.S. Bureau of Census, *1977 Census of Retail Trade* (Washington, D.C.: U.S. Government Printing Office, 1977).

Margins Versus Turnover   Retailers can be classified in regard to their average gross margin and rate of inventory turnover.[1] The gross margin shows how much gross profit (sales less cost of goods sold) the retailer makes as a percentage of sales. A 40 percent gross margin indicates that on each dollar of sales the retailer generates 40¢ in gross profit dollars. Inventory turnover refers to the number

1. For a more complete discussion of classifying retailers by margin and turnover, see Ronald R. Gist, *Retailing: Concepts and Decisions* (New York: Wiley, 1968), pp. 37–40.

of times per year, on average, that a retailer sells its inventory. Thus, an inventory turnover of twelve times indicates that, on average, the retailer turns its inventory once a month. As you will see in Exhibit 6.5, one can classify retailers into four basic types by using the concepts of margin and turnover.

Typically the low-margin/low-turnover retailer will not be able to generate sufficient profits to remain competitive and survive. Thus, there are few good examples of this type of retailer. On the other hand, the low-margin/high-turnover retailer is common in the United States. Perhaps the best examples are the discount department stores such as K-mart, Woolco, and Target or the full-line supermarkets such as Safeway, A & P, or Food Giant. High-margin/low-turnover retailers are also quite common in the United States. Furniture stores, TV and appliance stores, jewelry stores, and hardware stores are generally good examples of high-margin/low-turnover operations. Finally, some retailers find it possible to operate on both high margins and high turnover. As you might expect, this strategy can be very profitable. Probably the most popular example is the convenience food store such as 7-11, Circle K, Stop and Go, or Quick Mart.

The low-margin/low-turnover retailer is the least able of the four to withstand a competitive attack, because this retailer is barely profitable and thus as competitive intensity increases, profits will be driven even lower. On the other hand, the high-margin/high-turnover retailer is in an excellent position to withstand and counter competitive threats because of its attractive profit performance.

Location

Retailers can be classified according to location within the metropolitan area. This location can range from the central business district, to a shopping center, to a free-standing unit.

Historically, most retailers were located in the **central business district**

EXHIBIT 6.5
Retailers Classified by Margin and Turnover

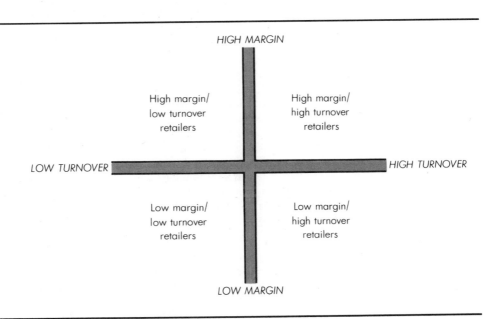

(CBD), which is the geographic point where most cities originated and grew up. This is also typically the point at which all public transportation systems converge. Many of the traditional department stores are located in the CBD along with a good selection of specialty stores, such as camera shops, luggage and leather stores, women's apparel shops, and jewelry stores. Stores located in the CBD draw their clientele from the entire metropolitan area and even from nonresidents. Naturally, they also focus efforts on workers and households located in or close to the CBD. In general, CBD's in the United States started to decline in the 1950s, but in the late 1970s many started to come alive again. This rebirth was due to such factors as rehabilitation of many downtown areas and migration of households back to the city from the suburbs due to rising transportation costs and an increasing disenchantment with suburban life.

Shopping centers are a popular location for stores.[2] The Urban Land Institute has defined four types of shopping centers, each with a distinctive function:[3]

1. **A neighborhood center** provides for the sale of convenience goods (foods, drugs and sundries) and personal services (laundry and dry cleaning, barbering, shoe repairing, etc.) for day-to-day living needs of the immediate neighborhood. It is built around a supermarket as the principal tenant. . . . The neighborhood center is the smallest type of shopping center and as a rule of thumb will have approximately 50,000 square feet in gross leasable space.

2. **Community center**—in addition to the convenience goods and personal services of the neighborhood center, this type of center provides a wider range of facilities for the sale of soft lines (wearing apparel for men, women and children) and hard lines (hardware and appliances). It makes greater depth of merchandise available—variety in sizes, styles, colors and prices. It is built around a junior department store, a variety store or discount department store as the major tenant, in addition to a supermarket. It does not have the full-line department store, though it may have a strong specialty store. In theory, the typical size is 150,000 square feet of gross leasable area, but in practice this size may vary.

3. **The regional center** provides for general merchandise, apparel, furniture and home furnishings in depth and variety as well as a range of services and recreational facilities. It is built around one or two full-line department stores of generally not less than 100,000 square feet. In theory, a typical size for definitive purposes is considered as 400,000 square feet of gross leasable area. The regional center is the second largest type of shopping center. As such the regional provides services typical of a business district yet not as extensive as the super regional.

4. **A super-regional center** provides for extensive variety in general merchandise, apparel, furniture and home furnishings as well as a variety of services and recreational facilities. It is built around at least three major department stores of generally not less than 100,000 square feet each. In theory, the typical size of a super regional is about 750,000 square feet of gross leasable area. In practice the size ranges to well over 1,000,000 square feet.

2. For some interesting insights into the future of shopping centers as viable locations, see "Shopping Center Futures" *Stores* 62(April 1980): 50–57.

3. Urban Land Institute, "The Dollars and Cents of Shopping Centers" (Washington, D.C.: Urban Land Institute, 1978), p. 294. Reprinted with permission.

The last location alternative available to the retailer is to locate as a **free-standing retailer.** Free-standing retailers generally locate along major traffic arteries. In fact, most cities have strips of free-standing retailers on most major traffic arteries. Most K-marts built since 1961 have been free-standing stores.

The location of a retailer is a determinant of the potential competition that will be faced. Generally, the closer two retailers are located (assuming they sell the same lines of merchandise) the more they will be in competition with one another. The most important thing about the geographic space between two retailers is the time and effort it takes a consumer to travel the distance. For example, a department store on the United States side of the Detroit River in Detroit may be close to another on the Canadian side in Windsor, but these two department stores would not be in as much competition with each other as two department stores within a mile of each other in suburban Detroit. It can be said that two retailers selling the same lines of merchandise will compete with each other to the extent that the consumer can shop at each with ease.

Size
Many retail trade associations classify retailers by sales volume or number of employees. The reason for classifying by size is that the operating performance of retailers will tend to vary according to their size. For example, the Retail Floorcovering Institute reports operating performance data by five sales volume categories (under $499,000; $500,000 to $999,999; $1 million to $1.9 million; $2 million to $4.9 million; and over $5 million). The National Retail Hardware Association classifies lumber and building materials stores into three categories by annual sales: under $500,000, $500,000 to $1 million, and over $1 million. For department stores, the National Retail Merchants Association categorizes stores into seven volume groups: $1–2 million; $2–5 million; $5–10 million; $10–20 million; $20–50 million; $50–100 million; and over $100 million. As you might expect, other retail trade associations provide similar breakdowns.

A MODEL OF RETAIL COMPETITION

Competition in retailing, as in any other industry, involves the interplay of both supply and demand. The student of retailing cannot appreciate the nature and scope of competition in retailing by studying only the type and number of retailers that exist (the supply factors). Rather, one must examine consumer demand factors in light of the supply of retail facilities. Thus, at this point it is appropriate to develop a formal framework for describing and explaining competition in retailing.[4]

The Competitive Marketplace   When retailers compete for customers, they compete on a local level. Retailers may compete nationally for financial capital, top executives, and college graduates, but for customers they compete locally. Why? Because

---

4. The framework is developed in elaborate detail in Charles A. Ingene and Robert F. Lusch, "A Model of Retail Structure," in Jagdish Sheth (ed.), *Research in Marketing* 5(1981): 101–64.

households will not typically travel beyond local markets to purchase the goods they desire. When they do travel beyond local markets, it is usually because their city or town is too small to support retailers with the selection of merchandise they desire.[5] But most cities of over 100,000 can provide the consumer with sufficient selection in almost all lines of merchandise. And in cities of less than 100,000, the household will need to travel to another town or city only for large purchases such as a new automobile, television, or furniture.

Market Structure   In terms of the four market structures economists use to describe competition in U.S. industry (pure competition, monopolistic competition, oligopolistic competition, and pure monopoly), retailing can be characterized as monopolistic and sometimes oligopolistic. As you will recall from microeconomics, the distinction between monopolistic competition and oligopoly lies in the number of sellers. Since each of the sellers in an oligopoly is large, any action by one is expected to be noticed and reacted to by the others. Conventional economic thought suggests that for this to occur, the top four firms have to account for over 60 percent of the market. For retailing in the United States this does not occur on a national level and seldom occurs on a local level. Exhibit 6.6 shows that the market share of the four largest national food store chains is less than 20 percent and that of the four largest general merchandise chains is less than 25 percent.

Earlier, however, we stated that retailers compete on a local, not national, basis. Obviously, retailing is much more concentrated within local markets than

EXHIBIT 6.6 **Total Sales of the Four Largest Firms in Two Retail Lines**	*FOOD STORES*		*GENERAL MERCHANDISE STORES*	
	Safeway Stores	$ 12,550,569	Sears, Roebuck	$ 17,946,000
	Kroger	7,828,071	K-mart	11,695,539
	A & P	7,469,659	J. C. Penney	10,845,000
	Lucky Stores	4,658,000	F. W. Woolworth	6,102,800
	Total, four largest	$ 32,506,299	Total, four largest	$ 46,589,339
	Total, all food stores	$187,652,400[a]	Total, all general merchandise, apparel, and furniture stores	$193,290,200[a]
	Four-firm concentration ratio	17.3%	Four-firm concentration ratio	24.1%

[a]Author's estimate based on linear extrapolation of *1977 Census of Retail Trade* data.

Source: Chain Store Age Executive (August 1979); U.S. Bureau of Census, *1977 Census of Retail Trade* (Washington, D.C.: U.S. Government Printing Office, 1977).

5. For a behavioral and segmentation analysis of those households that travel beyond local markets to shop, see the following pair of articles: Fred D. Reynolds and William R. Darden, "Intermarket Patronage: A Psychographic Study of Consumer Outshoppers," *Journal of Marketing* 36(October 1972): 50–54; and William R. Darden and William D. Perreault, Jr., "Identifying Interurban Shoppers: Multiproduct Purchase Patterns and Segmentation Profiles," *Journal of Marketing Research* 13(February 1976): 51–60.

the preceding national statistics suggest. Seldom, however, do the four leading retail firms in any of the 258 SMSAs in the United States account for more than 60 percent of the market. (**SMSAs** are Standard Metropolitan Statistical Areas, territorial units used by the Census Bureau that include cities of more than 50,000 people and their suburbs.)

Leonard Weiss notes that even where retailing becomes concentrated at the local level, there are several checks on the retailers' power:

> The country is full of automobiles, so most customers have large numbers of alternatives. Moreover, many modern retailers are becoming less specialized. The supermarket that sells nylons and the drugstore where you cannot find the drug counter are famous. Any seller who tries to maintain high prices is apt to find the grocers or the gas stations or someone equally far removed trying to take over his profitable lines. At any rate, there seems to be a continuous supply of new shopkeepers, ready to appear whenever prospects are good, and often even when they are not. It takes a good deal more to break into such fields as food retailing than it once did, but the cost of entry is still much lower than in most concentrated segments of manufacturing.[6]

The Demand Side of Retailing   Most retailers, then, face monopolistic competition, and thus we assume such a market structure in our model. (The model that follows would generally apply in oligopolistic competition as well.)

In a monopolistically competitive market, the retailer will be confronted with a negatively sloping demand curve. That is, as price, is lowered the consumer will demand a higher quantity. These statements may lead you to conclude that a typical retailer faces a demand function as shown in Exhibit 6.7 (page 144). However, the retailer does not confront such a curve.

The retailer faces a **three-dimensional demand function.** The three dimensions are (1) quantity demanded per household, (2) price at the retail store, and (3) distance from the household's place of residence or work to the store. Quantity demanded by a household is inversely related to prices charged and distance to the store.

Higher prices result in less demand, because households have limited incomes and many alternatives to allocate those dollars to. If a retailer raises prices, and all else remains unchanged, then households will try to shift some of their purchasing power to other retailers. Typically, if all or several retailers raise their prices this may not be the net effect. Also, if at the time the retailer raises prices consumer incomes are also rising, the effect may not be a drop in unit volume. But in these examples "all else" does not remain unchanged.

As the consumer lives farther away from the retailer the quantity demanded by the consumer will drop. This happens because it costs the consumer dollars and time to travel to a store. The larger these costs are, the less the consumer will purchase from distant retailers. In the model to be developed we will refer to these time and dollar costs as **transportation costs.** They will be comprised of three components: (1) the **actual dollar costs** of transporting oneself to the store and back; (2) the time involved, which is related to **oppor-**

6. Leonard W. Weiss, *Case Studies in American Industry* (New York: Wiley, 1971), pp. 222–23.

EXHIBIT 6.7
**Demand
Function
in a
Monopolistic
Competitive
Industry**

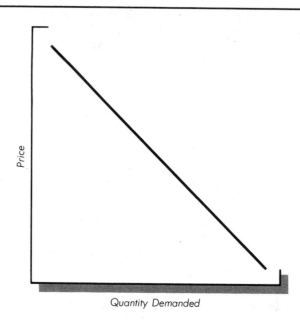

tunity costs (that is, what else could you be doing with your time and what value would you attach to those alternative activities?); and (3) the **psychic costs** of traveling to the store and back (that is, if traffic arteries or public transportation are very congested, then you may get frustrated and upset).

Exhibit 6.8 includes a graphical representation of a three-dimensional demand function confronting the typical retailer.[7] At this point you should spend a few moments studying this model.

From the three-dimensional demand model we can derive several key propositions that you, as a retail manager, will need to understand.

1. There is a **maximum demand price** that the retailer can obtain for the goods or services it offers the consumer. Refer to the three-dimensional demand model in Exhibit 6.8 to see where this maximum demand price is located. You should notice that the maximum demand price occurs only when the consumer's residence coincides with that of the store (an obviously unlikely occurrence) and when the retailer is willing to sell only a very small quantity of goods or services. Obviously, if the retailer desires to sell in large quantities to households located at increasing distances from the retailer's place of business then it must set its price below the maximum price it could theoretically establish.

2. There is a **maximum quantity** a consumer will demand from the retailer. This maximum quantity is obtained when the consumer lives very close to the store and the retailer's price on the good or service approaches zero. Notice where the maximum demand quantity is located on the three-di-

7. In the simple model to be developed we assume the retailer sells a single item. This need not be the case for the validity of the model to hold up; it is done only to reduce the amount of mathematics that we will need to incorporate into our discussion.

EXHIBIT 6.8
The Three-Dimensional Demand Model

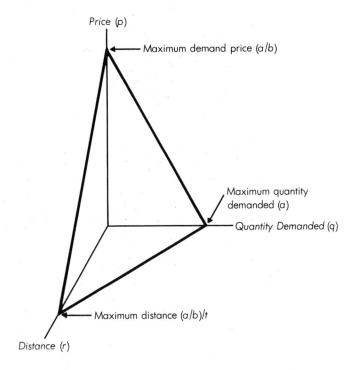

In functional form the three-dimensional demand model can be stated as follows:

$$q = a - bp - btr$$

where: q = quantity demanded
p = price per unit
t = round trip transportation costs per mile, which includes actual transport costs and time and psychic costs
r = the radius or distance from the consumer's home or work to the store
a, b = parameters that describe shape of the demand function

Illustrating the three-dimensional demand model with a specific example:

$$q = 10 - 2p - 2(.25)r$$

Then we can determine: (1) the maximum demand price, by setting q and r equal to zero

$$0 = 10 - 2p - 2(.25)0$$
$$2p = 10$$
$$p = 5,$$

note that this is equivalent to (a/b), or $(10/2) = 5$; (2) the maximum distance by setting p or q equal to zero,

$$0 = 10 - 2(0) - 2(.25)r$$
$$0 = 10 - 2(.25)r$$
$$r = 20,$$

note that this is $(a/b)/t$, or $(10/2)/(.25) = 20$; and (3) the maximum quantity demanded, by setting p or r equal to zero,

$$q = 10 - 2(0) - 2(.25)0$$
$$q = 10$$

note that this is a, or 10 in the model.

mensional demand model in Exhibit 6.8. Predictably, the retailer cannot operate profitably by selling the maximum quantity, since the revenues generated would be extremely low due to low prices and the necessity of selling only to households close to the store. In all probability the level of revenues generated would not cover the retailer's expenses.

3. There is a **maximum distance** the consumer will travel to shop at a retail store. This distance is obtained by allowing price and quantity to approach zero. Refer to Exhibit 6.8 to locate this point. The retailer will not typically attract customers from the maximum distance, since to do so would necessitate having to give merchandise or services away. Clearly this would be an unprofitable strategy.

The three preceding propositions should suggest to you that retailers cannot be profitable by setting prices at the highest possible levels, trying to sell the largest quantity of goods or services possible, or trying to attract households from the greatest distance possible. Retailers will find it necessary to set prices somewhere below the maximum possible price but above zero. This implies that they will not sell the maximum quantity nor attract consumers from the maximum distance. But where should they set prices? It seems reasonable that retailers would want to set prices to maximize profits. To do so, however, they need knowledge of their costs, and this involves an examination of supply factors.

The Supply Side of Retailing   Retailers cannot operate without incurring costs, which can be classified as fixed and variable. These costs are portrayed graphically in Exhibit 6.9. **Fixed costs** are those which the retailer incurs regardless of the quantity of goods or services sold. These costs are in most part related to the size of the

EXHIBIT 6.9   **Cost Functions in Retailing**

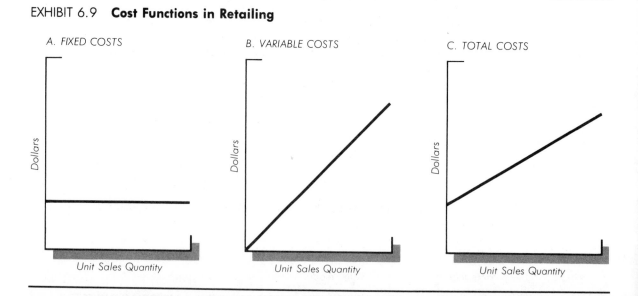

A. FIXED COSTS   B. VARIABLE COSTS   C. TOTAL COSTS

store and the costs of maintaining and financing it regardless of whether the store is open or closed. Examples of fixed costs in retailing include insurance, taxes, rent or lease payments, and security guards. **Variable costs** are those which increase proportionately with sales volume. The largest variable cost in retailing is the cost of the goods or services sold.

Without a doubt, all of the costs of operating a retail store cannot be categorized strictly into fixed and variable costs. **Semifixed costs** are constant over a range of sales volume, but past a crucial point they increase to a higher plateau and then again remain constant at another higher sales volume range. For example, labor may be viewed as semifixed (see Exhibit 6.10). Before the doors of the store can be opened each day, a staff of employees must be on hand, but as store traffic volume rises past a crucial point, more employees would need to be added, since the existing staff would be inadequate.

Regardless, however, of the exact form of the retailer's cost functions, it must examine the supply side of retailing in light of demand in order to set a profit maximizing price. In short, the principles of microeconomic price theory cannot be ignored.

The Profit-Maximizing Price   Let us assume that the retailer has established a price level at which to sell its goods or services. Having established a price and knowing its costs, the retailer could construct a break-even chart as in Exhibit 6.11 (page 148). The cost function is borrowed directly from Exhibit 6.9c and the total revenue function is obtained by multiplying the price the retailer has established by quantity Q. Note that Q is the total quantity the retailer sells and not the quantity (q) any individual household demands as portrayed in Exhibit 6.8. Let us examine how one might go about obtaining Q.

EXHIBIT 6.10
**Labor Cost
in Retailing**

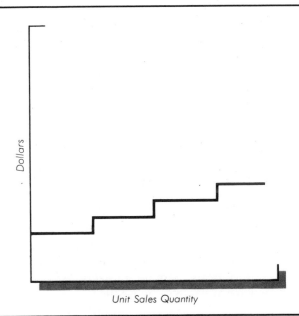

Unit Sales Quantity

EXHIBIT 6.11
**A Retailer's
Break-Even
Chart**

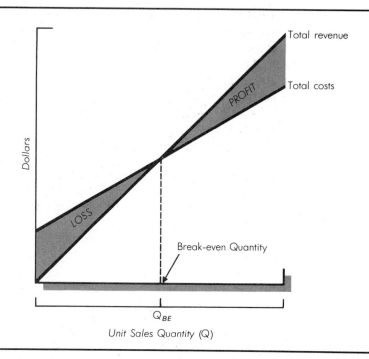

The key to obtaining Q is to recognize that the retailer will sell to more than one household. Thus, Q is simply the summation of the individual household demand curves (q) as shown in the three-dimensional demand model in Exhibit 6.8. As the retailer sets a lower price it will be able to attract customers from a greater distance. And the greater the density of households (households per square mile) the more households the retailer can attract to its store.

With an established price, the greatest distance a household will travel to a particular retail outlet can be defined as $(a/b - p)/t$, where a/b is the maximum demand price as earlier defined (see Exhibit 6.8) and p is the price the retailer has established and t is the transport cost (round trip cost per mile), which was also previously defined.

Let us construct a numerical example of the greatest distance a household would travel to purchase a particular item at a particular retail outlet. Assume that the retailer has established a price (p) of $5 per unit and that the maximum price (a/b) the household would pay is $10 per unit. Further assume that the round-trip transportation cost per mile (t) is $.50. From this information and our formula for the maximum distance $(a/b - p)/t$, we can easily compute the maximum distance a household would travel as $(10 - 5)/.50$ or 10 miles. Households would simply not travel beyond ten miles, because to do so they would spend more for the merchandise and the cost of transportation than the goods are worth to them. To illustrate this point, assume that the household traveled twenty miles to purchase the item. It would have spent $10 for transportation and $5 for the item for a total of $15, when the maximum demand price it was willing to pay was only $10.

We mentioned previously that the total quantity that a retailer sells is simply the sum of what all households purchase from the retailer. With an established price, the quantity demanded by an individual household will vary inversely with the distance from the retail outlet. In Exhibit 6.8, we portray the household's demand function given an established price. The maximum distance any household will travel is (r) or $(a/b - p)/t$ and the maximum quantity demand is $(a - bp)$. Exhibit 6.12 verifies the fact that as households are closer to the retailer's place of business (i.e., r^* approaches zero in Exhibit 6.12) then households will purchase a larger quantity from that retailer.

If we now sum all of the household demand functions (similar to those in Exhibit 6.12) for all households located at a distance from the store of up to (r^*) we will obtain Q or the total unit volume the retailer will sell. We can now take this Q and refer back to Exhibit 6.11 to see if it exceeds the retailer's breakeven quantity (Q_{BE}). If Q exceeds Q_{BE} then the price the retailer established was profitable; but, if Q fell short of Q_{BE} the established price was unprofitable.

In theory, it is possible for a retailer to establish a profit maximizing price if the retailer has knowledge of its cost functions and the demand functions of households in its trading area. The procedure would be similar to the procedure used in microeconomics when a manufacturer equates marginal cost with marginal revenue. When the profit maximizing price is established, it will imply that retailers will attract customers from a well-defined distance, which would be obtained by inserting the profit-maximizing price into the formula $(a/b - p)t$ that was previously outlined. To attract customers from a greater distance by cutting price would be unprofitable, since the marginal cost of doing so would exceed the marginal revenue generated.

EXHIBIT 6.12
A Household's Demand Curve at a Given Retail Price

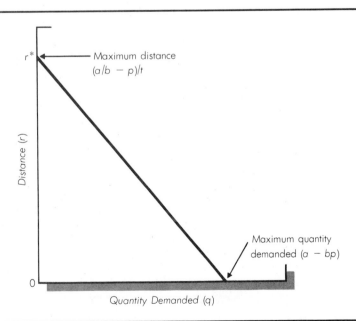

Nonprice Decisions   The retailer has at its disposal more than the price variable to influence the quantity it will sell and the resulting profit level. If store location is fixed, some of the more important nonprice variables are merchandise mix, advertising, special promotions, personal selling, and store atmosphere. These and all other nonprice variables are directed at enlarging the demand that the retailer faces. In fact, by using the three-dimensional demand model in Exhibit 6.8 as a frame of reference, we can show in Exhibit 6.13 the intended effect of nonprice variables in retailing. Pay particular notice to the fact that after successful implementation of a nonprice strategy, the maximum demand price consumers will pay, the maximum quantity they will demand, and the maximum distance customers will travel to shop at the retailer's store will all increase. How could the favorable shift in demand that was portrayed in Exhibit 6.13 have occurred? Here are some possible explanations:

1. The retailer could have altered its merchandise mix in the direction of higher quality shopping versus convenience goods. This would have increased the maximal demand price and thus increased the distance consumers would travel to shop for these goods, thereby enlarging the retailer's trade area.

EXHIBIT 6.13
**The Impact
of Nonprice
Strategies**

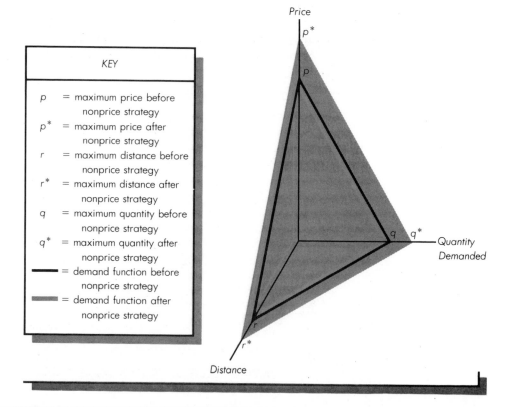

KEY

p = maximum price before nonprice strategy

p^* = maximum price after nonprice strategy

r = maximum distance before nonprice strategy

r^* = maximum distance after nonprice strategy

q = maximum quantity before nonprice strategy

q^* = maximum quantity after nonprice strategy

— = demand function before nonprice strategy

▓ = demand function after nonprice strategy

2. The retailer could have provided customers with free "park and shop" or "ride and shop" coupons, which would have effectively lowered the transportation costs of customers. The lowering of transportation costs would have increased the maximum distance the customer would be willing to travel, thereby increasing the retailer's trade area.

3. The retailer could have engaged in an extensive advertising campaign directed at persuading consumers to purchase more of the goods it sells. The net effect could have been an increase in the maximal quantity demanded.

The preceding analysis points out that all retail decision variables, whether they be price or nonprice, are directed at influencing demand. Of course, the profitability of the decisions will depend on the marginal cost of the action versus the marginal revenue it generates.

Competitive Actions In the model of retail competition, we saw that retailers attract customers from a limited geographic area and that as prices are lowered this area expands. But even at a zero price, households can only afford to travel a certain distance to purchase the goods and services retailers offer for sale. Therefore, in most cities there will be several, if not many, retailers in each line of retail trade. For example, the data presented in Exhibit 6.14 shows the number of retail establishments in eight lines of retail trade for representative cities of various population sizes.

When there are too many retail establishments competing for household patronage in a particular city, the profitability of retailing will suffer. Eventually, some retailers may even leave the market, as happened in 1976, when National Tea, a large retail food chain, closed all of its supermarkets in Chicago.

At the same time, if there are too few retailers competing for household patronage, then profits may be high enough to attract new retail competitors. Alternatively, existing retailers may be enticed to build more outlets or expand existing outlets.

Finally, the market would be in equilibrium in terms of number of retail

EXHIBIT 6.14 **Number of Retailers in Cities of Various Sizes (1977)**		*CITY SIZE*		
	LINE OF TRADE	*200,000*	*500,000*	*1,000,000*
	Hardware stores	20	58	71
	Department stores	12	24	47
	Grocery stores	175	342	886
	Motor vehicle dealers	207	285	707
	Furniture stores	55	166	360
	Drugstores	57	116	192
	Jewelry stores	42	61	159
	Florists	32	66	162

Source: U.S. Bureau of Census, *1977 Census of Retail Trade* (Washington, D.C.: U.S. Government Printing Office, 1977) and author's computations.

establishments if the return on investment is high enough to justify keeping capital invested in retailing but not so high to invite more competition.

A good measure of competitive activity in a market is the number of retail establishments per thousand households ($N/1,000H$). If we assume for the moment that the stores are of the same approximate size, then as the number of stores per 1,000 households rises, the degree of competition will intensify. This intensified level of competition will tend to lower the return on investment in retailing as illustrated in Exhibit 6.15. It can be seen that if $N/1,000H$ is at the level where the resulting return on investment is just enough to keep the capital employed in retailing, then the market is in equilibrium. This is at the point ($N/1,000H$)* and ROI* in Exhibit 6.15. When the number of stores per thousand households is below ($N/1,000H$)*, the return on investment will exceed ROI* and the market can be characterized as **understored.** However, if ($N/1,000H$)* is exceeded, the return on investment will fall below ROI* and the market will be characterized as **overstored.**

Competition is most intense in overstored markets, since many retailers are achieving an inadequate return on investment. These retailers face a major performance imperative and will therefore implement both price and nonprice actions in an all-out attempt to increase sales and profit levels. Since retailers operate in a relatively closed geographic market with a fixed number of households with limited income, any action by one retailer to increase its sales or profit level will warrant an action from competitors.

EXHIBIT 6.15
The Profitability of Under- and Overstoring

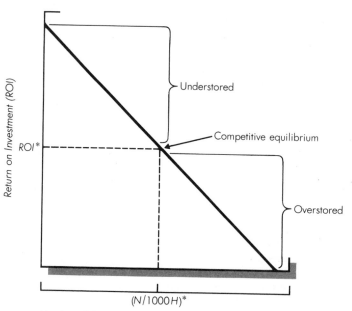

Number of Stores per Thousand Households (N/1000H)

Note: *ROI** is the return on investment that will just be enough to keep the capital employed in retailing (the equilibrium *ROI*).

The easiest and quickest actions to copy are those which are price based. If a retailer cuts price, many competitors will respond with a similar price cut. In many cases they have no choice if they want to keep their existing consumer franchise. Exhibit 6.16 gives an actual industry example of the profit effect of price competition. The example involves A & P, the second largest food retailer in the United States at the time, which engaged in a price-cutting strategy entitled *WEO*. WEO stood for "where economy originates" and was an attempt by A & P to gain back market share it had been losing to other large chains over a ten-year period. As shown in Exhibit 6.16, the profit effect of this strategy for both A & P and its competitors was disastrous.

EXHIBIT 6.16
The Economics of Price Competition

RETAILER	PROFITS AS A PERCENTAGE OF NET SALES			
	1970	1971	1972	1973
Chains with little A&P competition	1.4%	1.5%	1.5%	1.4%
Chains competitive with A&P	.9	.8	.2	.4
A&P	.9	.3	(.8)	.2

RETAILER	PROFITS AS A PERCENTAGE OF NET WORTH			
	1970	1971	1972	1973
Chains with little A&P competition	13.9%	14.8%	14.9%	14.3%
Chains competitive with A&P	9.9	8.7	2.3	4.8
A&P	7.4	2.2	(8.6)	2.0

Source: Bert C. McCammon, Jr., Robert F. Lusch, and Bradley T. Farnsworth, "Contemporary Markets and the Corporate Imperative: A Strategic Analysis for Senior Retailing Executives," presented at Seminar for Top Management in Retailing, Graduate School of Business Administration, Harvard University (June 1976), p. 9. Reprinted with permission of the authors.

Nonprice actions, however, are not as easy or quick to duplicate. A unique advertising program or merchandise mix cannot be copied without some lag in time, from several days to weeks or even months.

TYPES OF COMPETITION

Intra- and Intertype Competition   It is possible to merge the preceding discussion of competition in retailing with the classification schemes used by the Department of Commerce in conducting the Census of Retail Trade. **Intratype competition** occurs when any two or more retailers of the same type as defined in the Census of Retail Trade compete with each other for the same households.[8] As you might expect, this is the most common type of retail competition. We often

8. For a discussion of the concept of intratype competition applied to department stores, see Elizabeth C. Hirschman, "Intratype Competition Among Department Stores," *Journal of Retailing* 55(Winter 1977): 20–34.

refer to Safeway competing with Food Giant, or Sears competing with Penney's. Historically, most competition in retailing has been of this form.

Competitive pressures in the 1960s and 1970s, however, caused retailers of quite different types to sell many identical lines of merchandise. Witness for example, gasoline stations, convenience food stores, and supermarkets all selling milk, bread, and motor oil. Also, TVs have been sold through appliance stores, department stores, variety stores, and supermarkets. **Intertype competition** occurs when different types of retail outlets sell the same lines of merchandise and therefore compete for the same limited consumer dollars.

In Exhibit 6.17 light is shed on the economics of intertype competition in the health and beauty aid fields from 1963 to 1977. The data in this exhibit dramatically tell the story of the economics of intertype competition. In principle, as the types of retail firms that handle a particular merchandise line increase, gross margins will deteriorate.

EXHIBIT 6.17 **Health and Beauty Aids Gross Margins in Supermarkets (1963–77)**		GROSS MARGIN AS A PERCENTAGE OF SALES				*PERCENTAGE POINT CHANGE*
	PRODUCT CATEGORY	*1963*	*1967*	*1971*	*1977*	*(1963–77)*
	Baby needs	44.0%	38.5%	29.2%	24.7%	− 19.3
	Cosmetics	42.8	37.5	30.9	35.9	− 6.9
	Creams and lotions	40.1	35.9	32.5	24.8	− 15.3
	First aid	43.2	39.3	33.6	29.0	− 14.2
	Hair care	41.7	37.4	28.2	24.5	− 17.2
	Medications	38.8	31.6	26.6	28.5	− 10.3
	Men's toiletries and shaving preparations	37.6	33.6	26.5	22.4	− 15.2
	Oral hygiene	35.9	28.7	29.7	18.6	− 17.3

Source: Bert C. McCammon, Jr., Robert F. Lusch, and Bradley T. Farnsworth, "Contemporary Markets and the Corporate Imperative: A Strategic Analysis for Senior Retailing Executives" presented at Seminar for Top Management in Retailing, Graduate School of Business Administration, Harvard University (June 1976) p. 8. Reprinted with permission of the authors.

Another illustration of intertype competition is presented in Exhibit 6.18. This case study deals with the increasing number of retailers, especially supermarkets and drugstores, selling automotive accessories. As these examples show, intertype competition is beneficial to the consumer because of lower prices, but for retailers, the effect on profits can be disastrous.

Divertive Competition   Another concept that helps to explain the nature of competition in retailing is **divertive competition.**[9] It occurs when a retailer intercepts or diverts

9. The concept of divertive competition is discussed in Bert C. McCammon, Jack J. Kasulis, and Jack A. Lesser, "The New Parameters of Retail Competition: The Intensified Struggle for Market Share," In Ronald W. Stampfl and Elizabeth Hirschman (eds.), *Competitive Structure in Retail Markets: The Department Store Perspective* (Chicago: American Marketing Association, 1980), pp. 108–18.

customers from competing retailers. To comprehend the significance of divertive competition one needs to recognize that most retailers operate very close to their break-even point. For instance, supermarkets with their extremely low gross margins tend to have a break-even point of from 94 to 96 percent of current sales. General merchandise retailers with larger gross margins usually face a break-even point of 85 to 92 percent of their current sales. Both of these examples should be disquieting because they suggest that with a modest drop in sales volume the retailer would be operating in the red. The precise drop in sales volume needed to fall below break-even would depend on such factors as the retailer's cost structure, gross margin, current profit level, and a host of other factors.

This brief discussion suggests that retailers are susceptible to any downturn in sales. It logically follows that new retail entrants in a community do not have to get all the business. On the contrary, "all they have to do is *divert* or siphon off the 'plus' sales that existing firms need to operate profitably."[10] For example, super drugstores such as Skaggs, Longs, or Jack Eckerd divert sales from full-line general merchandise stores. Although these super drugstores may not carry as broad an assortment of merchandise as the general merchandise retailer, the assortment is attractive enough to capture the convenience

---

EXHIBIT 6.18
Intertype Competition in Automotive Accessories

Traditionally, the place to purchase automotive accessories was at your local service station, auto dealer, or auto parts store. Today this is no longer the case as more and more retailers are vying for the consumer's automotive dollars and as consumers are becoming more do-it-yourself oriented. Predictably, margins on auto accessories are rapidly deteriorating as competition intensifies.

The comments by the managers of some leading supermarkets and drug combos help to substantiate this observation:*

- Southwestern supermarket combo: "We can do quite a job with oil, an air filter, and an oil filter. I haven't seen anyone in the area touch us on price."
- Southeastern supermarket combo: "The first time out with Du Pont waxes on a rebate, you would have thought we were a national auto store."
- North Central drug combo: "I don't know how many units of Prestone II we moved in a three-day promotion, but we were cleaned out the second day at $3.29 per gallon."
- Midwestern supermarket combo: "We sold more than 2,000 cases of Ray Lube at a little over half a dollar a quart and $11.50 per case. We sold a lot of cases during this sale."
- Mountain States supermarket combo: "We ran a fog light a few months back and sold out at a really competitive price."
- Eastern drug combo: "We got rid of 1,800 cases of oil in a four-day period at 68 cents a quart."
- Southeastern supermarket combo: "We got under $4 for these steering wheel covers. I don't know how many we sold, but it was well over a thousand."

*Quotes taken from "More Hands Grab for the Automotive Dollar," *The Discount Merchandiser* (April 1980), p. 55.

---

10. McCammon, Kasulis, and Lesser, "The New Parameters," p. 110.

and time-constrained shopper. These super drugstores do an excellent job at diverting consumer dollars away from general merchandise retailers by reducing the consumer's dependence on these conventional retailers.

In Exhibit 6.19 we present a retail case study of the divertive competition that confronts the retail hardware industry. A careful reading of this case study should help reinforce the concept of divertive competition.

Competition for Market Share   Historically, retailers in the United States have been confronted with an ever-expanding market. The population was growing, real per capita incomes were constantly climbing, and the suburbs awaited new retail stores. However by the mid 1970s, the magic of growth vanished. By the early 1980s it was the consensus of retail analysts that the 1980s would be characterized by flat or, at best, moderate growth curves. Faced with the prospects of a constant market, retailers began to realize that growth could only be achieved by expansion of market share. Thus, they entered the 1980s by aggressively competing for market share.

Among the retail enterprises that have instituted continuing programs to monitor market share are Dayton-Hudson, K-mart, Sears, and J. C. Penney. In

---

EXHIBIT 6.19
The Economics of Divertive Competition

The concept of divertive competition has been outlined in relation to the retail hardware-home center industry in a recent issue of *Hardware Retailing*:

> Home centers have gone through a period of rapid expansion over the past decade, but many feel their growth curve is beginning to flatten out. As the industry matures, major markets become fully stored, secondary markets are occupied and outside companies rush to jump aboard the "hot" do-it-yourself bandwagon.
>
> Competition intensifies!
>
> Not only does direct competition heat up, indirect competition begins to form. Supermarkets begin to sell hardware, super drugstores get in on the act and specialty outlets like Color Tile and Wallpaper-To-Go move into the market and begin to divert do-it-yourself dollars.
>
> The flow of dollars away from a hardware/home center retailer may be so gentle that the owner may not even feel the pull. However, like the swimmer, there is a critical breakeven point at which the dealer ceases to record a black bottom line and begins penning it in red.
>
> Research by the National Retail Hardware Association shows that between 86% and 91% of a home center's current sales are needed to meet expenses. The exact breakeven level depends on the individual store.
>
> The critical point is only 9 to 14 percentage points below present volume. New market entries do not have to make a strong showing to dramatically hurt an existing business. All it takes is each of 5 or 6 fringe competitors to siphon $20,000 to $50,000— a couple of points—off the top and the home center is changed from being profitable, to breakeven or even to a loss operation.

Source: "High Break-Even Points, Indirect Competitors Dangerous," *Hardware Retailing* (January 1980), 119. Reprinted with permission.

addition, security analysts have recognized the close association between market share and financial performance. Consequently, Merrill Lynch, and Paine, Webber, Mitchell and Hutchins track market share by product category and by geographical area for each of the major general merchandise chains.[11]

Developing a Protected Niche   As competition intensifies in retailing, the retail manager will find it harder to be protected from competitive threats on the basis of the merchandise offered. Why? Because all retailers have access to the same merchandise. Therefore, retailers will find it more necessary in the future to develop a protected niche in the marketplace. A careful store positioning can be used to accomplish this. In **store positioning**, one identifies a well-defined market segment using demographic or life-style variables and appeals to this segment with a clearly differentiated approach. A notable example of positioning is The Limited, which appeals to career-oriented females, eighteen to thirty years of age, who are fashion oriented and upwardly mobile. The Limited's entire retail strategy—including store decor, merchandise, employees, background music, and prices—is geared to this segment.

Regarding positioning in retailing, Engel, Blackwell, and Kollat state:

> Positioning is closely related to segmentation and requires paying attention to the evaluative criteria of some market segment rather than trying to meet the criteria of the entire market. Stated simply, it is a marketing program that does not try to be all things to all people. While most stores have traditionally tried to stand for something in terms of price or fashion or service, the concept of positioning has been extended to reach different customers even *within* a store. Department stores may have 20 departments or "boutiques" closely correlated to demographic and life style segments rather than just three or four as in prior years.[12]

Most retail analysts contend that throughout the 1980s positioning in retailing will be a dominant competitive strategy.

RETAIL COMPETITION AND MILITARY PRINCIPLES

Some observers of the competitive free enterprise system have noted the similarity between principles of military strategy and competitive strategy.[13] There are seven principles of military strategy; they concern, respectively, (1) the objective, (2) coordination, (3) mass, (4) flexibility of maneuver, (5) security, (6) the offensive, and (7) surprise.[14] Familiarity with these principles is particularly helpful in understanding competitive behavior in retailing. Let us examine this notion in more detail.

11. McCammon, Kasulis, and Lesser, "The New Parameters," pp. 110–11.

12. From *Consumer Behavior*, 3rd edition, by James F. Engel, Roger D. Blackwell, and David T. Kollat. Copyright © 1978 by The Dryden Press, a division of Holt, Rinehart and Winston. Reprinted by permission of Holt, Rinehart and Winston.

13. An excellent discussion of military strategy can be found in Carl Von Clausewitz, *On War*, trans. J. J. Graham (London: Kegan Paul, 1918).

14. Philip Kotler, *Marketing Management: Analysis, Planning and Control*, 2nd ed. (Englewood Cliffs, N.J.: Prentice-Hall, 1972), pp. 250–52.

The **principle of the objective** states that there should be a well-defined and communicated objective that all relevant individuals in the retail enterprise should understand. In retailing, the principle objective is high financial performance. Since retailing is highly competitive, by striving for high financial performance the retailer is also serving society. Naturally, more than overall financial objectives must be established, since the retailer needs to manage parts of the business (merchandise lines, employees, buildings and fixtures, etc.). Nonetheless, objectives must be set and agreed on so that resources can be committed to achieving objectives.

The **principle of coordination** or unity of command states that all activities of the retailer must ultimately be orchestrated by one person. Someone must pull all things together. This person is typically the president or chief executive officer of the retail firm, and all responsibility ultimately rests on his or her shoulders. He or she must have the final decision on all matters of controversy, and all members of the organization must respect and follow this decision whether they agree or not.

The **principle of mass** suggests that the retailer should not spread its resources equally over the problems and opportunities it must address; it should concentrate them where they will do the most good. For example, if the retailer has a $100,000 annual advertising budget, it would not want to spread this amount equally over twelve months and on the various merchandise lines. It will instead concentrate on those months and products which would benefit the most. Similarly, a chain store does not spread its outlets evenly over geographic space but concentrates them in locations that offer the highest profit potential.

The **principle of flexibility** of maneuver states that the retailer should have contingency plans at its disposal. When the business environment turns out to be sufficiently different than anticipated, the retailer should be able to respond quickly and appropriately. Assume that the retailer had forecast a strong fourth quarter in terms of real economic growth but a mild recession occurred. If the retailer had a contingency plan, it would immediately know what competitive strategy to implement. It would waste little or no time attempting to develop an appropriate response. (Contingency plans are discussed more thoroughly in Chapter 9.)

The **principle of security** suggests that the retailer should hide or protect from competitors, information on its contemplated and forthcoming competitive actions. If the retailer is analyzing the possibility of locating a store in a community, it should not broadcast the news. If it is conducting consumer research in order to help develop a new store image, the results of that research should be guarded. If it has a clever method for improving inventory turnover, it should not freely reveal the method to competitors. Simply stated, the retailer should be secretive about its possible strategic and competitive behavior. At the same time though, it should try to obtain as much information as is legally possible about the strategies of competitors and their competitive behavior.

The **principle of the offensive** states that to become and remain an industry leader, the retailer must not only defend what it has but must be a pace setter. It must constantly challenge the market share of its competitors. If it settles on only protecting its current market share it would seem not to wish to grow faster than the market in general.

Finally, the **principle of surprise** recommends that the retailer mount the offensive when competition least expects it or when competition can least withstand intensified pressure. For example, if the retailer's competitors are experiencing poor financial performance or if they have just had a major shake up in the top management levels, then increased competitive effort may be quite effective in picking up market share points.

Although there is a profound similarity between military and competitive retailing principles there is also one major difference. In military strategy we typically want to defeat the enemy and win the war. In retailing, however, we seldom want to defeat or destroy the competitor. In fact, if the retailer consistently defeats its competitors then antitrust action may be forthcoming. However, there is little chance that the retailer will consistently defeat its competitors as long as it behaves ethically and legally. There are simply too many top-notch retail competitors to allow this to happen.

EVOLUTION OF RETAIL COMPETITION

Scholars studying retailing have developed several theories to explain and describe the evolution of competition in retailing. We will review five of them briefly.[15]

The Wheel of Retailing   Professor Malcolm P. McNair developed the wheel of retailing hypothesis to describe patterns of competitive development in retailing.[16] McNair stated in his hypothesis that new types of retailers enter the market as low-status, low-margin, low-price operators. This modest strategy allows these retailers to compete effectively and take market share away from the more traditional retailers. However, as they meet with success, these new retailers gradually acquire more sophisticated and elaborate facilities. This creates both a higher investment and a subsequent rise in operating costs. Predictably therefore, these retailers must raise prices and margins and they thus become vulnerable to new types of low-margin retail competitors, who in turn, go through the same pattern.

Not all retailing scholars agree with the wheel of retailing theory. Hollander notes that in both the United States and foreign retail environments

15. Space will not allow discussion of the views of all scholars that have written on the evolution of retail trade. Some notable articles that space does not allow us to comment on: A. C. R. Dressmann, "Patterns of Evolution in Retailing," *Journal of Retailing* 44(Spring 1968): 64–81; Arieh Goldman, "The Role of Trading-Up in the Development of the Retailing System," *Journal of Marketing* 39(January 1975): 54–62; and William J. Regan, "The Stages of Retail Development," in Reavis Cox, Wroe Alderson, and Stanley Shapiro (eds.), *Theory in Marketing* (Homewood, Ill.: Richard D. Irwin, 1974).

16. Malcolm P. McNair, "Significant Trends and Developments in the Postwar Period," in A. B. Smith (ed.), *Competitive Distribution in a Free High-Level Economy and Its Implications for the University* (Pittsburgh, Pa.: University of Pittsburgh Press, 1958).

there are nonconforming examples. In reference to retailing in the United States he states, "The department-store branch movement and the concomitant rise of planned shopping centers also has progressed directly contrary to the wheel pattern. The early department-store branches consisted of a few stores in exclusive suburbs and some equally high-fashion college and resort shops."[17] Furthermore, Hollander states in regard to retailing in underdeveloped countries that "The relatively small middle and upper-income groups have formed the major markets for "modern" types of retailing. Supermarkets and other modern stores have been introduced in those countries largely at the top of the social and price scales, contrary to the wheel pattern."[18] Hollander concludes that the number of nonconforming examples suggests that the wheel hypothesis is not valid for all retailing.

The Retail Accordion   Several observers of the history of retailing have noted that retail institutions evolve from outlets that offer wide assortments into specialized stores, and then return to the wide assortments to continue through the pattern once more. This contraction and expansion suggests the term *accordion*.[19]

In his history of Macy's of New York, Ralph Hower states:

> Throughout the history of retail trade (as, indeed in all business evolution) there appears to be an alternating movement in the dominant method of conducting operations. One swing is toward the specialization of the function performed on the merchandise handled by the individual firm. The other is away from such specialization toward the integration of related activities under one management or the diversification of products handled by a single firm.[20]

Retail historians have observed that in the United States retail trade was dominated by the general store up until 1860. The general store carried a broad assortment of merchandise ranging from farm implements to textiles to food. After 1860, due to the growth of cities and roads, retail trade became more specialized and was concentrated in the central business districts of cities. In the CBDs, department and specialty stores were the dominant competitive force. Both carried more specialized assortments than the general store. In the 1950s retailing began to move again to wider merchandise lines. Typical was the grocery store, which added produce and dairy products, and nonfood items such as kitchen utensils, health and beauty aids, and small household appliances. By the 1970s specialization in merchandise lines once again became a dominant competitive strategy. Kenderdine and McCammon observe,

> As consumer markets become more segmented, specialty stores will become increasingly important. This trend is already well advanced in a variety of product categories. Consider, for example, the explosive growth of such firms as Aaron

17. Stanley C. Hollander, "The Wheel of Retailing," *Journal of Marketing* 25(July 1960), p. 41.

18. Hollander, "Wheel of Retailing," p. 40.

19. Stanley C. Hollander, "Notes on the Retail Accordion," *Journal of Retailing* 42(Summer 1966): 29–40, 54.

20. Ralph Hower, *History of Macy's of New York 1858–1919* (Cambridge, Mass.: Harvard University Press, 1943), p. 73.

Brothers (artist's supplies and picture frames); Hickory Farms (specialty foods); The Limited (junior apparel); and Mervyn's (family apparel). In addition to these established chains, a new wave of "super" specialists has emerged. Included in this latter movement are such companies as Athlete's Foot, County Seat, Calculators, Inc., and the Gap. In short, specialty store retailing has become a high-growth sector of the economy.[21]

Natural Selection   The theory of natural selection in retailing is a direct descendant of Darwin's theory of natural selection, which has been popularized in the phrase "survival of the fittest." Basically, Darwin's theory states that a species that most effectively adapts to its environment is most likely to survive and perpetuate its kind. Applying this theory to retailing, Gist suggests,

> Retail institutions are economic species and the retail enterprise confronts an environment comprised of customers, competitors, and a fluctuating technology. We might, then, "transplant" the theory of natural selection into the context of retail institutional change and, to some extent, explain the success of some institutional species and the failure of others.[22]

Some observers of trends in retailing have noted that at times the American department store has had trouble rapidly and positively adapting to environmental change. For example, after World War II the conventional downtown department store dragged its feet, while growth in the suburbs was explosive. Delbert Duncan has observed,

> Those firms whose management did recognize the challenge of the changing social and economic forces, however, and established branches of various sizes and types to serve these new markets, made the necessary shift in organization structure to accommodate multi-unit operation, and adopted other innovations, have been richly rewarded. Moreover, in doing so, they helped to pioneer the development of the regional shopping center, one of the most important developments of the past two decades.
>
> Yet the measures adopted by the traditional department stores to meet the changing social and economic scene brought them face to face with problems not wholly anticipated. Moving from their long-established fortresses in downtown areas, they became vulnerable to the sharply increasing competition of other retailers quick to make innovations in policies and practices.[23]

In the late 1960s and throughout the 1970s consumer markets became more segmented. Department stores were slow to respond in a positive fashion. Consequently, many specialty stores experienced rapid growth because they were able and willing to design their total store offering to appeal to a select demographic or lifestyle group. Witness the growth during the 1970s of The

21. James M. Kenderdine and Bert C. McCammon, Jr., "Structure and Strategy in Retailing," in Henry W. Nash and Donald P. Robin (eds.), *Proceedings: Southern Marketing Association* (1975), p. 119.

22. Gist, *Retailing*, pp. 83–89.

23. Reprinted from Delbert J. Duncan, "Responses of Selected Retail Institutions to Their Changing Environment," in Peter D. Bennett *Marketing and Economic Development* (Chicago: American Marketing Association, 1965), p. 593.

Limited (appealing to the 18–30 year old career oriented, fashion conscious female), Radio Shack (appealing to the casual and serious electronics enthusiast), and Athlete's Foot (appealing to the casual and serious athlete). It was not until the mid to late 1970s that department stores began to recognize the magnitude of this challenge. Many responded by tailoring more than twenty departments within their stores to distinct groups. Consequently they became a group of minispecialty stores under one roof.

The Dialectic Process   A dialectic process of retailing was first proposed by Gist[24] and later validated by Maronick and Walker.[25] The dialectic process theory of retailing is based on Hegel's dialectic. According to Hegel, "Any idea, by the very nature of things, begets a negation of itself; the combination of the original idea, called the 'thesis,' with its negation called the 'antithesis,' results in a 'synthesis'—which, in turn, serves as the thesis when the process begins all over."[26]

A concise translation of Hegel's dialectic as applicable to competitive behavior in retailing has been made by Thomas Maronick and Bruce Walker.

> In terms of retail institutions, the dialectic model implies that retailers mutually adapt in the face of competition from "opposites." Thus, when challenged by a competitor with a differential advantage, an established institution will adopt strategies and tactics in the direction of that advantage, thereby negating some of the innovator's attraction. The innovator, meanwhile, does not remain unchanged. Rather, as McNair noted, the innovator over time tends to upgrade *or* otherwise modify products and facilities. In doing so, he moves toward the "negated" institution. As a result of these mutual adaptations, the two retailers gradually move together in terms of offerings, facilities, supplementary services, and prices. They thus become indistinguishable or at least quite similar and constitute a new retail institution, termed the synthesis. This new institution is then vulnerable to "negation" by new competitors as the dialectic process begins anew.[27]

To illustrate the dialectic process in retailing let us examine the evolution of competition in gasoline retailing as portrayed in Exhibit 6.20. In the early 1900s gasoline retailing was predominantly conducted by mom and pop gasoline retailers. These retailers generally charged high prices, offered personal service and credit, and also sold many nonautomotive products. They are thus labeled the thesis. The antithesis was the full-service gasoline station, which was able to offer lower prices due to its higher-volume operation. It also sold automotive accessories but few if any nonautomotive products. And, it emphasized automotive repair services. Severe competition from this antithesis destroyed many mom and pop stations.

The synthesis was the national brand service station:

24. Gist, *Retailing*, pp. 106–109.

25. Thomas J. Maronick and Bruce J. Walker, "The Dialectic Evolution of Retailing," in Barnett Greenberg (ed.), *Proceedings: Southern Marketing Association* (Atlanta: Georgia State University, 1975), pp. 147–51.

26. Thomas P. Neill, *Makers of the Modern Mind* (Milwaukee: Bruce Publishing Company, 1958), p. 298.

27. Maronick and Walker, "Dialectic Evolution," p. 147.

Gradually, these two institutions adopted features of the other, evolving into the type of gasoline retailer that dominated during the 1960s under national brand names such as Texaco and Standard. Price competition was avoided, many automotive maintenance and repair services were offered, and refreshments, sunglasses, and other nonautomotive products plus more credit plans were added by these institutions.[28]

The national brand service station was now the new thesis, and it begot its own antithesis—the discount gasoline station. This station eliminated frills and personal service as well as repair services. They emphasized pumping gasoline at the least possible cost. In the 1970s most national brand service stations scrambled to adopt the discount format.

As of the late 1970s the synthesis of the national brand service station and the discount gasoline station had not yet occurred. If this synthesis occurs in the 1980s what form might you expect it to take?

The Retail Life Cycle   The final framework we will examine for viewing the evolution of retail competition is the retail life cycle. Davidson et al. proclaim that this framework "argues that retailing institutions, like the products they distribute, pass

---

EXHIBIT 6.20   **The Dialectic Process Illustrated by Gasoline Retailing**

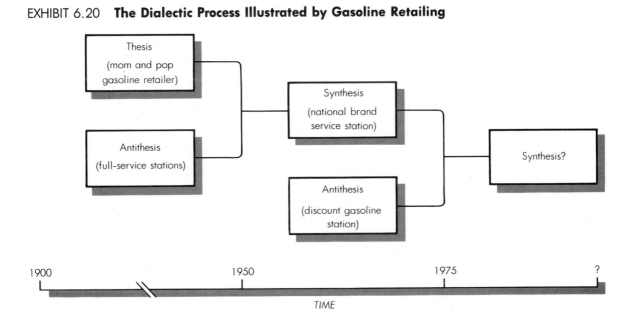

Source: Thomas J. Maronick and Bruce J. Walker, "The Dialectic Evolution of Retailing," in Barnett A. Greenberg (ed.), *Proceedings: Southern Marketing Association 1974 Conference* (Atlanta: Georgia State University, 1975), p. 148. Adapted with permission.

---

28. Maronick and Walker, "Dialectic Evolution," pp. 148–9.

through an identifiable cycle."[29] This cycle can be partitioned into four distinct stages: (1) innovation, (2) accelerated development, (3) maturity, and (4) decline. Each stage will be briefly discussed.

Innovation   This stage is typically given birth by an aggressive and bold entrepreneur who is willing and able to develop an approach to retailing that departs sharply from conventional approaches. Many times the approach is oriented to cost reduction, thus allowing the new wave of retailing to pass savings on to the customer (the supermarket in the early 1930s was able to operate on a gross margin of 12 percent, whereas conventional food outlets required 20 percent). However, at other times the innovative dimension centered on a distinctive product assortment, or shopping ease, locational convenience, advertising, or promotion. For example, the home improvement center, a retailing innovation of the mid-1960s, offered a better product assortment and more information than the conventional hardware store.

If the new advantage being offered is significant enough in the minds of consumers then sales will grow in the innovative stage. Profits in the innovation stage, however, will not be attractive and in fact may be nonexistent. In any new business there are operating problems that need to be solved. Also, high start-up costs and the absence of scale economies due to relatively low sales tend to put a damper on profits. But at the end of the innovation stage, sales begin to grow more rapidly and operating problems are overcome, therefore stimulating profit levels.

Accelerated Development   During development, sales and profit growth are explosive. Many new entrants arrive to share in the expanding receptivity of this new form of retailing. The market share of the innovators rises while that of conventional outlets is harmed. The firms that were astute enough to take part in the innovation stage are now expanding their number of outlets by entering new geographic markets:

> However, toward the end of the period these favorable factors tend to be counterbalanced by cost pressures that arise from the need for a larger staff, more complex internal systems, increased management controls, and other requirements of operating large, multi-unit organizations. Consequently, near the end of the accelerated development period both market share and profitability tend to approach their maximum level.[30]

Maturity   In maturity, market share stabilizes, and severe profit declines are experienced because of several problems. First, the managers have become accustomed to managing a high-growth firm that was simple and small, but now they must manage a large, complex firm in a stable market. Second, the industry has typically overexpanded. Selecting markets and building new stores

---

29. Reprinted by permission of the *Harvard Business Review.* From "The Retail Life Cycle," by William R. Davidson, Albert D. Bates, and Stephen J. Bass 54(November–December 1976): 89. Copyright © 1976 by President and Fellows of Harvard College; all rights reserved.

30. Davidson, Bates, and Bass, "Retail Life Cycle," p. 92.

takes a long planning horizon (twelve to thirty-six months). It is disheartening but inevitable that many stores planned in the accelerated development stage will open in the maturity state. Third, competitive assaults will be made on these firms by new forms of retailing (a bold entrepreneur starting a new retail life cycle).

Decline Although decline is inevitable, retail managers will try to postpone it by serious attempts to reposition, modify, or adapt the firm. When successful, these attempts can postpone the decline stage, but a return to earlier attractive levels of operating performance is not likely. Sooner or later decline will occur, and "the consequences are traumatic. Major losses of market share occur, profits are marginal at best, and a fatal inability to compete in the market becomes apparent to investors and competitors."[31]

A more complete profile of management activities throughout the retail life cycle is presented in Exhibit 6.21 (page 166). Try to identify the exhibit's bottom-line implications for retail managers. There are three primary implications:

1. Retailers should remain flexible so that they are able to adapt their strategies to various stages in the life cycle.
2. Since profits vary by stage in the retail life cycle, retail managers need carefully to analyze the risks and profits of entering the life cycle at various stages or expanding their outlets at various stages in the life cycle.
3. Retailers need to extend the maturity stage. Since retailers will have substantial investments in a particular form of retailing by the time of the maturity stage, they will have a vested interest in trying to work that investment as long as possible.

These three points are reinforced by the fact that the retail life cycle is growing shorter as is shown by the empirical data presented in Exhibit 6.22 (page 167). The downtown department store took eighty years to reach maturity, the variety store forty-five years, the supermarket thirty-five years, the discount department store twenty years, and the home improvement center a short fifteen years. Thus retail managers must recognize that high performance results can be achieved only over the long run by programming the firm to enter new lines of retail trade at appropriate points in time.

COMPETITION FROM NONSTORE RETAILERS

Industry analysts contend that between 1980 and 2000 nonstore retailers will become a major competitive force.[32] This may not be too surprising, since nonstore retailing is not revolutionary. For instance, Sears and Roebuck began in the mail-order business in the later half of the 1800s and Avon has always concentrated its efforts on nonstore retailing. Nonetheless, with accelerated

31. Davidson, Bates, and Bass, "Retail Life Cycle," p. 93.
32. Marcia Bielfield and Linda Nagel (eds.), *The Growth of Non-Store Retailing: Implications for Retailers, Manufacturers, and Public Policy Makers* (New York: Institute of Retail Management, New York University, 1978).

EXHIBIT 6.21 The Retail Life Cycle

AREA OR SUBJECT OF CONCERN	STAGE OF LIFE CYCLE			
	Innovation	Accelerated Development	Maturity	Decline
Market characteristics				
Number of competitors	Very few	Moderate	Many direct competitors, moderate indirect competition	Moderate direct competition, many indirect competitors
Rate of sales growth	Very rapid	Rapid	Moderate to slow	Slow or negative
Level of profitability	Low to moderate	High	Moderate	Very low
Duration of new innovations	3 to 5 years	5 to 6 years	Indefinite	Indefinite
Appropriate retailer actions				
Investment, growth, risk decisions	Investment minimization; high risks accepted	High levels of investment to sustain growth	Tightly controlled growth in untapped markets	Minimal capital expenditures and only when essential
Central management concerns	Concept refinement through adjustment and experimentation	Establishing a preemptive market position	• Excess capacity and "overstoring" • Prolonging maturity and reversing the retail concept	Engaging in a "run-out" strategy
Use of management control techniques	Minimal	Moderate	Extensive	Moderate
Most successful management style	Entrepreneurial	Centralized	"Professional"	Caretaker
Appropriate supplier actions				
Channel strategy	Develop a preemptive market position	Hold market position	Maintain profitable sales	Avoid excessive costs?
Channel problems	Possible antagonism of other accounts	Possible antagonism of other accounts	Dealing with more scientific retailers	Servicing accounts at a profit
Channel research	Identification of key innovations	Identification of other retailers adopting the innovation	Initial screening of new innovation opportunities	Active search for new innovation opportunities
Trade incentives	Direct financial support	Price concessions	New price incentives	None

Source: Reprinted by permission of the *Harvard Business Review*. Exhibit from "The Retail Life Cycle," by William R. Davidson, Albert D. Bates, and Stephen J. Bass 54 (November–December 1976), p. 92. Copyrighted © 1976 by the President and Fellows of Harvard College; all rights reserved.

EXHIBIT 6.22 **Life Cycle Characteristics of Five Retail Institutions**

INSTITUTION	APPROXIMATE DATE OF INNOVATION	APPROXIMATE DATE OF MAXIMUM MARKET SHARE	APPROXIMATE NUMBER OF YEARS TO REACH MATURITY	ESTIMATED MAXIMUM MARKET SHARE	ESTIMATED 1975 MARKET SHARE
Downtown department store	1860	1940	80	8.5% of total retail sales	1.1%
Variety store	1910	1955	45	16.5% of general merchandise sales	9.5
Supermarket	1930	1965	35	70.0% of grocery store sales	64.5
Discount department store	1950	1970	20	6.5% of total retail sales	5.7
Home improvement store	1965	1980 (est.)	15	35.0% of hardware and building material sales	25.3

Source: Reprinted by permission of the *Harvard Business Review.* Exhibit from "The Retail Life Cycle," by William R. Davidson, Albert D. Bates, and Stephen J. Bass 54 (November–December 1976), p. 94. Copyright © 1976 by the President and Fellows of Harvard College; all rights reserved.

communications technology and changing consumer lifestyles, the growth potential of nonstore retailing is explosive. Consequently, traditional retailers need continuously to monitor developments in nonstore retailing. In addition, traditional retailers need to be cognizant of the fact that the major nonstore competitors of the future will probably be new-wave retailers rather than traditional retailers changing their mode of operation. The evolutionary history of retailing has repeatedly shown this to be the case.[33]

Nature and Scope Nonstore retailers, as the name suggests, are retailers that do not consummate transactions in the store. The census of retailing classifies nonstore retailers into three major types:

1. **Mail-order houses,** establishments primarily engaged in the retail sale of products by catalog and mail order. Included are book and record clubs, jewelry firms, novelty merchandise firms, and the catalog divisions of large general merchandise retailers such as Sears, Penney's, Montgomery Ward, etc. Not included, however, are seasonal and special promotional catalogs

33. Eleanor G. May and Malcolm P. McNair, *The Evolution of Retail Institutions in the United States* (Cambridge, Mass.: Marketing Science Institute, 1976).

of conventional department stores such as Marshall Field, Lazarus, and Jordan Marsh.

2. **Automatic merchandising machine operators,** establishments primarily engaged in the retail sale of products by means of automatic merchandising units, also referred to as vending machines. This industry does not include coin-operated service machines, such as music machines and amusement and game machines, lockers or scales.

3. **Direct selling establishments,** primarily engaged in the retail sale of merchandise by telephone or house-to-house canvass. Included are individuals who are not employees of the organization they represent, and retail sales offices from which employees operate to sell merchandise from door-to-door. Examples include house-to-house selling of magazines, house delivery of milk and bakery goods, ice cream wagons, and party-plan merchandising (e.g., Stanley and Tupperware).

Davidson and Rogers have noted that the preceding classification is quite archaic, having been developed by the Department of Commerce prior to 1930.[34] Nonetheless, the Census Bureau persists in its use. Davidson and Rogers elaborate on the restrictive nature of this classification:[35]

> 1. **Mail order.** This was a term appropriate to the early days of Sears and Ward's, before they had retail stores. The terminology has persisted with remarkable tenacity, in spite of developments which have resulted in consumers being enticed to pick up catalogs at stores instead of receiving them by mail; orders being taken at catalog stores, at catalog order desks within stores, or by "800" phone numbers, rather than being sent by mail; and delivery by customer pick-up or by United Parcel Service rather than by mail (parcel post).
>
> 2. **Vending.** While commonly considered as nonstore, many vending machine operators have machines in stores, in employee lunch rooms, or rest-break areas and for consumer sales of single packs of cigarettes to prevent pilferage.
>
> 3. **Direct selling.** This method is commonly referred to as "house-to-house" or "door-to-door" selling. There was a time when the vacuum cleaner or hosiery salesperson actually went from door-to-door. While the vocabulary persists, the typical nonstore agent of a direct selling company does not walk the street but sells to selective prospects on a part-time basis (friends, fellow office workers, club members, church goers, bowling league acquaintances, etc.).

Exhibit 6.23 (on pages 170–71) highlights the inadequacy of the official census data on nonstore retailing. The shaded areas roughly show what the Census Bureau considers as nonstore retailing. If one considers Exhibit 6.23 as a more accurate reflection of the nature and scope of nonstore retailing, then

34. William R. Davidson and Alice Rogers, "Non-Store Retailing: Its Importance to and Impact on Merchandise Suppliers and Competitive Channels" in Marcia Bielfield and Linda Nagel (eds.), *The Growth of Non-Store Retailing: Implications for Retailers, Manufacturers, and Public Policy Makers* (New York: Institute of Retail Management, New York University, 1978), pp. 22–29.

35. William R. Davidson and Alice Rogers, "Non-Store Retailing: Its Importance to and Impact on Merchandise Suppliers and Competitive Channels," in Marcia Bielfied and Linda Nagel (eds.), *The Growth of Non-Store Retailing: Implications for Retailers, Manufacturers, and Public Policy Makers* (New York: Institute of Retail Management, New York University, 1978), p. 23. Reprinted by permission.

it is easier to accept the fact that nonstore retailing is becoming a significant competitive force.

Nonstore Growth   Taking the broad perspective of nonstore retailing, we can expect growth in this sector of retailing to be two to three times the rate of growth of retail sales in general. What factors will impede or accelerate this growth? An examination of the external environments of nonstore retailing can help us answer this question.

Economic Environment   Three major trends in the economic environment favor the growth of nonstore retailing. These trends relate to labor, capital, and inflation. Retailing has always been labor-intensive, and retailers have found it difficult to substitute capital for labor. As a result, the growth of labor productivity in retailing has been less than spectacular. Many forms of nonstore retailing such as mail-order and telecommunication retailing require considerably fewer labor resources per unit of output than more conventional forms of retailing.

Another trend relates to the skyrocketing cost of land and buildings that occurred in the 1970s and is projected to continue throughout the 1980s. This has predictably squeezed profit margins and return on investment in retailing. But an even more important capital consideration regards the inflexibility of stores, once located, to respond to changes in population. Building or leasing a store is a major long-range commitment, often extending twenty years or more into the future. The disquieting fact about this is that our population has become very fluid. Entire neighborhoods can experience substantial demographic changes in less than ten years. The nonstore retailer, however, can locate its warehouse or office in a lower cost area, thus avoiding high land and building costs, and similarly need not be nearly as concerned about the changing demographics of neighborhoods.

Inflation is the final economic trend that favors nonstore retailers. Consumer purchasing power has been eroded by inflation and thus the consumer is receptive to almost any reasonable method of saving on the cost of merchandise. Many forms of nonstore retailing, with their significant cost savings, have the potential to pass savings on to the customer.

Social Environment   Three significant trends in the social environment will be beneficial to nonstore retailers. First, the typical American household is being confronted more and more with a scarcity of time. The number of career-oriented wives has been on the rise since the late 1960s, and as a result many households don't have the time they once had to shop at stores. As incomes have risen, people have taken on many leisure activities such as tennis, skiing, boating, jogging, hiking, and camping, which they are more committed to doing than they are to shopping. It has been noted that for many consumers the ultimate store, in terms of convenience, would be in the home.[36] Second,

36. Peter L. Gillett, "Direct Marketing: Challenge and Opportunity in the 1980s," (working paper).

EXHIBIT 6.23 **Illustrative Types of Nonstore Retailing**

METHOD OF OPERATION	NONSTORE RETAILING SPECIALISTS	NONSTORE RETAILING AS A SUPPLEMENT TO CONVENTIONAL RETAIL STORE OR WHOLESALE ESTABLISHMENT OPERATIONS	NONSTORE RETAILING BY OTHERS
Catalog: general merchandise	Catalog divisions of Sears, Penney's, Wards, etc.	Seasonal and special promotional catalogs of conventional department stores such as Marshall Field, Lazarus, Higbee's, Bloomingdale's, Jordan Marsh, etc.	Catalogs of trading stamp companies, (S&H), premium companies in connection with sales incentive companies, etc.
Catalog: specialty	Catalog divisions of Lane Bryant, L. L. Bean, The Horchow Collection, J. C. Whitney, Figi's, The Talbots, etc.	Seasonal and special catalogs of specialty retailers such as Gump's, Bonwit Teller, Gattle's, Eddie Bauer, Sheplers, and resurrection of Abercrombie and Fitch by Oshman Sporting Goods.	Seasonal catalogs distributed to credit card customers by petroleum companies. In-flight shopping catalogs of major airline companies.
Direct advertising for telephone or mail orders and other forms of nonstore acquisition	Direct-mail solicitation by manufacturers or distributors such as New Process, Fingerhut, Bee Line, etc. Direct-response ads by nonstore specialists in magazines, newspapers, e.g., Walter Drake Club plans (books, records, cosmetics).	Department store and specialty store advertisements for mail or telephone order response in newspapers and magazines, by direct mail including bill stuffers, and by means of broadcast media.	Merchandise offers by magazines such as Apartment Life, Vogue, Playboy. Bank and Savings and Loan premium offers for new accounts. Merchandise promotional premiums to be redeemed by mail or newspaper coupons. Special item promotions by petroleum companies.
At-home personal selling	Residential door-to-door selling (Avon, Electrolux, Fuller Brush, etc.). Party plan selling (Stanley, Tupperware). "Pyramid" selling plans (Amway).	Outside salesmen of conventional retailers for products such as appliances, carpeting, draperies, home improvements, lawn services, etc.	At-home selling by publishers of encyclopedias and other book sets.
Electronic retailing	Merchandisers of gadgets, records, tapes, etc., not available in stores	Use of interactive cable TV as means of ordering merchandise (e.g., Qube Division of Warner Communications).	

METHOD OF OPERATION	NONSTORE RETAILING SPECIALISTS	NONSTORE RETAILING AS A SUPPLEMENT TO CONVENTIONAL RETAIL STORE OR WHOLESALE ESTABLISHMENT OPERATIONS	NONSTORE RETAILING BY OTHERS
Vending machines	Vending machine operating companies.	Vending machines as supplemental distribution by tobacco, candy, and novelty wholesalers.	Vending machines as supplemental distribution by bottlers of beverages, food processors or caterers.
Institutionalized or contract marketing of products formerly purchased as merchandise items in stores	Service retailing specialists who offer a complete system solution (Chemlawn, Barefoot Grass, Stanley Steamer, Carpet Cleaners).	Contract lawn or other home maintenance services offered by advertising or outside salesmen of store retailers, usually local.	Real estate developers offering residential units complete with appliances, carpeting, draperies, etc. Dispensing of pharmaceutical products in hospitals, nursing homes, and health maintenance organizations.
Borderline nonstore retailing situations	Duty-free shops at airports; concession stands at amusement parks and resorts; roadside stands of agricultural producers; auctions; merchandise sold at nonstore locations such as bowling alleys, golf clubs, tennis clubs, etc.; personal care products sold at barber shops and beauty salons, photo-finisher drive-through kiosks on the parking lots of retail premises; garage or yard sales of previously owned merchandise by relocating families, some handled by reselling experts; and catalog sales at wholesale prices to manufacturing plant employees through use of vendor catalogs.		

Source: William R. Davidson and Alice Rogers, "Non-Store Retailing: Its Importance to and Impact on Merchandise Suppliers and Competitive Channels," *The Growth of Non-Store Retailing: Implications For Retailers, Manufacturers, and Public Policy Makers* (New York: Institute of Retail Management, New York University, 1979), p. 24. Reprinted by permission.

---

research has indicated that store loyalty is on the decline.[37] Consumers are not tied to stores. In short, the eclectic shopper has arrived. Consequently, nonstore retailers with a concentrated effort, can attract customers from conventional retailers.[38]

Third, the consumer market is becoming more fragmented in terms of consumer and life style orientations. Everyone is trying to do his own thing. Nonstore retailers using selective mailings or cable TV can quite effectively target

37. Bert C. McCammon, Jack J. Kasulis, and Jack Lesser, "The New Parameters of Retail Competition: The Intensified Struggle for Market Share," paper presented at the 1979 Doctoral Consortium, American Marketing Association.

38. For a behavioral and demographic profile of the in-home shopper, see Peter L. Gillett, "A Profile of Urban in-home Shoppers". *Journal of Marketing* 34 (July 1970): 40–45; William H. Peters and Neil M. Ford, "A Profile of Urban in-home Shoppers: The Other Half," *Journal of Marketing* 36(January 1972): 62–64; Isabella C. M. Cunningham and William H. Cunningham, "The Urban in-home Shopper: Socioeconomic and Attitudinal Characteristics," *Journal of Retailing* 49(Fall 1973): 42–50; and Eric N. Berkowitz, John R. Walton, and Orville C. Walker, Jr., "In-home Shoppers: The Market for Innovative Distribution Systems," *Journal of Retailing* 55(Summer 1979): 15–33.

their messages. But they must be careful in doing so. As you will remember from our model of retail competition, stores can attract customers only from a limited geographic area. If they attract from a limited area, then they must not define their target too narrowly or else they might not be able to attract a sufficient number of households to generate adequate sales volume.

Technological Environment   E. B. Weiss and other prognosticators have long predicted that the future of the retail store will be seriously challenged by electronic in-home shopping.[39] Fifteen years ago the technology for electronic retailing was questionable. Today this is not the case. Interactive (two-way) CATV shopping systems linking a home terminal directly to the retail computer are technologically feasible. Also, recent developments in EFT (electronic funds transfer) have helped to overcome the payment and credit problems in telecommunications retailing.

Legal Environment   In nonstore retailing there are many potential legal problems. They are significant because so much trust is required between buyer and seller. If one behaves unethically, the other is likely to take legal action.

SUMMARY

Retailers can be classified in a variety of ways. Five of the more popular schemes are by SIC code, number of outlets, margins versus turnover, location, and size. None, however, sheds adequate light on competition in retailing.

A model of retail competition was developed to aid in illustrating certain principles of retail competition. This model suggested that retail competition is typically local; the retail industry is monopolistically competitive or oligopolistic; the demand side of retailing must consider the distance of the consumer from the store; both supply and demand factors must be examined in developing price and nonprice strategies; and an action by a retailer to increase its trade area is likely to elicit a response from competitors.

The economics of intra- and intertype competition, divertive competition, and the struggle for market share in retailing can affect retail profits. Therefore, retailers need to develop a protected market niche. One increasingly popular way to do this is by a store positioning strategy. In addition, if the retailer adopts certain principles of military strategy it will be better able to withstand competitive pressure.

Retail competition is both revolutionary and evolutionary. Five theories for viewing changing competitive patterns in retailing were reviewed. The wheel of retailing proposes that new types of retailers enter the market as low-status, low-margin, low-price operators. As they succeed, they become more complex, increasing their margins and prices and becoming vulnerable to new types of

39. E. B. Weiss, ''Electronic Stores Is Next Step in Today's Low-Cost Retailing,'' *Advertising Age,* June 2, 1972, p. 51.

low-margin competitors, who, in turn, follow the same pattern. The retail accordion theory suggests that retail institutions evolve from outlets offering wide assortments to specialized narrow assortment stores and then return to wide assortments to repeat the pattern. The theory of natural selection argues that those retail institutions that most readily adapt to a changing environment will prosper and others will not. The dialectic process of retailing suggests that each new form of retailing (called the thesis) begets a negation of itself (called the antithesis), which results in a blending of the two called a synthesis. The synthesis ultimately becomes the thesis and the process begins again. Finally, the retail life cycle theory tries to view the revolution and evolution of retail competition by arguing that retail institutions, like the products they distribute, pass through an indentifiable cycle during which the basics of strategy and competition change.

We conclude this chapter with a discussion of nonstore retailing, since industry analysts contend that this form of retailing will be a major competitive force in the future. Types of nonstore retailing were discussed, as well as the impact of the economic, social, technological, and legal environments on the growth of nonstore retailing.

QUESTIONS

1. What are the major obstacles and problems you see confronting nonstore retailers in their pursuit of a larger market share of the consumer's dollar?

2. Which of the following retailers would you expect to face the strongest competition: gas station, flower shop, women's apparel store, pet shop, discount department store? Why?

3. Pick a particular line of retail trade and identify what you believe will be the next turn in the wheel of retailing.

4. Would you expect large chain stores (those with 100 or more units) to continue to play an increasing role in retailing in the Unites States? Why?

5. Which retailer would you expect to face stronger competition: a free-standing shoe store or a shoe store in a regional shopping center that has six other shoe stores? Which would you rather own or manage?

6. Why are furniture stores able to attract customers from a greater distance than food stores?

7. Explain in your own words why retailers face a three-dimensional demand function. Do all retailers face a three-dimensional demand model?

8. Identify the weaknesses of the U.S. Bureau of the Census classification of retailers.

9. Given rapidly escalating energy costs, evaluate the competitive vulnerability of super regional shopping centers. What strategies might these large shopping centers develop to cope with rising energy costs?

10. Develop a list of expenses or costs for a department store and categorize them as fixed, variable, and semifixed.

PROBLEMS AND EXERCISES

1. Visit a local discount department store and attempt to identify the local retailers with which it would compete.

2. Consider two retailers—Alpha and Beta—in the same line of retail trade. Alpha currently has annual sales of $400,000 and fixed costs of $120,000 as well as variable costs which run 68 percent of sales. Beta has annual sales of $215,000 and fixed costs of $49,000. Variable costs for Beta are 66 percent of sales. Which of these two retailers is more susceptible to divertive competition?

3. Assume that you are in the market for a new Volkswagen. For the model equipped the way you want it you are willing to pay up to $8,900. The local Volkswagen dealer will sell you the model you want for $8,875. However, you notice an advertisement by a Volkswagen dealer located in a city 180 miles away. The ad prices the car you want at $8,595. Should you travel to the distant city to purchase the Volkswagen?

4. Pick a particular line of retail trade and attempt to determine if your community is overstored or understored in it. Note that you may do this on a subjective or objective basis, but be prepared to defend your position.

5. A supermarket chain in a city of 400,000 has been charged by the FTC with being a monopoly and price fixing. The chain has a 37 percent share of all food stores sales in this city. The FTC's position is twofold: a 37 percent market share allows one to control a market; and the chain always has the same price on milk, bread, beer, soda pop, and paper goods as its leading competitors, so it must be fixing prices. Using concepts presented in this chapter, develop some defenses for the supermarket chain.

SUGGESTED READINGS

Appel, David. "The Supermarket: Early Development of an Institutional Innovation." *Journal of Retailing* 48(Spring 1972): 39–52.

Day, George S., Allan D. Shocker, and Rejendra K. Srivastova. "Customer-Oriented Approaches To Identifying Product Markets." *Journal of Marketing* 43(Fall 1979): 8–19.

Goldman, Arieh. "Stages in the Development of the Supermarket." *Journal of Retailing* 51(Winter 1975–76): 49–64.

Granfield, Michael and Alfred Nicols. "Economic and Marketing Aspects of the Direct Selling Industry." *Journal of Retailing* 51(Spring 1975): 30–50, 113.

Hirschman, Elizabeth C. "A Descriptive Theory of Retail Market Structure." *Journal of Retailing* 54(Winter 1978): 29–48.

Lillis, Charles M., Chem L. Narayana, and John L. Gilman. "Competitive Advantage Variation Over the Life Cycle of a Franchise." *Journal of Marketing* 40(October 1976): 77–80.

"Socioeconomic Trends Cause High Growth in Nonstore Marketing Field" *Marketing News*, February 8, 1980, pp. 1, 3.

7

Overview *The purpose of this chapter is to examine the effect of the socioeconomic and technological environments on the retailing sector of the economy. We will show that the changing economic climate can significantly influence customer behavior and that changing demographics and life styles have created a customer who behaves somewhat differently than retailers have experienced historically. Finally, we will show that retail technology, both in new forms of retailing and in innovative equipment and fixtures, is continually changing the practice of retailing.*

Understanding the Socioeconomic and Technological Environments

Demographic Trends
Population
Geographic Shifts
Social Trends
Economic Trends

Psychographic Trends
General Trends
A Specific Study

Economic Factors
Interest Rates
Personal Income
Economic Turbulence

Technological Environment
New Forms of Retailing
Equipment and Fixture Innovations

Summary

WE HAVE SEEN that retailing does not operate in a closed environment. Retailers, in their decision making, must take into account the behavior of channel members, consumers, and competitors. We will now attempt to show that the retail decision maker must recognize and adapt to changes in the socioeconomic and technological environments. First we will discuss the demographic and psychographic trends in the socioeconomic environment, and then review economic factors. After that discussion, we will introduce and review forces in the technological environment.

DEMOGRAPHIC TRENDS

The model of retail patronage behavior in Chapter 5 was useful for understanding behavior of individual patrons. However, it is not useful in helping us to understand how general trends in the U.S. population might affect retailers in this country. To obtain this larger perspective, we must analyze demographic trends in the United States over the last several decades and, in a few cases, project them into the future.

Population

Population Growth Retailers have viewed an expanding population base as synonomous with the growth in retail markets. Unfortunately, this natural growth in markets is declining because families are having fewer children. In fact, many demographers believe that in the near future the U.S. fertility rate will approximate a "replacement level" (a level where the population would exactly replace itself in the absence of net immigration). If this is the case, then the population will stabilize at 269 million in the year 2030.[1] Of course, other assumptions about fertility will produce drastically different rates of population growth. For example, if you assume that the average female will produce 2.7 children over her lifetime, then the population by 2030 would be 393 million.[2]

Another very important influence on population growth is life expectancy. When people live longer, the population base gets larger over time; and people in the United States have been living longer. In 1950 the average male's life expectancy was 65.6 years, but by 1977 it was 69.3 years.[3] In 1950 the average female's life expectancy was 71.1 years, but by 1977 it had risen to 77.1 years.[4] Retail analysts should thus pay close attention to fertility rates and life expectancy levels in their long-range forecasting of market potential. This is especially true if the retailer caters specifically to young children or the elderly.

---

1. U.S. Bureau of the Census, *Statistical Abstract of the United States* (Washington, DC: U.S. Government Printing Office, 1979), p. 7.
2. *Statistical Abstract*, p. 7.
3. *Statistical Abstract*, p. 70.
4. *Statistical Abstract*, p. 70.

Age Distribution Retailers tend to appeal to different age groups in society. For example, furniture and appliance retailers obtain most of their patrons from the twenty-five to forty-four age segment, whereas patrons of record stores are mostly between fourteen and twenty-four, and children's apparel retailers obtain most of their customers from households with children under thirteen.

The retailer must realize that the distribution of the population by age is always changing, because fertility and mortality rates constantly change. To understand this phenomenon better, refer to Exhibit 7.1. Since most of the people who will be living in 1990 are alive today, it is possible to project what the age distribution will be in 1990. From Exhibit 7.1 we see that the groups that will experience the largest gains relative to 1978 are 25–34, 35–44, and over 65. Retailers who sell to these age segments will thus have the potential for significant growth in the late 1980s and early 1990s. For example, one would expect furniture retailers to do relatively well during this time frame, since

EXHIBIT 7.1 **Age Distribution of U.S. Population (1950–2000)**

YEAR	UNDER 5	5–13	14–17	18–24	25–34	35–44	45–65	OVER 65
1950	10.8%	14.7%	5.5%	10.6%	15.8%	14.2%	20.3%	8.1%
1978	7.0	14.4	7.6	13.2	15.5	11.2	20.1	11.0
1990	8.2	13.6	5.2	10.3	16.8	14.9	18.8	12.2
2000	7.1	13.8	6.3	9.4	13.1	15.7	22.5	12.1

Source: U.S. Bureau of the Census, *Statistical Abstract of the United States* (Washington, D.C.: U.S. Government Printing Office, 1979), pp. 8–9.

The growing number of elderly consumers offer retailers an expanding market. (Photo courtesy of Safeway Stores, Inc.)

people acquire most of their furniture when they are between twenty-five and forty-four.

Geographic Shifts

Shifting Geographic Center Retailers should be concerned not only with numbers of people, but where they reside, because consumers will not travel great distances to shop at a retail outlet. Consumers patronize local retail outlets (even though the local outlet may be part of a national chain). Because the U.S. population for the past 200 years has been moving toward the West and the South, growth opportunities in retailing have been greatest in these areas.

We can see the changing geographic center of the U.S. population in terms of north latitude and west longitude. In 1790, the geographic center was 23 miles east of Baltimore, Maryland. By 1900, it had moved to 6 miles southeast of Columbus, Indiana. By 1970 it was 5.3 miles east-southeast of the Mascoutah City Hall in St. Clair County, Illinois—not far from St. Louis. And on the basis of preliminary totals from the 1980 census, the new center is located in the community of De Soto in Jefferson County, Missouri, 40 miles southwest of the Gateway Arch in St. Louis.

In Exhibit 7.2, we see how rapidly four broad regions of the United States grew from 1960 to 1978. These statistics show that during this period, the South and West grew about twice as fast as the Northeast and Northcentral regions. Demographers contend that this trend will continue throughout the 1980s, with these effects: northeastern and northcentral retailers will experience a slower growing market for their goods and services; and national retailers such as Sears and Penney's will increasingly need to consider distribution centers (warehouses) in the South and West.

EXHIBIT 7.2 **Regional U.S. Population Growth (1960–78)**	*AREA OF COUNTRY*	*1960–70*	*1970–75*	*1975–78*

AREA OF COUNTRY	1960–70	1970–75	1975–78
United States	13.4%	4.8%	2.4%
Northeast	9.8	0.8	−0.8
Northcentral	9.6	1.9	1.1
South	14.3	8.4	3.8
West	24.2	8.6	5.8

Source: U.S. Bureau of the Census, *Statistical Abstract of the United States* (Washington, D.C.: U.S. Government Printing Office, 1979), p. 14.

City Life Most of the population of the United States resides in metropolitan areas of greater than 50,000 in population, which the Census Bureau calls **standard metropolitan statistical areas** (SMSAs). Most retail trade occurs in these SMSAs. Since 1940, the proportion of the population residing in SMSAs has increased dramatically, from 52.6 percent to 73.0 percent in 1977.[5] The percentage appears to have stabilized at this level. There were 279 SMSAs in 1977.

---

5. *Statistical Abstract,* p. 17.

On the other hand in the late 1970s and early 1980s, retailers witnessed a rapid growth in **secondary markets,** cities with a population of less than 50,000. Historically, most chain store retailers have ignored secondary markets, but as SMSAs began to stabilize and secondary markets continued to grow, retailers have started to exploit opportunities in these markets more systematically.

Mobility   In many countries, people are born, raised, married, and widowed, and die in the same city or immediate geographic area. Even in the United States, this has been true to some extent, but it is certainly not true of contemporary America. The United States population is extremely mobile. For example, between 1975 and 1978, 34.2 percent of the people in the United States changed residences.[6] At this rate, the total population, on average, would relocate every eight to ten years. This is important to retailers because they serve local markets and tend to cater to well-defined demographic groups. If the population moves, the retailer may find that its target market no longer resides in the immediate area.

Social Trends

Education   The average educational level of Americans is increasing. In 1978 the median years of school completed was 12.4 for all individuals over the age of 25.[7] This contrasted sharply with the level in 1940—8.6 years. There is a close correlation between formal education and consumer taste levels and expectations. Since educational levels for the population, in aggregate, are expected to continue to rise, retailers can expect consumers to become increasingly sophisticated and discriminating.

Divorce   There has been a rapid increase in the divorce rate in the United States over the last several decades. Between 1950 and 1978, the divorce rate nearly tripled.[8] We do not want to imply that divorces are a favorable trend, but when a divorce occurs, many retail purchases are stimulated, because a second household needs to be established almost immediately. This new household needs certain things such as a toaster, coffee maker, radio, and dishes and linens.

Unrelated Two-Person Households   The number of primary individuals in the United States grew 59.7 percent between 1970 and 1978. A **primary individual** is a household head living alone or with nonrelatives. In 1978, 46.3 percent of these primary individuals living with nonrelatives shared housing with a member (or members) of the opposite sex.[9] In fact, a significant number of those are people over 50 years of age. This trend is significant to the retailer because it represents a purchasing unit that is hard to understand by conventional household or family norms. The retailer as well as the social scientist has little un-

6. *Statistical Abstract,* p. 40.
7. *Statistical Abstract,* p. 145.
8. *Statistical Abstract,* p. 81
9. *Statistical Abstract,* p. 43.

derstanding of how joint decision making occurs or does not occur in such households.

Economic Trends

Income Growth   People or households do not represent markets unless they have purchasing power. Unfortunately, the trend in real income growth over the last twenty years has not been encouraging. The growth in disposable income per capita, after adjusting for inflation, has experienced several consecutive periods of decline. From 1960 to 1965 the growth was 16.9 percent; from 1965 to 1970, 14.8 percent; and from 1970 to 1975, 10.9 percent. If this trend continues into the 1980s, as expected, retailers will increasingly be competing for limited consumer dollars. In fact, the slowdown in income growth has created more competition from flea markets and factory outlet malls, which both have a strong price emphasis.

Employed Females   Over the last two decades females have become a dominant factor in the labor force. In 1960 37.1 percent of all females over the age of sixteen were in the labor force, but by 1978 the participation had risen to 49.3 percent.[10]

This trend is even more significant if we look at women from twenty-five to forty-four, the age when one would expect them to be raising families. In 1960, 33.1 percent of married women of that age, with a spouse present in the household, were in the labor force. By 1978 this had risen to 56.5 percent.[11] Incidentally, among single females of that age, 80.7 percent were in the labor force in 1978.

The significant rise in the number of working wives has protected many households from inflation and recession. In fact, many economists suggest that the working wife has been the nation's secret weapon against economic hardship. It is estimated that in families where both spouses work the wife contributes over 25 percent of household income.

The rise in the number of working women has many implications for retailers and marketers. Consider the following:[12]

- Working wives are often unable to shop during regular retailing hours. They might prefer that sales be held in the evening.
- Working women place a premium on a youthful appearance and on the "maintenance of self." Advancement in business is often associated with being young.
- Working women can justify economic expenditures for, and psychologically accept, expensive appliances and household equipment, such as microwave ovens and prepared foods, which may even reduce the wives' roles in important household tasks.
- Some shopping may be done by a "wife surrogate"—a daughter or son.

10. *Statistical Abstract*, p. 392.

11. *Statistical Abstract*, p. 399.

12. William Lazer and John E. Smallwood, "The Changing Demographics of Women," *Journal of Marketing* 41(July 1977), pp. 21–22. Reprinted with permission.

Shopping also becomes a shared activity, by husband and wife or the whole family. Saturdays, Sundays, and evenings become very important shopping times.

- The availability of household services beyond the usual morning and afternoon hours (e.g., repair services during weekends) will become increasingly important.
- Price for some products may become less important than convenience, availability, service, and time savings.

The preceding suggests that retailers can possibly build strategies based on the changing role of women in society.

PSYCHOGRAPHIC TRENDS

Changing demographics are not sufficient to explain changing consumption patterns in the United States; an understanding of psychographics is also fundamental. **Psychographics** is the examination of activities, interests, and opinions of the population or a meaningful segment of the population. It is also frequently referred to as **lifestyles.** Lifestyles can be defined "as the patterns in which people live and spend time and money."[13] Activities, interests, and opinions are defined by Reynolds and Darden as follows:[14]

> An **activity** is a manifest action such as viewing a medium, shopping in a store, or telling a neighbor about a new service. Although these acts are usually observable, the reasons for the actions are seldom subject to direct measurement.
>
> An **interest** in some object, event, or topic is the degree of excitement that accompanies both special and continuing attention of it.
>
> An **opinion** is a verbal or written "answer" that a person gives in response to stimulus situations in which some "question" is raised. It is used to describe interpretations, expectations, and evaluations—such as beliefs about the intentions of other people, anticipations concerning future events, and appraisals of the rewarding or punishing consequences of alternative courses of action.

General Trends   A discussion of psychographics can be phrased in terms of general or specific trends. One could profile the activities, interests, and opinions of the general populace about life in general, or, alternatively one could profile the activities, interests, and opinions of a specific populace about a specific aspect of life. An example of the latter would be a psychographic study of how middle-class households orient their lives to food shopping and consumption. After looking at general trends, we will show a specific example of psychographic research in the retail hardware industry.

Casualness   In the 1970s there was a dramatic increase in casualness. People began to drive pickup trucks to the opera; children in all social classes began

13. James F. Engel, Roger D. Blackwell, and David T. Kollat, *Consumer Behavior*, 3rd ed., (Hinsdale, Ill.: Dryden Press, 1978), p. 174.

14. Reprinted with permission from Fred Reynolds and William Darden, "Construing Life Style and Psychographics," in William D. Wells (ed.), *Life Styles and Psychographics* (Chicago: American Marketing Association, 1974), p. 87, published by the American Marketing Association.

wearing jeans to school; professors showed up to teach class in cutoffs and T-shirts; women went shopping in swimsuits. In short, people tried to reduce the effect of pressures surrounding them by dressing more casually.

Male-Female Role Flexibility   The distinction between male-female roles in society has become blurred. Women entered traditionally male jobs or careers (for example, we witnessed a dramatic rise in female bus drivers, sanitation workers, business executives, and police officers). At the same time, some males took on traditionally female jobs (the number of male nurses rose dramatically, and more males decided to stay home to cook and take care of the household as their wives became the breadwinners).

Rejection of the Work Ethic   Over the last two decades, the predominance of the protestant work ethic has dramatically declined in the United States. Many factory workers intentionally skip one day of work per week, and fewer executives are willing to work sixty hours or more a week. Medical doctors are refusing to see patients because they want more time to be with their families. The work force is becoming complacent and lazy and increasingly demands more rewards for less output.

Consumerism   The American consumer has decided to be a major force in the market system. Consumers have demanded and received, over the last twenty years, more reliable and safe products, fairer advertising and pricing, and better warranty protection. This trend will not change. In the 1980s consumers will continue to police business, specifically retailers.

Deterioration of Industrial Confidence   In the 1970s the American public showed substantially less confidence in institutions and an increasing distrust of government. Much of this distrust was latent, but became overt during the Watergate affair. Skepticism regarding business, religious, and educational institutions was perhaps based on feelings that these institutions were directed toward satisfying their goals rather than the public's wants and needs.

Management of Time Versus Money   Many households, especially multiple-income households, became more concerned with the management of time versus money. Money management obviously could not be ignored, but households frequently realized that it was not a question of whether they had the money to partake in an activity but whether they had the time to spend on it. For example, many two-income households are less concerned with whether they can afford a trip to Hawaii than with the possibility of coordinating their busy schedules to generate the time for the trip.

A Specific Study   In 1979 the Russell R. Mueller Retail Hardware Research Foundation released a major psychographic study on the changing do-it-yourself consumer.[15] The purpose of this study was to provide an empirical basis for developing market

15. Bert C. McCammon, Jr., et al., *The Changing Do-It-Yourself Consumer* (Indianapolis, Ind.: Russell R. Mueller Retail Hardware Research Foundation, 1979).

expansion strategies for the hardware or home improvement center retailer in the 1980s.

The research revealed five distinct do-it-yourself psychographic segments. Each will be briefly discussed and commented on in Exhibit 7.3 (pages 184–85).

ECONOMIC FACTORS

The economic environment in which retailers operate is complex. Few businesspeople (or government officials) understand the economic forces shaping society. In our brief overview we do not purport to reveal the complexities of this environment. Rather, we will focus on what we believe to be the three factors the retail executive should regularly monitor. They are interest rates, personal incomes, and economic turbulence.

Interest Rates
An **interest rate** is the price that is paid for the use of money. Consumers and retailers alike use other people's money to purchase merchandise. Consumers use credit cards or installment sales plans to purchase a large number of goods—especially major durables such as household appliances, furniture, and automobiles. Retailers use bank credit to help finance their heavy investments in inventory. To illustrate this point, consider that the typical new car dealer with a modest inventory of 200 cars has to finance between $1 and $2 million in inventory investment. At an interest charge of 15 percent from the lending bank, the daily interest expense to hold this inventory would be over $500.

Because the interest rate is the price of money and because the consumer uses this money to buy merchandise, the effective price of merchandise rises each time the interest rate rises. We know from basic economics that as the price of merchandise rises, the quantity demanded by consumers declines. Consider for example, a young family that is considering purchasing three rooms of furniture for their new home at a cash price of $4,000. If the total purchase price is financed at 12 percent over thirty months, the monthly payments would be $155; which would work out to a deferred payment price of $4,650 ($155 times 30). If the total purchase price is financed at 18 percent over thirty months, the monthly payments would be $165.96, which would work out to a deferred payment price of $4,978.80. Thus, because the price of money (the interest rate) went up, the deferred payment price of the merchandise also rose. Each time the interest rate rises, more and more potential customers are eliminated from the market because they cannot afford the purchase.

Therefore, retailers that sell merchandise typically purchased on credit need to be especially cognizant of interest rate fluctuations. Just as rising rates slash the size of the market, declining rates expand it.

Personal Income
We observed when examining demographic trends that the rate of increase in real per capita incomes in the United States has been declining. Nonetheless, the absolute increase in real per capital incomes continues to be positive. When consumer incomes rise, consumers need to decide how to allocate their increased income.

When incomes rise, not all retailers benefit equally. The obverse is also true: when consumer incomes decline, not all retailers are equally harmed. The rationale for this phenomenon is simply that not all purchases by consumers are essential.

A useful summary measure for capturing how consumers respond to changes in income is the **income elasticity of demand,** which is formally defined on page 185.

EXHIBIT 7.3
Do-It-Yourself Consumers

RELUCTANT DO-IT-YOURSELFERS

This segment comprises 35.9% of the market. Reluctant do-it-yourselfers are less than enthusiastic about undertaking home improvement projects, preferring to hire professionals even for minor repairs. For economic reasons, however, Reluctants are surprisingly active do-it-yourselfers.

Although Reluctants are only moderately price sensitive, they place considerable emphasis on store convenience and on a high level of in-store service. This segment also prefers to shop in stores that offer a wide variety and selection of products which are easy to locate on the selling floor. Because of their limited knowledge, Reluctants also place a premium on informal sales assistance. This segment, more than other segments, rely on TV commercials as a source of product information.

DEDICATED DO-IT-YOURSELFERS

The Dedicated segment comprises 21.3% of the market. Dedicated do-it-yourselfers are almost continuously involved in home improvement and repair projects. They are also aggressive and informed shoppers. They prefer to shop in stores that offer several brands in each product category, that carry hard-to-find items, and that offer creative advice on do-it-yourself projects.

Dedicated do-it-yourselfers are value sensitive and do not buy on impulse. This segment is composed of highly sophisticated customers with extensive product knowledge. Consumers in this segment enjoy shopping and typically compare prices and features before making purchases. The Dedicated do-it-yourselfer is a tough shopper with limited brand and store loyalty. Dedicated do-it-yourselfers rely more heavily than other segments on *Consumer Reports* and do-it-yourself magazines as a source of product information.

DISCRETIONARY DO-IT-YOURSELFERS

This segment comprises 17.9% of the market. Discretionary do-it-yourselfers tend to be moderately active home maintainers. This segment is more inclined to undertake routine repair projects than major home improvements. This, along with their substantially higher incomes, implies that Discretionary do-it-yourselfers view home maintenance and repair as one of many alternative uses of their leisure time.

Convenience of location is extremely important to the Discretionary segment when shopping for do-it-yourself products. Discretionary do-it-yourselfers also prefer to shop in stores that have uncluttered layouts and "accessible," informed personnel. Price considerations are of little importance to Discretionary shoppers, and thus, they tend to avoid price-oriented outlets. This segment does not shop for comparative prices nor do they respond to sale advertising. In general, consumers in this segment do not enjoy shopping since they view it as an infringement on their leisure time.

$$E_I = \left| \frac{\text{Percent change in quantity demanded}}{\text{Percent change in income}} \right|$$

The greater E_I is than 1.0, the more income elastic we say a particular line of merchandise is. The more E_I falls below 1.0, the less income elastic a merchandise line is.

Exhibit 7.4 shows measures of income elasticity for six broad merchandise

---

TRANSITIONAL DO-IT-YOURSELFERS

The Transitional segment is 11.9% of the market. Transitional do-it-yourselfers are the third most active segment and are strong believers in do-it-yourself home repair and improvement.

The primary consideration in shopping for hardware and lumber and building materials for this segment is price. Despite his interest in new products and ideas, the Transitional do-it-yourselfer's price orientation makes him a strong discount department store customer.

The Transitional segment is characterized by younger consumers, larger families, and lower incomes than other segments. These consumers are typically in the early stages of the family life cycle and must watch their expenditures carefully. Transitional do-it-yourselfers are willing to forego convenience and service, seeking out stores that offer low everyday prices and good sale prices.

Despite their income limitations, Transitionals tend to be impulse buyers, and they like to try new products. They are not sophisticated do-it-yourselfers, but are very much interested in becoming more knowledgeable about do-it-yourself products and applications. This segment also relies more heavily than most segments on circulars and TV commercials for product information.

ACTIVE DO-IT-YOURSELFERS

This segment comprises 13.0% of the market. Active do-it-yourselfers are knowledgeable and active home craftsmen. They place considerable emphasis on shopping convenience and buying from established "authoritative" stores.

Active do-it-yourselfers are only moderately price sensitive and do not buy on impulse. They are sophisticated customers with a high level of technical skill and in-depth product knowledge. They know which retailers and brands offer the "best value," and they tend to concentrate their purchases accordingly. In short, they are directional and expedient shoppers.

Comment: Note that the preceding psychographic profiles are situation specific. That is, they deal with how individuals view do-it-yourself home improvement activities. Situation specific psychographics are very useful to retailers because they relate specifically to the types of merchandise the retailer sells. Also, you should note that the profiles identified how responsive the different segments were to various retailer-controlled decision variables (i.e. price, advertising, in-store service, location and so on). This information allows the retailer to manipulate its decision variables to appeal to the segment it wishes to attract.

Source: Bert C. McCammon, Jr., et al., *The Changing Do-It-Yourself Consumer* (Indianapolis, Ind.: Russell R. Mueller Retail Hardware Research Foundation, 1979). Reprinted with permission.

categories. A careful examination of this exhibit reveals two important points. First, consumers vary considerably in how they allocate increased incomes to goods and services. For instance, they tend to allocate a more than proportionate amount of their increased incomes to medical care and recreation activities. In fact, this is one reason an increasing number of retailers are offering such things as optical and dental services within the store and selling recreation equipment (skis, tennis racquets, bowling balls, and so on). On the other hand, a less than proportionate amount of increased income is allocated to food, beverages, tobacco, clothing, accessories, and jewelry. This is because consumers can consume or use only so much food or clothing. Obviously, they may buy better cuts of meat or quality apparel, but still the degree of trading up is limited by the desire to allocate their increased income to other goods and services.

The second point to note in Exhibit 7.4 is that income elasticities change over time. That is, consumer tastes and wants do not remain longitudinally stable. For example, from 1960 to 1965 every 1 percent rise in disposable personal income produced a 0.61 percent rise in food, beverage, and tobacco sales; however by 1965 to 1970 the same increase in disposable income produced a 0.83 percent increase in sales of these items. And from 1970 to 1975 the same increase resulted in a 0.90 percent increase in food, beverage, and tobacco sales. During this fifteen-year time span, consumers began to eat out more and to eat more frozen, precooked meals—both of which were more expensive than conventional home-cooked meals. As you can see, retail analysts should regularly compute income elasticity measures in order to help identify changing consumer tastes. These measures should be as specific (by product and region) as possible, rather than as broad as those in Exhibit 7.4.

Economic Turbulence   The United States economy is becoming characterized by frequent swings in the business cycle. Economic turbulence has become one of the realities of contemporary American business. Because of this economic turbulence, some retail analysts have stated that retailers must learn to manage in a "roller coaster" economy.

In a roller coaster economy consumers become confused, because they don't understand the present economic situation. Because the economy is so volatile, they don't know if prosperity in the present will be with them tomorrow. As a result, they become pessimistic and more conservative in their purchasing activities.

At the same time, the retail decision maker has an increasingly difficult time deciding in what quantities to order merchandise. Since it takes some lead time to order and receive merchandise (usually from several weeks to months), the retail buyer can easily over- or under-commit the retailer for future merchandise. For example, the economy of a town may have been booming in May when the local jewelry store ordered a large shipment of gold chains. However, on June 14 the cosmetic factory in town, which employed the majority of the townspeople, cut production by 50 percent and indefinitely laid off 40 percent of the workforce. Do you think the jeweler will be able to sell all the gold

EXHIBIT 7.4		TIME FRAME		
Income Elasticity Measures for Six Merchandise Categories[a]	MERCHANDISE CATEGORY	1960 to 1965	1965 to 1970	1970 to 1975
	Food beverages, tobacco	0.61	0.83	0.90
	Clothing, accessories, jewelry	0.72	0.84	0.82
	Household operations (includes furniture, supplies, utilities, domestic service)	0.94	0.96	1.06
	Medical care	1.44	1.45	1.35
	Transportation	1.06	0.75	1.04
	Recreation	1.27	1.29	1.06

[a]The measure of income used is disposable personal income.

Source: Author's computations and U.S. Bureau of the Census, *Statistical Abstract of the United States* (Washington, D.C.: U.S. Government Printing Office, 1979), p. 440.

chains in a reasonable period of time when they arrive next week? The retail information system becomes a more important dimension of retailing in a roller coaster economy.

TECHNOLOGICAL ENVIRONMENT

Technology is the application of science in order to develop new methods or ways of doing things. In retailing, technology occurs in two broad areas: new methods of retailing and new equipment or fixtures used in retailing.

New Forms of Retailing   As we discussed in Chapter 6, the practice of retailing is continually evolving. New forms of retailing are born and old forms die out. This innovation in retailing is the result of a constant pressure to improve efficiency and effectiveness in the performance of the eight marketing functions and a continual effort to serve the consumer better. Perhaps this can best be seen through two detailed examples.

Grocery Retailing   In the 1970s the food industry witnessed three forms of innovation in grocery retailing: (1) warehouse stores; (2) limited item stores; and (3) combination stores.[16] The **warehouse store** was a no-frills, low-service, high-tonnage approach to grocery retailing (see Exhibit 7.5). Warehouse stores operate on a gross margin of 11–12 percent versus 20–24 percent for conventional supermarkets), and therefore offer the consumer significant price savings and good assortments. The **limited item store** was introduced by the Albrecht Company of West Germany. These stores are similar to warehouse stores in many operating characteristics (see Exhibit 7.5), but they carry fewer than 1,000

16. This section is based largely on "Continuing Evolution in Grocery Retailing," *The Nielsen Researcher* No. 2 (1980): 2–10.

Warehouse grocery stores offer consumers significant savings and retailers a higher return on investment than supermarkets. (Photo courtesy of Nash Finch Company.)

grocery items. Limited item stores offer the consumer lower prices, but the customer must be willing to trade off product assortment for this price saving. The **combination store** is the joining together of both a conventional supermarket and full line drug store (see Exhibit 7.5). These stores offer the customer one-stop shopping and lower cost in terms of time and miles traveled. They also do not sacrifice service and variety as do the limited item stores and warehouse stores.

It is difficult to predict which of these three innovations in grocery retailing, if any, will overtake the conventional supermarket. In the end, the consumer will be the judge. In retailing, in terms of new forms and types of retail trade, the consumer determines what is acceptable technology.

Computerized in-Home Shopping   With increasing sophistication in computer and telecommunications technology, new forms of retailing are emerging. They revolve around a computer used to facilitate transactions between the consumer and retailer. Let us look at several examples.

COMP-U-CARD of America, Inc., is a computerized shopping service that enables consumers to purchase name-brand appliances, cameras, furniture, fine china, silver, and even automobiles at 20 to 40 percent below retail.[17] Here is how this innovative system works. Suppose Mr. Randolf decides that he needs a new clock radio. He already knows that he wants a digital AM-FM

17. "COMP-U-CARD Helps 1.5 Million Shop by Phone," *Business Week*, September 10, 1979, pp. 58, 60.

EXHIBIT 7.5
Three Innovations in Grocery Retailing

LIMITED ITEM STORES

- Normally less than 1,000 items.
- Limited number of national brands and sporadic brand or item availability.
- Generally one brand and one size per item.
- Store hours limited.
- Items displayed in cut cartons.
- No individual item pricing.
- Little or no perishables.
- Customers do their own bagging.
- Generally 5,000–14,000 square feet of selling area.
- No check cashing.
- Little advertising.

COMBINATION STORES

- Generally range from 35,000 to 60,000 square feet.
- Full food mix including perishables.
- Features a pharmacy, health and beauty aids, toiletries, and all general merchandise normally carried by a super drug store.
- Ratio of food to drug usually 60–40.
- Average annual volume $13 million with some reaching $20 million or more.
- 25–30 percent of sales attributed to general merchandise.
- Common checkout area for food, drug, and general merchandise items.
- Average 13 checkouts with average weekly sales of $19,000 per checkout.

WAREHOUSE STORES

- Reduced gross margins, running as low as 11–12 percent.
- Reduced labor costs, usually under 4 percent of sales, or one half to one third that of a conventional supermarket.
- High unit sales; individual store tapes run as high as five times the supermarket average.
- Limited item selection; brands, sizes, and varieties carried by warehouse markets vary, but range from 1,000 to 8,000 items.
- Erratic brand or item availabilty.
- Special deal items; different brands will apppear and disappear as manufacturer deals come and go.
- Limited perishables; some warehouse markets carry fresh meat and push big cuts or large orders. Many carry frozen meat only—or none at all. Produce may be limited or in bulk only if available at all.
- Varied locations; warehouse stores emerged in fringe market areas drawing blue-collar workers, but many are now opening in large cities and drawing a cross-section of the population.
- Low construction costs; preexisting building or simple concrete block construction with minimum decor are generally preferred.

Source: "Continuing Evolution in Grocery Retailing," *The Nielsen Researcher* No. 2 (1980), pp. 4, 5, and 8. Reprinted with permission.

Panasonic and has looked up the model number. His next step is to call the toll-free COMP-U-CARD phone number and provide the product description. THE COMP-U-CARD employee who answers his call scans the electronic listings and quotes Mr. Randolf the current price and delivery time. Mr. Randolf makes the decision to buy and gives the employee his credit card number. A few days later, his order is confirmed by mail. COMP-U-CARD serves essentially as a broker in bringing consumers and retailers together. Consumers pay a membership fee and vendors are charged a 3 to 4 percent service charge.

Another innovative form of retailing has been developed by the Warner Amex Cable Communications of Warner Communications and American Express. The system, called QUBE, is an interactive video in-home shopping service.[18] Merchandise is displayed on TV screens in the home, and the consumer can push buttons to buy merchandise. The system was being tested in Columbus, Ohio, in the early 1980s. QUBE is essentially a cable TV catalog. Other conventional retailers, such as Sears, B. Dalton, Penney's, and Nieman-Marcus have been experimenting with in-home cable TV shopping.[19]

Retail analysts debate the potential of in-home shopping. Nonetheless, whether retailing in the future will occur more often in homes or in stores will largely depend on consumer reaction to the computer technology used for in-home shopping. In Exhibit 7.6 we profile the prospects of the widespread diffusion of nonstore retailing.

Equipment and Fixture Innovations

Innovations in retail equipment and fixtures are continually altering the nature and practice of retailing. Therefore, our discussion in this area will not be exhaustive; it will reflect only a sampling of innovations in equipment and fixtures in the late 1970s and early 1980s.

Cash Handling Systems

Many retailers that handle large amounts of cash, such as gasoline stations and convenience foodstores, are very susceptible to robbery. These retailers are therefore beginning to install cash-control systems, machines that allow employees to deposit excess cash. If the cash is needed for an especially large transaction then it can be retrieved after a preprogrammed time delay. The time delay is long enough (two to ten minutes) that would-be robbers are not willing to risk waiting around for the added cash. The 7-11 chain has reported that their cash-control system reduced by 45 percent the cash lost per robbery.[20]

Merchandise Handling Systems

Many chain-store retailers warehouse and distribute to their stores. These retailers have found that significant waste can

---

18. See "QUBE: The Ultimate Testing Vehicle," *Marketing News*, May 2, 1980, pp. 6, 7; and "Why TV Sets Do More in Columbus, Ohio," *Fortune*, October 6, 1980, pp. 67–73.

19. "Retailers Eye Cable-TV Catalogs," *Chain Store Age Executive* 56(July 1980): 13; and "Four Chains Plug Into 'Shop by TV' Test," *Chain Store Age—General Merchandise Edition* 56(January 1980): 50–51.

20. "New Cash-Handling System Protects 7-Eleven's Money," *Chain Store Age Executive* 56(April 1980): 73, 75.

EXHIBIT 7.6
Nonstore Retailing

Many retail analysts expect nonstore retailing to experience considerable growth in the future. Nonstore retailers, as the name suggests, are retailers who do not consummate transactions in the store. The most popular type of nonstore retailers is the mail-order house, but futurists envision consumers using in-home computer consoles to do much of their shopping. How would you evaluate nonstore retailing from a consumer's perspective?

We saw in our retail patronage model in Chapter 5 that consumers shop to buy, obtain information, socialize, and fulfill other personal needs. Nonstore retailing could be used to buy or obtain information, but we question its value in terms of socializing and filling other personal needs. However, if retailing gets to the point where consumers have in-home computer consoles to use for shopping, we would expect many of the consumer's information needs to be handled in the home. The entire process of searching for the desired item or items could be considerably simplified. And, if the consumer knows the exact brand wanted, the in-home console could be used to find which retailer has the best price on that brand.

Certain demographic and psychographic trends may also be favorable for the growth of nonstore retailing. Smaller cities and rural areas are experiencing relatively rapid growth. Consumers in these areas have less selection than those in a large city. They may, therefore, be attracted to mail-order merchandise or computer ordering that allows them to tap the merchandise selection at stores several hundred miles away. Also, the growth of the time-pressured household will benefit nonstore retailers. These households simply do not have the time or desire to shop. The ultimate in convenience to them would be in-home shopping.

occur in warehousing and distribution, and to help eliminate that waste they have sought the latest in technology in merchandise handling systems. For example, computer-designed, automated warehouse conveyor systems by Rapistan have significantly helped both K-mart and Safeway improve performance.[21] K-mart achieved a 33 percent faster turnaround in the order receipt to delivery cycle after installing a Rapistan system in its warehouse, and Safeway significantly increased the total throughput in its distribution center after installing a Rapistan system. In both situations, the cost of distribution was reduced.

Lighting Systems Many retailers are finding that with rapidly rising energy costs, investments in the latest technology in lighting systems can have high returns. In this regard, High Intensity Discharge (HID) lighting systems, consisting either of high-pressure sodium lamps or metal halide lamps, can offer improved quality of store light, reduced energy consumption, and decreased maintenance costs in relation to conventional fluorescent lighting.

Let us consider Best Products—a catalog showroom retailer.[22] Best's has installed HID lighting systems and found the following specific cost savings: (1) energy use per store was reduced by 65,000 watts annually ($9,100 savings); (2) selling floor maintenance of lighting decreased $1,664 per year; (3) warehouse

21. Rapistan advertisements in *Chain Store Age Executive.*
22. "Best Lightens Energy Usage with Switch to HID Systems," *Chain Store Age Executive* 56(March 1980): 65–66.

maintenance costs dropped $1,022 per year; (4) there were savings of 79¢ per air conditioning hour because of less heat given off from HID system than from fluorescent lighting; and (5) labor and wiring costs were cut in half, since 62 percent fewer light fixtures are needed than with fluorescent system.

Telecommunications   Retail executives can spend considerable time in travel: buyers to market; managers to branch stores; managers to distribution centers; and so on. A large amount of this travel can be reduced through telecommunications. Today it is possible for executives to communicate over the phone not just by voice but by sight. In fact, geographically dispersed executives can have a business meeting by teleconferencing. There are many teleconferencing systems available, but the top of the line is AT&T's picturephone meeting system (PMS) rooms.[23] In major cities AT&T has PMS rooms that accommodate up to six people. Having meetings in these rooms with executives in other cities can be a real cost saver. For example, an hour-long meeting between six executives in Atlanta and six in Boston, in PMS meeting rooms in each city, would cost $270. Compare that figure with the cost of transporting six people from one city to the other.

Retail analysts believe that retail headquarters and branch stores will soon be connected with full-motion, full-color video and audio teleconferencing systems.[24] This technological advance should improve efficiency as much as when retailers changed from using messenger boys to using telephones.

Distributed Data Processing   In the late 1970s and early 1980s, distributed data processing (DDP) experienced rapid growth. DDP involves two or more physically distinct processors that are functionally autonomous but are data dependent through a centralized computer.[25] Jointly they comprise a single system. A DDP system can enter, verify, and process data close to a user and transmit data between locations, thus eliminating the need to process all information centrally. In retailing DDP is occurring in three areas: (1) point of sale systems, (2) credit authorization and purchase order management, and (3) receiving and shipping merchandise from warehouses.[26]

> F. W. Woolworth, for instance, has installed a DDP system to control sending and receiving operations in its distribution centers in San Francisco; Greenville, S.C.; Denver, Pennsylvania; and Junction City, Kansas. Under the DDP system, merchandising, trafficking and accounting are still handled centrally, while the decentralized, Digital Equipment 11/70 processors at each of the distribution centers have complete control over sending and receiving merchandise.[27]

23. "Getting It Altogether with Teleconferencing," *Chain Store Age Executive* 56(October 1980): 41–42, 44.

24. Marian Burk Rothman, "Telecommunications Solutions for Keeping in Touch," *Stores* 62(January 1980): 68–70.

25. For a discussion of DDP in retailing, see Marian Burk Rothman, "Retail Technology: Customized vs. Packaged Approaches," *Stores* 62(January 1980): 56, 58.

26. "DDP Clicks with Chains," *Chain Store Age Executive* 56(October 1980): 46, 48.

27. "DDP Clicks," p. 46.

Video Ad System   Closed-circuit TV monitors are being installed over super-market checkout counters to transmit six one-minute programs of three-, five-, and ten-second commercials for major national advertisers. Advocates of video ad systems claim that they can deliver more impressions to a more qualifiable audience (one more likely to be in the target market) than prime-time network television, at one sixth the cost. This new method of advertising in the store gets to the customer while he or she is in the shopping mood and when the shopper is waiting in line with nothing else to do but watch the TV monitor.[28]

Scanning   One of the most significant technological developments in retailing during the 1970s was the development and implementation of the Universal Product Code (UPC). The UPC consists of twelve vertical bars that are placed on the package of all grocery products (except produce and meats). These twelve bars uniquely identify each product. Optical scanning machines at the checkout counter can be passed over the bars to compute the customer's bill automatically. Scanning has been a major profit producer for retail grocery stores by helping to increase worker productivity, because cashiers can work faster and because stockboys don't need to price each item. Also, shrinkage

28. "Two Supermarkets Test New Video Ad System; National Rollout Set for April, 1981," *Marketing News*, June 13, 1980, pp. 1, 5.

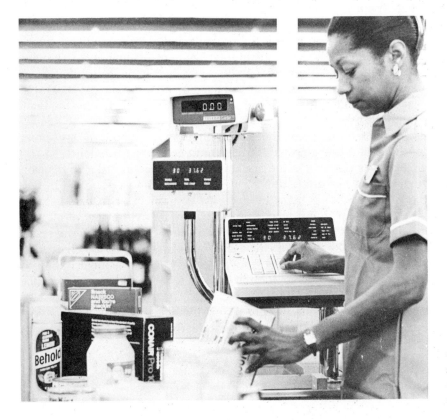

Electronic point-of-sale terminals give retailers up-to-the-minute information. (Photo courtesy of Fed Mart.)

has been reduced in the store, because the cashier is not able to undercharge friends or relatives. Some retailers are also selling the rich data they can capture with scanning. As one midwest grocery executive said: "We've already made several thousand dollars selling the information, and all we have to do is forward them our tapes. In turn, the data goes to the manufacturer, which eventually helps him give us more desirable products."[29]

An important benefit of scanning is the rich data that it does provide. The retailer can now quickly obtain item-movement data for any period of time it desires (weekly, daily, hourly, and so on). This data can be used to control inventory better; to determine the response to advertised specials; to assess the change in demand due to a price change; and to determine the sales effect of altering shelf space. In short, this data gold mine allows the grocery retailer to manage the store more analytically.[30]

SUMMARY

In this chapter we reviewed the major forces in the socioeconomic and technological environments that shape retailing in our society. We began with a discussion of major demographic trends, including population growth, age distribution, geographical shifts, city life, mobility, education, divorce, unrelated two-person households, income growth, and employed females. Then we reviewed psychographic trends. General psychographic or life style trends included increased casualness, male-female role flexibility, consumerism, deterioration of industrial confidence, and the management of time versus money. To illustrate that retailers need to conduct psychographic research that is unique to their line of trade we summarized a major study on the psychographics of the changing do-it-yourself consumer which was conducted for the retail hardware industry.

We also examined three economic factors that influence both the consumer and retailer: interest rates, personal incomes, and economic turbulence.

Technology was defined as the application of science in order to develop new methods or ways of doing things. In retailing, technology occurs in two broad areas: new methods of retailing and new equipment or fixtures used in retailing. It was not our intent to provide a comprehensive review of all new forms of retailing, but to demonstrate that innovation in retailing is the result of a constant pressure to improve efficiency or effectiveness in the eight marketing functions and a continual effort to better serve the consumer. We used two examples: the continuing evolution in grocery retailing, and the emergence of in-home computerized shopping. Our discussion of retail technology also consisted of a sampling of innovations in equipment and fixtures that were being adopted by retailers in the late 1970s and early 1980s.

29. "Hard Savings an MIS Statistic Now," *Chain Store Age Executive* 56(October 1980): 57.

30. For an easy-to-follow discussion of the uses of scanning data, see "Scanning Data . . . the Real World Applications," *The Nielsen Researcher* No. 4 (1978): 2–8.

QUESTIONS

1. In this chapter, we stated that innovation in retailing is "the result of a constant pressure to improve efficiency or effectiveness in the performance of the eight marketing functions and a continual effort to better serve the consumer." Do you agree or disagree with this statement? Explain why.

2. What demographic and economic trends do you see occurring in the United States that may help stimulate computerized in-home shopping?

3. Why is it more difficult for retailers to manage their enterprises in a roller coaster economy?

4. How does a demographic trend, such as an increasing number of working wives, affect retailing?

5. What strategies should retailers develop as a response to slower population growth in the nation?

6. As the proportion of the population over forty-five rises, what products or retailers will benefit the most?

7. Refer back to the retail patronage model in Chapter 5. How would you enter demographics and psychographics into this model?

8. Define income elasticity of demand. Is this concept of any use to retailers in developing strategy?

9. Using theories from the prior chapter, explain the continuing evolution of grocery retailing discussed in this chapter, being sure to explain the emergence of warehouse stores, limited item stores, and combination stores.

10. Discuss the interrelationships between demographic and psychographic trends. (This may best be handled by using examples.) Should retailers be more concerned with gathering data on demographic or psychographic trends?

PROBLEMS AND EXERCISES

1. Develop a scenario for retailing in 1990, assuming that real incomes between 1985 and 1990 do not rise and population growth is stagnant.

2. Interview several local retail executives to determine what actions they have taken to soften the effect of the energy crisis.

3. Obtain the most recent edition of the *Statistical Abstract of the United States*. Obtain current data for all the demographic and economic variables discussed in this chapter. Do you see any other data in the *Statistical Abstract* that may be useful to retailers in planning for the future?

4. Compare your life style with that of your parents. How does the difference influence the stores you shop compared to the stores shopped by your parents?

5. Review the last twelve to eighteen issues of *Chain Store Age Executive* and identify recent innovations in retail equipment, fixtures, and buildings.

SUGGESTED READINGS

Berry, Leonard L. "The New Consumer," in Ronald W. Stampfl and Elizabeth C. Hirschman (eds.). *Competitive Structure in Retail Markets: The Department Store Perspective* (Chicago: American Marketing Association, 1980), pp. 1–11.

Bucklin, Louis P., "Technological Change and Store Operations: The Supermarket Case." *Journal of Retailing* 56(Spring 1980): 3–15.

Hirschman, Elizabeth C. and Ronald W. Stampfl. "Role of Retailing in the Diffusion of Popular Culture: Micro-perspectives." *Journal of Retailing* 56(Spring 1980): 16–36.

"How Fingerhut Beat the Recession." *Fortune*, November 17, 1980, pp. 101–104.

Langeard, Eric and Robert A. Peterson. "Diffusion of Large-Scale Food Retailing in France: Supermarche et Hypermarche." *Journal of Retailing* 51(Fall 1975): 43–63, 80.

Pommer, Michael D., Eric N. Berkowitz, John R. Walton. "U.P.S. Scanning: An Assessment of Shopper Response to Technological Change." *Journal of Retailing* 56(Summer 1980): 25–44.

Stevens, Robert E., "Retail Innovations: A Technological Model of Change in Retailing." *Marquette Business Review* 19(Winter 1975): 164–168.

"Working Women Shake Up Traditional Values," *Chain Store Age—General Merchandise Edition* 56(March 1980): 48–53.

8

Overview *In this chapter, we will discuss the legal constraints on retail decision making. The discussion revolves around the legal aspects of decisions made on pricing, promotion, credit, products or merchandise, marketing channels, mergers and acquisitions, and buildings. Since decision making is discussed in detail in later chapters, you might find it useful to refer back to this chapter frequently.*

Understanding the Legal Environment

Pricing Constraints
Horizontal Price Fixing
Vertical Price Fixing
Price Discrimination
Deceptive Pricing
Below-Cost Pricing
Predatory Pricing
Price Controls

Promotion Constraints
Deceitful Diversion of Patronage
Deceptive Advertising
Bait-and-Switch Tactics
Substantiation and Retraction

Credit Constraints
Credit Disclosure
Credit Card Regulations
Credit Granting, Collections, and Billing

Product Constraints
Patents
Trademarks
Product Safety

Channel Constraints
Territorial Restrictions
Dual Distribution
Exclusive Dealing
Tying Arrangements
Franchise Distribution

Mergers and Acquisitions

Building Constraints
Zoning Regulations
Building Codes

Summary

THE PRECEDING CHAPTERS have suggested that the retailer is constrained by several uncontrollable external forces. One additional external force that must be discussed is the legal environment. In order to avoid costly legal blunders, the retail decision maker needs to understand the legal constraints to be faced. Thus, knowledge of the legal environment can aid the retail executive in profitably managing the retail enterprise.

Retailers cannot freely make decisions without regard for the laws society has established to regulate them and other business organizations. The *legal environment* consists of those local, state, and federal laws which limit the retailer's flexibility and freedom in making business-related decisions. Since local and state laws vary widely, the focus of this chapter will be on federal legislation that affects all retailers. Occasionally, we will comment on typical state or local laws but we will, in most part, leave it up to you to investigate thoroughly the legal constraints on retailing in your local community and state.

PRICING CONSTRAINTS

The price decision is the one that most frequently confronts retailers. Retailers continuously have to establish prices for the many items they offer to consumers. In doing this they have considerable, but not total, flexibility. Some of the constraining factors are summarized in Exhibit 8.1.

Horizontal Price Fixing When a group of competing retailers establish a fixed price at which to sell their merchandise, they are engaged in **horizontal price fixing.** For example, all retail grocers in a particular trade area may agree to sell eggs at $0.84 per dozen. Regardless of its actual or potential impact on competition or the consumer, this fixing of prices would violate section 1 of the Sherman Antitrust Act (1890), which states, "Every contract, combination in the form of trust or otherwise, or conspiracy, in restraint of trade or commerce among the several states, or with foreign nations is declared to be illegal."[1]

Since passage of the Sherman Act, the courts have viewed horizontal price fixing as a restraint of trade. Occasionally, retailers have argued that they operate locally, not "among the several states." This argument has generally been unsuccessful. Trade among the states—called **interstate commerce**—encompasses most retailers, because the merchandise retailers purchase typically originates in another state. Thus the courts tend to view retailers as involved in interstate commerce even if all of their customers are local. Also, most states have laws similar to the Sherman Act, prohibiting any restraints of trade such as horizontal price fixing on a strictly local level.

According to Owen M. Johnson, Jr., director of the Bureau of Competition for the Federal Trade Commission, horizontal price fixing is not unusual in

1. Sherman Act, 26 Stat, 209 (1980) as amended, 15 U.S.C. articles 1–7.

EXHIBIT 8.1
Pricing Constraints

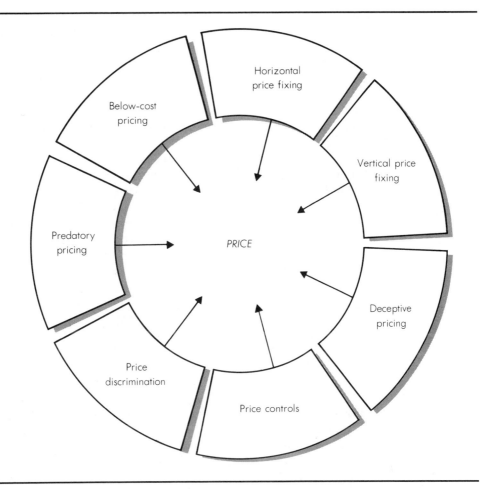

retailing.[2] One notable example involves Saks Fifth Avenue and I. Magnin and Company, who were indicted by a 1976 federal grand jury on charges of conspiring to fix prices on women's clothing from 1963 to April 1974. Each company, after pleading no contest, was fined $50,000.[3] In another situation, three of the largest supermarket chains in the Cleveland area were indicted by a federal grand jury for conspiring to fix food prices for two periods in the years 1976 through 1978.[4]

Vertical Price Fixing When a retailer collaborates with its supplier to resell an item at an agreed-on price, **vertical price fixing** has occurred. This is also often referred to as **resale price maintenance.** These agreements are illegal and have been viewed

2. "FTC's Retail Role Grows," *Chain Store Age Executive* 52(October 1976): 35.
3. "Saks, I. Magnin Hit on Pricing," *Chain Store Age Executive* 52(June 1976): 4.
4. "U.S. Panel Indicts 3 Food Concerns for Price Fixing" *Wall Street Journal*, October 13, 1980, p. 7.

as a violation of section 1 of the Sherman Act. For most of 1978, 1979, and 1980 the Federal Trade Commission investigated Bloomingdale's and thousands of the company's key suppliers for evidence of illegal resale price maintenance activities.[5]

Resale price maintenance does not suggest that manufacturers cannot recommend to retailers a price at which they would like to see an item sold. Rather, they cannot sit down and establish with the retailers a price for resale, nor can they legally threaten retailers with supply cutoffs if they do not sell at the recommended price.

From the mid-1930s to the mid-1970s resale price maintenance agreements in the United States were legal. These agreements were allowed by various **fair trade laws** enacted by the states, which were given exemption from antitrust prosecution by the Miller-Tydings Amendment (1937) and the McGuire Amendment (1950). However, in 1975 President Ford signed federal legislation repealing fair trade laws, and in March 1976 legal resale price maintenance came to an end.

Frequently, suppliers have sold to retailers on consignment. Under **consignment sales** the supplier retains title to the goods while the retailer has physical possession and attempts to sell or pay for the goods. Since, under such arrangement, the supplier has retained title, he has often used the arrangement to fix prices at the retail level. The courts have, however, consistently reduced a supplier's ability to control retail price. Regarding consignment sales, William Trombetta (deputy attorney general for New Jersey) has commented, "The courts are no longer concerned with technical niceties such as 'sale,' 'agency,' 'who has title,' and 'who assumes risk,' but rather with the significance of the effect of consignment, as a distribution practice, on competition."[6]

An example of the consignment scheme to fix prices involved General Electric.[7] Since the early 1920s, G.E. had sold approximately 75 percent of their lamps to retailers on consignment and set prices for resale to the consumer. Trombetta provides an insightful analysis of this very important precedent setting case.

> There were two major flaws in G.E.'s consignment scheme that can serve as guidelines for management in considering the reasonableness of an agency method of distribution. First, management must appreciate the court's increasing respect for the independence of a distributor dealing in a wide variety of goods, maintaining inventory, storing and delivering products, and providing repair service, notwithstanding the fact that he may be labelled a consignee. Second, [was] the scope of G.E.'s distribution system and the large number of retail outlets involved (G.E. had more than 40,000 consignees and more than 50 percent of the large lamp market). . . .[8]

5. "Bloomie's Price-Fix Probe to Expand?" *Chain Store Age—General Merchandise Edition* (April 1979): 100–101; "Bloomingdale's Crimps FTC Case with Latest Thing in Legal Tactics," *Wall Street Journal,* September 10, 1980, p. 27.

6. William L. Trombetta, "Distribution Practices Meet a Revitalized Sherman Act," in Robert F. Lusch and Paul H. Zinszer (eds.), *Contemporary Issues in Marketing Channels* (Norman Okla.: Distribution Research Program, University of Oklahoma, 1979), p. 117.

7. *U.S. v. General Electric Co.,* 358 F. Supp. 731 (S.D.N.Y. 1973).

8. Trombetta, "Distribution Practices," p. 118.

The implications of the G.E. case for retailers are quite clear. The courts favor viewing retailers as independent businessmen, even if they buy from suppliers on consignment. This is especially true if the consignor (supplier) has a large market share in the product being consigned. In such a situation, the retailer should be relatively free to establish prices independent of the consignor's actions or recommendations.

Price Discrimination   When two retailers buy identical merchandise from the same supplier but pay different prices we have **price discrimination.** Not all forms of price discrimination are illegal, and therefore we need to be careful in reviewing its legality.

Legal Definitions   Federal legislation addressed the legality of price discrimination in section 2 of the Clayton Act, which made certain forms of price discrimination illegal.[9] Section 2 was amended and strengthened with passage of the Robinson-Patman Act in 1936.[10] This act had two primary objectives:

1. To prevent suppliers from attempting to gain an unfair advantage over their competitors by discriminating among buyers either in price or in providing allowances or services.[11]
2. To prevent buyers from using their economic power to gain discriminatory prices from suppliers so as to gain an advantage over their own competitors.

The Robinson-Patman Act grew out of the struggle of small independent retailers to compete with chain-store retailers during the depression of the 1930s. During this time many small grocers, druggists, and other retailers were quite vocal in complaining to their senators and congressmen about how suppliers frequently discriminated in price between different customers. In fact, it was quite disheartening to these small retailers that suppliers would often charge chain stores even less than they did the wholesalers who sold to the small, independent retailer. Times, however, have changed, and the small, mom and pop grocer or druggist is almost nonexistent. In its place are a large number of well-organized chain-store organizations that aggressively compete with each other for market share and also large groups of independent retailers who have banded together in cooperatives to be able to have the purchasing economies of the large, chain-store organizations. Some scholars have thus argued that the Robinson-Patman Act should be repealed,[12] and FTC enforce-

---

9. Clayton Act, 38 Stat. 730 (1914), as amended, 15 U.S.C. articles 12–27.

10. Robinson-Patman Act, 49 Stat. 1526 (1936), as amended, 15 U.S.C. article 13.

11. Under the Robinson-Patman Act, references to *sellers* or *suppliers* and *buyers, purchasers,* or *customers* exclude the ultimate customer, the consumer. Thus, the buyer, purchaser, or customer is the retailer and the seller or supplier is the manufacturer or wholesaler. There is nothing illegal about a retailer charging different customers different prices for identical goods. For example, two households could go to a local Chevrolet dealer to buy an identical automobile and be charged different prices without any legal fault by the dealer. The Robinson-Patman Act protects competitors and not the final consumer.

12. Erwin A. Elias, "Robinson-Patman: Time for Rechiseling," *Mercer Law Review* 26 (1975): 689–736, and Rom J. Markin, Jr., "The Robinson-Patman Act: Regulatory Pariah," in Robert F. Lusch and Paul H. Zinszer (eds.), *Contemporary Issues in Marketing Channels* (Norman, Okla.: Distribution Research Program, University of Oklahoma, 1979), pp. 121–29.

ment of the act is at a minimum. Nonetheless, private treble-damage suits are not unusual.

For the retail manager, section 2 of the Robinson-Patman Act (actually section 2 of the amended Clayton Act) is the most important. Section 2(a) of the statute provides:

> That it shall be unlawful for any person engaged in commerce . . . to discriminate in price between different purchasers of commodities of like grade and quality . . . where the effect of such discrimination may be substantially to lessen competition or tend to create a monopoly in any line of commerce, or to injure, destroy, or prevent competition with any person who either grants or knowingly receives the benefit of such discrimination, or with customers of either of them. . . .

The retailer should recognize three things regarding this section of the act. First, the transaction must occur in interstate commerce, which the courts see as the case with virtually all retailers. Second, the actual competition does not have to be lessened, but the potential of a substantial lessening of competition must exist. Third, the retailer who knowingly receives the benefit of discrimination is just as guilty as the supplier granting the discrimination. Thus, retailers should not coerce their suppliers into giving them discriminatory discounts that would put them at an advantage over their competitors.

Within the recent past both Fred Meyer Company, a regional discount retailer in the Northwest, and Thrifty Drug Stores, a large California chain, have been charged by the FTC with attempting to get preferential treatment from suppliers.[13] In addition, the Great Atlantic and Pacific Tea Co. was involved in a five-year court battle with the FTC over buyer-induced discriminatory prices.[14]

Considerable attention has been given to the phrase "commodities of like grade and quality." What does this phrase mean? To begin with, commodities are goods and not services. This implies that discriminatory pricing practices in the sale of advertising space or the leasing of real estate are not prohibited by the act. For example, shopping center developers frequently charge varying rates for equal square footage depending on the tenant and the type of merchandise sold. In a case brought by Plum Tree, Inc. (a franchisor of a nationwide chain of retail shops), against N. K. Winston Corporation (a shopping center developer), Plum Tree charged the developers with price discrimination under the Robinson-Patman Act for charging different rents for equal space.[15] "Plum Tree contended that the commodities under the act are equivalent to leaseholds in shopping centers and that a landlord must charge equal rent for equal space. The court held that a lease for real property is not 'selling goods, wares, or merchandise.' "[16]

---

13. "Three Chains Rapped by FTC," *Chain Store Age Executive* 52(March 1976): 4.

14. Ray O. Werner (ed.), "Legal Developments in Marketing," *Journal of Marketing* 43(Fall 1979): 125.

15. *Plum Tree, Inc. v. N. K. Winston Corp. et al.*, Trade Cases, 74,245 (1972).

16. Joseph Barry Mason, "Power and Channel Conflicts in Shopping Center Development," *Journal of Marketing* 39(April 1975): 33.

"Like grade and quality" has been interpreted by the courts to mean of identical physical and chemical properties. This implies that different prices cannot be justified merely because the labels on the product are different. Therefore private labelling of merchandise does not make it different from identical goods carrying the seller's brand. However, if the seller can establish that an actual physical difference in grade and quality exists, then a differential in price can be justified.

Retailer's Defenses The preceding discussion may have led you to believe that the illegality of price discrimination is clear cut. This is not the situation. A variety of defenses are available to buyers and sellers charged with price discrimination. In principle these are:

1. A **cost justification defense,** which would attempt to show that a differential can be accounted for on the basis of differences in cost to the seller in manufacture, sale, or delivery arising from differences in method or quantities involved.
2. A **changing market conditions defense** would attempt to justify the price differential on the danger of imminent deterioration of perishable goods or on the obsolescence of seasonal goods.
3. An argument based on **meeting competition.** The seller can attempt to show that its lower price to a purchaser was made in good faith to meet an equally low price of a competitor.

Thus, the retailer that knowingly receives a discriminatory price from a seller (assuming the goods are of like grade and quality) should be relatively certain that the seller is granting a defensible discrimination based on any of the three preceding criteria.

Discrimination in Services Sellers are not only prohibited from discrimination in price; they are also banned from providing different services and payments to different retailers. These services and payments frequently include advertising allowances, displays and banners to promote the goods, in-store demonstrations, and distribution of samples or premiums. Sections 2(d) and 2(e) of the Robinson-Patman Act deal specifically with these practices and state that such services and payments or consideration must be made available on **proportionately equal terms** to all competing customers. Retailers have brought many more enforcement actions under these two sections than under section 2(a).

Two questions typically arise in interpreting these sections: (1) Who are competing customers? and (2) What is proportionately equal? Let us illustrate some of the technical difficulties in answering these questions.

A manufacturer of household cleaning detergents is providing a large supermarket chain with an advertising allowance of $0.50 per case purchased. The supermarket chain buys directly from the manufacturer. A small grocer who operates a single store in the ghetto of a large city also sells detergent produced by this manufacturer, but is offered no advertising allowance. This small grocer purchases all its merchandise through a local wholesaler and is six miles from the nearest store operated by the large supermarket chain. In reviewing this situation, the courts are most likely to be concerned with whether the small grocer and chain-store supermarket are competing customers.

It could be argued that the small grocer and chain grocer are not both customers of the detergent manufacturer, since the small grocer purchases from a wholesaler (therefore it is the customer of the wholesaler and not of the detergent manufacturer). Courts have generally not accepted this argument. **Competing customers** has been held to include those buying for resale from a seller's customer such as a wholesaler. Another argument might be presented: that the small grocer and chain grocer do not compete for the same customers. Expert witnesses may be brought in to testify that consumers typically do not travel more than two to four miles to purchase groceries—especially in an urban environment. Since the two respective stores are separated by six miles they could hardly be viewed as competitors. This argument, if carefully constructed and supported by empirical evidence and expert testimony, would be more likely to be accepted by the courts.

Let us now try to illustrate some of the ambiguity of the concept of proportionately equal terms. Assume that a cosmetics manufacturer offers to a department store in Chicago a cosmetics demonstrator for one eight-hour day per month. A small drugstore in Chicago also handles this line of cosmetics but sells only one eighth as much as the department store. The manufacturer believes that it would be impractical to furnish the drugstore a cosmetics demonstrator for one hour per month (a proportionately equal allowance). In fact, the drugstore retailer would also probably feel that this would be impractical. However, this does not relieve the manufacturer of its duty to the drugstore retailer for offering proportionate promotional service. The key point is that the service need not be the same. It could be, for example, the offering of a demonstration kit to the drugstore retailer, as long as both agreed this was an adequate substitute.

The same problem arises quite frequently in terms of advertising allowances offered retailers. A large appliance manufacturer may offer retailers an advertising allowance, which they can apply against any TV advertising they engage in. This is inherently unfair to the very small appliance retailer, because it cannot afford to advertise on TV, even if the manufacturer picks up part of the cost. A small retailer in this situation has the right to some alternative promotional allowance (perhaps an allowance to be applied to advertising in the newspaper or to be used for window displays or banners).

Synthetic Brokerages Another aspect of the Robinson-Patman Act with which the retailer needs to be acquainted is section 2(c). This important section prohibits the development of **synthetic brokerages** or any type of dummy brokerage payment. Any commission or allowance to a person directly or indirectly controlled by the buyer is prohibited. For example, occasionally a retailer who is buying through a broker will attempt to perform the broker's function by creating a synthetic brokerage company through which the retailer would place its orders. The manufacturer would be instructed by the synthetic broker to ship the goods directly to the retailer and subsequently to bill the retailer directly. The manufacturer would then remit to the broker a commission that would, in reality, end up in the hands of the retailer. Thus, the effective price that the retailer is paying for the goods is lower than the price competing retailers are paying who transact their business through legitimate brokers. Such arrangements involving synthetic brokers are a form of price discrimination and have been treated as per se violations of the Robinson-Patman Act.

Deceptive Pricing Retailers should avoid using a misleading price to lure customers into the store. Advertising goods at a price below what the retailer would be willing to take and advertising an item at an artificially low price and then adding hidden charges are deceptive pricing practices, which are unfair methods of competition. The Wheeler-Lea Amendment (1938) of the Federal Trade Commission Act (1914) made illegal all "unfair or deceptive acts in commerce." Not only is the retailer's customer being unfairly treated when the retailer uses deceptive pricing, but the retailer's competitors are being potentially harmed because some of their patrons may deceitfully be diverted to that retailer.

In 1977 the FTC charged the Kroger Company with deceptively advertising prices.[17] In Kroger's ads, called "Price Patrol," the chain compared its prices on selected products with those of Kroger's competitors. The FTC complaint alleged that the ads were deceptive in part because: (1) Kroger failed to disclose that meat, produce, and house brands were not included in the survey, (2) the Price Patrol survey was not methodologically sound, and (3) the results of the survey did not prove that shopping at Kroger, rather than competitors' stores, would result in lower overall expenditures.

Below-Cost Pricing Many states have sales-below-cost legislation that applies to the retail distribution of merchandise. The specific content of these laws varies, but generally they forbid the retailer from selling merchandise below cost plus some fixed percentage markup (6 percent is typical). Most of these state laws are unclear as to whether the retailer can give merchandise away or offer prizes or premiums as a form of price reduction.

State laws have been quite ineffective in preventing sales below cost. First of all, they generally require that a competitor lodge a complaint or institute a legal action against the retailer. Most retailers will not do this, because they also may sometimes sell below cost. A second problem has been that most statutes do not clearly define cost. Is a retailer's cost the cash price paid, the invoice price before a cash discount, the delivered price, the average price paid over a year minus any end-of-year rebates, the price less any advertising or promotional allowance, or something else? Because of the technicalities in defining cost, the litigation can become time-consuming and expensive.

Predatory Pricing If a retail chain charges different prices in different geographical areas in order to eliminate competition in selected areas, it is in violation of section 3 of

17. Ray O. Werner (ed.), "Legal Developments in Marketing," *Journal of Marketing* 42(Spring 1978): 117.

the Robinson-Patman Act. This section forbids the sale of goods at lower prices in one area for the purpose of destroying competition or eliminating a competitor, or sales of goods at unreasonably low prices for such purpose. The FTC's Bureau of Competition will generally investigate complaints about predatory pricing. For example, in 1976 they followed up on a complaint by a number of independent supermarkets in San Antonio, Texas that a supermarket chain's pricing in its San Antonio stores was predatory.[18]

Price Controls   Occasionally the U.S. government will enact wage and price controls in an attempt to control inflation. This has generally occurred only during war years, but price controls have been used in peacetime if inflation became a serious challenge to our standard of living. The controls can be either voluntary or mandated by law. The trend has been to have voluntary controls during peacetime, but this could change at any time (probably without much notice). Retailers need to anticipate mandatory price controls and develop contingency strategies for how they would profitably survive with a reduction in pricing flexibility.

In the late 1970s and early 1980s, voluntary price controls operated through the President's Council on Wage and Price Stability (COWPS). In spring 1980 the council "looked into" a series of sudden shelf-price increases by Ward's to determine if the chain had fallen out of compliance with price guidelines.[19] Although the council has made few investigations of retailers, retail executives should recognize the potential problems and bad publicity the council could create if they found a retailer to be making excessive price increases.

PROMOTION CONSTRAINTS

The ability of the retailer to make any promotion decision is constrained by two major pieces of federal legislation, the FTC Act (1914), especially section 5, and the Wheeler-Lea Amendment (1938) of the FTC Act. The retailer should be familiar with four promotional areas that are potentially under the domain of the FTC Act and the Wheeler-Lea Amendment. These areas are deceitful diversion of patronage, deceptive advertising, bait-and-switch tactics, and substantiation and retraction of advertising. Exhibit 8.2 depicts these four areas of constraint.

Deceitful Diversion of Patronage   If competitors publish or verbalize falsehoods about a retailer in an attempt to divert patrons from the retailer, then they are engaging in an unfair trade practice. The retailer would be afforded protection under the FTC Act but also could receive protection by showing that the defamatory statements were libel and slander. In either case, the retailer would have to demonstrate that actual damage had occurred. For example, assume that the

---

18. "FTC Probes Texas Price War," *Chain Store Age Executive* 52(August 1976): 4.
19. "Feds Aim Probes at Chains," *Chain Store Age Executive* 56(May 1980): 13.

EXHIBIT 8.2
**Promotion
Constraints**

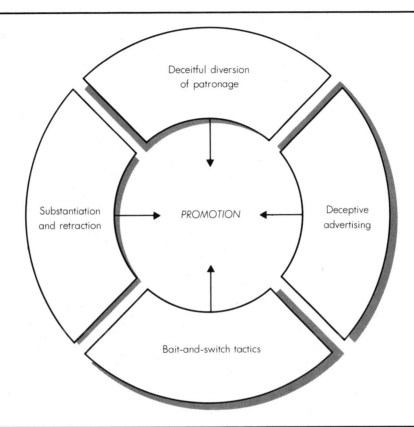

salespeople of Retailer *A* try to convince consumers coming into their store that Retailer *B* is a good-for-nothing crook who is out to cheat the public. If Retailer *B* could prove in a court of law that the defamatory statements were falsehoods and that it lost market share or patrons as a result of these statements, then Retailer *B* would be entitled to a settlement. The most difficult thing to demonstrate is the loss of patrons, and therefore cases involving the deceitful diversion of patronage are not common in retailing. Occasionally, however, they will surface, and therefore a retailer should not believe that it is free to say whatever it pleases (whether true or not) about a competitor. It is equally important that the retailer's sales force recognize this.

A form of deceitful diversion of patronage that occasionally occurs in retailing is **palming off.** Palming off occurs when a retailer represents merchandise as being made by a firm other than the true manufacturer. For example, consider an exclusive women's apparel retailer who purchases a group of nicely styled dresses at a bargain price and replaces their labels with those of a top designer. This is deception as to source of origin, and litigation can be brought under the FTC Act and the Wheeler-Lea Amendment. Also, if the designer's dress label is a registered trademark, protection would also be afforded under the major piece of federal trademark legislation—the Lanham Act (1946).

Deceptive Advertising   False or misleading advertising claims on the part of the retailer are illegal. It is often quite difficult to distinguish between what is false or misleading and what is simply "puffery," which retailers can use. For example, saying "this is an excellent buy, and you can't afford to pass it up" would probably be viewed as puffery, even though the product may not be an excellent buy by all standards, and you may be able to afford to pass it up! Probably most important for the retailer to recognize is that the FTC's concern is not with the intent of the advertiser but with whether the consumer was misled by the advertising. The good faith of the retailer or the absence of intent to deceive is immaterial. The retailer should also know that it cannot pass the blame for deceptive advertising to its advertising agency by arguing that they designed the advertisements and are the experts and thus they should be held liable. Since the retailer pays the advertising agency a fee, it is implicitly approving their work and saying that it likes the advertisements designed. Therefore, the retailer cannot claim ignorance.

From a practical perspective, the retailer should be concerned not only with its own advertising but also with that of manufacturers whose products it sells. If the manufacturer makes misleading statements, then the consumer will not only develop negative attitudes toward the manufacturer, but also toward the retailers who carry that manufacturer's products. There is also a legal liability, though. Retailers are also liable for deceptive co-op ads (which they and the supplier paid for). In a Supreme Court decision, Pay 'n Save, a west coast drug chain, was found liable for false and misleading advertisements of "X-11" diet pills. The ads were prepared by an advertising agency for Porter & Dietsch, the manufacturer of X-11. The Supreme Court ruled that Pay 'n Save's lack of knowledge of the false and misleading advertising claims was not a sufficient defense.[20]

Bait-and-Switch Tactics   A form of deceptive promotion that has been seen too often in retailing is **bait-and-switch advertising,** advertising merchandise at unusually attractive prices and, once the consumer is baited to come into the store, trying to persuade the customer that the low-priced model is not a good buy because of its poor quality or durability. Sears was ordered by the FTC to stop using bait-and-switch tactics in the sale of home appliances in 1976. The complaint charged "that Sears used 'bait and switch' tactics to sell appliances, advertising low-priced products and inducing customers to buy higher-priced goods by not stocking enough or disparaging the lower priced product once customers were in the store."[21] Although not many retailers have used bait-and-switch tactics, consumer advocates are eager to lump all retailers into this unethical category. In fact, partly as a response to fears of widespread bait-and-switching, several state legislatures have recently been pressing for laws that would make 100

20. "Pay 'n Save Loses Supreme Court Appeal," *Chain Store Age Executive* 56(July 1980): 10.
21. "FTC Fights Sears Settlement," *Chain Store Age Executive* 52(April 1976): 3; see also "Three Consent Orders Issued," *FTC News Summary,* May 6, 1977, p. 3.

percent stock availability mandatory on advertised merchandise.[22] If passed, such laws will undoubtedly cause serious problems for retailers and excessive costs to consumers.

Substantiation and Retraction   The FTC can request that the retailer substantiate its advertising claims about the safety, quality, or performance of its private label products.[23] In 1977 the FTC issued a complaint against Sears and its advertising agency for making deceptive and unsubstantiated claims for the cleaning performance of its Lady Kenmore dishwashers. Typical statements challenged in the ads were "The do-it-yourself dishwasher. No scraping. No pre-rinsing. . . ." According to the FTC, the firms had no reasonable basis for these claims, the demonstrations did not prove the alleged cleaning ability, and the claims were materially inconsistent with the owner's manual, which instructs consumers to presoak and firmly scour cooked or baked-on foods.[24]

If the FTC finds that a retailer has made false or deceptive statements in advertising, it may require that a new advertisement be made in which the former statements are contradicted and the truth stated. This is called **retractive advertising.** In 1979, the FTC issued a complaint requiring Montgomery Ward to run retractive advertising. According to the complaint, Ward gave consumers false and confusing information that may have led them to install wood stoves at unsafe distances from combustible walls. The proposed order required that Ward place full-page notices in its October 1979 house-clearance catalog and its Spring and Summer 1980 general catalog, offering to relocate wood-burning heaters to recommended distances from combustible walls.[25]

CREDIT CONSTRAINTS

In some lines of retail trade such as automobiles and furniture, most consumer purchases are on credit. The credit decision is important from both the retailer's and consumer's perspective. To the retailer, the ability to sell on credit represents an attractive sales tool, but it also is an investment of capital that could be used for other purposes (inventory, store expansion). To the consumer it is a means of acquiring goods without having the cash to immediately pay for them, but it also typically represents paying a significant premium over the price at which the goods could be purchased for cash. The legal aspects of credit decisions relate to three areas: (a) credit disclosure requirements, (b) credit card regulations, and (c) guidelines for granting credit and for collecting and billing. These are summarized in Exhibit 8.3.

22. Edward W. Smykay and Mary A. Higby, "The Impact of Full Stocking Laws on Retailing," in Lusch and Zinszer (eds.), *Contemporary Issues* pp. 131–34.

23. Robert E. Wilkes and James B. Wilcox, "Recent FTC Actions: Implications for the Advertising Strategist," *Journal of Marketing* 38(January 1974): 55–61.

24. Ray O. Werner (ed.), "Legal Developments in Marketing," *Journal of Marketing* 42(Summer 1978): 120.

25. Ray O. Werner (ed.), "Legal Developments in Marketing," *Journal of Marketing* 44(Spring 1980): 100.

EXHIBIT 8.3
**Credit
Constraints**

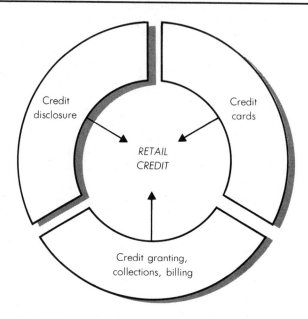

Credit Disclosure   Both the Consumer Credit Protection Act (CCPA) and Regulation Z adopted by the Federal Reserve Board of Governors attempt to "assure a meaningful disclosure of credit terms so that the consumer will be able to compare more readily the various credit terms available to him and avoid the uninformed use of credit."[26]

The CCPA is designed to remedy what Congressional hearings revealed to be unscrupulous and predatory creditor practices throughout the nation. Many of these unscrupulous practices were on the part of retailers attempting to hide the true cost of merchandise in unrealistically high credit terms. For example, the retailer might sell merchandise at a very low price but then tack on a high finance charge. Over the years, many retailers have used this tactic, making their profits on the financing, not on the merchandise. Another common practice was to find out how much the customer could afford to pay per month and then sell the merchandise on the monthly payments without revealing the true cost of the merchandise. Whenever enough retailers behave unethically, they wind up being regulated; this is why the CCPA and Regulation Z came into being.

In order to ensure that the consumer can make more informed purchases when using credit, the CCPA and Regulation Z require that the customer receive information on: the total cash price; the required down payment; the number, amounts, and due dates of payments; and the annual percentage rate of the credit charges.

26. *N. C. Freed Co., Inc. v. Board of Governors of Federal Reserve System* (CA2 NY) 473 F2d 1210.

Credit Card Regulations Contemporary retailers frequently accept credit cards as a form of payment. Although many retailers only accept national cards such as Master Card or VISA, other retailers, especially large, general-merchandise retailers such as Sears, offer and accept only their own charge plate. Ronald Anderson, drawing from the Truth in Lending Act Amendment (1976), the Consumer Credit Protection Act, and Regulation Z of the Board of Governors of the Federal Reserve Board, has summarized the following general rules that apply to retailers and their offering of credit cards:[27]

> 1. **Unsolicited credit cards.** The unsolicited distribution of credit cards is prohibited.
> 2. **Surcharge prohibited.** A seller (retailer) cannot add any charge to the purchase price because the buyer used a credit card instead of paying with cash or a check.
> 3. **Unauthorized use.** A cardholder is not liable for more than $50 for the unauthorized use of a credit card. In order to impose liability up to that amount the issuer (retailer) of the card must show that: (a) the credit card is an accepted card;[28] (b) the issuer has given the holder adequate notice of possible liability in such case; (c) the issuer has furnished the holder with a self-addressed, pre-stamped notification form to be mailed by the holder in the event of the loss or theft of the credit card; (d) the issuer has provided a method by which the user of the card can be identified as the person authorized to use it;[29] and (e) the unauthorized use of the card has occurred or may occur as a result of loss, theft, or otherwise.

We see, therefore, that retailers accept considerable risk when issuing credit cards. Retail executives need to be cognizant of the potential liability so that they can implement policies to control the firm's risk.

Credit Granting, Collections, and Billing Regarding credit granting, collections, and billing, retailers are heavily regulated. In terms of federal regulation, they must abide by the Equal Credit Opportunity Act, the Fair Credit Reporting Act, the Fair Billing Credit Act, and the Fair Debt Collection Practices Act. For retailers selling on credit, familiarity with these pieces of legislation is of paramount importance.

Equal Credit Opportunity Act The Equal Credit Opportunity Act attempts to reduce or eliminate credit discrimination, by making it unlawful to discriminate against an applicant for credit on the basis of race, color, religion, national origin, sex, marital status, or age; because all or part of the applicant's income

27. Ronald A. Anderson, *Business Law: Principles and Cases* (Cincinnati, Ohio: Southwestern, 1979), p. 112.
28. A credit card is "accepted" when "the card holder has requested and received or has signed or has used, or authorized another to use [it], for the purpose of obtaining money, property, labor, or services on credit." See Consumer Credit Protection Act, article 103(1).
29. Regulation Z of the Board of Governors of the Federal Reserve, as amended, provides that the identification may be "signature, photograph, or fingerprint on the credit card or by electronic or mechanical confirmation." See article 226.13 (d) Regulation Z.

is obtained from a public assistance program; or because the applicant has in good faith exercised any right under the Consumer Credit Protection Act. Furthermore, when a credit application is refused, the retailer must furnish a detailed written explanation to the applicant.[30]

Fair Credit Reporting Act Before granting credit, the retailer usually wants to know certain things about the applicant, often desiring more information than that given by the applicant on the application form. The retailer will probably purchase the needed information from a private credit bureau. The Fair Credit Reporting Act seeks to protect consumers from potential abuses in the retailer's use of credit bureaus.[31] If a customer believes that some of the information furnished to the retailer by the credit bureau was false, she has the right to discover the results of the credit investigation and usually may request a copy of the report the credit bureau sent the retailer. The customer can follow certain procedures to get the error corrected.

Fair Billing Credit Act It is not unusual for retailers to make errors in billing their customers. These errors are generally brought to the attention of the retailer by the customer. Under the Fair Billing Credit Act the consumer that believes an error has been made is advised to send the retailer a written statement and explanation of the error.[32] The retailer must investigate and make a prompt written reply to the consumer.

Fair Debt Collection Practices Act The retailer is prohibited from pursuing unreasonable collection methods. Improper methods of debt collection are prohibited by the Fair Debt Collection Practices Act and the Consumer Credit Protection Act.[33] Generally prohibited are sending bills that give the impression that a legal action has been taken against the customer and using extortionate methods of collection. In some cases, for instance, the retailer may be prohibited from informing the employer of the customer that the latter owes the retailer money.

PRODUCT CONSTRAINTS

A retailer's major activity is selling merchandise. Three areas of the law have a major effect on the products a retailer handles: patents, trademarks, and product safety. They are highlighted in Exhibit 8.4.

---

30. Equal Credit Opportunity Act, as amended, PL 93-495, PL 94-239, 15 USC article 1691 et seq.

31. PL 91-508, 15 USC article 1681 et seq. adding Title VI to the Consumer Credit Protection Act.

32. Fair Billing Credit Act, PL 93-495, Title III, 15 USC article 1601.

33. Fair Debt Collection Practices Act, added as Title VIII to the CCPA, PL 95-109, 91 Stat 874, 15 USC article 1692 et seq.

EXHIBIT 8.4
**Product
Constraints**

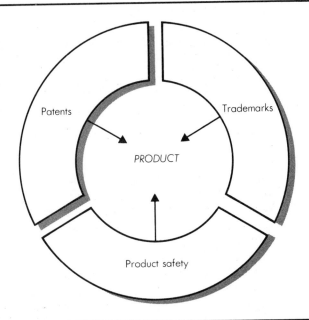

Patents

Trademarks

PRODUCT

Product safety

Patents

In mass retailing, the direct copying of popular product brands or lines is common. Retailers such as K-mart, Penney's, Woolco, and Sears often will copy an item that has been a commercial success. Their goal is to have the item produced at a lower cost so that they can offer it to the mass market at an attractive price. Society's acceptance of competition is so widespread in the United States that this practice is condoned unless a patent right is infringed on. A **patent** gives a seventeen-year legal monopoly for the marketing of a product or process to the patent holder. A person or company applying for a patent will typically receive it as long as it has completed all application forms properly. However, patent rights can be challenged in a court of law on the basis that the patent was on a product or process that didn't serve to advance the general well being or welfare of society.[34]

An insightful case in this realm involving a retailer was *Sears, Roebuck & Co.* v. *Stiffel Co.*[35] Stiffel developed a "pole lamp" that proved to be a commercial success. Sears then brought out a substantially identical lamp at a much lower price and Stiffel sued for unfair competition claiming that Sears had caused confusion in the trade as to the source of the lamps. The initial judg-

34. When patent laws were developed in the mid-1800s they were designed to grant patents only to processes or products that advanced the welfare of society. Since the patent office receives so many applications for patents, they have tended to approve applications as long as the application has been properly prepared. Thus, this generally leaves it up to the courts to decide the worthiness of the product or process. In short, most patents are not worth the paper they are written on.

35. *Sears, Roebuck & Co.* v. *Stiffel Co.*, 376 U.S. 225 (U.S. Sup. Ct. 1964).

ment was in favor of Stiffel, but Sears appealed and the U.S. Supreme Court reversed the decision. The Supreme Court stressed that a patent could not be given to an article that lacked the level of invention required to advance the welfare of society. They argued that the pole lamp sold by Stiffel was not entitled to a patent based either on design or mechanical features. Therefore, the pole lamp was in the public domain and Sears had every right to design and sell almost identical lamps. The fact that Stiffel originated the pole lamp and made it popular was irrelevant.

Trademarks

Retailers can often copy the products of manufacturers, but this does not imply that they can copy or use the trademark of the manufacturer. A **mark** is any word, symbol, or design, or a combination of these used to identify a product or service. If the mark identifies a product, such as a refrigerator or cereal, it is called a **trademark.** When it identifies a service, such as a car wash or restaurant, it is called a **servicemark.** These marks when registered with the appropriate federal agency are protected from use by others according to the Lanham Act.[36] Therefore, the retailer cannot copy the mark of another, and its own mark cannot be copied if it is properly registered. If a person or firm has the right to use a mark, it may prevent a competitor from duplicating or imitating the mark. The fundamental question in such litigation revolves around whether the public is likely to be confused by the mark of the imitator and believe it to identify the person or firm being imitated. When there is a sufficient danger of confusion, the court will prevent the imitator from using the particular mark.

Trademark rights can be lost if the mark loses its exclusive character by falling into the domain of the English language and becoming a generic label. For example, the terms *aspirin, nylon, cellophane, thermos,* and *shredded wheat* were once enforceable marks. But because they fell into the general language to describe product classes, the right to exclusive use was lost. However, before a mark falls into the public domain, legal battles are generally waged. It is probably not advisable for a retailer to try to be the first one to use a mark that it believes has fallen into the public domain. The free use of the mark should first be tested in a court of law.

Product Safety

Retailers are in a precarious position when it comes to product safety. Most retailers do not produce the goods they offer for sale but purchase them from wholesalers or manufacturers. Basically the retailer has little say about product quality or safety. You might therefore believe that retailers are not responsible for the safety of products they sell; this is definitely not the case.

According to section 15 of the Consumer Product Safety Act (1972) the retailer has specific responsibilities to monitor the safety of consumer products.[37]

Specifically, retailers (as well as manufacturers, other middlemen and importers) are required by law to report to the Consumer Product Safety Com-

---

36. Lanham Act, 15 USC articles 1050–1127.
37. United States Public Law 92–573, Consumer Product Safety Act (1972).

mission any possible "substantial product hazard." Furthermore, section 15 includes in the description of substantial hazards any failure to comply with an existing safety standard. Thus, a retailer may unknowingly violate the law by reselling products which do not conform to existing safety standards. Retailers may further violate the law by failing to repurchase non-conforming products which were sold after the effective date of a standard or for a number of other reasons.[38]

In one Consumer Product Safety Commission complaint, Sears was required to recall 70,000 allegedly hazardous household fans. Sears had to run national ads in hope of coaxing consumers to return the fans.[39]

Retailers are also responsible for product safety and performance under conventional warranty doctrines. Under the current warranty law, the fact that the ultimate consumer may bring suit against the manufacturer or processor in no way relieves the retailer from its responsibility for the fitness and merchantability of the goods. The disheartening fact that confronts the retailer is that in many states the buyer has been permitted to sue both the retailer and the manufacturer or processor in the same suit.

Retailers can offer express or implied warranties. **Express warranties** are the result of negotiation between the retailer and the customer. They may be either written into the contract or verbalized. They can cover all characteristics or attributes of the merchandise or only one attribute. An important point for the retailer (and its salespeople) to recognize is that an express warranty can be created without the use of the words "warranty" or "guarantee." For example, a car salesperson might tell a buyer, "Everybody we've sold this type of car to has gone at least 60,000 miles with no problems whatsoever, and I see no reason why you can't expect the same. I wouldn't be surprised if you will go 100,000 miles without any mechanical problems." This statement could create an express warranty. The court would be concerned with whether this was just sales talk ("puffery") or was a statement of fact or opinion by the salesperson.

Implied warranties are not expressly made by the retailer but are based on custom, norms, or reasonable expectations. There are two types of implied warranties (which overlap a bit): an implied warranty of merchantability, and an implied warranty of fitness for a particular purpose.

An **implied warranty of merchantability** is made by every retailer selling goods. By offering the goods for sale, the retailer implies that they are fit for the ordinary purpose for which such goods are typically used. The notion of implied warranty applies to both new and used merchandise. For example, imagine that a sporting goods retailer located close to a major lake resort sells used inner tubes for swimming and a patron purchases one. The tube bursts while the person is floating on it and the person subsequently drowns. This retailer may be held liable. Because of the potential legal liability that accom-

---

38. Barnett A. Breenberg, Danny N. Bellenger, and Dan H. Robertson, "An Exploratory Investigation of Retailers Undergoing Implementation of Federal Product Safety Regulations," presented to the Southwestern Marketing Association, March 25, 1977 (New Orleans).

39. "Feds Aim Probes at Chains," p. 13.

panies an implied warranty, many retailers will expressly disclaim at the time of sale any or all implied warranties. This is not always legally possible; some retailers will not be able to avoid implied warranties of merchantability.

The **implied warranty of fitness** for a particular purpose arises when the customer relies on the retailer to assist or make the selection of goods to serve a particular purpose. Consider a customer who is about to make a cross-country moving trip and plans to tow a 4 × 4, two-wheel trailer behind her automobile. She needs a pair of tires for the rear of the automobile and thus goes to a local tire retailer and asks the salesperson for a pair of tires that will allow her to tow the loaded trailer safely. The customer in this regard is ignorant and is relying on the expertise of the retailer. If the retailer sells the customer a pair of tires not suited for the job then the retailer is liable for breach of an implied warranty of fitness for a particular purpose. This is true even if the retailer did not have in stock a pair of tires to safely perform the job, but instead sold the customer the best tire in stock to do the job.

Consumer product warranties have frequently been confusing, misleading, and frustrating to consumers. As a consequence, the Magnuson-Moss Warranty Act was passed.[40] Under this act, anyone who sells a product costing the consumer more than $15 and gives a written warranty to the consumer is required to provide the customer with the following information:

1. The identity of the persons to whom the warranty is extended, if the written warranty can be enforced only by the original consumer purchaser or is limited to persons other than every consumer owner of the item during the term of the warranty.

2. A clear description of the products, parts, characteristics, components, and properties covered by the warranty; if necessary for clarity, those items excluded from the warranty must be described.

3. A statement of what the warrantor will do in the event of a defect, malfunction, or failure to conform with the written warranty, including those items or services the warrantor will pay for, and if needed for clarity, those items or services he or she will not pay for.

4. The point in time when the warranty begins (if it begins on a date other than the purchase date) and its duration.

5. A step-by-step explanation of the steps the consumer should follow to obtain performance of the warranty obligation and information regarding any informal dispute-settling mechanisms that are available.

6. Any limitations on the duration of implied warranties or any exclusions or limitations on relief, such as incidental or consequential damages; together with a statement that under some state laws the exclusions or limitations may not be allowed.

7. A statement that the warranty gives the consumer certain legal rights, in addition to his or her other rights under state law, which may vary from state to state.

---

40. Magnuson-Moss Warranty Federal Trade Commission Act, Public Law 93–637, 93rd Congress, 1975.

It is the retailer's responsibility to provide the prospective buyer with the written terms of the warranty for review prior to the actual sale. In this regard, the retailer has four options: clearly and conspicuously displaying the text of the written warranty near the product; maintaining binders of warranties readily available to consumers; displaying the warranty on the product package itself so that the text of the warranty is visible to the buyer; or placing a sign with the warranty terms visible near the products that are warrantied.

The FTC is policing retailers' adherence to the Magnuson-Moss Warranty Act. For example, in 1979 the FTC took action against the Korvette's department store chain for not properly making warranties available to consumers prior to the actual sale. Korvette's agreed to conduct a special training program to instruct its sales personnel about the availability and location of warranty information.[41] Even more illustrative of the FTC's posture was a new nationwide investigation of warranty practices that began in early 1980. This investigation started shortly after the FTC sent warnings to seventeen major chains, such as Sears, K-mart, Montgomery Ward, Woolworth, and Korvette's, pointing out that failure to disclose warranty terms could subject the firms to fines of up to $10,000 for each violation.[42]

CHANNEL CONSTRAINTS

Retailers are restricted in the relationships and agreements they may develop with channel partners. These restrictions can be conveniently categorized into five areas (see Exhibit 8.5 on page 218).

Territorial Restrictions As related to retail trade, **territorial restrictions** can be defined as attempts by a supplier, usually a manufacturer, to limit the geographical area in which a retailer may resell its merchandise. The courts have viewed territorial restrictions as potential contracts in restraint of trade and in violation of the Sherman Antitrust Act. Thus, even though the retailer and manufacturer may both favor territorial restrictions because of the lessening of intrabrand competition, the courts will often frown on such arrangements.[43]

What disturbs retailers is that the view of the courts on territorial restrictions has changed several times since the early 1960s, and thus it is difficult for the retailer and its suppliers to know what is legal and what is not. Let us review the changing view of the courts, beginning with the *White Motor* case.[44] White Motor Company had insisted that its dealers confine their sales to well-defined territories. The legality of this agreement was challenged, and in 1963

---

41. Ray O. Werner (ed.), "Legal Developments in Marketing," *Journal of Marketing* 44(Summer 1980): 112.

42. "FTC Still on Retailing's Case," *Chain Store Age Executive* 56(September 1980), p. 50.

43. **Intrabrand competition** is competition between two retailers selling the same brand, whereas **interbrand competition** would be between retailers selling different brands of the same product class. For example, one Chevrolet dealer engages in intrabrand competition with another Chevrolet dealer and in interbrand competition with a Ford dealer.

44. *White Motor* v. *U.S.*, 372 U.S. 253.

EXHIBIT 8.5
**Channel
Constraints**

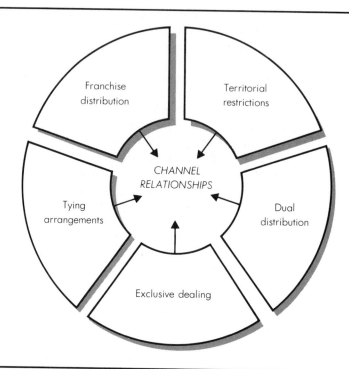

the Supreme Court admitted that it did not know "enough of the economic and business stuff out of which the arrangements emerge to be certain" about the appropriate decision.[45] As a result, the Supreme Court decided to send the case to a lower court to assess the competitive consequences of the territorial restrictions. Thus, the Supreme Court was implying by its behavior that territorial restrictions were not a per se violation of the Sherman Act. Before the lower court could make a decision, White Motor agreed to a consent order to stop the contested practice, but nonetheless, the message appeared to be to use **a rule of reason.** That is, territorial restrictions should be assessed on their individual merits in regard to their effect or potential effect on competition.

Four years later the Supreme Court decided the *Schwinn* case, which dealt with territorial restrictions Schwinn had placed on its distributors and franchised retailers.[46] The court stated that suppliers could not prevent middlemen who held clear title to goods from selling to anyone of their own choosing. Once title passed, the destination of goods could not be controlled. Not only Schwinn, but most other manufacturers were shocked by this ruling. In essence the court was stating that territorial restrictions on retailers for selling goods they have clear title to are a per se violation of the Sherman Act.

A decade later executives once again were surprised. In the *GTE Sylvania* case, the Supreme Court overruled the per se precedent of the *Schwinn* deci-

45. *White Motor v. U.S.*
46. *U.S. v. Arnold, Schwinn and Co.,* 388 U.S. 365.

sion.[47] The Court claimed it had acted too hastily. Continental TV (a retailer franchised by Sylvania) began to sell outside its defined territory and as a result Sylvania refused to continue selling them merchandise. Continental sued Sylvania for treble damages. Sylvania successfully argued that the promise of territorial protection for its dealers strengthened competition since it made the survival of their marketing system more likely. The Supreme Court accepted this argument and further proclaimed that territorial restriction should be decided on a case-by-case basis, thus reverting to the "rule of reason."

Dual Distribution   A manufacturer who sells to independent retailers and also through its own retail outlets is engaged in **dual distribution.** Thus, the manufacturer manages a corporately owned vertical marketing system that competes with independent retailers, which it also supplies through a conventional, administered, or contractual marketing channel. Retailers tend to get upset about dual distribution when the two channels compete at the retail level in the same trade area. For example, occasionally an auto manufacturer will open a dealership relatively close to an independent dealer it sells to. This can have a severe effect on manufacturer-retailer relationships. Independent retailers will argue that dual distribution is an unfair method of competition and thus in violation of the Sherman Act.

The courts have not viewed dual distribution arrangements as violations. In fact, they have reasoned that dual distribution can actually foster competition rather than reduce it. For example, the manufacturer may not be able to find a retailer to represent it in all trade areas, or the manufacturer may find it necessary to operate its own retail outlet to establish market share and remain competitive with other manufacturers. The courts will apply a rule-of-reason criterion. Thus, the independent retailer suing a manufacturer for dual distribution will have to convince the court that it was competed against unfairly and that therefore competition was damaged. The retailer's best bet would be to show that the manufacturer-controlled outlets were favored or subsidized (for instance, with excess advertising allowance or lower prices) to an extent that was detrimental to the independent retailer.

Exclusive Dealing   Retailers and their suppliers occasionally enter into exclusive dealing arrangements. In a **one-way exclusive dealing** arrangement, the supplier agrees to give the retailer the exclusive right to merchandise the suppliers' product in a particular trade area. The retailer, however, does not agree to do anything in particular for the supplier; hence the term one-way. A weak manufacturer will often have to offer one-way exclusive dealing arrangements to get shelf-space at the retail level. Truly one-way arrangements are legal.

A **two-way exclusive dealing** agreement occurs when the supplier offers the retailer the exclusive distribution of a merchandise line or product if in return the retailer will agree to do something for the manufacturer—usually not handle certain competing brands. Two-way agreements violate section 3 of

47. *Continental T.V., Inc. v. GTE Sylvania, Inc.*, 97 U.S. 2549.

the Clayton Act (1914) if their effect may be to substantially lessen competition or to tend to create a monopoly. Specifically, the courts have been concerned with three potential negative consequences of two-way exclusive dealing agreements. First, strong manufacturers may attract strong retailers and the strength of each reinforcing the other could lessen competition from smaller manufacturers and retailers. Second, since there are many more national manufacturers than there are retailers in any given smaller city, there would not be enough retail outlets for all manufacturers to be represented. Third, price competition at the retail level would be less, because intrabrand rivalry would be absent or severely restricted. The legality of two-way exclusive dealing agreements is determined case by case on a rule-of-reason basis, usually by considering the three preceding points.

Retailers must not try to coerce their suppliers into exclusive dealing agreements. This important point was highlighted in *Elder-Beerman Stores* v. *Federated Department Stores.*[48] The case can be summarized as follows:

> Elder-Beerman claimed that there was a conspiracy among Federated Department Stores and numerous suppliers to prevent it from getting access to certain premium-type merchandise. While there was some direct evidence of coercion on the part of certain suppliers, most of the evidence in regard to refusing to supply Elder-Beerman with merchandise reflected more of a business judgement nature. For example, Frigidaire explained that if it had sold refrigerators to Elder-Beerman, then Rike's, the Federated Department Stores' outlet in Dayton, would have sold other refrigerator lines to which it would have given substantial promotion, and this would have adversely affected Frigidaire's total sales in the Dayton market. . . .
>
> Hence, even though there was no proof that there were any separate agreements among suppliers and Rike's or any intent to eliminate Elder-Beerman as a competitor in the Dayton market, management would be wise to avoid conduct where its buyers say openly, or even suggest by implication to suppliers, that if the suppliers sell the line which the buyers desired as an exclusive to the competition, the buyer himself will no longer purchase the line. Managerial policies that countenance threats to withhold business to compel exclusives restrain trade unreasonably. Under no circumstances can a buyer ask that a specific competitor not be sold.[49]

Tying Arrangements   When a seller with a strong product or service forces a buyer (the retailer) to buy a weak product or service as a condition for buying the strong one, a **tying arrangement** exists. For example, a large national manufacturer with several very highly demanded lines of merchandise may force the retailer to handle its entire merchandise assortment as a condition for being able to handle the most popular merchandise lines. This is called **full-line forcing.** Alternatively, a strong manufacturer may be introducing a new product and in order to get shelf space or display space at the retail level it may force retailers to handle some of the product before they can purchase better-established merchandise lines.

Tying arrangements have been found to be in violation of section 3 of the

48. *Elder-Beerman Stores Corp.* v. *Federated Dept. Stores, Inc.,* 459 F. 2d 138 (6 Cir. 1972).
49. Trombetta, ''Distribution Practices'' pp. 115–16.

Clayton Act, sections 1 and 3 of the Sherman Act and section 5 of the FTC Act. The term or concept of tying, however, is not expressly mentioned in any of these acts. Tying is not viewed as a per se violation, but it will generally be viewed as illegal if a substantial share of commerce is affected. The point was made clear in *Standard Oil of California* v. *U.S.* (1949).[50] Standard operated in eight western states, where it was the largest seller of gasoline, with about 23 percent of the total gallonage. Sales by company-owned stations accounted for 6.8 percent of this total and by "independent," dealer-operated outlets 6.7 percent, with the remainder going to industrial users. Many of the independent dealers were required to contract to buy all their petroleum products and tires, batteries, and accessories from Standard. Supreme Court Justice Frankfurter argued that the real question revolved around whether the agreements "may be to substantially lessen competition" and whether this could be illustrated by simply showing that a substantial portion of commerce was affected or whether it had to be also proven that competitive activity had actually diminished or probably would diminish. The Court concluded that if the value of retail sales covered is substantial, then the contracts are unlawful, since they prevent competitors from using alternative ways to market products and thus reduce competitive activity.

Franchise Distribution   Since the early 1960s the number of franchised retailers has grown rapidly. Associated with this growth have been substantial legal difficulties between franchisors and franchisees.

In principle, a franchise is an arm's-length relationship between two independent parties, whose rights are determined by the contract existing between them. However, because of the imbalance of power in this relationship (the franchisor has much more), the franchisee should know that certain requirements the franchisor may try to impose will typically be viewed as illegal in a court of law. Basically, the legal system has attempted to equalize the balance of power between the franchisor and franchisee.

The franchised retailer should keep the following points in mind:

1. Although the franchisor may want the franchisee to set prices at a certain level, generally such agreements, if tested in a court of law, will be found in violation of the antitrust laws.
2. Requirements by the franchisor that the franchisee purchase materials and supplies from him when competitive goods of similar quality are available will be viewed as an illegal tying arrangement.
3. Geographic limitations may or may not be viewed as unlawful. A rule-of-reason approach must be considered as we earlier reviewed in the *GTE Sylvania* case.
4. Standards for operating procedures, quality control, and cleanliness are generally legal, since the franchisor has a legitimate interest in maintaining a consistent image in order to protect the name or reputation of the franchise.

50. *Standard Oil of California* v. *U.S.*, 337 U.S. 293 (U.S. Sup. Ct. 1949).

Franchises should be based on detailed contracts that clearly stipulate the obligations of franchisor and francisee. (Photo courtesy of Pizza Hut, Inc.)

Thus, the franchisor should not take undue advantage of the franchisee (through tying or price fixing) but the franchisee should also not take advantage of the franchisor (for instance, not following cleanliness standards).

One way that franchisors have taken advantage of franchisees was by unfair franchise termination. Traditionally, franchise contracts ran for a short period (typically a year) and the franchisor had maximal flexibility in cancelling the franchisee. Currently, however, most franchise contracts specify the causes for cancellation (failure to make payments, bankruptcy of franchisee, failure to meet sales quotas). Also, many franchise contracts now contain an arbitration provision that allows for a neutral third party to make a final and binding decision of whether a breach of contract has occurred and whether it was sufficient to justify cancellation of the franchise. In fact, termination is now quite difficult, because many states have statutes to protect franchisees from arbitrary termination.

Finally, fraud has occurred much too commonly in the sale of franchises to unsuspecting potential franchisees. Franchises have been sold to the small investor as "get-rich-quick" schemes and based on other misleading statements. Because of this practice, several states have enacted franchise investment laws. Under these laws, a franchisee who is deceived by misleading statements (typically in a prospectus) may sue for damages.[51]

MERGERS AND ACQUISITIONS

A fair number of retailers in the 1960s and 1970s were able to achieve explosive rates of growth by acquiring other retail enterprises. Notable examples include Dayton-Hudson and Lucky Stores. Merger or acquisition of another firm can present legal problems for the retailer. According to section 7 of the Clayton Act, an acquisition of stock or assets of a company where the effect may be to

51. Shelby D. Hunt and John R. Nevin, "Full Disclosure Laws in Franchising: An Empirical Investigation," *Journal of Marketing* 40(April 1976): 53, 62.

substantially lessen competition or tend to create a monopoly in any line of commerce in any section of the country is illegal. This section of the Clayton Act was strengthened by the Celler-Kefauver Act (1950).

Mergers or acquisitions are not per se violations but rather the courts use a rule of reason. Debate and arguments tend to revolve around three central issues.

1. What is the line of commerce involved? For example, is a women's apparel store in the same line of commerce as a men's apparel store or department store?
2. What is the relevant section of the country? Is a shoe retailer in Tucson that acquires a shoe retailer in Phoenix acquiring a firm in the same section of the country?
3. Is there a reasonable probability that anticompetitive effects will result from the merger?

In each of the preceding issues the concept of competition is crucial. We could restate our three questions thus: Do different types of merchandise compete? Do retailers in different geographic areas compete? Will practices that are likely to develop be anticompetitive?

The retail manager might find Exhibit 8.6 helpful in assessing the likelihood of legal problems surrounding a merger or acquisition. In this exhibit we can examine whether the acquisition or merger involved the same or a different line of commerce and the same or a different section of the country. At least four distinct possibilities exist.

The retailer could acquire or merge with a firm in the same line of commerce and in the same section of the country. A dominant furniture retailer in

EXHIBIT 8.6
Mergers and Acquisitions

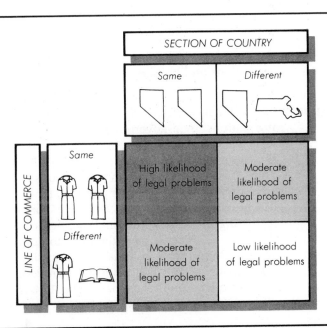

Seattle, Washington, might merge with or acquire another large furniture retailer in Seattle. Such mergers or acquisitions are very likely to be challenged either by existing competitors in that market or by the Justice Department's Antitrust Division. Of course, the challenge is more likely to occur if each firm has a large share of the market. In fact, the larger the market share of the firms involved in an acquisition or merger, the greater the likelihood of antitrust violations (irrespective of other facts surrounding the case).

Another alternative would be the acquisition or merger of two firms that represent different lines of commerce and are currently operating in different sections of the country. For example, a regional department store chain in the Southwest might acquire a modest-size petroleum distributor in Oklahoma City and Tulsa. In this situation, the likelihood of violating antimerger provisions of the Clayton or Celler-Kefauver Amendment is relatively small. The problem, of course, is that our example too clearly delineates the line of commerce and section of the country. What if a department store in the Southeast had stores only in cities of over 250,000 in population, and it acquired a chain of drugstores that operated in the Southeast but only in towns of less than 50,000 in population? Are the lines of commerce and sections of the country different? This is more typical of the questions the court will need to address.

The third and fourth alternatives in terms of acquisition or merger represent a moderate likelihood of antitrust violations. The third option would be to acquire or merge with a firm in the same line of commerce but a different section of the country (a supermarket chain in Colorado acquires a supermarket chain in South Carolina). The fourth option is to acquire a firm in a different line of commerce but in the same section of the country (a supermarket chain in Dallas acquires a retail sporting goods chain in Dallas).

BUILDING CONSTRAINTS

In constructing and remodeling their physical plant, retailers must stay within the guidelines of local ordinances. The most important of these are the zoning regulations and building codes.

Zoning Regulations   Retailers are typically confronted with many local zoning regulations. **Zoning** is an act by a governmental unit to impose restrictions on the use of land to foster the orderly growth and development of a city. Zoning subordinates the landowners' use of the property to the interest of the community at large. Thus, it is possible for zoning regulations to exclude retail enterprises in certain areas of the city. It would be possible, for example, to exclude gas stations from downtown shopping areas. Similarly, community growth could be limited by restricting the number of buildings that could be constructed per square mile. Retailers, as citizens, have the right to appeal to the local zoning agency for a variance to use land in a manner inconsistent with the zoning ordinance. But it is unusual to get such requests approved.

Although zoning is a local issue, federal government policies can have an effect. For example, many city officials have been arguing with the federal government over federal grants to projects that would be inconsistent with the goals of urban planners. Many cities have been trying to save or revitalize the central city. When the federal government makes grants for some interstate highways it can significantly hurt these efforts. As a result, the Carter administration established criteria for measuring federal grants in terms of their "urban impact"—do they help or hurt existing cities? A 1979 White House directive gives cities an opportunity to block a federal decision or grant that would help a suburban shopping mall if it would "result in damage to existing commercial areas."[52] Consider the following two examples:

- In Charleston, West Virginia, Transportation Department officials, backed by the mayor and downtown business interests, took a stand against giving a planned regional shopping mall—thirteen miles outside town—access to an interstate highway. The developer, Cafaro Company, of Youngstown, Ohio, subsequently joined in a downtown commercial development that was, in effect, an extension of the existing Charleston business district.
- In Dayton, Ohio, Transportation Department officials denied $80 million in federal highway funds to complete a major bypass around Dayton. Among the reasons cited for vetoing the proposed 13.5 mile segment of I-675 were "urban sprawl, energy consumption, damage to the central city economy, and dislocation of employment away from existing residential centers."[53]

Building Codes   Retailers also should familiarize themselves with local building codes. Building codes establish specifications regarding materials, method of construction, time to complete, and a variety of other guidelines. Thus, they can place considerable constraints on the type of materials used in the building and its appearance.

SUMMARY

The purpose of this chapter was to describe the multifaceted legal environment that confronts retailers in the United States. In this regard, we identified constraints on retailers' activities in seven broad categories: (1) pricing, (2) promotion, (3) credit, (4) products, (5) channel relations, (6) mergers and acquisitions, and (7) buildings. Within each of these broad constraints we summarized some specific activities that are regulated.

For example, with regard to pricing, we discussed horizontal and vertical price fixing, price discrimination, deceptive pricing, below cost pricing, predatory pricing, and price controls. Regarding promotion constraints we focused on four areas—deceitful diversion of patronage, deceptive advertising, bait-and-switch tactics, and substantiation and retraction. For retailer's credit activities, we focused on regulations dealing with credit disclosure, credit cards and credit granting, collection, and billing. When it came to reviewing product constraints, the topics of patents, trademarks, and product safety were discussed

52. "The Inner Cities Get an Antisuburb Weapon," *Business Week*, December 31, 1979, p. 36.
53. "Inner Cities Get Weapon," p. 36.

as they relate to retailing. Channel relations were also discussed in terms of the legality of territorial restrictions, and distribution, exclusive dealing, and tying arrangements. Also, some frequent legal issues in franchise distribution were highlighted. We discussed the retailer's potential legal problems in attempting to grow through merger or acquisition by reviewing antitrust provisions dealing with mergers and acquisitions.

Almost all of the preceding legal constraints were discussed in terms of federal legislation, since nearly all retailers must abide by federal laws. To review all the individual state laws we would need to write several more books. However, our discussion of building constraints was restricted to some broad generalizations about typical local zoning regulations and building codes.

QUESTIONS

1. Do you believe retailers will become more or less constrained by the legal environment in the future? Why?

2. A federal grand jury argues that because all major supermarkets in a town are selling milk at the same price there must be a conspiracy to fix prices. Agree or disagree and explain your reasoning.

3. Retail executives should abide by the philosophy "as long as it is legal, it is ethical." Agree or disagree and explain your reasoning.

4. How could two-way exclusive dealing arrangements be harmful to the consumer and competition?

5. Deceptive advertising and pricing harms not only the consumer but also competition. Agree or disagree and explain your reasoning.

6. Why should a retailer be familiar with the Robinson-Patman Act?

7. Why is sales-below-cost legislation usually ineffective?

8. What is deceitful diversion of patronage? Comment on the legality of it.

9. Discuss the concept of exclusive dealing. Are exclusive dealing arrangements in the retailer's best interest? Are they in the consumer's best interest?

10. Explain how a retailer could minimize its legal problems in mergers and acquisitions.

PROBLEMS AND EXERCISES

1. Obtain several recent copies of your local newspaper. Carefully go through the major advertisements and identify the ones you believe to be deceptive. Why are they deceptive?

2. Visit a local discount department store or appliance store. Analyze the extent to which product warranty information is available.

3. Are there any below-cost selling laws that apply to retailers in your state? If such laws do exist, what is their nature?

4. Obtain a copy of the franchise contract from a new auto dealer or fast-food restaurant. Carefully read the contract. Do you believe it is equally fair to both franchisor and franchisee?

5. Obtain copies of the last four issues of the *Journal of Marketing* and review the "Legal Developments in Marketing" section. What cases are discussed involving retailers? What are the major issues in the cases?

SUGGESTED READINGS

Barley, James R. "Territorial Restrictions and Distribution Systems: Current Legal Developments." *Journal of Marketing* 39(October 1975): 52–56.

Berry, Leonard L., James S. Hensel, and Marian C. Burke. "Improving Retailer Capability for Effective Consumerism Response." *Journal of Retailing* 52(Fall 1976): 3–14, 94.

Boddewyn, J. J. and Stanley C. Hollander (eds.). *Public Policy Towards Retailing: An International Symposium* (Boston: D. C. Heath, 1972).

Buc, Nancy L. "Retailers Liable for Ads Prepared by Resources." *Stores* 57(December 1975): 26.

Busch, Paul. "A Review and Critical Evaluation of the Consumer Product Safety Commission: Marketing Management Implications." *Journal of Marketing* 40(October 1976): 41–49.

Hendon, Ronald W. "Supermarket Chains' Responses to FTC's Regulation Concerning Out-of-Stock and Price Discrepancies in Advertised Food Specials." *Journal of Retailing* 52(Summer 1976): 13–22.

Hollander, Stanley C. "Consumerism and Retailing: A Historical Perspective." *Journal of Retailing* 48(Winter 1972–73): 6–21.

Howard, Marshall C. "Government, the Retailer, and the Consumer." *Journal of Retailing* 48(Winter 1972–73): 48–62.

Hunt, Shelby D. and John R. Nevin. "Tying Arrangments in Franchising." *Journal of Marketing* 39(July 1975): 20–26.

Krum, James R. and Stephen K. Keiser, "Regulation of Retail Newspaper Advertising." *Journal of Marketing* 49(July 1976): 29–34.

Matwes, George and Helen Matwes. *A Retailer's Guide to OSHA* (New York: Chain Store Age Publishing, 1976).

"Product Liability Crisis Grows." *Chain Store Age Executive* 53(March 1977): 9.

Trombetta, William L. and Albert L. Page. "The Channel Control Issue Under Scrutiny." *Journal of Retailing* 45(Summer 1978): 43–58.

9

Overview *The purpose of this chapter is to outline, in detail, the strategic planning process. In retailing the strategic planning process consists of five interrelated stages: definition of mission, definition of objectives, analysis of opportunities, strategy generation, and control of strategic fit.*

Developing Strategic Plans

CHAPTER 2 of this text was devoted to an overview of the retail planning and management process. In that chapter we emphasized the need for good strategic, administrative, and operations planning. Now we will discuss in more detail how to develop strategic plans in retailing. The review of the external forces to which the retailer must adapt in Chapters 4 through 8 provides a useful perspective from which a retailer can begin to develop a strategic planning orientation.

THE STRATEGIC PLANNING PROCESS

Strategic planning is the process of determining the general direction the retailer will take over a period of several years. In determining this general direction, the retailer needs to define its mission and objectives and then analyze opportunities in the marketplace for achieving them. It must then develop a strategy to capitalize on the most attractive opportunities. When the retailer's strategy is well matched with opportunities in the marketplace so as to maximally achieve its mission and objectives, the retailer will have obtained a strategic fit. Finally, the retailer's strategy will need to be assessed periodically to ensure that the strategic fit is in control. This brief overview of the strategic planning process is summarized in Exhibit 9.1.

Strategic planning in retailing has been receiving increased attention over

EXHIBIT 9.1
The Strategic Planning Process

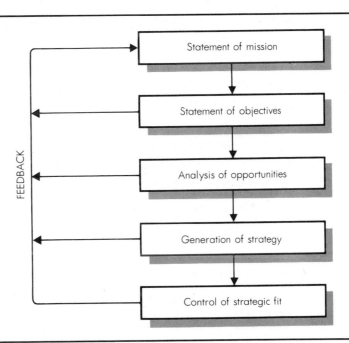

the last decade.[1] One of the major reasons for this is that retailers are starting to see the logic of long-range planning versus action-oriented, day-to-day planning. One executive noted in a presentation to the Retail Research Society:

> Most retailers are not strategic thinkers; they are action oriented, wanting to see real results in a short time frame. . . . There is no commitment by management to strategic planning. In most, but not all, retail companies, the time of top management is used inappropriately. Too often, it is devoted to short-term firefighting crisis management activities.[2]

Obviously, short-range problems must be solved, but at the same time, the retailer must not get so involved with these pressing problems that it loses a vision of where it is headed. Let us, therefore, turn to a more in-depth discussion of the strategic planning process in retailing.

STATEMENT OF MISSION

The retailer's **statement of mission** is its overall justification for existing. A retailer with a mission will find it much easier to survive and prosper than one without a mission. A retailer's mission should not be time- or merchandise-dependent. The statement of mission should be generic. That is, it should be stated so that it is just as applicable today as it will be in five, ten or even twenty years. And, it should not be stated as selling specific merchandise lines or brands.

The automobile dealer's mission is not to sell Chevrolet automobiles or even necessarily to sell automobiles. Rather, it is to help fulfill some basic needs of the customer—probably a need for personal transportation. The logic is not complex. Very simply, the retail customer does not patronize a retail establishment to purchase products or services but to buy need fulfillment. Two more examples may further clarify this point. Most beauty shops are patronized not to get one's hair cut or rearranged but to acquire a feeling of beauty or the hope for more recognition. The supermarket is not patronized to purchase food but to provide substance to satisfy physiological and often psychological needs.

In Exhibit 9.2 we provide several examples of how retailers in particular lines of trade might state their missions. These are not intended to illustrate how all retailers, in these respective lines of trade, should view their missions. They only help to convey that a retailer's mission should be stated generically. When its mission is stated generically, the retailer will not need to change its mission every time the environment changes. Thus, the mission will provide a long-run perspective and guiding force for all strategic plans.

1. For three articles that discuss the increasing importance of strategic planning in retailing, see Bert Rosenbloom, "Strategic Planning in Retailing: Prospects and Problems," *Journal of Retailing* 56(Spring 1980): 107–20; Robert D. Buzzell and Marci K. Dew, "Strategic Management Helps Retailers Plan for the Future," *Marketing News*, March 7, 1980, pp. 1, 16; and Allan L. Pennington, "Do's and Don'ts of Retail Strategic Plans," *Marketing News*, March 7, 1980, pp. 5, 17.
2. Arnold Becker, "Development of Retail Store Strategies," paper presented at Retail Research Society meeting, New York, June 29, 1977.

EXHIBIT 9.2
**Retailers'
Statements
of Mission**

Our mission is to help make ordinary women feel beautiful.

—Retail apparel chain

Our primary mission is to help people of all ages experience and enjoy literature.

—Retail book chain

Our primary mission is to help people better express their feelings toward others.

—Retail card and gift store

Our primary objective is to help households protect their investments in transportation.

—Automotive repair shop

STATEMENT OF OBJECTIVES

The retailer's mission, by its nature, is broad, providing general direction for the firm. More specific direction is obtained by the **statement of objectives.** The objectives that retailers may establish for themselves may conveniently be categorized into three groups:

1. **Financial objectives** are those which can be stated in monetary or economic terms. These are objectives that directly relate to the dollars and cents of retailing.
2. **Societal objectives** are phrased in terms of helping society fulfill some of its needs.
3. **Personal objectives** relate to helping people employed in retailing fulfill some of their needs.

Let us examine each set of objectives in more detail.

Financial Objectives   Retailers can establish many financial objectives, but they can all be conveniently fitted into categories of profitability, productivity, and market position.

Profitability Objectives   Profit-based objectives deal directly with the monetary return a retailer desires from its business. The most frequently encountered profit objectives in a retail enterprise are:

1. **Return on sales.** The retailer's return on sales is defined as net profit divided by net sales. This ratio is also frequently called the **profit margin.** A retailer's return on sales depicts what percentage of the average dollar of sales is profit.
2. **Return on assets.** A retailer's return on assets is defined as net profit divided by total assets. This ratio depicts what percentage of the average dollar invested in assets is returned in profit.
3. **Return on equity.** Net profit divided by owner's or stockholder's equity is the definition given to return on equity or return on net worth. It shows the percentage profit return on each dollar invested in equity.

4. **Earnings per share.** This ratio is defined as total earnings available to common stockholders divided by shares of common stock outstanding. It shows the profit that each share of common stock has earned.

All profit-oriented retail enterprises establish some form of profit objective. The specific profit objectives developed will play an important role in evaluating potential strategic opportunities.

Productivity Objectives Productivity objectives state how much output the retailer desires for each unit of resource input. The major resources at the retailer's disposal are space, labor, and merchandise; and productivity objectives for each may be established.

1. **Space productivity.** This measure is defined as net sales divided by total square feet of retail floor space.[3] A space productivity objective states how many dollars in sales the retailer wants to generate for each square foot of store space.
2. **Labor productivity.** This measure is defined as net sales divided by number of full-time equivalent employees. A labor productivity objective reflects how many dollars in sales the retailer desires to generate for each full-time equivalent employee.
3. **Merchandise productivity.** Net sales divided by average dollar investment in inventory is the definition given to merchandise productivity. This measure is also frequently called **inventory turnover.** Specifically, this objective states the dollar sales the retailer desires to generate for each dollar invested in inventory.

Productivity objectives are vehicles by which a retailer can program its business for high-profit results. For instance, it would be impossible for a supermarket chain to achieve a respectable return on assets while experiencing dismal space, labor, and merchandise productivity. In short, productivity is a key determinant of profit in retailing.[4]

Market-Position Objectives These objectives establish the amount of dominance the retailer has in the marketplace. The most popular measure of market position in retailing is **market share** (retailer's total sales divided by total market sales), or the proportion of total sales in a particular market that the retailer has been able to capture. In developing measures of market share in retailing, one must pay particular attention to delineation of the geographic and line-of-trade markets. For instance, if we desire to compute the market share of a supermarket chain in Tucson, Arizona, we would not state the total sales of that chain in the Tucson area in relation to total retail sales in southern Arizona, but in relation to total food store sales in the Tucson area.

In most cases a strong market position is a correlate of profitability in re-

---

3. In this discussion, whenever we refer to *net sales* we are talking about *annual* net sales.
4. Hirotaka Takeuchi, ''Productivity Analysis as a Resource Management Tool in the Retail Trade,'' Ph.D. dissertation, University of California, Berkeley 1977.

tailing. Research conducted by the Strategic Planning Institute for twelve of the top retailers in the United States has shown that profitability is clearly and positively related to market share.[5] Thus, market position objectives are not pursued for their own sake but because they are a key profit path.

Societal Objectives Sometime in the early 1970s, a significant number of retailers began to establish societal objectives. Societal objectives are generally not as specific or as quantitative as are financial objectives but they do highlight the retailer's concern with broader issues in our world. There is no agreed-on or widely circulated list of societal objectives in retailing. The following list, based on personal observation, discussions with retail executives, and analysis of many annual reports, includes the most frequently encountered objectives.

1. **Employment objectives.** Employment objectives relate to the provision of employment opportunities for the members of the retailer's community. Many times they are more specific, relating to hiring the handicapped, social minorities, or students.
2. **Payment of taxes.** Paying taxes is the retailer's role in helping finance societal needs that the government deems appropriate. The author once knew a retailer who had as his stated objective to have the privilege of paying taxes in the highest possible tax bracket. Implicitly he was saying that if he could be so successful that he had to pay high taxes, then he wouldn't mind it.
3. **Consumer choice.** A retailer may have as an objective to compete in such a fashion that the consumer will be given a real alternative. A retailer with such an objective desires to be a leader and innovator in merchandising and thus provide the consumer with choices that previously were not available in the trade area.
4. **Equity.** An equity objective reflects the retailer's desire to treat the consumer fairly. The consumer will not be unnecessarily price-gouged in case of merchandise shortages. Consumer complaints will be handled quickly, fairly, and equitably. The retailer will inform the consumer, to the extent possible, of the strengths and weaknesses of its merchandise.
5. **Benefactor.** The retailer may desire to underwrite certain community activities. For example, many department store retailers make meeting rooms available for civic groups to gather. Other retailers help underwrite various performing arts. Still others provide scholarships to help finance the education of the young.

Personal Objectives The final set of objectives that retailers may establish is personal. The personal objectives can relate only to the owners or top level executives in the firm, or they may reflect all employees of the retail establishment. Once again, no standard list of personal objectives exists in the literature. We have observed, however, that retailers tend to pursue three types.

5. Buzzell and Dew, "Strategic Management Helps Retailers," p. 16.

1. **Self-gratification.** Self-gratification has as its focus the needs and desires of the owners, managers, or employees of the firm to pursue what they truly want out of life. For example, an individual may have opened up a sporting goods store because she enjoyed being around athletically oriented people. This individual is also an avid amateur golfer and skier, and by operating a sporting goods store she is able to combine pleasure with work. Basically, this individual is experiencing and living the life she really wanted even though the profit potential may have been higher in another line of trade.

2. **Status and respect.** All humans strive for status and respect. In stating this type of objective, one recognizes that the owners, managers, or employees need status and respect in their community or within their circle of friends. Recognizing this need, the retailer may, for example, give annual awards to outstanding employees. Or when promotions occur, favorable coverage may be sought in local newspapers or trade journals such as *Stores* or *Chain Store Age.*

3. **Power and authority.** Objectives based on power and authority reflect the need of managers and other employees to be in positions of influence. Retailers may establish objectives that give buyers and department managers maximal flexibility to determine their own destiny. They are given the power and authority to allocate scarce resources such as space, dollars, and labor to achieve a profit objective. Having the power and authority to allocate resources makes many of these managers feel important and gives them a sense of pride when they excel because they know they controlled their own destiny.

Exhibit 9.3 is a synopsis of the financial, societal, and personal objectives that retailers can establish in the strategic planning process. Clearly revealed in this exhibit is the fact that all retail objectives, of whatever type, must be consistent with the overall mission of the retailer. The retailer's objectives must reinforce its mission.

Three Recommendations   Philip Kotler has stated that as a general rule an organization's objectives be realistic, quantitative, and consistent.[6] Retail organizations are no exception to this general rule.

Realistic   Objectives should be developed so that they are within the realm of reason. To state during a recessionary year that a moderately successful supermarket chain in Detroit, Michigan, is going to increase sales by 50 percent is a little hard to digest. There is nothing wrong with being optimistic, but the optimism should not be overdone. Some overstatement of what you may believe to be a reasonable objective may help stimulate effort by managers and employees, but an unrealistic objective will tend to frighten them off rather than motivate them. Furthermore, if the retailer continually states unrealistic objectives then employees will quickly begin to discount any objectives that are

6. Philip Kotler, *Marketing Management: Analysis, Planning and Control,* 4th ed. (Englewood Cliffs, N.J.: Prentice-Hall, 1980), pp. 69–70.

EXHIBIT 9.3
**Retail
Objectives**

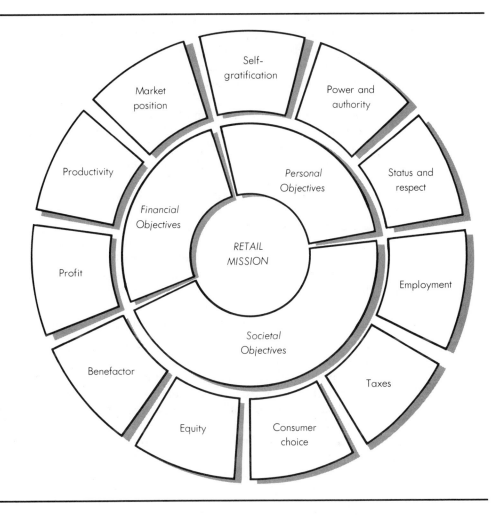

established for them. If the retailer has the environment it has anticipated, it should have a reasonable chance of achieving the objectives that it established.

Quantitative   Objectives that are quantitative are better than those stated in nonquantitative terminology. Performance in achieving stated objectives can be more accurately measured if specific quantities are initially formulated.

To illustrate, assume a retailer stated that one of its primary objectives was to increase return on net worth over the next three years. At the close of the three-year period the retailer's financial statements show that return on net worth increased from 10 percent in the first year to 10.4 percent in the year just ended. Did this retailer attain its objective? Mathematically it did, because obviously 10.4 percent is greater than 10 percent. But what if the retailer really had in mind a much more significant increase—say in the 14 to 16 percent range? Then, the objective was not achieved. Unless a precise quantitative goal was established earlier, the degree of achievement of that objective will be difficult to assess.

Of the three types of retail objectives that were elaborated earlier, the financial ones can be most readily stated in quantitative terms. Societal and personal objectives are much more difficult to state quantitatively, but the task is not impossible. See if you can develop quantitative measures of some of the personal and societal objectives that were discussed earlier in this chapter.

Consistent   A third criterion of good retail objectives is consistency. We have seen that the retailer will state not one, but many objectives. The potential exists for some of these objectives to be internally inconsistent. Early in the strategic planning process, the retailer must ensure that this inconsistency not occur.

For example, the retailer who states a financial objective of maximizing return on assets and a societal objective of maximizing consumer choice, introduces a glaring inconsistency. If the retailer truly wanted to maximize consumer choice then it would need to offer many brands or product lines, and these would not generate high enough margins or rates of inventory turnover to aid the retailer in maximizing its return on assets. Clearly these two objectives, as many others, can exist only in tradeoff relationships. Maximizing the two of them is simply not an option.

Eight basic tradeoffs confronting any company have been enumerated:[7]

1. Short-term profits versus long-term growth.
2. Profit margin versus competitive position.
3. Direct sales effort versus market development.
4. Penetration of existing markets versus the development of new markets.
5. Related versus nonrelated new opportunities as a source of long-term growth.
6. Profit versus nonprofit goals (that is, social responsibilities and personal goals).
7. Growth versus stability.
8. Riskless environment versus high-risk environment.

Each of the tradeoffs needs to be explicitly considered in the retailer's attempt to develop strategic plans. The relative emphasis to be placed on each of these conflicting objectives needs to be decided early in the strategic planning process. If these conflicts are not sorted out early, there will be problems in implementation and execution of retail plans.

ANALYSIS OF OPPORTUNITIES

Once the retailer has firmly established its mission and objectives, it must attempt to identify and analyze opportunities on which it can develop strategy. The key to identifying opportunities is analysis of external forces. This, in turn, can be facilitated by futures research. **Futures research** is analysis of future environments the firm might confront.

7. Robert Weinberg, "Developing Management Strategies for Short-Term Profits and Long-Term Growth," presented in a seminar sponsored by Advanced Management Research, Inc., New York City, September 29, 1969.

External Forces The external forces that need to be carefully examined are those we discussed in Chapters 4 through 8. These forces, none of which the retailer has much control over, are the behavior of members of the marketing channel, the behavior of consumers, the behavior of competitors, the socioeconomic environment, the technological environment, and the legal environment. The retailer needs to analyze them for two reasons. First, because they are all largely uncontrollable, *and therefore* the retailer will need to adapt to them. Second, the retailer needs to translate threats emanating from these external forces into opportunities and subsequently into strategies.

The notion that environmental threats can be translated into opportunities is highlighted in Exhibit 9.4, which shows how specific environmental trends

EXHIBIT 9.4 Environmental Threats Can Be Retail Opportunities

TREND	THREATENED RETAILER	OPPORTUNITY
Increasing proportion of households eating food out of the home (social-environmental trend)	Grocery stores	Grocery store managers should view this as an opportunity to develop in-store delis, expanded frozen food departments, and an increased assortment of food items that are easy and quick to prepare but that compare favorably to food sold at fast-food restaurants.
Decline in birth rate (social-environmental trend)	Toy stores	Toy store managers should view this as an opportunity to broaden their market base to appeal to adults by adding sophisticated toys and games.
Casual wear for a wide variety of occasions (social-environmental trend).	Formal wear stores	The manager of the retail formal wear store should view this as an opportunity to put increased emphasis on the rental versus the outright purchase of formal wear.
Rising costs of personal transportation (economic-environmental trend).	Regional shopping centers	This presents the manager of a regional shopping center with the opportunity to use the shopping center as a regional recreational area in order to attract people for social motives, for instance, allowing people to camp in their motor homes in the parking lot or having an art show or boat show in the mall.
Rising minimum wage (legal-environmental trend).	All retail stores	Presents the retail manager with increased incentive to explore new methods and techniques for improving labor productivity.
In-home ordering of merchandise via computer (trend in technological environment)	General merchandise retailers	Presents the traditional general merchandise retailer with the opportunity to offer both in-home and in-store shopping services and therefore obtain a significant advantage over the new retail firms that offer only in-home purchasing services.
Growth of low-cost warehouse food stores	Grocery stores	Offers the manager of a traditional grocery store the opportunity to strongly differentiate itself on nonprice variables such as friendliness of employees, store decor, and customer service.

in the legal, socioeconomic, technological, and competitive environments in the early 1980s posed not only threats to specific lines of retail trade but also significant opportunities. For example, one trend in the social environment was the increasing proportion of households eating food outside the home. Most grocery store managers perceived this as a threat to their livelihood. But astute and adaptive managers viewed this trend as an opportunity to develop in-store delis, to expand frozen food departments, and to increase the assortment of food items that are easy and quick to prepare.

The Role of Futures Research   The discipline of futures research may have a considerable effect on the retailer's ability to assess future retail environments. However, this effect can occur only if retail executives understand and feel comfortable using the tools and techniques of futures research. First, however, it is important to recognize that futures research is not research to predict the future. The future is too complex to be predicted accurately, and the retail analyst needs to realize this. Instead, the retail analyst can use futures research to achieve the following more modest objectives:

1. To make explicit the assumptions the retail manager holds about future retail environments.
2. To anticipate alternative futures.
3. To trace possible consequences of important current and past developments.
4. To shape and guide current strategies that might affect the future.

A **futurist**—a person who works in futures research—holds the view that the future is partially controllable if it can be anticipated.

In order to conduct futures research, futurists use at least three types of research methods. These methods have been borrowed from economics, mathematics, statistics, and management and have been adapted in order to gather perceptions systematically and to formulate projections about the future. The

The rise of two-income families simultaneously benefited fast-food outlets and threatened grocery retailers. (Photo courtesy of Pizza Hut, Inc.)

basic methods can be grouped as authority methods, conjecture methods, and mathematical modeling.

Authority Methods Perhaps the oldest method of obtaining an outlook for the future is to elicit the views of an **authority.** Ancient and modern history are replete with examples of persons being consulted because of the "sense" they possessed about the future. The Greeks had their oracles, rulers in the Middle Ages conferred with wizards, and various American and African tribes utilized medicine men. Astrologers, the group perhaps with the most staying power, have been popular throughout recorded history.

Just as the ancients and primitives contacted those with the "second sight," one frequently employed method in the retail world is to solicit the views of a single expert or authority. In essence, the **sole-source authority method** consists of drawing on the insights of an expert to forecast likely developments. For instance, a supermarket chain might call on a leading retail academician to draft a report on the future of food retailing. The educator then uses his expertise and existing information to project developments in the macro environment that the supermarket firm will probably face.

The **polling method,** an extension of the sole-source method, uses a group of experts instead of only one. The underlying belief here is that several heads are better than one. Using more than one person to assess the future retail environment provides the following advantages:

1. A group of experts can generate and analyze more alternative futures.
2. A broader set of facts can be relied on, more opinions can be expressed, and sometimes more estimates of the future can be developed.
3. Specialists as well as generalists can be utilized in areas of high importance in order to help synthesize facts, refine opinions, and secure estimates.

One method for polling experts that has received considerable attention over the last decade in many disciplines is the **Delphi techinique,** which was developed at the Rand Institute.[8] Essentially, Delphi is used to attain a consensus of opinion from a group of experts without having the experts confront each other, but still allowing them to know the opinions of the other experts involved. In futures research this usually involves having a group of experts independently estimate the likelihood of some future events. The results are then tabulated, and the participants are asked if they desire to revise their estimates in light of the initial estimates given by the other experts. This procedure can be repeated through several rounds. Experiments have shown that, over repeated trials, the range of responses will decrease and that the group response, or median, will move in the direction of the most likely answer.[9]

The Delphi technique can be used within the field of retailing to help the firm assess future retail environments. Of extreme importance to the retail-oriented firm are the social, competitive, legal, economic, and technological

8. Norman Dalkey and Olaf Helmer, "An Experimental Application of the Delphi Method to the Use of Experts," *Management Science* 9(April 1963): 458–67.

9. Olaf Helmer, *Social Technology* (New York: Basic Books, 1966).

environments. Experts from each of these areas, coupled with a few general-ists, could enable the firm to use a Delphi technique to assess likely future environments.

Conjecture Methods   The second major category of futures research methods, conjecture methods, are reasoned and systematic efforts to identify and de-scribe alternative futures that may be pertinent to a forecast topic. Two com-monly used conjecture methods are scenario construction and future histories. Conjecture methods employ authorities to develop ideas about the future, but in these methods the participants develop whole pictures, whereas in authority methods they produce speculated facts.

A **scenario** is a background narrative that describes an alternative future. The scenario can be thought of as a description of some future point in time, a prehistory, so to speak. Hence, a scenario dealing with technology in retailing in 1995 might posit a period of fantastic new developments including a crop of new technology that will alleviate many of the retail productivity problems of the late 1970s and early 1980s. In sharp contrast, an alternative scenario might describe 1995 as a period when an antitechnology backlash by society grew to fruition and drastically reduced the amount of technological innovation in re-tailing to a level below that of 1980.

Scenario construction is of value to retail executives because familiarity with many alternative scenarios will prevent management from experiencing **future shock** if a reasonable facsimile of one of the scenarios occurs. For ex-ample, if either of the foregoing scenarios were to occur, the typical retailer would be affected substantially. The retailer who is aware of possible future consequences will be able to react to the future in a more positive manner.

One strong advantage of scenario construction to retail organizations is that it provides an excellent vehicle for allowing retail executives within the organization to plan for the future unselfishly. Typically in the planning pro-cess, retail executives will try to protect their individual departments because each executive is likely to continue to manage the same division or department over the next year or two. However, if the executives are asked to construct a scenario for the retailer for fifteen years from today, they will do so very open-mindedly. This is due to the simple fact that they do not plan to be in the same administrative position fifteen years from today and therefore, will not try to protect their domain. The fifteen-year scenarios then can be translated into shorter-range plans, which are necessary to achieve or avoid the contemplated scenarios.

A **future history,** like a scenario, is a narrative conjecture technique based on facts and assumptions. In contrast to a scenario, however, the future history traces the course of developments and events over a time interval in order to explain how a particular set of circumstances set forth in a scenario developed. Thus, whereas a scenario might portray department store retailing in 1995, a future history might begin with computerized banking in 1985, leading to a mass system of cashless financial transactions by 1990, and finally to an auto-mated, cash-free department store in 1995. Three key elements in the formu-lation of a future history are the enumeration of heavy trends, the development of coupling events, and the analysis of branch points.

Heavy trends are those which will have a large effect on the future. For example, the trend in the cost of private transportation, if it continues, will drastically alter the structure of retail trade in urban areas. Consumers will be less willing to search for their ideal bundle of goods and will tend to make fewer shopping trips. An excellent source for developing awareness of potential heavy trends is the Trend Analysis Program sponsored by the Institute of Life Insurance.

In the development of future histories, careful consideration should be given to the coupling of events. **Coupling of events** refers to the manner in which the occurrence or nonoccurrence of one event affects the likelihood of a subsequent event. For instance, a retailer might ask, "What will be the effect of continual declines in real household purchasing power over a five-year period [the antecedent event] on the average length of time that households keep a durable good such as a TV, car, sofa, etc. [the consequent event]?"

In considering coupling of events, one is forced to identify **branch points**. These are events whose occurrence or nonoccurrence will affect the retailer's future significantly. For example, a major branch point for food retailers might be the successful development of a pill that provided 100 percent of a person's total nutritional requirements.

Mathematical Modeling   The final futures research method to be discussed is **mathematical modeling**. A model is an abstraction of reality. Therefore, mathematical model building is the construction of mathematical relationships that portray relationships found in the real world of retailing. The primary advantage of these models is that they can be used to help one understand, as well as forecast, the events with which they deal. In futures research, however, models are more concerned with understanding a system than with forecasting. In retailing, models could be constructed of relatively small sectors of activity—such as a single retailer's sales—or they can be constructed for large sectors of retail activity—such as total monthly or quarterly retail sales in the United States.

Mathematical models can be classified as static or dynamic. **Static models** are those which ignore time as a variable, whereas **dynamic models** consider time as an independent variable. Because retailers in their planning activities are concerned with future time, they naturally tend to deal with dynamic models more. Dynamic models can be of two basic types—deterministic or stochastic. **Deterministic models** operate under conditions of certainty (i.e., the retail model builder assumes it knows the parameters of the model). With these deterministic models, the futurist is able to arrive at a specific forecast of the future (i.e., the model will forecast the future to take on one value).

As a simplified example, consider that a local department store retailer is attempting to forecast sales for 1990. The retail model builder might develop a model that links retail sales to such factors as trade-area population, number of competitors, average household discretionary income, and cost of personal transportation. In addition, interactions between these factors might need to be modeled. A deterministic model would state a very rigid relationship between retail sales and these factors; it might state that for every 1 percent increase in average household discretionary income, retail sales would increase by 0.84 percent. The important point here is that 0.84 percent is assumed with certainty. The model thus will be able to forecast a single-value figure for retail sales in 1990, such as $7.9 million. In all probability, this estimate will be wrong, because the assumption of certainty in regard to the functional relationship between retail sales and the four causal factors is unrealistic.

Herein lies the major weakness of deterministic models: they assume certainty about an uncertain future. However, deterministic models have the strong advantage of being easier to construct than stochastic models and they cost less to computerize. When deterministic models are used by retail analysts, typically the output is subjectively adjusted in consideration of the uncertainty inherent in future environments.

Stochastic models operate under conditions of risk and, therefore, the parameters of the model take on a series of possible values rather than only one value. As a consequence, the forecast of the future takes on a series of values. Consider the example of the department store retailer outlined previously. Now the retail researcher is uncertain as to the exact relationship between retail sales and the hypothetical causal variables. In such a case, the causal factors should be treated as random variables. That is, if average household discretionary income increases by 1 percent, the researcher may hypothesize that retail sales may increase by anywhere from 0.69 percent to 0.90 percent. By treating the causal variables as random, the retail researcher is able to generate a series of projections for retail sales in 1990 ranging from $6.8 million to $8.3 million, with an expected sales volume of $7.9 million. This will give the researcher not only a level of sales to expect in 1990, but also the level of uncertainty that surrounds that projection. Obviously this type of forecast is more useful and realistic; in addition, it is less likely to be misleading.

Naturally, mathematical models in retailing are not as simple as the preceding illustrations indicate. In fact, mathematical models in retailing can consist of multiple equations versus merely a single equation.

Selecting the Best Opportunity   By using the techniques previously outlined, the retailer will, in all probability, be able to generate many attractive opportunities. The difficult task, then, becomes deciding which to pursue. The opportunities must be narrowed down, since all firms have limited resources and cannot pursue all opportunities. Instead, the retailer must select the opportunity or opportunities that offer the best prospects for fulfilling the retailer's mission and accomplishing its objectives.

THE GENERATION OF STRATEGY

So far, we have addressed how the retail planner might assess and adapt to the external forces, but not how the retail planner develops good retail strategies. Good retail strategy must be based on the information that was gathered on the external forces.

Generating ideas on which to build a retail strategy can be the most demanding part of planning. This is because the generation of ideas cannot usually be accomplished through a precise series of scientific steps; it is a creative process. As we showed in Chapter 1, however, the creative process is quite similar to the scientific or analytical process and therefore, the development of ideas can be approached in an orderly manner.

Sometimes ideas pop into the head of the retail planner, but more often they must be developed through creative thinking techniques, which are conscious and deliberate procedures. There are at least five main techniques at the retailer's disposal for facilitating the generation of ideas for new and innovative strategies: (1) brainstorming, (2) attribute listing, (3) morphological-synthesis, (4) checklist, and (5) synetics. All of these techniques are useful in most of the stages of the creative problem-solving process outlined in Chapter 1. For a brief discussion of each of these techniques refer to Exhibit 9.5.

EXHIBIT 9.5
Techniques of Creative Thinking

BRAINSTORMING

In this technique the participants freely toss out ideas, which are recorded but not discussed by the group as they are suggested. The purpose is to obtain the greatest number of ideas possible, even wild ones, for the greater the number of ideas, the greater the chance of obtaining one or more that is innovative.

ATTRIBUTE LISTING

This method is used to improve something that already exists. It involves listing or itemizing the important attributes of the item needing change, then considering each separately as a source of potential change or improvement.

MORPHOLOGICAL-SYNTHESIS

The purpose of this technique is to produce as many combinations of attributes as possible. To do this, two or more attributes are chosen, then specific values of these attributes are listed and combined in different ways to potentially yield a new or better combination.

CHECKLIST

In this procedure the group members consider each item on a prepared list as a possible source of innovation in respect to a given problem. By discussing the given solutions, the group members have an opportunity to expand the list with other possibilities.

SYNETIC

This method uses metaphors and similes, especially those drawn from nature. There are three types of synetic problem solving.

1. *Personal analogy:* Group members imagine themselves to be one of the problem objects, then try to figure out how they would change to solve the problem.
2. *Fantasy analogy:* Members are encouraged to propose ideal, although sometimes far-fetched solutions such as using insects, animals, or machines to solve problems.
3. *Free-association word meaning:* Group members are asked to react to a specified stimulus word before they are told about the specific problem they need to solve; thus preparing the subconscious mind for the problem.

A Detailed Example   The White Knight Supermarkets, Inc., is holding a planning meeting to develop a list of as many alternative long-range strategies as possible. This is the third such meeting, the first two yielding little more than jangled nerves. This meeting promises to be different because the company president has brought in Sharon Riley, an expert in creative problem-solving techniques, to lead the discussions. In addition, at the request of Ms. Riley, the president has brought in three households that are representative of the White Knight customers—a young married couple with no children, in which both husband and wife have professional careers; a couple in their late thirties with two teenage daughters and the wife not employed outside the home; and a retired couple living on a small pension and social security payments.

Ms. Riley was introduced to the group. The top management of the White Knight Supermarkets, Inc., eyed her suspiciously, wondering how an outsider could possibly be of any help to them. She began the meeting by using a technique called *brainstorming.* Sharon got the ball rolling by posing the following question: "What will a supermarket be like in 1996?" After a long pause (because nobody wanted to be first) the responses shown below started to emerge:

- Supermarkets in 1996 won't be any different than they are now.
- They will be larger.
- They will be fully automated, with the shopper having only to push buttons and pay.
- They will handle no cash, since purchases will be automatically deducted from the customer's bank account.
- They will be smaller and more specialized.
- They will be almost nonexistent, because consumers will shop by cable TV and have groceries delivered to their homes.
- We won't need supermarkets because people will use vitamins and food pills for nourishment.
- Stores will be life-style oriented—there will be convenience markets catering to the person on the go, back-to-nature stores that sell only fresh foods or pure ingredients with no preservatives, low-cal stores for people on diets, and low-sodium stores for people with salt restrictions.

Many other ideas emerged from this brainstorming session, and as a result the creative juices really began to flow.

As the number of new ideas began to taper off, Sharon broke in with the following question: "It is difficult for us to visualize the future, isn't it? You're right, we may not even have supermarkets in the future, but then again, we might. What are the attributes that make a supermarket what it is?" (Now Sharon was using the technique called *attribute listing.*) The attributes that the group members listed were

Prices	Hours of operation
Quality of meats	Product mix
Parking	Layout
Personnel	Services
Atmosphere	Location

After this list of attributes was generated, Ms. Riley asked the group how each attribute could be modified to make supermarkets better in the future. Most of the suggestions were in reference to product mix and layout.

The third technique, morphological-synthesis, was then introduced to the group. "We've got a list of attributes, now we need the specific values for those attributes," announced Sharon. "If, for example, I asked you what services were important to the grocery shopper, what would you reply?" The participants answered: check cashing, package pick-up, speedy check out, coupon and food stamp acceptance, and ease of locating merchandise.

"OK then, you need to come up with the specific values that are important to you for each of the attributes named earlier. Then combine these attributes and values in as many combinations as possible and maybe a new combination of attributes or values will emerge as being superior to all the others. It is sometimes helpful to list the attributes and values in a grid," replied Ms. Riley.

After a break, the group reassembled, thinking they had already come up with all possible new ideas, but Sharon wasn't through with them yet. "Remember the list of store attributes we developed earlier?" she asked as she held up a long list, "Well, from it I have compiled a checklist of attributes that we will examine." "We're looking for sources of change and innovation," she said as she handed each of the group members a questionnaire like the one shown in Exhibit 9.6. A short discussion followed as each participant's response was read.

EXHIBIT 9.6
White Knight Checklist

Question: We want to make some improvements in our existing stores in the areas of convenience and atmosphere. What suggestions can you make for each item on the checklist?

Checklist	Convenience	Atmosphere
1. Aisles	_____	_____
2. Checkouts	_____	_____
3. Services	_____	_____
4. Lighting	_____	_____
5. Personnel	_____	_____
6. Layout	_____	_____
7. Decor	_____	_____
8. Parking	_____	_____

The synetic technique was introduced next, and the enthusiasm began to build. Sharon introduced three types of synetic techniques. The personal analogy is used to stimulate the thought process. Sharon began, "I am a White Knight Supermarket. How can I be better or more efficient?" Everyone laughed. "No, really," she replied, "How can I change? Put yourselves in my position. You are supermarkets, or better yet, let's divide into smaller parts. There are twelve of you; each will become one of these things and design yourself to be better. Here is the list: main entrance, meat counter, checkout counters, frozen foods cases, fresh fruit and vegetable display, canned foods area, specialty goods and foods section, and bakery. Now get to work and improve yourselves." The person who "became" the checkout area showed originality by picturing a self-unloading shopping cart that plugged into a computer terminal register, which totaled the sale and automatically subtracted it from the customer's bank account. The groceries would then be packaged by a robot and sent out via conveyer belt to the customer's auto.

"What about the store personnel? Picture the ideal worker and tell me what this employee is like," Sharon asked, introducing the fantasy analogy. Someone answered, "The ideal worker would always be: on time, friendly, energetic, reliable, and willing to work without being paid. For that matter, why have people work at all? Why not train animals to do it, or machines. That's it, we should have robots to do all the labor-intensive jobs such as stocking, marking, checkout, and packing. That way people wouldn't have to do those things."

The third type of synetic method, free-association word meaning, proved to be a real eye opener. Sharon asked the group members to free associate to the word "Mexico." The group responded with the following list: warm and sunny, bright colors, cactus, good food, big hats, burros, mariachi bands, old, handicrafts, friendly people. The group members, however, were confused. "What does Mexico have to do with a supermarket?" someone asked. Ms. Riley replied, "You need to develop a new atmosphere for your foreign food department." Almost immediately the group members began to create. "I know," said one, "Let's build a foreign market area within our supermarket and put all the Mexican things together, all the Oriental, all the French, all the German, and build little stalls for each and decorate them to look like the country."

"We could even sell the plants and notions that go with the particular atmosphere," added another.

"I've got it!" a third chimed in, "but it would take some doing. Rather than just stalls for each country, we could create complete 'atmospheres.' For example, a Mexican food section could play mariachi music, be painted bright colors, be decorated with cactus and big straw Mexican hats and have a warm, sunny dry climate. A German area might play polka music, feel cool, smell like german chocolate cake, and be surrounded by mountain peaks and window boxes full of geraniums."

"I understand," added another. "You're right, that would take a lot of work, but it's worth looking into. Can you imagine how much more exciting grocery shopping could become?"

The synetic technique was so successful at generating new ideas that the group did not want to quit. The group members were excited with the results of their meeting, but more importantly they realized that the skills they had learned could be used in all their problem-solving situations.

As the final step in the process, Ms. Riley had each participant write a scenario of the White Knight Supermarket of the future based on the ideas that had been generated during their meeting, and send it to her. When all are received, the group will be called together once again to read and discuss their scenarios. The White Knight executives will then strategically plan the future of their company.

The White Knight example has been presented as a detailed example of the various methods of creative thinking and how they can be applied. It does not mean that in order to solve problems and plan future strategies all these techniques should be used, or that they should be used in the manner described here. It would be up to retail managers to decide which technique to use and how to use it.

Core and Contingency Strategies In the strategy generation stage, a mainstream strategy should be developed, which will become the **core strategy**. This core strategy should blend well with the configuration of external forces that management expects to be most likely. This naturally involves making assumptions about future environments, a necessary process, not only for the development of the core strategy, but also for the selection of contingency strategies. A **contingency strategy** is one that the firm has readily on hand in case the most likely configuration of environmental factors does not occur.

Each contingency strategy is designed for an alternative set of environmental factors. Contingency strategies are important since the most likely set of environmental events is difficult to predict. If expectations of the environment do not materialize, then contingency strategies can be quickly substituted and implemented. Thus, the retailer avoids future shock if an alternative scenario occurs.

Consider a general merchandise retailer who has carefully assessed the environment and concludes that the most important elements in the environment that could affect business are population and consumer income trends. Population is expected to level off over the next ten years and real income will increase. As a result, a core strategy referred to as incremental positioning has been developed. This is shown in Exhibit 9.7. This strategy consists of maintaining present market position in terms of geographical areas and income groups served, but incrementally positioning the firm in the marketplace to attract people with higher incomes and from a larger geographical area.

EXHIBIT 9.7
Hypothetical Core and Contingency Strategies

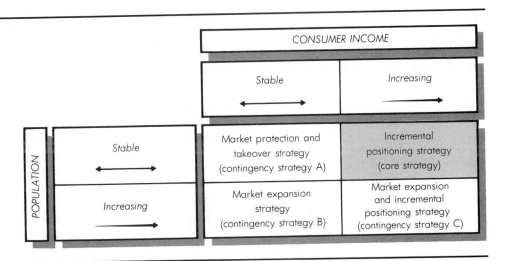

		CONSUMER INCOME	
		Stable ↔	Increasing →
POPULATION	Stable ↔	Market protection and takeover strategy (contingency strategy A)	Incremental positioning strategy (core strategy)
	Increasing →	Market expansion strategy (contingency strategy B)	Market expansion and incremental positioning strategy (contingency strategy C)

Alternatively, the company has developed three contingency strategies, as follows (see Exhibit 9.7):

1. Contingency strategy A is to be implemented if population remains stable as expected but income fails to rise as anticipated. In such a scenario, one could expect fierce competition, since markets would not be growing. The firm would adopt a market protection and takeover strategy, consisting of defending present market position while preying on and finally taking over weaker competitors that cannot weather the increased pressures.

2. Contingency strategy B is to be implemented if population increases as expected, but income remains stable. This scenario would call for a market expansion strategy consisting of opening additional outlets to serve an increasing population.

3. Contingency strategy C is to be implemented if income increases as expected but unexpectedly population also increases. Under such a favorable scenario the retailer would pursue a market expansion and incremental positioning strategy. The company would open new outlets to serve an increasing population and incrementally position its stores to appeal to a slightly higher income group while still being careful not to lose their core market.

As a result of the alternative futures that this hypothetical general merchandise retailer has identified, it should be able to change quickly from its core strategy to a contingency strategy if the need arises. It should not need to waste time thinking about the consequences of operating in an unanticipated environment. In today's turbulent environment, contingency strategies cannot be overemphasized. In developing these contingency strategies, the retailer should be sure to allow himself flexibility at all points and not just at the beginning. He should have contingency strategies that spin off the core at various points, so that once he has begun implementing the core strategy and finds the environment changed, he needn't go back to the beginning to start implementing a contingency strategy. Visualize it as a road with many forks in it at different points—the principle is to maintain flexibility along the road, not just at the beginning.

The Role of Market Segmentation Whatever strategy the retailer develops, it will need to decide which group of consumers to focus its efforts on. Because all consumers are not homogeneous in their wants and preferences, the retailer needs to focus its efforts, thereby using its resources more efficiently and better achieving its financial objectives. The president of Federated Department Stores has stated, "Customers don't fall into just a few broad groups. Markets are becoming increasingly fragmented as more people search for their own identity and answers. These attitudes are resulting in great diversity of desires, demands, lifestyles, and values."[10] And Eleanor May, a leading retail academician, says, "A long-established goal of being 'all things to all people' is not possible in today's consumer market. A store must decide which segments of the market

10. Presentation to the New York Society of Security Analysts, November 21, 1974, p. 6.

it is serving, or wants to serve, and then attempt to match the store to the need of these consumers."[11] The retail manager must develop an effective market segmentation strategy that will complement the retailer's overall retail strategy.

Market segmentation is the process of breaking or dividing a heterogeneous group of consumers into more homogeneous smaller groups. The smaller groups will be quite different from one another but members within any given group will be quite similar. Ideally, the members of the different market segments respond differently to a retailer's merchandise and service offering. In essence, this argues that their demand elasticities for different retail decision variables will be different. For example, the retailer might find the respective segments varying in how responsive they are to lower prices, increased advertising, and higher levels of customer services.

Demographic Segmentation Retailers can segment their market by using **demographic** variables, which describe the population characteristics of the market. Common demographic variables used to segment retail markets are age, ethnic group, income, education, sex, geography, family life cycle, and social class.

Age can be a good variable to segment many retail markets. For instance, most records are purchased by people between twelve and twenty-four. Stereo retailers receive a disproportionate amount of their business from people eighteen to thirty-four years of age. Home improvement centers often cater to those in the thirty- to fifty-year-old bracket.

Ethnic group is another possible segmentation variable. Many grocery stores cater to local ethnic groups and design merchandise assortments to cater to the ethnic dishes these groups frequently prepare. Occasionally clothing stores will focus their efforts on certain ethnic groups. For example, in El Paso and Tucson, there are clothing stores that appeal solely to Mexican-Americans.

Income can often be used as a segmentation variable. Exclusive restaurants often cater to the high-income household. Every large city seems to have an exclusive department store that appeals to upper-income households, as Memphis has Goldsmith's:

> Goldsmith's, and Goldsmith's alone in Memphis, caters to middle, upper-middle, and upper-income brackets on a broad and aggressive scale—especially the latter two groups. Goldsmith's competition for these income groups, two of which are hardly fazed by either recession or inflation, is virtually nonexistent among Memphis mass retailers. Sears, for example, which vies for many of the same customers as Goldsmith's, was hurt more by the recession and inflation because its middle and lower-income customers were feeling the pinch. Additionally, Sears in Memphis has had to cope with K-mart.[12]

Education level occasionally can be used to partition the retailer's market. Consumption of most products or retail services is not a function of educational

11. Eleanor G. May, "Practical Applications of Recent Retail Image Research," *Journal of Retailing* 50(Winter 1974–75): 19.

12. "Goldsmith's Tying a Ribbon on Oak Court Showpiece," *Memphis Commercial Appeal*, September 12, 1976, p. 5.

attainment, but there are notable exceptions. For example, book stores generally cater to more highly educated individuals.

Sex, when used to segment a retailer's market, can be approached from two perspectives. First, one can base merchandise appeal on one sex. This would be applicable to bridal stores, for example. Second, one could segment on the basis of whether the wife or husband makes the most purchase decisions. Thus, a menswear store might try to appeal to females if it thought a significant group of wives made clothing decisions for their husbands.

Geography can also be approached from two perspectives. First, the retailer must decide which area of the country to focus efforts on. Major geographic areas include Pacific, Mountain, West North Central, West South Central, East North Central, East South Central, South Atlantic, Middle Atlantic, New England. Second, the retailer must decide where to concentrate its efforts within an area. Options include the central business district, the central city (non-CBD), and the suburbs. All retailers must explicitly or implicitly focus on some geographic segment. Everytime a store is located, the retailer is making a decision to cater to a geographic market. Since the location decision is so crucial in retail planning and management, we will devote Chapter 12 exclusively to it.

Family life cycle refers to the changes in family composition over time that substantially alter family needs, decision making, and market behavior. The six stages of the family life cycle, developed by William Wells and G. Gubar, follow (note that three stages have two subphases):[13]

1. The bachelor stage; young, single people
2. Newly married couples; young, no children
3. The full nest I; young married couples with dependent children
   a. Youngest child under six
   b. Youngest child six or over
4. The full nest II; older, married couples with dependent children
5. The empty nest; older, married couples with no children living with them
   a. Head in labor force
   b. Head retired
6. The solitary survivor; older, single people
   a. In labor force
   b. Retired

The retailer will find that households in each of the preceding six stages exhibit different wants and preferences. Households in the bachelor stage are heavy buyers of basic household furnishings; those in the empty nest stage tend to purchase more tasteful furniture and nonnecessary appliances. Obviously therefore, furniture retailers would find that family life cycle would be a useful segmentation variable.

Social class refers to relatively permanent and homogeneous divisions in a society in which individuals or families share similar values, lifestyles, inter-

13. Reprinted with permission from William D. Wells and G. Gubar, "The Life Cycle Concept in Marketing Research," *Journal of Marketing Research* 3(November 1966): 355, published by the American Marketing Association.

Retailers can achieve success by skillfully focusing on one of the stages of the family life cycle. (Photo courtesy of Safeway Stores, Inc.)

ests, and behavior. In the social structure of the United States, six social classes (based on income, wealth, education, and occupational prestige) are typically identified: upper-upper, lower-upper, upper-middle, lower-middle, upper-lower, and lower-lower. Retailers can direct their overall retail strategy to a particular social class. For instance, K-mart and other discount department stores tend to target efforts on the lower-middle and upper-lower social classes. Stores such as Bergdorf Goodman in New York and Nieman Marcus in Dallas focus on the lower-upper and upper-middle classes.

Behavioral Segmentation   Retail managers can also use behavioral variables to segment the market. The two most popular are consumer lifestyles and the benefits consumers seek.

Lifestyles refer to how consumers live and spend their time and money. One can talk of consumers in terms of labels that capture their major orientation toward life—the "swinger," the "risk taker," the "career-oriented individual," the "back-to-nature enthusiast." To illustrate further, Christie Paksoy has provided a lifestyle profile of the retail-catalog shopper:[14]

> Retailers desiring to capture the segment of the catalog market which most frequently utilizes mail order catalogs would be wise to stress the ease and timesaving aspect of catalog purchasing in promotional campaigns. Furthermore, since frequent catalog shoppers also tend to be more innovative, these shoppers would be expected to perceive less risk associated with catalog buying. However, frequent catalog buyers would also be inclined to demand more variety and novelty in product lines offered by mail order retailers. On the other hand, since less frequent catalog buyers appear to be more store loyal and more likely to make credit purchases, retailers seeking to cultivate this market must develop marketing strategies unique to infrequent catalog shoppers.

14. Christie Paksoy, "Life Style and Psychographic Analysis of Catalog Shoppers," in Karen Hull (ed.), *Consumers in an Era of Shortages and Inflation* (Kansas City, Mo.: American Council on Consumer Interests, 1975), p. 70.

Retailers are increasingly developing strategies that appeal to well-defined life-style segments. For instance, Radio Shack appeals to the electronics enthusiast, Standard Brand Paint Stores to the active do-it-yourself home decorator, and The Limited to the upwardly mobile, career-oriented female.

Retailers can also segment their markets on the basis of the **benefits** consumers most want from retailers. Some consumers may attach importance to low prices; others, to friendly and courteous employees. Some may want broad merchandise assortments; still others may attach most importance to the quality of merchandise. Convenience food stores such as 7-11 and Circle K appeal to consumers who attach a high importance to time and place utility.

We have seen that the retailer has many alternative variables on which to segment its market. However, it is not restricted to using only one variable. For example, the furniture retailer could segment its market by stage in family-life cycle and by social class. Consequently, it might decide to focus its effort on the full nest II and empty nest stages of the life cycle and upper-middle and lower-upper social classes.

Effective Segmentation   Philip Kotler notes that, regardless of the variables used to segment the market, there are three requirements for effective segmentation:

1. **Measurability,** or the "degree to which the size and purchasing power of the resulting segments can be measured."
2. **Accessibility,** or the "degree to which the resulting segments can be effectively reached and served."
3. **Substantiality,** or the "degree to which the resulting segments are large and/or profitable enough to be worth considering for separate marketing attention."[15]

Some of these variables produce segments that are much easier to measure than others. Consider age versus lifestyle. With census data, the retailer can easily determine how many people within the trade area are in various age brackets. But if the retailer wanted to know how many people in its trade area pursued a "casual" lifestyle, no ready source of data would be available. There would not even be an agreed-on definition of the variable—"casual" lifestyle. Therefore, an attempt to segment on this variable would be more difficult than to segment according to age.

In the same vein, some segmentation variables produce segments that are easier to gain access to than others. For example, twelve to eighteen year olds can be reached by advertising on popular radio stations. But how does a retailer direct its advertising at upper-social class households? Do they tend to listen to or watch different TV programs, or read different parts of the local newspaper? Unless the retailer can readily obtain access to a market segment, then the segmentation strategy will not be totally effective.

Finally, the retailer needs to be concerned with the substantiality or size of the segment. Does it offer sufficient profit potential? A menswear retailer could

15. Kotler, *Marketing Management*, pp. 205–6.

decide to focus its retailing efforts on midgets, but the number of midgets in its trade area might not justify such a segmentation strategy.

CONTROL OF STRATEGIC FIT

Strategic planning by the retailer will be useless unless the retailer is committed to a systematic process, like the RIS discussed in Chapter 3, of controlling its strategic fit. If the retailer develops a plan that is in tune with the contemporary retail environment and implements that strategy, but then fails to monitor the retail environment, the strategy may, over time, become inappropriate. As the environment slowly changes, the retailer will occasionally need to alter its strategy so that it stays in tune with the environment. Consider, for example, McDonald's, which initially focused its strategy on providing low-cost, quick and tasty lunches for workers and low-cost dinners for families. Over time, more households had two working spouses and thus McDonald's expanded its strategy to appeal to working families that need a quick, low-cost, and nutritious breakfast.

KEY MISTAKES IN STRATEGIC PLANNING

Many retailers have failed at strategic planning because they focused on the trappings of strategic planning rather than its substance. This is the conclusion of Allan Pennington, vice president of Corporate Development at Dayton-Hudson Corporation, who has identified seven key mistakes that retail executives make in strategic planning:[16]

1. Thinking that strategic plans are an extension of financial plans. . . . Strategic plans and financial plans must be linked, but in the right sequence. Financial plans should follow the strategic plans and be merely the quantitative expression of the strategy.
2. Confusing strategy and objective. [What we want to accomplish is not the strategy. The statement that "our strategy is to operate on a 20 percent gross margin" is not a strategy, but an objective. The strategy is how to accomplish what we want to accomplish.]
3. Expecting consultants to plan. . . . Consultants can play a very important role. They can help define the process of planning, interpret the external environment, serve as a devil's advocate, and provide research and perspective. But they cannot assume the responsibility of the content of a company's strategy. This must fall upon the shoulders of those accountable for the execution of the plan—top management.
4. Reliance on staff experts. . . . "Staff experts" can't provide any better plans than inside consultants, and for the same reasons.
5. Reliance on quantitative tools. . . . Just as financial plans can obscure the quality of strategic plans, so too can formulas, models, and other mechanistic devices which take the focus off direction, commitment, and execution. These

16. Allan L. Pennington, "Do's and Don'ts of Retail Strategic Plans," *Marketing News*, March 7, 1980, p. 5. Reprinted with permission.

tools, if they are used at all, should be employed as an adjunct to an effective planning process, not as the core of one.

6. In the strategic planning process too many retailers focus too sharply on expansion and diversification and ignore their base business. [Refer to Exhibit 9.8 for an actual example of how a diversification strategy can fail.]

7. Taking too narrow a perspective. . . . Placing planning in too narrow a perspective results in strategic inconsistencies that are difficult or expensive to correct. A common example is the development of a rapid expansion program that is inconsistent with the financial structure of the company.

We believe the preceding mistakes identified by Pennington are the central causes of strategic failure in retailing.

SUMMARY

This chapter was devoted to a discussion of the strategic planning process in retailing. The three chapters to follow will concern administrative planning, and the remainder of chapters in this text (13 through 19) will focus on operations planning in retailing.

The strategic planning process consists of the retailer's matching its mission and objectives to external opportunities. From these opportunities strate-

---

EXHIBIT 9.8
The Failure of a Diversification Strategy

Diversification was a strategy that appealed to many retailers in the 1960s and 1970s. However, few retailers found the high profits in diversifying that they thought existed. One notable example was Genesco. In the 1950s Genesco had been a leading shoe manufacturer and retailer, but, not satisfied with their success, they began a fifteen-year period of massive diversification. By 1970 they had become the largest apparel company in the United States, with sales of $1.2 billion.

Unfortunately, profits began to tumble in the 1970s. Genesco developed a habit of acquiring apparel operations and letting them fail, by not retaining the entrepreneurs who built them. The net result was that their diversification spree had led to a $170 million loss in a five-year period during the mid 1970s.

To reverse the red ink that flowed from the diversification strategy, Genesco began to retreat to its traditional base—shoe retailing. By early 1980 they had already sold or closed fifty of the eighty companies they had acquired in their diversification spree and in so doing cut sales by $500 million. For example, Genesco closed 480 S. H. Kress & Company stores; closed twenty women and children's clothing manufacturing divisions; sold Bonwit Teller and Whitehouse & Hardy (a pair of specialty apparel chains); and closed six shoe manufacturing operations. After twenty years of being sidetracked, Genesco is finally realizing that shoe retailing is their hope for the future.

Source: Based on data from "Genesco: An Apparel Empire Returns to Its Retailing Base—Shoes," *Business Week,* June 23, 1980, pp. 90, 95, 99; corporate press releases; Genesco Company, *Annual Report* (1970 to 1980).

gies must be generated. Finally the strategies must be controlled to ensure that they stay in tune with external environments.

Futures research can help the retailer identify significant trends in the external environments. The most common types of futures research tools are going to authorities, getting conjectures on possible alternatives, and using mathematical models. Once the environments have been assessed for significant trends and opportunities, the retailer must generate possible strategies. Techniques that can be used to facilitate the generation of retail strategies include brainstorming, attribute listing, morphological synthesis, checklist, and synetics. Each was discussed through a single comprehensive example involving a hypothetical retailer—the White Knight Supermarkets, Inc.

The retailer must identify the strategy that it expects to be most in tune with the anticipated future environment and the retailer's mission and objectives. This strategy will be labeled the core strategy. But since the environment is turbulent and uncertain, the retailer must also develop contingency strategies. They will help the retailer avoid future shock if the environment does not unfold as planned.

Whatever retail strategy is pursued, the retailer must focus on well-defined consumer segments. For this reason, we discussed market segmentation as it applies in a retail setting. The retailer also needs to control its strategic fit by regularly monitoring the external environments and adjusting the strategy as the environment warrants. Finally, the retailer must be careful to avoid the major causes of strategic failure in retailing.

QUESTIONS

1. Does strategic planning become more or less important as uncertainty in the external environments increases?

2. The retailer could simplify matters in the strategic planning process if it stated only profit objectives. Agree or disagree and explain why.

3. In analyzing opportunities the retailer should develop a strategy for that opportunity which offers the highest expected return on investment. Agree or disagree and explain why.

4. Is strategic planning or day-to-day management of the store more important?

5. How many contingency strategies should a retailer develop?

6. How might the strategic planning process be influenced by the personalities of the executives involved?

7. To what extent should the retailer analyze the legal environment when developing strategic plans?

8. Strategic planning is an exercise in creative thinking versus analytical problem solving. Agree or disagree and explain why.

9. Identify and briefly discuss the steps in the strategic planning process.

10. Why are quantitative objectives preferable to qualitative objectives? Should a retailer have no qualitative objectives?

PROBLEMS AND EXERCISES

1. Construct a scenario for department store retailing in the year 2000.

2. Visit several women's or men's apparel stores in your community and attempt to assess the demographic segment they appeal to.

3. Assume that you plan to open a sporting goods store in your community. Develop a strategic plan for your proposed store.

4. Gather together a group of four to six class members and use several of the techniques for creative thinking discussed in this chapter to develop a new approach or a strategy for a retail florist.

5. Do a literature search on either Sears, Penney's, or K-mart for the last five to seven years. Analyze and assess the extent to which their strategy has changed over this time.

SUGGESTED READINGS

Blackwell, Roger D. "Successful Retailers of '80s Will Cater to Specific Lifestyle Segments." *Marketing News* (March 7, 1980): 3.

Davidson, William R. "To Understand Retailing in 1980s, Analyze Firms' Responses to Trends." *Marketing News* (March 7, 1980): 1, 12, 13.

Lusch, Robert F. and Gene R. Laczniak. "Futures Research for Managers." *Business* 29(January–February 1979): 41–49.

Mayer, Morris L., Joseph Barry Mason, and Morris Gee. "A Reconceptualization of Store Classification as Related to Retail Strategy Formulation." *Journal of Retailing* 47(Fall 1971): 27–36, 96.

Pessemier, Edgar A. "Store Image and Positioning." *Journal of Retailing* 56(Spring 1980): 94–106.

Soldner, Helmut. "Conceptual Models for Retail Strategy Formulation." *Journal of Retailing* 52(Fall 1976): 47–56, 96.

Case

J. Robert Foster
University of Texas at El Paso

Chartwell Liquor Imports, Ltd.

CHARTWELL LIQUOR IMPORTS, LTD. is a major importer of Canadian whiskies in the United States. It buys Canadian whiskies in bulk and bottles them in the United States under the Royal Oak label, in contrast to other importers, which have the liquor bottled in Canada. Bottling in the states allows Chartwell to market its brand at a much cheaper price than some of the other leading brands. Mr. Ev Mallory, the manager of distributor relations, has become increasingly concerned about what he perceives as a lack of promotional effort on the part of its wholesaler distributors in the United States and the indifference of local retail liquor store dealers to Chartwell's point of purchase material. These concerns have been magnified by the changing sales patterns in the liquor market.

BACKGROUND

Market Changes   Americans have moved away from their traditional pattern of hard purposeful drinking to a style reflecting greater moderation and more varied drinking patterns. Per capita consumption of alcoholic beverages has stabilized in recent years after a steep rise during the 1960s. By 1978 consumption amounted to just under 0.7 gallons per person, or the equivalent of twelve fifths of 86 proof spirits. In addition Americans consume twelve and one half fifths of wine and twelve and one half fifths of beer for every person fourteen years of age and older. While this seems like a lot, actually the United States ranks sixteenth in per capita consumption among twenty-seven other countries.

Note: Reprinted with permission of the author. This case was prepared as a basis for class discussion rather than to illustrate appropriate or inappropriate handling of retail situations.

Sales of domestic whiskies, the mainstay of the distilled spirits business, have fallen off dramatically in the past five years with a drop of almost 30 percent in blended whiskies and 16 percent in bourbons. Americans are drinking more wine, and products the industry calls *white goods,* vodka, rum, gin, and tequila. Imported whiskies have experienced a much slower sales increase than characteristic of the 1960s. Scotch whiskey sales have grown by only 8 percent since 1972. Canadian whiskies however, have grown by 30 percent, but the traditional leaders among the Canadian imports—Seagrams VO and Canadian Club—have lost ground to cheaper bottled-in-America brands. Canadian whiskies imported in bulk (and then bottled in the United States) have grown substantially from only about 2 million cases in 1966 to 11 million cases in 1976. This has been led by such brands as Brown Foreman's Canadian Mist, Heublein's Black Velvet, Seagram's Lord Calvert Canadian, and Chartwell's Royal Oak brand. The marketers of these bulk imports have been able to persuade the public that their brands are really just about as good as those bottled imports that sell for 20–30 percent more. Much of the overall growth in Canadian whiskies that has taken place has been at the expense of sagging American blended whiskies, whose customers appear to be abandoning them for the bulk imports, brands they perceive as being similar in character and price though possessing more prestige.

Channel of Distribution   The starting point in the channel of distribution for Canadian whiskey is the distillery, which performs the function of producing the liquor and aging it over a period of years in large charred wooden barrels that can only be used one time. Unlike other foreign distilleries, who then bottle the finished goods and send them to market, the makers of Royal Oak ship the finished good in bulk to the import selling agent, Chartwell Liquor Imports, who takes on the responsibility of bottling the product in the United States. As with other imported brands of Scotch and Canadian whiskies, there is only one selling agent representing the brand for the entire United States. After the product is bottled by Chartwell, it is then sold to regional wholesalers throughout the United States.

The wholesalers are a primary element in the channel of distribution for Royal Oak and other brands of distilled spirits. Wholesalers are characterized by the exclusive lines that they carry. Once a wholesaler has established a relationship with a particular distillery or selling agent, such as Chartwell, that supplier does not sell to any other wholesalers in that area. But a wholesaler can contact other distilleries to carry their lines if previous commitments have not been established. The wholesaler then makes sales calls on the retail liquor store, provides credit, uses its own trucks to provide delivery, and takes the risk of damaged bottles.

Historically, most distillers and import selling agents have put their promotional money and efforts into persuading distributors to order as much liquor as they could possibly handle. The distributors in turn had to be aggressive in selling to retailers. The success of many brands has been built as much by the efforts of enterprising wholesalers as it has been by the distillers' own efforts to reach consumers. Consequently, distillers spend about three times more on promotions to the trade than they do on consumer advertising. Most of the trade promotion has been in the form of old-fashioned salesmanship, with the personality of the local wholesaler's salesman determining the success of getting the product on the retailer's shelf. Price-discounting to the trade has also been another popular promotional device. The industry has been characterized by **loading-up,** or forcing retailers to carry slow moving brands in order to get an allotment of a best selling brand. These practices of trying to use salesmanship, price-discounting, and loading-up to obtain distribution have resulted from the fact that there are more brands on the market than can be effectively sold. Currently two thirds of the industry's total case sales are accounted for by sixty top brands, all of which sell some 600,000 or more cases a year. The other third of case sales is spread among a roster of several thousand brands, which may either be regionally popular or private label products. But many brands simply gather dust on cluttered shelves because their makers are reluctant to give up anything that contributes to total sales volume.

The changing nature of the liquor market—the decline in per capita consumption—has brought about some rather dramatic changes in the marketing of liquor. Major U.S. distillers have pruned many unprofitable brands in order to concentrate their efforts on profitable labels. The industry leader has discontinued some 15 brands in recent years, and one distiller has eliminated no fewer than 250 marginal or money losing brands, leaving it with a present product line of 50 brands. With the larger advertising budgets needed to promote the fewer brands, the industry has also begun to raise prices in pace with rising costs. Distillers have been traditionally concerned with their case sales. They refuse to risk market share by charging higher prices for fear that competitors would simply hold their prices and take business away. Nor could distillers bring themselves to abandon trade discounts as a means of increasing market share even though individual brands were not making money in the first place. The situation has begun to change as the industry's leading distillery has begun to raise prices an average of 5 percent in keeping with cost increases, and has doubled its spending on advertising in recent years.

Another dramatic change in the marketing of liquor is the changing relationship of distillers and wholesalers. Rather than regarding wholesalers merely as a pipeline for distribution of goods, distillers are beginning to look to them for marketing information, either through advisory councils made up of distributors or by greater use of market research to obtain information on market trends and local performance. Typically this research has examined the wholesaler's reputation for service, sales effort, and the management of promotions.

CURRENT SITUATION

In an effort to improve Chartwell's marketing activities, Ev Mallory commissioned a marketing research study in six adjoining southeastern cities to assess the perceptions of retailers carrying the Royal Oak brand toward their supplying wholesalers. Each of these retailers allocated their purchases of Canadian whiskey and other liquor products among three principal wholesale suppliers, each of whom represented a principal importer of Canadian whiskies. Each wholesaler stocked an assortment of the principal importer's line in a variety of different package sizes. Since the retailers operated establishments with limited selling space, they exercised considerable discretion in selecting the brands and package sizes they purchased from each of the three wholesale suppliers. Consequently, the retailer became a focal point in the channel for efforts by both wholesalers and distillers seeking to secure availability for their brands. This placed the retailer in an excellent position to judge the channel performance of these suppliers.

The Study

Twenty dimensions of wholesaler service were singled out as indicators relative to the retail customer. These dimensions centered on management knowledge and integrity, pricing and discounts, service responsiveness, delivery, and sales representation. Each retailer interviewed was asked to rate whether the twenty items always, usually, infrequently, or rarely applied to each wholesaler. If the retailer's experience did not allow him to judge a particular item attribute, he was given the option to indicate a don't know answer.

Retailers were also asked to rate nine items applying to the point-of-purchase display efforts of the three importers who each supplied only one of the wholesalers. Point-of-purchase display effort was selected as the major dimension of each importer's attempt to secure influence in this particular retail market. Basically, the only face-to-face contact with an importer that a retailer ever experienced was when the importer's representatives called to provide displays, display assistance, and merchandising suggestions. While product reputation and national advertising were recognized as important dimensions of the importer's efforts at influence, these attributes are reinforced at the retail level by point-of-purchase displays designed to stimulate immediate buying action from the retailer's customers. The dimension of point-of-purchase display effort was divided between the adequacy of the display material and the performance of the importer's display representative in the local market.

The sample for the study was selected from a list of 249 retailers located in six medium-sized southeastern cities. The largest percentage of sales in this trading area was located in these six cities. Suitable interviews for analysis were obtained for 157 retail stores out of a total number of 177 selected for inclusion in the sample. The response rate for the rating of the manufacturer's display services was appreciably lower, since a number of the smaller stores made little use of display materials because of lack of space.

The Findings

The results of this study were analyzed by using a straight scaling and ranking procedure to identify how similarly retailers rated each wholesaler and its respective supplier. In order to obtain a comparison among the three competing wholesale firms, the following scaling technique was employed to compile the individual ratings of the 157 retailers interviewed. Each response category was assigned a numerical value between 1 and 4. "Rarely" was assigned a scale value of 1; "infrequently," 2; "usually," 3; and "always," 4. Because the "don't know" responses were small, they were proportionally allocated to the other four categories. In the case of one item, dealing with whether or not the wholesaler's salesman pushed weak brands too hard, the scale values were reversed to keep the higher scale values as being most favorable. An overall mean score was obtained for each of the three wholesalers by multiplying the number of responses for each response category by the numerical scale value, summing the scores, and dividing the sum by the total number of responses. The higher the scale score received, the more favorable was the assessment of that aspect of the wholesaler's service by all of the retailers.

Exhibit 1 presents the mean values for each item for the three wholesalers. The data clearly indicate the high overall favorability of Chartwell's wholesaler over the other two.

EXHIBIT 1 **Ratings of Wholesalers**	WHOLESALER FUNCTION	CHARTWELL'S WHOLESALER	COMPETITOR A's WHOLESALER	COMPETITOR B's WHOLESALER
	Salesman is friendly and a pleasure to do business with.	3.80	3.79	3.73
	Salesman shows up when he's supposed to.	3.79	3.72	3.71
	Handles special orders promptly.	3.75	3.62	3.62
	Consistently meets delivery promises.	3.73	3.61	3.66
	Delivery is made at right time of day or week.	3.67	3.56	3.66
	Delivery driver unloads and stacks cases in right spot.	3.66	3.68	3.71
	Handles complaints satisfactorily.	3.65	3.57	3.49
	Keeps their word to the retailer.	3.64	3.68	3.60
	Billing system is accurate.	3.64	3.55	3.57
	Gives good service on returns and breakages.	3.64	3.48	3.37
	Driver parks truck so as not to block customers.	3.59	3.55	3.60
	Knows what's going on in the business.	3.56	3.56	3.50
	Salesman follows up on the retailer's request.	3.56	3.50	3.51
	Keeps retailer informed about discounts.	3.51	3.52	3.37
	Keeps retailer from being out-of-stock.	3.50	3.49	3.48
	Offers special deals at the right time of the year.	3.43	3.39	3.34
	Gives good discounts when retailer buys several cases.	3.38	3.49	3.39
	Salesman provides good ideas and advice about what will sell.	3.29	3.29	3.19
	Treats all retailers equally.	3.22	3.04	2.96
	Salesman pushes weak brands too hard.	3.14	3.10	3.01

EXHIBIT 2
Ratings of Importers Display Service

IMPORTERS' SERVICES	CHARTWELL	COMPETITOR A	COMPETITOR B
Display man is a pleasure to deal with.	2.71	2.74	2.81
Displays are colorful with sales appeal.	2.66	2.69	2.80
Display man makes good use of time in store.	2.67	2.71	2.76
Displays are available at right time of year.	2.60	2.64	2.75
Display man knows what's going on in business.	2.60	2.62	2.69
Ample supply of display materials available.	2.59	2.62	2.67
Display man calls when he's supposed to.	2.44	2.46	2.56
Displays are practical to use in store.	2.43	2.49	2.55
Displays are appropriate in size.	2.40	2.47	2.47

The same scaling technique was used in comparing the display service provided by importers. Here, however, responses were assigned numerical values ranging from 3 for "always" to 1 for "rarely," since only three response categories were obtained.

The higher the mean score, the more important or favorable was that aspect of the importer's service as perceived by the retailers. Exhibit 2 presents the average scale scores for each of the importers identified as being the supplier of a particular wholesaler.

DISCUSSION QUESTIONS

1. Evaluate the effect that changes in the market for liquor and changes in industry marketing practices are likely to have on retail package stores.

2. What conclusions can you draw from Chartwell's research study of retailers' perceptions?

3. What areas of Chartwell's wholesaler service and sales promotion effort need improvement?

TG&Y (A)

IT IS not unusual for northern retailers to view southern retailers as slow-moving and relatively unaggressive competitors. This observation obviously does not apply to TG&Y. From 1970 to 1976, TG&Y's compound annual growth in sales was 19.3 percent, which was surpassed only by S. S. Kresge's compound growth of 22.2 percent. By the end of 1976, TG&Y executives were optimistically looking forward to 1977—the year in which they expected annual dollar sales to surpass the $1 billion mark.

BACKGROUND

No one would deny that the company has made significant strides in its forty-year history. In the mid-1930s, R. E. Tomlinson, Less Gosselin, and R. A. Young pooled their resources and opened the first store under the TG&Y banner in Norman, Oklahoma. Norman was a small college town—home of the University of Oklahoma. No one at the time could have foreseen that by 1958 TG&Y would have close to 150 stores and sales of close to $30 million, or that by 1976 they would have 935 stores and sales approaching $1 billion.

The goal for the early 1980s was even more provocative. Simply stated, this goal was to reach $2 billion in sales. If successful, TG&Y would be the first retailer in the history of United States commerce to reach $2 billion in sales in less than fifty years. To accomplish this goal, the firm would need 350 to 400 additional stores and would need to achieve an average sales per store of $1.5 million.

Note: Reprinted with permission of the author. This case was prepared as a basis for class discussion rather than to illustrate appropriate or inappropriate handling of retail situations. Much of the information and data in this case is based on "TG&Y: Retailing's Next Billionaire: Harnessing the Sunbelt's New Energy," *Chain Store Age—General Merchandise Edition* (December 1976): 40–194.

TG&Y stores operate in the census of retailing classification labeled general merchandise retailing (SIC 53). When the company was initially founded, and throughout much of its history, it operated small variety stores. However, by the 1970s, this was no longer the case; the stores grew in size and merchandise mix. Almost all of the new outlets range in size from 30,000 square feet to more than 100,000 square feet. In this latter category, the company has only one store, in Oklahoma City—the corporate headquarters. Most of the larger stores have from 30,000 to 60,000 square feet. These stores are called "TG&Y Family Centers" and merchandise lines range from toys, fabrics, electrics, hardware, lawn and garden, wearing apparel, health and beauty aids, candy, automotive accessories, and plants to cards and stationery. The Family Center stores have generally been highly successful.

Since 1960 TG&Y has been a subsidiary of City Products Corporation. In the mid-1960s, Household Finance Corporation (HFC) acquired City Products Corporation and with it the City Products retail empire, one of the largest diversified retail organizations, with annual sales in excess of $2.5 billion. The empire consists of TG&Y, Ben Franklin Stores, White Stores, Coast-to-Coast Stores, Von's Supermarkets in Southern California, and several regional retail furniture chains.

In the past, TG&Y was able to finance its rapid growth with relative ease through its HFC and City Products connections. Recently, however, it has been largely able to finance its own growth. Nonetheless, HFC is still a valuable asset to TG&Y. HFC helps to finance accounts receivable, and City Products relies on HFC's staff of forty in Washington, D.C., to keep TG&Y alerted to activities of the Federal Trade Commission and recent legal developments in such areas as warranties and product safety.

Seven straight years of explosive growth characterized the time frame 1970–76. During this period, sales had nearly tripled, and for most of this period TG&Y opened at least one new store per week.

TG&Y operates a total of 935 stores in thirty states from coast to coast, but since 1970 most of the growth was derived from new store openings in sixteen sunbelt states. For example, of the over 9 million square feet added since 1970, nearly three fourths was in those sixteen states. In addition, expansion was in the direction of the large outlets called the Family Centers. These centers were typically between 30,000 and 60,000 square feet. Currently there are over 300 Family Centers that cover the sunbelt from coast to coast (the Carolinas and Florida to Southern California).

Expansion in the sunbelt from 1970 to 1976 was a wise strategic move. During this time, retail sales in the sunbelt grew 50 percent more rapidly than in the rest of the United States.

CURRENT SITUATION

Within the last few years, the management of TG&Y has shifted its store-location focus from the perimeters of markets over 100,000 in population (Phoenix, Amarillo, Little Rock, Tulsa, Albuquerque, etc.) to smaller markets of as little as 5,000 to 10,000 in population (secondary markets). Many of the prime secondary markets are county seat towns. With the location of a 30,000 to 60,000 square foot TG&Y Family Center, these towns frequently become major shopping districts—drawing from rural surrounding areas of up to forty miles away. Secondary markets are attractive for a variety of reasons: less competition, lower building and land costs, lower taxes, fewer zoning problems, and lower labor costs.

Two prototype stores located in secondary markets are stores number 1321 and 1345. Each is briefly profiled below:

- *Store 1321.* Located in Marianna, Florida (population 6,741), the county seat of Jackson County (population 34,434). The TG&Y Family Center in Marianna is 38,000 square feet. The store was opened in October 1972 and almost immediately was generating sales of $70 per square foot on an annual basis. Store number 1321 is one of the top performing Family Centers in the TG&Y organization.
- *Store 1345.* Located in Quincy, Florida, which is the county seat of Gadsden County (population 39,000). The per capita income of Quincy is a low $6,000. The TG&Y Family Center is 40,000 square feet. The store has not yet been opened a full year but it has been marked a success. First-day sales exceeded $40,000 and first-month sales were $250,000. The Family Center is quickly becoming the dominant retailer in the area with shoppers traveling from miles around to shop in Quincy, whereas previously they traveled to a larger town or city.

The Golden Southeast   According to the firm's real estate analysts, the hottest area for future retail growth is the Southeast. By the early 1980s they foresee that this area could comprise a third of company-wide sales. Over the next five years, TG&Y could obtain two thirds of its growth in the Southeast. The company estimates that there are 300 opportunity sites in Florida, 100 in Georgia, and 50 in South Carolina. Not all of these sites will be capable of profitably supporting a TG&Y Family Center, but the fact remains that the potential is overwhelming in the Southeast.

Pricing for Market Share   Increasingly, TG&Y Family Centers were beginning to compete head to head with discounters. Although TG&Y never thought of itself as a discounter, it couldn't ignore the reality of price competition in the marketplace. If it was confronted in the same market by a K-mart, Woolco, Wal-Mart, or similar discount chain, it simply had to be price competitive. Therefore, on a company-wide basis, in the mid 1970s, TG&Y adopted a strong price emphasis policy. In principle, TG&Y guaranteed the consumer that it would be competitive item for item with all competition.

A major part of the pricing strategy is an emphasis on fast markdowns. If an item or line does not move quickly, then the price is slashed. The company will not allow merchandise to sit on the floor for inordinate periods of time. An illustration can be obtained from store number 1321, one of the prototype secondary market stores previously profiled. In that store, fabrics are on a six-week cycle. In the first week a fabric could start at $2.97 per yard, and in each subsequent week it would be marked down. By the sixth week the price would be down to $1.27 per yard. It is hoped, of course, that all the fabric will be sold before the sixth-week price of $1.27 is reached. Part of the philosophy behind this markdown is the efficient use of space. If TG&Y can move merchandise 50 percent more quickly than competitiors move merchandise, then they can do the same annual sales volume in 40,000 square feet that competitors do in 60,000.

Consumer Research   Traditionally, TG&Y operated small variety stores, and in fact, in 1976 the majority of stores were still these smaller variety stores. As the company began to open Family Centers in markets where the firm traditionally had only variety stores, the possibility existed for the consumer to become confused by the chain's new image. But consumer research conducted by Grey-North involving 6,000 consumers in early 1976 in six major markets (Oklahoma City, Wichita, Kansas City, Shreveport, Mobile, and Jackson) was greatly reassuring. The typical shopper was willing to accept the new Family Center image. Some specific findings are presented in Exhibit 1.

EXHIBIT 1
Selected Results of Grey-North's Survey

The survey covered three phases and involved 6,000 consumers in early 1976 in the following markets: Oklahoma City, Wichita, Kansas City, Shreveport, Mobile, and Jackson. Among the results were the following:

- 93% of those surveyed had shopped in a TG&Y Family Center during preceding year.
- Over two thirds ranked TG&Y as the "best" or "next best" store to buy fabrics, yarns, and notions.
- 57 percent ranked TG&Y as the "best" or "next best" place to shop for housewares, toys, and games.
- Only one third think of TG&Y as the place to shop for adult apparel and shoes.
- One half of TG&Y shoppers are "heavily committed" to shopping at TG&Y.
- TG&Y ranked ahead of competitive discounters and other general merchandise chains in: convenient locations; quick-moving check-outs; friendly sales personnel, and broad merchandise selection.
- One quarter of the "heavily committed" TG&Y shoppers have annual family incomes in excess of $15,000.
- 56 percent of the "heavily committed" TG&Y shoppers have annual family incomes in excess of $10,000.
- Six of ten TG&Y shoppers have a family of five persons or more.

Source: Findings reported in "TG&Y: Retailing's Next Billoinaire— Shoppers Tell It Like It Is," © *Chain Store Age—General Merchandise Edition* (December 1976): 58–59. Lebhar-Friedman, Inc., 425 Park Ave. N.Y., NY 10022. Reprinted with permission.

DIMENSION	1970	1975	1980 (est.)
EXHIBIT 2 **TG&Y Planning Data** Number of Family Centers	136	342	600
Family Center sales as percentage of total TG&Y sales	39%	61%	80%
Family Center space (in million square feet)	8.6	15.4	21.0
Merchandise mix			
Hardlines	41%	36%	35%
Variety lines	29	25	20
Soft lines	30	39	45

Source: Adapted from *Chain Store Age—General Merchandise Edition* (December 1976): 42–43, 46.

The Future

J. M. Newgent, executive vice president, has stated "We don't plan to put new stores in any region on a quota basis. We go where the hottest opportunities are."[1] The firm also plans to concentrate on Family Centers and to give an added push on soft goods while selectively cutting back on hardlines and variety lines. Data in Exhibit 2 shed additional light on where the company may be in 1980.

DISCUSSION QUESTIONS

1. Evaluate TG&Y's growth strategy.

2. Why are big outlets in small towns necessary? Why not smaller outlets in small towns?

3. What would happen to TG&Y's plans if Household Finance Corporation decided to use TG&Y as a vehicle to generate cash?

4. What additional information does TG&Y need to better develop their growth strategy?

1. "TG&Y: Retailing's Next Billionaire," p. 56.

Case

James M. Kenderdine
University of Oklahoma

Jack J. Kasulis
University of Oklahoma

TG&Y (B)

WHILE TG&Y's GROWTH during the middle 1970s was at a rate above average, there were some disturbing clouds on the horizon. Several "new wave" discount chains were beginning to compete with the company. Norman, Oklahoma, was representative of the situation. In 1977 TG&Y had three stores in Norman—one large Family Center store (75,000+ square feet), one small Family Center store (40,000+ square feet), and one variety store (4,000+ square feet). In the early 1970s TG&Y dominated the general merchandise trade in this city. In fact, TG&Y was so successful that its two direct competitors—Arlans and Clarks—eventually closed their doors. However, two new competitors entered this market that seemed to have the potential to interfere with the company's plans for the 1980s, not only in Norman but elsewhere. These were Wal-Mart and Target.

BACKGROUND

Wal-Mart was a regional discount chain which had originated in Arkansas in 1962, and by 1977 it had grown to over 400 stores in the ten states surrounding Arkansas. Originally Wal-Mart had focused on secondary market locations for its stores—preferring to locate in small county seat towns where the company would be the largest nonfood retailer in the market. By 1977 the company had begun to invade the suburbs of the large metropolitan markets in this same region. In the fall of 1977 Wal-Mart announced plans to open an 80,000 square foot discount store in Norman. The location of this store would be about twenty

Note: Reprinted with permission of the authors. This case was prepared as a basis for class discussion rather than to illustrate appropriate or inappropriate handling of retail situations.

miles from TG&Y's corporate headquarters. Most important, it was located about one mile from Norman's large TG&Y Family Center and one half mile from the variety store.

Target Stores, a division of Dayton-Hudson Corporation, was a smaller discount chain (sixty-four stores in 1977) headquartered in Minnesota. It had begun head-to-head competition with TG&Y in the early 1970s when it had acquired the vacant Oklahoma stores of Arlan's. In the Oklahoma City area, for instance, Target had opened five discount department stores on the same day—overnight becoming a significant factor in that market. One of these stores was located in Norman directly across the street from the site of the proposed Wal-Mart store (which was to be opened in a vacant store that had been a Clarks discount department store.)

The competitive strategies of Target and Wal-Mart differed significantly: Target had positioned itself as a "fashion discount store"—bright graphics in the store, a "clean" merchandising policy that featured wide aisles, diverse store fixtures, and a minimum of in-store signs and banners. National brands were featured in hard goods, and appeared in the soft goods area. The soft goods emphasis was on fashion-oriented merchandise. The store's newspaper advertising was clean, made excellent use of color, and dramatized price as well as fashion.

The Wal-Mart store had an interior with smaller aisles. In many cases, these small aisles were actually extra wide aisles whose centers were occupied by a solid line of 4' × 4' sale tables—each with a large, brightly colored sign above it describing the values available. Wal-Mart stores made extensive use of in-store signs and banners and high displays (to the point that it was sometimes quite difficult to see one end of the store from the other end). Wal-Mart also featured national brands in all areas of the store—soft goods as well as hard goods. The soft goods carried by the stores were more price-oriented than those carried by Target. Like Target and TG&Y, advertising dollars were concentrated in the local newspaper. However, national brands were emphasized more, and the advertisements tended to mention a greater number of products per newspaper page than did those of Target stores.

TG&Y fell between the strategies of Target and Wal-Mart. Store interiors were less cluttered than those of Wal-Mart, but they made more extensive use of signs and banners than did Target's stores. Store fixturing was not as elaborate as that found in Target, and merchandise displays were not as high or as highly packed as those in Wal-Mart units. Except for hardware and sporting goods, TG&Y did not feature national brands to the extent that Wal-Mart did, nor did their soft goods have the fashion image held by Target. TG&Y's advertising was price-oriented—"your best buy is at TG&Y"—though the company pursued a competitive pricing strategy rather than one of aggressive price leadership. The company favored the use of coupons for sale items in their newspaper advertising.

Wal-Mart opened their Norman store in November 1977, about six weeks after they made the decision to enter the Norman market. (The short lead time was possible because of the vacant Clark's location.) The entrance of a vigorous, new competitor into the Norman market at the height of the Christmas selling season prompted responses from both Target and TG&Y. Both companies sent teams of "price checkers" to the nearest Wal-Mart Stores during the six-week period to gather prices on all Wal-Mart's merchandise. Both stores used this price information during the two weeks just before the Wal-Mart opening to reprice their Norman stores; on some small electric appliances, for example, prices at both Target and TG&Y dropped by as much as 20 percent in that two-week period, although the average price reduction was probably closer to 10 percent. Both stores also increased their newspaper advertising.

The crowds of shoppers at the Wal-Mart exceeded almost everyone's expectation: a major traffic jam developed at the intersection where both Target and Wal-Mart were located—with some shoppers parking in the Target lot and walking across the street to the new Wal-Mart. One Wal-Mart official at the opening said that his company expected to do "about $75 per square foot" the first full year of operation, and to have that figure up "in the neighborhood of $120 per square foot by the third year." According to Wal-Mart's research, he said, "nobody owns the market in Norman, and we intend to do just that."

CURRENT SITUATION

Recognizing that the entrance of Wal-Mart into the Norman market set the stage for a confrontation between Target, Wal-Mart, and TG&Y, a group of researchers at the University of Oklahoma (located in Norman) began a longitudinal study of the market impact of the store's opening in the weeks before the new Wal-Mart unit opened its doors. During November 1978 they did a second study designed to measure both the market shares (for selected products) and consumer images of the major retail competitors in the Norman market. Exhibits 1, 2, and 3 contain information from the research. Exhibit 1 contains information on store market share for selected product categories.

Exhibit 2 summarizes the results of a telephone survey of a random sample of consumers in Norman. The respondents were given a series of phrases describing each of the stores, and then asked to evaluate the store on each dimension. If the store was evaluated as substantially worse than other stores, the store was given a rating of zero. If it was substantially better than other stores it was given a rating of ten. Evaluations between the extremes were given values between zero and ten. Thus, when comparing two stores, the one with the higher average score is the one with the better evaluation.

The "Item importance" measure in Exhibit 2 shows how important that particular store characteristic was to the consumer. It was a score from 0 ("of no importance") to 10 ("of great importance"). Thus, the higher the importance score, the more important that characteristic was to the survey sample. The overall store evaluation was a separate rating, also based on a scale that ran from 0 to 10, with 10 being the highest possible rating a consumer could give a store. In both of these cases, the item with the higher score was perceived by the survey sample to be more important or to be better.

Exhibit 3 (page 272) contains information on the frequency of shopping at each of the listed stores. The exhibit summarizes data from the telephone survey and indicates the percentage of responses for each category given.

EXHIBIT 1   **Market Share by Store for Selected Product Categories**

PRODUCT CATEGORY	TARGET	TG&Y	WAL-MART	SEARS	PENNEY'S	OTHER[a]
Health and beauty	32%	6%	5%	NA	NA	57%
Boys' clothing	11	5	3	29%	14%	38
Girls' clothing	14	4	3	26	16	37
Women's clothing	4	1	2	12	10	71
Men's clothing	4	1	2	15	14	63
Fabrics and sewing	2	37	3	1	2	55
Stationery	13	24	2	1	2	59
Electronics	9	2	13	18	1	57
Hardware	10	11	4	20	1	54
Housewares	25	8	8	7	2	50
Domestics	12	5	2	19	18	44
Records	12	9	12	NA	NA	67
Photography	23	15	21	13	9	19
Toys	37	25	10	4	1	23
Sporting goods	25	14	4	7	2	48
Auto goods	24	7	3	10	1	55
Small appliances	27	10	5	16	1	41

[a]"Other" category includes all other stores.

EXHIBIT 2   **Store Profiles**

DESCRIPTIVE PHRASE	ITEM IMPORTANCE	WAL-MART	SEARS	PENNEY'S	TARGET	TG&Y
Low everyday prices	8.41	7.39	6.14	6.48	7.50	6.82
Shelves fully stocked	7.73	7.38	7.27	7.08	7.85	7.64
Fashionable clothing	7.67	4.54	6.68	6.61	5.22	4.86
Helpful employees	8.46	5.95	6.82	6.82	5.71	6.36
Variety and selection	8.43	7.00	6.92	6.50	7.58	7.35
Clean and attractive	8.55	6.61	7.97	7.00	7.41	7.11
Quality merchandise	9.18	6.19	7.76	7.39	6.81	6.78
Easy to shop	8.18	6.54	7.22	6.95	7.40	7.35
Good sale prices	8.69	7.71	7.05	6.89	7.80	7.26
Speedy checkout	8.32	6.38	6.79	7.09	5.78	6.56
Convenient location	7.58	7.29	6.87	6.94	7.23	7.78
Easy to return or exchange	8.02	6.95	8.05	7.65	7.69	7.26
Variety of national brands	7.36	6.72	5.88	5.86	7.26	7.22
Overall store evaluation	—	6.61	7.27	6.76	7.44	7.19

SHOPPING FREQUENCY	TARGET	TG&Y	WAL-MART	SEARS	PENNEY'S
2–3 times a week	9.1%	12.4%	4.3%	2.7%	2.4%
Once a week	23.3	29.6	11.9	9.4	5.9
2–3 times a month	30.3	24.7	13.5	22.0	14.5
Once a month	19.0	18.5	14.8	23.1	19.4
Less than once a month	12.6	10.2	15.9	26.6	27.4
Shopped once	2.7	1.1	11.9	4.6	7.5
Never shopped	2.9	3.5	27.8	11.6	22.8

EXHIBIT 3 Shopping Frequency by Store

DISCUSSION QUESTIONS

1. What competitive position does TG&Y have in the Norman market?

2. What are the competitive strengths and weaknesses of TG&Y?

3. How would you evaluate the success of the competitive strategy of TG&Y?

4. If you were TG&Y management, what would you do now?

Case

David Karp
Loyola Law School (Los Angeles)

Von's Grocery Company

FOOD RETAILING in the United States is characterized by extremely large stores that offer a wide variety of both food and nonfood products. Although true today, this has not always been the case. Prior to the depression of the 1930s the industry was dominated by a great many small stores, each serving a small trading area. Two factors combined to create this situation. In the first place, there was not enough business in these small areas to support two or more stores. Secondly, most consumers walked to the local store almost daily. Thus, the trading area for a store was determined by the radius within which a customer could walk to the store and return home carrying a bag of groceries. The limited number of customers patronizing any one store allowed an owner or manager to become very familiar with them. They were therefore able to safely offer credit, as well as other services like home delivery and extensive in-store service.

BACKGROUND

Change and Innovation   Along with the 1930s came technological changes that had a tremendous impact on the retail food industry. The first of these changes was the development and subsequent widespread use of the electric refrigerator. The precise temperature control allowed by the refrigerator made it possible to store perishables for a longer time than had been allowed by the unreliable icebox. A second development was the refinement, ready availability, and increasingly

Note: Reprinted with permission of the author. This case is to be used as a basis for class discussion rather than as an illustration of appropriate or inappropriate handling of a retail situation. The author would like to thank Dr. Robert F. Lusch of the University of Oklahoma for his guidance and patience, and Terry L. Childers of the University of Wisconsin-Madison for his helpful comments.

common use of the automobile. Ownership of a car allowed more and more households to save traveling time as well as provide ease of transport for the greater quantity of groceries they could stock the new refrigerator with.

The depression of the thirties also had an effect on food retailing. Squeezed by the depression, consumers became extremely price conscious. This price sensitivity, combined with the mobility and low cost of travel made possible by the automobile, caused a greater willingness to travel farther to shop for low-priced groceries.

The depression also created a situation which begged for innovation in the retail food industry. The stagnant economy forced many businesses to retrench or close down. As a result many small factories and warehouses across the country were left vacant. Food suppliers were also hard hit, and began to offer large quantity discounts in an attempt to boost sales. For the first time, producers of packaged foods used advertising in order to stimulate their sales volume. Another significant development was the introduction of the consumer-sized package, which replaced the crates and barrels that had been used in the past.

Capitalizing on these conditions, entrepreneurs in New York, New Jersey, and California simultaneously developed a major innovation in food retailing, the supermarket. These early supermarkets took advantage of consumer's newfound mobility and desire to obtain low-priced groceries by locating farther away from the consumer than had been possible in the past. These stores were located in vacant factories and warehouses that were available at low rents. Several other factors also contributed to lowering consumer prices in these supermarkets. All of the new stores were stocked with items that had been purchased at rock-bottom prices from struggling distributors. Services were drastically reduced, most notably in-store service. This was made possible by advertising and the new consumer-sized packages. Presold on the items that they desired, shoppers merely had to walk up and down the store aisles to select the appropriate ones. As a result, fewer employees were needed and labor costs were cut to a minimum. The elimination of services like credit and home deliveries also contributed to a reduction in operating expenses. Consequently, supermarkets operated on the basis of low gross margins and high sales volume. The large volume of sales generated by a supermarket permitted margins to be cut from the traditional 30 percent (or higher) to about 10 percent. No neighborhood grocer could ever hope to offer goods at similar prices.[1]

Phenomenal Growth   Not surprisingly, supermarkets became extremely popular. This popularity triggered an explosive growth rate in the number of new supermarkets. It is interesting to note that this first growth spurt was fed not by large chain organizations, but by independents and new entrants in the field. Following World War II the revolution continued as an even more widespread changeover to supermarkets took place. Where the old neighborhood stores had been rather tiny affairs, the new supermarkets ranged from 5,000 to 10,000 square

---

1. Louis P. Bucklin, *Competition and Evolution in the Distributive Trades* (Englewood Cliffs, N.J.: Prentice-Hall, 1972), pp. 85–86.

feet. In 1952 one source estimated that supermarkets were responsible for 39 percent of all retail food sales. During the 1960s there was further growth in store size, with the new stores ranging from 15,000 to 20,000 square feet. The same source cited previously estimated that in the mid-sixties supermarket sales approached 70 percent of U.S. retail food sales.[2] This postwar explosion in the number of supermarkets was triggered by the increasing number of chains that converted to supermarket operations. By 1963, 57 percent of all supermarkets in the United States were chain stores.[3] Even as the number of supermarkets increased, the total number of food stores in the United States declined.[4] Evidence of this decline in the total number of stores can be seen in Exhibit 1.

EXHIBIT 1   **Store Population and Sales (1940–63)**

YEAR	NUMBER OF STORES			DOLLAR SALES (billions)		
	Independent	Chain[a]	Total	Independent	Chain[a]	Total
1940	405,000	41,350	446,350	$ 5,830	$ 3,180	$ 9,010
1945	365,000	33,400	398,400	10,000	5,350	15,350
1950	375,000	25,700	400,700	16,950	10,140	27,090
1955	324,000	18,800	342,800	25,155	14,260	39,415
1960	240,000	20,050	260,050	32,150	19,550	51,700
1963	210,000	21,000	231,000	34,075	24,125	58,200

[a]Through 1951, chains were considered to be firms operating four or more stores; after 1951, chains were those operating eleven or more stores.

Source: Adapted from the *Progressive Grocer 46th Annual Report of the Grocery Industry*, p. 11.

THE LOS ANGELES TRADING AREA

Following World War II, Los Angeles, California, and its fringes experienced a large increase in population. The combined populations of Los Angeles and Orange counties (which together comprise the Los Angeles trading area) rose by 2.5 million during the period 1953 to 1961. This expansion brought the areas total population to 6.8 million. As a result, Los Angeles became the nation's second largest city. Los Angeles experienced the same evolutionary trends in the food industry as did the rest of the country. While the number of supermarkets grew rapidly, the number of food stores of all types declined. The experience of the Safeway chain is illustrative of this phenomenon. The total number of Safeway stores in Los Angeles fell from 1,000 (small stores) in 1930 to 147 (supermarkets) in 1964.

2. Bucklin, *Competition and Evolution*, p. 87.
3. Bucklin, *Competition and Evolution*, p. 104.
4. Louis W. Stern and Adel I. El-Ansary, *Marketing Channels* (Englewood Cliffs, N.J.: Prentice-Hall, 1977), p. 41.

Von's Grocery Company   Von's traced its origins back to a small business started by the Von der Ahe family in 1932. By 1959 the firm had become the third largest grocery chain in Los Angeles, with sales of $85 million. In 1957 Von's posted a profit margin (net income divided by total sales) of 2.1 percent and a rate of return on assets (net profit divided by total assets) of 12.7 percent. By 1958 these figures had shifted to 2.3 percent and 10.8 percent. Von's distributed its merchandise to twenty-eight Von's stores through a corporate warehouse located in Los Angeles.

Shopping Bag Food Stores   In 1959 Shopping Bag was Los Angeles's fifth largest chain with sales totaling $79 million. Slightly older than Von's, Shopping Bag had opened as a single store in 1930. Figures for 1957 show that Shopping Bag experienced a profit margin of 1.6 percent, and a rate of return on assets of 6.6 percent. Unfortunately for Shopping Bag, 1958 saw these figures decline to 0.9 percent and 3.2 percent respectively. Shopping Bag's thirty-six stores were supplied through a central warehouse which, along with the corporation's headquarters, was located in El Monte, California. During the late 1950s Mr. Hayden, the company's president and major stockholder, realized that Shopping Bag was faced with a problem due to its lack of managerial talent, and the fact that there was no qualified replacement for him should he retire.

The Merger   On March 25, 1960, following negotiations between the two firms, Shopping Bag was merged into Von's Grocery Company. Upon this, Von's sold its Los Angeles warehouse and took over the Shopping Bag facilities in El Monte. The merger pushed Von's into the number two position in the area in both dollar sales and in number of stores operated, with 7.5 percent of all sales and 1.4 percent of the grocery stores in Los Angeles.

On March 25, 1960, the United States Department of Justice tried to prevent the merger by filing a complaint in District Court and asking for a temporary restraining order, which would prevent the merger from taking place until a decision could be reached on the case. On March 28 the latter request was denied. Later, on June 13, a Justice Department request for an injunction requiring Von's and Shopping Bag to operate as separate entities pending the outcome of the trial was denied by another district judge. Finally, on December 15, 1961, the Justice Department was frustrated again as one more district judge denied their motion for summary judgment. By motioning for a summary judgment, the Justice Department hoped that its case was so obvious that the judge would make his decision without going through the entire trial.

The Department of Justice suit claimed that the merger violated Section 7 of the Clayton Antitrust Act, which states:

> That no corporation engaged in commerce . . . shall acquire the whole or any part of another corporation engaged also in commerce, where in any line of commerce in any section of the country, the effect of such acquisition may be substantially to lessen competition or create a monopoly.[5]

---

5. *United States v. Von's Grocery Company*, 233 F. Supp. at 1479.

ISSUES

Von's and Shopping Bag stores were located in the Los Angeles metropolitan area, which was considered to be comprised of Los Angeles and Orange counties. Annual grocery sales for the 4,842 square mile area were approximately $2.5 billion, or roughly $368 per person. Total retail sales totaled about $9.1 billion.

Effect of the Merger Von's stores were located primarily in the southern and western portions of the region, while Shopping Bag stores were found mainly in the northern and eastern sections. In the few areas where the two firms competed directly there were also other competitors. Six other chains and many independents also operated stores that were available for customers to patronize if they chose. By virtue of the merger, Von's began to operate stores in areas where it had not competed in the past. In fact, only one fourth of the combined sales of the two firms represented sales in areas where Von's and Shopping Bag had competed directly. For the most part the merger resulted in an increase of the breadth of Von's operations rather than in intensifying its depth of coverage in areas already serviced by Von's stores. Therefore, the merger could be characterized as 25 percent market intensification, and 75 percent market extension.

Many products could possibly be considered in determining what would be the relevant line of commerce for the purposes of this case. Among the products considered were: groceries, meat, produce, bakery goods, dairy products, delicatessen products, frozen foods, fruits, vegetables, sundries, household supplies, and drugs.

During the trial, the District Court heard testimony from an expert witness (a marketing consultant) who had worked for Ralph's, Market Basket, and Food Giant, as well as several other of the area's leading grocery chains. The witness told the court that customers chose their primary grocery store on the basis of many attributes. Some of these characteristics were prices, store appearance, size, variety of brands, parking, location in a shopping center versus a free-standing store, store reputation, meat quality, produce quality, cleanliness, and efficient checkout service. His research also indicated that shoppers felt supermarkets usually offered what they desired and that the old-fashioned corner grocery store did not. The consultant also stated that the average consumer was willing to travel ten minutes (about four miles) to reach a store, as well as to pass other stores in order to shop at a preferred one. Research also showed that there were usually two to ten stores located within a convenient distance from the average shopper's home.

Competitive Environment In 1948, the four largest firms in the Los Angeles metropolitan area were responsible for 25.9 percent of the region's sales; the top eight totalled 33.7 percent; the top twelve, 38.8 percent; and the top twenty 43.8 percent. Ten years later, in 1958, these figures had shifted to 24.4 percent, 40.9 percent, 48.8 percent, and 56.9 percent respectively. Following the Von's–Shopping Bag merger, the market share picture changed once again. The top four firms totalled 28.8 percent; the top eight, 44 percent; and the top twelve, 50 percent of all grocery sales. Within this group of leading firms, Safeway, the leading chain, saw its market share drop from 14 percent in 1948 to 8 percent in 1958. The share of the top two firms combined also declined: from 21 to 14 percent. Between 1952 and 1958 the total market share of the third, fourth, and fifth largest chains also fell.

The dynamic nature of competition in the retail food business can be expressed in figures illustrating entry and exit of firms in the area. The composition of chains can be used to illustrate this fact. Seven of the top twenty chain-store firms in 1958 were not even in existence as chains ten years earlier. During the nine years between 1953 and 1962 the number of large chains (with ten or more stores) grew from 96 to 150.

Between 1953 and 1962 there were 269 different grocery chain organizations operating in Los Angeles at one time or another. Of these organizations, 208 were two- or three-store chains. Most of these small chains were outgrowths of successful single-store firms. Many of these successful small chains were owned and managed by former executives of the large chains. After gaining experience and expertise they would go into business for themselves, in competition with their former employers. In one case it only took four years for one such owner to build a chain of seven stores. During the same nine-year period, new chains appeared 173 times, while 119 chains either went out of business (66), were acquired (25), or reduced their scope of operations to a single store (28).

Merger activity among supermarket chains was common in the area, both before and after that of Von's and the Shopping Bag (see Exhibit 2 and Exhibit 3 on page 280). Between 1949 and 1958 nine of the top twenty chains acquired 126 stores from their competitors. Analysis of these mergers shows that of the 126 stores acquired, 40 percent (48 stores representing sales of $71 million) were acquired by Fox (number nine in 1958), Yor-Way (number 11), and McDaniels (number 20). All three of these firms later went bankrupt, possibly as the result of overexpansion, undercapitalization, or mismanagement. There was no activity involving chains and single-store firms between 1960 and 1963.

Single-store firms also competed with the chains for the consumer's food dollar. In 1950 there were 5,365 single-store firms in the area (including small grocers and supermarkets alike). This figure declined to 3,818 in 1961, and still further, to 3,590 in 1963. The only year for which data exist on entry and exit of single-store firms into or out of the area is 1960. During that year, 128 stores opened their doors for the first time and 132 firms went out of business.

Retail Cooperative Groups   All independent grocers were eligible for membership in a retail cooperative group. A retail cooperative is an organization created by retailers in order to help them to gain the benefit of purchasing items in large quantities at low prices. They were first formed during the 1930s as the independent's response to the appearance of chain stores. These cooperatives were operated democratically by the member retailers as a wholesale company serving the member stores.[6]

6. Stern and El-Ansary, *Marketing Channels*, p. 402.

	YEAR	ACQUIRING FIRM	ACQUIRED FIRM	NUMBER OF STORES
EXHIBIT 2 **Food Store Acquisitions (1954–61)**	1954	Kory's Markets	Carty Brothers	8
	1956	Fox Markets	Desert Fair	4
	1957	Food Giant	Panorama Markets	3
			Toluca Markets	2
		Mayfair	U-Tell-Em Markets	10
		Piper Mart	Bi-Right & Big Bear	3
	1958	Alpha Beta	Raisin Markets	13
		Food Giant	Clark Markets	10
		Fox Markets	Iowa Pork Shops	11
		Mayfair	Bob's Supermarket	7
		Pix	Patton's Markets	3
		Yor-Way	C. S. Smith	5
	1959	Lucky	Hiram's	6
		Pix	S & K Markets	2
			Shop Right Markets	3
	1960	Piggly Wiggly	Rankin's Markets	4
		Von's	Shopping Bag	37
	1961	Better Foods	Border's Markets	3
		Food Giant (and others)	McDaniel's Markets	16

Source: Adapted from *United States* v. *Von's Grocery Co.*, 86 S. Ct. at 1483.

At the time of the merger, three cooperatives were operating in the Los Angeles area: Certified Grocers of California, Ltd., Spartan Cooperative, and Orange Empire. These cooperatives were able to supply their members with a wide variety of grocery products and other items. For example, Certified distributed over 13,000 items, including dry groceries, frozen foods, delicatessen products, housewares, and appliances. Although neither Certified, Spartan, or Orange carried fresh meat, fresh produce, or some dairy products, the evidence demonstrated that independents could and did compete effectively with the chains in the purchase of these items. As a result of their membership in the cooperatives, many owners of small firms not only felt that they could compete for sales with large chains, but that a large chain might be at a disadvantage when competing with the smaller firms. The court heard testimony from several such owners. One said:

> I have often been asked if I could compete successfully against this sort of competition [a chain store next to his and two others within one mile]. My answer is and always has been that the question is not whether I can compete against them, but whether they can compete against me.[7]

Another owner said of the chains that:

7. *United States* v. *Von's Grocery Company*, 86 S. Ct. at 1494.

EXHIBIT 3
Food Store Acquisitions (1961–1964)

YEAR	ACQUIRING FIRM	ACQUIRED FIRM	NUMBER OF STORES	SALES (thousands)
1961	Acme Markets	Alpha Beta	45	$ 79,042
	The Boys Markets	Kory's	5	10,000
	Food Giant[a]	McDaniel's	9	21,500
	Mayfair	Yor-Way	1	1,500
		Alpha Beta	1	1,700
1962	Mayfair	Schaubs Market	1	1,800
		Fox Markets	1	2,200
	Ralph's	Imperial Supreme	1	916
1963	Food Fair	Fox Markets	22	44,419
	Kroger	Market Basket	53	110,860
	Mayfair	Bi-Rite	1	2,569
		Dale's	1	2,200
		Food Giant	1	1,700
1964	Albertson's	Greater All-American	14	30,308
	Mayfair	Gateway	4	8,000
		Patton's Markets	4	10,400
	Ralph's	Cracker Barrel	1	1,000
	Food Giant[a]	McDaniel's	7	18,350
	Total		172	$348,464

[a]Von's claimed that this acquisition didn't take place in 1961, but that McDaniel's seven stores were bought by Food Giant in 1964 (also shown in table).

Source: Adapted from *United States* v. *Von's Grocery Co.* 86 S. Ct. at 1484.

When they grow too large they are actually easier to compete with. . . . If I had a choice I would rather operate a store near a chain unit than another independent.[8]

A third owner stated:

Competition in the grocery business is on a store by store basis and any aggressive and able operator like myself can out-compete the store of any of the chains because of personalized service, better labor relations, and being in personal charge of the store and seeing that it is run properly.[9]

Future Competition   The court was also told of new competitors moving into the retail food business. Discount houses were beginning to offer groceries at this time, as were newer forms of retailers such as deli-liquor stores and drive-in dairies. Even though these trends had been detected, it was still early to make any prediction about their possible impact on the industry.

8. *U.S.* v. *Von's,* 86 S. Ct. at 1494.
9. *U.S.* v. *Von's,* 86 S. Ct. at 1494.

THE DECISION

The Justice Department had based its case on the decrease in the number of stores that had occurred even as the population of the Los Angeles area increased.[10] Von's argued that the merger did not violate Section 7 because the Los Angeles retail grocery business was competitive before the merger, after the merger, and may continue to be so in the future.[11] On September 14, 1964, the district court issued its decision on this case.

DISCUSSION QUESTIONS

1. In what line of commerce and section of the country are Von's and Shopping Bag operating in the eyes of the court? Do you think this is relevant in a marketing sense?

2. Did the big chains, like Safeway and Von's, have a detrimental effect on the prosperity of small independent grocers?

3. Did Von's gain monopoly power as a result of the merger? Is this an appropriate consideration in the light of the portion of Section 7 that is relevant to this case?

4. Place yourself in the position of the district court judge. How would you have ruled on this case? Why?

10. *U.S. v. Von's*, 233 F. Supp. at 981.
11. *U.S. v. Von's*, 86 S. Ct. at 1482.

III

ADMINISTRATIVE PLANNING AND MANAGEMENT

10

Overview *In this chapter we show that financial capital is needed to fuel a retailer's strategy. In this regard, we discuss both start-up capital and recurring capital needs. We will illustrate the need for good analytical decision making in the area of financial capital planning and management.*

Financial Planning and Management

ALL RETAIL ENTERPRISES need capital. Consider, for instance, that in 1979 Sears had $16.4 billion in financial capital invested; K-mart, $5.6 billion; Safeway, $3.1 billion; and Federated Department Stores, $3.3 billion. These are only a few examples, but they help illustrate the need for financial capital in retailing.

In a new venture, capital is needed to commence operations and to help carry the enterprise through several operating periods until a profitable level of sales is achieved. On the other hand, an established firm will need capital if it desires to grow. Most disquieting is the fact that as rates of inflation rise the amount of capital needed merely to maintain the existing level of sales rises dramatically.

Therefore, we see that financial capital is an important resource that must be planned and managed in order for the retailer's strategy to be implemented effectively. Without adequate financial capital, the best strategy is worth little.[1]

The specific form of the retailer's strategy will help determine the retailer's need for capital. If a department store's strategy is in part composed of a self-service policy, additional capital will need to be invested in fixtures and self-selection displays so that shoppers can easily select merchandise without sales assistance. Or, if a furniture retailer's strategy, in part, consists of free delivery and liberal credit, capital is needed for delivery equipment and financing accounts receivable. A menswear retailer whose strategy, in part, is to have a very broad and deep assortment of menswear naturally has a slower rate of inventory turnover and thus an increased need for capital to finance merchandise.

START-UP CAPITAL

Let us begin our discussion of capital planning and management by assuming that you are the entrepreneur of a new venture. You have developed a good strategy and now must acquire the capital needed to make the strategy a reality. The key components of start-up capital are inventory investment, accounts receivable investment, fixed assets, negative cash flow before break-even is achieved, and contingency funds.

Inventory Investment   The capital that will be needed for inventory will be a function of the retailer's planned annual sales volume and its rate of stockturn. For our present purposes we will define **stockturn** as annual sales divided by average inventory investment. Retail trade associations such as the Retail Floorcovering Institute and the National Retail Merchants Association provide industry averages for stockturn by size of store. For all lines of retail trade there are similar trade associations that make available to industry members such statistics.

Once the retailer acquires the industry average stockturn, that number

---

1. Poor use of financial capital will lead to poor performance indicators, which can be used as early warnings of retail failure. For example, see Subhash Sharma and Vijay Mahajan, "Early Warning Indicators of Business Failure," *Journal of Marketing* 44(Fall 1980): 80–89.

needs to be adjusted subjectively depending on whether a quick or slow turn is part of the retailer's strategy. The next step is to estimate total annual sales. This, as you might expect, is no easy task. The major determinants of sales will be the retailer's location, size of store, and prices established. In later chapters we will discuss these determinants in more detail. Finally, if you divide the expected annual sales by the rate of stockturn you will arrive at average inventory investment at its retail value. To arrive at inventory at cost you would need to multiply the average inventory at retail times the cost of goods sold as a percentage of sales.

In mathematical form, we have the following relationship:

$$I = \frac{S}{T} \cdot C$$

where:

I = required inventory investment (at cost)
S = expected annual dollar sales
C = cost of goods sold as a percent of sales
T = expected rate of annual stockturn

A careful study of this mathematical relationship will show that it can be quite useful in planning required inventory investments.

Let us look at an example. You have decided to start a floorcovering store and have developed strategy in a manner similar to that outlined in the first part of this text. The typical rate of stockturn for a floorcovering retailer is 9.1 times annually. Your strategy is to offer a wide selection of high-quality carpets at relatively high prices, and you therefore expect your stockturn to be 7.5 times. Given your location, size of store, and pricing, you expect to generate annual sales of $1.25 million. Simple computation will provide you with average inventory investment. Dividing the expected annual sales of $1.25 million by the expected stockturn of 7.5 times yields $166,667. This number, however, reflects retail value. If we assume that the cost of merchandise will be 65 percent of sales, then the average inventory investment at cost would be 0.65 × $166,667 or $108,334.

Accounts Receivable Investment   Accounts receivable are dollars that are owed to the retailer by its customers. This customer debt arises when the retailer sells to customers on credit instead of for cash. Most new retail enterprises do not have the capital to finance customer purchases, therefore, they sell for cash or find a way to sell on credit that doesn't require their capital (they accept bank credit cards). In Chapter 14, we will discuss the credit decision from a more detailed, day-to-day perspective. The concern at this point is how to determine how much capital the retailer will need to finance accounts receivable. The relative amount of investment in accounts receivable is a direct outgrowth of the strategic plan.

If the strategic plan can be successfully carried out without providing retailer-financed credit to customers, then the expected accounts receivable investment can be set at zero. For some lines of retail trade—gasoline service stations, restaurants, greeting card shops, and supermarkets—this may be reasonable. But in many other cases the retailer will find that some customer purchases will need to be financed. This is not unusual, for example, in jewelry stores, furniture and appliance stores, and high-fashion, high-priced apparel stores.

When customer purchases need to be financed, the two key questions are: What percentage of customer purchases needs to be financed? and How long will customers take to pay? The higher the percentage of customers requiring credit, the greater the investment in accounts receivable required. Similarly, as customers take longer to pay, more investment in accounts receivable will be required. Retail trade associations can provide industry norms on each of these variables.

A useful formula for determining the expected level of investment in accounts receivable is:

$$A = (S \cdot R \cdot P)$$

where:

A = expected investment in accounts receivable
S = expected annual dollar sales
R = percentage of sales made on credit
P = proportion of a year it takes a typical credit customer to pay its bill

In words, then, the expected investment in accounts receivable is found by multiplying expected annual sales, percentage of sales made on credit, and proportion of a year it takes a typical credit customer to pay its bill.

Let's continue the example of the floorcovering store that you are contemplating opening. Let us assume that expected annual sales are $1.25 million (as previously mentioned); that 45 percent of the customers are expected to purchase on credit; and that the typical customer's bill will be paid in one month. The capital required to finance accounts receivable will be: ($1,250,000) × (45%) × (1/12), or $46,875.

Fixed Assets

The capital needed for the building, land, fixtures, and equipment depends greatly on whether these resources are purchased outright or leased. Most new retailers will lease the building and land. However, they may need to make improvements for which they require capital. Perhaps the parking lot will need resurfacing or the storefront redesigning. Also, permanent fixtures may need to be added; new lighting, carpeting, or partitions may be necessary to have the store convey the appropriate image. These improvements are called **leasehold improvements** and become the permanent property of the lessor on expiration of the lease, although they were paid for by the lessee. In addition, there are nonpermanent (portable) fixtures and equipment such as cash registers, clothing racks, and mannequins, that require capital but can be taken by the lessee when the lease expires.

Capital deployed into fixed assets, whether by a direct capital investment or a lease, represents a commitment to a strategy that is not easily changed. Current-asset decisions regarding inventory and accounts receivable can be al-

Retailers need to invest in fixed assets, either building a new building or refitting an existing structure. (Photo courtesy of Circle K Corporation.)

tered and assets redeployed quite quickly, but fixed-asset decisions bind a retailer to a particular strategy well into the future.

The prices of various fixed assets are relatively well established in the market. Therefore, if the retailer can decide on the mix of fixed assets needed, it can derive a reasonably accurate estimate of what those resources will cost.

In our continuing floorcovering example, let us assume that you will lease the building and land. Certain leasehold improvements are necessary that will cost an estimated $23,000. In addition, fixtures and equipment are estimated to cost $27,000. Thus, the total investment in fixed assets is estimated at $50,000.

Expected Negative Cash Flow Seldom will a new retail venture be able to break even in less than three months. In fact, it is not unusual for it to take from six to twelve months to build the business to a profitable level. During this time, the enterprise will be experiencing **negative cash flow,** which in reality is an investment of capital to reach break-even. A significant part of this negative cash flow will be the cost of supporting the entrepreneur's cost of living. The entrepreneur will find it necessary to continue to make house payments and car payments, meet food expenses, and so on. These expenses cannot be covered by nonexistent profits, and therefore start-up capital must be used.

To estimate the expected cash flow, the executive should develop a proforma cash flow statement for each of the first twelve months. To start with, this statement should show all sources of **cash inflows,** typically consisting of cash sales plus collections from prior months' credit customers. Next, all cash outflows should be subtracted. Major **cash outflows** would include payments for merchandise; cash expenses such as rent, heat, and wages; and other cash payments such as taxes, dividend payments, and long-term debt payments. When cash outflows are subtracted from cash inflows, the result is cash flow for the month. And, when one month's cash flow is added to the prior months' cash flow, we arrive at **cumulative cash flow.**

With a new retail venture, the cumulative cash flow is likely to be negative for several months, if not longer. In Exhibit 10.1, we show a standard form used in retailing to compute cumulative cash flow.

In our continuing retail floorcovering example, let us assume that for the first four months of operation you have negative cash flows of $8,000, $5,000, $3,000, and $1,000. Mathematically, therefore, the cumulative negative cash flow that would need to be funded with start-up capital is $17,000.

Contingency Funds Mistakes or errors are a certainty when planning capital resources for a new retail venture. Sales may not materialize as planned; operating expenses may be higher than anticipated; the air conditioner or roof may need fixing.

EXHIBIT 10.1 **Cash Budget Worksheet**

MONTH	CASH INCOME (1)	MERCHANDISE PAYMENTS (2)	CASH EXPENSES (3)	OTHER CASH OUTLAYS (4)	CASH FLOW (1—2—3—4)	CUMULATIVE CASH FLOW
January						
February						
March						
April						
May						
June						
July						
August						
September						
October						
November						
December						

For these contingencies, the retailer needs to have a reserve of capital to draw on. Contingency funds of 15 to 20 percent of the total capital requirements are recommended. The lower the contingency funds, the greater the risk of insolvency if the business doesn't develop as expected or as quickly as expected. On the other hand, if contingency funds are too high then the retailer may have too much capital sitting idle.

Let us once again return to the floorcovering example. The combined capital requirements for inventory, accounts receivable, fixed assets, and the expected operating loss are $222,209. If we take 15 percent of this amount for contingency funds, we arrive at $33,331 as the reserve for contingencies.

SOURCES OF START-UP CAPITAL

As you have seen in our retail floorcovering example, the capital needed to start a relatively small retail venture can be significant. Let us now see how you might acquire this start-up capital.

Equity Capital

In any start-up retail enterprise equity capital must be a significant source. **Equity capital** is that which the owner of the firm contributes. In point of fact, it will be almost impossible for a retail enterprise to get started if the entrepreneur is not willing to contribute some capital. If the entrepreneur has a partner, then additional capital can be obtained from the partner.

When the retail enterprise is organized as a corporation, it is possible to sell stock in the company to raise equity capital. This, of course, expands the number of owners of the firm and dilutes the control the entrepreneur can have over the direction of the enterprise. The president reports to the board of directors, who represent the owners; the president works for the owners.

In most new retail ventures, 35 to 50 percent of the capital should be equity capital. If the equity capital is less than 35 percent, the entrepreneur is being placed in a very risky position. Any significant error in overestimating the demand potential or underestimating expenses could quickly create losses that could erode the limited amount of equity capital and eventually force the firm into bankruptcy.

Debt Capital

The typical sources of debt capital are supplier financing, bond financing, bank and financial institution financing, and the government through the Small Business Administration.

Supplier Financing Merchandise suppliers typically sell to retailers on credit. It is not unusual for retailers to get from thirty to fifty days to pay for merchandise. These terms are of course more difficult for the beginning retailer to obtain—but nonetheless, some supplier financing is a good possibility. The use of supplier capital for financing inventory investments can be a significant help. For example, if the retailer plans to turn inventory six times per year (or once every sixty days) and if supplier terms are thirty days net, then one half of the retailer's investment in inventory can be financed by suppliers.

Bonds   A second source of start-up capital is the sale of company or corporate bonds. **Bonds** are typically sold in denominations of $1000 and have maturities that usually range from five to thirty years. They often pay a fixed interest rate per year based on the face value of the bond. Thus, a 9¼ percent, $1,000 face value bond would pay $92.50 per year in interest. No principal is usually paid on the bond until it matures, at which point the retailer would pay the face value of the bond to the bondholders. Bondholders must be paid the interest due to them on a regular basis and the principal when it becomes due. They have priority over stockholders in receiving any payment due to them. If the retailer is unable to make these payments, the bondholders may force it into bankruptcy.

Banks and Financial Institutions   Banks and financial institutions can be another source of financial capital. Banks can provide loans that help finance inventories. They also lend money to purchase land, buildings, and equipment and in turn frequently take a lien or mortgage on the property.

Insurance firms also act as financial institutions when they help to finance a large amount of the fixed assets in retailing through large real estate operators. For example, many suburban shopping centers and downtown retailing properties are owned or financed by life insurance companies.

Sales finance companies are another form of financial institution that can provide capital. They provide financing by buying for cash the retailer's accounts receivable at a discount of their face value. Banks also will provide this type of financing. In either case, it can significantly speed up the retailer's cash flow.

Small Business Administration   Finally, there are government sources of capital available through the Small Business Administration (SBA). According to SBA guidelines, a small business can be quite sizable according to conventional standards. Generally, a company with assets of less than $5 million is considered a small business, but those with considerably more can be as well. Securing SBA funds, however, is not an easy matter. A five- to ten-year forecast of the retailer's market and a detailed organizational structure of the enterprise are needed. Furthermore, the long-range financial objectives must be stipulated and qualifications of the principal executives must be stressed.

RECURRENT CAPITAL NEEDS

Retail enterprises need financial capital not only to commence operations but also to continue them. Capital is needed on a recurring basis for things such as payment of dividends to the owners, paying off debt, increasing current assets in order to support a higher level of sales, and acquiring fixed assets to replace old ones or to support a higher level of sales. Let us briefly explore each need.

Current Assets   As sales grow, the need arises for increased levels of inventory, accounts receivable, and cash to support the increased business.

Inventory   If we refer back to the equation on page 287, which gave the determinants of required inventory investment, we will be able to show the effect of rising sales on required inventory investments in retailing. Assume a retailer has annual sales of $600,000, a stockturn of 5 times, and cost of goods sold as a percentage of sales of 70 percent. Mathematically, the required inventory investment would be:

$$\frac{S}{T} \cdot C = \frac{600,000}{5} \cdot (70\%)$$
$$= \$84,000$$

Now, if sales over the next year grow by 15 percent to reach a level of $690,000, then the new required inventory investment would be:

$$\frac{S}{T} \cdot C = \frac{690,000}{5} \cdot (70\%)$$
$$= \$96,600$$

Thus, we see that a growth in sales of 15 percent results in an increased inventory investment (assuming stockturn and cost of goods as a percentage of sales remain unchanged) of $12,600. Incidentally, this is a 15 percent growth in inventory investment. This illustrates an important principle of retail management. Any increase in sales requires an identical percentage increase in inventory investment (this assumes stockturn and cost of goods as a percentage of sales remain unchanged).

Furthermore, this suggests that in times of rapid inflation, retailers are confronted by major increases in inventory investments simply to maintain the same level of real dollar sales.[2] That is, for example, if furniture prices are rising at a 12 percent annual rate, then a furniture retailer will need to increase inventory investment by 12 percent per year just to maintain the same physical volume of inventory. Therefore, retailers have a major need for recurring capital to replenish and expand inventory. For instance, in 1979, Melville Corporation, a diversified specialty retailer, increased its investment in inventory over the prior year by $47.8 million.[3]

Accounts Receivable   The equation on page 288 will provide us with a vehicle for analyzing the need to increase investments in accounts receivable. Recall that accounts receivable are used to finance customer purchases on credit. Let us work with the data for the same hypothetical retail firm that we used for our inventory exercise. This retailer has annual sales of $600,000 and makes 50 percent of all sales on credit; its typical credit customer takes 13 weeks to pay.

2. R. Fulton MacDonald, "What's Impacting Retail Profitability—And How Can We Plan for the Eighties?" *Retail Control* 45(March 1977): 3–4.
3. Melville Corporation, *Annual Report* (1979), p. 12.

Using our previous formula, what is this retailer's average level of investment in accounts receivable?

$$(S \cdot R \cdot P) = (600,000 \cdot 50\% \cdot 13/52)$$
$$= \$75,000$$

As we did in the inventory exercise, let us assume that sales grow by 15 percent over the following year, and all else will remain constant. At the end of the following year, what would this retailer have invested in accounts receivable?

$$(S \cdot R \cdot P) = (690,000 \cdot 50\% \cdot 13/52)$$
$$= \$86,250$$

This translates into an increase of $11,250 or 15 percent. Another principle of retail management is illustrated. An increase in sales requires an identical percentage increase in accounts receivable investment (this assumes that the percentage of sales made on credit, and the proportion of a year it takes a typical credit customer to pay its bill, remain unchanged).

Cash   Arguments similar to those presented for inventory and accounts receivable can be presented regarding the need for increased cash balances as sales volume expands. However, many retailers are developing sophisticated cash management systems that substantially reduce the need to expand cash balances as volume expands. In Chapter 14 we will review some of these systems.

Fixed Assets   As equipment and fixtures used in retailing depreciate and wear out, they must be replaced. Disquieting to many retail executives was the rate of inflation experienced during the 1970s and early 1980s, which pushed the cost of replacing existing fixtures and equipment to levels substantially above their historical costs. For example, a 100,000-square-foot department store may have paid $50,000 for carpet and floorcoverings in 1975 when the store first opened. Five years later, when the carpeting and floorcoverings needed replacing, the cost would have approached $100,000. Similar inflation was experienced in cash registers, display racks, wall coverings, and heating and cooling systems.

Retailers not only are faced with the continuing need to replace worn-out fixtures and equipment but sometimes must replace fixed assets that are in good working order but are obsolete. In this regard, electronic point-of-sale cash registers have outdated mechanical cash registers, necessitating removing the registers even though the old mechanical cash register may still be in fine working condition. Since the cost can easily reach $10,000 per terminal, to retrofit a store, such as a supermarket, with electronic point-of-sale terminals obviously requires a significant capital expenditure.

In addition, the retailer's strategy may call for expanding the number of stores in operation. These planned stores will need financial capital to become a reality. As an example, consider Wal-Mart Stores, Inc.—an expansion-oriented, discount department store headquartered in Arkansas. Between 1976 and 1980 Wal-Mart added 151 stores, or approximately one store every two weeks. To expand at this pace, Wal-Mart needed over $150 million just for increased investments in fixed assets.[4] Another example of the need for expansion capital is provided in Exhibit 10.2.

Dividends

The payment of dividends to stockholders or the withdrawal of profits by owners is another significant use of capital in retailing. Stockholders or owners invested in the retail enterprise for the potential return it would provide. In the short run, they may be satisfied with reinvesting profits to help the company expand further. Sooner or later, however, they will want to receive more immediate returns in terms of dividends.

Retailers can be big dividend payers. In 1979 Avon Products, Inc., paid a cash dividend of $2.75 per share. In total, Avon paid $164.6 million in dividends in 1979, which was 65.7 percent of their total 1979 profits.[5]

Reducing Debt

When retailers obtain capital by issuing bonds or by borrowing from banks or other financial institutions they should realize that the debt must, at some point, be repaid. It is not our concern how it will be repaid but merely to stress the point that a recurring need for capital in retailing is to repay existing debt.

In any given year, debt repayments can be large. In 1979 Service Merchandise Company, Inc., the nation's second largest catalog showroom merchandiser, reduced long-term debt by $12.3 million.[6]

EXHIBIT 10.2
Capital to Grow

The amount of financial capital that large retailers need to grow can be staggering. For instance, Dayton-Hudson in their 1980–84 capital investment budget projected they would need $1.64 billion.

The Dayton-Hudson store empire consists of Hudson's, Dayton's, Diamond's, John A. Brown (all department stores); Target, Lechmere, and Mervyn's (all low-margin, general merchandise stores); and B. Dalton and Dayton Hudson Jewelers (specialty stores). Logically, Dayton-Hudson is placing the most expansion capital behind those stores with the most attractive return on investment. The top three performers are Target, Mervyn's, and B. Dalton. Target will grow from 80 to 175 stores; B. Dalton will expand from 422 to 862 stores; and Mervyn's will move from 60 to 118 stores.

Because Dayton-Hudson desires to grow at such a rapid pace, it cannot generate all of its growth capital internally. The company will, therefore, need to increase its financial leverage as it takes on additional debt. Predictably, this higher financial leverage places Dayton-Hudson in a more risky position if it confronts a softening of demand in the future.

Source: Based on data from "Dayton-Hudson Unveils $1.6 Billion Growth Plan," *Chain Store Age Executive* 56(March 1980): 31–33.

---

4. Wal-Mart Stores, Inc., *Annual Report* (1980).
5. Avon Products, Inc., *Annual Report* (1979), p. 29.
6. Service Merchandise Company, Inc., *Annual Report* (1979–80), p. 14.

SOURCES OF RECURRENT CAPITAL

The retailer, then, has major needs for recurrent capital. How are those needs met? To obtain the needed capital for continuing expenses, as for starting up an operation, the retailer can turn to inside or outside sources.

Internally Generated   Capital that can be generated through the normal operations of the firm is called internally generated capital. The major sources of internally generated capital are profits, depreciation tax shelters, tax deferrals, and improved working capital productivity.

Profit   The most obvious and dominant source of recurring capital in retail enterprises is **profit** from operations. Retailers must generate a profit in order to be able to survive and increase their businesses. In addition, steady and predictable profits help the retailer convince lenders and potential investors that the retail organization is financially sound.

The role of profits in providing capital for growth is illustrated in Exhibit 10.3, which graphically depicts the profit-capital cycle in retailing. In this simple model, we start with the net worth or owners' investment and add debt and other liabilities to obtain the retailer's total assets. These assets are used to attract and support patronage and thus result in some level of sales volume. From the sales are subtracted costs and expenses to arrive at net profit. The net profit provides additional funds for growth of the owners' investment and the cycle is repeated.

EXHIBIT 10.3
**The Profit-
Capital Cycle**

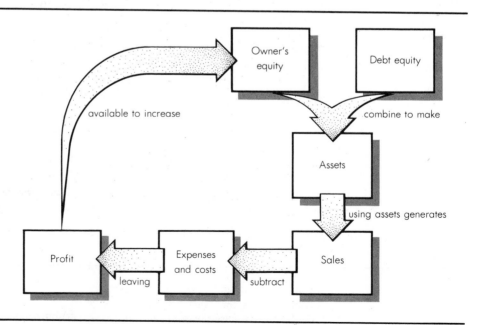

EXHIBIT 10.4 **Depreciation as a Tax Shield**		DEPRECIATION USED	DEPRECIATION NOT USED
	Sales	$200,000	$200,000
	Cost of goods sold	100,000	100,000
	Gross profit	$100,000	$100,000
	Less: operating costs		
	Operating expenses	25,000	25,000
	Depreciation expense	25,000	—
	Net taxable income	$ 50,000	$ 75,000
	Taxes	22,500	33,750
	Net income after taxes	$ 27,500	$ 41,250
	Capital flow		
	Profit	$ 27,500	$ 41,250
	Depreciation	25,000	—
	Total	$ 52,500	$ 41,250

Note: The difference in total capital flow of $11,250 is due totally to the reduction of taxes by $11,250 when depreciation is used. This is equivalent to the tax rate times the depreciation expense of $0.45 \times \$25,000$, which equals $11,250.

Depreciation Tax Shelters In the retailing industry, as well as in other industries, **depreciation** can be a source of recurring capital. This occurs because depreciation is a noncash expense and can therefore allow the organization to cut its tax bill. To illustrate this interesting and sometimes puzzling phenomenon, let us construct an example.

In Exhibit 10.4 we show a pair of income statements for a retailer. One income statement assumes the retailer has annual depreciation expenses of $25,000; the other assumes no depreciation expense. In all other aspects the two income statements are identical, and in both cases the tax rate is 45 percent. When depreciation is used, the net income after taxes is $27,500; without depreciation, net income is $41,250. Thus, at first glance you might conclude that when no depreciation is used more capital would be internally generated. This conclusion would be false. To obtain the total capital internally generated, we need to add the noncash depreciation expense to after tax profits, providing a total capital flow of $52,500 when depreciation was used and $41,250 when depreciation was not used. In short, we see that the capital flow was $11,250 higher when depreciation was used, equal to the difference in taxes paid under the two situations. Specifically, every dollar of depreciation expense reduces taxes by the tax rate times the depreciation expense. In the case at hand, the depreciation expense of $25,000 multiplied times the 45 percent tax rate created $11,250 in tax savings.

Tax Deferrals Federal and state tax laws allow for taxes to be deferred when certain accounting procedures and techniques are used. Certainly we cannot review all the ways that taxes can be deferred. This is a topic for an entire course. Instead, we will merely provide you with enough concrete evidence to show that one can generate capital through tax deferrals.

When taxes are deferred they are simply pushed into future years, at which time they will be paid. Nonetheless, if the retail firm is able to postpone paying taxes it can use the capital it would have used to pay taxes for other needs. Tax deferrals can thus be a significant source of recurrent capital in retail enterprises. The Limited deferred taxes of $1.4 million in fiscal 1978; $2.8 million in 1979; and $3.2 million in 1980.[7] Obviously, The Limited has been quite successful at generating capital through creative tax deferral techniques.

During periods of rapid inflation the **last-in, first-out** method of inventory valuation—called **LIFO**—can be a good technique for deferring taxes. Before we demonstrate this point, you will need to understand how inventory valuation effects profit. With LIFO inventory valuation, the most recently purchased goods (last in) are assumed to be the items sold (first out). If we assume rising prices, then the costs of goods sold are stated at the most recent prices we paid for merchandise, and alternatively inventory is valued at the oldest prices. Thus items in inventory are given a lower price than cost of goods sold. Since inventory is given a low valuation and cost of goods sold a higher valuation, the retailer's reported profits are lower than if the values were reversed. And lower profits result in lower taxes.

Regardless of whether the retailer used LIFO or not, however, the actual facts remain unchanged. That is, the retailer still has the same physical inventory on hand. How could it be otherwise? If a retailer has ten television sets of a given model—the first five of which were purchased at $200 and the last five at $215—and five are sold, then the cost of goods sold under LIFO would be $1,075 and the ending inventory would be $1,000. On the other hand, if LIFO was not used and **FIFO (first-in, first-out)** was used, the cost of goods sold would be $1,000. In either case, there are still five TV sets at the end of the period and they are the same TV sets. There is only a difference in accounting technique.

In Exhibit 10.5 we see how switching from FIFO to LIFO inventory valuation helped Vornado, Inc. (a multimillion-dollar chain-store retailer) defer taxes and thus generate needed capital. Specifically, Vornado increased its internally generated capital in 1974 by $6.7 million by merely changing inventory accounting procedures. The change lowered the book value of inventories by $13.2 million, which subsequently increased cost of goods sold by the equivalent amount. This resulted in lower reported profits, reducing the 1974 tax bite to $1.1 million versus the $7.8 million it would have been if Vornado had stuck with FIFO inventory accounting.

Working Capital Productivity   A final method for generating funds internally is to increase working capital productivity.[8] The two most important sources in

    7. The Limited Stores, Inc., *Annual Reports* (1978, 1979, 1980).
    8. "Finding Money on the Inside" *Chain Store Age Executive* 54(February 1978): 24–25.

EXHIBIT 10.5
Income Statement for Vornado Under LIFO and FIFO (1974)

	THOUSANDS OF DOLLARS	
	FIFO	LIFO
Total revenue	$900,322	$900,322
Cost of goods sold		
Beginning inventory	161,354	161,354
Purchases	614,153	614,153
Ending inventory	150,174	136,919
Total cost of goods sold	$625,333	$638,588
Gross margin	$274,989	$261,734
Operating expenses	258,194	258,194
Net profit (before taxes)	$ 16,795	$ 3,540
Income taxes	7,804	1,089
Net profit (after taxes)	$ 8,991	$ 2,451
Capital flow		
Profit	$ 8,991	$ 2,451
Reduction in inventory value	—	13,255
Total	$ 8,991	$ 15,706

Note: The difference in total capital flow of $6,715 is due totally to a lower tax bill of $6,715, which was caused by changing the inventory valuation to increase the cost of goods sold and thus lower profit.

Source: Vornado, Inc., *Annual Report* (1974).

this regard are inventory productivity and accounts receivable productivity. To show how they can help generate capital, we will need to use the equations that we developed early in the chapter. Please glance back at these formulas so you will be familiar with them (pages 287 and 288).

The key to generating capital through inventory management is to increase stockturn. In Exhibit 10.6, we show the effect on financial capital of improved stockturn for a hypothetical retailer. This retailer, with annual sales of $1 million, is able to generate $22,033 in capital by improving stockturn from 6.1 times annually to 7.5 times annually.

The key to generating capital through accounts receivable management is decreasing the average time it takes to collect from credit customers. In Exhibit

EXHIBIT 10.6
Generating Capital Through Increased Stockturn

1.	Total retailer sales (S)	$1,000,000
2.	Typical stockturn (T)	6.1 times
3.	Cost of goods as a percent of sales (C)	72%
4.	Total inventory investment $[(S \cdot C)/T]$	$ 118,033
5.	Attainable stockturn (T^*)	7.5 times
6.	Necessary inventory investment $[(S \cdot C)/T^*]$	$ 96,000
7.	Capital generated through improved stockturn (4 − 6)	$ 22,033

10.7, we examine the same hypothetical retailer as in Exhibit 10.6. We see that by getting credit customers to pay their bills on average in eleven weeks instead of thirteen, $19,231 can be generated in capital by reducing the average investment in accounts receivable.

EXHIBIT 10.7			
Generating	1.	Total retailer sales (S)	$1,000,000
Capital Through	2.	Percent of sales made on credit (R)	50%
Better Accounts	3.	Proportion of a year it takes a typical credit cus-	
Receivable		tomer to pay his or her bill (P)	(13/52)
Management	4.	Total accounts receivable investment ($S \cdot R \cdot P$)	$ 125,000
	5.	Attainable proportion of a year it takes a typical	
		credit customer to pay his or her bill (P^*)	(11/52)
	6.	Necessary accounts receivable investment ($S \cdot R \cdot P^*$)	$ 105,769
	7.	Capital generated through improved accounts re-	
		ceivable management (4 − 6)	$ 19,231

Externally Generated   Retailers can also externally generate capital for their recurring needs. The major ways of generating capital externally are selling stock, issuing bonds, borrowing from banks or other financial institutions, and obtaining supplier financing. All of these ways were discussed under start-up capital earlier in this chapter.

The retail enterprise that is already well established will generally find it easier to acquire external capital sources than will the new venture retailer. However, the ability to raise additional external capital to finance future growth will also be directly related to the quality of the retailer's balance sheet and income statement.[9] The higher the quality of the retailer's financial statements, the easier it will be to sell stock at an attractive price, issue bonds with lower interest yields, borrow money from the bank and other financial institutions, and get suppliers to provide attractive credit terms.

When the general market level of interest is high, the borrowing of financial capital is generally unattractive regardless of the retailer's credit rating. In January 1981, when the prime interest rate reached 21.5 percent, capital was not borrowed unless it was severely needed.

Similar logic applies to the stock market when it is in a depressed state. When stock prices are tumbling it is not wise to raise capital by selling stock in the firm. This is because the retail enterprise that sells stock in a depressed market will be selling at a low price in relation to what it can obtain when the market recovers.

---

9. For a discussion of ratios used to assess income statements and balance sheets, see Herbert Mayo and Bert Rosenbloom, "Ratio Analysis for the Small Businessmen," *Journal of Small Business Management* (January 1975): 5–8.

PORTFOLIO MANAGEMENT

Imagine yourself as a wealthy individual with $5 million to invest. How would you invest this money? What proportion would you place in stocks, bonds, real estate, gold, silver, or art? This decision is essentially a portfolio decision.[10] All retailers face a similar decision regarding their financial resources.

Here are some of the portfolio decisions a retailer faces: What proportion of the total financial capital should be in fixed versus current assets? Of the current assets, what proportion should be devoted to accounts receivable versus inventory? Of the inventory assets, what proportion should be invested in each of the merchandise lines? The portfolio decision also relates to the retailer's strategy for growth. For example, if, in order to pursue growth goals, the retailer has several available markets to build new stores in, what should be the proportion of stores in each market?

Risk and return are the two key elements in portfolio management. **Return** can be thought of as some measure of return on investment and **risk** can be viewed as the amount of variance in your expectations of a return around your mean, or average expected return. In portfolio management, risk and return are traded off, so that higher risks should result in higher expected returns. Success or failure is determined according to the combination of risk and return. A reasonable goal is to arrange the portfolio so as to achieve a target return while minimizing risk.

What are the elements in the portfolio? For retail enterprises they are types of stores, types of products, location of stores, or types of departments within the store. The retail executive must decide on the proper mix within each category to minimize risk for a given target return or maximize return for a given target risk level. The key is to diversify into different groupings. Let us develop a simplistic example to help illustrate the economics of portfolio management. Our example will deal with diversifying stores by location.

Imagine a retail shoe chain that plans to expand by adding two stores over the next year. This retailer has learned that under normal circumstances it takes three months for a new store to reach break-even. If break-even is not reached in six months, the store will be closed at a cumulative loss of $200,000—most of which was for leasehold improvements and lease cancellation fees. Typically, when a store fails or succeeds it is largely due to the competitive and demographic characteristics of the market. The probability of this store's failing is 0.08 or 8 chances in 100.

If the retailer decides to locate both of the new stores in the same city, there will be 8 chances out of 100 that it will have two stores failing, for an expected loss of $0.08 \times 400,000$ or $32,000. But, if it decides to locate the two stores in separate cities then the probability of them both failing is 0.08×0.08

10. For an excellent discussion of how principles of portfolio management can be applied in a retail setting, see William R. Davidson and Nancy E. Johnson, "Portfolio Theory and the Retailing Life Cycle," in Elizabeth C. Hirschman and Ronald W. Stampfl (eds.), *Theory in Retailing: Traditional and Nontraditional Sources* (Chicago: American Marketing Association, 1981), pp. 51–63.

or .0064. Here the expected loss would be 0.0064 × 400,000 or $2,560. Therefore, by diversifying by location, the risk of losing a large sum of money has been reduced.

Let us elaborate on this example. Assume a successful store has an expected profit of $100,000. If both stores are located in a single city then the probability of success is 0.92 (1.00 − 0.08) for an expected profit of 0.92 × $200,000 or $184,000. On the other hand, if they are located in separate cities the probability that both would be successful is 0.92 × 0.92 or 0.8464, which would result in an expected profit of 0.8464 × $200,000 or $169,280. But to this we must add the probability that one would be successful and one would fail: 0.92 × 0.08 or 0.0736; this would result in an expected loss of 0.0736 × (100,000–200,000) or $7,360. Since the cities are unique, the reverse could also happen: instead of the first being successful and the second being a failure; the first could be a failure and the second successful. The expected loss would be the same ($7,360).

Summarizing, we would have:

	Single City	*Two Cities*
Both fail	.08(− 400,000) = ($32,000)	.0064(− 400,000) = ($2,560)
Both succeed	.92(200,000) = $184,000	.8464(200,000) = $169,280
First succeeds, second fails	N/A	.0736(− 100,000) = ($7,360)
First fails, second succeeds	N/A	.0736(− 100,000) = ($7,360)
Total expected profit	$152,000	$152,000

Diversification—expanding into the two cities—has lowered the risk while keeping the expected return unchanged. Thus, diversification reduces the instability of returns. Notice that diversification reduced the likelihood of large losses but also lowered the likelihood of large gains; however, the expected return remained the same. The reduced likelihood of significant gains is a small price to pay for the reduction in the chances of a large loss.

The same principles that we have just outlined can be applied to merchandise portfolios, department portfolios, and type of store portfolios. For instance, a chain of discount department stores may wish to diversify in order to lower its risk or increase its return. Discount department stores are in the mature stage of their life cycle, and returns are generally average. By diversifying into growth areas, such as nonstore retailing (direct mail or computerized shopping), long-term returns may be increased. This same discount department store may wish to diversify by department. Perhaps it could add some growth departments, which might consist of service departments such as an in-store legal clinic, dental clinic, or savings and loan office. Alternatively, it may find it profitable to further diversify its merchandise mix within existing departments. For instance, it may add some high-profit but high-risk fashion items to its women's apparel department.

SUMMARY

The purpose of this chapter has been to discuss the need for planning and managing financial capital in retailing. The need for financial capital is a direct outgrowth of the retailer's strategy. A change in strategy will always translate into some change in financial resources—either in the amount or in the mix.

An entrepreneuer starting a new retail enterprise will need capital for a variety of purposes. The more important are inventory investment, accounts receivable investment, fixed asset investment, investment in expected negative cash flow, and contingency funds. This same entrepreneuer can obtain start-up capital from equity capital—such as the entrepreneuer's personal funds, contribution of funds from a partner, or sale of stock—and debt capital such as supplier financing, bank and financial institution lending, sale of bonds, and government financing through the Small Business Administration.

Not only the start-up retailer needs capital; so does the established retailer. It needs capital on a recurring basis for increasing current assets to support high levels of sales; to replace worn-out and technologically obsolete fixtures and equipment; to open more stores; to pay dividends; and to repay debt. This capital can be obtained either internally or externally. The major sources of internally generated capital are profit from operations, depreciation tax shelters, tax deferral accounting techniques such as LIFO inventory valuation, and increased productivity of working capital. External sources of capital involve sale of stock, additional use of debt instruments, or more supplier financing of inventory.

Retailers should attempt to build a portfolio of assets (composed of types of stores, merchandise, departments, and locations) so as to achieve a target return while minimizing risk. The key to risk minimization is diversification of assets.

QUESTIONS

1. Would it require more inventory and accounts receivable to support a supermarket doing $4 million in annual sales or a furniture store doing $4 million in annual sales? Why?

2. A retailer that leases or rents space instead of owning it is using less capital. Agree or disagree and explain why.

3. Develop a list of factors that would influence the amount of contingency funds a start-up retailer should have on hand.

4. When a retailer's cost of goods sold as a percentage of sales rises, and all else remains unchanged, it will need more capital to invest in inventory. Why is this so?

5. What are the key factors influencing how much capital a retailer will need to invest in accounts receivable?

6. Profitable retailers may not be liquid. Agree or disagree with this statement and explain why.

7. Can retailers always defer taxes by shifting from FIFO to LIFO inventory accounting?

8. Elaborate on the effect rising prices have on the need to generate capital in retailing.

9. Is the concept of portfolio management more important to start-up retailers or ongoing retailers attempting to expand their businesses?

10. How might the start-up capital required to open a franchised fast-food restaurant differ from that required to start an independently owned and operated restaurant?

PROBLEMS AND EXERCISES

1. Hatfield's is a locally owned and operated furniture store in a moderate-size city in Illinois. Annual sales are $870,000 and cost of goods sold as a percent of sales is 62%. Stockturn (sales ÷ average inventory) is 3.6 times annually. If sales increase to $920,000, annual stockturn reaches 4.5 times, and all else remains constant, what will be the increase or decrease in the average inventory investment?

2. Obtain a copy of the annual report to stockholders for a large, publicly held retailer. Some possibilities are Kroger, Sears, Roebuck, A&P, Southland Corporation, K-mart, and J. C. Penney. For their most recent fiscal year assess how they generated capital and how they used that capital.

3. The Yellow Jersey is a sporting goods store in California that specializes in jogging and running wear and equipment. The owner of the store is contemplating opening another store in the same city. Explain how the manager should go about estimating the capital required to establish a second outlet. Where do you recommend the capital be obtained?

4. Hatfield's, the store in Problem 1, sells 68 percent of its merchandise on credit. The typical customer takes 8 weeks to pay its bill. What is Hatfield's average investment in accounts receivable? If Hatfield's increases sales by 20 percent and all else remains unchanged how much more will it need to invest in accounts receivable? What if sales do not increase but the typical credit customer takes an extra week to pay?

5. Identify a line of trade in which you would like to open a store in your community. Attempt to itemize the things you would need capital for in order to open your store. Where would you obtain the capital?

SUGGESTED READINGS

Clifford, Donald K., Jr. "Growth Pains of the Threshold Company." *Harvard Business Review* 51(September–October 1973): 143–54.

Davidson, William R. "Life Cycle, Portfolio Management Maximizes Retail Wealth." *Marketing News*, August 22, 1980, p. 14.

Entenberg, Robert D. "Planning for Financial Requirements." In *Effective Retail and Market Distribution* (Cleveland: World, 1966), pp. 194–206.

Singhvi, Surendra S. "A Model for Corporate Growth." *Mergers and Acquisitions* (Spring 1975): 10–15.

Smalter, Donald J. "The Keys to Growth Power." *Managerial Planning* 21(January–February 1973): 1–10.

11

Overview *In this chapter we will examine the role that human resources play in retail enterprises. We will try to show that to carry out a strategy successfully, it is necessary to have the proper number and mix of human resources. Thus, the retailer must plan for human resources, it must acquire human resources, it must train and develop human resources, it must compensate human resources, and it must organize its human resources.*

Human Resource Planning and Management

Planning for Human Resources
Task Analysis
Long-Range Analysis
Short-Range Analysis

Human Resource Acquisition
Competition
Sources
Screening

Training and Development
New Employees
Existing Employees

Human Resource Compensation

Organizing Human Resources
Organizing Modes
Which Mode?
Organizing Around Functions
Organizing Around Merchandise
Organizing Around Location
Multi-Mode Organizations
Branch-Store Organizations
Chain-Store Organizations
Ownership Groups

Summary

IN RETAIL ENTERPRISES, as in all other organizations, human resources make things happen. Human resources are energy resources that help propel the firm. Since good human resources, just as good energy resources, are in short supply, the retailer must plan and manage them properly. By doing so, the retailer will be able to unlease additional human energy and thus push the retail enterprise to higher plateaus of performance. Therefore, the proper planning and managing of human resources is a key correlate of high performance retailing.

Retailers use different methods for planning and managing human resources. There are many approaches, philosophies, and perspectives. To the student and the retail manager attempting to learn more about retailing, this may be disturbing. Nonetheless, there seems to be some common core of knowledge regarding planning and managing human resources in retailing; and it is that common core which will be the focus of this chapter.

PLANNING FOR HUMAN RESOURCES

As we said in Chapter 9, planning is deciding today what to do in the future. Thus, planning for human resources involves deciding now what human resources will be needed later. Both existing retailers and entrepreneurs wishing to establish a retail enterprise must engage in human resource planning.

Assume that you and your spouse have just opened a sporting goods store. You feel that you can staff the store with the help of your younger brother, a senior in high school. However, if you expect your business to grow, sooner or later you will need additional human resources beyond your immediate family—either that, or your offspring will need to multiply rapidly and grow quickly.

Task Analysis A logical starting point for human resources planning in retailing is task analysis. **Task analysis** involves simply identifying all of the tasks the retailer needs to perform and breaking those tasks into jobs. Three steps should be followed: identifying the functions within the marketing system that the retailer needs or wishes to perform; identifying the tasks that need to be performed within each function; and mapping the tasks into jobs.

Marketing Functions In Chapter 4, we stressed that the retailer needs to view itself as a part of a larger marketing system. We suggested that the retailer is but one institution in a marketing channel, which, as a system, must perform eight marketing functions: buying, selling, storing, transporting, sorting, financing, information gathering, and risk taking. Since the eight functions can be shifted and divided, no single institution in the marketing channel will typically perform all of a function.

The starting point for good human resource planning is for the retailer to decide which and how much of the eight marketing functions it will perform.

The investment in human resources is important for retailers: helpful, efficient employees project a good store image to consumers. (Photo courtesy of Sears.)

As it assumes more of each function, it will require more human resources.

For example, large, chain-store retailers perform more marketing functions than small retailers and will therefore require more human resources. For instance, the large chain store may:

1. Perform more of the buying function by having buying offices in major cities throughout the world
2. Perform more of the selling function by heavily advertising and promoting merchandise on TV and radio and in the newspapers and magazines
3. Perform more of the storage function by operating its own warehouse
4. Perform more of the transportation function by having its own trucks
5. Perform more of the sorting function by buying in large quantities and breaking bulk and in some cases doing its own packaging
6. Perform more of the financing function by establishing a subsidiary to finance consumer purchases or by helping to finance small manufacturers
7. Perform more of the information gathering function by developing a department of consumer research and long-range planning
8. Perform more of the risk-taking function by designing and developing specifications for products and then contracting with manufacturers to produce them

Identifying Tasks   Once you have established the amount of each marketing function to perform, you must identify all of the tasks that will need to be performed. Functions are broad classifications of activities; tasks are specific activities. For example, selling is a function that may involve the tasks of customer contact, customer follow-up, advertising in newspapers, and pricing merchandise.

Exhibit 11.1 provides a list of typical tasks that most retailers perform. Note that the number is large and heterogeneous—ranging from transporting goods to cleaning the floors and windows of the store.

Mapping Tasks into Jobs   The final step involves the mapping of tasks into jobs. You will want a job to be comprised of a relatively homogeneous set of tasks. Since the tasks are heterogeneous, you will need to find those which are most similar (least heterogeneous) and group them together. The smaller the retail organization, the less this will be possible. Witness the "mom and pop" store in which the owner does everything—purchasing supplies and merchandise, preparing financial statements, contacting customers, even cleaning the windows.

As stores grow in size and add more employees, specialization can occur. For example, in Exhibit 11.1, we may see that as a retailer grows, the tasks of granting credit, billing customers, paying bills, and preparing financial statements will be placed in the hands of an accounting or financial clerk. Similarly, the tasks of handling customer complaints, repairing and altering merchandise, and gift wrapping may be placed in the hands of a director of customer services. When the retailer was smaller, these two sets of tasks may have been handled by the same person, even though they were heterogeneous. At the other extreme, if the retailer gets large enough, each task may be performed by a separate individual and ultimately there may be many employees handling a single task. For instance, Sears needs hundreds of employees just to bill customers, and thousands more just to purchase merchandise.

Long-Range Analysis   On a long-range time horizon (two to five years), the major driving force behind human resource requirements will be the retailer's projected growth in sales volume and number of stores. This is not to suggest that human resource

---

EXHIBIT 11.1 **Typical Tasks Retailers Perform**				
Searching for merchandise	Following up on customers	Contacting customers	Doing customer research
Packaging	Handling customer complaints	Transporting inbound merchandise	Preparing press releases
Gift wrapping			
Advertising	Cleaning store	Transporting outbound merchandise	Preparing financial statements
Purchasing supplies	Controlling inventory		
Purchasing merchandise	Hiring and firing employees	Paying bills	Storing merchandise
Granting credit	Training employees	Handling cash	Preparing merchandise statistics
Billing customers	Selling	Altering merchandise	
Building merchandise assortments	Supervising employees	Repairing merchandise	Maintaining the store
	Displaying merchandise	Forecasting sales	Providing store security
Pricing merchandise			

requirements are unilaterally a function of growth in sales and number of stores. Frequently, the growth in sales and number of stores depends on the availability of good human resources. This is especially true when a chain-store retailer's growth is not constrained by its capital or market opportunities but by the availability of qualified assistant store managers to promote to the position of store manager. And, of course, every new store that is opened by a chain-store retailer needs not only a store manager but an assistant manager and a multitude of other supervisory employees.

In analyzing long-range growth trends, you should pay particular attention to the speed and predictability of growth, the geographical dispersion of growth, and the amount of growth related to line-of-trade diversification. Each of these has significant implications for human resource planning.

Growth Speed and Predictability The more rapid the growth, the more difficult it will be to manage human resources. Fast-growing retail enterprises create both opportunities and problems in regard to human resource planning. Rapid growth creates many opportunities for existing retail employees, because possibilities for promotion and advancement are numerous. At the same time, it can create a host of problems. Naturally, for every retail employee promoted, another has to take his or her old job. In addition, not every employee who thinks he or she deserves a promotion will receive it, creating tension in the organization. In some situations, no employee may be ready for the promotion, and thus an outsider may be hired—again possibly creating internal tension and perhaps hostility. The more rapid the growth, the more often such problems will arise.

To a considerable extent, these problems can be overcome if the retailer feels fairly confident that strong growth will occur over the next two to five years. Then the retailer can start early to groom and prepare its current employees for increased responsibility. Of course, there is some downside risk to this process if the expected growth does not occur. In that case, the retailer has prepared a select group of employees for significant increases in authority and responsibility but no new positions opened up because growth did not materialize. An employee that has been prepared for a key management position and doesn't get it will most likely seek out such a position somewhere else.

Geographic Diversification If growth is expected to occur through geographic diversification, then a problem arises in regard to the frequent necessity of transferring employees to stores in different geographical areas. Consider a retailer that has saturated one city with its stores and thus, to achieve continued growth, begins to build stores in other cities or towns. Each new store will need a host of managers. A good potential pool for these new managers is the employees in existing stores. However, not all talented employees will jump at a promotion if it involves a geographic move. This is especially true if the area seems to be an unattractive place to reside or raise a family.

Diversification into a new geographic area may also be accompanied by a different labor environment. For instance, in larger cities and on the West Coast, retail employees are more likely to be unionized. Furthermore, in larger cities wages may be significantly higher due to more intense competition from other industries (manufacturing, wholesaling, and banking, to name a few).

Line-of-Trade Diversification   The retailer that plans to diversify into other lines of retail trade will face additional problems. Especially important will be the problem of deciding which, if any, present employees can adapt to a different line of retail trade. Although the basics of retailing are constant across lines of trade, the specifics are quite different. There is no assurance that a manager of a supermarket can manage a women's apparel store or a jewelry store. In general, the higher the position in the organization, the less this will be a problem. The controller or president of a supermarket chain should be able to perform similar functions for a women's apparel chain or jewelry chain. But, as we get down to more day-to-day operations, this will less likely be the case.

Once the three preceding factors—speed and predictability of growth, geographic diversification, and line of trade diversification—have been identified then a human resource audit should be performed.

Human Resource Audit   A **human resource audit** is a careful examination, by top management or an outside consultant, of the strengths and weaknesses of all employees. Lower-level employees such as sales clerks, janitors, and delivery persons might be placed in groups and evaluated as a whole. This, however, need not be the approach. A small retailer may want to carefully evaluate the prospective management abilities of each employee, keeping in mind that many salesclerks, janitors, delivery persons, and other low-level employees have moved on to become store managers, vice presidents, and presidents or owners of their own stores or even retail chains.

An evaluation of each person holding a middle or top management position should be made. Where does each excel, perform poorly, and need improvement? What are the desires and goals of each manager? What have been their track records? How fast have they progressed, and how motivated and talented are they? Do they desire to continue to move up in the organization? How flexible are they (are they willing to make a geographic move for a promotion)? These are only a sampling of the questions that the audit should answer.

From this audit, management should be able to develop a profile of the number and quality of employees at the lowest levels in the organization that are potential first-line managers, and the number of subsequent managers at each stage in the organizational hierarchy that offer the potential for continued advancement. By comparing this profile with long-range growth needs, the retailer should be able readily to identify the human resource areas that need the most attention.

The retailer that can identify its weak points through a human resource audit, can begin to correct the situation by training and developing existing employees. By foreseeing, for example, a significant need for more store managers within the next two to five years, a retailer could start today to train and develop those employees who exhibit the drive and potential to advance to the rank of store manager.

Short-Range Analysis   Human resources need to be planned not only on a long-range basis, but also over a short range. Such a horizon is usually less than one year and in many cases may be weekly, monthly, or seasonal. The retailer should forecast any short-run swings in sales and then adjust human resource inputs appropriately.[1] For instance, if a retailer forecasts a recession in the third and fourth quarters, then all hiring may immediately cease, so that if the recession materializes, no employees will need to be fired or laid off.

It is wise to analyze any recurring seasonal trends. If the retailer always does a strong business during the Christmas season then plans should be made to have adequate human resources during this period each year. Similarly, if the retailer always experiences more traffic on Friday and Saturday, it should plan to have the human resources to serve this increased traffic.

Periodic and predictable increases in short-run demand for human resources can be handled either by utilizing part-time employees or by having existing employees participate in job sharing. Part-time employees for peak periods such as Christmas or weekends can help the retailer serve more customers. However, the peak business can often be handled by having existing employees share jobs, such as having managers waiting on customers, or by having some employees work longer work weeks.

HUMAN RESOURCE ACQUISITION

Few retailers will be able to operate continually without sooner or later needing to acquire additional human resources.[2] Present employees may quit, be fired, become terminally ill, or even die. Also, we showed in the first part of this chapter, retailers may need additional employees because of growth.

Competition   Retailers must first remember that human resources are acquired in a competitive marketplace. Good employees are not waiting around to be hired, and seldom will they come pounding at your door. In fact, when a good worker or manager is looking for employment, he or she will seldom think of contacting retail firms, simply because of the reputation many retailers have for low wages. Therefore, retailers must aggressively seek out and recruit good employees; by so doing, they must compete for labor resources.[3]

1. For an example of short-run human resource planning, see R. Dale Von Riesen, "Toward Staffing Optimality in Retail Selling," *Journal of Retailing* 49(Winter 1973–1974): 37–47.

2. Frequently there is not sufficient top management talent within the organization and thus even top executives must be recruited. See "Going Outside for Top Execs," *Chain Store Age Executive* 52(August 1976): 13–15.

3. For a discussion of human resource acquisition related to department stores, see Irving Burstiner, "Current Personnel Practices in Department Stores," *Journal of Retailing* 51(Winter 1975–1976): 3–14, 86.

Sources   What are the sources from which retailers can obtain human resources? The following six are the most common: walk-ins, employment agencies, schools and colleges, former employees, advertisements, and recommendations.

Walk-ins During periods of high unemployment, retailers will have many walk-ins seeking employment. These walk-ins can be a source for clerical, sales, and custodial positions, but seldom are they a source for managerial or supervisory employees. Also, it should be mentioned that when walk-ins are most frequent—during periods of high unemployment—retailers need additional human resources least. Nonetheless, it is good practice to keep a file of applications filled out by walk-ins, since it is a low-cost method of acquiring a list of potential employees.

Employment Agencies Using the services of public or private employment agencies is another possibility. All states provide public employment services, which are typically available free of charge to both jobseekers and employers. In the past, however, the quality of these services has not been high. Their ability to provide a good pool of prospective managerial or white-collar employees is generally poor. They can, however, be a reasonable, if not good, source for unskilled employees. At the same time, they are an excellent source for minority, handicapped, and veteran employees. This can help the retailer meet its commitment to help achieve a national policy of equal employment opportunities for all persons.

Private employment agencies are generally a much better source for managerial and white-collar employees. The reputations and skills of these agencies, however, vary widely. All of them charge a fee to either the retailer or the job applicant when the applicant is hired. Thus, you should be especially cautious of those agencies more interested in getting a fee than in obtaining a good fit between applicant and employer.

Some private employment agencies specialize in recruiting retail executives. Two examples are Retail Executive Search, Inc., based in Chicago and Retail Recruiters based in New York City. Both are good sources for suitable candidates for top management retail positions.

Schools and Colleges Many candidates for potential employment may be completing formal educational programs. They could be completing high school, junior college, college, or even graduate school. All graduates are potential candidates, but they do possess differing levels of talent, skills, knowledge, and expectations.

Many high schools have Distributive Education Clubs of America (DECA) chapters. High school students that belong to DECA take courses that relate to retailing, such as bookkeeping and merchandising. They also, while in school, work part-time for local retailers. These high school graduates provide an excellent source for operating-level employees. Many of them have the basic talent, skills, and ambition to become shift managers or assistant department managers within a one- or two-year period. High schools do not have placement bureaus; therefore the best way to attract good high school graduates with an interest in retailing is by developing a good working relationship with the teachers of business-related courses or with advisors of the local DECA chapter.

Graduates of junior college programs in business administration or retailing are an additional source of human resources. The job of recruiting these graduates is somewhat easier because almost all junior colleges have a placement bureau, which facilitates the interviewing and selection process. Many junior college graduates have some retail experience and because of their college training, can begin in some low-level supervisory role, such as assistant night manager of a store.

Retailers can also recruit graduates of four-year college programs. If the retailer decides to move in this direction, it should be willing to make a significant commitment in terms of added financial resources to attract and hire a given number of employees. Not only do four-year college graduates expect and receive higher starting salaries, but the cost of recruiting them can be significant. Not every city or town has a four-year college, and if there is a college in town it may not train the type of graduates the retailer desires. Thus, the retailer will need to send a representative (recruiter) to screen candidates on campus. Once candidates are screened, a select few will be invited to visit the retailer, with the retailer picking up the travel and lodging cost. If things go well, the retailer will extend an offer to one or several applicants. Probably not all, and in some cases none, will accept, simply because the top college graduates will have several offers. The net result is that all of the costs of recruiting should be related to the number of hires. If a retailer has openings for three people in a management training program and visits two campuses for two days to interview a total of thirty students, and then invites five to company headquarters and subsequently hires two of them, and if the cost of all of this recruiting was $3,600, then the cost per hire was $1,800—not an insignificant amount. Incidentally, most college graduates will expect to start immediately as a management trainee or assistant buyer.

A select group of retailers have recently experimented with the hiring of MBA graduates. The available evidence suggests that results have been mixed. Too often these graduates expect to progress through the organization and become vice presidents or presidents of retail organizations within a few years. This is most often not possible—but given the right MBA and right retail organization, it is not impossible.

Former Employees The retailer should keep a tab on former employees who performed well. In many cases, the retailer valued these employees, but at the time simply did not have the flexibility to promote them. Since retail organizations are always changing, there may come a time when a position is open for which this former employee would be excellent. It is not uncommon for a person to leave one retail organization as an assistant buyer to take a job as buyer at another retail organization and return to the initial retailer several years later as divisional merchandise manager.

Advertisements Obviously, one may attempt to get a pool of applicants for a particular job by placing advertisements in the classified ad section of the local newspaper. Retailers will often advertise for salesclerks, cashiers, and janitors in this fashion, and occasionally, they will seek buyers and managers in this way. In the mid-1970s a Houston department store placed an ad for assistant buyers in the classified section of the newspaper and had a good response. Ads can also be placed in retail trade journals such as *Chain Store Age* or *Stores* or in magazines with a more specific orientation, such as *Hardware Retailing* or *Progressive Grocer*. Trade journal advertising is most useful if the search is for a middle or top management position, because they provide a low-cost means of reaching retail executives across the nation.

Recommendations A final source of future employees is the recommendations of current employees. These employees may have acquaintances or friends with an interest in applying for the jobs that are open. This source is good for filling jobs at all levels in the organization. Salesclerks as well as store managers and vice presidents may know of others seeking employment at a variety of ranks or positions.

Screening

Regardless of the specific source of job applicants, they should all be subject to a formal screening to sort the potentially good from the potentially bad employees. As with any screening, some degree of error is unavoidable. That is, the retail personnel manager may classify an applicant as a potential loser when in reality the applicant would be excellent for the job. On the other hand, the applicant may be classified as a potential winner and be hired, but turn out to be a real loser. Nonetheless, fewer of these errors should occur with screening than with no screening at all.

Retailers tend to vary in the amount of screening they use. In principle, there are five screens that the applicant can be put through; they are displayed in Exhibit 11.2. The total applicant pool for a particular job is progressively reduced as the applicants are subjected to each screen. This process will be illustrated as each screening device is briefly discussed.

EXHIBIT 11.2
The Employee Screening Process

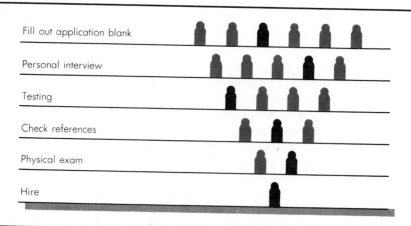

Fill out application blank

Personal interview

Testing

Check references

Physical exam

Hire

Application Blanks   As a matter of procedure, all applicants should be asked to fill out an application blank. The application blank should try to capture conveniently and compactly the individual's personal characteristics and history. Commonly asked for information includes age, sex, education, marital status, physical disabilities, employment history, and previous job responsibilities. This basic information will help screen out, at a relatively low cost, any applicants that do not possess the basic characteristics they need to have to qualify for the job.

Information should not be used in a discriminatory way to unfairly screen out applicants because of age, sex, marital status, or other personal characteristics. Many times, however, certain personal characteristics or attributes will legitimately disqualify a person. For example, if the retailer is seeking a night security guard to protect its property, it should be able to eliminate individuals with physical disabilities that would prevent them from effectively performing the job responsibilities and tasks of a night security guard.

Some retailers have developed weighted application blanks.[4] These have statistical weights assigned to different types of information to reflect how well the respective pieces of information can predict success on the job. Two advantages accrue in the use of such applications. First, the retailer can better process the information on the application blank to determine which of the applicants offer the most promise. Second, the retailer can ensure that it does not unfairly discriminate against individuals because of personal characteristics.

Personal Interview   Those applicants who possess the basic characteristics needed to perform the job should be personally interviewed. This important step should allow you to assess how qualified the applicants are for the job. By its very nature, an interview is subjective; but in a well-structured interview one can obtain information or at least gain insight into the attitudes, personality, motives, and job aspirations of the interviewee.

Many interviewers overlook the fact that the interview should be a two-way communication process. Not only does the retailer want to gather information on the applicant, but the applicant may desire information on the retailer. Allowing time for the applicant to ask questions is essential if the retailer is competing for the talents of highly recruited applicants. In fact, part of the interview time may actually be used by the interviewer to try to sell the applicant on the retailer.

Testing   Sometimes formal tests will be administered to those applicants who received favorable ratings in their personal interviews. These tests may involve skill tests for jobs that require proficiency in certain tasks—the retailer hiring clerical staff may be concerned with typing ability or ability to take shorthand. Other characteristics, such as intelligence, interests, leadership potential, or personality traits, may be measured with paper-and-pencil tests. For instance, the Ghiselli Self-Description Inventory has been administered to applicants for

4. Robert F. Hartley, "The Weighted Application Blank Can Improve Retail Employee Selection," *Journal of Retailing* 46(Spring 1970): 32–40.

store management positions.[5] This test measures a variety of individual traits such as supervisory ability, initiative, self-assurance, perceived occupational level, decision-making approach, and sociometric popularity.

When tests are used in screening, the retailer needs to be especially concerned about any bias or discrimination inherent in those tests. The Equal Employment Opportunity Commission (EEOC), which enforces the Civil Rights Act of 1964, has been concerned about some of the tests used in employment screening. For example, many intelligence and interest tests are culturally biased and thus can cause the retailer to discriminate in the hiring of racial minorities. If the retailer is going to use tests, it should go to the added effort to ensure, as much as possible, that the testing instruments are not biased.

References   As a general rule, you should not ask for or check the references the applicant has provided until the applicant has been screened or filtered through the preceding stages. If references are obtained and verified on all initial applicants, the cost would be excessive. It is more cost-effective to obtain and check references after most applicants have been eliminated from consideration.

When references are obtained and checked, the retailer should try to assess the honesty and reliability of the applicant. The reason for leaving the prior place or places of employment should also be investigated. Finally, the retailer should be interested in finding out what type of person will vouch for the prospective employee.

Physical Examination   The final step in the screening process is the physical examination. Not only will the retailer want some information on the applicant's physical capabilities as related to the physical tasks of the job, but will also need to have on file any preexistent medical problems. This will help to minimize expensive liability claims in the future if the employee were to argue that a medical condition was job-related. If the retailer can show that the condition existed before the present job, there will be less risk of legal liability.

If the individual passes all of the screens, he or she might be offered the job, but not necessarily. Several applicants may pass all the screens, but there may only be one current vacancy. In this case, the retailer will need to match each of the remaining applicants to the job description in an attempt to identify the best candidate. This candidate will be extended an offer and, the retailers hope, will accept, and thus be hired.

TRAINING AND DEVELOPMENT

Human resources, both new and existing, should receive training and development if the retailer wishes a good return on its investment. Training and development are consistent with the concept of human resource planning. Re-

---

5. Jan P. Muczyk, T. H. Mattheiss, and Myron Gable, "Predicting Success of Store Managers: A Forced Choice Personality Test Refined by Discriminant Analysis," *Journal of Retailing* 50(Summer 1974): 43–49, 104.

call that human resource planning was deciding in the present what would be the human resource requirements in the future. Training and development fit nicely into this scheme because they provide a vehicle for enhancing the quality of both old and newly acquired human resources so that they will better be able to meet the future needs of the organization.

New Employees In the not-too-distant past, most retailers would subject new employees to either of two types of training. Both of them on-the-job and informal in their approach, they were the sink or swim method and the sponsorship method. Today, however, many retailers use some type of formal training method.

Sink or Swim Sometimes the new employee is thrust into the job and has to learn in any way possible or else quit or get fired. Although this sink or swim method eliminates all direct training and development costs, it generates high indirect costs. For example, new employees will make costly mistakes in attempting to learn. These mistakes cost the retailer money, not the employee. Also, employee turnover will be excessive, which increases payroll costs as a percentage of sales. Therefore, although the sink or swim method looks deceptively low in cost, it, in reality, is quite expensive.

Sponsorship The sponsorship method of information training involves assigning the new employee to a present employee who is performing or has performed the job for which the new employee was hired. The existing employee becomes the sponsor of the new employee and directs, guides, advises, and watches over the new employee until the tasks associated with the job are learned.

If good sponsors are selected, this can be a quite effective and low-cost method of training and development. The biggest problem is that the method's success depends greatly on the talents and interpersonal skills of the sponsor. The sponsor may know how to perform the tasks of the job quite well, but if these skills cannot be communicated to the new employee then the result could be disastrous. Nonetheless, for the small retailer with limited resources to invest, sponsorship may be the best method.

Formal Programs Formal training and development programs for new employees consist of exposing all new employees for a given type of job to a prescribed set of learning methods or materials. These materials can be spread over several hours or days (in the case of training new retail salesclerks) all the way to one or two years (in the case of training buyers or department managers). The different types of methods and materials that are used can be categorized as follows:

1. The **lecture method** works best when the retailer has large groups to train (for example, 100 part-time employees for the Christmas season at a large department store). This method is effective when the lecturer is dynamic and well organized.
2. The **lecture-discussion method** also works well with large groups, but not

if they have more than fifty individuals. It is more effective than the straight lecture method, since it allows participants to seek clarification on concepts and encourages involvement by inviting participation.

3. The **multimedia method** complements lectures with films, slides, video-tapes, overhead projections, and flip charts. These should complement the lecturer and not be a substitute.

4. The **programmed instruction method** uses programmed materials to guide students through step-by-step, self-learning exercises. The trainee is given material in small steps and must continually respond and then is informed if the response is appropriate.

5. Computer-based retail **simulation games** allow the trainee to experience a simulated retail environment. The trainee can get feedback on how it is performing in the simulated environment. Frequently, trainees compete against each other in the computer game to see who can perform the best.

6. **Role-playing** consists of placing the trainees in contrived real-life situations and having them act out their responses.

7. **Case-analysis** involves providing the trainees with detailed descriptions of problems that have confronted actual retailers. The trainee is then asked to develop and recommend a course of action.

Existing Employees   Besides training new employees, the retailer will often find it advantageous to further train and develop key existing employees.[6] A systematic, and well-developed program can help the retailer prepare certain employees for increased future responsibility. Such a program can also assist in screening employees to determine which ones are sufficiently motivated to learn new material required by greater responsibility. The author knows of one large retail chain that put a group of twenty-five middle managers through a rigorous set of executive development courses offered at several universities in order to assess which of the managers had good potential for advancement and which ones thought retailing was getting too complex and analytical and thus were not willing to put out the effort to achieve further promotions.

Various methods are used to expose existing employees to new material and to help them acquire additional knowledge and insights. A brief description of ten of the most frequently used methods will follow.

Job Rotation   Job rotation involves assigning the retail employee to other jobs in the organization for three to twelve months. The employee should thus develop a better understanding and broader perspective of the total retail system.

Special Assignments   The employee is given a special assignment that is intended to be not only of value to the retailer, but also a learning experience for

6. "Focus on Mid-Management Needs: Study Lists Eight Essentials" *Stores* 59(January 1977): 28–29.

the employee. For instance, the assignment could involve an evaluation of the retailer's policy toward employee theft or a feasibility study for a new store.

Staff Assistant   The promising employee is assigned as the assistant to a top-level executive. These assignments are typically for three months to a year and provide the employee with a perspective on the complexities and problems of managing a retail organization.

Reading Material   Selected books, trade journals, articles, or trade association studies can be circulated to key employees who are being cultivated for higher-level positions in the organization.

In-House Courses   The retailer can offer in-house courses on selected topics such as management by objectives, retail arithmetic, and personal selling techniques. These courses can be taught by company trainers or by hired consultants or teachers.

Outside Short-Courses   Frequently, short courses are offered by educational institutions, trade associations, or private training and consulting firms on a variety of specialized topics. There are many courses available, and the key is to carefully select the ones that will be beneficial to the employee's career development.

College Degree Programs   Many colleges are increasingly offering evening and weekend programs that make it possible for retail employees to earn a college degree in business administration. Retailers, in many cases, will offer tuition refund programs to encourage their employees to pursue such degree programs.

Advanced Management Programs   Many prestigious higher education institutions such as Stanford, Harvard, and MIT offer intensive in-residence programs. These programs vary considerably in length from several weeks to a year. Material covered is quite sophisticated, and the pace of instruction is rapid.

Trade Conferences   All major retail trade associations have regular conferences at which they usually have many workshops on selected topics conducted by industry experts. Professional associations such as the American Marketing Association also have annual conferences, which some retailers may find informative.

Correspondence Courses   Many courses that are retailing-related (basic accounting, finance, business law, marketing) are available through correspondence. Such home-study courses require that the trainee is highly committed to learning and can accomplish the learning task with little supervision and guidance.

HUMAN RESOURCE COMPENSATION

As all businesspeople know, human resources are not free goods. They are expensive, and in retailing their cost typically represents 50 percent of operating expenses. We will not discuss how to control labor expenses, but merely highlight some important aspects about compensating human resources.

Compensation is one of the major variables in attracting, retaining, and motivating human resources. The quality of employees that can be attracted, whether as salesclerks or executives, is directly proportional to the compensation package offered. The better the human resource, the higher the price. Naturally, other things besides compensation are important to employees, but compensation still stands out as the most important aspect in most employees' feelings of job satisfaction.

It is impossible to retain good employees unless they receive competitive compensation. In this regard, the retailer needs to realize that if it invests more money in training and developing employees, these employees will actually increase in value, not only to the retailer, but also to competitors who may try to hire them. Thus, as the retailer invests money to train and develop employees, it must also make a commitment to provide them with more compensation, or the retailer will be training and developing employees for its competitors.

Compensation plans in retailing can have up to three basic components: a fixed component, a variable component, and a fringe benefit component.[7] The **fixed component** typically is composed of some base wage per hour, week, month, or year. The **variable component** is often composed of some bonus that is received if performance warrants it. Salesclerks may be paid a bonus of 1 percent of sales above some established minimum; department managers may receive a bonus based on the profit performance of their department. Workers in restaurants often receive tips, a variable component that the retailer does not control. Finally, a **fringe benefit package** may include such things as health insurance, disability benefits, life insurance, retirement plans, automobiles, and financial counseling.

Each of the three components helps the retailer to achieve a different human resource goal. The fixed component helps it to ensure that its employees have a basic source of income to meet their most basic financial obligations. As such, it helps to fulfill the employees' need for **safety**. The variable component allows the retailer to offer its employees an incentive for higher levels of effort and commitment. As such, it helps to fulfill a need among employees for **special recognition** in return for high performance. The fringe benefit component allows the retailer to offer employees **security** and **prestige**. Retail employees have a need to be protected and cared for when they are faced with difficult times or when they become too old to provide for themselves. Also, certain employees (especially executives) have a need for prestige and status.

The best combination of fixed, variable, and fringe compensation components depends on the person, the job, and the retail organization. There is no

7. Raymond B. Krieger, ''Employee Benefits: Beyond the Fringe?'' *Tempo* (Touche Ross & Co.) vol. 28, no. 1 (1974): 20–24.

set formula. Some top retail executives prefer mostly salary, others thrive on bonuses, still others would rather have more pension benefits. The same holds for salesclerks. Therefore, the compensation package needs to be tailored to the individual.

ORGANIZING HUMAN RESOURCES

If you were the owner-manager of a retail organization, you could not merely plan for and hire human resources and then let them run loose to do their own thing. Doing so would create havoc! Rather, you would need to organize them to work efficiently toward the organization's objectives and goals. For this, you would need an organization structure.[8]

An organization structure is an arrangement of human resources in terms of lines of authority and responsibility. There are, of course, formal and informal organization structures. The **formal organization structure** represents the way employees *should* behave in terms of lines of authority and responsibility. The **informal organization structure** depicts how the employees within the retail organization *actually do* behave in terms of lines of authority and responsibility.[9] All retail enterprises have both formal and informal organization structures—and both are useful.

Organizing Modes Retailers tend to organize their human resources around three modes: functions, merchandise lines, and geography. Organizing around **function** would involve delineating the functions the retailer performs (buying, selling, transporting, storing) and structuring the human resources so that there are specific tasks, responsibilities, and lines of authority regarding the performance of the functions. Organizing around **merchandise lines** would involve a similar process. What are the major merchandise lines to be handled (produce, meats, etc.)? How should the human resources be structured to perform tasks related to each of the lines while receiving the appropriate levels of responsibility and authority? To organize around **geography,** one might ask: What are the major geographic areas in which tasks need to be performed? Which human resources should perform these tasks in each geographic area?

Which Mode? How does one decide which mode is best suited for a specific retail enterprise? The answers to three other questions will help you answer this fundamental question.

1. What is the retailer's target market?
2. Where do decisions need to be made?
3. What is best for employees?

8. Many of the thoughts in this section are based on Dalton E. McFarland, *Management Principles and Practices*, 4th ed. (New York: Macmillan, 1974).

9. For detailed discussion of informal organization, see McFarland, *Management Principles and Practices*.

Target Market All retail organizations serve customers or markets. These customers or markets provide the transactions that help make the retailer profitable or unprofitable. Whether human resources are organized around functions, merchandise, or geography, the human resources will ultimately be concerned with retaining and attracting new customers to the retail enterprise. Therefore, the retailer must carefully define its target market if it is going to design a good retail organization structure that is customer oriented.

Decision Making Where will most of the decisions be concentrated? If we are referring to a 200-unit women's apparel chain with the units spread over thirty states, then it is likely that many decisions will have to be made at each location or region. Such a retailer might organize around geographic regions. On the other hand, decision making in a local department store may center on its departments and their respective merchandise lines. That store might therefore organize around merchandise lines. Other retailers, whose decisions most often concern functions, might organize around functions.

Employees Which organizing mode would be best for employee morale, productivity, and protecting or facilitating the retailer's investment in human resources? Let us assume that a local sporting goods retailer is growing rapidly and expects to open five stores in nearby cities over the next three years. If this retailer is organized around merchandise lines, then it may not be developing its human resources so that middle managers (merchandise managers) can become store managers in the near future. This retailer needs to develop a group of managers that understand all of the functions within the retail enterprise; therefore a merchandise line organization may not be its best organization structure.

As another example, consider a retailer organizing its human resources so that each person performs a specialized function and nothing else. This specialization may, in theory, increase productivity, but if it is too extreme employees may become bored, and morale and productivity may be harmed. Consider dividing the retail salesclerk's function into greeting customers, assisting customers, persuading customers, and collecting payment from customers. If a separate clerk was employed for each subfunction, then regardless of how much productivity could increase in theory, the practical problems of employee boredom and morale would block the theoretical productivity gains.

Organizing Around Functions Regardless of how retailers organize around functions and the number of functions that are formally incorporated into the organization structure, the basic tasks that need to be performed in retailing still remain. For example, assume you are the owner/manager of a local hardware store. In your organization you may formally recognize only one function—to manage the store. In principle, however, in your small retail organization you will have as many tasks and related functions to perform as there are formally delineated in the organization charts of some of the largest retail organizations in the free world.

Illustrations will be provided of one-, two-, three-, four-, and five-function retail organization structures. Keep in mind that there is a direct correlation between the size of the retailer and the number of functions formally recognized in the organization structure.

One-Function Organization Exhibit 11.3 shows a typical organizational structure of small, single unit retailers. The small, local, two- to four-employee hardware store, record store, drugstore, gasoline station, or floral shop is a good example. As illustrated in Exhibit 11.3, these organizations are headed by a store owner or manager, who is most often the same person. Reporting directly to the manager/owner is a head salesperson; this connotes that the major func-

EXHIBIT 11.3
**One-Function
Retail
Organization**

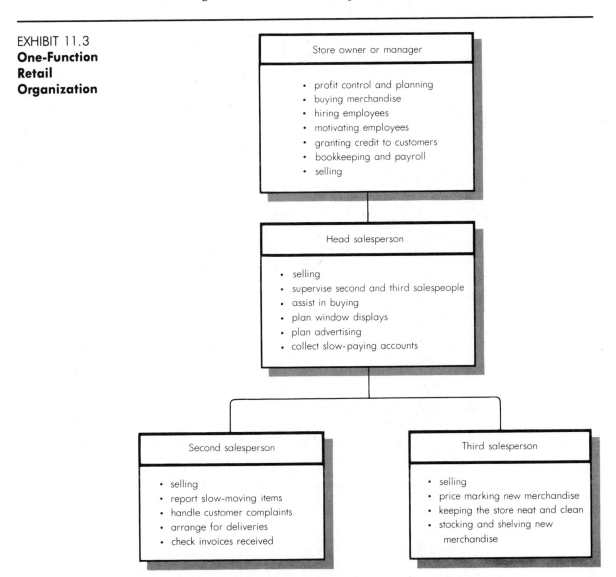

Store owner or manager

- profit control and planning
- buying merchandise
- hiring employees
- motivating employees
- granting credit to customers
- bookkeeping and payroll
- selling

Head salesperson

- selling
- supervise second and third salespeople
- assist in buying
- plan window displays
- plan advertising
- collect slow-paying accounts

Second salesperson

- selling
- report slow-moving items
- handle customer complaints
- arrange for deliveries
- check invoices received

Third salesperson

- selling
- price marking new merchandise
- keeping the store neat and clean
- stocking and shelving new merchandise

tion of the retail organization is to sell merchandise. Almost all small retail enterprises, when initially established, will find themselves organizing around the selling function. Reporting to the head salesperson are two employees, labeled the second and third salespeople (obviously, there could be more).

With the typical one-function retail organization, the selling function appears to be dominant and pervasive. This is somewhat misleading, though, because as we mentioned earlier, all retail organizations, regardless of size, must perform the same basic tasks and jobs. If we were to examine the duties assigned to each of the individuals in the basic one-function retail organization, we would see this truth more clearly. Refer to Exhibit 11.3 to examine the duties of each employee.

Two-Function Organization   As retail organizations grow, they may find that the basic one-function organization structure has become obsolete. With an increase in size, a modest degree of specialization can be obtained by establishing a two-function organization structure. Typically when this occurs, the two functions that are formally delineated are merchandising and operations.

Each function is handled by units headed up by managers; reporting to both the merchandise and operations manager would be a set of subordinates, each of whom would be assigned certain duties. In general, however, the merchandise manager would be responsible for all activities related to the buying and selling of merchandise, whereas the operations manager would be responsible for activities related to maintaining the store in good working order and performing tasks that assist in serving customers (delivery and stocking merchandise). With the two-function organization, the owner/manager would still retain primary responsibility for profit control and planning but would probably have some assistants to help in record keeping.

Three-Function Organization   Once again, the driving force for adding more functional specialization is growth. As the retailer grows, the amount of paperwork and record keeping actually grows more than proportionately. Tighter financial controls are needed as the number of employees grows, because the opportunity for embezzlement and theft of merchandise grows rapidly. It is not surprising therefore, that the next function to be formally added to retail enterprises is financial control, performed by a unit under the supervision of the financial control manager.

The financial control manager would relieve the owner/general manager of much of the work associated with profit planning and control. Notice, however, that the general manager or owner is still responsible for the overall profit performance of the retail enterprise. But by delegating some control to a financial control manager, the general manager/owner will have more time to concentrate on long-range strategic planning and growth goals.

Four-Function Organization   When retailers become sufficiently large to formalize a fourth function in their organization structure, it most often is promotion. Large retailers will spend a lot of money on promotion (advertising, public relations, window displays). A local department store doing $10 million in annual sales (which is not highly unusual) and spending 3½ percent of sales on promotion would be spending $350,000 annually. Such an expenditure might warrant the addition of a promotion manager to the organization structure. The four functions—financial control, merchandise, operations, and promotions—are now each being performed by separate units, with each unit headed by a manager. The four managers, all with equal status, report directly to the owner or general manager.

Complex Structures Our preceding discussion has intentionally been simplistic so that we could allow you to visualize how retail enterprises might change their organization structures as they grow. If we had shown you the retail organization structure portrayed in Exhibit 11.4 (see page 326), you wouldn't have been able to see the forest for all the trees. Exhibit 11.4 presents a complex organization structure for a large, corporately owned, general-merchandise store.[10] The skeleton of this organization structure is our basic four-function organization: the financial control manager, merchandise manager, promotion manager, and operations manager head the four functions and each reports to the general manager. At this point, however, the organization becomes more complex.

The general manager is not the owner, because we are dealing with a corporately owned organization; therefore, the stockholders are the owners. Between the stockholders and the general manager are a board of directors, president, and vice president. Both the president and vice president tend to concentrate on strategic and administrative planning matters, with a staff to assist and advise. The president's staff includes an executive secretary, a legal counselor, and a treasurer. The vice president has an executive secretary, research director, and director of planning on his or her staff.

You will also be able to see complexity in the number of subordinates reporting to each of the four functional managers. Still, however, we have not shown all of the complexity of a retail organization. For example, the accounts payable manager who reports to the assistant controller would have a staff of several people, or even, in a retailer as large as Sears, over a hundred accounts-payable clerks. And notice we only show the subordinates for one division merchandise manager, whereas each would have a number of buyers and department managers reporting to her.

Organizing Around Merchandise Retailers who offer a wide variety and assortment of goods will sometimes organize their enterprise around the main merchandise categories they handle. By organizing around distinct merchandise categories, the retailer is implying that separate merchandise categories require unique managerial skills, and that these skills are more crucial than skills in managing specific functions. Exhibit 11.5 shows a basic, merchandise-oriented, retail organization for a home improvement center. Reporting directly to the store

10. This view of the complex organization is based on the writing of Paul M. Mazur, *Principles of Organization Applied to Modern Retailing* (New York: Harper, 1927).

EXHIBIT 11.4   **Complex Organization for a Large, Corporate-Owned, General-Merchandise Store**

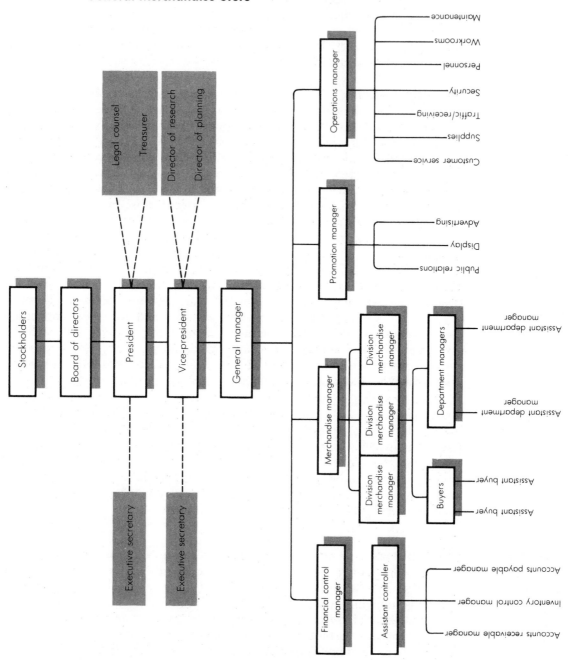

Parts of this exhibit are adapted from Paul M. Mazur, *Principles of Organization Applied to Modern Retailing* (New York: Harper, 1927), frontispiece.

owner or general manager are a lawn and garden manager, a lumber and building materials manager, a paint and wall covering manager, a hand and power tool manager, and a hardware, plumbing, and electrical supplies manager.

Organizing Around Location   A retail enterprise that has a large number of stores spread over a broad geographic area will often find it advantageous to structure its organization around geographic locations. It does this in order to be able to quickly address operating problems on a regional or local level. Having good managerial talent in each region, with the appropriate amount of responsibility and authority, means that decisions can be made more rapidly. The basic location-oriented retail organization structure is shown in Exhibit 11.6 (on page 328).

Multi-Mode Organizations   Retailers need not only organize around a single mode—functions, locations or merchandise categories—but may organize their human resources around several modes. Two examples are the functional-location organization structure and the locational-merchandise organization structure. These two examples are depicted in Exhibit 11.7 (page 329) and Exhibit 11.8 (page 330).

EXHIBIT 11.5
Merchandise-Oriented Retail Organization

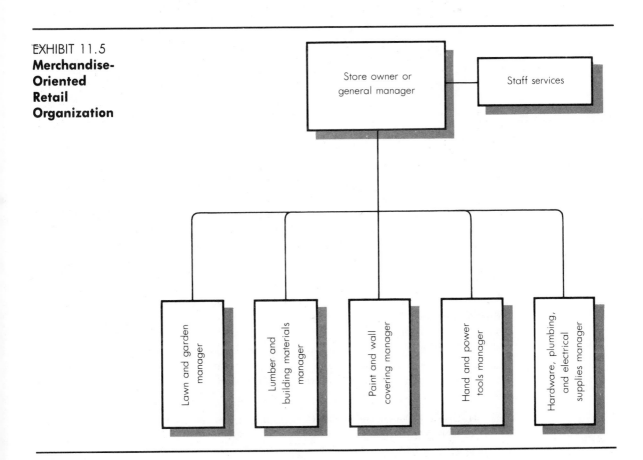

Store owner or general manager

Staff services

Lawn and garden manager

Lumber and building materials manager

Paint and wall covering manager

Hand and power tools manager

Hardware, plumbing, and electrical supplies manager

EXHIBIT 11.6
**Location-
Oriented
Retail
Organization**

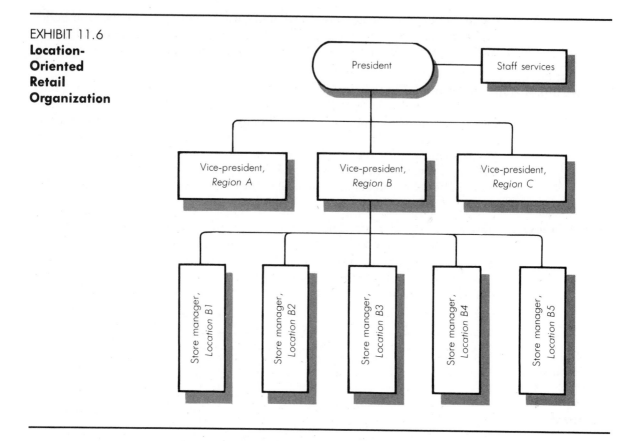

Branch-Store Organizations   When a single-unit retailer decides to add a second store in the same city, it typically refers to this as a branch store. In fact, the first several stores a retailer adds in its base city are often called branch stores. These branch stores represent coordination and control problems. There is no best way to handle these problems in terms of organization structure, but several alternatives are available. Delbert Duncan and Stanley Hollander call these the "brood hen and chick" organization, the "separate store" plan, and the "equal store" structure.[11]

Brood Hen and Chick   When a retailer first begins to expand by opening new stores, and when these new stores are substantially smaller than the parent store, the brood hen and chick plan is often followed. In principle, the parent store operates the branch. Each key executive at the parent store performs or supervises the functions of related personnel in the branch. For example, the

11. Delbert J. Duncan and Stanley C. Hollander, *Modern Retailing Management*, 9th ed. (Homewood, Ill.: Richard D. Irwin, 1977) pp. 190–91.

EXHIBIT 11.7   **Functional-Locational Retail Organization**

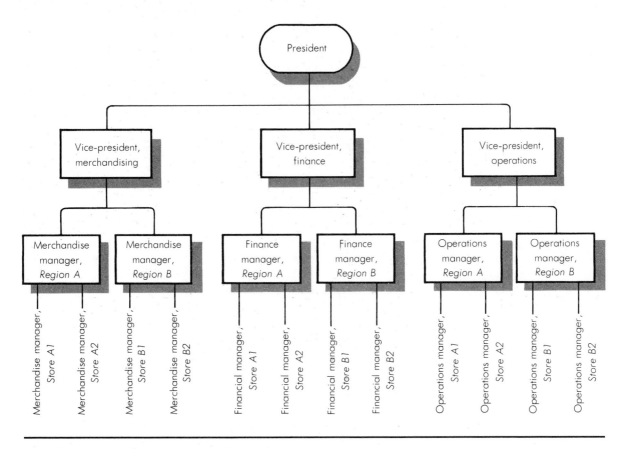

financial control manager of the parent store is also the controller of branch operations.

Separate Store   If too many branches are added or if the branch becomes too large, the workload on the executives at the parent store will become too heavy. At this point, the retailer may create a separate management group and staff for the branch. However, if each branch has its own management group and staff, there may easily result a duplication of efforts and therefore an inefficient use of human resources.

Equal Store   It is possible to move in the opposite direction from that which we outlined above, that is, all major management functions may be centralized at a single headquarters. The management group and staff at headquarters will treat all stores as equal in terms of organizational status. The first store is given no special treatment or attention merely because it was the parent. The major

EXHIBIT 11.8
**Locational-
Merchandise
Retail
Organization**

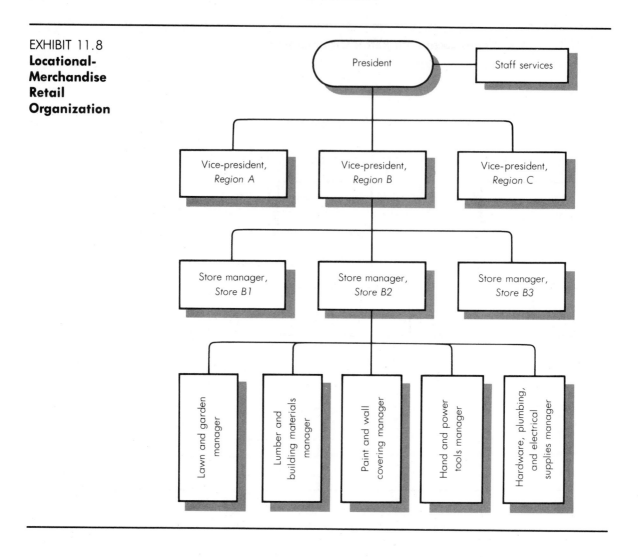

problem under this plan is that many of the unique problems of the individual stores—parent or branch—can not be given special attention, because most decisions are centralized and made at headquarters.

Chain-Store Organizations   Most of the concepts already discussed will apply to chain-store organizations. The major point to keep in mind is that chains have eleven or more outlets and therefore problems of coordination and control become crucial. However, there is no precise pattern for organizing chain-store enterprises. The structure developed by a particular chain depends on the organizational philosophies of top management, merchandise lines carried, and whether the chain is national, regional, or local.

In organizing chain-store enterprises two special problems should be considered: how to coordinate and control decisions, and how to separate buying and selling.

Coordination and Control   The central problem in organizing chain-store enterprises is one of coordination and control of individual stores. In fact, what we want to do with the organization structure is to create a system in which a network of stores, each with human and economic resources, will work smoothly. As the chain store grows in size, this becomes a more difficult feat.

Most chain stores have developed an extremely centralized organization structure in which all major decisions for all stores are made at the chain headquarters. In short, the store managers merely make sure that policies, procedures, and directives from headquarters are followed. The system becomes a bureaucracy, with store managers responding to memos from headquarters and filling out numerous reports (daily, weekly, monthly) to keep headquarters aware of the store's performance. Obviously, chain stores will vary in the degree to which they are centralized. But all are going to be more centralized than decentralized in order to be able to cope with the major problem of coordination and control.

In order to facilitate coordination and control in a chain-store enterprise, the central management will often have a large number of staff personnel who are specialists in a number of key functional decisions. Staff personnel could include:

- Consumer research specialists
- Merchandise statistics specialists
- Real estate specialists
- Legal counselors
- Public relation specialists
- Tax planning specialists
- Human resource specialists
- Pension plan specialists
- Consumer advocate advisors

Obviously, only the size and complexity of chain-store enterprises can justify this type of management specialization and investment in human resources. In fact, there is often even a specialist in human resource management.

Buying and Selling   The second major problem in designing chain-store organization structures is whether to separate buying and selling. In other words, should buying be totally centralized—with headquarters buying all the merchandise for all the stores—while the stores are responsible for selling the merchandise? By centralizing all buying, the chain store can obtain significant buying economies because it can purchase in large quantities. The problem with this approach is that all stores get a standard merchandise mix that, by definition, will not be tailored to the trade area of each store. This is obviously less of a problem for supermarkets than for fashion apparel chains. But in either situation, it is a problem.

Some chain-store organizations have responded to this problem by allowing local stores to purchase up to a certain percentage (possibly 20 percent) of their own merchandise. This still gives each store, regardless of location, a core of standard merchandise, but it allows some tailoring of the merchandise mix to local demands and preferences. The major problem is that as each local store is allowed to buy a higher percentage of its own merchandise, the presentation of a consistent image for the chain's stores becomes increasingly difficult. For example, a person who generally shops at a store of chain X in Georgia may not recognize the chain's store in Michigan.

It is still the dominant industry practice in chain-store retailing to centralize decisions and to do 100 percent of the buying at headquarters and most of the selling on a local level. Any selling at the headquarters relates to designing or placing national or regional advertisements and occasionally managing local advertising.

Ownership Groups   Ownership groups are retail enterprises that have purchased previously independent retailers and in some cases other retail chains. The ownership group allows individual stores to maintain their prior image and management and merchandising procedures. Any changes that are made typically relate to centralizing certain staff services, such as legal services or long-range planning. Examples of ownership groups are Federated Department Stores, Carter Hawley Hale Stores, Allied Stores Corporation, Cities Stores Company, Dayton-Hudson Corporation, and Mercantile Stores Company. Federated, for instance, owns Bloomingdale's in New York, The Boston Store in Milwaukee, Bullocks-Magnin Company in California, Shillito's in Cincinnati, Abraham and Straus in Brooklyn, and fifteen other store groups, mostly local department stores.

Ownership groups, as opposed to chain-store organizations, allow their stores to be relatively autonomous. One important area in which they are not autonomous is expansion—opening new outlets, adding additional space, or remodeling. Basically, this is the situation because all positive cash flow goes to headquarters and the top management of the ownership group will allocate capital back to the respective divisions according to need and the long-range plans that each division has developed in consultation with the ownership group. Obviously, therefore, some divisions will receive more financial capital than they generated, and others less. This is because some divisions, based upon their location, image, or other strategic advantage, will be better positioned for profitable growth opportunities.

SUMMARY

Our discussion of human resource planning and management focused on five major dimensions: planning for human resources, human resource acquisition, training and development, human resource compensation, and organizing human resources.

To properly plan for human resources, the retailer should first identify the myriad of tasks that need to be performed. A useful frame of reference is the marketing functions. Which functions and how much of each does the retailer desire to perform? Each function can then be broken into tasks, with the tasks into jobs.

In long-range planning, the retailer should carefully examine its projected speed of growth and the predictability of this growth. It should also carefully examine its plans to diversify geographically or by line of trade. Finally, it should conduct a human resource audit. In short-run human resource planning, the retail executive should attempt to forecast any weekly, monthly, or seasonal swings in sales activity and then adjust human resource inputs appropriately.

Human resource acquisition occurs in a competitive labor market. There are many available sources of applicants; the more common include: walk-ins, employment agencies, schools and colleges, former employees, advertising, and recommendations from existing employees. Once the applicants are obtained, they must be properly screened. We suggested a five-step screening process: application, personal interview, testing, reference check, and physical examination.

Expenditures on training and development are an attempt by the retailer to increase its return on investment in human resources. Training methods for new employees include the sink or swim method, the sponsorship method, and formal training programs. Techniques used to train and develop existing employees include: job rotation, special assignments, staff assistant, reading material, in-house courses, outside short courses, college degree programs, advanced management programs, trade conferences, and correspondence courses.

Compensation is crucial to attracting, retaining, and motivating retail employees. A good compensation program includes a fixed component to provide income, a variable component to motivate employees, and a fringe benefit component to provide security and prestige.

Retailers can organize their enterprises around functions, merchandise lines, or geographic location. Some of the larger retail enterprises will organize around more than one. In deciding which way to organize, the retailer should ask, What is my target market? Where do decisions need to be made? and What is best for my employees?

We discussed alternatives for organizing branch stores, including the brood hen and chick organization, the separate store plan, and the equal store structure. We also commented on organizing problems associated with chain-stores and ownership groups.

QUESTIONS

1. What are the various methods of compensating retail employees? Which method would be best for a salesperson? a store manager? a retail controller?

2. How might the training needs of a supermarket retailer be different from those of a camera store retailer?

3. Why do retailers need an organization chart?

4. What problems arise when retail employees become too specialized?

5. Discuss the alternative methods for organizing branch stores.

6. How might a nonstore retailer such as a direct-mail, general-merchandise retailer organize differently than a conventional department store?

7. How can better organization of human resources increase labor productivity?

8. What are the major problems in centralizing the buying function in a chain organization?

9. What are the advantages and disadvantages of paying salespeople in a furniture store strictly on a commission basis?

10. Are the problems facing a personnel manager in a retail institution any different from the problems confronting a personnel manager in a factory?

PROBLEMS AND EXERCISES

1. Obtain an employment application form from a local retailer. What questions are asked on this form? Why do you think these questions are asked?

2. Interview several friends, acquaintances, or classmates that have worked in a retail organization. What are their perceptions of the competitiveness of wages and the quality of training and development?

3. Find out from your campus placement office which retailers interview college students on campus. What do these retailers have in common? Write to each company for a copy of its annual report to stockholders. Which companies look like the type you might like to work for when you graduate?

4. Interview a friend or acquaintance that works for a retailer. How do the formal and informal organizations vary? In other words, are there people who have more influence than the organization chart or their position in the organization would suggest? What lines of communication have developed outside the formal organization chart?

5. Develop a job application form for a department store.

SUGGESTED READINGS

Hallon, Charles J. and Myron Gable. "Information Sources in Retail Employment Decision-Making Process." *Journal of Retailing* 55(Fall 1979): 58–74.

Harvey, Reed and Robert Smith. "Need Satisfaction for Retail Management." *Journal of Retailing* 48(Fall 1972): 89–95.

Spivey, W. Austin, J. Michael Munson, and William B. Locander. "Meeting Retail Staffing Needs via Improved Selection." *Journal of Retailing* 55(Winter 1979): 3–19.

Sutherland, Dennis J. "Managing by Objectives in Retailing." *Journal of Retailing* 47(Fall 1971): 15–26.

12

Overview   *In this chapter we will develop a locational decision-making paradigm showing the steps a retail analyst should go through in selecting a good retail location. Our purpose is to expose you to some of the complexities and many of the questions that a retail decision maker will need to face in order to determine the best site for a new store.*

Location Planning and Management

A RETAILER'S LOCATION is the third in the trichotomy of major resources needed before operations can be commenced. You might not think of location as a resource, but it is a crucial one. Resources are fundamentally things that can be drawn on for assistance in taking care of some need. All retailers have a need to generate revenue, and any retailer's location is its fundamental resource in determining the potential revenues it can generate. This is true because any given location will draw patrons only from some finite distance or geographic area.

In a good location, a retailer can generate high levels of revenue; thus the value of that location as a resource is high. On the other hand, a poor location will produce low levels of revenue—regardless of the retailer's pricing, promotion, and customer service decisions—making the value of that location low. Therefore, location is appropriately viewed as a resource and thus best discussed under the administrative portion of the retail planning and management model.

Location is a crucial determinant of the retailer's ability to achieve high performance results. Let us identify some of the underlying reasons why location is so important.

1. A location decision is both a large and long-term commitment of resources, and it will reduce a retailer's future flexibility. Regardless of whether the retailer leases or purchases, the location decision implies some degree of permanence.
2. The location decision will have implications for the merchandise the retailer handles, the prices it sets, and the promotion programs it establishes. Once the location is established, the store's potential customers have been identified, which limits the retailer's merchandising, pricing, and promotion alternatives.
3. A retailer's growth goals often imply that more new locations should be established.
4. Since the environment that encompasses any given location will change over time, the value of a location may deteriorate, requiring some action on the part of management.
5. The location is also important to consumers and society, since it influences consumer travel costs.

As a potential retail decision maker you should therefore appreciate the scope and importance of the location decision.

DECISION-MAKING PARADIGM

In Exhibit 12.1, we present the paradigm for decision making on location. As you can see, the paradigm has six distinct steps and a continuous feedback loop.

EXHIBIT 12.1
**Location
Decision-Making
Paradigm**

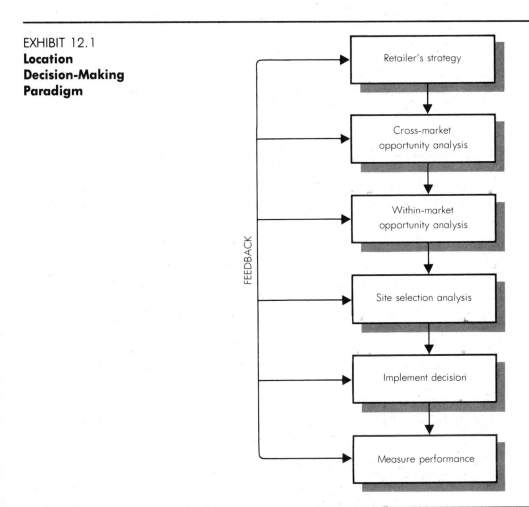

The paradigm depicts a process, which logically begins with defining the retailer's strategy. Once the strategy is defined, the retailer performs a cross-market opportunity analysis, which consists of identifying the markets (cities or towns) that represent the most attractive opportunities for carrying out that strategy. Next, the retailer must perform a within-market opportunity analysis, identifying the most attractive sites within each of the most attractive markets. Subsequently, the process moves to selection of the best site from those identified as most attractive. More than one site may be selected depending on the retailer's growth goals, capital, and human resources. The process then moves to implementation of the location decision, which involves such things as purchasing the site and construction of a new building, if needed. The last step is measuring performance, which consists of evaluating whether the location is performing up to or beyond expectations. Associated with each of the preceding steps in the process is a feedback mechanism that allows for the adjustment of prior decisions as new information is received.

You should note that the paradigm is not specific to line of trade but applies to any line. In addition, the paradigm does not unrealistically assume that the retailer has already decided on the city or town in which it would like to conduct business. Finally, the paradigm is normative in that it suggests how retail decision makers should make good location decisions. The fact that the paradigm may not fully capture how retail decision makers currently select locations should not be disturbing. Our goal is to illustrate how to achieve high performance results, and not how to behave like the typical industry retailer. With these points in mind, let us delve into each of the steps in the paradigm in more detail.

DEFINING A STRATEGY

In Chapter 9 we discussed the strategic planning process. In this process the retailer matched its mission and objectives with opportunities emanating from behavioral trends and the socioeconomic, technological, and legal environments. The outcome was development of a strategy that capitalized on opportunities and allowed the retailer to achieve its mission and objectives. We saw that an important component of any retailer's strategy was market segmentation or the identification of its target market.

The retailer's strategy will thus be the first major variable to consider in location decisions. The rationale for this is straightforward. A retailer's strategy will severely limit the number of alternative locations that need to be explored—and this is good because it makes locational decision-making more efficient.

Assume that you are a proprietor of two Scandinavian furniture stores in two separate cities in Pennsylvania. You have experienced considerable success and your goal is to become the dominant retailer of Scandinavian furniture in Pennsylvania by 1990. Furthermore, your financial objective is to achieve a return on equity of 25 percent and a growth in total earnings of 40 percent per year. Analysis of your two existing stores and industry data suggests that the best target market for Scandinavian furniture stores is small households with above-average income and education, living in cities over 100,000, and with a head of household between 24 and 45 years old. Obviously, these requirements limit the number of cities or towns you must analyze. First, you could ignore all cities not in Pennsylvania. Second, you could ignore all cities in Pennsylvania under 100,000 in population. Third, for those cities over 100,000 population within Pennsylvania, you would be concerned only with those which have a significant number of small households with above-average income and education and in which the head of household is twenty-five to forty-five.

Exhibit 12.2 gives another example of how location decisions and strategy are intertwined. This case study shows that location decisions may involve the elimination of locations, as well as their addition.

EXHIBIT 12.2 **Store Pruning**	Occasionally, although it may be disheartening, the best strategy for a chain-store retailer is to retreat and prune its poorest performing stores. In all retail chains there is considerable variability in the profit performance of stores. It is not uncommon for the top 20 percent of the stores to produce 80 percent of the retail enterprise's profit. Often by pruning stores, the chain can increase its overall profitability dramatically.

Store pruning is precisely the strategy that Liberty House of California pursued in the late 1970s. The company cut 52 percent of its department stores. Many of the Liberty House Department Stores were spread too far apart—from the Northwestern to Southwestern United States. Since stores were as far away as Texas and Washington, the company could not achieve economies of scale in advertising and administration. Also, many of the stores were in poor locations.

Liberty House of California retrenched by slashing the number of stores to ten—all in northern California. The net result was an acceleration of profits by 78 percent to $24 million for the fiscal year ended December 31, 1979.

Source: Based on data from "Liberty House's Big Pruning," *Chain Store Age Executive* 56(May 1980): 65.

CROSS-MARKET OPPORTUNITY ANALYSIS

The cross-market opportunity analysis, the second step in the location paradigm, is an attempt to identify the most attractive markets the retailer could locate within. The markets considered are those consistent with the retailer's strategy. In Exhibit 12.3 we present a retail case study dealing with market selection. It points out the extreme importance of market selection to retailers in the mature stage of the retail life cycle.

A trio of locational theories and concepts is especially useful for shedding light on the need to conduct a cross-market analysis. The first is central place theory and second is retail gravity theory, both of which were developed by scholars working independently of one another in the late 1920s and early 1930s. A third is retail saturation.

Central Place Theory   In 1933 Walter Christaller published *Central Places in Southern Germany.*[1] A central place is a center of commerce composed of a cluster of retail institutions—typically what today is called a village, town, or city. Central place theory was based on a ranking of communities according to the assortment of goods available in each. At the bottom of the hierarchy were communities that represented the smallest central places. They provided the most basic assortment of goods and services—the necessities of life. As one went up the hierarchy, one would find larger central places, which carried all of the goods and

1. Walter Christaller, *Central Places in Southern Germany,* trans. Carlisle W. Baskin (Englewood Cliffs, N.J.: Prentice-Hall, 1966).

EXHIBIT 12.3
**Market
Selection**

When planning for growth through entering new markets, retailers must identify the most attractive markets and those which are stagnant. This is extremely important to retailers in the mature stage of the retail life cycle, such as supermarkets.

In selecting markets, retailers must realize that to enter a market profitably they will often need to build several stores in a single market. This is necessary to obtain scale of economies in distribution and administration. It also enables the retailer to obtain a significant market share in order to be a major competitive force in the marketplace.

An illustration of market selection involves Winn-Dixie, a $5 billion supermarket chain based in Jacksonville, Florida. In 1979 Winn-Dixie had an estimated 35 percent of the Fort Worth market. Dallas was selected for expansion because it was a growth market—population growth in Dallas was among the top in the nation—because it was close to Fort Worth, where Winn-Dixie was already established, and because Winn-Dixie has a major warehouse in Fort Worth, which could easily service the new Dallas stores. To obtain an immediate presence in Dallas, Winn-Dixie had fourteen stores under construction in early 1980 and had nine more on the drawing board.

Source: Based on data from "Winn-Dixie Targets Booming Dallas Market for Expansion," *Chain Store Age Executive* 56(February 1980): 39–40.

services found in lower-order central places plus more specialized ones that were not as necessary to a basic existence.

To obtain goods and services, households surrounding the central places would need to travel there. Thus, consumer travel becomes crucial in determining the location of central places. In fact, Christaller illustrated how central places would be established in a geographic space in order to minimize aggregate travel costs for the consumer. The more basic the good or service, the shorter the distance the consumer would need to travel to purchase it. On the other hand, for specialized goods and services, the typical household could expect to travel a great distance, since only the larger central places would have them.

Although Christaller developed his theory to describe the location of retail activity in Southern Germany in the 1930s, the validity of his theory has been demonstrated by at least three independent, empirically based research studies in the United States over the last three decades.[2] All three agreed that among the first twenty lines of retail trade to locate in a community, the following nine would appear, and in this order:

1. Gasoline service station
2. Grocery store
3. Restaurant

2. Brian Berry and William Garrison, "The Functional Bases of the Central Place Hierarchy," *Economic Geography* 34(April 1958): 146–149; J. Hurlebaus and R. Fulton, "Community Size and the Number of Businesses and Services," *Tennessee Survey of Business* 3(1968); and Joseph Barry Mason, "Threshold Analysis as a Tool in Economic Potential Studies and Retail Site Location: An Illustrative Application," *The Southern Journal of Business* 8(August 1972): 43.

4. Physician
5. Insurance agency
6. Beauty salon
7. Real estate agency
8. Auto parts dealer
9. Furniture store

Furthermore, two of the three studies agreed that the following five functions would also locate in the top twenty:

10. Automobile dealer
11. Lawyer
12. Hay-grain and feed store
13. Women's ready-to-wear
14. Dry cleaner

What are the implications of central place theory for cross-market opportunity analysis? There are three:

1. Not all communities will be able to support all types of retailing activity. The more basic or necessity-oriented goods that the retailer is selling (gasoline and food), the more communities it must consider as potential markets to enter. If it is selling very specialized goods such as furs and jewelry, then it need only consider the larger communities.
2. It tells the retailer the types of retail activity that a growing community will most likely need in the future. For example, a small community with only a gasoline service station and a grocery store will next need a restaurant as it continues to grow. Thus, central place theory can help the retailer identify the communities or markets that will be most in need of its type of retailing activity.
3. The theory tells us that a single trip to a higher-order central place will replace the need to make separate trips to lower-order centers. This suggests that the larger central places will do a disproportionately larger amount of business. Households from smaller surrounding communities, when they travel to a larger central place, will be able to purchase not only specialized goods and services, but also basic ones. The implication is simply that large central places tend to be more attractive in terms of potential demand.

The preceding points suggest that central place theory can provide insights into cross-market opportunity analysis.

Retail Gravity Theory   In 1929 William Reilly developed the **law of retail gravitation**, dealing with how large urbanized areas attracted customers from smaller communities serving the rural hinterland.[3] As its name implies, Reilly's law mimics the grav-

---

3. William J. Reilly, *Methods for Study of Retail Relationships* (Austin, Tex: The University of Texas, Bureau of Business Research), Research Monograph, No. 4, 1929.

itational law of physics. In it, mass is replaced by population and distance remains distance. The most popular version of Reilly's law is as follows:[4]

$$D_y = \frac{D_{xy}}{\left(1 + \sqrt{\dfrac{P_x}{P_y}}\right)}$$

where:

D_y = distance from which community Y can attract households
D_{xy} = distance separating communities X and Y
P_x = population of X (the larger community)
P_y = population of Y (the smaller community)

Consider the population and distances separating communities A, B, C, and D in Exhibit 12.4a. Community A is the largest, with a population of 240,000 and it is surrounded by three smaller communities. Community B is 18 miles away and has a population of 14,000; Community D is 5 miles away and has a population of 30,000; and Community C is 14 miles away and has a population of 21,000. We will assume that the roads on Exhibit 12.4a are the only ones connecting the smaller communities with the larger Community A.

Reilly's law will allow us to determine the distances from which each of the smaller communities will be able to attract households. The converse of this is the distances from which Community A will be able to attract households in the direction of the smaller communities, B, C, and D.

For example, if we consider Communities A and B we would have:

$$D_B = \frac{18}{\left(1 + \sqrt{\dfrac{240,000}{14,000}}\right)} = 3.5 \text{ miles}$$

Thus, Community B is able to attract households from 3.5 miles in the direction of Community A. Since A and B are 18 miles apart, we could also conclude that A could attract customers from 14.5 miles (18 − 3.5) in the direction of B.

Applying the same equation, but using the relevant data on Communities C and D yields:

$$D_C = \frac{14}{\left(1 + \sqrt{\dfrac{240,000}{21,000}}\right)} = 3.2 \text{ miles}$$

$$D_D = \frac{5}{\left(1 + \sqrt{\dfrac{240,000}{30,000}}\right)} = 1.3 \text{ miles}$$

Thus, Community C can attract households from 3.2 miles in the direction of A, and D can attract households from 1.3 miles in the direction of A.

4. This formulation of Reilly's law was developed by P. D. Converse in "New Laws of Retail Gravitation," *Journal of Marketing* 14(January 1949): 379–384.

In Exhibit 12.4b we show that we can connect the three points that we just determined. The result is Community *A*'s **general trading area,** a geographically delineated area that surrounds a community, from which households that reside in that area would generally be willing to travel to the community to purchase goods and services.

In Exhibit 12.4b, you will notice that Community *A* can draw from a relatively large distance in the direction of *B, C,* or *D.* This is because Community *A*'s "mass" or population is large, which makes it more of a "magnet" to pull people from the hinterlands. Actually, however, the population is not the attractive force, but rather the large assortment of goods and services that are associated with large population centers. As a community grows in population, it develops a larger assortment of goods and services, and thus it becomes more of a central place as noted by Christaller. This causes more households to be attracted to the community to do their shopping.

What is the major implication of Reilly's law for cross-market opportunity analysis? When the retail analyst is evaluating different markets (communities) in which to locate, special consideration must be given to the population of the community in relation to the populations and distances of communities that surround it. This is important because it determines the general trading area of a community and the households that can be attracted to a community to shop.

EXHIBIT 12.4
A Community's General Trading Area

A. Distances of Communities A, B, C, and D

B. Distances Community A Can Attract Customers

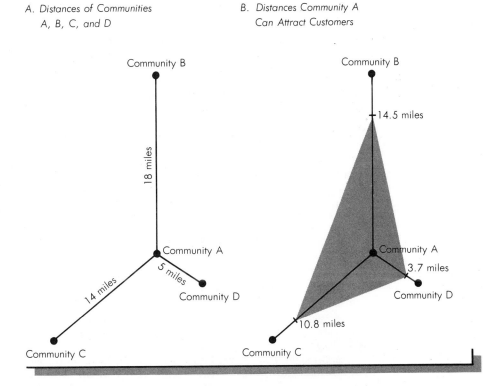

Saturation Theory   The third theoretical concept that can help shed light on cross-market opportunity analysis is retail saturation. William Applebaum and Saul Cohen define **store saturation** as follows:[5]

> Store saturation of a market is a condition under which existing store facilities are utilized efficiently and adequately meet customer needs. Saturation exists for a given type of store, when a market has just enough store facilities of a given type to serve the population of the market satisfactorily and yield a fair return to the owners on their investments without raising prices to the customer to achieve this return. When a market has too few stores to provide satisfactorily the needs of the customer, it is under-stored. When a market has too many stores to yield a fair return on investment, it is over-stored. Saturation as defined here, implies a balance between the amount of existing retail store facilities and their use (which in turn is a reflection of need).

A possible indicator of under- versus over-stored markets is the **index of retail saturation** (IRS).[6] The IRS can be defined as follows:

$$IRS_1 = \frac{H_1 \cdot RE_1}{RF_1}$$

where:

IRS_1 = index of retail saturation for area one
H_1 = number of households in area one
RE_1 = retail expenditures for a particular line of trade per household in area one
RF_1 = square feet of retail facilities for a particular line of trade in area one

When the IRS takes on a high value, it indicates that the market is not saturated, and therefore a potentially attractive opportunity exists. When it takes on a low value, it indicates a saturated market, which precludes the potential of a significant opportunity.

On careful inspection of the IRS formula, you should notice two things. First, the IRS informs the retail analyst that market-entry decisions should be based on supply and demand factors. In fact, the IRS is simply the ratio of aggregate household demand ($H_1 \cdot RE_1$) to aggregate retail space supply (RF_1). The higher the ratio of aggregate demand to aggregate supply, the more attractive the market opportunity. Second, the IRS is essentially a measure of average sales per square foot of the existing retail establishments in the market. With this statistic the analyst can derive an estimate of profits by working with known gross margin and operating expense ratios for the industry.

Often when American retailers face saturated markets at home, they can

5. William Applebaum and Saul B. Cohen, "Trading Area Networks and Problems of Store Saturation," *Journal of Retailing* 37(Winter 1961–62): 35–36. Reprinted with permission of the *Journal of Retailing.*

6. Bernard LaLonde, "The Logistics of Retail Location," in William D. Stevens (ed.), *1961 Full American Marketing Association Proceedings* (Chicago: American Marketing Association, 1961), p. 572.

take their retailing concepts and strategies to foreign markets that may not be saturated. In Exhibit 12.5 we present a case study on Wickes Corp., which illustrates this point.

Probably the major implication of the concept of retail saturation for cross-market opportunity and analysis is the explicit need to recognize demand and supply factors in analyzing markets. Thus, let us turn to the identification of the major demand and supply factors that were not explicitly recognized in the IRS.

Demand Factors The major demand factors that should be carefully analyzed, in addition to retail sales per household (as defined in the IRS), are household and community characteristics. Household characteristics include its income, age profile, and size. Community characteristics include its life cycle, population density, and mobility.

Household Income The average household income and the distribution of household incomes can significantly influence demand for retail facilities. As average household income rises, the community will exhibit a greater demand for luxury goods and a more sophisticated demand for necessity goods. Consider the demand for food. Regardless of household income, as long as it is above the poverty level, individuals will consume the same approximate number of calories, or quantity of food. At low incomes, however, they may consume pinto beans, hot dogs, and bread; and at the higher income level they may eat asparagus, sirloin steak, and fancy dinner rolls.

The distribution of household incomes in a community can also influence the demand for retail facilities. If all households in a community had an identical income (an unlikely phenomenon) then the same type of retail facility within any given line of trade would probably appeal to all households. There would be no opportunity to segment the market based on income. For example, if all households had relatively low incomes, then an upscale, high-price, fashion-oriented women's apparel store would face little opportunity, even though there might be a need for an additional women's apparel store. On the other hand, if the average household had a low income, but there were also a fair number of households with high incomes, then there might exist some potential for such a store.

Household Age Profile The age composition of households can be an important determinant of demand for retail facilities. In communities where households tend to be young, the preferences for stores may be different than in communities where the average household is relatively old. For example, in communities with a disproportionate number of young households, the demand for restaurants will be heavily oriented toward the fast-food type, whereas in communities with a disproportionate number of older households, the demand will be more oriented to leisurely dining. Similarly, age will help determine the demand for a wide range of retail facilities such as furniture stores, jewelry stores, and apparel stores.

EXHIBIT 12.5
Foreign Market Selection

A United States retailer searching for attractive markets to enter should not limit its search to domestic borders. Oftentimes, when a retail innovation catches on in the United States, communities get saturated with the new innovation. At this point, the retailer may find that the innovation may be right for introduction into a foreign market.

Consider Wickes' entry into the Netherlands in 1969 with the home improvement center concept—a supermarket of hardware and lumber catering to the do-it-yourself home-remodeling customer. At the time of entry, the European market was relatively unexploited. Within five years, the concept had caught on and several European retail companies had jumped into the field. But Wickes still found enough understored communities to allow it to open forty-five home improvement centers in the Netherlands, Belgium, Holland, England, and West Germany. And by the late 1970s the European operations were earning a 30 percent return on assets, which was twice their United States average. Facing an overstored European market in the 1980s, the company is considering entering Brazil. Brazil has few building supply retailers and represents a substantial unexploited market.

Source: Based on data from John Quirt, "Wickes Corp.'s Retailing Triumph in Europe," *Fortune*, August 13, 1979, pp. 178, 184.

Size of Household If we hold income and age constant and change the size of the household, we will be able to identify another determinant of the demand for retail facilities. To illustrate, consider two young households with moderate incomes but in which one household contains a husband and wife, and the other a husband, wife, and three children. For the second household, the moderate income loses much of its power, because of the larger household size. This will influence the distribution of retail expenditures between food stores, apparel stores, furniture stores, restaurants, auto dealers, and so on. This in turn will influence the demand for retail facilities in general as well as the demand for specific types (e.g., discount department store versus full-service, conventional department stores). To illustrate this point further, place yourself as the head of a household with an income of $26,000 and consider how you would spend that money if you had no children, and then if you had three children.

Community Life Cycle Communities tend to exhibit growth patterns over time. It has been suggested that:

> Over a span of time, growth patterns of communities may be of four major types. These include the pattern of rapid growth, the pattern of continuous growth, the pattern of relatively stable growth, and the pattern of decline. The rapid growth pattern can be found largely in communities located along the Gulf Coast, in the Southwest, and in the West. The continuous growth pattern is appearing in communities that are developing new industries and expanding established industries. The slow or constant level growth pattern can be found when a city has developed an established economy that remains in a relatively stable position. The dimin-

Wickes Corp. found opportunity for profitable expansion abroad. (Photo courtesy of Wickes Corp.)

ished or declining growth pattern is often associated with the exhaustion of resources or a shift in technology.[7]

The retailer should try to identify the communities that are in a rapid or continuous growth pattern, since they will represent the best long-run opportunities.

Population Density   The population density of a community can be defined either as the number of persons per square mile or number of households per square mile. In either case, empirical research suggests that the higher the population density, the larger the average store in terms of square feet and thus the fewer the number of stores that will be needed to serve a population of a given size.[8] Therefore, it is important that retailers consider the population density of the various markets they are evaluating.

Mobility   The easier it is for people to travel, the more mobile they will be.[9] When people are mobile they are willing to travel greater distances to shop, and therefore there will be fewer, but larger stores in the community. Thus, in a community whose households are highly mobile, there will be a need for fewer retailers than in a community whose mobility is low. Mobility cannot be directly determined, but there are readily available surrogate indicators. One popular indicator is number of automobiles per household. As this number rises, the household becomes more mobile. Other indicators are the availability of public transportation and the amount of traffic congestion. Households may

7. Rom J. Markin, Jr., *Retailing Management*, 2nd ed. (New York: Macmillan, 1977), p. 150.
8. Charles A. Ingene and Robert F. Lusch, "A Model of Retail Structure," in Jagdish Sheth, *Research in Marketing* 5(1981): 101–64.
9. Mobility can be viewed as both a household characteristic and a community characteristic. We chose to treat it as a community characteristic because the design of the community, the availability of public transportation, and the cost of operating an auto in any given area are determinants of mobility and are themselves characteristics of the community.

have cars, but if the roadways are inadequate to handle the quantity of traffic, then congestion will hamper household mobility. Thus more stores are needed, and they should be spaced closer together.

Supply Factors   The IRS formula used an aggregate measure of supply, mainly total square feet of retail facilities (by line of trade) in a community. Although this is a useful indicator, there are many others—square feet per store, square feet per employee, growth in number of stores, and quality of competition.

Square Feet per Store   It will be helpful if the retail analyst has data on the square feet per store for the average store in the communities that are being analyzed. This will indicate whether the community tends to have large- or small-scale retailing. And, of course, this is important in terms of assessing the extent to which the retailer's standard type of store would blend with the existing structure of retail trade in the community. We do not mean to imply, however, that a retailer consider locating only small stores in communities that presently tend to have small stores, etc. Rather, if there currently are only small stores in a community, then before entering with a large store, the retail analyst should make certain that the demand factors previously discussed would support a large establishment.

Square Feet per Employee   A measure that combines two major supply factors in retailing—store space and labor—is square feet of space per employee. A high number for this statistic in a community is evidence that each employee is able to handle more space. This could be due to either a high level of retail technology in the community or more self-service retailing. Since retail technology is fairly constant across communities, any difference in square feet per employee is most often due to level of service being provided. In communities currently characterized by retailers offering a high level of service, there may be a significant opportunity for new retailers that are oriented toward self-service.

Growth in Stores   The analyst should look at the rate of growth in the number of stores over the last one to five years. When the growth is rapid, then on average the community will have better-located stores with more contemporary atmospheres. More recently located stores will coincide better with the existing demographics of the community. Also their atmosphere will better suit the tastes of the marketplace, and they will tend to incorporate the latest in retail technology. All of these factors hint that the strength of retail competition will be greater when the community has recently experienced rapid growth in number of stores.

Quality of Competition   Our three supply factors have reflected the quantity of competition. An analyst also needs, however, to look at the strength or quality of competition. He or she should attempt to identify the major retail chains or local retailers in each market and evaluate the strength of each. Answers to questions such as the following would be insightful: What is their market share or profitability? How promotion- and price-oriented are they? Do they tend to react to new market entrants by cutting price, increasing advertising, or improving customer service?

A Recap   The discussion we have pursued of central place theory, retail gravity theory, saturation theory, and demand and supply factors should provide you with a frame of reference for cross-market opportunity analysis. More complete statistically based frameworks are available, but they are beyond the scope of this text.[10] Perhaps the most important point to keep in mind is that before a retailer selects a location, it should first identify the communities (markets) that represent attractive opportunities. The data necessary to do this type of analysis is available in the following publications: *Census of Retail Trades, County and City Data Book, Census of Housing and Population, Sales Management's Survey of Buying Power,* and *Editor & Publisher Market Guide.*

WITHIN-MARKET OPPORTUNITY ANALYSIS

Once you have identified the top-ranking markets in terms of opportunity, you will need to perform a more detailed analysis of each market. We will refer to this as a **within-market opportunity analysis,** which should consist of an evaluation of the density of demand and supply within each market, by census tract or other meaningful geographic area, and should be augmented by an identification of the most attractive sites that are available for new stores within each market.

Demand Density   The extent to which potential demand for the retailer's goods and services is concentrated in certain census tracts or parts of the community is called **demand density.** To determine the extent of demand density, the retailer needs to identify what it believes to be the major variables influencing its potential demand. The variables identified should be standard demographic variables, since readily available data will exist on them. Let us construct an example.

A retailer is evaluating the possibility of locating in a community whose geographical boundaries are shown in Exhibit 12.6. It is comprised of twenty-three census tracts. The community is bordered on the west by a mountain range, on the north and south by major highways, and on the east by railroad tracks. The retailer has decided that three variables are especially important in determining the potential demand: median household income of over $22,000; households per square mile in excess of 1,200; and average growth in population of at least 3 percent per year over the last three years. In Exhibit 12.6, we have mapped the extent to which these three conditions are met for each of the twenty-three census tracts in the community undergoing evaluation, and thus

10. See "Selecting a Store Site, the Computer Way," *Chain Store Age Executive* 57(March 1981): 45–48.

you can easily visualize the density of potential demand in each tract. You should note that only three tracts (6, 10, 17) meet all three conditions; only four (1, 5, 11, 16) meet two of the three conditions; five (8, 9, 14, 15, 18) meet only one condition; and eleven (2, 3, 4, 7, 12, 13, 19, 20, 21, 22, 23) meet none of the conditions.

Demand-density maps similar to the one in Exhibit 12.6 are available at a modest cost from DATAMAP, Inc. which is a location consulting firm based in Minneapolis. DATAMAP generates these maps by computer. The retail analyst could also construct such maps by hand.

EXHIBIT 12.6
**Demand
Density
Map**

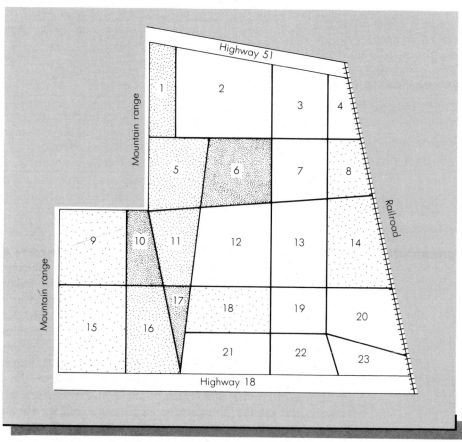

KEY:

Three Variable Demand Density Map
Variable 1 = median income over $22,000
Variable 2 = households per square mile greater than 1,200
Variable 3 = average growth in population over
               last 3 years in excess of 3% per year

Number of variables met

	0		2
	1		3

Supply Density The demand-density map allows you to identify the areas within a community that represent the highest potential demand. But the location of existing retail establishments should also be mapped. This will allow you to examine the **density of supply** or the extent to which retailers are concentrated in different census tracts.

Exhibit 12.7 shows the density of stores in the community we saw in Exhibit 12.6. Examination of Exhibit 12.7 reveals that two census tracts (10 and 17) out of the three most attractive ones have a lack of stores. Also, in the

EXHIBIT 12.7
Store Density and Site Availability Map

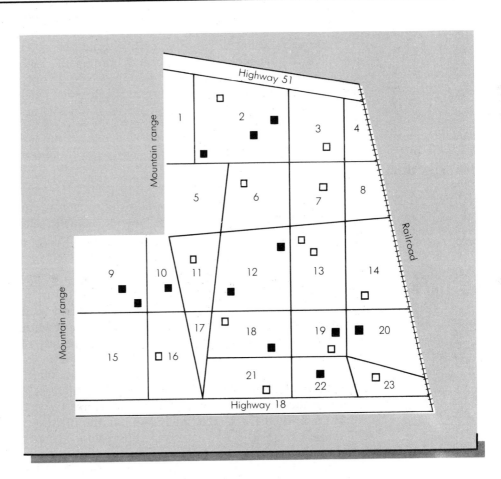

KEY:

□ = current store

■ = available store site

census tracts with fairly attractive demand density (two of the three conditions met) there are currently no retail outlets (see tracts 1 and 5).

Site Availability Simply because demand outstrips supply in certain census tracts does not immediately imply that stores should be located in those census tracts. Sites must be available.

A map should be constructed of available sites in each community being analyzed. We have done this in conjunction with the supply density map in Exhibit 12.7. The only available site in the top six census tracts (in terms of demand density) is in census tract 10. In tracts 1, 5, and 17, which currently have no retail outlets, no sites are available, which may explain the present lack of stores in these areas: perhaps these tracts are zoned totally for residential use.

Although Exhibit 12.7 seems to show only one good potential site, there may exist several more. Census tract 9 borders the high-density tract 10, in which there are no present stores and in which only one site is available for a new store. Tract 9, however, has two available sites. Furthermore, tract 12 has an available site that is close to the borders of tracts 11 and 17, which are both attractive but lack available sites.

SITE-SELECTION ANALYSIS

On completing the within-market opportunity analysis, you will have identified the top-ranking sites in each market. Now, it is time to select the best. A retailer may select several sites, but only if its growth strategy and its financial and human resources warrant it.

The 100 Percent Location In principle, every retailer should attempt to find a 100 percent location for its store: "The essence of this idea is that there is a location that is the best possible (most optimum) site for every store within a given shopping district. Generally, this is the location with the greatest amount of the kind of traffic desired."[11] The retail manager should be careful to note that what may be a 100 percent site for one store may not be for another. The best location for a supermarket is not the best location for a discount department store. Further, he or she should realize that if two or more stores view the same site as a 100 percent site, then the retailer willing to pay the highest price for the site will determine its use. This is what is called in resource economics the highest and best use.

How is the 100 percent location or site identified? Unfortunately, there is no firm answer to this basic question. There is, however, general agreement on the types of things that the retail location analyst should consider in evaluating sites: the nature of the site, traffic characteristics, type of neighbors, size of trade area, and pro-forma strategic profit model.

11. Markin, *Retailing Management*, p. 177.

Nature of Site   Is the site currently a vacant store, a vacant parcel of land, or the site of a planned shopping center? Many of the available retail sites will be vacant stores. This is because 10 to 15 percent of stores go out of business each year. You should realize, however, that many of the reasons for a retailer's failure at a given location may make that site inadequate for another store. This is especially true if the prior occupant of the store was in the same line of retail trade. If Supermarket A fails at a particular store site, then the probability is significantly increased that Supermarket B will also fail at that site.

When the retail site is a vacant parcel of land, the retailer needs to investigate why it is vacant. Why have others passed up the site? Was it previously not for sale or was it priced too high? Or, is there some other reason?

Finally, the site may be part of a planned shopping center. In this case, the retailer can usually be assured that it will have the proper mix of neighbors, adequate parking facilities, and good traffic. Sometimes, of course, the center has not been properly planned, and the retailer needs to be on the outlook for these special cases.

Traffic Characteristics   The traffic that passes a site, whether it be vehicular or pedestrian, can be an important determinant of the potential sales at that site. However, more than traffic flow is important. The retailer must also determine whether the population and traffic are of the type desired. For example, a retailer of fine furs and leather coats may be considering two alternative sites—one in the central business district and the other in a group of specialty stores in a small shopping center in a very exclusive residential area. The CBD site may generate more aggregate traffic, but the alternative site may generate more of the right type of traffic.

The retailer should evaluate two traffic-related aspects of the site. The first is the availability of sufficient parking, either at the site or nearby. One of the advantages of shopping centers is the availability of adequate parking space. In fact, most shopping centers are designed to have a 4-to-1 ratio of parking space to selling space. If the site is not a shopping center then the retailer will need to determine if the parking space will be adequate. It is difficult to give a precise guideline for the space that will be needed. Generally, it is a function of four factors: size of the store, frequency of customer visits, length of customer visits, and availability of public transportation.

A second traffic-related aspect the retailer should consider is the ease with which merchandise can be delivered to the store site. Are the roadways wide enough for delivery by semi-trailers? If important, is there a railway close by? The cost of having merchandise delivered can rise significantly if the traffic arteries to the store are not adequate.

Type of Neighbors   What are the neighboring establishments that surround the site? There can be good and bad neighbors. And what is a good or bad neighbor depends on the type of store that one is considering operating at the site. Suppose that you plan to open a children's apparel store and are considering a pair of alternative sites. One site has a toy store and a gift shop as neighbors. The other site has a bowling alley and an adult book store as neighbors. Obviously, you know who the good and bad neighbors are.

A good neighboring business will be one that is compatible with the retailer's line of trade. When two or more businesses are compatible, they can actually help generate business for each other. For example, a paint store, hardware store, and auto parts store located next to one another may increase total traffic and benefit them all.

The **principle of compatibility** has been formalized by Richard Nelson as follows:

> Two compatible businesses located in close proximity will show an increase in business volume directly proportionate to the incidence of total customer interchange between them, inversely proportionate to the ratio of the business volume of the larger store to that of the smaller store, and directly proportionate to the sum of the ratios of purposeful purchasing to total purchasing in each of the two stores.[12]

This relationship can be more explicitly summarized as follows:

$$V = I\,(V_L + V_S)\left(\frac{V_S}{V_L}\right)\left(\frac{P_L}{V_L} + \frac{P_S}{V_S}\right)$$

where:
V_L = volume of larger store
P_L = purposeful purchasing in larger store
V_S = volume of smaller store
P_S = purposeful purchasing in smaller store
V = increase in total volume of two stores
I = degree of interchange

Size of Trade Area   Earlier in this chapter we discussed the general trading area of a community. Our attention will now shift to how to determine and evaluate the trading area of specific sites within markets. In short, we will attempt to estimate the geographic area from which a store located at a particular site will be able to attract customers.

It is relatively easy to define the trading area of an existing store. All that is necessary is to interview current customers of the store to determine where they reside. But for a new store the task is not so easy. There is a fair amount of conventional wisdom that has withstood the test of time about the correlates of trading area size, which can be summarized as follows:

1. Stores which sell convenience goods versus shopping or specialty goods have smaller trading areas.

---

12. Richard L. Nelson, *The Selection of Retail Locations* (New York: F. W. Dodge, 1958), p. 66. A **purposeful purchase** is one made by a shopper who, when interviewed, states that a visit to the store was a major purpose of the shopping trip. Total purchases, of course, include incidental and impulse purchases as well.

2. As consumer mobility increases, the size of the store's trading area increases.
3. As the size of a store increases then its trading area increases, because it can stock a broader and deeper assortment of merchandise, which will attract households from greater distances.
4. As the distance between competing stores increases their trading areas will rise.
5. Natural and manmade obstacles such as railroads, rivers, mountains, and freeways can abruptly stop the boundaries of a trade area.

One of the most accepted approaches to defining and estimating a store's trade area has been developed by David Huff.[13] Huff has defined a **trading area** as "A geographically delineated region, containing potential customers for whom there exists a probability greater than zero of their purchasing a given class of products or services offered for sale by a particular firm or by a particular agglomeration of firms."[14] Thus, a trade area can be thought of as a series of demand gradients or zones in which as the distance from the retailer increases, the probability of a household purchasing or shopping there declines. In Exhibit 12.8 (page 356), this way of viewing a trade area is graphically presented. The demand gradients or contours are for shopping center J_1. "If the retail trading areas of shopping centers J_2 and J_{14} had also been calculated and superimposed over the trading area of J_1, it would be seen that parts of each shopping center's trading area envelop parts of the others."[15]

The probability of any particular household shopping at a retail site (whether it be a single store or shopping center) can be calculated with the following formula:[16]

$$P_{ij} = \frac{S_j/T_{ij}\lambda}{\sum_{j=1}^{n}(S_j/T_{ij}\lambda)}$$

where:

P_{ij} = the probability of a household at a given point of origin i traveling to a particular retail center j

S_j = the size of retail center j (measured in terms of the square footage of selling area devoted to the sale of a particular class of goods)

T_{ij} = the travel time involved in getting from a household's travel base i to a given retail center j

λ = a parameter which is to be estimated empirically to reflect the effect of travel time on various kinds of shopping trips

n = number of competing retail centers or stores

With this formula, the retailer can calculate the size of its trading area in terms

13. David L. Huff, "Defining and Estimating a Trading Area," *Journal of Marketing* 28(July 1964): 34–38.
14. Huff, "Defining and Estimating," p. 38.
15. Huff, "Defining and Estimating," p. 37.
16. Huff, "Defining and Estimating," p. 36.

EXHIBIT 12.8
**Retail
Trading Area
Shown by
Probability
Contours**

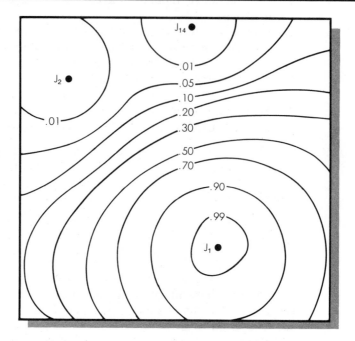

Source: Reprinted with permission from David L. Huff, "Defining and Estimating a Trade Area," *Journal of Marketing* 28(July 1964): 37, published by the American Marketing Association.

of expected number of households that will be attracted to the retail site.[17] This can be done by summing the number of households in each demand gradient by the probability of their shopping at the retail center. More specifically, we would have:[18]

$$TA_j = \sum_{i=1}^{n} (P_{ij} \cdot H_i)$$

where:

TA_j = the trading area of the particular firm or agglomeration of firms; that is, the total expected number of households within a given region who are likely to patronize j for a specific class of products or services

P_{ij} = the probability of an individual household residing within a given gradient i shopping at j

H_i = the number of households residing within a given gradient i

17. The Huff model has been extended to include image and other competitive variables. For example, see John R. Nevin and Michael J. Houston, "Image as a Component of Attraction to Intraurban Shopping Areas," *Journal of Retailing* 56(Spring 1980): 77–93; and Thomas J. Stanley and Murphy A. Sewell, "Predicting Supermarket Trade: Implications for Marketing Management," *Journal of Retailing* 54(Summer 1978): 13–22, 91, 92.

18. Huff, "Defining and Estimating," p. 38.

Naturally, there are other approaches to determining trade areas.[19] The preceding discussion was merely intended to acquaint you with the need to determine the potential trade area of a proposed store at a particular site.

Pro-Forma Strategic Profit Model The final step in site-selection analysis is construction of a pro-forma strategic profit model for each possible site. From Chapter 2, you might recall that the strategic profit model was comprised of three crucial variables: profit margin (net profit divided by net sales), asset turnover (net sales divided by total assets), and financial leverage (total assets divided by owner's equity). When the profit margin is multiplied by the rate of asset turnover, the result is return on assets. Subsequently, when the return on assets is multiplied by the financial leverage ratio, the result is return on owner's equity.

For the purpose of evaluating sites, the financial leverage ratio is not important. This is because the leverage ratio is a top-management financing decision, which represents how much debt the retail enterprise would be willing to assume. Most likely, the question of how to finance new store growth has already been answered or at least contemplated. The retailer should have determined that it has the capital or can obtain the capital to finance new store expansion. It is therefore reasonable and appropriate to evaluate sites on their potential return on assets and not return on equity.

If the retailer is to evaluate sites on their potential return on assets then it will need at least three estimates: total sales, total assets, and net profit.

Total Sales The sales that can be generated from a proposed store at a particular site are not easy to estimate with precision. Quantitative techniques, such as regression, may be employed,[20] but in practice, the estimation is often done less rigorously. Whatever the procedure, however, the retail analyst should consider all of the factors discussed earlier as part of the within-market opportunity analysis and site-selection analysis. Of the array of topics under these headings, the most important in estimating sales is the potential trade area of the site.

Given a well-defined trade area, the retailer will know how many potential households it will be able to attract to its store. It can then estimate the annual sales it will make to a typical household that patronizes the store. This estimate could be developed from past experience in similar settings, from industry averages, or from formal quantitative techniques.[21] If you then multiply the expected number of households that can be attracted to the store by the expected annual sales per household, you will obtain estimated total annual sales.

19. William Applebaum, "Methods for Determining Store Trade Areas, Market Penetration, and Potential Sales," *Journal of Marketing Research* 3(May 1966): 127–41.

20. G. I. Heald, "The Application of the Automatic Interaction Detector (A.I.D.) Program and Multiple Regression Techniques to the Assessment of Store Performance and Site Selection," *Operations Research Quarterly* 23(December 1972): 445–57.

21. Charles A. Ingene and Robert F. Lusch, "A New Frame of Reference for Managing Retail Profitability," in *Proceedings of the Sixth International Research Seminar in Marketing* (Gordes, France, June 5–8, 1979).

Let us consider an example. A supermarket retailer is evaluating a site expected to have a trade area comprised of 3,600 households. The retailer estimates that annual sales per household will be $1,600. Its expected total annual sales are therefore $5.76 million (3,600 × $1,600).

Total Assets   The retail analyst must next estimate total dollar investment needed to conduct business at the site. If the site is to be purchased and a store constructed on it, these costs must be considered. The cost of sites can vary considerably, as can the cost of constructing similar buildings on alternative sites. Also, the estimated costs of inventory, fixtures, lighting, and parking, must be determined. In addition, if the store is not expected to break even for several months or longer, then the anticipated losses should be considered as asset dollars or capital needed to commence operations. In short, the retailer must estimate the total capital needed to begin operations. Generally, the estimate of capital (asset dollars) is much more accurate than the sales estimate, because the retailer can obtain fairly firm data on what various assets will cost to acquire.

In the supermarket example previously used, let us assume that the total capital needed to start operations is $1.9 million. This includes the cost of the land, building, fixtures, parking lot, inventory, and other working capital. If the retailer estimated annual sales at $5.76 million; it follows that its expected rate of asset turnover is 3.03 times ($5,760,000 ÷ $1,900,000).

Net Profit   If the retailer has done a good job at estimating total sales and assets then the estimate of net profit should not be too difficult. Conceptually, net profit is total sales less fixed and variable costs. Fixed costs, you recall, are those which remain constant regardless of the level of sales; variable costs change in proportion to sales.

Most fixed costs in retailing are related to the size of the store, which is in turn tied to the magnitude of the total assets. As the store becomes larger, it requires more employees to be on hand each day, it takes more energy to heat and cool the store, it requires higher interest costs to finance capital, it incurs higher insurance premiums, and it incurs more dollars of depreciation.

The major variable expense will be the cost of merchandise sold. Obviously, as more is sold, the total cost of merchandise becomes higher. There is often a fairly linear relationship between cost of merchandise and sales. Therefore, if the retailer can estimate how much the goods cost as a percentage of sales, then it can easily estimate the total cost of goods sold by multiplying the cost of goods sold percentage by the estimated total sales.

Several other expenses may be expected to vary with total sales (for example, some labor and advertising expenses). Past experience or industry standards can give the retailer a reasonable estimate of operating expenses that vary with sales. These expenses can also be stated as a percentage of sales.

In our supermarket example, we established that the supermarket had expected sales of $5.76 million and would need $1.9 million in assets. Let us now assume that the annual fixed costs of operating the supermarket are estimated to be $471,000. Furthermore, the cost of goods sold is expected to be 78.7 percent of sales. In addition, other variable operating expenses are estimated at 9.4 percent of sales. Through analysis of these numbers we can determine the expected net profit:

$$
\begin{aligned}
\text{Net Profit} &= \text{Sales} - \text{Fixed costs} - \text{Variable costs} \\
&= \$5,760,000 - \$471,000 - (0.787 + 0.094)(\$5,760,000) \\
&= \$214,440
\end{aligned}
$$

The overall profit margin (net profit divided by sales) would thus be 3.72 percent or ($214,440 ÷ $5,760,000).

Return on Assets The computation of return on assets is straightforward if sales, assets, and net profit have been estimated. The appropriate data can be inserted into the following return on assets model:

$$
\left(\frac{\text{Net profit}}{\text{Total sales}}\right) \times \left(\frac{\text{Total sales}}{\text{Total assets}}\right) = \left(\frac{\text{Net profit}}{\text{Total assets}}\right)
$$

For each site being evaluated, the necessary data to compute expected return on assets should be collected.

Using our supermarket example, we can compute the expected return on assets as:

$$
\left(\frac{\$214,440}{\$5,760,000}\right) \times \left(\frac{\$5,760,000}{\$1,900,000}\right) = \left(\frac{\$214,440}{\$1,900,000}\right)
$$
$$
(0.0372) \times (3.032) = (0.11286)
$$

If the supermarket is located at the site under consideration, it can be expected to have a profit margin of 3.72 percent and a rate of asset turnover of 3.03 times, which will yield a 11.29 percent return on assets. Notice that all of these numbers are before taxes. Thus, assuming a 50 percent tax rate, the return on assets would drop to less than 6 percent. This is hardly an attractive return on assets given the cost of capital and rates of inflation facing most supermarket retailers. The retailer should probably continue to search for a better site.

DECISION IMPLEMENTATION

We see from the location-planning paradigm presented in Exhibit 12.1 that, after all relevant sites have been analyzed and the best selected, the next step is to implement the decision. The first hurdle in implementing the decision is negotiation to purchase or lease the site or building. If negotiations fail to be satisfactory then the retailer may have to revert to an alternative site that might not offer such an attractive return on assets. But, this may be preferable to overpaying for the site, since this would drive down the expected return on assets.

After negotiations are complete and the site has been leased or purchased then it must be prepared for use. This could involve constructing a new store on the site, remodeling of an existing building, or possibly only painting and cleaning.

While the site is being prepared for use, the retailer should develop a detailed operating plan for at least one year. This would involve developing the merchandise and credit plan, the pricing and markdown plan, the advertising plan, the plan for personal selling, and detailed plans for all other day-to-day activities that will need to be done to keep the store operating smoothly. The details of operations planning are discussed in Chapters 13 through 19.

Once the operating plans have been developed, the initial phases will need to be implemented. That is, merchandise will have to be ordered and placed in the store, employees hired, advertising scheduled, and a myriad of other things will need to be done before the doors can officially be opened for business.

MEASURING PERFORMANCE

At last, the site is a reality and the store is open and operating. In the early weeks of operation, careful attention needs to be given to sales performance. Are sales materializing at the level anticipated? If not, what is the cause? Is it a management or merchandising failure or is it due to having selected a poor site? If the performance is attributable to poor management or merchandising then corrective action needs to be taken as soon as possible. If a poor site was selected then the retailer can only hope to learn from its error. However, if the retailer carefully plans new locations (as we have suggested) then errors in site location should be minimal.

After the first month or two of operations, the retailer will want to analyze not only its sales performance but also its expense performance. If any expenses are not in line with expectations then an investigation of the deviation will be worthwhile. The cause of the deviation is typically either poor expense control or poor initial planning. Quite frequently, since the expense estimates are approximate (because of no prior experience in operating at the site), the cause will be poor expense planning. But, if the cause is poor management control of the expense item, then corrective action should be taken as quickly as feasible.

SUMMARY

This chapter was organized around a location paradigm that depicted a decision-making process consisting of six steps: review of the retailer's strategy, cross-market opportunity analysis, within-market opportunity analysis, site-selection analysis, decision implementation, and measurement of performance.

In deciding on a location, retailers should first reflect on their overall strategy with particular attention to market segmentation. This should be the first step because a well-defined target market will cut down on the number of alternative locations the retailer will need to analyze, making location decision making more efficient.

The second step is to conduct a cross-market opportunity analysis that attempts to identify the most attractive communities to locate within. In this regard, three location theories and concepts provide useful insights: central place theory, retail gravity theory, and the concept of retail saturation. In addition, a cross-market analysis should carefully weigh retail demand and supply factors in each market under evaluation.

The third step is to perform a within-market opportunity analysis of each of the more attractive markets identified in the preceding step. This analysis should consist of an evaluation of the density of demand and supply within each market, by census tract or other meaningful geographic area. Coupled with this should be an identification of the sites that are available for new stores in the most attractive areas within each market.

Next, the retail location analyst should conduct a site-selection analysis of the top-ranking sites in each market. The goal is to select the best site or sites. The consensus among retail site analysts is that the following should be considered: nature of the site, traffic characteristics, type of neighbors, size of trade area, and pro-forma strategic profit model.

After all the relevant sites have been analyzed and the best selected, then the decision must be implemented. The last step in the process is an ongoing one, measuring the sales, expense, and profit performance of the store once it begins operations. Any significant deviations from expectations should be investigated and corrective action taken.

Finally, the entire location decision-making paradigm has a continuous feedback mechanism. This mechanism allows for the adjustment of prior decisions as new information is received.

QUESTIONS

1. Identify the factors you would consider as most important in locating a fast food restaurant. Compare them with the factors you would use in selecting a site for a furniture store.

2. Why are discount department stores such as K-mart usually not located in large shopping centers?

3. Give an example of how a retailer's advertising policy would be influenced by the location decision.

4. Explain the Huff model. What are its advantages and disadvantages?

5. What is the index of retail saturation? How can it be used in making a location decision?

6. How can the strategic profit model be used to assist in location decisions?

7. When retailers want to expand their number of store locations, should they always consider cross-market opportunity analysis?

8. Explain the concepts of demand density and supply density. Why are they important to retail decision making?

9. What are the factors that determine the general trading area of a community?

10. Refer to the location decision-making paradigm in Exhibit 12.1 and discuss the significance of and rationale for the feedback loop in it.

PROBLEMS AND EXERCISES

1. For a pair of SMSAs of your choosing, attempt to gather as much secondary data on food stores as possible. Consider both supply and demand factors. For example collect at least the following data: (a) average square feet per store, (b) square feet per employee, (c) growth in stores, (d) average household income, (e) average household size, (f) population density, (g) age profile of population, and (h) population growth over the last five to ten years. Compare these SMSAs on the data you gather. Identify the opportunities for grocery retailers in each SMSA.

2. Using Reilly's law, construct a general trade area for your community.

3. You plan to open a store in your community to sell office supplies and equipment (including small computers) to individuals that have offices in their homes. What would be the best location for this store in your community?

4. Compute the expected return on assets for a proposed supermarket with the following characteristics:

4,400 households in trade area
18,000 total square feet of store space
Expected annual sales per household of $1,400
Land costs of $280,000
Construction costs of $36 per square foot
Costs to develop land $38,000
Inventory investment per square foot of $8
Equipment and fixture costs of $400,000
Gross margin of 23.4 percent
Operating expenses (variable) of 12.4 percent of sales
Fixed operating costs per year (including depreciation) of $340,000

What other factors, besides expected return on assets, should be considered in deciding whether to build the proposed supermarket?

5. Compute the index for retail saturation for the following three markets. The data is for department stores.

	A	B	C
Retail expenditures per household	$510	$575	$610
Square feet of retail space	600,000	488,000	808,000
Number of households	112,000	91,000	147,000

Which market is most attractive? What additional data would you find helpful in assessing the attractiveness of the three markets?

SUGGESTED READINGS

Cort, Stanton G. and Luis V. Dominguez. "Cross Shopping as Incremental Business in Concentric Growth Strategies." *Journal of Retailing* 53(Winter 1977–78): 3–16, 96.
Kinney, William R., Jr. "Separating Environmental Factor Effects for Location and Facility Decisions." *Journal of Retailing* 48(Spring 1972): 67–75, 94, 95.
MacKay, David B. "A Microanalytic Approach to Store Location Analysis." *Journal of Marketing Research* 9(May 1972): 134–40.

MacKay, David B. and Richard W. Olshavsky. "Cognitive Maps of Retail Location: An Investigation of Some Basic Issues." *Journal of Consumer Research* 2(December 1975): 197–205.

Rosenbloom, Bert. "The Trade Area Mix and Retailing Mix: A Retail Strategy Mix." *Journal of Marketing* 40(October 1976): 58–66.

Rudelius, William, Robert F. Hoel, and Roger Kerin. "Assessing Retail Opportunities in Low-Income Areas." *Journal of Retailing* 48(Fall 1972): 96–114.

Case

Donald J. Bowersox
Michigan State University

M. Bixby Cooper
Michigan State University

Douglas M. Lambert
Michigan State University

Donald A. Taylor
Michigan State University

W. T. GRANT COMPANY

ON FEBRUARY 6, 1976, the committee of secured creditors, composed of six bankers and five merchandise suppliers, voted 7–4 for liquidation of W. T. Grant. Thus, the doors were closed on the nation's seventeenth largest retailer. The collapse of W. T. Grant Company represents the biggest retailing failure in the history of the United States, and the closing of Grant's 1,073 retail stores meant that 80,000 employees lost their jobs. The demise of the giant retailer, whose 1973 sales were $1.8 billion, is a classic example of mismanagement. Facing changing channels of distribution at the retail level, Grant countered with vigorous expansion in the absence of management information systems, controls, well-conceived performance measures, or a management team trained in basic merchandising principles.

BACKGROUND

The first W. T. Grant store was opened in Lynn, Massachusetts, in 1906 by William T. Grant, who invested his entire savings of $1,000. Grant, aged 30, had more than a decade of retailing experience and believed that there was a

Note: From *Management in Marketing Channels* by Donald J. Bowersox, M. Bixby Cooper, Douglas M. Lambert, and Donald A. Taylor. Copyright © 1980 McGraw-Hill, Inc. Used with the permission of the McGraw-Hill Book Company.

market for a retailer offering prices in the range above those of the five-and-ten-cent stores such as Woolworth's and Kresge's, but below those of the expensive department stores. The concept was a success and first-year sales of $99,000 were achieved.

Between 1907 and 1917, twenty-nine stores were added and sales reached $4,511,000. The chain grew to 157 stores by 1927 with sales of $43,744,000. However, in 1924, the founder gave up active management for the position of chairman of the board, which he held until 1966. Grant built a successful retail giant on the sales of basic, staple merchandise such as infants' wear, children's wear, white goods, and curtains and draperies, which had provided the basis for growth.

The year 1966 represented W. T. Grant Company's sixtieth year and the chain boasted 1,104 "Friendly Family Stores in 46 States" and sales of $920 million. In 1968, sales passed the $1 billion mark and the company made the following statements in the annual report:[1]

> Credit service is available at all stores, with approximately 25% of all sales being sold on credit.
>
> Over half of the present company stores have been opened during the last 10 years. There has been a rapid increase in the size of the average store opened. These newer stores, free-standing and in shopping centers, are complete promotional department stores offering broad merchandising assortments and services.
>
> Over half the stores have restaurants.
>
> More than one-third offer major appliances and have outside garden shops.
>
> There are over 60 auto service centers.
>
> 17 appliance service centers inspect, deliver, install, and service our "Bradford" brand of appliances.
>
> Five major distribution centers warehouse and deliver merchandise to the stores.

Net earnings for the year were almost $38 million and management made the following projection.[2]

> Having reached this significant milestone of one billion dollars in sales, the company will continue to build a bigger and stronger company for the benefit of Grant customers, stockholders, vendors, and employees.

A CRITICAL CHANGE IN TOP MANAGEMENT

On June 27, 1966, on the occasion of his ninetieth birthday, William T. Grant resigned as a director and chairman of the board. He was replaced by his brother-in-law, Edward Staley, formerly vice chairman of the board. Staley, a long-time Grant employee, was president of the company from 1952 to 1959. Louis C. Lustenberger remained as president, a position he had held since

1. W. T. Grant Company 1968 *Annual Report*.
2. [1968 *Annual Report*].

1959. However, a number of organizational changes took place that would shape the future destiny of the firm. For example, in October 1966, Harry E. Pierson, former president of Pacific Coast Properties, Incorporated, and prior to 1960, a Grant real estate attorney and negotiator, was elected vice president, store expansion. Also, effective February 1, 1967, James G. Kendrick, formerly sales and store expansion vice president, again became president of Zeller's Limited, Grant's Canadian subsidiary. Kendrick was previously president of Zeller's Limited from 1958 until 1964. Richard W. Mayer, financial vice president and treasurer, who had set up the company's credit operation and had held the positions of national credit manager and treasurer, became sales vice president. John G. Curtin, formerly president of Zeller's Limited from 1965 to 1967, was elected financial vice president and treasurer.

Effective February 1, 1968, Louis C. Lustenberger, president of the company since August 25, 1959, retired under the terms of the employees retirement plan. Under his direction, W. T. Grant's sales had more than doubled and earnings had increased from $9,850,000 to over $32,000,000. In addition, new Grant stores had tripled in size, and total selling area had more than doubled. In the 1967 fiscal year, W. T. Grant Company set all-time records in both sales and earnings.

Lustenberger's choice for his successor was James G. Kendrick, then president of Zeller's Limited. Kendrick had joined Grant's store management program in 1935 after completing his education at the University of Minnesota. However, Lustenberger and Staley, the chairman of the board, had long been rivals on whether Grant was competing for the same market as K-Mart or if its target market was the same as Ward's and Penney's. Kendrick had openly disagreed with Staley over the direction of the company's expansion program. He believed that store interiors should be upgraded to match the change in merchandise mix. By changing store interiors, Kendrick felt they would create a consumer image that would be consistent with the objective of selling better merchandise. Staley, on the other hand, wanted to keep opening costs per store to the barest minimum and was against upgrading the interiors.[3] Also, Staley was not about to let Lustenberger's retirement slip by without strengthening his own position. Consequently, "a Staley man," Richard W. Mayer, was elected as Grant's ninth president on August 27, 1968.

THE STALEY-MAYER EXPANSION YEARS

Under the direction of the Staley–Mayer management team, Grant began an ambitious expansion program that "placed a great strain on the physical and human capability of the company to cope with the program. These were all large stores we were opening—6 million to 7 million square feet per year—and the expansion of our management organization just did not match the expansion of our stores."[4]

---

3. Based on information obtained from James G. Kendrick during a telephone conversation on December 19, 1977.

4. James G. Kendrick in "How W. T. Grant Lost $175 Million Last Year," *Business Week* (February 24, 1975), p. 75.

During the six years from 1968 to 1973 inclusive, Grant opened 410 new stores, enlarged an additional 36, and in the process spent $117,284,000 ([Exhibit] 1 contains a summary of Grant's store growth from 1964 through 1973). The new stores ranged in size from 60,000 square feet to Grant City "super-stores" of 180,000 square feet. The smaller stores were built in neighborhood and convenience shopping centers and the big stores were either free-standing or in medium-sized malls, with Sears, Ward's, or a discounter as coanchor.

The merchandise mix in the larger stores emphasized major appliances, televisions, stereo equipment, automobile accessories, furniture, sporting goods, and camera equipment. Major appliances and televisions were sold under Grant's private label, called Bradford. While this was similar to the Sears position with its Kenmore line, it was in contrast to K-Mart's strategy of marketing a line of major appliances under the Whirlpool brand name.

By the early 1970s the average store stocked over 21,000 items, 71 percent of which were private label goods. Family fashions, which had once contributed about one-half of Grant's annual sales volume, represented less than 25 percent of sales in the early 1970s. In an effort to stimulate sales of big-ticket items, credit sales were emphasized. One former finance executive said: "We gave credit to every deadbeat who breathed."[5] Credit sales continued to account for as much as 25 percent of Grant's sales volume.

THE BEGINNING OF THE END

The year 1969 represented a significant turning point for Grant. It marked both the eighth consecutive year of improved sales and profit and the last year that such a claim could be made. A summary of selected financial data covering the years 1969 through 1973 is contained in [Exhibit] 2. Although sales increased by almost 53 percent from 1969 to 1973, credit accounts receivable rose 62 percent, merchandise inventories more than doubled, short-term and long-term

EXHIBIT 1 **Store Growth Program, 1964–73**	YEAR	NUMBER OF NEW STORES OPENED	NUMBER OF STORES ENLARGED	CAPITAL EXPENDITURES	STORE CLOSINGS	NET NUMBER OF STORES AT YEAR END
	1973	77	4	$23,537,000	96	1,189
	1972	92	5	26,983,000	52	1,208
	1971	83	5	26,476,000	31	1,168
	1970	65	8	15,995,000	44	1,116
	1969	52	3	13,668,000	49	1,095
	1968	41	11	10,625,000	35	1,092
	1967	24	13	7,792,000	42	1,086
	1966	51	11	14,856,000	35	1,104
	1965	27	13	7,846,000	31	1,088
	1964	31	12	5,262,000	20	1,092

Source: W. T. Grant Company Annual Reports.

5. "Investigating the Collapse of W. T. Grant," Business Week (July 19, 1976), p. 61.

EXHIBIT 2 **W. T. Grant Company: Selected Financial Data, 1969–73**

	1973	1972	1971	1970	1969
Sales	$1,849,802,346	$1,644,747,319	$1,374,812,791	$1,254,131,857	$1,210,918,068
Cost of merchandise sold, buying and occupancy costs	1,282,944,615	1,125,261,115	931,237,312	843,191,987	817,671,347
Interest expense	51,047,481	21,127,084	16,452,635	18,874,134	14,919,228
Net earnings	8,429,473	37,787,066	35,212,082	39,577,087	41,809,300
Per common share	.59	2.70	2.51	2.87	2.99
Dividends paid per preferred share	3.75	3.75	3.75	3.75	3.75
Dividends paid per common share	1.50	1.50	1.50	1.50	1.40
Employee compensation and benefits	434,368,156	397,133,721	336,311,735	295,882,263	271,650,884
Cents per sales dollar	23.5	24.1	24.5	23.6	22.4
Accounts receivable, net	598,798,552	542,751,365	477,324,069	419,731,126	368,267,131
Merchandise inventories	450,636,556	399,532,793	298,676,170	260,492,329	222,127,620
Store properties, fixtures and improvements	100,983,800	91,419,748	77,173,498	61,832,352	55,310,732
Short-term commercial notes and bank loans	453,096,715	390,033,500	237,740,700	246,420,216	182,132,200
Accounts payable for merchandise	58,191,731	60,973,283	Unavailable	80,681,456	70,853,108
Long-term debt	220,336,000	126,672,000	128,432,000	32,301,000	35,402,000
Net worth	323,738,431	334,338,566	325,745,094	302,036,424	290,688,499
Income from retail operations before taxes[a]	1,502,000	59,901,000	59,059,000	69,806,000	78,598,000
Cents per sales dollar	.08	3.64	4.30	5.57	6.49
Percent earned on net worth	2.6%	11.3%	10.8%	13.1%	14.4%
Inventory as a percent of sales	24.4%	24.3%	21.7%	20.8%	18.3%
Cost of goods sold as a percent of sales	69.36%	68.42%	67.74%	67.23%	67.52%
Accounts receivable as a percent of sales	32.37%	33.00%	34.72%	33.47%	30.41%
Square feet of store space at year end	56,224,000	50,618,000	44,718,000	38,157,000	33,855,000
Sales per square foot	32.90	32.49	30.74	32.87	35.77
Dividends paid—common	20,828,989	20,806,653	20,793,621	20,426,251	19,279,815
Dividends paid—preferred	293,054	344,709	345,813	395,031	456,858

[a]1973 Annual Report, Comparative Statement of Operations, p. 27.

debt combined more than tripled, and earnings per share fell from $2.99 to $0.59. Perhaps even more significant, income before taxes from retail operations fell from $.0649 per dollar to $.008 per dollar of sales.

As early as 1971, significant dangers were evident. Sales per square foot reached an abysmal $30.74, less than one-half the rate achieved by Grant's major competitors. Return on net worth was 10.8 percent, down from 14.4 percent, and inventory and credit accounts receivable were increasing as a per- ·cent of sales. Also, short-term and long-term debt increased 68 percent on sales increases of 13.5 percent over 1969 levels. Alarmed by the direction in which the company was moving, former president Lustenberger and Raymond H. Fogler, also a past president and a Grant director, tried unsuccessfully to mobilize the outside directors. A former board member said: "The outside directors had to become more active if they were going to fulfill their responsibilities as company directors."[6]

THE 1973 ANNUAL REPORT

On October 1, 1973, Edward Staley retired as chairman of the board of directors and became chairman of the executive committee. Mayer became chairman of the board and chief executive officer, and Harry Pierson was elected president and chief operating officer, effective February 1, 1974. These changes were no doubt related to the 1973 performance of the firm.

Sales for 1973 increased to $1,849,802,346, but profits fell 78 percent to $8,429,473, the lowest profit since 1961 when sales were $574,502,000. Short-term commercial notes and bank loans and long-term debt reached $673,432,-715, more than twice the net worth. It is interesting that on profits of less than $8.5 million, the company continued to pay dividends in excess of $21 million.

In the 1973 annual report, Mayer and Pierson addressed the issue of the company's lack of image at the consumer level.[7]

> During the last six years your Company opened 410 large stores of over 50,000 square feet, enlarged 36 successful stores, and closed 307 smaller units. In view of the decline in earnings in 1973, you might well ask . . . WHY?
>
> Retailing is synonymous with change. Selling methods, size and types of stores, and lines or departments of merchandise change as the demands of the American Consumer dictate. The Management of your Company recognized this inevitable shift from smaller, limited stores to larger "full line" stores and committed itself to the complete restructuring of the Company.
>
> As this proceeded, a frequent question asked was "We do not understand or recognize your image." Ten years ago, the Company had been "understood and recognized" as a large chain of Variety Stores. Our image was clear. We sold limited price items in smallwares, wearing apparel and soft goods for the home. Times changed and retailing changed . . . to the one stop, complete store of over 50,000 square feet which we call Grant City and that is the direction your Company followed.

6. "How W. T. Grant Lost $175 Million Last Year," *Business Week* (February 24, 1975), p. 74.
7. W. T. Grant Company 1973 *Annual Report*, p. 2.

To convert a chain of approximately 1,000 successful limited variety stores to a Company with approximately half of its units composed of Grant City or "full line" stores, while at the same time adding all of the necessary back up services, merchandise distribution centers, data processing, and major appliance ware-housing, home delivery and service in a relatively short span of time was not easily accomplished. Our image may have become blurred. We do have both small and large stores. This has to be. Ten years ago, from Maine to California, Grant operated small stores with limited merchandise assortments. Today in hundreds of communities the Grant City store is recognized as a store with complete assortments of merchandise for the home and family. Our Grant City stores may not yet have the general acceptance of some of our major competitors, but we firmly believe our quality is good, our pricing and values excellent and that our reputation and acceptance as a Grant City full line store improves each year. We are still relatively new to the full line store field, but we intend to stay—and to improve each year.

In this letter to Stockholders we will cover more fully the factors influencing operations in 1973 and our prospects for the future.

In addition, Mayer used the opportunity to attempt to justify the ill-fated credit system which he had expanded, promoted, and directed for a number of years.[8]

In 1946, the Company first introduced a credit service to aid its customers to purchase wanted merchandise and pay on an installment plan. The stores were small and stocked with merchandise limited in lines and price. The credit coupon book was selected as the most practical method as these coupons could be used as cash and the customer did not have to wait for individual sales slips on each item purchased. It gave us a method of granting credit without incurring the expense of a sophisticated credit system to keep customer credit limits under control. For smaller stores, this type was not only popular with customers—but it was tailor-made for the simplified operation of this small unit. However, as the Company developed new full-line Grant City stores, customers indicated a preference for the revolving credit charge plan. In addition, governmental regulations have made it increasingly difficult and expensive to administer the coupon-type credit plan. Primarily, in recognition of the customer preference for revolving credit charge accounts, this plan was promoted in 1973, and this emphasis will continue in the future. This change from the credit coupon book plan produces less service charge revenue and is more expensive to operate. During 1973, although credit sales were $45,000,000 higher, service charge revenues were down by over $7,000,000. On the other hand, our experience in the past year indicates that Grant City customers prefer the revolving credit charge and will purchase more merchandise with this plan.

In spite of the looming financial disaster, Grant continued with its expansion plans for 1974 and its diversification into catalog showroom stores:[9]

In 1973 the Company opened 77 new stores and enlarged 4 existing units, for an additional 5,606,000 square feet of new store space. In addition, construction of the new 475,000 square foot Distribution Center in Windsor Locks, Connecticut, was completed in late Fall 1973.

8. [1973 *Annual Report*], pp. 2–3.
9. 1973 *Annual Report*, p. 4.

In 1974, we will open approximately 45 new stores and enlarge 1 unit for approximately 3,000,000 square feet. The reduction, both in number of stores and square footage from 1973 levels, is due to developers encountering difficulty in securing necessary materials to complete centers on schedule, inability to start some projects because of the high cost of interim financing, and the increased time required to be spent before beginning a project in satisfying environmental control requirements. It is our estimate at this time that the 1975 program will be of the same magnitude as 1974, or smaller, and management feels that this is a more workable program in view of present conditions. This will, of course, reduce pre-opening costs and the additional funds required for investment in capital expenditures, inventories and to carry customer receivables, from the peaks of the last few years.

The program of closing older Grant stores, typically of a smaller size, was accelerated in 1973 with 96 closings. All expenses pertaining to this program were charged to the year of closing. Since the closing of unprofitable stores not only reduces investment in inventory but eliminates the burden of operating costs, this program will be continued in 1974.

In 1973, GranJewel, the company's joint venture participation in catalog showroom retailing with Jewelcor, opened 11 stores and purchased Edison Jewelers and Distributors Co. of Fort Worth, Texas, which operates 4 units. In 1974, an additional 7 catalog showroom stores are planned.

Mayer and Pierson concluded their message to the stockholders as follows:[10]

We will continue opening full-line Grant City stores and will continue to expand our revolving credit charge account plan. This year, the economy will be uncertain, but Management will continue to take aggressive steps to strengthen its entire operation, whether in limited or full-line Grant City Stores. We will continue to change the Company to meet the demands of customers. In the final analysis, our customers will determine the success of the Company. We feel that Customers are aware of the positive changes that are occurring and that, as a result, the acceptance of the Grant City stores—as full line stores—will continue to increase.

[Exhibit] 3 contains a list of Grant directors as of the 1973 year-end.

CRISIS MANAGEMENT AT GRANT

The dismal 1973 financial performance was followed by a $10 million loss for the first 6 months of 1974. Effective June 30, 1974, Richard Mayer resigned as chairman and chief executive officer of Grant's and Edward Staley resigned as a director. Fogler and Lustenberger also resigned from the board. One former director made the following observation about the reorganization:[11]

. . . it is a pretty safe bet that Staley's resignation would not have been forthcoming if his old foes didn't leave, too.

On September 3, 1974, James G. Kendrick became chairman and president of W. T. Grant after leading Zeller's Limited for a total of approximately 13

10. [1973 *Annual Report*,] p. 5.
11. "How W. T. Grant Lost $175 Million Last Year," *Business Week* (February 24, 1975), p. 76.

EXHIBIT 3   **Grant Directors as of 1973 Year-End with Company Affiliations**

Richard W. Mayer	Chairman of the Board and Chief Executive Officer
Harry E. Pierson	President and Chief Operating Officer
Edward Staley	Chairman of the Executive Committee
A. Richard Butler	Executive Vice President—Merchandising
Joseph W. Chinn, Jr.	Director and Chairman, Consulting Committee, Wilmington Trust Company
Raymond H. Fogler	Retired, former President of W. T. Grant Company
John D. Gray	Chairman of the Board and Chief Executive Officer, Hart, Schaffner & Marx
Joseph Hinsey	Partner, White & Case
James G. Kendrick	President and Chief Executive Officer of Zeller's Limited
E. Robert Kinney	President and Chief Operating Officer of General Mills, Inc.
John J. LaPlante	Personnel Vice President
Robert A. Luckett	Corporate Service Vice President and Comptroller
Louis C. Lustenberger	Retired, former President of W. T. Grant Company
DeWitt Peterkin, Jr.	Vice Chairman of the Board, Morgan Guaranty Trust Company of New York
Charles F. Phillips	President Emeritus, Bates College
Clarence W. Spangle	Executive Vice President of Honeywell, Inc.
Asa T. Spaulding	Consultant to Boyden International Group, Inc., of Los Angeles

years of impressive sales and profit growth. He believed that the most critical problems facing him were: (1) to increase the company's sales per square foot, (2) to revise significantly the merchandise program back to the basic lines that the company had built its reputation on, (3) to reduce the substantial losses associated with the company's credit operation, and (4) to revise and strengthen its financial policies and controls.[12]

One of Kendrick's first accomplishments was refinancing the short-term notes with a $600 million line of credit with 143 banks headed by Morgan Guaranty Trust Company. Three banks put up $300 million, eleven banks doled out about $200 million, and the remaining $100 million came from 129 banks. Grant used its 50.2 percent interest in Zeller's Limited and $600 million in credit accounts receivable as collateral.

Kendrick planned to reduce the company's reliance on private label merchandise and to replace an inventory of slow-selling items with fresh, new, wanted merchandise. With rising credit delinquencies, Grant began accepting BankAmericard and Master Charge sales. In addition, nervous suppliers had to be assured that Grant would continue to pay its bills since the American Credit Indemnity Company had canceled its credit insurance policy.[13] In an effort to gain immediate consumer support, $6 million was budgeted for television advertisements in thirty-five major markets in fall 1974.

12. Based on a telephone interview with James G. Kendrick on December 19, 1977.
13. "It's Get-Tough Time at W. T. Grant," *Business Week* (October 19, 1974), p. 46.

In spite of these changes, Grant suffered losses in 1974 of $175 million on sales of $1.7 billion. Contributing to the massive loss were credit losses of over $90 million, $24 million in store closing expenses, heavy interest charges, and a substantial markdown budget. Also, Grant filed suit against three former real estate employees, including John A. Christensen, former real estate vice president, for taking what Kendrick described as "hundreds of thousands of dollars in bribes in connection with store leases."[14]

THE COLLAPSE

In 1975, Kendrick began a program to close another 126 stores and the maturity date on Grant's agreement with the banks was extended from June 1975 to March 31, 1976. To satisfy the banks, Robert Anderson, former vice president of Sears, was hired as president and chief executive officer in April 1975 for a guaranteed salary and pension totaling $2.5 million. At this point, any anxious supplier could have brought down the company by filing a Chapter X proceeding.

By October 1975 losses were mounting and Grant was having great difficulty obtaining merchandise from suppliers. As a result, the company filed under Chapter XI. Under Chaper XI, stores west of the Mississippi River were closed and plans were initiated to reduce further the number of stores to 359 in the Northeast. However, questionable financial data and an uncertain future resulted in liquidation:[15]

> The final blow came when the consultants cautioned the creditors that it would take six to eight years to determine whether Grant would survive. The bankers favored liquidation and were hungrily eyeing the $320 million in cash accumulated from store closings and liquidations. Trade creditors, by contrast, were uncertain. They were fully secured and doing business with Grant. But on Feb. 6, the committee voted 7–4 for liquidation.

EPILOGUE

In December 1977, former president Kendrick was asked whether he believed in September 1974 when he returned to Grant's from Zeller's that he could save the company. He replied: "I would not have accepted the job if I had not. However, at that point in time I was not aware of just how bad the credit situation was." In addition, Kendrick was asked whether he could have accomplished his objectives if he had been named president 7 months earlier (on February 1, 1974, Pierson became president). Keeping in mind the impending legal cases, he observed that, with the benefit of 20/20 hindsight, it might be possible for some people to reach that conclusion.

14. "How W. T. Grant Lost $175 Million Last Year," *Business Week* (February 24, 1975), p. 74.
15. "Investigating the Collapse of W. T. Grant," *Business Week* (July 19, 1976), p. 62.

QUESTIONS

1. What channel decisions do you see in the W. T. Grant Company case?

2. When did it become evident that Grant was headed for financial trouble? What were the danger signs? What measures of financial performance would have provided management with additional useful information?

3. What were the primary causes of the bankruptcy of the W. T. Grant Company?

4. What role did the American Credit Indemnity Company play in the collapse of the W. T. Grant Company? The decision to private label big-ticket items? Grant's credit department?

Robert F. Lusch
University of Oklahoma

Blair's Floorcovering

OVER THE LAST ELEVEN YEARS Stephen Blair has catapulted Blair's Floorcovering from a small one-person operation to an over $1 million business with a staff of ten employees (including Stephen). Stephen, now approaching his thirty-fifth birthday, is having visions of transforming Blair's into a chain of floorcovering stores.

BACKGROUND

Stephen is the sole owner of Blair's and proud of it. He single-handedly started the firm, in a midwestern town of 81,000 people, in February of 1969 immediately after completing a two-year program at a local junior college. Before college, Stephen spent four years in the Air Force and during those four years managed to save $4,000. After completing college, Stephen had close to $5,000 and with that and a $2,500 loan from a local bank he started Blair's Floorcovering. One month later he married Sally Tiedeman.

Originally Blair's was located in a fifty-year-old 1,500-square-foot building near a warehousing district. The rent was cheap but retail customers were few and far between. In those early years, Stephen would often leave the store for Sally to tend and he would go out to search for customers. He built quite a business calling on local builders, and by year end 1970 was selling 40 percent of the carpet being installed in new houses in the area. Selling to builders resulted in slender margins, but they were adequate to cover out-of-pocket expenses.

Note: This case was prepared as a basis for class discussion rather than to illustrate appropriate or inappropriate handling of retail situations. Data in this case are heavily based on Bert C. McCammon, Jr., Robert F. Lusch, and Ray R. Serpkenci, *1979 Management Report: 1978 Operating Results Study, Floorcovering Retailers* (Norman, Okla.: The Retail Floorcovering Institute and Distribution Research Program, University of Oklahoma, 1979) and are used with permission of the authors.

Blair's ended 1970 with sales of $130,000. In addition, by year end 1970 Stephen had repaid the $2,500 bank loan. All of this was accomplished with only one part-time employee in addition to Sally's help.

The following year sales approached $200,000. During this year Stephen added another employee and made a significant effort to capture a portion of the retail market. Several thousand dollars were put into radio and newspaper advertising and the retail market responded favorably.

In late 1971 Stephen spotted an old building on the outskirts of town that was for sale. The building was on the major highway leading to town. The price was reasonable, but unfortunately the building was in poor condition. Sally was strongly against purchasing the building. She argued with Stephen: "You're crazy to try to buy that building. The roof leaks and it is five times the size of our present building. We simply don't need that much space to sell a couple hundred thousand dollars of carpet." Stephen replied, "I don't care. We must own our own building. How can we ever get ahead by paying rent to someone else. Anyway, who cares if it costs $85,000 as long as we can borrow most of the money?" Sally interrupted, "We've paid rent on our house since we've been married. If you don't want to pay rent and if you want to own something then let's buy a house. With the baby due in six months we really need a house of our own more than that old run-down building!" Stephen didn't reply. The conversation was over. Sally hoped that she had made her point clear.

Two days later when Stephen came home from work he informed Sally that he had put a $6,000 down payment on the building. For a few years it was rough. Sales grew, but Sally was right, the building was too large. It was not until 1976, when sales surpassed the half-million-dollar mark, that space was beginning to be efficiently utilized. In 1979, when sales passed $1 million, the building decision finally seemed right.

CURRENT SITUATION

By 1979 Stephen and Sally had their own home and two children. Things looked splendid. Blair's Floorcovering made over $12,000 in profit for 1979 and that was after Stephen drew a $15,200 salary for himself. Sales were in excess of $1 million, with 42 percent coming from the building contract market and 58 percent from residential retail sales.

Stephen had worked hard to get his business to the $1 million sales level. His next goal was to start a chain of floorcovering stores. He had determined that within a 100-mile radius of his base operation there were twenty towns between 30,000 and 60,000 in population—none of which had their own floorcovering store.

The plan was quite simple. Stephen would convert his existing outlet into a warehouse that would supply all stores. With one truck and driver, he felt that supplying up to twenty stores within a 100-mile radius would be no problem. Since his existing outlet would be converted to a warehouse, Stephen

	YEAR	SALES
EXHIBIT 1 **Sales Growth Profile (1969–79)**	1969	$ 82,000
	1970	130,000
	1971	197,000
	1972	231,000
	1973	260,000
	1974	257,000
	1975	408,000
	1976	548,000
	1977	711,000
	1978	903,000
	1979	1,114,000

planned to build a new retail outlet for his existing business or possibly try to rent a vacant building for the time being.

The first additional outlet—besides the warehouse and Stephen's own new outlet—would be opened in a town thirty miles to the southeast. The population of this town is 41,000 and Stephen's brother-in-law, Scott Stern, would be the manager. Scott recently married Stephen's younger sister. Scott is a high school graduate and has been managing the produce department in a local supermarket for the last two years.

Stephen feels he could open at least one new outlet per year over the next ten years. By the time he reaches age forty-five, Stephen would like to have ten or more outlets, with total sales surpassing $5 million.

Stephen doesn't want any partners. He wants to be the owner and ultimate decision maker. Scott recently suggested, "Why don't we form a partnership on the store you want me to manage? I've been able to save $7,500, which I was planning to use as a down payment on a house, but that can wait." Stephen immediately rejected this suggestion: "I need people not capital. I can get all the money I need from the bank. I've never been late on a payment, even though sometimes it has been extremely close." Stephen has a good credit standing with the largest bank in the county. He had a revolving line of credit of $75,000 at two points over the prime rate—presently at about 14 percent. In addition he has a long-term note with an outstanding balance of approximately $86,000. This note has an interest rate of 10 percent.

In January of 1980 Stephen set up an appointment with his banker. At the meeting he presented Jack Black, vice president of commercial loans, with his idea of transforming Blair's Floorcovering into a full-fledged chain store enterprise. Stephen talked of ten stores in ten years as a reasonable goal. Jack Black appeared to be taken by surprise. He seemed to hesitate—no reassurance was forthcoming. Stephen spoke again: "Don't you see how we can both make money on this deal?" Jack firmly responded, "Stephen, you're a valuable customer but your balance sheet and income statement will simply not justify expansion at this time. To open even one additional outlet you will need at least $30,000, and that is if you can find a store to rent rather than purchase." Stephen stood up, "Mr. Black, I've built Blair's to over $1 million in sales without defaulting on any loans and you say my balance sheet and income statement are too weak!" Jack responded in a soft and reassuring voice, "Don't get irrational, Stephen. We can work something out, but first sit down and let me tell you something." Stephen reluctantly sat down, although still uneasy. "With sales of $1 million you should be walking home with a lot more than $25,000 per year. You may have built sales, but your profit performance is dismal. Take my advice, Stephen, try to squeeze more profit out of your current operation and then let's sit down together in another year or two and discuss your expansion plans more seriously."

Stephen went home that evening disgusted and had trouble sleeping that night. He was going to show Jack Black that now was the time to expand and not in another year or two. The next day at the office he ran across in some old mail, a copy of the *1979 Operating Results Study of Floorcovering Retailers* prepared by the Retail Floorcovering Institute (RFI). While breezing through the report, Stephen saw a section of the report entitled "High Performance Retailing." In this portion of the report a typical high-profit floorcovering retailer in the $1 million range was profiled in terms of operating performance. Relevant data from this profile are presented in Exhibits 2 to 4 with comparable data on Blair's Floorcovering.

EXHIBIT 2
Operating Statements for Blair's and a High Performance Floorcovering Retailer

ITEM	BLAIR'S	HIGH PERFORMANCE FLOORCOVERING RETAILER
Net sales	100.00%	100.00%
Cost of sales	70.58	70.28
Gross margin	29.42%	29.72%
Operating expenses		
Payroll	12.82%	15.90%
Advertising	2.99	2.81
Samples	.33	—
Utilities and telephone	1.71	.65
Rent or occupancy	3.98	1.44
Depreciation (trucks, fixtures, and equipment)	.44	.41
Bad debt losses	—	.30
Interest paid	1.64	.66
All other	3.53	2.62
Total operating expenses	27.44%	24.79%
Operating profits	1.98%	4.93%
Net other income	(.33)	(.52)
Net profits (before taxes)	1.65%	4.41%
Net profits (after taxes)	1.10%	2.95%

EXHIBIT 3 **Balance Sheets for Blair's and a High Performance Floorcovering Retailer**	ITEM	BLAIR'S	HIGH PERFORMANCE FLOORCOVERING RETAILER
	Assets		
	Current assets		
	Cash (including marketable securities)	10.39%	10.30%
	Accounts receivable	30.00	39.38
	Inventory	45.42	40.47
	All other	1.29	—
	Total	87.10%	90.15%
	Fixed assets	12.90	9.85
	Total assets	100.00%	100.00%
	Liabilities and net worth		
	Current liabilities		
	Accounts payable	23.80%	23.33%
	Notes payable	13.43	7.78
	Customer deposits	4.87	—
	All other	5.93	4.34
	Total	48.03%	35.45%
	Long-term liabilities	21.05	—
	Net worth	30.92	64.55
	Total liabilities and net worth	100.00%	100.00%

When Stephen was driving home that evening he was pondering how he could use this data to show Jack Black how his performance was respectable or, alternatively, how he could use data in this report to better program Blair's to achieve high performance results. When he got home, Scott Stern was there. Sally had told Scott about the turn down by the bank. Scott blurted, "Stephen, I want you to know that I still have the $7,500 if you want to form a partnership on that new outlet."

EXHIBIT 4 **Productivity Ratios for Blair's and a High Performance Floorcovering Retailer**	ITEM	BLAIR'S	HIGH PERFORMANCE FLOORCOVERING RETAILER
	Net sales per dollar invested in inventory	$ 5.94	$ 10.55
	Net sales per square foot	128.99	168.32
	Net sales per full-time salesperson[a]	222,806	364,695
	Net sales per full-time employee[a]	111,403	136,761
	Net sales per dollar invested in assets	2.70	4.30

[a]Two part-time employees equal one full-time employee.

DISCUSSION QUESTIONS

1. Is Blair's financially able to grow and become a multiple-outlet operation?

2. Using the data from the Retail Floorcovering Institute, identify Blair's major operating problems.

3. Should a partnership with Scott Stern be formed?

4. What do you think Blair's income statement and balance sheet should look like in order for Jack Black to lend Blair's more money?

5. Can you develop a strategy that would allow Blair's to generate enough capital internally to finance new outlets?

6. Would you say that Blair's problems are in most part strategic, administrative, or operating? (Refer to the retail planning and management model in Chapter 2.)

William A. Staples
University of Houston at Clear Lake City

Robert A. Swerdlow
Lamar University

Case

Burnside Furniture and Appliance Centers, Inc.

IN JUNE of 1976, Thomas and James Burnside were confronted with a major operating decision that would affect the future development of their furniture and appliance business. The decision centered on whether or not to add a fourth store in the southern section of Des Moines, Iowa. Thomas, as president and financial officer, was reluctant to open a new store, although James, serving as vice president with responsibility for marketing operations, thought the time had come for an additional Burnside Furniture and Appliance Center.

BACKGROUND

In September 1948, Alexander Burnside opened a retail furniture store in Des Moines. Mr. Burnside had previously been employed as a furniture salesperson by a large department store. The store on the east side of Des Moines initially carried furniture only. Although the first few years were very difficult, by 1953 Mr. Burnside believed that financial stability had occurred. In 1959, due to the growth of Des Moines and the success of the east side store, Mr. Burnside opened a second store on the north side of Des Moines. It was at this time that Mr. Burnside decided to add appliances to the product mixes of both of his stores.

During the 1960s, the two Burnside Furniture and Appliance Centers were

Note: Reprinted with the permission of the authors. This case was prepared as a basis for class discussion rather than to illustrate appropriate or inappropriate handling of retail situations.

very successful. It was during the 1962–65 period that Alexander Burnside brought his two sons, Thomas and James, into the daily operation and management of his retail stores. Thomas and James were both college graduates and had received degrees in business administration from the University of Iowa and Drake University, respectively. Thomas had majored in finance; James was a marketing major.

Due to the large number of people employed in insurance, publishing, and state government, Des Moines continued to grow during the 1960s. The major growth of Des Moines was occurring in the western section of the city. In a joint decision, Thomas and James Burnside concurred with their father that a third furniture and appliance center should be opened on the west side of town. In 1969, this idea became a reality.

During the early 1970s, all three stores continued to prosper, although the sales of the first outlet had stabilized and the major sales growth was occurring in the newest (west side) store followed by the outlet in north Des Moines. In 1973, Alexander Burnside retired from the day-to-day operation of the business, although he did retain his position as chairman of the board of the corporation. Thomas Burnside was appointed president of the company with James serving as vice president.

CURRENT SITUATION

In 1976, Thomas and James Burnside were faced with a decision of whether or not to establish their fourth furniture and appliance center, on the south side of Des Moines. While the population of Des Moines had grown during the 1970–75 period, the growth rate was not as high as for the 1950s and 1960s. While the total population had not grown dramatically, there was a major growth area. Due to new real estate developments, the southern section of Des Moines had attracted a high number of young families with children. The new residents of the south side also were above average with respect to years of education, income levels, and percentage of head of households with white-collar occupations. James Burnside believed that this group should be a prime target for their business and thus suggested that a new store should be opened on the south side. Thomas Burnside was somewhat skeptical of the idea due to the slowed overall growth rate of Des Moines. He believed that major attention should be directed at furthering the development of the three existing stores, where sales were beginning to level off.

James and Thomas Burnside decided that an informal market analysis of the south side was in order. Due to his marketing background, James took a leadership role in assembling some secondary information for further study. Exhibit 1 shows the boundaries of the south side area. The boundary on the north was the C&M Railroad, while the east side was marked by the Des Moines River. The western and southern borders were marked by Interstate 80 and State Highway 28, respectively. By consulting the Des Moines Chamber of Commerce's Research Division, James was able to determine the estimated 1975 median household incomes for the southside census tracts. Census records revealed that all of the census tracts on the south side were either in the upper-

or middle-income tracts for the entire city. An analysis of city building permits isolated the fact that the major building areas during the early 1970s had been in the south, west, and northwest sections of Des Moines. In addition, the Des Moines Planning and Zoning Commission was able to supply James with their estimate of the population growth for Des Moines for the 1970–90 period.

James Burnside, after assembling the data, reanalyzed the past location decisions with respect to the store on the north and west sides of Des Moines. He determined that there were special levels of household incomes, building permit growth, and population changes that must be considered. The critical values were $13,400 in household incomes, 3 percent in average annual building permit growth, and 10 percent population growth rate for 1970 to 1990.

James also realized that in order for him and Thomas to make a complete assessment of the situation an analysis of the competition and available store sites was in order. Exhibit 2 presents an analysis of the southside area with respect to store density and site availability. The competition on the south side was diverse in that there were appliance stores, furniture stores, plus combination furniture and appliance outlets. In addition, a large department store chain, Adler's, which carried furniture and appliances, had a store in the shop-

EXHIBIT 1
Demand Density Map

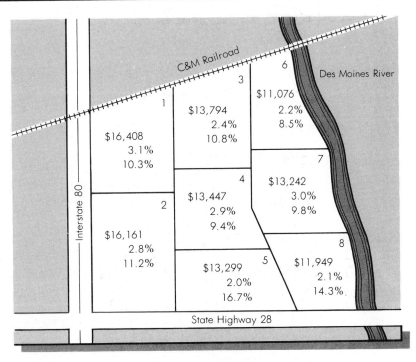

Top number   = 1975 median household income
Middle number = average annual growth in building permits
                         over last five years (1970–75)
Bottom number = projected population growth rate (1970–90)

EXHIBIT 2
**Store Density
and Site
Availability
Map**

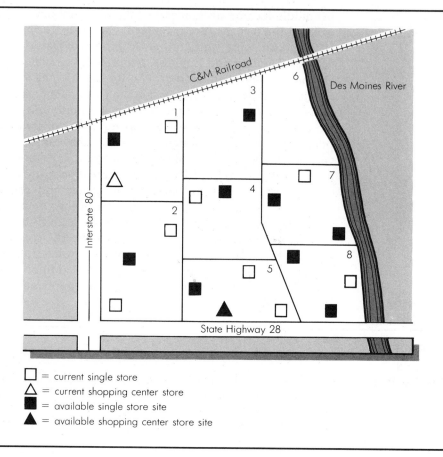

☐ = current single store
△ = current shopping center store
■ = available single store site
▲ = available shopping center store site

ping center off Interstate 80. Another major competitor would be Odom Appliances, which had two stores on the south side. James Burnside knew of at least nine furniture or appliance outlets that could provide strong competition for a new store in the area under consideration.

DISCUSSION QUESTIONS

1. How would the demographic characteristics of the population on the south side affect the demand for furniture and appliances?

2. Evaluate the census tracts in Exhibit 1 with respect to the criteria outlined by James Burnside. Which tracts appear to be appropriate for further consideration?

3. What effects would the boundaries of the southern section of Des Moines, Iowa, have on a retail business?

4. What store sites in Exhibit 2 appear to be most promising?

5. If the next step was to select a specific site for a fourth store, what additional factors should Thomas and James Burnside consider?

Robert F. Lusch
University of Oklahoma

Scope Pharmacies, Inc.

Ms. JANE HOOVER is the president and principal stockholder of Scope Pharmacies, Inc. Currently she is in a quandary over how to reorganize the corporation so that it will be able to continue its rapid growth. In six years the firm has grown from a single-unit pharmacy to a group of five pharmacies. Ms. Hoover is finding it increasingly difficult to manage and control the five stores.

BACKGROUND

In 1972, Jane Hoover graduated from college with a degree in pharmacy and immediately took a job as a pharmacist for Walgreen Drugs. It didn't take Jane long to recognize that the day-to-day activities of a pharmacist were not very exciting and challenging. Jane frequently found herself daydreaming about operating her own drugstore.

In April of 1974, while visiting a friend in a nearby city, Jane accidentally ran across a small drugstore that was for sale. The present owner had operated the store for twenty-two years and was nearing retirement. The store was located in a neighborhood shopping center and was easily accessible to many households within eight blocks of the store. Luckily for Jane, the owner was having difficulty finding a buyer, and thus she was able to purchase the store (which had a five-year lease remaining) for the book value of the inventory (which was $60,000) and $10,000 for fixtures and equipment. The owner was willing to finance most of the $70,000 purchase price, and thus Jane was able to purchase the drugstore with only $7,500 of her own funds. Thus by June 1974 Jane was in business for herself.

Jane operated the drugstore with the help of two part-time clerks while she served as the full-time pharmacist. Although the new venture did not free her of her role as a pharmacist, she was enjoying the new venture since there

Note: This case was prepared as a basis for class discussion rather than to illustrate appropriate or inappropriate handling of retail situations.

were many other duties to perform besides filling prescriptions. The accounting records had to be kept, employees supervised, merchandise bought and priced, and sales promotions planned. Not surprisingly, she quickly found herself taking night courses at a local university in the fields of accounting and marketing.

By October 1975 Jane had spotted another small drugstore for sale. It was also located in a neighborhood shopping center. The price was $110,000 but the owner would not finance any of the purchase price. Jane acquired outside capital by incorporating and selling stock to friends and acquaintances who had been impressed with how well she had managed the first store. She was also able to convince the existing owner of the store to take $10,000 of the purchase price in stock of Scope Pharmacies, Inc.

The first store was turned over to a manager and the new store was managed by Jane. Also at this point Jane added a part-time bookkeeper to handle the records for both stores.

In 1977, 1978, and 1979 a total of three more drugstores were acquired—all from individual proprietors desiring to get out of the drugstore business. The two most recently acquired stores were located in a city of 47,000 people which was twenty-one miles from the first three stores. Stores acquired in 1977, 1978, and 1979 were financed through retained earnings and issuing stock in Scope Pharmacies, Inc., to the prior owner. Every time a store was acquired, Jane would become the manager and turn the store she was presently managing over to a new manager.

CURRENT SITUATION

As 1980 ended, Jane began to recognize that she did not have the time to keep a close watch over all the stores. At the beginning of 1978, she had hired a full-time assistant to help her with the buying and in late 1978 added a full-time accountant. But still there were too many problems occurring that required her special attention and that were taking her away from managing her store. Jane also wished she had more time to follow up on other possible drugstore acquisitions. Recently she heard of a small group of four drugstores for sale in a city fifty-four miles away.

The income statement and balance sheet for Scope Pharmacies, Inc., are provided in Exhibits 1 and 2. These financial statements reflect the composite performance for all five stores as of the end of 1980. All five stores were located in neighborhood centers and were 4,000 to 5,000 square feet in size. Approximately 40 percent of sales were prescription drugs and the remainder was divided among the following product categories: health and beauty aids, magazines, books, newspapers, tobacco, candy, greeting cards, and small gifts ($5–$25). Each store carries 9,500 items. An item is defined as one size of one product. For example a bottle of vitamin pills containing 200 tablets was considered as one item, even though there may be a dozen bottles in stock of that size and description.

Drugstores are complicated in terms of legal regulations. There are state

EXHIBIT 1
Scope Pharmacies, Inc., Income Statement (1980)

ITEM	DOLLARS	PERCENT
Net sales	$2,420,663	100.0
Cost of goods sold	1,575,852	65.1
Gross margin	844,811	34.9
Operating expenses		
Wages	455,085	18.8
Rent	60,517	2.5
Advertising	29,048	1.2
Utilities and phone	31,469	1.3
Insurance	24,206	1.0
Legal and professional fees	12,103	.5
Delivery	9,683	.4
Repairs	26,627	1.1
Interest	21,786	.9
Bad debts	7,262	.3
Miscellaneous	70,199	2.9
Total expenses	$ 747,985	30.9
Profit (before taxes)	96,826	4.0
Taxes	36,794	1.5
Profit (after taxes)	$ 60,032	2.5

and federal laws which druggists must comply with since they handle products with dangerous ingredients. Also licenses need to be obtained from the State Board of Pharmacy. In addition, some dangerous drugs need to be ordered by serial number and regularly inventoried and reported to government agencies.

EXHIBIT 2
Scope Pharmacies, Inc., Balance Sheet (1980)

ASSETS		LIABILITIES AND NET WORTH	
Current assets		Current liabilities	
Cash	$ 30,103	Accounts payable	$112,041
Accounts receivable	96,827	Notes payable	44,955
Inventory	387,306	Other	35,964
Other	68,163	Total	$192,960
Total	$582,399	Long-term liabilities	$118,274
Fixed assets		Net worth	$380,384
Equipment	79,209		
Leasehold improvements	30,010	Total liabilities and net worth	$691,618
Total	$109,219		
Total assets	$691,618		

DISCUSSION QUESTIONS

1. What are the advantages and disadvantages of a multiple-store organization?

2. How should Scope Pharmacies, Inc., be reorganized to improve control and give Jane the time she needs to direct the corporation?

3. Write job descriptions for any new personnel you might add to Scope Pharmacies, Inc.

4. Analyze the financial performance of Scope Pharmacies, Inc.

5. Does Jane Hoover have a strategy for Scope Pharmacies, Inc.?

IV

OPERATIONS PLANNING AND MANAGEMENT

13

Overview *This is the first chapter in a set of seven that deal with operations planning and management. This chapter will focus on the management and planning of merchandise investments. The planning and control of merchandise in terms of both dollars and units will be our major focus.*

Merchandise Planning and Management

Merchandise Management Personnel
General Merchandise Manager
Divisional Merchandise Manager
Buyer
Department Manager
Merchandise Support Staff

Planning and Control

Dollar Merchandise Planning
Basic Stock Method
Percentage Variation Method
Weeks' Supply Method
Stock-to-Sales Method

Dollar Merchandise Control

Unit Stock Planning
Who Will Plan?
Optimal Merchandise Mix
Constraining Factors
Model Stock Plan
Conflicts in Unit Stock Planning

Unit Stock Control
Periodic Unit Control Systems
Perpetual Unit Control Systems

Evaluating Merchandising Performance
Stockturn
Profit Measures
Gross Margin Return on Inventory

Summary

THE ANALYSIS, planning, acquisition, and control of inventory investments in a retail enterprise is **merchandise management.** Analysis comes into play because the retailer needs to analyze consumer demand in order to make good merchandise management decisions. Planning occurs because merchandise to be sold in the future must be bought before that time. Acquisition happens because the merchandise needs to be procured from suppliers or manufacturers. Finally, control of the large dollar investments in inventory is important to ensure an adequate financial return on merchandise investments.

If you decide to pursue a career in retailing, you cannot avoid some contact with activities related to merchandise management. This is because merchandising is a day-to-day operating decision in all retail enterprises. As inventory is sold, new merchandise needs to be purchased, displayed, and sold once again. Clearly then, in retailing, merchandise management is pervasive.

Merchandise management not only is essential to retailing, but actually is its largest component in terms of dollars invested. Exhibit 13.1 dramatizes this point. Retailers, on average, invest approximately 38 percent of their total asset

EXHIBIT 13.1
The Composition of Assets in Retailing (1979)

TOTAL ASSETS (100%) = $262.6 billion

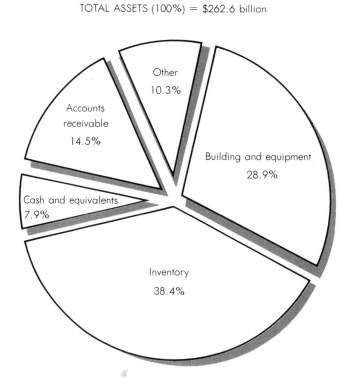

Source: Federal Trade Commission, *Quarterly Report on Manufacturing, Mining, and Trading Companies* (Washington, D.C.: U.S. Government Printing Office, 4th quarter, 1979).

dollars in inventory. In 1979, for all retailers in the United States, this translated into $100.9 billion. Predictably therefore, retailers that do a superior job at managing inventory will make substantial progress toward achieving high performance results. If a retailer does a poor job at managing inventory, however, then close to 40 percent of the business is being mismanaged, making it impossible to achieve high performance results.

In retailing, profits are not produced by investments in bricks and mortar but by wise investments in inventory. Obviously, bricks and mortar are required, because the retailer usually needs a place to store and display merchandise and conduct continuing operations. Empty stores, however, do not produce sales dollars. To produce revenue, the retailer needs merchandise.

An orientation toward serving consumer needs and wants at a profit should be the major underlying principle in merchandise management. This principle needs to be embraced because merchandise purchased will have to fill some consumer demand in the retailer's trade area or the merchandise will not sell or will have to be sold at a loss.

In Chapters 5 and 7, which dealt with consumer behavior and the socioeconomic environment, we developed a host of concepts intended to help you be consumer oriented in retail decision making. A glance back to these chapters may be helpful.

MERCHANDISE MANAGEMENT PERSONNEL

The personnel necessary to perform the merchandise management function in a large retail chain are displayed in Exhibit 13.2. We give the personnel needed for a large retail chain to show all the personnel that may be needed. However, in many small retail establishments, a single person may perform all the activities we will discuss.

General Merchandise Manager In most large retail organizations there will be a general merchandise manager who would probably hold the rank of vice president. Because this person has a high position in the organizational hierarchy, he or she will not get involved in day-to-day merchandise management problems. Rather, this executive would more likely be involved with quarterly, seasonal, or annual planning, budgeting, and controlling of merchandising activities.

Divisional Merchandise Manager Reporting to the general merchandise manager would be several divisional merchandise managers. They will be responsible for particular lines of merchandise. For example, in a department store there may be divisional merchandise managers for menswear apparel, furniture and home furnishings, hardware, televisions and stereos, womenswear, and so on.

Divisional merchandise managers, regardless of the size of the retail organization, will have four basic duties:

1. Forecasting sales for the forthcoming budget period. This involves estimating consumer demand, and therefore the manager must understand and

assess the competitive and socioeconomic environments that were detailed in Chapters 6 and 7.

2. Translating the sales forecast into dollar inventory levels. To do this effectively, the merchandise manager needs to know what inventory levels are necessary to support the level of sales that has been forecast.

3. Inspiring commitment and performance on the part of the buyers and department managers. The buyers will need to procure the right types of merchandise, and the department managers will need to do a good job in moving the merchandise.

4. Assessing merchandising performance. This is necessary in order to provide control and to maintain good performance or improve on it in forthcoming budget periods.

Notice that the duties of the divisional manager cannot be accomplished without the help and assistance of both buyers and department managers. Let us now look at what their duties are.

Buyer The buyer has three primary duties.[1] By doing them well, the buyer can significantly contribute to overall store profitability.[2] These three tasks are listed below:

1. To work with the divisional merchandise manager in arriving at dollar inventory levels. The buyer has considerable insight into the market and should share this insight with the merchandise manager.

2. To convert the dollar inventory plans into unit plans. Specifically, the buyer needs to decide what mix of merchandise to procure with the dollars that have been allocated.

3. To procure the merchandise. The buyer must visit the marketplace to purchase the goods and negotiate terms of purchase (price, credit, delivery).

Department Manager The final players in the merchandise management process are the department managers. They are responsible for certain merchandise lines on the selling floor, and they have four central tasks:

1. To work with the buyer on the unit inventory plan, especially regarding merchandise assortments. Since department managers are closer to the customer than buyers are, they should have a better feel for the specific type of merchandise that will sell well.

2. To lead, motivate, and guide the sales personnel. The sales personnel need to know their merchandise and how to present and sell it to the customer.

1. David J. Rachman, ''The Organization Structure of the Retail Firm: The Buyer's Role,'' in R. Patrick Cash (ed.), *The Buyer's Manual* (New York: National Retail Merchants Association, 1979), pp. 29–42.

2. Claude R. Martin, Jr., ''The Contribution of the Professional Buyer to a Store's Success or Failure,'' *Journal of Retailing* 48(Summer 1973): 69–80.

EXHIBIT 13.2   **Merchandise Management Personnel for a Retail Chain**

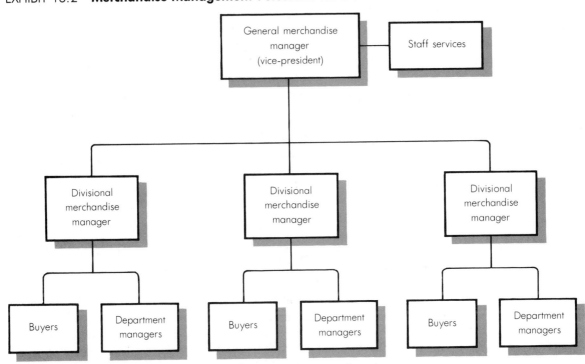

3. To monitor changing consumer tastes and wants for the merchandise lines being sold. On a recurring basis, the department manager needs to examine what the customer wants.
4. To make certain that customers are properly served. Customer complaints, suggestions, questions, or praise must be properly handled.

If the department manager does a good job of performing these tasks, then the retailer will be more assured of achieving good merchandise management performance.

Merchandise Support Staff   The four major players we have profiled will often require special assistance in performing their respective tasks. If they happen to be in a small retail organization, then even if they need assistance, they frequently must do without it. This may even be the case in some larger retail organizations. However, in an increasing number of larger retail organizations, staff personnel are available who can substantially facilitate the merchandise management cycle. They generally provide six types of services:

1. **Comparative data services** offer merchandise managers, buyers, and department managers comparisons of store offerings in the respective trade

area. The most frequent comparisons are of price, service, style, quality, and assortment.

2. **Consumer research services** offer tailored research based on consumer responses or behavior patterns. Such research includes trade area delineation studies, store image studies, and competitive store ratings and segmentation research.

3. **Fashion analysis services** can help coordinate buying and selling efforts by providing seasonal fashion forecasts, techniques for identifying dead fashions early, advice on fashion portrayal in advertising and display, and direction for the development of fashion shows for customers.

4. **Sales and inventory analysis services** typically are provided by the accounting or controller's office and provide timely information on product movement, markdowns, returns and allowances, and gross margins. This information is crucial in determining if merchandising objectives are being achieved.

5. **Product testing services** are provided in some of the largest retail chains. This service allows the buyer to assess the actual physical characteristics or performance of a product before making a commitment for more substantial purchases. As such, this service helps to ensure that the retailer's customers are receiving the best merchandise for their dollars.

6. **Training services** allow for the training of new personnel in the merchandise management cycle (assistant buyers and assistant department managers). There is also continuing education of existing personnel so they can be advanced to more responsible and authoritative positions within the merchandise management cycle.

Although all retailers are not able to provide the above services (due to size constraints), the underlying principle, that merchandise needs specialized services in many areas, cannot be ignored.

PLANNING AND CONTROL

A major aspect of merchandise management involves planning. Since it takes time to buy merchandise and have it delivered and displayed, it becomes essential to plan. The merchandise manager needs to decide today what merchandise on hand will look like in several weeks, months, or even a year from now.

If planning occurs, then it is only logical that control be exercised over the merchandise dollars or units that are planned. A good control system will help ensure profitable investments.

Because of the importance of these topics, the rest of this chapter will focus on dollar merchandise planning and control and unit merchandise planning and control.[3]

3. For distinction between these two types of planning and control, see "Item Control Compared to Dollar Control," *Hardware Retailing* 130(April 1975): 39.

DOLLAR MERCHANDISE PLANNING

Although the merchandise manager may obtain the inputs of buyers and department managers, he or she is ultimately responsible for dollar planning of merchandise investments. How might a merchandise manager plan these investments? There are a variety of methods, but a sales forecast is essential to all of them. A sales forecast is needed for at least each of the months for the next buying season and potentially for each of the next twelve months.[4] Once sales have been anticipated, there are four methods for planning dollars invested in stocks.

Basic Stock Method   The **basic stock method** (BSM) of dollar planning will have as its foundation a baseline or fixed level of dollar inventory investment regardless of expected sales volume. On top of this foundation will be a variable element that increases or decreases at the first of each month in the same dollar amount as sales are expected to increase or decrease. The BSM uses the following formula to compute the planned dollar investment in inventory for the beginning of each month:

$$I_i = S_i + \left[\left(\sum_{i=1}^{n} S_i/t \right) - \left(\sum_{i=1}^{n} S_i/n \right) \right]$$

where:

I_i = retail value of inventory for beginning month i
S_i = forecasted dollar sales for month i
t = desired stockturn level per season or year
n = number of months in season or year

Do not let the formula for the BSM scare you off. Let us look at a numerical example. Assume you are the owner of a small menswear store in your community. You need to plan dollar inventory investments for next month and have the following forecasted sales:

Month	Forecasted Sales
1	$12,000
2	14,000
3	16,000
4	17,000
5	20,000
6	18,000
7	18,000
8	12,000
9	14,000
10	13,000
11	15,000
12	18,000

4. Some of the problems in forecasting in turbulent times are discussed in Howard Eilenberg, "Coping With Economic Uncertainty," *Retail Control* 43(October 1974): 2–14.

Assume that n, the number of selling months, is 12, and that t, the desired level of stockturns per season, is 4. From these data and the BSM formula, you can compute the retail inventories to have on hand at the beginning of the next twelve months. Let us compute the planned dollar inventory for the first month. (Remember that $\Sigma_{i=1}^{12} S_i$ means the sum of the forecasted dollar sales for months 1–12; in this case, $187,000.) The desired inventory would then be:

$$I_1 = \$12,000 + [(\$187,000/4) - (\$187,000/12)]$$
$$= \$12,000 + [(46,750) - (\$15,483)]$$
$$= \$12,000 + [\$31,167]$$
$$= \$43,167$$

Notice that the foundation or baseline inventory is the amount in brackets—that is $31,167—and the variable element is the $12,000. The dollar inventory planned for the second month will rise in direct proportion to the increase in sales for the second month over the first month. Referring to the previous list, we find that second-month sales are expected to rise by $2,000 to a level of $14,000. Thus, we would expect the BSM formula to tell us to raise dollar inventories by $2,000 from the first month's level of $43,167 to $45,167. By plugging the appropriate numbers into the BSM formula this statement is verified:

$$I_2 = \$14,000 + [(\$187,000/4) - (\$187,000/12)]$$
$$= \$45,167$$

Now see if you can compute the planned dollar inventory investments for the remaining ten months for this hypothetical menswear retailer.

The basic stock method of planning dollar inventories fails to perform adequately when stockturn is greater than twelve times a year. Under such a scenario, the foundation or basic stock

$$(\sum_{i=1}^{n} S_i/t) - (\sum_{i=1}^{n} S_i/n)$$

will actually become negative. This is obviously nonsense. Thus, when stockturn is greater than six times per year, you should use weeks rather than months in the basic stock method equation.

Percentage Variation Method   A second commonly used technique for planning dollar inventory levels is the **percentage variation method** (PVM). This method postulates that the percentage fluctuations in monthly stock from average stock should be half as great as the percentage fluctuations in monthly sales from average sales. Here is the percentage variation formula:

$$I_i = 1/2 \cdot (\sum_{i=1}^{n} S_i/t) \cdot \left[1 + S_i/(\sum_{i=1}^{n} S_i/n)\right]$$

where:

I_i = retail value of inventory for beginning of month i
S_i = forecasted dollar sales for month i
t = desired stockturn level per season or year
n = number of months in season or year

The PVM utilizes the same components as the BSM, and thus they can be expected to have similarities. In fact, the PVM will give the same results as the BSM when a stockturn of six times per year is planned. When higher stockturns are planned, however, the PVM will give stocks that fluctuate less than those found by the BSM.

At this point it might be helpful to use the preceding menswear example to determine planned dollar stock for the first month using the PVM formula. The result you should obtain is as follows:

$$
\begin{aligned}
I_i &= 1/2 \cdot (\$187{,}000/4) \cdot [1 + \$12{,}000/(\$187{,}000/12)] \\
&= 1/2 \cdot (\$46{,}750) \cdot [1 + .770] \\
&= \$41{,}374
\end{aligned}
$$

With a little effort, you should be able to use the PVM formula to determine planned dollar stocks for the remaining eleven months for our hypothetical menswear retailer.

Weeks' Supply Method A third method for dollar stock planning is the **weeks' supply method** (WSM). It is one of the simpler methods and uses this formula:

$$
I_i = \sum_{j=1}^{52/t} S_j
$$

where:

I_i = retail value of inventory for beginning of month i
S_j = forecasted sales for week j
t = desired stockturn level per year

Basically, the WSM formula states that stocks should be set equal to a predetermined number of weeks' supply. The predetermined number of weeks' supply is directly related to the stockturn desired. In the WSM, dollar stocks vary in proportion to forecasted sales. Thus, if forecasted sales double, dollar stocks will also double.

To illustrate the WSM, let us examine a hypothetical floorcovering retailer. Assume that it wants to program its operation for a stockturn of 6.5 times per year. Thus, the amount of inventory to have on hand as of March 1 is

$$
I_{\text{March 1}} = \sum_{j=1}^{52/t} S_j
$$

Since stockturn (t) is equal to 6.5, then (52/6.5) equals 8. Therefore,

$$
I_{\text{March 1}} = \sum_{j=1}^{8} S_j
$$

This simply means to sum the forecasted sales for the eight weeks beginning March 1. If the forecasted sales for each of those eight weeks are $10,000, $12,000, $11,000, $13,000, $10,500, $11,500, $12,000, and $9,000, then the sum of these is $89,000. This then becomes the planned dollar inventory for March 1.

Stock-to-Sales Method   The final method for planning dollar stocks is the **stock-to-sales method** (SSM). This method is quite easy to use but requires one to have the **beginning-of-the-month stock-to-sales ratio.** This ratio tells the retailer how much dollar stock to have on hand at the beginning of the month to support that month's dollar sales. A ratio of 6.1, for example, would tell the retailer that dollar stocks at the beginning of the month should be 6.1 times as great as expected sales for that month.

Stock-to-sales ratios can be obtained from internal or external sources. Internally, the statistics can be obtained if the retailer has designed a good accounting system and has properly stored historical data so that it can be readily retrieved. Externally, the retailer can often rely on retail trade associations such as the National Retail Merchants Association or the Menswear Retailers Association. These and other trade associations collect stock-to-sales ratios from participating merchants and then compile, tabulate, and report them in special management reports or trade publications. Exhibit 13.3 provides an example of beginning-of-the-month stock-to-sales ratios that the National Retail Merchants Association releases to the department store industry.

With available beginning-of-the-month stock-to-sales ratios, the merchandise manager can compute dollar stocks with this equation:

$$I_i = S_i B_i$$

where:

I_i = retail value of inventory for beginning of month i
S_i = forecasted dollar sales for month i
B_i = beginning of the month stock-to-sales ratio for month i

EXHIBIT 13.3
Beginning-of-the-Month Stock-to-Sales Ratios for Department Stores (1978)

		ANNUAL STORE SALES			
MONTH	Under $1 Million	$1–3 Million	$5–10 Million	$10–20 Million	Over $20 Million
February	6.40x	5.85x	6.14x	5.10x	5.79x
March	4.85	5.63	4.30	5.08	4.52
April	6.62	5.32	5.50	5.98	5.05
May	5.98	5.25	4.90	5.06	5.13
June	5.58	4.91	5.39	5.55	4.50
July	5.90	5.32	5.42	6.20	5.18
August	5.66	4.92	5.15	5.75	4.90
September	5.74	5.18	5.00	5.06	4.15
October	6.70	5.00	5.15	5.86	4.80
November	6.93	5.11	4.65	5.20	4.25
December	3.45	2.68	2.60	3.06	2.14
January	7.07	6.46	6.30	6.47	5.67

Source: National Retail Merchants Association, *Department Store and Specialty Store Merchandising and Operating Results of 1978* (New York: Financial Executives Division, National Retail Merchants Association, 1979), p. xix. Reprinted by permission of the National Retail Merchants Association.

It simply tells the merchandise manager to take the forecasted sales for the appropriate month and multiply it by the appropriate beginning of the month stock-to-sales ratio to arrive at planned dollar stocks. Assume, for example, you are the merchandise manager for a large department store (sales in excess of $20 million annually) and are planning the dollar inventory to have on hand at the beginning of March. March sales are forecast to be $2.1 million. You refer to Exhibit 13.3 and pull out the appropriate beginning-of-the-month stock-to-sales ratio, which for stores over $20 million in volume is 4.52 for the month of March. Using the SSM equation, you multiply the $2.1 million sales forecast by the stock-to-sales ratio of 4.52 and obtain a $9.49 million planned dollar stock level for the beginning of March (I_i = $2.1 million × 4.52).

DOLLAR MERCHANDISE CONTROL

Once the dollar merchandise to have on hand at the beginning of any month is planned by the merchandise manager, it becomes essential to ensure that the buyer does not make commitments for merchandise that would exceed the dollar plan. In short, the dollars planned for merchandise need to be controlled. This control is accomplished through a technique called **open-to-buy**. The open-to-buy represents the dollar amount that a buyer can currently expend on merchandise without exceeding the planned dollar stocks previously discussed. At the start of any given month, the buyer will not necessarily be able to purchase a dollar amount equal to the planned dollar stocks for that month. This is the case because there may be some inventory already on hand or on order. To illustrate this point more succinctly, let's see how to compute open-to-buy:

1. End-of-month planned retail stock
2. Plus planned sales for month
3. Minus stock on hand at retail
4. Equals planned purchases at retail
5. Minus commitments at retail for current delivery
6. Equals open-to-buy at retail

Taking this open-to-buy formula, we can continue our previous department store example. In that example we arrived at planned dollar stocks for the beginning of the month of March of $8.4 million. If we are currently at February 1, and plan February sales to be $1.6 million, presently have $6.9 million in inventory, and have $1.7 million due to arrive in the next three weeks, then what is the buyer's open-to-buy? The answer is $1.4 million, arrived at as follows (all figures in this example are in millions):

Planned stock end of February (same as beginning of March)	$8.4
Plus planned February sales	1.6
Minus current stock on hand	6.9
Equals planned purchases	3.1
Minus merchandise on order for delivery	1.7
Equals open-to-buy at retail	$1.4

Without careful monitoring of open-to-buy, the buyer is likely to commit more dollars than the firm is able to absorb financially.

UNIT STOCK PLANNING

The dollar merchandise plan is only the starting point in merchandise management. Once the merchandise manager has decided how many dollars can be invested in inventory, the dollar plan needs to be converted into a unit plan. On the sales floor, dollars are not sold, but items. The assortment of items that will comprise the merchandise mix must then be planned.[5]

Designing the optimal merchandise mix involves a complex decision for which there exists no standard methodological solution. The final mix will be determined by a combination of creative and analytical thought processes. Consider, for example, a grocery store manager attempting to allocate $250,000 in inventory dollars among 4,000 to 6,000 individual items. On a strict analytical basis, the manager might try to allocate the $250,000 to the thousands of possible items in order to maximize the combined contribution of all the items to total store overhead and profits. It does not take a genius to conclude quickly that without knowledge of the demand functions for each of the items, the preceding task could not be accomplished using only analytical techniques. Thus, creative thought processes must accompany analytical thinking in attempting to design the optimal merchandise mix.

Who Will Plan?   The unit plan should be developed with the input of several parties. The merchandise manager sets dollar limits that the plan must fall within, but the buyer and department manager will do most of the detail work. Knowing what merchandise is available from competing vendors (suppliers) makes the buyer important. However, equally important is the department manager, who is closest to demand, the consumer. An optimal merchandise mix cannot be developed unless these three parties cooperate and share their knowledge and insights. Of course, in the small, one- or two-person store, the unit plan will be the result of the input of probably only one individual. In such a setting, that person will need to question his or her own decisions, since others will not be on hand to check the consistency of logic and the assessment of both the supply and demand factors in the market.

Optimal Merchandise Mix   Exhibit 13.4 shows the three dimensions of the optimal mix: variety, breadth, and depth. Each of these dimensions needs to be defined; however, we need first to define merchandise line. A **merchandise line** consists of a group of products that are closely related because they are intended for the same end use (all televisions); are sold to the same customer group (junior miss womenswear); or fall within a given price range (budget womenswear).

Variety   The variety of the merchandise mix refers to the interrelatedness of the product lines represented. The lines could be interrelated because they

5. Frank Burnside, ''Merchandise Assortment Planning,'' in R. Patrick Cash (ed.), *The Buyer's Manual* (New York: National Retail Merchants Association, 1979), pp. 245–71.

EXHIBIT 13.4
**Dimensions of
and
Constraints on
Optimal
Merchandise
Mix**

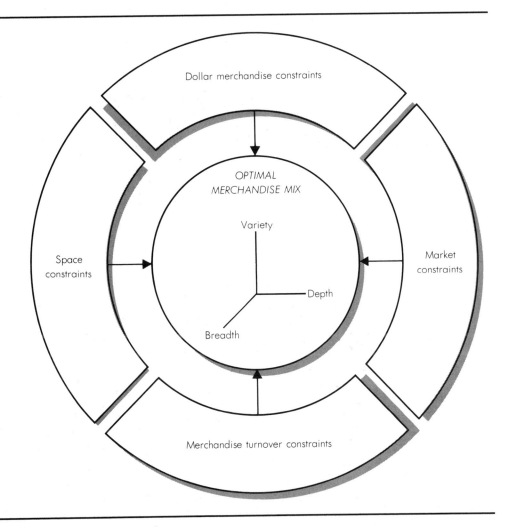

have similar end uses. For example, televisions and stereos are both used for home entertainment and thus are highly interrelated, whereas food and televisions are not related since they do not have similar end uses. In conventional supermarkets the product lines are typically very interrelated—dry groceries, produce, meats, frozen foods, beverages are all intended to be used for the same consumer end, nourishment. However, some supermarkets are deviating from this conventional mode and increasing merchandise variety by stocking portable TVs, stereos, plants, casual clothing, and automotive supplies. One can also increase variety by adding product lines that are sold to different customer groups or in different price ranges. See if you can think of several examples in this regard.

Breadth   Merchandise breadth refers to the number of product lines that are found in the merchandise mix. No account is taken of the lines' interrelatedness. Thus a bakery store may be thought of as having a good breadth if it has pastries, breads, cakes, and cookies; and at the same time a discount department store can be thought of as having good breadth if it stocks toys, apparel, garden equipment, televisions, household appliances, and giftware. The bakery store's lines are broad but very interrelated; the discount department store's are broad but not very interrelated.

Depth   Merchandise depth refers to the average number of items within each line of the merchandise mix. For instance, if televisions are the line, the depth could be characterized by how many of the following items are carried: black and white versus color, various screen sizes, various cabinet types, and so on.

Constraining Factors   With these definitions in mind, we can now refer back to Exhibit 13.4 to observe the four constraining factors that influence the design of the optimal merchandise mix.

Dollar Constraint   The dollars available for investment in merchandise can be expended to increase merchandise variety, depth, or breadth or some combination thereof. But seldom will there be enough dollars to emphasize all three dimensions. If the decision is made to emphasize variety, it would be unrealistic to expect also to have a lot of breadth and depth.

For instance, assume for the moment that you are the owner/manager of a local gift store. You have $30,000 to invest in merchandise. If you decide that you want a lot of variety in gifts (jewelry, crystal, candles, games, cards, figurines, ashtrays, clocks, and radios) then you obviously could not have much depth in any single line, such as crystal glassware.

Space Constraint   The retailer must also deal with space constraints. If depth or breadth is wanted, space is needed. If variety is to be stressed, it is also important to have enough empty space to separate the distinct merchandise lines. For example, consider a long counter containing cosmetics, candy, fishing tackle, women's stockings, and toys. This would obviously be an unsightly and unwise arrangement. As more variety is added, empty space becomes necessary to allow the consumer to clearly distinguish among distinct product lines.

Turnover Constraint   As the depth of the merchandise is increased, the retailer will be stocking more and more variations on the product to serve smaller and smaller segments. Consequently, inventory turnover will deteriorate. One does not have to minimize variety, breadth, and depth to maximize turnover, but one must know how various merchandise mixes will affect inventory turnover.

Market Constraints   Market constraints should also affect decisions on variety, breadth, and depth of the merchandise mix. The three dimensions have a profound effect on how the consumer perceives the store, and consequently on the customers the store will attract. The consumer perceives a specialty store as one with limited variety and breadth in terms of merchandise lines but considerable depth within the lines handled. An individual searching for depth in a limited set of merchandise lines such as formal menswear will thus be attracted to a menswear retailer specializing in formal wear. On the other hand, the consumer perceives the general merchandise retailer such as Penney's or Sears as a store with lots of variety and breadth in terms of merchandise lines, but with more constrained depth. Therefore, someone who needs to make several purchases across several merchandise lines, and who is willing to sacrifice depth of assortment, would be more attracted to the general merchandise retailer.

Comment We see that the constraining factors make it almost impossible for a retailer to emphasize all three dimensions. Even Marshall Fields' flagship store in downtown Chicago, with over 2 million square feet and over $50 million in inventory, is not able to offer the broad and deep assortments within certain merchandise lines that some specialty stores (such as jewelry, luggage and camera stores) are able to offer. On a practical basis, you simply can't have it all. Some customers will walk out of the store emptyhanded because the store didn't have what they wanted or could afford. No retailer can avoid this completely. However, if you are going to lose customers, lose the less profitable ones by properly dimensioning your merchandise in terms of variety, breadth, and depth within the dollar, space, turnover, and market constraints.

Model Stock Plan   After you decide the relative emphasis to be placed on the three dimensions of the merchandise mix, you need to decide what merchandise lines and items to stock. This can be an overwhelming task for the novice, but even for the experienced retailer it is time consuming and often frustrating. Units are usually planned using a model stock plan. The model stock plan represents the precise items and their respective quantities that should be on hand for each merchandise line. A separate model stock plan needs to be compiled for each line of merchandise.

Exhibit 13.5 shows a hypothetical menswear retailer attempting to develop a unit plan for men's shirts. It has already conducted a dollar plan and has allocated $12,000 at retail for men's shirts. Since the average retail price of a shirt for the store is $12, 1,000 shirts will need to be stocked. The model unit plan will reveal how many shirts of each kind the retailer should keep in stock. While the exhibit only shows the breakdown within one attribute (casual shirts), the same procedure would be followed for all types.

The first thing the menswear retailer should do is attempt to identify what attributes cause customers to purchase shirts. Exhibit 13.5 shows that the retailer has identified six atributes: (1) type of shirt (dress, casual, sport, or work), (2) size, (3) sleeve length, (4) collar type, (5) color, and (6) fabric. Are any key attributes left out? What about price? If customers shop for shirts by price point, then price should also be a product attribute.

EXHIBIT 13.5 **A Partial Model Unit Plan for Men's Shirts**

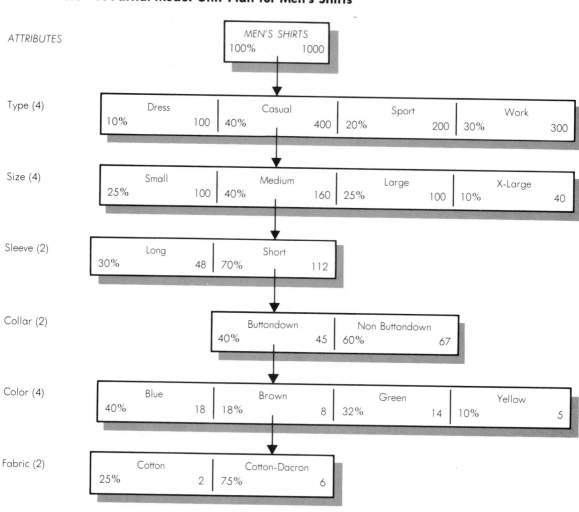

ATTRIBUTES

| MEN'S SHIRTS |
| 100%   1000 |

Type (4)

Dress		Casual		Sport		Work	
10%	100	40%	400	20%	200	30%	300

Size (4)

Small		Medium		Large		X-Large	
25%	100	40%	160	25%	100	10%	40

Sleeve (2)

Long		Short	
30%	48	70%	112

Collar (2)

Buttondown		Non Buttondown	
40%	45	60%	67

Color (4)

Blue		Brown		Green		Yellow	
40%	18	18%	8	32%	14	10%	5

Fabric (2)

Cotton		Cotton-Dacron	
25%	2	75%	6

The second step is to identify the number of levels under each attribute. The retailer in Exhibit 13.5 has selected four types of shirts to stock, four sizes, two sleeve lengths, two collar types, four colors, and two fabrics.

In relation to the first two steps in the construction of a model stock plan, a basic principle of merchandise management can be identified: Stocking requirements will grow explosively as more product attributes and expanded levels are offered on each attribute. If the retailer offers four shirt types, four sizes in each type, two sleeve lengths, two collar styles, four colors, and two fabrics, then it will have to stock 512 shirts ($4 \times 4 \times 2 \times 2 \times 4 \times 2$), just to stock one unit of each. More importantly, if the retailer now decides to offer two price points instead of one, the stocking requirements double to 1,024 items. But alas, we started out this example knowing our menswear retailer could only stock 1,000 shirts. Obviously the retailer has a problem if it wants to feature six or seven attributes and several levels on each attribute.

The preceding discussion illustrates the need for a basic tradeoff in merchandise management. As more attributes are featured, the probability is increased that a product on hand will match the customer's needs and purchasing power. However, there is a cost associated with increasing this probability—the cost of carrying the additional inventory. At some point, the carrying cost of the additional inventory required to increase the probability of purchase is greater than the profit obtained from those additional unit sales. This reinforces our earlier point, that the retailer will have to allow some customers to walk out of the store empty-handed.

The third step in developing the model stock plan is to allocate the total dollars or units to the respective item categories. There is an optimum allocation if the model unit plan has recommended quantities for each item that are in direct proportion to market demand patterns. If the plan reflects this optimum, then by comparing actual stocks with model stocks one can easily determine if the stocks are out of balance. The more actual stocks mirror the model stock plan, the more the stocks will be balanced; and balanced stocks maximize sales potential. Stocks that are out of balance will cause customers to walk out of the store without the item they came to purchase. Worse yet, they might walk out with a product that is not well suited to their needs; that will hurt the retailer's long-run business.

But how can a retailer determine that the recommended quantities for each item are in direct proportion to market demand patterns? The most useful thing to do is to analyze past sales records. Exhibit 13.6 shows the sales experience of our hypothetical menswear retailer in reference to the last 500 shirts sold. This exhibit, derived from past sales records, shows the demand density for different types and sizes of shirts. This simple analysis forms the basis of planning unit stocks in the model plan. Changing the data in Exhibit 13.6 to percentage form, we can see that 10 percent of our shirt sales were dress, 40 percent casual, 20 percent sport, and 30 percent work. Furthermore, of the casual shirts, 25 percent were small, 40 percent medium, 25 percent large, and 10 percent extra large. The percentage derived from such a sales analysis can then be used in the model stock plan (Exhibit 13.5). Thus, in this example, past sales will be used to indicate future demand density. As such, of the 1,000 shirts we plan to stock, 100 will be dress, 400 casual, 200 sport, and 300 work. These numbers are obtained simply by multiplying the 1,000 shirts by the percentages obtained in the sales analysis. In the past, 10 percent of the shirts sold were dress shirts, so we will plan to stock 100 dress shirts, which is 10 percent of 1,000. A similar procedure is conducted to determine how many to stock in each size, sleeve length, collar type, color, and fabric.

One should not always allow past sales results to determine future stocking patterns. In the past, quantities not in proportion to demand patterns may have been stocked, and in fact sold—but probably at a loss. However, the pure sales statistics will not reveal this. In addition, new products that come into the market may feature attributes previously not stocked, and the demand for

EXHIBIT 13.6
**A Sales
Analysis of
Men's Shirts**

	SIZE			
TYPE	Small	Medium	Large	X-Large
Dress	XX	XXXX	XXX	X
Casual	XXXX XXXX XX	XXXX XXXX XXXX XXXX	XXXX XXXX XX	XXXX
Sport	XXXX X	XXXX XXXX X	XXXX X	X
Work	XXXX XXXX	XXXX XXXX XXX	XXXX XXX	XXXX

KEY:
Each X = 5 shirts

these may be so hot that the item must be stocked in order to compete. Strict analysis of past statistics cannot dictate your model stock plan. Use insight and creative power where appropriate.

So far, we have ignored the problems of a person opening his or her first store. Such a person will have no past sales records to rely on. In this situation, does one use gut feelings and creativity in developing a model stock plan? Certainly not! Of the three steps, the first two pertain as much to the entrepreneur as to any existing retailer. However, for the third step, one will not have any historical sales records to study. It will be necessary to obtain trade or other external sources on consumer purchasing patterns. For example, in the food industry, one could consult the Towne-Oller Index, which measures actual sales and sales rank of each product and shows the number of different products needed to meet the demand of a certain percentage of the buying public for that particular product line. For instance, one might see that if 80 percent of the demand preferences for mouthwash is the desired goal, the four leading brands would need to be stocked.

Conflicts in Unit Stock Planning   Unit stock planning is an exercise in compromise and conflict. The conflict is multidimensional because everything cannot be stocked. The dimensions of conflict are presented in Exhibit 13.7. The conflicts are summarized below.

1. *Maintain a strong in-stock position on genuinely new items while trying to avoid*

EXHIBIT 13.7
**Conflicts
in Building
a Model
Stock Plan**

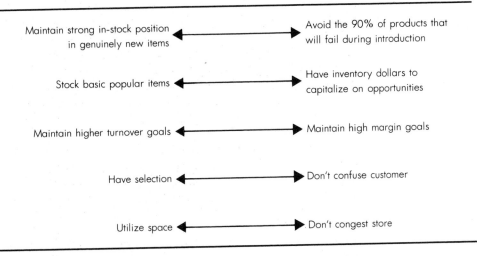

Maintain strong in-stock position in genuinely new items ⟷ Avoid the 90% of products that will fail during introduction

Stock basic popular items ⟷ Have inventory dollars to capitalize on opportunities

Maintain higher turnover goals ⟷ Maintain high margin goals

Have selection ⟷ Don't confuse customer

Utilize space ⟷ Don't congest store

the 90 percent of new products that fail in the introductory stage. The retailer will want to have on hand the types of new products that customers will be satisfied with. If the consumer is sold a poor product, it hurts the retailer as much as the manufacturer. The problem becomes one of screening out poor products before they reach the customer. Any screening device, however, has error; we might end up stocking some losers and turning down winners. Thus, a basic conflict arises.

2. *Maintain an adequate stock of the basic popular items while having sufficient inventory dollars to capitalize on unforeseen opportunities.* Many times, if we fill out the model stock with recommended quantities, there is little if any money left to hold for the super buy that is just around the corner. But, if we hold out that money and cut back on basic stock, we may lose customers, and also that super buy may never surface.

3. *Maintain high merchandise turnover goals while maintaining high margin goals.* This is perhaps the most glaring conflict. Almost always, items that turn over more rapidly have thinner profit margins. Therefore, trying to build a unit plan that will accomplish both objectives will surely be frustrating.

4. *Maintain adequate selection for customers while not confusing them.* If customers are confronted with too many close alternatives, they will not be able to make up their minds and will leave the store emptyhanded and frustrated. On the other hand, if the selection is inadequate, the customer will again leave emptyhanded. Thus, a delicate balance needs to be struck between too little and too much selection.

5. *Maintain space productivity and utilization while not congesting the store.* Take advantage of buys that will utilize the available space, but avoid buys that cause the merchandise to spill over into the aisles. Unfortunately, some of the best buys come along when space is already occupied.

As should be readily evident at this point, unit stock planning is no easy task.

UNIT STOCK CONTROL

The systematic analysis of stocks on hand in order to ensure that items are replenished as needed and kept in balance with the model stock plan is **unit stock control.** In addition to keeping stocks in balance and providing information on when to order, unit control also provides timely information on fast and slow sellers. This information will be instrumental in deciding which items to mark down or place special promotional effort behind. Unit control systems are of two major types: periodic and perpetual.

Periodic Unit Control Systems   A **periodic unit control system** involves counting, or taking an inventory of the items in stock. Obviously, since an actual count is required, one can usually not take a physical inventory daily. The exception of course would be for the retailer selling rare gems, coins, artwork, or other items of high value and limited quantities.

By taking a physical inventory, it is possible not only to analyze what is on hand, but also to determine what was sold since the last inventory. This is possible using the following formula:

$$S = I_a + P - I_b$$
where:
- S = unit sales
- I_a = last inventory
- P = purchases
- I_b = current inventory

Since a physical inventory can be quite time consuming, methods have been developed to make the task more manageable. It is possible, for example, to take the physical inventory over several weeks or even every week of the month by counting the inventory in separate merchandise classes. For example, a womenswear retailer could count sportswear items during the first week of each month, dresses and evening wear during the second week, underclothing and bedtime wear during the third week, and outerwear and accessories the fourth week. The periodic inventory method can thus be a continuous process. Another way of facilitating the counting is to equip the people taking the count with electronic devices into which they can enter data. The data are recorded on a magnetic tape and can then be transmitted to a computer.

Often one must decide how often a physical inventory should be taken. There is no standard answer. The more frequent the inventory, the more useful the data. But taking the inventory often can be unnecessarily expensive, and there may also be some physical limitations on how quickly it can be taken. One may not be able to take it rapidly enough to meet the information requirements. In this case, the retailer should consider adopting a perpetual unit control system.

Perpetual Unit Control Systems   A **perpetual unit control system** involves tabulating units sold each day and subsequently updating inventory records. Book inventory at any point is equal to the former book inventory plus subsequent receipt of units, less units sold. Perpetual systems provide the most timely inventory data possible.

In order for a perpetual system to operate, someone needs to retrieve the sales information. This retrieval can occur in one of five basic ways. First, on each transaction, a sales invoice can be issued on which a description of the item or an item code is recorded. The salesclerk or cashier can save these invoices each day and at the end of the day record them in a permanent inventory record. Second, a detachable stub could be part of the price ticket on each item. When the item is sold, the stub is torn off and deposited in a locked box. At the end of the day, these stubs are sorted and transcribed to a permanent inventory record. A third method involves taking the stub of a cash register receipt and writing on its reverse side what was sold. The receipts are then sorted daily and the relevant data transferred to permanent inventory records. The fourth method involves the cashier keeping a tally in a ledger book of everything that is sold. The ledger can be the permanent inventory record. The final method would involve an electronic cash register in which the clerk would punch a code that identified each item sold. The cash register would be linked to a computer, and the book inventory would be instantaneously adjusted for each item sold. Thus at any point in time the retailer could determine the units on hand by accessing the computer's storage.

An advantage that the perpetual unit control system has over periodic systems is the ability to detect stock shortages. One can compare the book inventory obtained with a physical count of stock on hand. If the book inventory is greater than the physical count of inventory, then some of the stock is missing and has possibly been stolen.

EVALUATING MERCHANDISING PERFORMANCE

So far we have ignored evaluating the merchandising function's performance. To address this area, we will need to introduce several new concepts.

Stockturn

In retailing, **stockturn**, which also may be called inventory or merchandise turnover, is a key to profitability. The stockturn concept tries to capture how long inventory is on hand before it is sold. Items with a high stockturn are on hand a short time; those with a low stockturn are on hand longer.

Retailers have at their disposal four ways to measure stockturn:

1. (Net sales) ÷ (average inventory at retail)
2. (Cost of merchandise sold) ÷ (average inventory at cost)
3. (Units sold) ÷ (average units in inventory)
4. (Net sales) ÷ (average inventory at cost)

Methods 1, 2, and 4 are the most frequently used. Method 3 can be misleading unless units are measured in homogeneous groups. The other methods are better for combining heterogeneous groups of items, because each item can be weighted by its dollar value.

The relationship between stockturn and both sales and inventory levels can be shown by taking method 1 and analyzing it in more detail. For example, it can be shown that:

5. Net sales = (stockturn) × (average inventory at retail)
6. Average inventory at retail = (net sales) ÷ (stockturn)

Method 5 shows that if a retailer is capable of achieving a given stockturn—say six times—and has an average retail inventory of $100,000, then that retailer has the capacity to generate $600,000 in annual sales (6 × $100,000). Method 6 could be used to determine inventories needed to support an expected sales volume with a fixed stockturn goal. If the retailer has forecast sales of $500,000 and experience has shown that a stockturn of four times is reasonable to expect, then the retailer would need to have average inventories at retail of $125,000 ($500,000 ÷ 4 = $125,000).

At the outset we emphasized that stockturn was a key to profits in retailing. It is, however, not true that higher stockturns will indefinitely increase profits; and the lowest stockturns will not necessarily result in the lowest profits. This point can be brought into sharper focus by examining the advantages and disadvantages of rapid stockturn, outlined in Exhibit 13.8.

Rapid stockturns enable the retailer to reduce certain expenses. Central to this proposition is a relationship uncovered in method 6—the more rapid the stockturn, the lower the average inventory required. Lower inventories will obviously require less capital, and thus the retailer's interest expense will be lower. At the same time, associated with lower inventories will be lower levels of required insurance coverage, lower inventory taxes on year-end inventories, and a lower cost of space to store the inventory. On the other hand, a rapid stockturn can increase expenses. With smaller average inventories on hand, the retailer must order more frequently and in smaller quantities, resulting in lost quantity discounts and in higher transportation rates. The costs of correspondence, clerical work, and handling will also rise, since more orders will need to be processed over a season or year.

Thus, at one extreme, if the retailer places one large order per year, order placement costs will be low, but since average inventories will be high, the associated inventory carrying costs will be high.[6] At the other extreme, if the

EXHIBIT 13.8 **Advantages and Disadvantages of a Rapid Stockturn**	ADVANTAGES	DISADVANTAGES
	Reduction of certain expenses (carrying costs)	Increase in certain expenses (ordering costs)
	(a) Interest	(a) Correspondence
	(b) Insurance	(b) Handling of merchandise
	(c) Merchandise taxes	(c) Clerical
	(d) Space charges	(d) Transportation
	Increased sales due to rapid flow of new merchandise	(e) Lost quantity discounts
		Danger of lost sales due to thin stocks

6. Donald E. Edwards, "Is Your Sales Dollar Being Consumed by Inventory Holding Costs?" *Journal of Retailing* 45(Fall 1969): 55–68ff.

retailer orders every week, the ordering costs will be high, but the average inventories and the costs associated with carrying them will be relatively low.[7] This basic relationship is portrayed in Exhibit 13.9.

The rate of stockturn influences not only the supply side of retailing (cost functions), but also demand (sales or revenue functions). A rapid stockturn can increase sales; but a rapid stockturn can also result in lost sales due to decreased stocks and the customer not being able to find the merchandise which is best suited to his or her needs.

This discussion thus demonstrates the importance of the stockturn concept to merchandise management. Programming a store to operate on the optimal rate of stockturn is a difficult, but necessary, task in propelling the retailer toward the goal of high performance results. However, stockturn is not the only possible measure of performance.

Profit Measures   The ultimate test of merchandising performance should not be a productivity measure such as stockturn, but a profit criterion. The retailer could have excellent stockturns by giving the merchandise away—but that is not the name of the game. As we stated in Chapter 1, the role of the retail executive is to manage demand and supply factors in order to achieve a return on investment sufficient for survival and future growth. We have also said that inventory investments influence supply (cost) functions and demand (sales) functions.

EXHIBIT 13.9
Inventory Carrying and Placement Costs as a Function of Order Quantity

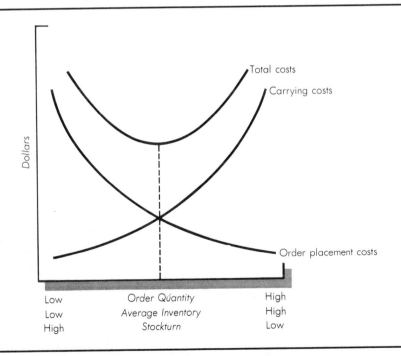

Low	*Order Quantity*	High
Low	*Average Inventory*	High
High	*Stockturn*	Low

7. One of the most significant costs associated with low inventories is stockout costs; see C. K. Walter and John R. Grabner, "Stockout Cost Models: Empirical Tests in a Retail Situation," *Journal of Marketing* 39(July 1975): 56–60.

Thus we need to see how inventory can help the retailer achieve profit objectives.

How profitable are a retailer's merchandising decisions? To answer this, we need to define profit. Merchandise managers may use three measures of profitability when assessing merchandising performance.

1. **Gross profit,** defined as net sales less cost of goods sold. This measure is good if there are no expenses besides the cost of merchandise that can be directly related or traced to the merchandise. For example, it may not be possible to directly tie any advertising or sales expenses to particular lines of merchandise.

2. **Contribution profit,** defined as net sales less cost of goods sold and any expenses that are directly traceable to the goods. In this case, items such as advertising expense can be related to specific product lines.

3. **Operating profit,** defined as net sales less cost of goods sold, direct expenses, and a share of all indirect expenses the retailer incurs. This method is not good unless the indirect expenses can be equitably allocated. Typically, however, they cannot, since it is difficult to allocate such expenses as the president's salary or clerical and office expenses to merchandise lines without doing it on an arbitrary basis.

All three profit figures can be related to a sales base, to obtain profit margin statistics like these:

Gross margin = (gross profit) ÷ (net sales)
Contribution margin = (contribution profit) ÷ (net sales)
Operating margin = (operating profit) ÷ (net sales)

Of the available profit measures, gross margin is the most widely used in the retail trades to assess merchandising performance. There are two reasons for this. First, it is the most accurate number to work with, since both sales and cost of merchandise sold can be measured by merchandise line, or even merchandise item, with minimal error. This is a significant advantage over the contribution margin and operating margin methods, since both of them require decisions as to which expenses, besides cost of merchandise, should be subtracted from net sales. Second, many industry trade associations regularly report data on gross margins by merchandise line, making it possible for the retailer to compare its performance to the experience of others. Consider for example, the gross margin data by merchandise line for home improvement centers (Exhibit 13.10). These data, provided by the National Retail Hardware Association, allow the home improvement retailer to compare its gross margin performance in eleven merchandise lines with that of similar retailers.

Gross Margin Return on Inventory   Gross margin return on inventory **(GMROI)** incorporates into a single measure both stockturn and profit.[8] It can be computed as follows:

$$\frac{\text{Gross profit}}{\text{Net sales}} \times \frac{\text{Net sales}}{\text{Average inventory at cost}} = \frac{\text{Gross profit}}{\text{Average inventory at cost}}$$

8. Daniel J. Sweeney, "Improving the Profitability of Retail Merchandising Decisions," *Journal of Marketing* 37(January 1973): 60–68.

EXHIBIT 13.10		GROSS MARGIN RATIO (percent)		
GMROI Ratio by Merchandise Line for Home Improvement Centers (1976–78)	*MERCHANDISE LINE*	*1976*	*1977*	*1978*
	Lawn and garden	30.6	30.8	30.9
	Housewares	33.1	31.2	29.5
	Hand and power tools	32.1	32.1	33.5
	Paint and paint sundries	35.5	35.0	37.3
	Sporting goods and outdoor	26.4	27.8	33.4
	Plumbing and heating	33.7	33.5	35.6
	Electrical supplies	33.2	33.5	36.0
	Hardware	35.9	34.6	34.5
	Major appliances	26.2	29.3	23.7
	Lumber and building materials	24.2	26.9	26.0
	Automotive supplies	33.3	31.3	37.5
	Other merchandise lines	<u>30.5</u>	<u>32.7</u>	<u>32.5</u>
	Composite	31.2	31.6	32.5

Source: Based on data from *1979 Bottom Line* (Indianapolis, Ind.: Home Center Institute, 1979) and earlier issues.

In this simple model the gross margin ratio is multiplied by stockturn to obtain gross margin return on inventory. Thus, if a particular merchandise line has a gross margin of 30 percent and a stockturn of 6 times a year, then GMROI is $1.80 ($0.30 \times 6 = \$1.80$). That is, for each dollar invested in inventory, on average the retailer obtains $1.80 in gross profit annually. These gross profit dollars can be used to pay store operating expenses and help yield a profit for the retailer.

The GMROI model is not complex but it does tell us three things:

1. The principal goal in managing merchandise investments (inventory) should be a **return on investment** goal—specifically gross margin return on inventory investment. Gross margin and stockturn are not goals; they are worth pursuing only to the extent that they enhance GMROI.
2. There are two principal decision making areas in merchandise management. The first is **gross margin management** and the second is **stockturn management.**
3. Merchandise managers who effectively interrelate gross margin management and stockturn management will be able to achieve **high performance results.**

One of the advantages of using the GMROI framework for merchandising decisions and performance evaluation is that an increasing number of retail trade associations are regularly reporting statistical data on GMROI by merchandise lines. This makes it possible for retailers to gauge their performance against industry norms. For example, Exhibit 13.11 gives GMROI data by merchandise line for home improvement retailers. These data allow the home improvement center to gauge its performance in terms of return on inventory

EXHIBIT 13.11
GMROI by Merchandise Line for Home Improvement Centers (1976–78)

	GMROI		
MERCHANDISE LINE	*1976*	*1977*	*1978*
Lawn and garden	$1.56	$1.43	$1.83
Housewares	1.27	1.59	1.22
Hand and power tools	1.30	1.41	1.58
Paint and paint sundries	1.86	1.81	2.06
Sporting goods and outdoor	.79	1.46	1.11
Plumbing and heating	1.56	1.53	1.59
Electrical supplies	1.56	1.60	1.74
Hardware	1.56	1.89	1.53
Major appliances	1.22	1.33	1.00
Lumber and building materials	1.63	2.07	2.23
Automotive supplies	1.47	1.38	1.71
Other merchandise lines	1.81	1.45	.99
Composite	$1.47	$1.58	$1.55

Source: Based on data from *1979 Bottom Line* (Indianapolis, Ind.: Home Center Institute, 1979) and earlier issues.

investment. Exhibit 13.11 shows that in 1978 lumber and building materials had the highest GMROI ($2.23), and that the line with the lowest GMROI was major appliances with a GMROI of $1.00. Obviously, all other things being equal, housewares were much more attractive as an inventory investment than major appliances.

SUMMARY

Merchandise management is the analysis, planning, acquisition, and control of inventory investments and assortments in a retail enterprise. An understanding of the principles of merchandise management is essential to good retail management. In all such decisions the consumer should be considered. Serving consumer needs and wants at a profit should be the major underlying principle in merchandise management.

In a small retail enterprise, one person will typically perform all activities related to the analysis, planning, acquisition, and control of merchandise. However, in a large retail organization, such as a chain store, several parties will be involved. There may be a general merchandise manager, divisional merchandise manager, buyer, department manager, and merchandise support staff.

A major part of merchandise management is planning. The retailer needs to plan, first, the dollars to invest in inventory and, second, the units of merchandise to purchase with these dollars. These two forms of planning are called dollar merchandise planning and unit stock planning. Obviously, planning should be followed by control. In merchandise management there are two forms of control. Dollar merchandise control is accomplished by a technique called "open-to-buy," whereas unit stock control is obtained by use of periodic and perpetual unit control systems.

Good retail management of the merchandising function can not occur unless the retailer's merchandising performance can be evaluated. Evaluative techniques include stockturn and profit measures. A useful model for combining these measures is the GMROI (gross margin return on inventory) model.

QUESTIONS

1. Compare the strategic profit model (introduced in Chapter 2) with the GMROI model. How might the GMROI model be improved?

2. Explain "open-to-buy." How can it be used to control merchandise investments?

3. What are the advantages and disadvantages of a rapid stockturn (inventory turnover)?

4. Can you identify any unique problems in merchandise management and planning for nonstore retailers, such as mail-order firms or door-to-door selling companies?

5. Why are both dollar merchandise planning and unit stock planning necessary in merchandise management?

6. How can the retail information system, discussed in Chapter 3, be used in merchandise planning and management?

7. Discuss the importance of the consumer and retail patronage behavior in making merchandise management decisions.

8. What type of staff personnel may be used to facilitate the merchandise management cycle?

9. Under what condition will the percentage variation method (PVM) of planning dollar inventory levels produce the same result as the basic stock method (BSM)?

10. What are the major constraining factors in the design of the optimal merchandise mix?

PROBLEMS AND EXERCISES

1. Visit two different stereo retailers and compare them in terms of merchandise variety, breadth, and depth.

2. Compute the ratios in the GMROI model for the three product lines identified below.

Merchandise Line	Sales	Average Inventory at Cost	Gross Profit
A	$120,000	$35,000	$31,000
B	$130,000	$34,000	$42,000
C	$115,000	$50,000	$38,000

3. Herb's Hardware is attempting to develop a merchandise budget for the next twelve months. To assist in this process, the following data have been developed. The target stockturn is 4.8 and forecasted sales are shown on page 418.

Month	Forecasted Sales
1	$27,000
2	26,000
3	20,000
4	34,000
5	41,000
6	40,000
7	28,000
8	27,000
9	38,000
10	39,000
11	26,000
12	28,000

Develop a monthly merchandise budget using the basic stock method (BSM) and the percentage variation method (PVM).

4. A buyer is going to market and needs to compute its open-to-buy. Here is the relevant data: planned stock at end of March is $319,000 (at retail prices); planned March sales are $149,000; current stock on hand (March 1) is $274,000; merchandise on order for delivery is $17,000. What is the buyer's open-to-buy?

5. A retailer has a target GMROI for a particular merchandise line of $1.44 and believes that it can competitively price the line to obtain a gross margin of 32 percent. What must its target stockturn on this line be? (We will define stockturn as net sales divided by average inventory at cost.)

SUGGESTED READINGS

Berens, John S. "A Decision Matrix Approach to Supplier Selection." *Journal of Retailing* 47(Winter 1971–72): 47–53.

"Planning and Budgeting for Effective Retail Merchandise Management." *Journal of Small Business Management* 16(January 1978): 1–6.

Quinn, John P. "Creating an Effective System of Retail Inventory Control." *Certified Public Accountant* 41(October 1971): 761–65.

"Return on Inventory Investment Is Vital." *Stores* 59(February 1977): 35.

Wilson, Cyrus C. and Charles D. Greenidge. "Classification Profitability." *California Management Review* 12(Fall 1969): 53–61.

Wingate, John W., Elmer O. Schaller, and F. Leonard Miller. *Retail Merchandise Management* (Englewood Cliffs, N.J.: Prentice-Hall, 1972).

14

Overview *In this chapter we will review the importance of credit and cash planning and management in retail enterprises. We will discuss the different types of retail credit a retail enterprise can offer and the major credit decisions a retailer must make: the credit policy decision, the credit granting decision, and the credit collection decision. We will also discuss the control of cash resources through cash budgeting.*

Credit and Cash Planning and Management

WHEN MONEY doesn't work it doesn't count.[1] Stop and think about this. Very simply, retailers sitting on bags of money will not achieve optimum profits, but by investing this money, so that it will work, they will produce profits.

Money is an important supply variable in retailing, since all retailers need money to conduct operations. There are two money variables that we will focus on in this chapter: (1) the cash the retailer will need on hand and in safeholding to continue operations in an uncertain environment; and (2) the amount of credit that it will need to grant customers in order for it to be competitive and stimulate consumer demand.

IMPORTANCE AND MAGNITUDE

In our economic system, cash and credit are essential. All members of the marketing channel, including consumers, need cash or credit to function. Ex-

EXHIBIT 14.1 **The Flow of Goods and Services and Money and Credit**

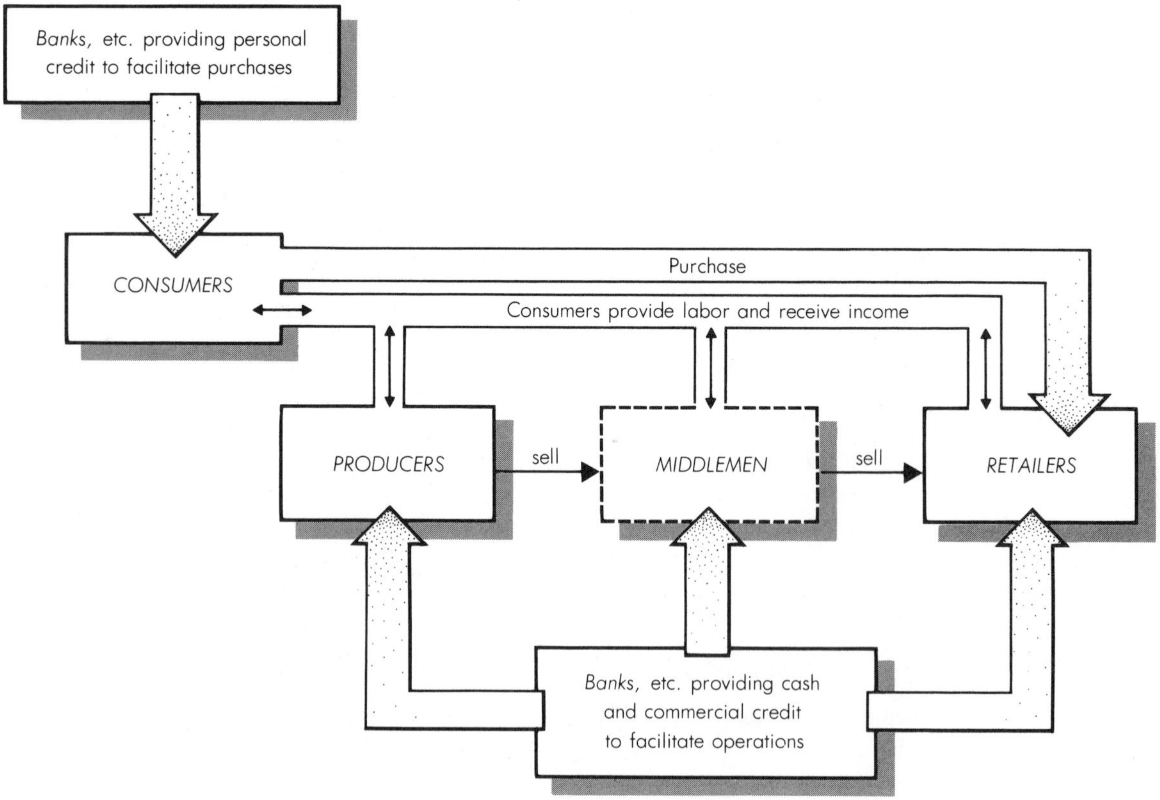

1. Recent advertisement for CNA Financial Corporation

hibit 14.1 helps to illustrate this point. In this exhibit we can trace the flow of goods and services versus the flow of money and credit. Goods will flow from manufacturers through the marketing channel to retailers and then on to consumers. As these goods travel through the channel, cash and credit are exchanged for them. Thus, in a real sense, we can view cash and credit as lubricants that help move goods through the marketing channel into the hands of consumers.

Exhibit 14.1 should be carefully studied since it conveniently portrays, in a somewhat simplified fashion, the pervasiveness of credit in our economy. Consider, for example, that most consumers would rather use credit than cash to pay for merchandise. This preference may be due to either greater convenience or necessity. At the same time, since retailers are holders of consumer credit, they must finance their inventories and other working capital requirements with the use of business credit from financial institutions and their suppliers (wholesalers and manufacturers). And, in turn, manufacturers and wholesalers need to borrow capital to finance their operations.[2] To get a flavor of the magnitude of cash and credit in the retail system in the United States, Exhibit 14.2 provides a cash and credit profile of retailers.

This chapter will deal exclusively with consumer credit since the credit the retailer can obtain from suppliers was discussed in Chapter 10. Here, we will examine the five major elements in the consumer credit management process: (1) establishing a credit policy, (2) determining the type of credit to offer, (3) deciding whether or not to grant the credit, (4) credit collections, and (5) using credit to generate demand.

CREDIT POLICY

All retailers must develop a consumer credit policy to guide them in managing and controlling their investments in accounts receivable. At one extreme, this policy could be to grant absolutely no customer credit (a cash-only policy). This would represent the ultimate in financial conservatism. At the other extreme,

EXHIBIT 14.2 **A Cash and Credit Profile of Retailers (December 31, 1979)**	ITEM	DOLLAR AMOUNT (billions)
	Cash on hand and in banks	$18.387
	Cash invested in government and other securities	2.294
	Credit outstanding to customers	38.172
	Borrowing from banks	
	Due in one year	13.423
	Due in more than one year	17.184
	Borrowing on credit from suppliers	39.464

Source: Federal Trade Commission, *Quarterly Report on Manufacturing, Mining, and Trading Companies* (Washington, D.C.: U.S. Government Printing Office, 4th quarter, 1979).

2. Robert H. Cole, *Consumer and Commercial Credit Management*, 5th ed. (Homewood, Ill.: Richard D. Irwin, 1976), p. 34.

you could give credit to any and all customers. Obviously this would be very liberal and probably much too risky. Needless to say, the optimum consumer credit policy would in all likelihood be somewhere between these two extremes.

The best consumer credit policy depends on many factors, which are presented in Exhibit 14.3. We will discuss each factor and its effect on credit policy.

Competitive Intensity   In general, the less competition there is in a line of retail trade, the less pressure there will be to establish a liberal credit policy. If there is little competition, there is less rationale for taking on a high-credit risk customer just to close the sale. If there is a high degree of competition, the retailer will often find it necessary to be more liberal in granting credit.

Profit Margins   The more liberal the credit policy, the higher the proportion of bad debts as a percentage of sales. Thus, the higher a retailer's profit margin, the more liberal it can afford to be in extending credit. With thin profit margins, a liberal credit policy becomes increasingly risky.

EXHIBIT 14.3
**Factors
Influencing
Retail
Credit Policy**

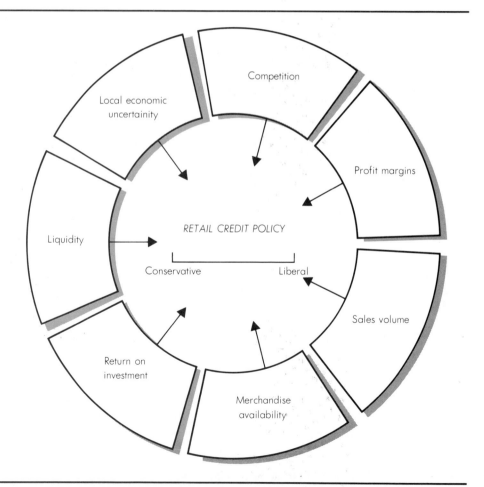

Sales Volume   If a retailer has a low sales volume, near its break-even point, then a liberal credit policy will be risky. When a retailer is operating close to its break-even point, then losses arising from extending credit too liberally could seriously harm its cash flow. It follows that a retailer with a sales volume well above break-even will be more able to afford a liberal credit policy.

Merchandise Availability   A liberal credit policy, to stimulate sales, can be quite helpful to the retailer who has plenty of merchandise available for sale. But when merchandise supplies are low, a more conservative credit posture would be more profitable. In severe merchandise shortages, retailers may require customers to put a cash deposit on the item before they order the merchandise. In this situation, credit provided by the retailer is typically out of the question.

Liquidity   If liquidity is poor then the retailer may be forced to establish a very conservative policy. With inadequate liquidity, a retailer cannot afford to take the risk of customers defaulting on their payments. On the other hand, high liquidity will tend to foster more liberal credit policies.

Economic Uncertainty   The less the certainty, the greater the need for conservative policies. But with a fair degree of certainty surrounding the local economy, more liberal credit policies will be justified.

Return on Investment   Whatever the credit policy decided on, the retailer needs to know how it will affect return on investment. Specifically, will the credit policy help to stimulate sales? Then, will the higher sales cover the added cost of the credit operation and still generate a sufficient return to help bolster the retailer's overall return on investment?

With the inflationary pressures in the 1970s and legal limits on interest rates, many retailers were faced with the disheartening fact that their credit operations were net losers. This trend continued into the 1980s. Exhibits 14.4 and 14.5 dramatize this point. Exhibit 14.4 provides an assessment of the return on assets Sears obtained from its credit operation between 1972 and 1976. The returns ranged from −1.9 percent to a high of 2.6 percent, but were all extremely low by contemporary financial standards.

Exhibit 14.5 shows the economics of accounts receivable elimination at F. W. Woolworth Company in the 1975–76 period, when Woolworth almost totally eliminated its credit operations. The result was a dramatic improvement in asset turnover, a more conservative use of financial leverage, and a small incremental increase in return on net worth. Selling without retailer-financed credit was more profitable than selling with retailer-financed credit.

TYPES OF RETAIL CREDIT

Retailers that decide to offer credit to their customers can select from three major types of retail credit. They are retail revolving credit, retail installment credit, and retail open charge.

EXHIBIT 14.4
Income Statement for Sears' Credit Operation

INCOME STATEMENT ITEM	INCOME AMOUNT (millions)				
	1972	1973	1974	1975	1976
Credit income	$549	$594	$649	$683	$729
Expenses					
Credit sales expense	275	296	322	356	406
Uncollectable accounts	42	45	52	56	56
Interest	155	268	345	255	244
Total expenses	472	609	719	667	706
Net profit (before taxes)	77	(15)	(70)	16	23
Accounts receivable balance (average during the year)	$2,981	$3,350	$3,670	$3,864	$4,134

Source: Reprinted by permission of D. Van Nostrand Company from *Retailing and Its Environment,* by Albert Bates, 1978.© 1979 by Litton Education Publishing Company.

Revolving Credit   The most common form of retail credit is **revolving credit.** With this type of credit, the customer is given a specific credit limit. Very credit-worthy patrons are provided with a higher credit limit than less credit-worthy patrons. After the customer is billed, a short grace period in which to pay without incurring a finance charge is given. If the customer does not wish to pay the entire bill, a specified minimum payment is required. The outstanding balance, which is not paid, is subject to a monthly finance charge. Finally, the customer is allowed to purchase additional merchandise in the amount of his or her credit limit minus what is currently owed on past purchases.

With the adoption of a revolving credit plan, the retailer is implicitly making a decision to commit capital to help finance consumer purchases. This capital can be obtained from a variety of sources. The retailer could reinvest the earnings of the firm to help increase accounts receivable and thus increase the amount of credit that can be provided to patrons. Unfortunately there are many competing demands on reinvested earnings: as sales grow, inventory levels must be increased; occasionally stores need to be remodeled, new equipment purchased, and often new stores opened. Thus, often retailers will find it necessary to obtain capital externally to help finance their revolving credit plans.

On an external basis, loans can be obtained from banks or other financial institutions. Naturally, retailers will need to pay interest on these loans and therefore must be capable of generating sufficient profits from their revolving credit plans (either through increased sales or interest charges to customers on their credit balances) to justify the interest payments.

A second way to obtain capital from banks or other financial institutions is to sell, or **factor,** the accounts receivable. When this is done, the accounts receivable must be sold at a discount. The discount will be a function of the financial institution's assessment of the degree of risk in the retailer's portfolio of credit customers. If the financial institution is fairly certain that all or nearly all of the retailer's credit customers will pay, then the discount may be only a

EXHIBIT 14.5	KEY BALANCE SHEET ACCOUNTS (thousands)		
Accounts Receivable Elimination at Woolworth's (1975–76)	Item	1975	1976
	Accounts receivable	$ 229,700	$ 18,200
	Inventory	914,100	1,026,100
	Total assets	2,173,100	2,092,800
	Short-term debt	92,000	0
	Current liabilities	603,600	502,600
	Long-term debt[a]	492,800	446,700
	Total liabilities	1,167,900	1,016,000
	Net worth	1,005,200	1,076,800

[a]Including portion currently due

STRATEGIC PROFIT MODEL[b]

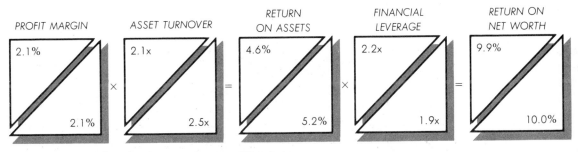

PROFIT MARGIN		ASSET TURNOVER		RETURN ON ASSETS		FINANCIAL LEVERAGE		RETURN ON NET WORTH
2.1%	×	2.1x	=	4.6%	×	2.2x	=	9.9%
2.1%		2.5x		5.2%		1.9x		10.0%

[b]1975 figure on top; 1976 on bottom

Source: Albert D. Bates, "The Internalization of Retail Strategy," presented at Symposium on Distribution Strategies for the 1980s, the Distribution Research Program, University of Oklahoma, January 1979. Reprinted with permission of the author.

few percent. If the probability is moderate or high that a fair number of customers will not pay, then the discount would be considerably higher (10 to 15 percent or more). In Exhibit 14.6 we present a case study on the economics of inflation and the need to factor accounts receivable.

An increasingly popular method of financing retail revolving credit plans is the adoption of a bank credit card plan. As is shown in Exhibit 14.7, bank credit card plans have grown explosively since the late 1960s. On a national basis, the two most popular bank cards are Master Card and VISA.

A bank credit card plan is, in principle, a revolving credit plan where the total risk and management of the plan is undertaken by a bank or affiliated group of banks. The bank assesses credit applications and decides who are the credit-worthy applicants. Also, the bank establishes the credit limit for each cardholder. A cardholder can charge merchandise purchases at participating merchants, generally, with a twenty- or thirty-day grace period after billing to pay the bill with no finance charge. A cardholder who chooses to not pay the entire bill must make a minimum payment and then is billed a finance charge, typically 1-1/2 percent of the outstanding balance. These plans allow the retailer

EXHIBIT 14.6
**Inflation
and Accounts
Receivable
Management**

When inflation accelerates to a double-digit rate, consumers increasingly purchase merchandise on credit. The reason for this is quite simple: Retailers generally face interest ceilings in terms of what they can charge their credit customers. Typically, this ceiling is 18 percent annually. Thus, when the rate of inflation approaches or exceeds 18 percent, consumers prefer to purchase on credit since they can pay back the retailer in the future with cheaper dollars.

The tendency for consumers to purchase more heavily on credit during inflationary periods causes the retailer's accounts receivable to grow faster than sales. Consequently, the need for working capital expands more rapidly than the retailer's ability to generate it internally. In short, the retailer needs to borrow to finance accounts receivable. However, when inflation is high the prime rate is similarly high, and therefore borrowing money at a 15 to 20 percent prime is relatively unattractive. Retailers confronted with this situation will generally sell their accounts receivable. For instance, J. C. Penney sold $272 million of receivables to Citicorp in the spring of 1980, when the prime rate was approaching 20 percent. This transaction was the largest one in United States banking history between a single bank and a single company.

> John Kuehn, vice president of finance and administration for Unishops Inc., [believes] that as the prime rate increases it becomes less attractive for a retailer to handle its own receivables. "If I can generate $150 million by exchanging one asset for another, it's a good reason for selling [receivables]," says Kuehn.

Source: Based on data from "Rising Prime Rate Causing Sales of Accounts Receivable," *Chain Store Age Executive* 56 (May 1980), p. 46.

to finance sales on credit, because the retailer can take the sales receipts to the bank sponsoring the credit card plan and get a direct deposit to its account less a discount. The discount the merchant must pay is typically between 1 and 6 percent and depends on the types of merchandise, the potential volume of business the bank can do with the merchant, and the potential profitability to the bank.

EXHIBIT 14.7
**Growth of
Bank
Credit Card
Plans
(1967–78)**

END OF YEAR	VOLUME (in millions)
1967	$ 1,351
1970	5,127
1972	7,183
1973	9,092
1974	11,077
1975	12,310
1976	14,355
1977	18,365
1978	24,362

Source: U.S. Bureau of the Census, *Statistical Abstract of the United States,* 100th ed. (Washington, D.C.: U.S. Government Printing Office, 1979), p. 538.

Installment Credit Frequently used in the sale of durable goods (automobiles, TVs, furniture, appliances) is **installment credit,** usually granted the customer for a single purchase, although sometimes several items may be involved—for example a new refrigerator and microwave oven. Payment is over a fixed period of time, generally on a monthly basis. A finance charge is also a standard feature. In addition, the credit is usually secured by some form of legal agreement that allows the organization granting the credit some mode of formal recourse if the consumer fails to pay.

Few households can purchase all their durable goods for cash. Most automobiles are sold on installment credit and much furniture and many appliances and other home furnishings are sold on installment credit.

Although department stores, furniture stores, household appliance stores, and automobile dealers are instrumental in creating most installment loans or credit, they tend themselves to carry or hold only a small portion of this credit, as Exhibit 14.8 shows. It can readily be seen that retailers carry only about 8 percent of the outstanding installment credit. The more significant holders of installment credit are commercial banks, finance companies, and credit unions. In the most recent years for which we have data, credit unions and commercial banks have become more significant holders of installment credit, whereas finance companies have declined in importance.

EXHIBIT 14.8
Holders of Installment Credit (1950–79)

YEAR	COMMERCIAL BANKS	FINANCE COMPANIES	RETAIL OUTLETS	CREDIT UNIONS	OTHER
1950	42.6%	34.2%	18.7%	3.9%	0.6%
1960	41.5	34.2	14.0	8.7	1.6
1970	46.2	26.2	13.2	12.3	2.1
1975	48.1	20.9	10.6	14.9	5.5
1976	48.3	20.1	9.9	16.1	5.6
1977	48.6	19.5	10.2	16.3	5.4
1978	49.4	19.7	9.0	16.7	5.2
1979	49.4	20.9	8.1	16.3	5.3

Source: U.S. Bureau of the Census, *Statistical Abstract of the United States,* 100th ed. (Washington, D.C.: U.S. Government Printing Office, 1979), p. 537.

The reason retailers hold such a small portion of installment credit is that they can get better returns on their scarce capital by investing it in other areas, such as inventory, equipment, remodeling, or new stores. Thus, they tend to shift the credit burden to financial institutions.

Retailers can shift the credit function to commercial banks either directly or indirectly. Under a **direct** basis, only two parties are involved—the retailer's customer and the bank. The bank, through its own advertising and promotion programs, solicits credit-worthy customers to make loans to. Credit policy, whether it be conservative or liberal, is determined solely by the bank. And the bank assumes all the burden for evaluating credit applicants, granting credit, and assuming the risk of default.

The **indirect** method involves three parties: the bank, the retailer, and the retailer's customer. Under this arrangement, the retailer is responsible for taking the credit application from the customer and making an initial evaluation. If the retailer approves the credit application, it is passed on to the bank, which in turn can either reject or accept it. If it is accepted, the retailer is paid by the bank (less a discount) and the retailer's customer gets a payment book. Obviously, this method requires that the bank assume greater risk since it cannot personally evaluate the retailer's customer but must rely on paper. Therefore, as far as the bank is concerned, the retailer's paper is only as good as the retailer. If the retailer has a good track record for bank applications (sending customers who are credit worthy) then the bank will be more likely to accept the paper the retailer sends.

Retailers, when working with banks under this indirect method of financing, generally work under one of three plans. Cole describes these plans:

1. **Full recourse**   Under the full recourse plan, dealers sell or sign over to the bank installment sale paper that they have originated. Dealers do this with their unconditional guarantee. They accept full responsibility for the paper should the purchaser become delinquent. In the event of default on the part of the consumer, the dealer will repurchase the obligation from the bank for the balance due at that time. The full-recourse arrangement is often requested by a dealer because of the lower bank discount rate generally associated with it. This is particularly true when there is relatively little risk connected with the consumer. Under this plan the dealer is responsible for the balance due, reconditioning, and resale of the product.

2. **Nonrecourse**   Under the nonrecourse plan of purchase, dealers are not contingently responsible for the credit failure of the customer. Dealers are relieved of all liability of the paper sold to the bank, except that they warrant the genuineness of the paper, terms of sale, title, and so forth. Under this plan, the commercial bank assumes the full responsibility of retaking, reconditioning, and reselling the product.

3. **Repurchase**   Under the repurchase plan, in case of consumer default on the terms of the contract, dealers are responsible for buying back the property for the unpaid balance after it has been retaken from the installment buyer. The property repossessed by the bank must be delivered to the dealer's place of business within a specified number of days after maturity of the oldest unpaid installment. As a general rule, the bank has ninety days to locate the property and return it to the dealer.[3]

In addition to shifting the credit function to commercial banks, retailers often shift the function to sales finance companies. Sales finance companies are specialists in buying consumer installment contracts from retail dealers and in providing wholesale financing at competitive rates to these dealers.[4]

Sales finance companies are primarily in the business of purchasing con-

3. Robert H. Cole, *Consumer and Commercial Credit Management*, 5th ed. (Homewood, Ill.: Richard D. Irwin, © 1976), p. 147. Reprinted with permission.
4. Cole, *Consumer and Commercial Credit Management*, p. 150.

sumer installment contracts from retail dealers and also in providing financing of the dealers' inventories. If the retail dealer is using a sales finance company then the customer will fill out an application for credit, and if the dealer decides to accept the application, an installment sale contract will be completed. In turn, the contract may be offered to a sales finance company if the retailer does not care to hold it to maturity. The sales finance company may perform a credit investigation to ensure that all papers are in order, and if everything appears to be in order, will purchase the contract from the retailer. At this point, the customer's account is opened and he or she is notified to make payments directly to the sales finance company. Like shifting the financing function to commercial banks, the purchase of these contracts by the sales finance companies can fall under three plans: full recourse, nonrecourse, and repurchase.

Open Charge

Open-charge credit has been very popular in the United States, but today it is increasingly difficult to find retailers using this form of credit plan (see Exhibit 14.9). **Open-charge credit** involves setting a credit limit for each customer and allowing him or her to purchase on credit up to this limit in any given month. At the close of a month or other thirty-day period, the customer is billed and is expected to pay the bill in full. Generally, finance charges are not involved but may be imposed if payment is unreasonably late. Although, as pointed out in Exhibit 14.9, open-charge credit is declining in the aggregate economy, it is still very popular among small retailers.

EXHIBIT 14.9
Retail Open-Charge Credit (1950–79)

YEAR	OPEN-CHARGE CREDIT (billions)	TOTAL CONSUMER CREDIT (billions)	OPEN-CHARGE AS PERCENTAGE OF TOTAL
1950	$4.9	$25.6	19.1
1960	7.2	65.1	11.1
1970	9.2	143.1	6.4
1975	11.5	223.3	5.2
1976	12.7	249.0	5.1
1977	11.0	289.4	3.8
1978	11.7	339.9	3.4
1979	11.7	355.0	3.3

Source: U.S. Bureau of the Census, *Statistical Abstract of the United States,* 100th ed. (Washington, D.C.: U.S. Government Printing Office, 1979), p. 537.

THE CREDIT GRANTING DECISION

Regardless of whether retailers decide to offer revolving, installment, or open-charge credit, they themselves will often need to assess the credit worthiness of individual customers. Of course, if they decide to restrict their credit operations to bank credit cards then this important decision is taken off their shoulders. The credit granting decision is basically one of balancing risk versus reward. The potential rewards are the higher sales that selling on credit will generate. The risks are from granting credit to patrons who may default on payments. Thus, the retail credit manager has a difficult balance to maintain between expected rewards versus risks.

The Credit Decision Matrix   To visualize the rewards versus risks, you can think of the retail credit manager's credit granting decision in terms of the decision matrix presented in Exhibit 14.10. In this exhibit we see that the credit manager, when assessing each credit applicant, can either grant or deny credit. At the same time, we see that in reality (which no one knows for certain) the applicant either will pay the bill or will not pay the bill. As a result of this interplay between the retail credit manager's decision and reality, four outcomes are possible—two of them good and two bad.

If the credit manager grants credit to the applicant and if the applicant is indeed one who will pay, then a good decision has been made (cell 1 in the matrix). The applicant should purchase more goods from the retailer, since credit is available. Thus, as many good decisions as possible of this type will help improve the retailer's profitability.

A second type of good decision is the one in which the credit manager denies credit to the applicant and the applicant in reality will not pay (cell 4 in the matrix). As many good decisions of this type as possible will prevent the retailer from having an excess of bad debts.

Unfortunately, when the retail credit manager is denying credit applicants, it is not known for certain if a particular applicant will or will not pay. The credit manager must make the best decision possible with the information that is available. Occasionally, therefore, the credit manager may decide to deny credit to an applicant who in reality would pay (cell 3). One should readily see

EXHIBIT 14.10
**Credit
Manager's
Decision Matrix**

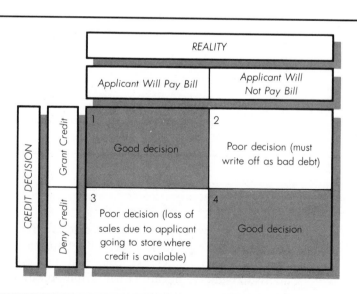

that this is a poor decision; the retailer will lose sales because the applicant will patronize another store.

The last possibility also represents a poor decision (cell 2). In this case the retail credit manager grants credit to the applicant but in reality the applicant will not pay. As a result, this unworthy credit applicant is able to purchase merchandise on credit but never pays for it, forcing the retailer to write off the customer's account balance as a bad debt. This decision causes the retailer to lose money.

In reference to the retail credit manager's decision matrix (Exhibit 14.10), we can now emphatically state that the credit manager will want to maximize the good decisions (cells 1 and 4) and minimize the poor decisions (cells 2 and 3). He or she does this by carefully studying all the relevant information on the credit applicant.

Evaluation of the Application   Traditionally, applicants for credit have been evaluated on three Cs: character, capacity, and collateral. *The Dun and Bradstreet Handbook of Credit and Collection* defines **character** as "the sincerity with which a customer undertakes a trade obligation and the determination he will have to see that obligation through."[5] Important factors that reflect on an applicant's character are attitude, past credit history, and what others (for example, an employer) say about his or her character.

Capacity refers to how able the credit applicant is to pay any bills incurred. Generally, objective factors can be used to assess capacity. These objective factors may include such things as the amount and regularity of income and the demands on this income, such as family size and fixed payment obligations. Other factors include length of employment, probability of continued employment, and the health of the applicant and those the applicant must support.

Collateral is the third C, and it refers to the resources of the customer at the time of sale. Collateral also can usually be evaluated objectively. Included in this evaluation are whether the applicant's residence is owned or rented, and if owned the amount of equity in the residence; ownership of stocks and bonds, savings accounts, personal possessions (cars, appliances, furniture); and investments in other income-producing assets.

Some authorities have identified a fourth "C," **common sense.**[6] They persuasively argue that the credit manager must use common sense in looking at intangible factors when assessing the tangible aspects of a credit application. Such a factor is the employment status of the applicant. Suppose the applicant is unemployed because of a personal injury but expects to be rehabilitated within a short time. Before the injury, the applicant had worked for a single company for sixteen years and had never defaulted on any loans or retail credit purchases. However, this information may not come out on a first examination, and therefore a perfectly reliable credit risk may be denied credit because of

5. Harold T. Redding and Cuyon H. Knight III, *The Dun and Bradstreet Handbook of Credit and Collections* (New York: Thomas Y. Crowell, 1974).

6. Gilbert A. Churchill, Jr., John R. Nevin, and R. Richard Watson, "The Role of Credit Scoring in the Loan Decision," *The Credit World* (March 1977), pp. 6–10.

being unemployed. Such a mistake can cause hard feelings that cause the customer to stop patronizing the retailer.

Retail credit managers can obtain the information they need by a direct field investigation of the application to ensure its accuracy. This, however, could be very time-consuming and expensive. More frequently the credit manager will use the services of a local retail credit bureau.

Retail credit bureaus, since they are specialists, can actually provide credit information at a lower cost than if the retailer collected it. This is possible since the cost of collecting the information can be spread over many users. Local retail credit bureaus are set up with the primary objective of providing credit information to retail merchants and other legitimate users of credit information. They centralize credit information from the records of almost all credit granters in the community and by also examining facts that are contained in public records. Retailers using the services of a local credit bureau are charged either a flat membership charge per month, a charge based on use, or a flat membership charge plus a variable charge based on use.

Large retail chains selling nationally may find it useful to use the services of a national retail credit bureau. The three major national credit bureaus are TRW Credit Data; Equifax, Inc.; and Trans Union Systems Corporation.

How does the retail credit manager combine the information about an applicant's character, capacity and collateral to arrive at a decision on whether to grant or deny credit? Traditionally, credit managers have subjectively combined all the relevant factors to arrive at a decision. Thus it was fairly predictable that two different credit managers working with the same information would arrive at differing decisions, because of their personal prejudices and biases. This problem has been overcome through a technique called **credit scoring**:

> Credit scoring is a system for assigning numeric values to specific demographic characteristics which reflect risk; for example, so many points for owning a home, so many for having a savings account. The point values for each applicant are accumulated, and the credit decision is based on this total score.[7]

Credit scoring has grown in importance since the Federal Equal Credit Opportunity Act of 1975, which provided that any person denied credit could demand a written statement justifying the denial. Using a credit scoring system, the retailer can consistently justify denials. Sears, Penney's, and Montgomery Ward all use computerized credit scoring to evaluate credit applications.

Exhibit 14.11 (see page 434) shows a hypothetical credit scoring system. The numerical values associated with various demographic characteristics are obtained through a statistical technique called multiple discriminant analysis.[8] Here, however, the important thing is this:

> Properly constructed credit scoring systems recognize that no single characteristic is likely to be a perfect predictor of a person's loan behavior. Rather, one must

---

7. Churchill, Nevin, and Watson, "The Role of Credit Scoring," p. 6.
8. Gilbert A. Churchill, Jr., John R. Nevin, and R. Richard Watson, "The Role of Credit Scoring in the Loan Decision." Reprinted with permission from the March 1977 issue of *The Credit World*, official publication of the International Consumer Credit Association, St. Louis, Missouri.

look at the totality of characteristics which describe an applicant and must somehow aggregate these characteristics into a composite profile—the credit score. Simple addition . . . is not appropriate because the characteristics are not independent of one another. A person who is older is also likely to have been on the job longer, and is more likely to own a home. What is needed is a method for simultaneously considering the various characteristics with due allowance for their overlapping nature. This is the province of multivariate statistical techniques.[9]

The multivariate statistical technique will not only give the credit manager the point values for the demographic characteristics in Exhibit 14.11, but will also yield a total score cutoff point. For example, if the cutoff point is 110, then applicants that score below 110 appear to be poor credit risks and those above, good risks. Obviously, scores far below 110 are more likely to indicate poor risk. But the credit manager should combine common sense with this score: are there any extenuating circumstances?

Using the decision matrix in Exhibit 14.10 we can say that a good credit-scoring system is one that allows the retail credit manager to maximize good credit decisions and minimize poor decisions.

CREDIT COLLECTIONS

Earlier in our discussion of retail credit management, we established the need for a retailer to develop a credit granting policy. We stated that this policy could be viewed along a conservative–liberal continuum. The retailer also needs to develop a credit collection policy, which can be viewed on a strict–lenient continuum. A retailer that has a strict policy will quickly apply pressure to delinquent credit customers. A very strict collection policy can create extremely negative feelings toward the retailer. At the lenient end of the continuum, delinquent customers are given a free ride for a while and then if they still fail to pay they are gently pressured. When gentle pressure fails, more harsh tactics are utilized.

Credit granting and credit collection policies need to be viewed collectively. In Exhibit 14.12, it is readily evident that the combination of credit granting and credit collection policies results in four distinct credit philosophies.

Tight Credit   A tight credit philosophy will involve very tough credit screening in hope of granting credit to those who are credit-worthy and in conjunction being very strict with those who do not immediately pay. With this philosophy, the retailer could lose a lot of goodwill on two counts. First, since the credit screening is tough, the retailer runs a high risk of turning away someone who deserves credit. Many times the credit-worthy person who has been denied credit will feel hostility toward the merchant and will criticize him or her to friends and acquaintances. Second, a strict screening means that most credit customers will in reality be very good risks, but, if the merchant immediately gets after them

9. Churchill, Nevin, and Watson, "Credit Scoring," p. 9.

EXHIBIT 14.11
**Hypothetical
Credit Scoring
System**

APPLICANT CHARACTERISTICS	ALLOTTED POINTS
Home phone	
Yes	36
No	0
Own or rent	
Own	34
Rent	0
Other finance company	
Yes	−12
No	0
Bank credit card	
Yes	29
No	0
Applicant occupation	
Professional and officials	27
Technical and managers	5
Proprietor	−3
Clerical and sales	12
Craftsman and nonfarm-laborer	0
Foreman and operative	26
Service worker	14
Farm worker	3
Checking or savings account	
Neither	0
Either	13
Both	19
Applicant age	
30 or less	6
30+ to 40	11
40+ to 50	8
Over 50	16
Years on job	
5 or less	0
5+ to 15	6
Over 15	18

Source: Gilbert A. Churchill, Jr., John R. Nevin, and R. Richard Watson, "The Role of Credit Scoring in the Loan Decision." Reprinted with permission from the March 1977 issue of *The Credit World*, official publication of the International Consumer Credit Association, St. Louis, Missouri.

when they are a little late in paying, they will understandably be upset. As a consequence, goodwill will suffer appreciably. Since a tight credit philosophy will be costly in terms of lost goodwill, few retailers will practice such a philosophy.

EXHIBIT 14.12
**Credit Granting
and Collection
Philosophies**

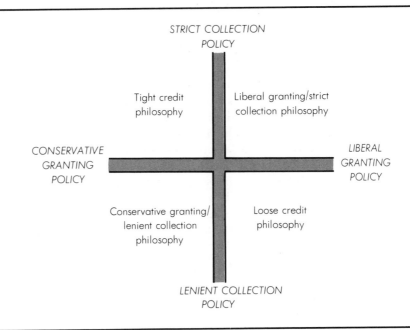

Loose Credit A loose credit philosophy will not cost much in goodwill, but may still be expensive. Such a credit philosophy will utilize a relatively lax screening. Thus, few credit applications will be denied, but as a consequence many credit customers will not pay or will be unable to pay. In addition to a lax screening, a loose philosophy will entail a lenient collection policy. Thus, people who are not credit-worthy and don't intend to pay are treated leniently. This ends up being expensive, since many bad debts will have to be written off the retailer's books. Because a loose credit philosophy can be quite expensive, it is not often used by retail firms.

Liberal Granting and Strict Collection In the contemporary retailing environment, a liberal granting and strict collection philosophy is most common. With this philosophy, the retailer will maintain goodwill in the credit granting stage by granting most applicants credit and therefore giving them a chance to prove their credit worthiness. But the retailer uses a strict collection policy to minimize its bad debt losses.

Conservative Granting and Lenient Collection The conservative granting and lenient collection philosophy is also frequently found. The logic behind this philosophy is to minimize giving credit to poor risks to avoid bad debts. Since the retailer may deny credit to an applicant who in fact deserves it, some goodwill may be lost. At the same time, the retailer feels that if the applicant gets by the tough credit screening, then in all probability he or she will pay. Therefore, if the customer is late in paying, the retailer will be lenient because it does not want to lose any goodwill from such a customer. Thus, the retailer is willing to sacrifice some loss of goodwill in the credit granting stage but will try to avoid any loss of goodwill in the credit collection process.

Collection Stages   Regardless of whether the credit collection policy is strict or lenient, the actual collection system should involve several stages in which nonpayers are treated with increasing pressure. As pressure is increased, fewer and fewer nonpayers will remain delinquent on their accounts. At the outset it is important to note that as pressure is increased, the risk of harm to the store's goodwill also rises dramatically. Above all, the credit manager needs to use his fourth C—common sense. Perhaps the customer is very wealthy and has not paid because she has been in Europe vacationing and thus has not received her mail for eight weeks. Although there is no way the credit manager should know this fact, the stark reality remains that if this customer is pressured, she is likely to not patronize the store in the future.

Cole has suggested a four-stage credit collection system in which low-cost collection procedures that preserve goodwill are replaced by harsher and more costly collection procedures.[10]

Impersonal Routine   The impersonal routine stage begins after the established credit period for remitting payment has expired. If the credit manager has done a good job screening credit applicants then most credit customers will never enter this or later stages. Many debtors who enter this first stage simply have not received the notice in the mail, have honestly overlooked paying the bill, are temporarily short of funds, or are simply careless or procrastinators. They should be treated gently, since most will pay if they are given a slight nudge. Some devices available at this stage are second and third statements or simple form letters that merely remind the debtor of nonpayment.

Impersonal Appeal   Generally, the impersonal routine will not cause all debtors to become current. Those which remain delinquent should be moved to the impersonal appeals stage:

> In this stage, the form letters used are no longer of the routine impersonal type but take on more of the character of appealing to 'anything wrong?' or 'tell-us-your-story' tone, or to the pride of the customers in meeting their credit responsibilities, or to their sense of fair play.[11]

It is also common at this stage to use the telephone, a telegram, or letters sent special delivery or by registered mail. Debtors in this stage can be of the same type as those in stage one but also may involve those who have overbought, have had an accident or similar misfortune, or have a dispute over their account balance.

10. Cole, *Consumer and Commercial Credit Management,* pp. 372–73.
11. Cole, *Consumer and Commercial Credit Management,* p. 376.

Personalized Appeal When a debtor has not responded to either of the two preceding stages then treatment must become more harsh. He or she will therefore receive the third treatment—a personalized appeal. The credit manager or someone on the credit staff may personally interview the debtor or make a personal telephone call. Often the debtor will be informed by a personalized letter that his or her employer or the local retail credit bureau will be informed of the delinquency. Debtors in this stage can be similar to those in previous stages but also may include potential insolvents or frauds who have no intention of paying.

Drastic or Legal Action There will still remain some customers who did not respond to the pressure in the first three stages. These debtors must receive more drastic or legal action. In prior stages, the retailer's goodwill was fairly well protected and the nonpaying customer was treated gently. Now it's time to play hardball! Possible courses of action are repossession, legal suit, garnishment or wage assignment, or use of a collection agency. For customers at this fourth stage who are sincere, an extension agreement (allowing them more time to pay) might be considered. Another possibility for the sincere debtor is a **composition arrangement.**

> Under this arrangement a group of creditors agree to accept a reduced amount as settlement of their indebtedness in full. This scaling down is done only in those cases in which the debtor is honest and sincere and entirely free from any taint of fraud. Obviously, such an arrangement enables the debtor to recover a debt-free position, while the creditors may have been fortunate in receiving x cents on the dollar of their indebtedness without any more drastic action.[12]

CREDIT CONTROL

It is not uncommon for a retailer's investment in accounts receivable to be 15 to 20 percent of total assets; because of this, it is important that retailers have control. Control can be obtained by several methods, but we will discuss two of the more popular ones—the days-outstanding method and the aging-of-accounts method.

Days Outstanding The method called **days-outstanding** shows the number of days of credit sales that are uncollected. If the days of credit outstanding are more or less than normal, then an investigation is necessary to determine if the cause of the abnormal behavior can be justified. To understand this method, we must understand the concept of accounts receivable turnover. **Accounts receivable turnover** can be defined as follows:

12. Robert H. Cole, *Consumer and Commercial Credit Management*, 5th ed. (Homewood, Ill.: Richard D. Irwin, © 1976), p. 379. Reprinted with permission.

$$T_{ar} = \frac{S_c}{I_{ar}}$$

where:

T_{ar} = annual accounts receivable turnover
S_c = annual credit sales
I_{ar} = average annual investment in accounts receivable

Therefore, if annual credit sales are $1 million and the average annual investment in accounts receivable is $150,000 then accounts receivable turnover is 8.0 ($1,200,000 ÷ $150,000). A retailer that has a rapid rate of accounts receivable turnover has fewer days outstanding than a retailer characterized by a slower rate of turnover. The exact relationship between accounts receivable turnover and days outstanding can be defined as follows:

$$\frac{360}{\text{Annual accounts receivable turnover}} = \text{Days of credit sales outstanding}$$

The 360 assumes the retailer is working on a 360-day year.

Exhibit 14.13 shows how the days-outstanding statistic can be used to control investments in accounts receivable. In this exhibit, the days outstanding for the beginning of each month are plotted to see if they fall within certain

EXHIBIT 14.13
**Control Chart
for Days Credit
Outstanding**

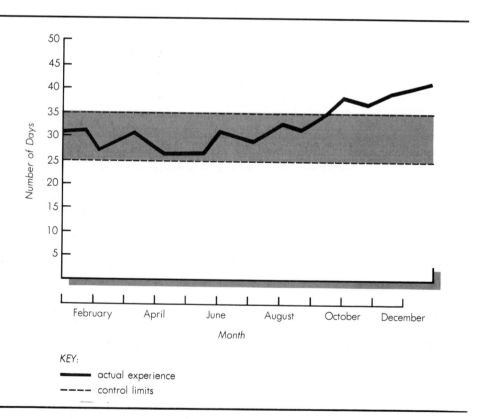

KEY:

▬▬ actual experience

- - - - control limits

preestablished control limits. The control limits are derived from prior experience. That is, in prior years the days of credit outstanding at the beginning of each month have fallen within the control limits 95 percent of the time. It can be seen in Exhibit 14.13 that from September through December, the days outstanding have consistently fallen above the upper control limit. This implies that the retailer is turning over its investment in accounts receivable too slowly. As a consequence, the investment in accounts receivable is too high, and if this practice continues, the firm's liquidity position will be harmed.

One should exercise caution in making any decision based on this information. The information merely tells the manager that, according to historical standards, the investment in accounts receivable is out of control. There may, however, be a satisfactory explanation for the higher than normal days of credit outstanding. Perhaps the employees of the major employer in town are on strike. As a result they have not received a regular pay check for ten weeks and are postponing paying as many bills as they possibly can. Within a few days, the strike should be settled and within a month or two thereafter the payment patterns of credit customers should be back to normal and the accounts receivable investment should fall back into the normal control bounds.

Aging of Accounts Receivable   The **aging method** allows the retailer to classify all credit purchases on the basis of the time that has elapsed since the purchase occurred. If the retailer can contrast the age distribution of these unpaid credit purchases with a standard, it can assess performance in the credit function.

In Exhibit 14.14 we see the age of a hypothetical retailer's credit accounts. By comparing this retailer's actual performance to the industry standard in the last column, we can see that the major problem lies in the accounts that are 31 to 90 days old. In this category, there are too many slow payers.

EXHIBIT 14.14   Aging of Accounts Receivable (as of January 31, 198x)

MONTH OF SALE	AGE OF ACCOUNT (DAYS)	PROPORTION OF TOTAL RECEIVABLES (ACTUAL)	CUMULATIVE PROPORTION (ACTUAL)	PROPORTION OF TOTAL RECEIVABLES (STANDARD)	CUMULATIVE PROPORTION (STANDARD)	PERFORMANCE[a]
January	0–30	40%	40%	40%	40%	0%
December	31–60	20	60	30	70	−10
November	61–90	18	78	15	85	−7
October	91–120	15	93	10	95	−2
Prior months	121+	7	100	5	100	0

[a]Computed by subtracting cumulative standard from cumulative actual. A negative variance is bad; it denotes what percentage of accounts are older than standard. A positive variance is good; it denotes what percent of accounts are younger than standard.

In order to use the aging method effectively, the retailer needs to establish a standard aging pattern. The pattern can be based on either historical patterns or the retailer's desired state of affairs. For example, the retailer may desire a certain aging pattern in order to maintain the firm's current ratio (current assets divided by current liabilities) within a certain range.

CREDIT AS A DEMAND GENERATOR

Although credit is often viewed as a supply variable, it does have an important effect on demand. In fact, the astute retailer will manage its supply of credit in order to generate demand. If credit cannot generate additional demand for the retailer then investments in it are unwise.

The driving force behind a retailer's sales volume is the number of customers that can be attracted (and the amount those customers will spend with the retailer). Without a doubt, the use of credit will allow the retailer to attract more customers, and these credit customers are attractive in three ways. Credit customers are more store-loyal, they have larger transaction sizes, and they are less price conscious.

Because credit customers are attractive, promotion should be important to the operation of a retail credit department. At least three promotional targets exist. Promotion can be directed at soliciting new accounts. In this regard the retailer would want to get credit into the hands of households that represent the most intense demand for its merchandise. Next, promotion should be directed at reactivating inactive accounts. Special attention needs to be paid to previously active accounts that for some reason have become dormant. Finally, promotion should be directed at selling more merchandise to present credit customers. Sending them special catalogs, presale notifications, and the like can help stimulate purchases and increase store loyalty.

PROFITABLE CREDIT MANAGEMENT

Retail credit involves risks and rewards. This has been illustrated at several points throughout our discussion. The risks, however, can be undertaken only if the rewards are sufficiently attractive. Retailers do not offer credit because it performs a useful function in our society and economy. It is good for society and the economy, but retailers offer credit because it leads to increased profits. Very simply, investments in accounts receivable can help a retailer achieve its target return on assets as dramatized in the strategic profit model.

Exhibit 14.15 shows a conceptual framework for evaluating investment in accounts receivable. First is the identification of the additional sales generated by offering credit. Although this number may be difficult to obtain, a reasonable estimate is possible. Next, the costs of offering credit and any other costs that are variable with sales need to be identified. Costs of credit may include credit investigation costs, billing costs, bad debt expense, cost of account solicitation, space and supplies costs for the credit department, and equipment costs. Other costs that vary with sales may be cost of merchandise and a portion of wages and salaries. The result of subtracting incremental costs from incremental sales is the profit or loss from offering credit. If we divide this profit or loss by the retailer's investment in accounts receivable, we obtain the return-on-accounts-receivable investment.

If a retailer estimates that it has generated additional sales of $400,000 annually from offering credit and that the costs associated with this are $300,000 then the profit from offering credit is $100,000. If this retailer has an average accounts-receivable investment of $80,000, then its return on accounts receivable is 125 percent (100,000 ÷ 80,000). This high return can therefore be used to cover many of the retailer's fixed expenses and overhead and also contribute toward the retailer's overall return-on-assets goal.

RETAIL CASH MANAGEMENT

The preceding material highlighted the widespread use of credit in the retail sector of the economy. In fact, not only do most retailers sell on credit, most purchase from suppliers on credit. However, they still need cash to conduct day-to-day operations. To illustrate, some customers will pay cash for merchandise and may need change. The retailer may also need cash for items such as postage stamps and other small, day-to-day operating supplies.

Not only should the retailer keep cash on hand, but it should also have some other form of liquid assets. **Liquid assets** are those which can be quickly converted to cash if the need arises. They will be needed because unpredictable events will arise that require cash. For example, perhaps the roof begins to leak and needs immediate repair. Or, perhaps the retailer runs across a special closeout offered by a national manufacturer on a major brand—but a truckload must be purchased and cash must be paid on delivery. Obviously the retailer cannot be expected to have enough cash in the cash register to pay for these unexpected events, but liquid assets should be available.

The demand for cash and liquid assets can be categorized into three major types:

1. **A transactions demand:** This demand arises from the normal need to make change when selling to cash customers and the need to meet day-to-day expenses. On a periodic basis, suppliers need to be paid, employees compensated, services and operating supplies paid for, and taxes paid to the government.
2. **A precautionary demand:** This demand is a function of the unpredictability of the timing of cash outflows and inflows in the retail enterprise.

EXHIBIT 14.15 **Return on Investment in Accounts Receivables**

The retailer doesn't know precisely, for any given week or month, how much will be sold and how much cash will be received from customers for merchandise they purchased in prior months. Nor does the retailer know precisely when unexpected expenses will occur (e.g., the leaky roof).

3. **A speculative demand:** Although retailers should not be in the business of speculating, some will hold cash or other liquid assets in hope of trying to capitalize on price movements in merchandise. They will try to buy heavy when prices are soft and sell when prices are strong. A large, national TV and stereo chain, for example, may observe that prices at the factory are dropping for TVs because of a general economic slowdown and a softening of consumer demand. This retailer, viewing the downturn as temporary, may buy enough TVs to last ten months (where it typically buys for three). When the economy picks up in a few months, the retailer will expect to profit from this strategy. However, if the economy doesn't pick up it will lose—perhaps heavily. For most retailers speculation is too risky.

In the United States, retailers tend to have most of their liquid assets in cash to meet transaction demands. Other liquid assets are held to meet precautionary demands. Few funds are held for the express purpose of speculation.

An aggregate profile of retailers' investment in cash and other liquid assets is presented in Exhibit 14.16. These aggregate statistics tend to reflect how retailers invest in liquid assets. As can readily be seen from the exhibit, retailers invest approximately 7.9 percent of their total assets in liquid assets. Most of this investment is in the form of cash or demand deposits (checking accounts), which comprise roughly 5.3 percent of total assets. Cash and demand deposits are held mostly for transactions demand, with a small portion held as a precaution. The remaining liquid assets are, in most part, invested in time deposits, government securities, and commercial and finance company paper, all of which can be quickly converted to cash if necessary. These liquid assets are

---

EXHIBIT 14.16
A Profile of Investment in Cash and Other Liquid Assets in Retailing (1979)

ASSET ITEM	DOLLARS (millions)	PERCENTAGE OF TOTAL ASSETS
Cash and demand deposits	13,936	5.30
Time deposits	4,324	1.64
Deposits in banks outside U.S.	127	0.04
U.S. Treasury securities	489	0.19
Federal agency securities	53	0.02
Commercial and finance company paper	988	0.38
State and local government securities	150	0.06
Foreign securities	45	0.02
Other short-term securities	569	0.22
Total liquid assets	20,681	7.87

Source: Federal Trade Commission, *Quarterly Report on Manufacturing, Mining and Trading Companies* (Washington, D.C.: U.S. Government Printing Office, 4th quarter, 1979).

approximately 2.6 percent of total assets and are being held, in most respects, as a precaution.

THE RETAIL MERCHANDISE—CASH CYCLE

Cash is always flowing in and out of the retail firm, mostly as a direct result of the purchase and sale of merchandise. To help visualize this cash flow, let us refer to Exhibit 14.17, which shows the retail merchandise-cash cycle. In it we can see the flow of cash out of the firm to pay for merchandise, and into the firm as customers pay for their merchandise purchases.

EXHIBIT 14.17 **The Retail Merchandise-Cash Flow Cycle**

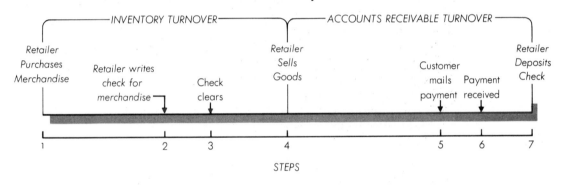

The retail merchandise-cash cycle has seven steps. Between each of these steps, time elapses. As will be seen in a moment, between some of these steps the retailer will want a relatively long time to elapse, and between other steps, a relatively short time.

The first step is the purchase of goods from suppliers. At this first step, the retailer seldom has to pay any cash, since most merchandise will be purchased on credit. The more attractive the payment terms obtained from the supplier, the later step 2 will occur. Thus, the more attractive the payment terms, the longer the retailer can postpone paying cash from the firm's reservoir of liquid assets. Under such a scenario, the supplier is, in effect, financing part of the retailer's investment in inventory. In principle, the longer the payment terms the retailer receives, the more the supplier is financing the retailer's inventory investments.

Step 2 in the cycle is the issuing of a check by the retailer to pay for the merchandise. In general, retailers should issue checks in time to take advantage of any cash discounts suppliers offer. For example, if the supplier offers terms 2%/20, net 40, then the retailer can get a 2 percent cash discount if the bill is paid within twenty days, but the full invoice amount must be paid within forty days. If the retailer doesn't take the 2 percent cash discount then the extra twenty days of inventory financing is costing 2 percent. Since twenty days is

1/18 of a year, this inventory financing is annually costing 36 percent (2% × 18). As long as the retailer can borrow from the bank at less than 36 percent, it is better to pay within twenty days and receive the 2 percent cash discount.

Although the retailer has written and mailed the check at step 2, it has not, in principle, used any resources until the check finally clears the bank. That is, the supplier must receive the check, record it in the ledger, and deposit it in the bank; and the bank then must present it to the retailer's bank for collection. When this occurs, we are at step 3 in the cycle. All of this could take a couple of days, and during this time the retailer still has use of the funds. The time between the retailer's writing a check and the check's clearance is called the **float.** Many large retail chains will try to maximize their float, even though the banking community and the Federal Reserve System frown on such practices. A large retail chain could be writing several million dollars in checks daily. If it can average a float of two days then it has $5 million to $6 million in extra liquid assets to work with.

The fourth step in the retail merchandise-cash cycle is the actual selling of merchandise. We have seen that the retailer wants to maximize the time between step 1, the purchase of goods, and step 3 when the check clears for payment of these goods. Of course, the retailer wants to maximize this time without foregoing any attractive cash discounts or violating any laws. On the other hand, the retailer wants step 4 to occur as soon as possible after step 3, simply because between steps 3 and 4, it is financing the investment in inventories. The goods have been paid for but they are still sitting on the sales floor or in the warehouse. The key to speeding up step 4 is inventory turnover. The quicker the merchandise is turned, the closer the sale will be to the time the retailer will have to relinquish some liquid assets to pay for the merchandise. What we have witnessed up to this point has been an exercise in using supplier's funds versus the retailer's liquid assets. This is simply good retail management.

At the fourth step in the retail merchandise-cash cycle, the retailer has sold the merchandise, but in many cases has received no cash, since the sale may have been on credit. Time will, therefore, elapse before the fifth step. At step 5 the customer mails a check to the retailer. The time between purchase and mailing the check will in most part be a function of the credit terms the retailer establishes. If the retailer gives the customer thirty days to pay without penalty (that is, no interest charge) then the elapsed time between steps 4 and 5 will at least be in the vicinity of thirty days.

Since the postal system takes time to deliver mail there will be some time elapsed between step 5, when the customer mails payment, and step 6, when the retailer receives the check in the mail. If the retailer is a national chain, then the elapsed time between steps 5 and 6 could be several days, because the customers are dispersed over a wide geographic area and the central collection point will on average be a long distance from the customer. Consider, for example, a national retailer that collects an average of $500,000 daily from credit customers. If the average time it takes for the customer's check to reach the retailer is three days, then $1.5 million (3 × 500,000) in funds are tied up in the mail and cannot be used.

In the final step in the retail merchandise cash cycle, the retailer deposits the customer's check. Again, time could elapse between step 6 (receiving the check) and step 7 (depositing the check). The check could be received but spend a couple of days sitting in the retailer's bookkeeping department waiting to be posted to a ledger acccount. Until the checks are deposited, the retailer cannot use these funds. For example, if the retailer has an average of two days of credit customers' checks sitting in the bookkeeping department, and if an average of $500,000 per day is collected, then $1 million in potentially liquid funds are frozen and cannot be used.

Many large, national retail chains have developed effective systems for shortening the time between steps 5 and 7. The most popular strategy is a form of **concentration and lock box banking.** Using this strategy, the retailer establishes a number of regional or local collection points. In each of these locations there is a post office box to which the customer mails its payment. This cuts the average time from when the customer mails payment (step 5) and when the retailer receives the payment (step 6). For each location, the retailer employs a local bank, which has a key to the post office box, to pick up the checks on a regular basis. Pickup by the bank is at least daily and often three or four times a day. The bank will then xerox copies of all checks and send these copies to the retailer so they can be posted to ledger accounts. At the same time, it can process the checks so the retailer can obtain, for immediate use, the funds which those checks represent. At the end of each business day, the local banks will wire all funds obtained in such a fashion to the retailer's national bank, which is usually at corporate headquarters. Thus, all local accounts are concentrated daily into a single, national bank account. Notice that having the local banks process the checks before the retailer posts them to its ledger and then concentrating all the funds collected on a local level is an attempt to shorten the time between when the checks are received (step 6) and when the checks are deposited to the retailer's bank accounts (step 7).

By using lock box and concentration banking, the national chain-store retailer can typically speed up the retail merchandise-cash cycle by a few days. For a retailer collecting several million dollars per day from credit customers, the consequence of such a strategy would be to free up as much as $10 million in liquid assets for more productive uses.

There are two other advantages to a lock box system. First, since the retailer will be able to process the checks more quickly and ultimately present them to the customer's bank for collection sooner, there will be less chance that checks will bounce. Second, since the bank posts the checks before the retailer does, there will be less chance of theft on the part of the retailer's employees. They simply cannot develop a scheme to cash the checks themselves if the bank picks up the checks from the post office box and immediately posts them to the retailer's bank account. Finally, you should be aware that banks do not provide lock box and concentration banking services free. Often there is a fee involved or the requirement that the retailer hold some level of compensating balances at the local banks.

The retail merchandise-cash cycle helps to illuminate two important principles of retail management, shown on page 446.

1. As the retailer obtains more attractive accounts-payable terms from suppliers and turns inventory more quickly, it will need to invest less of its own capital in inventory.
2. As the retailer offers more attractive accounts-receivable or credit terms to customers and turns inventory more slowly, it will need to invest more funds in inventory and accounts receivable.

Carefully study Exhibit 14.17 to verify these principles.

CONTROL OF CASH

Retailers need to control the flow of cash into and out of the firm. If the retailer allows cash balances to plot their own course, then, without a doubt, it will end up in a precarious position. The reason for this is that the demand for cash by the retailer—to pay for supplies, labor, and merchandise—will seldom coincide with the supply of cash obtained as customers pay for merchandise. Central to the control of cash by the retailer is an understanding of working cash balances and the cash budget.

Working Cash Balance   At any point in time, the retailer's cash balance can be viewed as follows:

$$C_t = C_{t-1} + R_{t-1} - D_{t-1}$$

where:

C_t = cash balance at time t
C_{t-1} = cash balance at beginning of period $t-1$
R_{t-1} = cash receipts during period $t-1$
D_{t-1} = cash disbursements during period $t-1$

If receipts (R) and disbursements (D) occurred at approximately the same time and if they were highly predictable, then the problems in managing the cash balance (C) would be relatively simple. In such a predictable situation, the retailer would program its cash balance to be close to zero. All excess inflows of cash would be invested in assets capable of earning a financial return (more inventory, securities, bonds, accounts receivable, buildings, etc.). In retailing, however, events are not totally predictable and the timing of disbursements does not match the timing of receipts. Managing the cash balance is therefore no easy task for the retailer.

In Exhibit 14.18 we see cash balances rising and falling due to the differences between receipts and disbursements at any given time. If receipts exceed disbursements at some point (time) then the cash balance rises. If disbursements exceed receipts, the cash balance declines.

If disbursements exceeded receipts by a large amount and if the cash balance were not controlled, it would theoretically become negative. At the other extreme, if receipts continued for an extended period of time to exceed disbursements, then the cash balance would get unreasonably large. This is where control comes into play. The retailer must decide what minimum and maximum

EXHIBIT 14.18
**Fluctuations
in a Retailer's
Cash Balance**

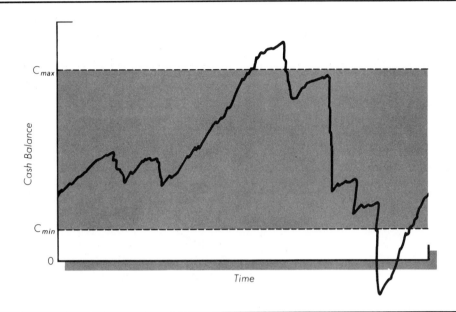

working cash balance it will want to have. In Exhibit 14.18 the minimum is referred to as C_{min} and the maximum as C_{max}. When the cash balance rises above C_{max}, the retailer will transfer the excess funds to income-producing assets—perhaps treasury bills. When the cash balance drops below C_{min}, the retailer will transfer funds to the cash account by selling income producing assets—possibly treasury bills. If the retailer has no income-producing assets to sell, it may borrow from the bank. Generally, the more uncertainty in receipts and disbursements, the higher both C_{min} and C_{max} will be set.

Appearing in the finance literature are models for determining the optimal C_{max} and C_{min}.[13] In most part, these models look at the opportunity costs of having too much cash sitting idle versus the high transaction costs of having low cash balances. Notice that if cash balances are too low, the retailer will need to sell securities more frequently, which will result in a fixed transaction cost on each sale. Consequently, therefore, we see that a tradeoff is involved, as shown in Exhibit 14.19.

Cash Budget

To control cash balance, retailers use a **cash budget,** which shows the timing of the retailer's cash disbursements and receipts and how they affect the retailer's cash balance. The cash budget can be a useful tool for determining when to transfer cash resources to income-producing liquid assets such as treasury bills. At the same time, the retailer can use it to pinpoint when it will be necessary

13. William J. Baumol, "The Transactions Demand for Cash: An Inventory Theoretic Approach," *Quarterly Journal of Economics* 66(November 1952): 545–56; M. H. Miller and D. Orr, "A Model of the Demand for Money by Firms," *Quarterly Journal of Economics* 80(August 1966): 413–35.

EXHIBIT 14.19
**Retailer's
Optimal
Cash Balance**

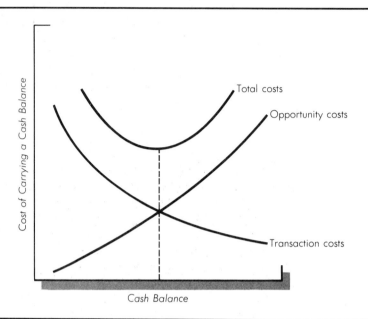

to borrow funds or sell income producing liquid assets in order to avoid negative cash balances.

To illustrate the cash budget concept, a retailer's hypothetical monthly cash budget is presented in Exhibit 14.20. It shows that the retailer can probably transfer funds during March–July into income-producing liquid assets. However, from August to November, funds will have to be transferred out of income-producing assets or possibly borrowed. But by the end of December, the retailer should have a cash balance of $188,000—significantly above the cash balance of $22,000 it had at the start of the year.

As dramatized in Exhibit 14.20, retailers will periodically have excess cash, which they will find profitable to invest. In investing idle cash, retailers need to pay particular attention to three factors: default risk, maturity, and marketability.

Default risk refers to the likelihood that interest on principal might not be paid on time (or ever). If a retailer is willing to assume a larger risk of default, then it can obtain a higher expected yield. But since retailers are not in the business of speculating, they will want to avoid securities of high or even modest default risk. A retailer's safest bet may be federal government securities such as treasury bills.

Maturity refers to the period of time over which interest and principal must be paid. Generally, the longer the maturity, the greater the risk because, with a fixed interest–bearing security, a change in the market interest rate will influence the price at which the security can be sold before the maturity date.[14]

14. If the market interest rate is below the fixed interest on the security, the security can be sold at a premium, but if the market interest is above the fixed interest in the security, then the security will have to be sold at a loss.

EXHIBIT 14.20 **A Twelve-Month Cash Budget (thousands)**

	JAN.	FEB.	MAR.	APR.	MAY	JUNE	JULY	AUG.	SEPT.	OCT.	NOV.	DEC.
Beginning cash balance	$ 22	$ 6	$ 60	$127	$120	$149	$119	$126	$ 63	($ 14)	($ 16)	($ 98)
Cash disbursements												
Merchandise	218	80	110	260	190	235	190	200	220	210	300	80
Labor	28	26	27	29	30	31	31	28	29	29	31	33
Supplies	5	4	5	5	6	7	7	6	6	6	6	6
Rent	6	6	6	6	7	7	7	7	7	7	7	7
Miscellaneous	3	3	4	3	4	4	4	4	5	5	5	5
Total	260	119	152	303	237	284	239	245	267	257	349	131
Cash receipts												
Cash sales	60	30	80	90	91	108	71	38	75	70	100	200
Collection on credit accounts	180	140	135	200	170	142	172	140	110	180	160	210
Other	4	3	4	6	5	4	3	4	5	5	7	7
Total	244	173	219	296	266	254	246	182	190	255	267	417
Net increase (decrease)	(16)	54	67	(7)	29	(30)	7	(63)	(77)	(2)	(82)	286
Ending cash balance	6	60	127	120	149	119	126	63	(14)	(16)	(98)	188

And as the maturity lengthens, there is a higher probability that the retailer will need to sell the security before maturity.

A security is said to be **marketable** or highly liquid if it can be sold quickly in large amounts at a price that can be determined in advance within narrow limits. If it takes a long time to sell the asset and the price the retailer can receive is very uncertain, then the security is not very liquid or marketable.

Most retailers find some form of short-term government securities, especially treasury bills, very attractive. They are relatively short-term (maturities may be as short as thirty days). They have a low default risk, since they are backed by the U.S. Treasury. Finally, they are very liquid or marketable, since they can be sold on any Monday through Friday (excluding national holidays) in almost any quantity at a quoted price.

SUMMARY

We showed that cash and credit are instrumental components of the American economic system, the marketing channel, the household, and the retail firm. Proper cash and credit management is also a prerequisite for high performance.

The retailer must manage and control consumer credit. In doing so, it must establish a credit policy. The policy can range from very conservative (giving little credit) to very liberal (giving almost anyone credit). Factors influencing the retailer's credit policy are competitive intensity, profit margins, sales volume, merchandise availability, liquidity, certainty regarding the local economy, and return on investment. Once the credit policy is established, the retailer must select the type of credit to offer—retail revolving credit, retail installment credit, or retail open charge. In managing consumer credit, the retailer must continually make credit granting decisions. To aid in this time-consuming process, it is advisable to develop a credit scoring system.

Retailers also need to develop a credit collection policy. Such a policy can be strict or lenient. But whatever the policy, the retailer must increasingly apply pressure, the longer accounts remain delinquent. We discussed various techniques for properly applying pressure.

Since the retailer may have from 15 to 20 percent of its assets invested in accounts receivable, its investments in credit must be controlled. Two methods for controlling accounts receivable were discussed: the days-credit-outstanding method and the aging-of-accounts method. Retailers need always to keep in mind that investments in accounts receivable should be justifiable on a profit basis. The retailer should grant credit only if it is a profitable use of assets; otherwise dollars should be invested where they can get a higher return on investment. Related to this perspective is the notion that credit, although a supply variable, can be an important demand generator if properly managed.

We also discussed the management of cash balances, and to illustrate the flow of cash in a retail setting, we presented the retail merchandise-cash flow cycle. This model showed how cash is converted into merchandise and then how merchandise is converted back into cash. As with accounts receivable, cash must be controlled. The two techniques that were presented for the control of cash were the working cash balance model and the cash budget model. Both present helpful concepts for the retail manager in search of ways to better control dollars invested in cash.

QUESTIONS

1. What is the relationship between credit granting policy and credit collection policy?

2. Explain how a retailer's profit margin should influence its credit policies.

3. How is the decision to maintain a certain cash balance similar to the decision to maintain merchandise inventories at a certain level?

4. Explain how credit can be used to increase a retailer's market share.

5. If you were the president of a local department store, how would you judge the effectiveness of your credit department?

6. How is the granting of credit likely to influence a retailer's prices?

7. Discuss several methods the retailer can use to conserve its use of cash.

8. What problems may a retailer face in developing a cash budget?

9. How does credit management influence cash management?

PROBLEMS AND EXERCISES

1. Visit a local retailer that grants credit and ask the credit manager what steps the firm takes in collecting delinquent accounts. See if you can get copies of some of the types of letters it mails to delinquent customers. Evaluate the harshness of these letters.

2. The Tennis Shop has annual credit sales of $600,000 and an average accounts-receivable balance of $78,000. What is the average figure for days of credit sales outstanding?

3. Sid's Appliance Center is evaluating the profitability of its credit operation. Annual sales are $1.4 million, of which $712,000 are credit sales. The retailer estimates that 20 percent of the customers who purchase on credit would purchase with cash, if credit were not available. The retailer's cost of goods sold is 67.5 percent of sales. Cost of selling on credit is estimated to be 6 percent of credit sales. The retailer's average investment in accounts receivable is $189,000. Evaluate the profitability of this retailer's credit operation.

4. Donna's Dimensions (a dress shop) has monthly fixed cash expenses of $40,000. In addition, variable cash expenses (for labor, supplies, etc.) are 7 percent of sales. Cost of goods sold averages 68 percent of sales; however, merchandise is paid for one month after it is purchased. In any month 39 percent of sales are for cash and the rest are equally collected over the subsequent two months—except that 1 percent of credit customers never pay. Sales and purchases over the next twelve months are planned to be:

Month	Sales	Purchases
Jan	$120,000	$ 40,000
Feb	$118,000	$ 80,000
March	$149,000	$150,000
April	$181,000	$120,000
May	$179,000	$128,000
June	$178,000	$ 88,000
July	$140,000	$ 93,000
Aug	$142,000	$150,000
Sept	$180,000	$138,000
Oct	$122,000	$128,000
Nov	$198,000	$ 94,000
Dec	$212,000	$ 50,000

In November and December of the just-completed year, sales were $171,000 and $192,000 respectively. Purchases in December were $46,000. The cash balance at the end of December was $7,100. Develop a cash budget for the next twelve months. At what points will the retailer need to borrow?

5. The Carpet Shop has annual sales of $1,470,000, and 40 percent of these sales are on credit. The average rate of accounts receivable turnover is 11.7 times. What is the average accounts receivable balance? If the average days of credit sales outstanding dropped by four, what would happen to the average accounts receivable balance?

SUGGESTED READINGS

"Cash Management: The New Art of Wringing More Profit from Corporate Funds." *Business Week*, March 13, 1978, pp. 62–66.

The Changing Universe of Retail Credit (New York: Institute of Retail Management, New York University, 1980).

Hartman, Bart P. and Dan C. Smith. "Improving Credit Collection Responses." *Management Accounting* 61(August 1979): 18–21.

Hirschman, Elizabeth C. "Differences in Consumer Purchase Behavior by Credit Card Payment System." *Journal of Consumer Research* 6(June 1979): 58–66.

Hirschman, Elizabeth C. and Jac L. Goldstucker. "Bank Card Users: A New Market Segment for Regional Retailers." *Business Topics* 25(August 1977): 5–11.

Morley, James E., Jr. "Cash Management—Working for the Extra 1% or 2%." *Management Accounting* 60(October 1978): 17–22.

Myers, G. Robert and David V. Burchfield. "Sustaining In-House Credit." *Stores* 58(February 1976).

Roy, H. J. H. and E. M. Lewis. "Overcoming Obstacles in Using Credit Scoring Systems." *The Credit World* (June 1970).

Searby, F. W. "Using Your Hidden Cash Resources." *Harvard Business Review* 46(March–April 1968): 71–80.

15

Overview   *In this chapter, we will study the retailer's planning and management of fixed assets—its buildings and fixtures. We will discuss the major factors to consider in selecting a building and whether to lease or buy it. In addition, we will spend considerable time discussing the layout of selling and nonselling space. Since buildings and fixtures can consume substantial energy, we will also discuss energy management.*

Building and Fixture Planning and Management

THROUGHOUT HISTORY, retailers have needed a place to transact their business, and a means of displaying their merchandise to prospective customers. In contemporary retailing, the picture that usually comes to mind when we say "a place to transact business" is a building. However, this need not be the case. The building can be a multistory department store in a large city with marble pillars, plush carpet, wide aisles, and a high energy bill. Or, it can be merely a small stall or enclosed roadside stand. In fact, the place needn't be a building at all; nonstore retailing is accomplished without a building. However, most retailers do require a building, so we will limit our discussion to retailers that use a building.

The fixtures in contemporary retailing include a wide variety of display tools. They can range from antique buffets and hutches to modern chrome and glass shelves; from the long, tall shelves in a grocery store to an old blanket lying on the earth covered with pottery, baskets, or jewelry. But, whatever form the building and fixtures take, they are important ingredients in high performance retailing. The role of this chapter is to help the student of retailing better appreciate the challenges and problems in managing buildings and fixtures.

A CAPITAL ALLOCATION PROBLEM

Capital allocation is the distribution of the total funds a retailer has decided to commit to a store among the available options. It is a problem because the number of available dollars is limited, and usually there are more places to use those dollars than the retailer can manage. All of us know the problem of trying to pay all the bills, put money into savings, and still have some discretionary funds. The problem is similar for the retailer who also has to distribute its funds to several need areas and still leave enough to cover the day-to-day business expenses. In making this allocation decision, the retailer will need to choose between the following alternatives: fixed versus current assets, selling space versus parking space, selling space versus nonselling space, and store space versus fixtures.

Fixed Versus Current Assets   Building and fixture decisions in retailing inherently involve capital allocation decisions. The total capital available to the retailer must be allocated between current assets (cash, inventory, and accounts receivable) and fixed assets (building, land, fixtures, and equipment). The allocation is necessary because no retailer has an unlimited source of capital and because the potential sales a retailer can generate in a trade area will justify only a given level of capital investment. For example, if the potential sales in a trade area of a furniture store in Atlanta, Georgia, are $3.8 million then it would be highly unlikely that the retailer could invest $30 million, $10 million, or even $2 million to capture that sales level. The level of capital that can be invested in retailing has some limit. But, given that limit, the retailer must then decide on the amount to invest in fixed versus current assets.

Obviously, if 100 percent of the capital is devoted to fixed assets, the retailer will have no merchandise to sell or cash and credit resources to facilitate transactions. It will need to shift some of the available capital toward current assets. On the other hand, if the retailer has invested 100 percent of the capital in current assets, then it will have merchandise and cash and credit resources to facilitate transactions, but no buildings or fixtures to store and display the goods and conduct sales transactions. At this extreme, the balance needs to be shifted in the direction of fixed assets. Should the balance of current-to-fixed be 50/50, 40/60, 60/40, or some other ratio? The answer will be different for each line of trade and even for each firm within a line of trade. However, one general rule is that the proportion of current assets should be greater than the fixed assets. This is primarily because the retailer is in business to sell merchandise rather than bricks and mortar. In fact, it is not unusual for 75 percent of assets in retailing to be current assets.

Even when the retailer has decided how much to invest in fixed assets, the capital allocation decision is not complete. The retailer will also need to determine the mix of current assets (cash, accounts receivable, and inventory) and the mix of fixed assets (space and fixtures). We have already discussed the current assets of cash, accounts receivable, and inventory and therefore our present focus will be on fixed assets.

Store Space Versus Parking Space   The larger the square footage of a store, the more people will be attracted to that store. In most (but not all) areas of the country, customers will travel to a store by automobile. Consequently, adequate parking facilities should be made available. If, for example, a 28,000-square-foot supermarket is constructed in suburban Dallas on a 30,000-square-foot piece of land, then regardless of how good its location, business will be tragic. The reason? Customers would not have a place to park, so they would not patronize the store. Thus, we again have a balancing act for the retailer to manage; the size of the building, the size of the piece of land, and the amount of parking space all have to be compatible. If too much land is allocated to parking space, too much is being spent on land that isn't being used. On the other hand, if there are too few parking spaces, building space cannot achieve its potential, because inconvenienced consumers will patronize another retailer. You can probably recall driving to a store or shopping center only to become frustrated because you haven't been able to find a place to park. What was your reaction when this happened? Most of us would develop a negative attitude toward that store or shopping center and then drive on to a store that had adequate parking. The negative attitude toward the first store would then influence our future patronage.

Selling Space Versus Nonselling Space   Just as the piece of land needs to be divided into store space and parking space, the store space needs to be divided into selling and nonselling space. Typically, nonselling space will be required for such things as offices, merchandise receiving, employee lounges and restrooms, and storage. The question is, how much of the total space should be committed to such uses? In answering it, we must keep in mind that nonselling space does not stimulate or create sales. It is used only to support sales. Any sales volume will require a certain amount of nonselling space to support it. The retailer should allocate enough space to support activities such as receiving and marking merchandise, clerical or office work, and inventory storage, so that the work can be done efficiently. However, once the point of efficiency is passed, valuable store space is being wasted. Again, the retailer has a balancing decision that is not simple to make.

Store Space Versus Fixtures   Large store space will require not only a large investment in space, but also a large investment to pay for fixtures to cover the space. If the retailer spends all its dollars on space, then the building will be of little use unless the merchandise can be stacked on the floor and business transacted out of the retailer's back pocket. There would be no shelves, counters, or racks to display the merchandise and there wouldn't even be a cash register or money box in case a sale was made. Even the accounting would have to be done by hand rather than by computer or other mechanical system. This sounds ludicrous; however, if the retailer didn't make allocations for fixtures, it might be the only way business could be transacted. Many times retailers have built stores that were larger than they could afford to fit with fixtures and equipment. This has usually resulted in inefficiency. At other times, retailers have "over-fixtured" stores by cramming so many fixtures and so much equipment into the floor space that the store looked crowded and unkept. This allocation is also inefficient and unprofitable.

THE BUILDING DECISION

As previously mentioned, the building a retailer selects is a key determinant in the achievement of high performance results. In fact, the building can be so important to success that it can make or break an otherwise average retailer.

Image Dimension   The building is more than just bricks and mortar. And, although location is of prime importance, the actual building and all of its characteristics must be considered by the retailer. For instance, studies might indicate that the perfect spot for a new children's clothing store is the northeast corner of Tenth Avenue and Park Place. All location theory may point to this corner as being right, so Little Village opens such a store in the big red building already on the site. The retailer is pleased to have found a site with an existing building, and since the location theory points to that location, the store is certain to be a big success. However, Little Village fails within just a few months due to a lack of customers. What went wrong? There are a lot of possible explanations, but perhaps the big red building had the wrong image for a children's store. Was it barnlike, or warehouse-like? Was it old and shabby? Was it dirty and smelly? Or, was it the fact that several months earlier a gang of drug dealers had been found using the big red building as a front? Whatever the cause, the building itself could have contributed to the failure.

The preceding discussion suggests that a retail building projects an image. The **image** of a building is the character as perceived in the mind of the public. The image as perceived by the retailer may be quite different from the image perceived by the public. In the preceding example, for instance, the retailer viewed the big red building as a children's clothing store. However, the customers obviously saw it as something else, something out of character with children. Without a doubt, the character or image of a building can be a selling tool.

The building's image projects beyond the front door of the building to the entire external appearance of the structure and its compatibility with contiguous buildings and parking areas. If given the choice, most of us would buy food at a supermarket that is new, brightly lighted, and sparkling clean rather than at an old, rundown, dimly lit store with a dark, dirty parking lot. Similarly, it might be fun to visit a swap meet or flea market to enjoy the carnival-like atmosphere and search for bargains, but most of us would not trust our expertise enough to purchase diamonds, works of art, or major appliances at these places. We would, instead, seek out the retailers whose stores convey the image of trust and stability. Retailers must remember that these virtues can be conveyed through the building.

Bolen captures the importance of the building as a selling tool: "The store is the package which contains the merchandise. If that package does not attract, entice or at least interest the customer, the product will not sell. A good design helps sell the product. A poor design will not."[1]

If the store is to be viewed as a package that sells, it will be necessary to plan the package to allow it to convey the proper image. The **atmosphere** of a building is its tone or mood, or formally its psychological environment. The atmosphere can be controlled to build the image. Seldom does an atmosphere just happen. Consider the case of Water Tower Place in Chicago.[2] According to its codevelopers, Edgar Shook and Carl D. Guldager, the unique elegance of the building itself is the contributing factor to the overall atmosphere. The entire building is well planned and totally coordinated—even down to using the same typeface for lettering all signs. The overall atmosphere is quite elegant, and its image most favorable. Creating the right atmosphere will be discussed later in the chapter.

Size Requirements How large a building does the retailer need? In general, the size requirements of a store depend on location, type of merchandise handled, and amount of capital available to invest in a building.

Location When speaking of size in relation to location, one can typically expect buildings in cities to be smaller than buildings in suburban areas. In a city, especially in the central business district, land is very expensive, and therefore the amount of space that can be devoted to an average retail outlet will be

1. William H. Bolen, *Contemporary Retailing* (Englewood Cliffs, N.J.: Prentice-Hall, 1978), p. 99.

2. "Marketing Water Tower Place—A $2 Million Job," *Buildings* (April 1979): 54.

smaller than if the land costs less. For example, in a city of 250,000, it is not unusual for an acre of land in the CBD to be worth $1 million. This high cost of land creates pressure to use land efficiently. Oversized stores quickly become unprofitable.

Also, because of cost and availability of land, stores located in the Northeast are, on average, smaller in terms of square feet than stores in the West or Southwest. Here, the most important factor is availability of land. In the Northeast, almost all of the prime land is already developed, some buildings standing there for over 100 years. Thus, to build a large new store not only requires the costs of construction, but the costs of moving or tearing down the existing buildings. Sometimes, as in Boston, the buildings have been standing in some areas of the city for centuries. Rather than removing them, it has been the practice to renovate them. In other cities, the central business district has been completely razed and rebuilt, creating a new, modern CBD. The land is still expensive, however. One answer to this space problem in the past has been to build up rather than out. By having a multistory building, a retailer can acquire enough square footage without using a large amount of land. This practice will probably continue as the cost of land increases and the amount of usable land decreases.

Size may also be determined by whether the building is located in a shopping mall or is free standing. In a shopping mall, space is much more expensive because of all the services the malls provide shoppers, such as air conditioning and heating, lounge areas, public restrooms, shopping lockers, and public display space for shows and civic groups. The retailer cannot afford as large a store in a mall because of all these added costs. However, the mall retailer may not need as much space as the free-standing retailer because of the added services. For example, parking facilities are spread out, each store doesn't need to provide restrooms and janitorial services, and low-profit, low-volume departments can often be eliminated without upsetting the customer if the merchandise is carried elsewhere in the mall.

Finally, retailers with several outlets in a single metropolitan area can have, on average, smaller stores because they can consolidate such things as accounting services, purchasing, and merchandising storage. With some of the new computer systems, a store may even centrally control such things as temperature and light, and security.

Type of Merchandise   It quite obviously takes considerably less room to display and sell $1 million of diamonds than $1 million of furniture or appliances. Some merchandise, such as appliances, stereos, TVs and electronic games, and cameras, will require demonstration space. Other merchandise, such as frozen food or cut flowers, might require a controlled environment. Clothing requires fitting rooms, and shoes need a lot of storage space.

The type of merchandise affects not only the amount of space needed to display the goods, but also the space needed for aisles and checkout areas. Supermarkets, discount stores, and home improvement centers generally need to devote more space to these areas than bookstores, tobacco shops, or record stores do.

Capital Available   The final influence on the size of a building is the retailer's capital constraint. Retailers need to realize that in obtaining capital for a building, lenders are generally less concerned with the building itself than with its location. Many readers are probably familiar with the fundamental principle of real estate: there are three things that sell property—location, location, and location! This principle is very important to the moneylenders the retailer deals with. Lenders will be very concerned with the prospects of reselling the building in case the retailer does not succeed. The lenders also look at the selling space rather than the total space, because it is the selling space that will generate the profits to pay back the loan.

New Versus Old Building   Retailers must decide between constructing a new building and occupying an old building. A new building may be ideal in terms of enabling the retailer to design a total atmosphere into the building, construct the proper amount of space in the desired form, and have energy efficiency. However, a new building can be much more expensive than an existing building.

The problem with an old building is that one cannot just occupy it. It usually needs to be renovated or at least remodeled in order to take on the right character and fill the retailer's specific needs. Renovation and remodeling costs can often make an old building more expensive than a new building of similar size. However, this need not be the case. The key is careful planning and assessment of the alternative costs and opportunities before committing to either an old or new building.

The following useful insights on renovating an old building for retail use are offered by Mel Kaufman:[3]

1. The structure of old buildings may yield interesting and sometimes unexpected opportunities such as floors 12" thick, steam heat radiators which can be electronically controlled, and unique display possibilities.
2. Old buildings are, on the average, not as mechanically sound as new ones.
3. Sometimes entire systems (heating, cooling, plumbing, etc.) have to be replaced because of obsolescence yet the new systems don't necessarily fit the old places.
4. Old buildings are difficult to air condition unless they were originally built with that capability because there is rarely enough space for duct systems and central plants which leads to inadequacy, hot spots, and high utility bills.

Thus it can be seen that there are some downside risks involved in renovating old buildings. One encouraging signal, however, is the 1978 Investment Tax Credit Act, which provides special tax incentives for rehabilitating buildings for productive uses.[4]

Lease Versus Buy   Since the capital outlay required for construction can be substantial, many retailers choose to lease their space. In fact, high interest

3. Craig Henrieh, "Mel Kaufman and His Rules on Rehab," *Buildings* (June 1979): 63–66.

4. For more information on the 1978 Tax Investment Credit Act, see "Tax Incentives Encourage Renovation," *Buildings* (June 1979): 143.

rates and high construction costs have put ownership almost out of sight for the small retailer. Generally, specialty stores that seek only mall locations haven't any choice; they have to lease. Department stores, on the other hand, are more able to construct their own building. According to some developers, bankers, accountants, and retailers, in the long run it may be advantageous to build because of depreciation write off and property appreciation. In the short run, however, it is probably cheaper to rent. On the other hand, because of new accounting rules that mandate capitalization of leases (putting them on the books as if they were owned), it may no longer be less expensive for the retailer to lease instead of own.

Dale A. Feet, senior retail consultant at Price Waterhouse & Co., stresses that it is wrong to try to weigh just the cost of leasing against the cost of ownership. One should also consider what the property is likely to be worth at the end of the lease. If there is a strong probability of great appreciation within the lease time, it may be advantageous to borrow money and build and own the property. On the other hand, Feet says,

> If you own the store and the neighborhood has deteriorated, you're stuck with the building. . . . How much is a retailer willing to lay out today to have a building with an unknown value 25 years hence? It means taking today's value minus the estimated value 25 years from today, comparing it with the cost of leasing, and bringing these both back to today's present value.[5]

One of the common pitfalls of leasing space in new malls or recycled buildings is the need to build your own interior, even though the finished product is owned by the landlord. An example of this was Kay Jewelers, a Virginia-based chain that often had to install or pour its own floors and walls before it ever got around to putting in fixtures. Granted, this way the lease cost is usually less and the store interior becomes customized, but if the retailer leaves after the lease expires, everything except the portable fixtures must be left behind. It all belongs to the landlord, for the retailer has no equity in the floors and walls it builds.

Most rates for the lease of a building for retail use involve a fixed dollar charge per year that is typically based on square footage. In addition, a charge is usually made on a specified percentage of sales volume with a guarantee from the retailer of some minimum sales volume. For example, a grocery store retailer may lease a 22,000-square-foot building for $70,000 annually plus 1.25 percent of annual retail sales with a minimum guaranteed sales volume of $2 million. Thus, on retail sales up to $2 million, the annual rent would be $95,000, and for any volume above $2 million, the retailer would pay 1.25 percent of the volume.

If the retailer chooses a mall location, the lease costs may be more than expected. Costs of a mall lease often include minimum rent, merchants association dues, maintenance charge for the common area, real estate taxes, HVAC (heating and cooling of common area), a sprinkler system charge, and a per-

---

5. "Retailer's Question: Is It Better to Lease or to Own?" © *Chain Store Age Executive* 56(March 1980): 34–35. Lebhar-Friedman, Inc., 425 Park Ave. N.Y., NY 10022. Used by permission.

centage of sales charge. The decision of whether to lease or buy is important and should be thoroughly studied by the retailer before a commitment is made.

SELLING SPACE LAYOUT

The space within the store must be efficiently and effectively utilized. To accomplish this a retailer must design a store layout. Brown and Davidson define **layout** as: "The arrangement of selling and nonselling departments, aisles, fixtures, displays and equipment in the proper relationship to each other and to the fixed elements of the building structure."[6] Our discussion of layout will be broken into selling space and nonselling space decisions.

Traffic Patterns

Traffic is the most important aspect of selling space layout decisions. By cleverly stimulating more traffic within the store, retailers will expose shoppers to more merchandise and will cause them, therefore, to purchase more. The basic idea of a good layout is to route customers through the entire store in their search for goods, while keeping the goods they are looking for easy to locate.

The area near the store entrance will get the heaviest consumer traffic; thus it should be viewed as the most valuable space. A general rule is to place interesting merchandise within view of the entrance to draw in customers, thereby building traffic. The rest of the store layout should be planned to continue pulling the customer further into and on through the store. Commenting further on traffic, Larry Redinbaugh suggests,

> Traffic should be deliberately routed through the areas which will induce the most merchandise comparison and stimulate purchases. Usually higher priced items are placed near the rear of the store so that the customer must walk past all the goods. By putting the high priced things at the back, the customer has already seen the lower priced goods and is more ready to appreciate the features of the higher priced goods.[7]

This forced traffic pattern of low price to high price is especially useful in high-fashion apparel, household appliances, and furniture.

Here are some other basic principles of retail layout as related to traffic flow:

1. Aisles need to be kept wide enough that they are easy to get through even when customers stop to examine merchandise.
2. Aisles need to be kept short enough so that the customers aren't forced to go through a maze of goods to reach a specific item at the end of the aisle.
3. The entrance should be kept free of obstacles or clutter that may interefere with the flow of customers into or out of the store.
4. Try to visualize how the traffic should move to reach the entire store, then arrange the fixtures, displays, and aisles to help route the traffic this way.

6. William R. Davidson and Paul L. Brown, *Retailing Management*, 2nd ed. (New York: Ronald Press, 1960), p. 114.
7. Larry Redinbaugh, *Retail Management* (New York: McGraw-Hill, 1979), pp. 187–88.

5. Place staple goods in more remote areas of the store, because the traffic patterns will move to them.
6. Place impulse goods in high-traffic areas.
7. Place frequently purchased goods in easy-access areas.

Shoplifting Prevention   A retailer should also lay out its selling space in order to help prevent shoplifting. Although shoplifting may not seem to be a major problem to the ordinary retailer at first glance, statistics show otherwise. Bob Curtis, a security specialist, suggests in his book *Security Control: External Theft* that in self-service stores, shoplifting creates 35 to 45 percent of total inventory shortages. In department stores, 25 to 35 percent of total losses may be attributed to shoplifting.[8]

Some layouts will minimize vulnerability to shoplifters. One of the most important considerations when planning the layout of a retail store is visibility of the merchandise. Most shoplifting takes place in fitting rooms, blind spots, aisles crowded with extra merchandise, or behind high displays. As a general rule, display fixtures should be no taller than eye level, thus enabling employees to see over the top into the next aisle. Fitting rooms should not give the dishonest customer a secure place to steal. Instead, they should be designed so that employees can easily keep an eye on everyone and everything that goes in or comes out of the area. The manager's office is often stuck in a dark unused corner, out of sight and out of mind. However, for a one-story building this office can be an excellent deterrent to shoplifting if it is placed in an obvious area above floor level, where the manager can easily see the entire store.

8. For a very thorough discussion of the problem of external theft, see Bob Curtis, *Security Control: External Theft* (New York: Chain Store Publishing, 1978).

Bookstores often place discount items on special tables set in the aisles to catch the eye of passing shoppers. (Photo courtesy of SuperValu Stores.)

Another consideration when planning the general layout of a retail store is the merchandise characteristics. Small, expensive items that are easily palmed or pocketed, should be placed in locked display cases rather than on open displays, and anything put near stockrooms, fitting rooms, public restrooms, or exits should be less attractive to the ordinary shoplifter.

The checkout area should be located where it is most efficient and where the employees can watch the exit. The checkout also needs to be speedy, because the customer left waiting in a long, slow line is more likely to pocket a few items and walk out.

Atmosphere

We have already mentioned that the building must be designed to project an image. Similarly, the layout of the space within the building must reinforce this image. If the external appearance invites the customer to enter but the internal layout doesn't reinforce the projected image, the customer will develop a poor impression and may immediately turn around and exit. To prevent that, the retail manager needs to develop an understanding of how the image of a store is determined through the atmosphere of the selling space. Some of the main determinants of the selling space atmosphere are the type and density of employees, merchandise, fixtures, sound, and odor, which all combine with the visual factors to create the store atmosphere. This relationship is shown in Exhibit 15.1. Notice how all of these factors help to create the store atmosphere, which in turn determines the customers' sensory perceptions and the image the store projects.

EXHIBIT 15.1
The Image Star

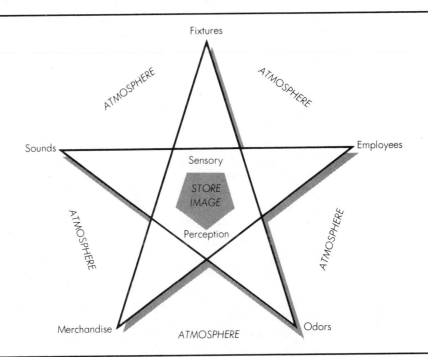

Employee Type and Density   Major determinants of the store atmosphere and image are employee type and density. The type of employee refers to the employees' general character. For example, are they neat and well dressed? Old or young? How compatible are the employees with the merchandise? The employer needs to be careful not to discriminate in hiring practices, but he or she should try to match the employees with the merchandise and store atmosphere. Employees can be outfitted to help reinforce an atmosphere; they can wear western clothing in a western wear store, or sportswear in a sporting goods store. In addition, employees with special characteristics can enhance the overall atmosphere of a store. Some maternity shops have found success in hiring pregnant women to supplement the regular sales force. Sears has been applauded for using larger-sized models in the catalog to show the larger-sized clothing. This appeal could carry over to the store sales force as well. As a general rule, the type of employee should be consistent with the atmosphere and the image the retailer is trying to project.

Density of employees refers to how many store employees there are per 1,000 square feet of selling space. Self-service stores such as K-mart or Safeway have fewer employees per 1,000 square feet of selling space, which yields an atmosphere of do-it-yourself and casualness. If the retailer has too low an em-employee density, customers with a problem may not be able to find the assistance they need and will therefore develop a negative opinion of the store. But, if there is too high an employee density, the customer may get the impression that the retailer is prosperous and that the employees are idly standing around waiting to prey on the customers. Have you ever been about to enter a store only to notice the employees standing around watching the door? If there weren't any or many customers in the store, did you find yourself deciding not to enter? Customers don't like to feel like they are walking into a den of wolves. The key in regard to employee density is to have enough to give the level of service desired. By doing so, the retailer is usually projecting the right image.

Merchandise Type and Density   Type and density of merchandise also determine a retailer's image. If a furniture retailer wants to project a high-quality and high-status image, then its lines of furniture must reinforce this. The merchandise density (the merchandise displayed or shelved per 1,000 square feet) is also crucial. Our furniture retailer could not project the high-quality and high-status image if the furniture was packed into the store so that only one person could squeeze down an aisle. Merchandise density can be increased by stacking merchandise very high, possibly even right up to the ceiling. Again, however, a furniture retailer that does this would not project a high-quality, high-status image.

Fixture Type and Density   The type and density of fixtures depends largely but not entirely on merchandise type. The type of fixture simply refers to the physical makeup of the fixtures. Are they chrome and smoked-glass showcases, standard metal shelves, antique wooden buffets, or old, cast-iron bathtubs? All the fixtures should be consistent with the overall theme or atmosphere. For instance, if a retailer wants the store to look like an old English pub, the fixtures used should be made of wood and antique brass rather than chrome or Chinese lacquer.

The retailer is sometimes tempted to take advantage of a good deal on fixtures that don't complement the decor. These good deals can wreck the continuity needed to achieve the high-status image many of these retailers seek. However, since nationally retailers spend between $3.91 and $9.53 per square foot on fixtures it is necessary to weigh the fixture costs against the potential atmosphere damage.

Certain decorator pieces can add an immeasurable amount to the store's atmosphere if they are wisely selected. This is especially successful in specialty stores, such as using Scandinavian furniture and lights in a shop that specializes in Scandinavian housewares and gifts.

Buskirk and Buskirk suggest that retailers be imaginative when planning fixtures.[9] Retailers should explore sources other than the traditional, ready-made store fixtures. Not only can the cost be less, but the result can be the difference between an average store and a unique one. Some sources to explore are local cabinetmakers, metalworkers, welders, and antique and second-hand dealers. Large retailers and chain stores, however, usually find it necessary to rely on standardized fixtures to obtain consistency throughout the country. But even these retailers can usually add a bit of local atmosphere through a few special accent pieces.

The density of fixtures refers to the number per 1,000 square feet of selling space. Stores can be over- or under-fixtured. If the store is over-fixtured, the customer may become confused as to what the retailers' business actually is. Picture, for example, a menswear retailer using the following for display: antique dressers and tables on which shirts and sweaters are piled, a display of antique pipes and guns on two walls, antique books in shelves bordering two other walls, the shelves also containing merchandise such as cuff-links, ties and belts, turn-of-the-century bicycle flanked by mannequins dressed in 1890s attire in the front display window. The density of antique fixtures and accents is so high that the customer may wonder if the retailer is selling men's clothing or antiques.

On the other hand, stores can be under-fixtured. Picture a hardware store with all the merchandise sitting on the selling floor in crates, boxes, and a few old wooden tables. Such a store tends to look old, run-down, and highly inefficient. It would be difficult for the do-it-yourself shopper to find the items on his or her shopping list. Imagine having to search through all the boxes to find thirty finishing nails, #001 sandpaper, a small can of walnut stain, and a paintbrush. Think how much easier it is to find these items in a hardware store that is well laid out, with adequate fixtures for displaying the merchandise. The proper density and type of fixture can turn a disorganized, inefficient store into quite the opposite.

Sound Type and Density The type of sound and its density can influence the atmosphere of the store positively or negatively. Sounds can be pleasant or

9. Richard H. Buskirk and Bruce D. Buskirk, *Retailing* (New York: McGraw-Hill, 1979), p. 154.

unpleasant to the typical customer. An unpleasant or wrong sound (from the shrill pitch of a dentist's drill to the roar of jet planes) can detract from, and even destroy the atmosphere the retailer is trying to build, by getting on the customers' nerves. Noises like these are usually from external sources over which the retailer has little control, except for sound deadening insulation and counter-noise or internally produced sounds that muffle the unpleasant noises. Wrong noises in one place, however, can be considered pleasant in other circumstances or places. For example, the sound of balls rolling, pins falling, and people laughing and joking are all pleasant inside a bowling alley; but these same sounds inside Neiman Marcus or a jewelry store would be inconsistent with the desired atmosphere and therefore wrong.

A right, pleasant sound can, in turn, draw attention to the merchandise. Clocks ticking and chiming, wind chimes blowing in the breeze, music boxes playing, and of course, in their respective places, stereo equipment, radios, and television sets being demonstrated can all be right sounds that will actually draw the customer's attention to the merchandise.

The third type of sound, alluded to earlier, is **counter-noise.** This is background sound piped into the store to cover up other sounds and to overcome dead quiet, which can also be distracting. The most widely used counter-noise is background music heard in elevators, retail stores, offices, and restaurants.

Sound density refers to the strength or the loudness of the sounds. Since background music is used so much by retailers, it is one of the most important sounds for the retailer to control. It helps to eliminate unwanted sounds and at the same time to pace employees, but the music can be so loud that it is irritating, or so soft that it is useless. Thus, the loudness of the music must be appropriate for the in-store environment the retailer is trying to create. Another important consideration when discussing music is the type. This, too, is important to the atmosphere and must be consistent, whether Bach, Loretta Lynn, or Kiss. It is sometimes hard for the retailer to realize that even though he or she can listen to E. Power Biggs playing toccatas and fugues for hours on end, the customers may not be able to tolerate the music for more than five minutes; and it surely wouldn't be appropriate in a feed and grain store.

Odor Type and Density   Also important in atmosphere building and in making the selling space maximally productive is odor. If the space does not smell right then the merchandise will not sell to its true potential. The right type of odor makes the customer anxious to purchase the product. The taste buds react to some odors to the point that people can actually taste some things just by smelling them. Examples are chocolate, fresh bread, oranges, popcorn, and coffee. Other odors stimulate other reflexes; musk oil used in perfumes and aftershaves is supposed to be sexually arousing. Odors also can be helpful in creating a pleasant mood. The smell of flowers in a florist; perfume at a cosmetic counter; cookies at a bakery; fudge and nuts at a candy store; scented candles in a gift shop; leather in a leather goods department; and tobacco in a pipe store; these odors are all consistent with the merchandise and helpful in stimulating a desire for it.

Just as there can be wrong sounds, there can also be wrong odors, which can actually drive the customer away from making a purchase. Examples of wrong odors include musty carpets, cigarette smoke, strong fabric dyes, rodent and insect problems, lingering fire damage odors, gasoline, and even paint and cleaning supplies if improperly located. Next-door odors, like outside sounds, can also be a problem for the retailer. These odors need not be unpleasant, just inconsistent—such as the smell of chocolate and nuts drifting into a health food store, or the overly medicated scent of a doctor's or dentist's office in a bakery. The odor must be the right one to be conducive to a purchase.

As was the case with the other influences of atmosphere, the density (strength) of the odor must be considered along with the type. If the odor is the wrong type, the retailer should try to diminish its strength with air filtration systems. For the right odors, density should be high enough to stimulate the purchase of merchandise but subdued enough that it isn't distracting or irritating to the customer. For example, the scent of perfume around the cosmetic counter may stimulate the demand for perfume or other cosmetics. However, too strong a scent may be overpowering or even irritate allergies, thus driving the customers from the area.

Visual Factors Visual factors also help determine the atmosphere that encompasses the selling space. Most important is the overall appearance as seen through the eyes of the customer. This will be the combined effect of several of the factors we have discussed—employee type and density, fixture type and density, and merchandise type and density—as well as of several factors still to be discussed—color combinations, lighting, and floor covering.

Color can create a mood and focus attention. For example, displaying diamonds on blue, red, or black velvet shows them better than putting them against pink, yellow, or white velvet.

Colors themselves have moods which it is helpful to understand. Red, yellow, and orange are considered by the artist as warm colors, and as such they are used when a feeling of warmth and closeness are desired. Many restaurants use these colors along with candlelight and fireplaces to help create a mood. Blue, green and violet are considered cool colors and are used to open up closed places and create an air of elegance and cleanliness. These colors do well in dark hallways, restrooms, infant departments, and other areas the retailer wishes to make appear larger or lighter. Browns and golds are considered earth tones, and blend with everything. They also convey a warmth to the surroundings.

The degree of lighting can also change the atmosphere. Consider a well-lighted gift shop compared with one that is dimly lit. On examining trade journals, you will readily notice numerous ads for different types of lighting. Each type has its purpose, and the retailer needs to determine what his or her lighting needs are, then seek the fixtures to fill those needs. For example, jewelry, especially diamonds and other precious stones, is best displayed under high-intensity spotlights, and cosmetics under no-glare natural lighting. Some lighting may cause colors to appear different than they look in natural sunlight; a customer purchasing a pair of navy blue socks may return them the next day because they looked black in the store rather than navy.

The type and colors of the floorcoverings are also important to the overall appearance and atmosphere of a retail store. Do the rest of the determinants indicate a subdued, functional flooring, a shiny parquet, or a plush carpeting? The floorcovering, as with the other influences on atmosphere, must be consistent with the customer's desired overall visual perception, without using too much capital.

Demand Stimulation As we have shown, proper investments in buildings and fixtures can actually be investments in stimulating demand. That is, the building is more than a place to store the merchandise, and fixtures are more than vehicles for displaying the merchandise. The building and fixtures should also bring the customer and the retailer closer together. They can be strong motivators in getting potential customers to make a purchase by inviting them into the store to look around.

In Exhibit 15.2, we present a case study of how buildings can be used to stimulate retail demand. The key is to incorporate the proper sights, sounds, and smells into the retail space.

EXHIBIT 15.2 **Demand** **Stimulation**	Retailers can use their buildings to stimulate demand by incorporating into their store space the proper sights, sounds, and smells. There are a variety of enterprises that specialize in advising retailers on how to use sight, sound, and smell to stimulate demand:*

- Minnesota Mining & Manufacturing Co. supplies background music that is specially arranged to put people in the mood to purchase. Muzak Corp. offers similar services to retailers.
- International Flavors & Fragrances, Inc. has successfully reproduced the aroma of hot apple pie, chocolate-chip cookies, fresh pizza, baking ham, and french fries. Timed-release aerosol cans of these artificial odors can be purchased for $25 to $30. These devices release scents into the shopping mall, tempting customers to buy.
- Don Watt & Associates Ltd., a Toronto-based consulting firm, has found how to use color to convey certain images in a retail setting and thus stimulate demand.

    *Examples taken from "Sight, Smell, Sound: They're All Arms in Retailers' Arsenal," *Wall Street Journal*, April 17, 1979, pp. 1, 27.

Layout Types After the retailer has made atmospheric decisions regarding colors, floorcovering, and fixtures, the type of layout must be chosen. This refers to the actual arrangement of the fixtures, merchandise, stockroom, and other features of the store's interior. There are basically two types of layout, grid and free flow, as well as several variations on these two basic types.

Grid Layout The **grid layout** is one in which all the counters and fixtures are at right angles to each other, thereby forming a maze. This type of layout is most often used in supermarkets, drug stores, variety stores, and discount department stores. Exhibit 15.3 shows a grid layout used in a supermarket.

EXHIBIT 15.3
**Grid Layout
in a
Supermarket**

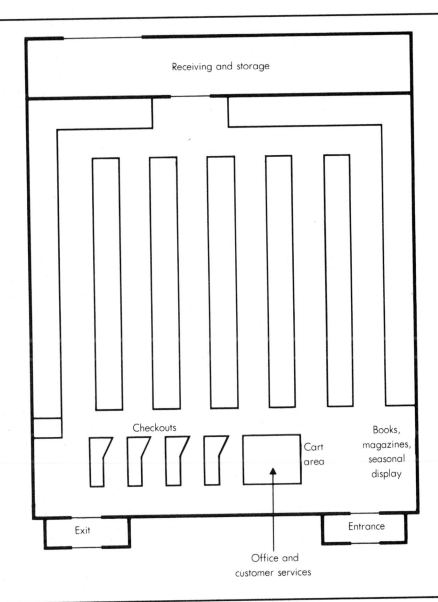

Notice how the layout itself seems to move the customer through the maze of merchandise from the entrance to the exit.

Free Flow Layout   The second main type of layout is the **free flow**, in which the fixtures and merchandise are grouped into patterns or left free standing, thereby creating an unstructured traffic pattern. Many of the fixtures used in the free-flow system are irregularly shaped, such as circles, horseshoes, arches, and triangles. The aisles are usually wide and curving and leave little more than walking areas between merchandise displays.

EXHIBIT 15.4
**The
Free-Flow
Layout**

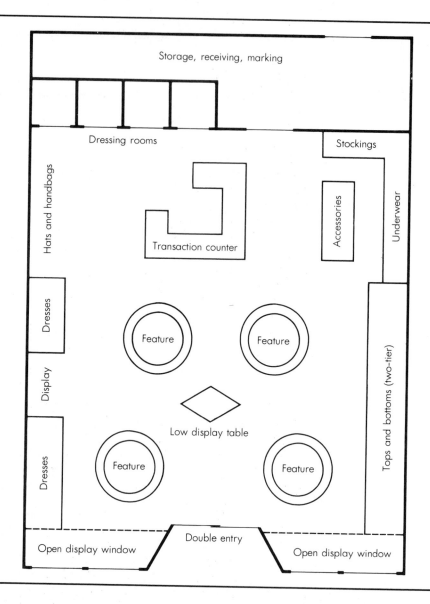

The free-flow layout is often used in specialty stores, boutiques, gift stores, and some apparel stores. Exhibit 15.4 shows a free-flow layout used in a junior apparel shop.

A chart highlighting the advantages and disadvantages of both the grid and the free-flow methods of layout is shown in Exhibit 15.5.

Some Variations Two subtypes of layout also need mentioning. The first is used mainly for fast-food chains, ticket agencies, and other businesses whose major concern is moving customers in and out rapidly. It is called the **standard layout** and consists of an entrance, a counter, a checkout area, and an exit.

Wickes, the home improvement retailer, uses a supermarket-like grid layout, as do many discount stores. (Photo courtesy of Wickes Corp.)

The second subtype, which is picking up support from retailers, is the **boutique layout.** Usually a form of free-flow layout, the boutique layout creates "mini-stores" within a larger store. Each of the mini-stores is aimed at a specific target group and is often a grouping of merchandise from a single designer or company. The boutique layout works best for retailers in gift shops, high-status department stores, and any field where specific designers or names are known. Exhibit 15.6 shows a womenswear store using the boutique layout arranged according to designer.

At this point, it is important to note that there is no right or wrong layout pattern for every retailer or retail classification. The layout must depend on other variables, like the type of merchandise, size and shape of the building, and the atmosphere desired by the retailer.

EXHIBIT 15.5 **Advantages and Disadvantages of Grid and Free-flow Layouts**	TYPE	ADVANTAGES	DISADVANTAGES
	Grid	1. Low cost 2. Customer familiarity 3. Merchandise exposure 4. Ease of cleaning 5. Simplified security 6. Possibility of self-service	1. Plain and uninteresting 2. Limited browsing 3. Stimulation of rushed shopping behavior 4. Limited creativity in decor
	Free-flow	1. Allowance for browsing and wandering freely 2. Increased impulse purchases 3. Visual appeal 4. Flexibility	1. Loitering encouraged 2. Possible confusion 3. Waste of floor space 4. Cost 5. Difficulty of cleaning

EXHIBIT 15.6
**The
Boutique
Layout**

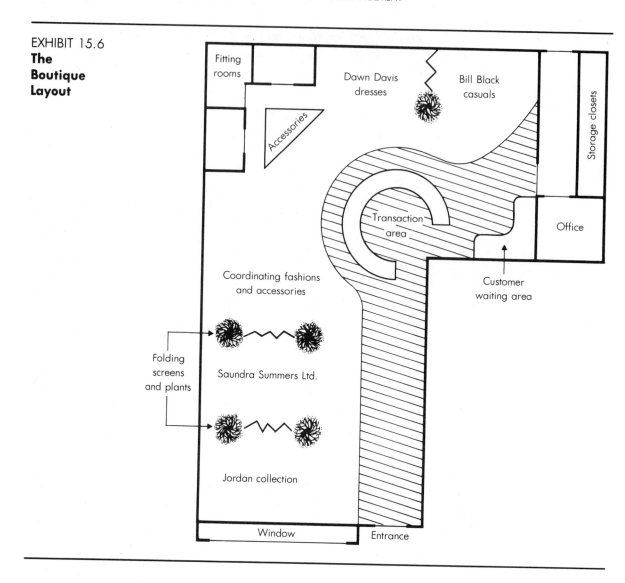

Selling Space Productivity

The retailer cannot achieve high performance results unless selling space is used productively. In order to ensure selling space productivity, the retail manager must employ measures to assess selling space performance.

Productivity Measures

Any productivity measure relates output to input. Regarding selling space productivity, the input is obviously the amount of selling space, which is typically measured in square feet. However, the output can take on a variety of measurements. The most commonly used measures of output are net sales, gross profit, contribution profit, and operating profit. Retail managers may use these four measures of output when assessing space productivity:

1. **Net sales** will reflect the total dollar sales (less any returns and merchandise allowances) that are created in the selling space.

2. **Gross profit** is defined as net sales less cost of goods sold. This measure is good if no expenses besides the cost of merchandise can be directly related or traced to the selling space where the goods were sold. For example, it may not be possible to directly tie any advertising expenses to particular selling space areas within the store.

3. **Contribution profit** is defined as net sales less cost of goods sold and any expenses that are directly traceable to the space in which the goods were sold. In this case, items such as advertising and labor expenses can be directly related to specific selling areas. For instance, newspaper ads for bowling balls can be directly allocated to the sporting goods department of a department store.

4. **Operating profit** is defined as net sales less cost of goods sold, direct expenses, and a share of all indirect expenses that the retailer incurs. This method is not good unless the indirect expenses can be equitably allocated to the respective selling areas within the store. Typically, only the cost of renting or maintaining the selling space can be equitably allocated according to the square footage occupied by each selling area; other expenses, such as the salaries of top management or clerical and office expenses, can be allocated only on an arbitrary basis.

Utilizing these output measures and accepting square footage of selling space as the appropriate input measure, we can identify four possible measures of selling space productivity:

1. **Sales per square foot of selling space** equals net sales divided by square feet of selling space. This ratio shows, on average, how much in annual net sales dollars the retailer generated for each square foot of selling space.

2. **Gross profit per square foot of selling space** equals total gross profit divided by square feet of selling space. This simple measure reflects how many gross profit dollars a retailer generates, on average, for each square foot of selling space.

3. **Contribution profit per square foot of selling space** equals total contribution profit divided by square feet of selling space. A more stringent measure of space productivity than the prior two measures, it reveals how much in contribution profit dollars were generated, on average, for each square foot of selling space.

4. **Operating profit per square foot of selling space** equals total operating profit divided by square feet of selling space. The most stringent measure of space productivity, this measure captures the dollars of operating profit that were generated, on average, for each square foot of selling space.

Due to the nature of the relative output measures just defined, the most accurate measure of selling space productivity is contribution profit per foot of selling space. Nonetheless, the sales per square foot and gross profit per square foot measures dominate, because many retail trade associations regularly report these measures in their operating results studies. For example, Exhibit 15.7 profiles composite selling space productivity measures for home improvement retailers across twelve departments. These statistics, and similar ones supplied by other retail trade associations, provide the retail manager with useful benchmarks by which to gauge selling space productivity.

EXHIBIT 15.7
Composite Selling Space Productivity Measures for Home Improvement Centers (1979)

DEPARTMENT	SALES PER SQUARE FOOT OF SELLING AREA	GROSS PROFIT PER SQUARE FOOT OF SELLING AREA
Hardware	$117.91	$40.09
Hand and power tools	115.09	39.36
Plumbing, heating and cooling	114.25	40.10
Electrical supplies	104.64	36.94
Paint and paint sundries	111.74	39.67
Lumber and building materials	171.83	45.02
Lawn and garden	92.60	27.22
Housewares	90.34	26.29
Automotive supplies	96.83	28.18
Major appliances	89.05	20.93
Sporting goods and outdoor living	93.20	29.36
Other departments	117.37	34.98

Source: Based on data from *1980 Bottom Line* (Indianapolis, Ind., National Retail Hardware Association, 1980), p. 12, and author's computations.

Space Reallocation After the retail manager has evaluated the space productivity for various departments or areas of the store, the question of reallocating selling space may arise. Can the selling space be reallocated to increase overall store performance? Overall store performance could be increased if the average contribution profit per square foot could be raised. However, it would not necessarily increase if sales per square foot of selling space rose or if gross profit per square foot of selling space rose. Why? Because the increase in sales per square foot could be the result of giving more space to merchandise that was easy to sell but not as profitable as the displaced merchandise—thus lowering overall profits. Similarly, if gross profit per square foot is increased, overall store performance will not necessarily improve. The reason for the increase may be that the merchandise that is given more space may have a higher gross margin; however, it may require more than a proportionate increase in direct expenses to handle and sell it. For example, an expanded jewelry department may increase gross margin per square foot, but if added employees are needed to keep an eye on the jewelry to prevent excessive thefts, and if more advertising is needed to sell more of the jewelry, the **contribution profit per square foot** could actually decline.

EXHIBIT 15.8 **Contribution Profit per Square Foot of Selling Space**

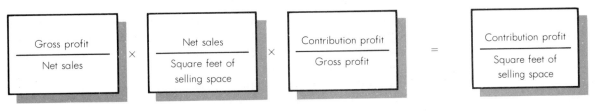

The preceding discussion can be summarzed with the equation presented in Exhibit 15.8. As the equation shows, contribution profit per square foot of selling space is equal to the multiplicative effect of: (1) gross margin percentage, (2) sales per square foot, and (3) the ratio of contribution profit to gross profit. This last ratio shows how much shrinkage occurs in gross profit as a result of the need to expend additional dollars to sell the merchandise. A ratio of 1.0 indicates no direct expenses were incurred to sell the merchandise—a highly unlikely event. A ratio of less than 1.0, say 0.8, would show that gross profit dropped by 20 percent $(1.0 - 0.8)$ in order to sell the merchandise. The important point to remember is that if overall performance is to rise then the multiplicative effect of these three variables must increase contribution profit per square foot of selling space.

Assume that within a department store the management is contemplating taking some selling space away from the gift department and giving it to the fabric and notions department. Currently, the gift department has a gross margin of 40 percent, sales per square foot of $80, and a ratio of contribution profit to gross profit of 0.75. Therefore, its contribution profit per square foot is $(0.40)(\$80)(0.75) = \$24$. Since the gift department has a total of 2,800 square feet, its total contribution profit is $\$24(2,800) = \$67,200$. The fabric and notions department currently has a gross margin of 34 percent, sales per square foot of $92, and a ratio of contribution profit to gross profit of 0.88. Its contribution profit per square foot is $(0.34)(\$92)(0.88) = \$27.53$. This department has 2,200 square feet, which results in total contribution profit of $\$27.53(2,200) = \$60,566$. Management observes that for each square foot of selling space, the fabric and notions department is generating $27.53 in contribution profit, whereas the gift department is generating only $24 per square foot. Therefore, management decides to equalize department size by taking 300 square feet from the gift department (making it 2,500 square feet) and adding it to the fabric and notions department (bringing it up to 2,500 square feet). What will be the profit effect of this decision?

To answer this question, the retail manager needs to look beyond the current contribution profit per square foot for each department, since the three determinants of contribution profit per square foot might change. In short, as more square feet are added to fabric and notions, will the present gross margin be able to be maintained, the sales per square foot remain constant, and the contribution profit to gross profit ratio remain unchanged? Probably not. To sell more fabric and notions it may be necessary to be more price competitive, and thus the gross margin may decline. It is also unlikely that the average sales per square foot would rise or even remain constant, since the fabric and notions that would be added would tend to be the more marginal types because the existing space would already be devoted to the best selling fabrics and notions. As a consequence, sales per square foot would probably decline. Whether there would be any change in the contribution profit to gross profit ratio would be difficult to say. If proportionately more advertising and wages are incurred as a result of an expanded fabrics and notions department, then a decline in the ratio would occur.

Let us assume, then, that the net impact was a drop in gross margin from 0.34 to 0.32, a drop in sales per square foot from \$92 to \$90, and a drop in the contribution profit to gross profit ratio from 0.88 to 0.87. Consequently, the new contribution profit per square foot is $(0.32)(\$90)(0.87) = \$25.06$. And, the total contribution profit for the fabrics and notions department is $(2,500)(\$25.06) = \$62,650$, as compared to \$60,566.

What might you expect to happen to the space productivity of the gift department? It is possible that each of the three ratios would move in the opposite direction as in the scenario outlined above. Since the gift department has to eliminate 300 square feet, it will need to drop certain gift lines. One would expect the manager of that department to drop lines that have the lowest gross margins, the lowest sales per square foot, and the most direct expenses—those which would reduce most heavily the ratio of contribution profit to gross profit. Assume that the actual changes were an increase in gross margin from 0.40 to 0.42, an increase in sales per square foot from \$80 to \$81, and an increase in the ratio of contribution profit to gross profit from 0.75 to 0.76. The new contribution profit per square foot would be $(0.42)(\$81)(0.76) = \$25.86$. The total contribution profit of the gift department would be $2,500(\$25.86) = \$64,650$.

Has the overall effect on the department store been positive? Before the reallocation of space, the combined contribution profit of the gift and fabric departments respectively was $\$67,200 + \$60,566 = \$127,766$. After the reallocation, the combined contribution profit was $\$64,650 + \$62,650 = \$127,300$. Thus, rather than an increase, there was a marginal drop in overall store performance. The reallocation of departmental space was an unnecessary, and actually unprofitable, exercise. This, of course, did not have to be the situation. The key to remember is that space allocation decisions should not be made on the basis of only the existing average contribution profit per square foot of selling space. The retail analyst has to ask how space productivity might change as a result of reallocating space within the store and this requires examining potential changes in: (1) sales per square foot, (2) gross margin percentage, and (3) the ratio of contribution profit to gross profit.

Recently, due to rapid inflation, many retailers have attempted to improve space productivity by leasing their unproductive space to other firms. In Exhibit 15.9, we present a case study that illustrates this point.

EXHIBIT 15.9 **Inflation and Space Management**	Record high rates of inflation in the United States in the late 1970s and early 1980s prompted retailers to try to achieve higher productivity growth in order to help offset the ravages of inflation. One avenue they took in their pursuit of productivity growth was better space management. In essence, retailers attempted to get more sales out of each square foot or cubic foot of space. To accomplish this, several retailers leased unproductive space to other enterprises. This allowed these retailers to retain their most productive space and at the same time obtain a predictable return on their unproductive space. Consider the following cases:*

- "J. C. Penney is subletting space in a number of its Treasury discount stores as part of a concerted effort to turn that operation into the black."
- "Korvettes has disclosed plans to sublet more than 13 percent of its total store space, also an effort to make that chain profitable."
- "Woolco has carved out 20,000 to 30,000 square feet in eight of its Woolco stores in the southwest to create room for its new J. Brannam apparel stores, and also as a part of a planned Woolco cutdown program."

*Examples from "High Costs Convince Chains to Sublet, Cut Store Space," *Chain Store Age Executive* 56 (May 1980), p. 47.

NONSELLING SPACE LAYOUT

The efficient design and layout of nonselling space is as important as the design of selling space. Unfortunately, many retailers ignore this fact, believing that the only stimulator of space productivity is selling space layout. All space must be properly allocated and designed in order to maximize space productivity. Also the design of selling and nonselling space are interdependent. Consider, for example, storage space for reserve stock. In general, the reserve stock should be located near the selling area, because customers don't like to be left alone for a long time while the employee searches for items from stock. If left alone too long, the customer will leave, the sale will be lost, and sales per square foot of selling space will suffer.

The retailer will need space for up to four nonselling needs: office space and equipment, merchandise receiving and handling space and equipment, storage or warehouse space and equipment, and customer service space and equipment. For all four areas, the key is to allocate adequate space so the job to be done in that space can be performed efficiently without wasting space.

Office Space and Equipment The design of office space and environments is a science in itself. Many consulting firms actually specialize in the efficient layout of the office. These firms also can assist retailers in selecting the proper type of equipment for performing clerical functions. With today's sophistication of office equipment (computerized typewriters, copying machines, mail sorters and minicomputers), the retailer typically needs the professional advice of someone other than the equipment salesperson.

It should be recognized that office space, like selling space, has an atmosphere. The retailer should try to create a work atmosphere that stimulates productivity. In principle, the office could be bare of carpet, wall decor, background music, and efficient lighting. It could consist of a dark, drab corner with a few metal desks and chairs and filing cabinets. However, this atmosphere may make the office so unpleasant that the clerical staff will spend as much time as possible away from their desks. Clerical employees are hardly efficient workers when they are in the employee lounge or restroom, running personal errands, making personal phone calls, or even wandering around the stockroom or selling space. They are productive only when they are working. Therefore, the retailer needs to create an office atmosphere that is cheerful enough to take the dreariness out of the day, yet subdued enough to retain a work atmosphere.

Receiving and Handling   The retailer will need to have some means of handling incoming merchandise. For some types of retailer (a grocery store for instance) this need will be significant and frequent; for others (as for a jeweler) it will be relatively minor and infrequent. A retailer with a frequent and significant amount of incoming merchandise, needs considerable planning of merchandise receiving and handling space. To illustrate, consider that a full-line grocery store will need to build receiving docks to which forty- to sixty-foot semi-trailers can be backed up. Similarly, space may be needed for a small forklift to drive between the truck and the merchandise receiving area to unload the merchandise. Subsequently, the merchandise will need to be moved from the receiving area, where it may be counted and marked, to a storage area—either on the selling floor or in a separate location.

The point at which incoming merchandise is received can be a high theft point. The retail manager needs to design the receiving and handling area in order to minimize this problem. Several frequently used theft methods that take place in the back room are mentioned below. Some involve the retail employees themselves, others involve outsiders.

- **Vendor collusion** includes the types of loss that occur when the merchandise is delivered. Typical losses involve the delivery of less merchandise than is charged for, removal of good merchandise disguised as old or stale merchandise, and stealing other merchandise from the stockroom or off the selling floor while making delivery. This type of theft often involves both the delivery people and the retail employee who signs for the delivery with the two splitting the profit.
- **Employee theft.** Some employees have the notion that free merchandise is part of their pay. Although some of the stolen goods come from the selling floor, a larger percentage is pilfered from the stockroom to the employee lounge and lockers, where it is kept until the employees leave with it at quitting time.
- **Customer theft** is also a problem at this point, although not usually to as high a degree as shoplifting. Stealing merchandise from the stockroom and receiving area may be easier than taking it from the selling floor for several

reasons. First, much of the back room merchandise is not ticketed, so it is easier to get it through electronic antishoplifting devices. Second, once the thief enters the stock area, there is very little antitheft security. Most security guards watch the exits and fitting rooms. Third, there is usually an exit in the immediate area of the stockroom through which the thief can carry out the stolen goods. In more recent times, these exits have been wired to set off an alarm when opened without a key, helping curb thefts somewhat.

The retailer must be aware that there is an excellent opportunity for receiving, handling, and storage thefts to happen. Therefore, steps should be taken to help cut down on these crimes. The retailer cannot watch the employees every minute to see whether or not they are honest, but some surveillance is helpful. Fourteen rules for controlling receiving-area thefts are enumerated in Exhibit 15.10.

Storage or Warehousing   The amount of storage space the retailer will need will be related to the physical dimensions of the merchandise and the safety stock level needed

---

EXHIBIT 15.10
Rules for Controlling Receiving Area Thefts

1. Make periodic, unannounced checks of receiving and stock areas to observe.
2. Keep receiving and marking areas locked at night and any time during the day when not supervised.
3. Keep the area clean and orderly. Not only does this appearance indicate that management cares about the merchandise, it also makes losses easier to spot.
4. Do not allow *anyone* at *any time* to exit across the receiving dock where merchandise can easily be picked up and carried to a car.
5. Do not allow merchandise to leave the receiving room before it is processed.
6. Receiving room employees should not be permitted to bring personal property such as packages, large handbags, or anything in which merchandise could be concealed, into the receiving area.
7. Check the receiving dock at the end of the day for merchandise left on the dock, purposely or otherwise.
8. Check case counts and randomly spot-check item counts.
9. Do not allow receiving checker to be interrupted during receiving and checking. To do so, allows the dishonest employee or delivery person an ample opportunity to take goods.
10. Only allow authorized receiving personnel to have possession of invoices.
11. Supervise the handling of goods taken from the store by vendors as being stale, soiled, returns, or empty.
12. Do not permit outside resource delivery people to have access to any of the inside areas of the store or receiving operation.
13. Place delivered merchandise in a proper location from the start so it can be checked, marked, assembled, and inventoried in one step.
14. Do not allow the receiving room to be unlocked and cleaned at night.

Source: Adapted from Bob Curtis, *Security Control: Internal Theft* (New York: Chain Store Publishing Corp., 1977), pp. 251–52. Reprinted with permission of Chain Store Publishing Corp. and the author.

to maintain the desired rate of stock turnover. For example, furniture is bulky and thus requires considerable storage space; and grocery items turn over frequently, so more merchandise is needed than can be displayed on the shelves. The safety stock level is not specific to the line of merchandise. It depends more on the retailer's willingness to lose a sale if merchandise is out of stock.

Retailers will also need to decide what equipment to use to store merchandise. The retailer could have employees physically carry the merchandise from delivery trucks and stack the boxes and cartons on the floor of the stockroom. In most cases, however, this scenario would be fairly inefficient and also costly when the retailer is probably paying those employees anywhere from five to fifteen dollars per hour. Thus, in most cases, some type of equipment will be used to increase productivity in this area. For instance, rather than having the employees carry incoming merchandise, there are numerous types of carts especially made for this purpose. Also, instead of stacking the cartons and boxes directly on the floor of the stockroom where they must remain packed and risk being damaged, the merchandise can be unpacked, checked, inventoried, and ticketed, then placed on shelves or in bins until needed. By doing this, one can increase the amount of merchandise stored per square foot by decreasing the amount of packing materials and, as noted earlier, a tidy, well-ordered stock area is less tempting to dishonest employees. Trash compactors can be helpful by compressing the packing clutter.

Customer Services   Space will also need to be allocated to allow for the performance of customer service functions. This includes space for restrooms, check cashing, dressing rooms, elevators, stairways, gift wrapping, handling of complaints, processing of credit applications, and payment of bills, among other things. Space devoted to customer services can help stimulate or reinforce selling efforts, but the primary and immediate purpose is not for selling. For example, well-designed restrooms can give a favorable impression, which can help reinforce future selling efforts. On the other hand, a customer's perception of a dirty restroom can carry over and cloud his or her perception of the entire store.

It is important for the retailer to realize that it is not in the business of providing customer services. Although some customer services are necessary, they are not the purpose of the retailer. Therefore, the space devoted to them should be in relation to how these services can help to support the selling efforts; the retailer should decide how much space is actually necessary versus how much it would like to devote to these services.

As we indicated before, the customer's perception of the store depends on, among other things, its visual effect. Therefore, when discussing the customer service areas, it is important to blend these areas with the desired atmosphere of the store. For example, a discount department store might get by very well using barren fitting rooms with small mirrors and flimsy curtains. However, putting those same fitting rooms into a bridal shop would be totally inconsistent with the store's image and would adversely affect the consumer's perception of the store.

ENERGY MANAGEMENT

On the contemporary retail scene, one of the major operating concerns of retail managers is energy management. Since the management of energy is intertwined with building and equipment decisions, it will be covered in this chapter.

Marshall Sauls, vice president for property management for Rich's in Atlanta, has stated, "The price of utilities today is more than rent in many cases."[10] This suggests that the retailer take a closer look at energy management. In some cases, this closer look is actually being forced upon retailers. Massachusetts, for example, has adopted the first state energy conservation plan of the nation. Under this plan, retail centers of over 100,000 square feet are required to conduct lighting audits of their stores and to reduce lighting levels to comply with the new state guidelines. It should be noted, however, that reduced wattage doesn't have to mean reduced lighting, due to advances in more energy efficient light fixtures.

In addition to the encouragement from the government, the retailer is also getting encouragement from other sources. Consider the following examples:

- Aetna Life & Casualty recently adopted a new plan concerning its company real estate investments, many of which are in retail buildings. Aetna has developed an energy plan that includes solar collectors, weatherstripping, insulation, and caulking, which can significantly reduce a building's operating costs. The resulting savings will then be reflected in the building value from which the loan amount or purchase price will be determined. Aetna is requiring each new building to have an energy budget established by a certified design engineer.[11]
- York (a division of Borg-Warner Corporation) is offering to finance the incremental cost of all energy-efficient commercial and industrial air-conditioning products selected in place of low-first-cost equipment. A computer comparison is made of the two units to determine savings based on many variables including project life, tax depreciation, income tax rates, debt percentage, mortgage interest rate (for incremental investment), target rate of return, energy costs, and anticipated energy inflation rate. The financing is available to all building owners and developers with good credit ratings. Loans are on a five-year basis.[12]

Retail managers and store planners can incorporate energy savings into the five areas discussed on the following pages.

Size

Obviously, larger stores use more energy than small stores (if everything else is the same). However, the number of square feet in a building is not the only consideration when discussing store size. Other factors that need to be consid-

10. Marcia Powell, "Reducing Operating Costs," *Stores* 59(January 1977): 32.
11. "Energy," *Buildings* (April 1979): 34.
12. From *Buildings* (May 1979): 41.

ered are the building's shape and its relationship to the sun. Passive solar collection can substantially add to the temperature inside a building if there is a massive south or west exposure. In some climates, however (e.g., southern Arizona), it may be more advantageous to eliminate some passive solar heat by using architectural overhangs, awnings, heat retarding exterior treatments, and landscaping. It is also advantageous to keep a building within a temperature range, rather than creating hot spots due to uneven solar heat.

Insulation   Adding insulation is one of the cheapest ways of conserving energy. The best insulation decisions can be made when the building is being constructed, when the floors, walls, and ceilings can be properly assessed and fitted with insulation. It is difficult to state any firm rules in regard to insulation needs, since the amount will depend on such factors as the climate and tightness of construction. Also, the type of insulation that can be used is generally regulated by local building and fire codes.

Entrance and Window Design   A significant amount of energy can be saved through the proper design of the entrance. For example, it should be positioned away from prevailing winds, either at an angle or in a recess. In addition, the doors should be as airtight as possible to retain the warm or cold air within the building. Often a set of two doors will be used to create an air lock. This is especially helpful in the cold, windy northern states. Most department stores and supermarkets have a second set of doors about ten to twelve feet beyond the outside doors.

Windows can also be a significant source of heat gain or loss. Insulated or thermopane glass is helpful in this regard. Also, recessed windows that are used for display can do more than create interesting design. They can also provide a structural overhang for sun control and cut down on heat loss and gain.

Space Allocation   The key to using space allocation to conserve energy is to realize that different spaces require more or less heating or cooling. For example, many of the non-selling space needs such as storage, handling, receiving, and restrooms do not require as much heating or cooling as do selling areas. Therefore, if the retailer used these areas as buffer zones around the perimeter of the store, energy could be saved.

Lighting   Retailers use a lot of lighting, and thus the opportunity for energy conservation in this area is great. One of the major cost reduction areas has been store parking lots. Even the small, single-unit retailer can decrease energy costs in parking lot lighting. However, the savings for a shopping center or large department store can be even more significant. Consider the following examples.

- Clearwater Mall (Clearwater, Florida). In this mall the parking lot lights were changed from mercury vapor to high-pressure sodium lamps. Since the change was made, the cost of parking lot lighting has decreased approximately 75 percent.

• Dayton-Hudson's Westland Center (Michigan). The lights in parking areas have been changed from mercury vapor to metal halide lamps. This change increased illumination 1.5 times without increasing electrical consumption.

Recently, some large shopping malls have gone to a high-rise, clustered lighting strategy. Clusters of ten luminares are placed on tall poles often approaching 120 feet. They have been proven more efficient than shorter poles with fewer luminares. One excellent example of high-rise cluster lighting efficiency is shown by comparing two shopping centers in the Dallas area that have roughly the same parking lot size. Six Flags Mall used ninety 60-foot poles and Red Bird used twelve 120-foot poles, called supermasts, with clustered luminares. Red Bird's exterior lighting costs were 50 percent less. Exterior maintenance costs dropped as well, because the supermasts have easy-to-service, self-lowering luminares, which eliminate costs of $20–$40 per hour to maintenance people who would have to go up in buckets to service the lights.

In reducing lighting costs within the store, the key is to realize that different areas of the store require different types and degrees of lighting. For example, for office and clerical tasks, fifty-footcandle lighting with low glare is appropriate, whereas for corridor, washrooms, and lobbies, only five- to ten-footcandle lighting is necessary. Similarly, different types of merchandise require different types and degrees of lighting (as we discussed under lighting fixtures and equipment).

Chain Store Age Executive reports in its August 1979 section on support systems that there is a trend toward more energy efficiency concerning store lighting:

> The push toward reduced general illumination is demonstrated by P. A. Bergner, a Peoria, Ill., based department store chain, which has halved its general lighting levels, from 80 footcandles to 40 footcandles, by gradually cutting out incandescents.
>
> From a design standpoint, less general illumination enables a store to accent merchandise effectively without squandering light, according to Arthur Everhart, Bergner's VP-Store Planning.[13]

A general rule of retailing is that the level of lighting is directly related to the quality of the merchandise and how much attention the retailer wishes to draw to it.

Electrical and Power Controls   During the 1970s, a wealth of computer technology was applied to the development of energy control systems. Computerized systems constantly monitor indoor and outdoor temperature and make adjustments in the heating and cooling levels used in the building. They can also be used to turn on, turn off, or dim lighting automatically according to conditions within the store; and they can do many other tasks.

13. "New Systems Brighten Interior Lighting Picture," © *Chain Store Age Executive* 55(August 1979): 137. Lebhar-Friedman, Inc., 425 Park Ave. N.Y., NY 10022. Reprinted by permission.

There are two main types of energy management systems. The **central processor system** will control power usage for several locations from one central computerized unit. It is often used by retailers that have several branch stores within one general area. The **stand-alone system** is self-contained and monitors and controls power usage at a single location. These systems have been shown to cut energy consumption by as much as 30 percent. For example, a system that controls air conditioning can allow the retailer to cool the building with natural outside air when the outside temperature is below 66°. At temperatures between 66° and 73°, the outside air continues to be used, because it takes less energy to cool air that is 73° or below, than to recirculate and cool the 74° air inside the building.[14] The same concept is used for heating the building; and some computerized systems can actually recirculate air through lighting systems, which partially heat it before it reaches the heating unit, thus cutting the amount of energy required to raise the air temperature for recirculation.

Other Possibilities   Several other energy cost-cutting programs are used by retailers throughout the country. Bullock's of northern California has put a fabric roof on its 148,000-square-foot San Jose store, permitting natural sunlight to light the store's interior. With the material's 250-footcandle transmission capability, the store is expected to save $24,000 or 480 kilowatt hours over the amount spent on lighting with a conventional roof.

Solar power is another possibility for helping to cut down on conventional energy consumption. Used mostly in the Sunbelt, it has been mainly experimental so far, but with more technological advances, solar energy may be a valuable asset to the cost-conscious retailer. Even in areas outside the Sunbelt, the use of solar energy is being tried. An example is the Montgomery Ward catalog distribution center in Sharonville, Ohio, which opened in 1980. Among its new features are solar energy panels that are expected to provide up to 75 percent of its salesroom and office heat.[15]

SUMMARY

In this chapter we dealt with the building and fixture decisions the retailer faces. Since the building can be a demand stimulator, it is more than merely a place to transact business. It is a vehicle for bringing the customer and retailer closer together.

Whenever the retailer must decide how to allocate funds for building and fixtures, it must perform a balancing act with such factors as fixed assets versus current assets, store space versus parking space, selling space versus nonselling space, and store space versus fixtures. The retailer should try to allocate more funds to the current assets (cash, inventory, and accounts receivables) than to fixed assets (building, land, fixtures, and equipment) because its business is selling goods. However, it needs enough fixed assets to ensure efficiency. This amount varies considerably among retailers.

14. "Energy," *Buildings* (November 1979): 84.
15. *Chain Store Age Executive* 56(March 1980): 13.

The retailer should make adequate parking facilities available for its customers. Since nonselling space does not directly create or stimulate sales, it needs to be allocated wisely. The retailer needs to determine how much space is needed to accomplish the nonselling tasks efficiently and allocate only that amount of space to them. There should be enough fixtures to efficiently display the merchandise, but not so many that the store becomes crowded.

A poor image can damage the retailer. Besides the building's image, the retailer must also consider size, location, merchandise, the amount of capital available, the building's age, and whether to lease or buy it.

The store layout is the arrangement of selling and nonselling departments and their merchandise, fixtures, and equipment. Selling space layout was discussed in terms of traffic patterns, shoplifting prevention, and atmosphere. The main determinants of the selling space atmosphere are the type and density of employees, merchandise, fixtures, sound, and odor, which all combine with the visual factors to create the store's atmosphere and image.

There are two main methods of laying out the store's interior. The grid layout—often used by grocers, drugstores, variety stores, hardware stores, and discount department stores—is characterized by counters and fixtures at right angles, forming rows. The free-flow layout allows the fixtures and merchandise to be artistically grouped, creating an unstructured traffic pattern. It is successful in department stores, apparel stores, and gift stores. Two subtypes of layout are the standard layout and the boutique layout.

Selling space productivity is one means of achieving high performance results. Four output measures were defined: net sales, gross profit, contribution profit, and operating profit. Using those measures, we identified four productivity measures: sales per square foot of selling space, gross profit per square foot of selling space, contribution profit per square foot of selling space, and operating profit per square foot of selling space. These ratios help the retailer make space allocation and reallocation decisions.

The nonselling space discussion highlighted the arrangement of office space and equipment, merchandise receiving and handling space and equipment, storage space and equipment, and customer service space and equipment.

A final section was about energy management and its effect on the building decision, an increasingly important topic. Energy was discussed in relation to the building's size, insulation, entrance and window design, space allocation, lighting, and electrical controls and power.

QUESTIONS

1. How does store layout influence shoplifting?

2. What factors influence store atmosphere?

3. How is the building and fixture decision in retailing an exercise in capital allocation?

4. What is "traffic" and how is it important in the store layout decision?

5. How should a retail manager evaluate selling space productivity?

6. How would building and fixture decisions be different for nonstore retailers than for conventional retailers?

7. How do high inflation rates affect the decision to lease or own a building?

8. Discuss the interrelationships among the retailer's building, image, and atmosphere.

9. How are building decisions related to merchandise thefts?

PROBLEMS AND EXERCISES

1. Visit several different menswear or womenswear stores and evaluate their atmosphere in terms of the factors identified in this chapter.

2. Evaluate the space productivity of the following four departments in a department store.

	A	B	C	D
Sales	$394,000	$611,000	$304,000	$791,000
Square feet	5100	7200	6000	9400
Gross margin	31%	29%	42%	34%
Advertising	$21,000	$54,000	$11,000	$24,000
Wages	$30,000	$50,000	$18,000	$81,000

3. Interview a manager of a large shopping mall (preferably a regional mall) about the rents charged various retailers in the mall. What services are included in the rent? Why do some locations in the mall demand a higher rent per square foot?

4. Visit several gift and card shops in your community and compare their selling space layouts. Attempt to take the best features from each and design a layout for a new gift and card shop.

5. Fred's IGA Supermarket is considering allocating 800 additional square feet to frozen foods, taking the space from dry groceries. These are the changes Fred expects to occur after this change:

	Dry Groceries		Frozen Foods	
	Before	After	Before	After
Square feet	7,000	6,200	1,200	2,000
Sales	$1,210,000	$1,108,000	$250,000	$360,000
Gross profit	278,300	265,000	77,580	100,400
Contribution profit	208,300	199,700	46,548	58,232

Should Fred allocate more space to frozen foods? What other factors should be considered?

SUGGESTED READINGS

"Designing for More Creative Use of Space." *Chain Store Age Executive* 46(November 1970): 28–29.

"Fewer Frills, Less Space to Reduce Costs." *Chain Store Age Executive* 56(December 1980): 45–58.

Guffery, Hugh J., Jr., James R. Harris, and J. Ford Laumer, Jr. "Shopper Attitudes Toward Shoplifting and Shoplifting Preventive Devices." *Journal of Retailing* 55(Fall 1979): 75–89.

"How Major Departments Pull Traffic Through the Store." *Progressive Grocer* 55(January 1976): 72.

Markin, Rom J., Charles M. Lillis, and Chem L. Narayana. "Social-Psychological Significance of Store Space." *Journal of Retailing* 52(Spring 1976): 43–54, 94, 95.

"Store Design from the Operations Viewpoint." *Stores* 51(May 1969): 50–51.

"Where Store Designers Can Help in Cutting Energy Costs." *Stores* 59(January 1977): 36.

16

Overview *In this chapter, we will examine the retailer's need to make price decisions. Both demand- and supply-oriented pricing concepts are discussed. In conjunction, we will also discuss planning markups and the management of markdowns.*

Price Planning and Management

PERHAPS the most frequent decision that confronts the typical retailer is merchandise pricing. The decision is often made several times for each item or group purchased by the retailer, since the initial price may have been too high, necessitating markdown in order to move the goods. In addition, the price decision helps to determine the total revenues the retailer will generate. And, of course, the total revenues must be large enough to cover the cost of the merchandise, operating expenses, and, one hopes a fair profit.

INTERACTIVE PRICE DECISIONS

Pricing decisions should be interactive. Specifically, the decision to price an item at a certain level should interact with the retailer's decisions on lines of merchandise carried, location, promotion, credit, customer services, and the store image the retailer wishes to convey.

Merchandise

You should not set prices without carefully analyzing the attributes of the merchandise being priced. Does your merchandise have attributes that differentiate it from similar merchandise? What is the value of these attributes to the consumer? Consider, for example, the menswear retailer who has purchased 100 men's suits for the fall selling season. What are the attributes of these suits (sizes, colors, type of fabric, cut or style, brand label, quality of workmanship, quality of fabric)? How does the consumer value these attributes? Is a Hickie Freeman label more valuable than a Crickett label or a Johnny Carson label? Is good workmanship worth more? Are better quality fabrics worth more? The answers to all these questions are not obvious; they depend on the market the retailer is serving. In Tucson, Arizona, 100 percent wool fabrics would have little value to the typical menswear customer; in Boston they would. In Grosse Pointe, Michigan, the value of a Hickie Freeman label would be high, but in poorer sections of Detroit the value would be zero.

Location

The location of the retail store will have a significant effect on prices that can be charged. The closer the store is to competitors with identical or similar merchandise, the less pricing flexibility it will have. The distance between the store and the customer is also important. Generally, if the retailer wants to attract customers from a greater distance, it must lower the prices it establishes on its merchandise lines. This is because of increasing travel costs consumers incur when they are located farther from the store. These high travel costs cut into the amount the customer is able or willing to pay for the merchandise, thus causing the retailer to lower prices to attract those customers.

Promotion

In the next two chapters we will illustrate how promotion can be a significant demand generator. Here we will show how pricing can generate demand.

However, pricing and promotion decisions are not independent.[1] If the retailer promotes heavily and is also very price competitive, it may get a cumulative increase in demand greater than the high promotion and lower price strategies would produce independently. Imagine, for example, the retailer establishing low prices but not promoting them in the marketplace. Or, imagine heavy promotion but no cut in prices. Obviously each will generate demand, but the interactive and cumulative effect of both would be much greater.

Credit

For a given price level on merchandise, the retailer selling on credit will often be able to generate greater demand than the retailer not selling on credit. Conversely, the retailer selling merchandise on credit may be able to charge a slightly higher price than the retailer not selling on credit and still generate the same demand as the noncredit retailer. Credit-granting retailers often charge higher prices, as shown by the recent move of some retailers to offer special discounts for cash-bearing customers.

Customer Services   Retailers that offer many customer services (delivery, gift wrapping, sales assistance) tend to have high prices. A decision to offer many customer services will automatically increase operating expenses and thus prompt management to establish higher retail prices. Consequently, customer service decisions interact heavily with pricing decisions.

1. Joseph N. Fry and Gordon H. McDougall, "Consumer Appraisal of Retail Price Advertisements," *Journal of Marketing* 38(July 1974): 64–67.

Pricing must be consistent with store image: while K-mart can discount books, a department store with a different strategy might not. (Photo courtesy of K-mart Corporation.)

Store Image   One of the most frequent cues the customer receives from a store is its prices. Prices aid the customer (either consciously or unconsciously) in developing an image of the store. If an exclusive, high fashion women's apparel store started to discount the merchandise heavily, it simply would not be the same store in the eyes of the customer. The merchandise, store decor, personnel may remain unchanged, but the change in price strategy will significantly alter the overall store image. Thus, price policies and strategies interact with store image policies and strategies.

DEMAND-ORIENTED PRICING

When establishing prices, retail decision makers should be demand oriented. They should conscientiously take into account customers and their wants, needs, preferences, and ability to purchase the merchandise.

A frame of reference for the demand-oriented retailer is the three-dimensional demand model in Exhibit 6.8. That model suggested that the retailer pay particular attention to population density, consumer travel costs, and the maximum demand price.

Population Density   Since retailers attract patrons from a spatial area, they should be concerned with the number of potential patrons in that area. In high-population areas, the retailer will not have to draw customers from as great a distance in order to generate a given level of total revenue. Thus, there will be less need to lower prices to attract customers from greater distances. Of course, such a strategy may still be profitable.

Assume that you are a retailer operating in a city with a population density of 3,000 households per square mile and you are currently attracting patrons from a two-mile radius of your store. The area within your trade area would be equal to πr^2 (the formula for the area of a circle) or (22/7)4, which equals 12.57 square miles. Therefore, the potential number of households in your trade area is 12.57 × 3,000 or 37,710. Assume now that you could lower prices sufficiently to attract households from a 2.5-mile radius; then your trade area would be 19.64 square miles, and the number of potential households in the trade area would be 58,920. See if you can show how these numbers were obtained. Notice that by increasing the radius by half a mile, the number of potential households in the trade area rose by over 50 percent.

Consumer Travel Costs   The three-dimensional demand model tells us that consumer travel costs are important determinants of shopping at retail stores. In terms of retail shopping behavior, consumer travel costs consist of the actual dollar costs of transporting oneself to the store and back, the time involved, which is related to opportunity costs (what else could you be doing with your time and what would be the value you would attach to those alternative activities?), and the psychic costs of traveling to the store and back. The retailer needs to know that lower prices can be used to offset the negative effect of all three of these travel costs on quantity demanded. Let us explore the price implication of each type of travel costs.

Actual Dollar Transport Cost   Consumers demand goods that offer certain form utility, which the consumer can possess at a certain location (i.e., that offer possession and place utility). To obtain the possession utility, the customer needs to travel to the store. Usually, to obtain the place utility, the consumer needs to transport the good back home (he or she will usually not wish to consume the good at the store). Now let us assume that the customer would be willing to pay $15 for the item in order to obtain the total package of form, place, and possession utility. If the customer is five miles from the store (ten miles round-trip) and the cost per mile of travel is $0.20 then the actual travel cost would be $2.00. Thus, if the retailer had a price on the item above $13, this consumer would not purchase the item.

Opportunity Transport Cost   Travel takes time, and time is money to an increasing number of households in the United States. As the number of two-income households increases, time will become even more scarce for many households. If the household spends time on traveling to shop, it will not be able to engage in other leisure-time activities. Thus, households attach an opportunity cost to their time. Consider once again the consumer who is willing to pay $15 for an item. The round-trip distance to the store is ten miles and it takes an hour to visit the store and purchase the item. Actual travel costs are $0.20 per mile and the opportunity cost per hour is $2.75. In this case, the highest price the customer would pay would be $10.25.

Psychic Travel Costs   Traveling may also involve psychic costs or benefits. On the cost side of the equation, travel may be punishing. Consider, for example, travel to a store in a metropolitan area where the traffic arteries or public transportation is very congested and indeed at some points quite dangerous. On the other hand, the travel may represent net psychic benefits. Consider, for example, the first warm day after a dreadfully cold winter on which the consumer decides that an afternoon drive to a regional shopping mall, on a quiet back country road, would actually be enjoyable. These psychic travel costs (or benefits) are difficult to measure, but they will influence how much the consumer would be willing to pay to acquire an item.

Pricing Implications   All of these components of consumer travel costs have implications for retail price policies. Consider the following suggestions, which are derived from the preceding discussion:

1. Offering customers "shop and park" or "shop and ride" coupons effectively lowers the price to consumers and can be a strong force attracting customers to the store.
2. One might offer to pay the customer's gasoline cost to the store and back home if he or she comes from a distant area to shop at the store. An appliance and stereo retailer in Madison, Wisconsin, offers customers who present a driver's license from Milwaukee, $5 for gasoline expenses.

3. Offer special discounts for multiple-item purchases, since this encourages the customer to economize on time—a scarce resource.
4. Try to design the store so that there is a net psychic benefit from visiting it. In essence this is the logic behind the theatrical atmosphere of department stores such as Nieman Marcus. Customers receive a net psychic benefit from visiting Nieman Marcus, and thus they are willing to pay more for an item.

A Note on Nonstore Retailing One of the most significant advantages of nonstore retailing from the customer's perspective is the absence of travel costs. Thus, nonstore retailers should be able to demand a higher price for merchandise similar to that offered by traditional retailers. This assumes that, on all other dimensions, the customer would view the nonstore and traditional retailer the same. Since nonstore retailers tend to have lower operating costs than traditional retailers and since the customer would be willing to pay them a higher price per unit, nonstore retailers have the potential of becoming a major competitive threat in the near future.

Maximum Demand Price The **maximum demand price** is the highest price (inclusive of all transportation costs) that a consumer would be willing to pay for one unit of the product. What factors tend to make the consumer willing to pay a higher maximum demand price for an item? There are two basic determinants. The first is the utility or satisfaction the customer expects to get from the product. This boils down to the attributes of the product and the value the consumer attaches to each attribute. The second is the consumer's income or budget. How much money at this time does the consumer have to allocate to the purchase of goods and services?

Surprisingly, the retailer can have an influence over each of the preceding determinants. The crucial concern on product attributes is what the customer expects, and consumers' expectations are heavily influenced by the information they collect. The retailer's promotion program is an important source of the information. Regarding the consumer's budget, the retailer can influence it by providing credit—buy now, pay later!

Demand Elasticity A concept that aids retail decision makers in being demand oriented is demand elasticity. **Demand elasticity** is product-specific and refers to the change in quantity demanded that is due to a change in a demand determinant. Formally it is defined as follows:

$$E = \left| \frac{\Delta Q}{\Delta D} \right|$$

where:

E = demand elasticity
ΔQ = percentage change in quantity demanded
ΔD = percentage change in demand determinant

There are three basic categories of demand determinants: environmental, household, and managerial.

Environmental Demand Determinants Demand determinants that are beyond the control of the individual household and the individual retailer are called environmental. Examples include traffic congestion, weather patterns, and population density. Environmental demand determinants can have either a positive or a negative effect on demand, depending on the product type and the direction of change in the demand determinant. Consider, for example, weather patterns and the demand for snow tires, swimsuits, or overcoats. In fact, weather can have a major effect on the demand for almost all goods, because bad weather keeps people indoors and makes shopping trips less likely. Many retailers subscribe to weather service forecasts to help them plan for downturns or upturns in demand.

Household Demand Determinants   Determinants that characterize the household can affect demand. Typical household characteristics are size, age of members, and income. Try to consider what the change in demand for a record store might be if more households with teenage children moved into the trade area.

Managerial Demand Determinants   Any variable that is under the control of the retailer and can influence demand is a managerial demand determinant. Some of the more common are promotion, credit, customer services, and price. By treating price as a demand determinant, we come to the concept of demand elasticity of price. This is the percentage change in quantity demanded divided by the percentage change in price. Formally, it can be defined as follows:

$$E_p = \left| \frac{\Delta Q}{\Delta P} \right|$$

where:

E_p = demand elasticity of price
ΔQ = percentage change in quantity demanded
ΔP = percentage change in price

If the demand elasticity of price coefficient takes on a value less than 1.0, then demand is **price inelastic.** A 1 percent change in price results in a less than 1 percent change in quantity demanded. If demand is price inelastic, a cut in price will yield a drop in total revenues, and a rise in price will yield an increase in total revenue. On the other hand, if the coefficient is greater than 1.0, demand is **price elastic.** A 1 percent change in price results in a more than proportionate change in quantity demanded. Thus, a drop in price will raise total revenues and a rise in price will lower total revenues. Notice that this is merely a review of basic microeconomic price theory.

Let us develop an example of demand elasticity of price. Assume that a retailer has an item priced at $10 and sells 100 units a month; this would result in sales of $1,000 ($10 × 100). If demand elasticity of price is 1.5 and if price is cut by 10 percent, then what will happen to total sales? Using the equation on page 494, we could derive the percentage of change in quantity demanded: 15 percent. As a result, the quantity demanded would rise from 100 to 115 and price would fall from $10 to $9. The new sales volume would be $1,035 ($9 × 115), which is an increase from the previous month's sales volume of $1,000.

SUPPLY-ORIENTED PRICING

Retail decison makers should study and analyze their supply or cost curves when establishing and changing prices. Typical cost curves for a retail store were presented in Chapter 6; you might wish to take a moment to review them. For our purposes we can view costs in retailing as fixed and variable.

Cost Curves

Fixed costs are those which do not change in the short run as a result of an increase in volume. Most retailers have relatively high fixed costs, which include telephone, heat, light, cooling, insurance, taxes, rent, and wages for most types of employees. The presence of high fixed costs in retailing suggests that retailers have high break-even points. The logic of this can be made clearer if you consider that to open a store each morning one needs to have a staff of employees on hand, the lights and heating or cooling operating, and so on. All of these costs must be incurred regardless of whether any customers enter the front door.

Variable costs are those which change in proportion with volume. The major variable cost in retailing is that of the merchandise sold. Another might be some portion of wages, since retail salesclerks are often paid on commission.

Profit

In a sense, desired profit represents a cost. The profit the retailer desires can be viewed as a cost on the use of its capital and payment for taking risks. In other words, profit can be thought of as an opportunity cost. If a retailer took its capital and invested it in a relatively safe fashion (U.S. Treasury securities) how high a return could it obtain? Desired profit should equal this return plus a premium for taking risks.

Regardless of the specifics, the basic fact remains that the retailer cannot use its capital or that provided by stockholders or creditors without programming into its supply function a fair return on that capital. In short, profit is a necessary cost of doing business.

Markup Equation Using supply-oriented pricing, the retailer should begin with the following basic markup equation.

$$R = C + M$$

where:

C = dollar cost of merchandise per unit
M = dollar markup per unit
R = selling price per unit

In other words, if the retailer has a cost per unit of $10 and a dollar markup of $5, then the price per unit is $15.

Markup Methods   In the retail trades, markup is typically not discussed in terms of dollars but in terms of percentage. Two methods exist for computing markup percentages, and they differ in terms of the base on which the markup is computed. They are the cost-based markup method and the retail-based markup method.

Cost-Based Markup   This cost-based method uses the following formula:

% markup based on cost = $(R - C)/C$

Since price (R) is always planned to be higher than cost (C), the percentage of markup on cost will always be greater than the percentage of markup on retail. Using the previous example with R = $15 and C = $10, the markup would be 50 percent.

Retail-Based Markup   The formula for percentage of markup on retail is:

% markup based on retail = $(R - C)/R$

If R = $15 and C = $10, the markup on retail would be 33.3 percent. This helps to confirm our point that markup on retail is always less than markup on cost. In actual practice, most retailers use a retail-based markup. Occasionally, however, one will find a retailer computing markup percentages based on cost.

Relating Retail- and Cost-Based Markups   Both methods of computing markup percentages use two pieces of information: price per unit (R) and cost per unit (C). Therefore, the two methods must be related. The formula for relating them is:

$$\text{\% markup on retail} = \left(\frac{R - C}{C}\right) \times \left(\frac{1}{1 + \dfrac{R - C}{C}}\right)$$

If you have a 50 percent markup on cost, the preceding formula would yield the following percentage of markup on retail:

$$(0.50)\left(\frac{1}{1 + 0.5}\right) = 0.333 \text{ or } 33.3\%$$

Similarly the formula for relating percent markup on cost to percent markup on retail is as follows:

$$\text{\% markup on cost} = \left(\frac{R - C}{R}\right) \times \left(\frac{1}{1 - \dfrac{R - C}{R}}\right)$$

If you have a markup on retail of 33.3 percent, the preceding formula would yield this markup on cost:

$$(0.333) \left(\frac{1}{1 - 0.333} \right) = 0.50 \text{ or } 50\%$$

In Exhibit 16.1, markup on retail is converted to equivalent markup on cost. Note that as the markup on retail gets closer to 100 percent markup on cost grows rapidly.

EXHIBIT 16.1
Markup on Retail Converted to Markup on Cost

MARKUP ON RETAIL (%)	EQUIVALENT MARKUP ON COST (%)
10	11.1
20	25.0
30	42.9
40	66.7
50	100.0
60	150.0
70	233.3
80	400.0
90	900.0
95	1900.0

Using Markup Formulas   Although quite simple in concept, the basic markup formulas will enable you to determine more than the percentage of markup on a particular item. Let us work with the markup on retail formula to illustrate how an interesting and frequently occuring question might be answered. If I know that a particular type of item could be sold for $8 per unit and that I need a 30 percent markup on retail to meet my profit objective, then how much would I be willing to pay for the item? Using our equation for markup on retail, we have:

$$\% \text{ markup on retail} = \frac{R - C}{R}$$

$$0.30 = \frac{8 - C}{8}$$

$$C = \$5.60$$

Therefore, you should be willing to pay $5.60. If the item cannot be found at $5.60 or less, it is probably not worth stocking.

Initial Versus Maintained Markup   Up until this point we have assumed that the retail price per unit is the price we initially established as well as the price at which the item was sold. The **initial** or **planned markup** was implicitly assumed to be equal to the **maintained** or **achieved markup.**

To assist in illustrating this point, let us formally distinguish between the initial and maintained markup, which we can do by using the equations on top of page 498.

$$\text{Initial markup} = \frac{\text{Asking price} - \text{Cost}}{\text{Asking price}}$$

$$\text{Maintained markup} = \frac{\text{Actual price} - \text{Cost}}{\text{Actual price}}$$

Assuming that the actual price is less than the asking price, then the maintained markup will be less than the initial markup.

Maintained markups are often less than the initial markup for three reasons. First is the need to reconcile supply and demand. Most markup formulas are supply- and cost-oriented and pay little, if any, attention to demand factors. When the price established by markup formulas is higher than consumers are willing to pay for the item, then markdowns on the merchandise must be offered the customer. Second are stock shortages. Shortages occur from thefts by employees or customers, but in either case the net result is a zero dollar actual price for the merchandise. Third are employee and customer discounts. Employees may be given discount privileges after they have worked for the retailer a stipulated period of time. Also, certain customer groups (for example senior citizens) may be given special discount privileges. Exhibit 16.2 provides some examples of typical markdowns and stock shortages for selected merchandise lines in department stores.

PLANNING INITIAL MARKUPS

A principle of good retail price management is that markups should be planned. Initial markup planning will increase the retailer's ability to cover its expenses while making a reasonable profit. The planning of initial markups should be keyed to a storewide markup or pricing policy.

Storewide Price Policy   Three storewide price policy alternatives are available to the retailer: (1) pricing at the market, (2) pricing above the market, and (3) pricing below the market.

Pricing at Market   Retailers who decide to price at the market are pursuing an average markup policy. These retailers are pricing at the prevailing market prices for particular merchandise lines in particular lines of trade. In Exhibit 16.3 some typical markups are presented for various merchandise lines in department stores. Most retailers that price at the market have no unique competitive edge and thus often have little choice but to price at the market level.

Pricing Above Market   An above-market pricing strategy is a high markup strategy. To use this strategy successfully, retailers need a high level of nonprice competitive differentiation.[2]

2. William R. Davidson and Alton F. Doody, *Retailing Management*, 3rd ed. (New York: Ronald Press, 1966), p. 461.

EXHIBIT 16.2
Typical Markdowns and Stock Shortages for Department Stores with Sales over $1 Million

MERCHANDISE LINE	MARKDOWNS (INCLUDING EMPLOYEE DISCOUNTS)	STOCK SHORTAGES
Men's footwear	9.7%	1.3%
Women's and misses' suits	28.9	5.9
Bridal and formal	14.9	2.5
Women's dresses	20.9	2.1
Maternity clothing	13.8	2.0
Fine jewelry and watches	5.6	2.8
Men's furnishings	8.6	1.6
Televisions	5.9	1.2
Toys	8.6	2.5
Luggage	6.2	1.7
Sporting goods	13.7	5.0
Glassware	8.0	4.4
Houseware	7.6	1.8
Towels	6.6	1.0

Source: *Merchandising and Operating Results of 1978* (New York: Financial Executives Division, National Retail Merchants Association, 1979), pp. 2–26.

This differentiation can be evidenced by any or all of the following factors: location advantage, high standards of personal selling service, strong emphasis on broad assortments, unusually attractive store atmosphere, reputation for fashion leadership, exclusiveness of merchandise lines, special promotional at-

EXHIBIT 16.3
Typical Initial Markups for Department Stores with Sales over $1 Million

MERCHANDISE LINE	MARKUP
Men's footwear	48.7%
Women's and misses' suits	49.7
Bridal and formal	49.0
Women's dresses	49.5
Maternity clothing	50.8
Fine jewelry and watches	48.4
Men's furnishings	49.4
Televisions	25.2
Toys	40.3
Luggage	48.3
Sporting goods	42.0
Glassware	50.2
Houseware	42.5
Towels	47.8

Source: *Merchandising and Operating Results of 1978* (New York: Financial Executives Division, National Retail Merchants Association, 1979), pp. 2–28.

tractions such as premiums or trading stamps, service at hours when most other stores are closed, and special customer services such as liberal credit, free alterations, and home decoration advice.[3]

Pricing Below Market A below-market pricing strategy is a low-markup approach to price setting.[4] Successful use of this strategy is contingent on low operating costs and rapid inventory turnover. Also, customer services and other expense-creating niceties must be kept to a minimum. When utilizing the below-market strategy, price will often become the most distinctive attribute of the store.

Recently a host of retailers have focused on selling top-of-the-line womenswear substantially below regular prices. They have been able to do this by using low markups and also by buying merchandise at extremely attractive prices. The case study in Exhibit 16.4 illustrates this.

EXHIBIT 16.4
Off-Price Buying

New York City is a haven for experts in retail and wholesale buying. One such expert is Ruth Britten, a principal in Arthur B. Britten Associates Ltd. Britten's specialty is in acquiring top-of-the-line womenswear for clients during the prime selling season for discounts of from 30 percent to 70 percent. In addition, she has had little problem in acquiring merchandise from some of the best-known names on Seventh Avenue.

Britten's clients pay 5 percent of the cost of merchandise purchased as a fee for the buying service. Since labels are left on all garments, the clients also agree not to use the brand or designer names in their advertising. With the increase in off-price branded merchandise gaining momentum in apparel retailing, Arthur B. Britten Associates Ltd. can expect a bright future.

Source: Based on data from "Ruth Britten: Expert in Off-Price Buying," *Chain Store Age—General Merchandise Edition* 56(January 1980): 69.

Initial Markup Equation No longer can retailers casually arrive at a decision to mark up merchandise by a given percentage. Markup percentages of high performance retailers are not derived out of thin air or based on tradition; they are planned. The planning of initial markups can be facilitated by use of the following equation:

$$\frac{\text{Initial markup}}{\text{\% on retail}} = \frac{\begin{array}{c}\text{Operating expenses} + \text{Net profit} + \text{Alteration costs} \\ - \text{Cash discounts} + \text{Markdowns} + \text{Stock shortages} \\ + \text{Employee and customer discounts}\end{array}}{\begin{array}{c}\text{Net sales} + \text{Markdowns} + \text{Stock shortages} + \text{Employee} \\ \text{and customer discounts}\end{array}}$$

We can simplify this equation if we know that markdowns, stock shortages, and employee and customer discounts are all reductions from initial asking

---

3. Davidson and Doody, *Retailing Management*, p. 461.
4. Bruce J. Walker, "Decision Sequence for Retail Pricing," *Retail Control* (June–July 1978): 8.

prices, and further that the sum of operating expenses and net profit are equal to gross profit. Restating the equation in simpler terms yields:

$$\text{Initial markup \% on retail} = \frac{\text{Gross profit} + \text{Alteration costs} - \text{Cash discounts} + \text{Reductions}}{\text{Net sales} + \text{Reductions}}$$

Regardless of which equation is used, in order to plan the initial markup, the retail executive must plan the following items: net sales, operating expenses, net profit, alteration costs, cash discounts from suppliers, markdowns, stock shortages, and employee and customer discounts.

At this point, a numerical example might be helpful. Assume that a retailer plans to achieve net sales of $1 million and expects operating expenses to be $270,000. The net profit goal is $60,000. Planned reductions include $80,000 for markdowns, $20,000 for merchandise shortages, and $10,000 for employee and customer discounts. Alteration costs were expected to be $20,000, and cash discounts from suppliers were expected to be $10,000. What is the initial markup percentage that should be planned? What is the cost of merchandise to be sold?

The initial markup percentage can be obtained by using the preceding equation:

$$\text{Initial markup \% on retail} = \frac{\$27,000 + \$60,000 + \$20,000 - \$10,000 + \$80,000 + \$20,000 + \$10,000}{\$1,000,000 + \$80,000 + \$20,000 + \$10,000}$$
$$= 40.54\%$$

The second question (What is the cost of merchandise sold?) can also be answered. We know that the gross profit is the operating expenses plus net profit ($330,000). This gross profit is equivalent to net sales less cost of merchandise sold, where cost of merchandise sold includes alteration costs and where cash discounts are subtracted. Thus, in the problem at hand, we know that $1 million less cost of merchandise sold (including alteration costs and subtracting cash discounts) is equal to $670,000. Since the alteration costs are planned at $20,000 and cash discounts at $10,000, the cost of merchandise is equal to $660,000 (670,000 − 20,000 + 10,000).

We can verify our result by returning to the basic initial markup formula: asking price minus cost divided by asking price. The asking price is the planned net sales of $1 million plus planned reductions of $110,000 ($80,000 for markdowns, $20,000 for shorts, and $10,000 for employee and customer discounts). The cost is the cost of merchandise before the alteration costs and prior to cash discounts, or $660,000. Using the basic initial markup formula, we obtain ($1,110,000 − $660,000) ÷ $1,110,000, or 40.54 percent. This is the same result we achieved earlier.

The preceding computations resulted in a markup percentage on retail for merchandise lines storewide. Obviously, not all lines or items within lines should be priced by mechanically applying this markup percentage. Rather, you will want to price the mix of merchandise lines in such a fashion that a storewide markup percentage is obtained. To achieve this, some lines may be priced with considerably higher markups and others with substantially lower markups than the storewide average that was planned using the initial markup planning equation. It will be helpful to explore some of the common reasons for varying the markup percentage on different lines or items within lines.

Price Lining

One of the major reasons for deviating from the average storewide markup is that potential customers may fall into different purchasing power zones. For example, a customer for a men's suit might be willing and able to purchase one in a high ($250+), moderate ($100 to $249), or low (below $100) price zone. A **price zone** is, therefore, a range of prices for a particular merchandise line that appeal to customers in a certain demographic group. The demographic groups are most often socioeconomic. On the other hand, a **price line** is a specific price within a price zone at which a representative stock is carried.

Our menswear retailer might carry two lines of men's suits in the high price zone, one at $319 and another at $289; two lines in the moderate price zone, one at $219 and one at $159; and two lines in the low price zone, one at $99 and another at $79. With a little reflection, one can see that when the retail price has been established it will be difficult to ensure that the storewide average markup will occur in all situations. Take for example a desired storewide average markup of 50 percent and the $219 price line. The mathematics of this example would imply that the cost of the $219 suits should be $109.50. But, as you might expect, it will be next to impossible for buyers to buy all suits that could be priced at $219 for exactly $109.50. Some suits can be purchased for less than the $109.50 and others for somewhat more. Therefore you will want to establish a **cost range** for each retail price line. Thus, for the price line of $219 men's suits, the cost range might be from $100 to $120, which represents a markup of from 54.3 percent to 45.2 percent. It is, however, possible for the average markup to be much higher than planned. For example, if the buyer finds a super buy on men's suits (they could sell at $219 but cost $78), then the markup would be 64.4 percent.

Price lining as an element of price policy has much to offer. Perhaps foremost is the ease that it offers for setting prices on merchandise. The retailer needs to decide which price line purchased merchandise falls into; once this is done, the price has been established. At the same time, price lining offers advantages in inventory and promotion management. With price lining, fewer stocks can be carried, and therefore inventory turnover will be higher. Also, the consumer will learn more rapidly what the retailer has to offer, and therefore promotional dollars will be more effective. At the same time, the salesperson's job is made easier because price coordination of merchandise in different lines is facilitated. For example, the man purchasing a suit from the $219 price line can quickly be shown dress shirts in a moderate price range.

We have shown what price lining offers the retailer, but the consumer can also benefit. His or her decision-making process is simplified, because the number of alternative price lines to consider is minimized.

As you might expect, price lining is not without its drawbacks. It offers the buyer less flexibility, because price lining coupled with percentage markup targets implies that the buyer must buy in established cost zones. Also, in a market with rapidly rising or falling prices, the established price lines become quite unrealistic. If prices continue to escalate, it may become impossible to find a man's suit at $79 regardless of whether there exists a strong demand at the $79 price or not.

A third problem with price lining is that it may be difficult for the customer to trade up if the price jumps between price lines are sizable. In the example we gave earlier, the customer that is not satisfied with the quality of a $99 suit must take a $60 jump to get to the $159 price line. For many customers, this jump may be too large. The customer may leave in hope of finding a suit elsewhere that is better than the $99 suit, but does not cost $159. Sears, Roebuck has recognized the importance of establishing price lines that allow the customer to easily move up the spending scale and at the same time allow Sears to minimize its inventory investment.

> Where a leading department store will stock 250 to 300 china patterns, Sears . . . simply can't afford the duplication. A mere 25–30 designs—from traditional down to plastic at $10.99 a set—must do the job. But the limited selection is carefully planned on a system of price points or levels, that will cover the whole range and gently, but inexorably, encourage the customer to step up in the spending scale. . . . In the words of Sears' jargon, the customer is moved from "good" to "better" to "best."[5]

A fair amount of conventional wisdom has developed in retailing circles about price lining.[6] Without exception, retailers agree that price lines must be competitive with the offerings of other retailers. Next, most retailers would agree that the greatest unit volume for a merchandise category should be enjoyed at a middle price zone, and thus stocking requirements should be heaviest at the middle price zone. In fact, if the retailer discovers that the high price zone is selling the best, there is compelling evidence that an even higher price zone should be established. The third point of conventional wisdom is that the dollar jumps in price lines in the high price zones should be greater than those in the medium and lower price zones. Finally, it is generally suggested that price lines carried in related departments should be correlated, since this will allow customers to put together assortments within their purchasing range. In other words, a store carrying $219 suits should have $20 shirts and $10 ties; a store carrying $99 suits should have $10 shirts and $5 ties.

Leadership Pricing   Many retailers use a technique called **leadership pricing**, establishing a price on an item at a markup significantly lower than the demand warrants for that item. In short, retailers are establishing a price below the one that would allow

---

5. "Why Sears Stays the Number 1 Retailer," *Business Week*, January 20, 1968, p. 66.

6. For an excellent discussion of price lining and some conventional wisdom surrounding it see John W. Wingate, Elmer O. Schaller, and F. Leonard Miller, *Retail Merchandise Management* (Englewood Cliffs, N.J.: Prentice-Hall, 1972), pp. 96–111.

profits to be maximized on that item. There is compelling logic behind this technique. The retailer anticipates that the low price on the item will build store traffic and thus help to generate sales of related items. As a consequence, although the profits on the leadership-priced item may be low, the profits store-wide are expected to rise, because of the increased sales of related items.

There are several keys to the successful use of leadership pricing. First, there must exist the possibility for low-markup goods to attract customers who will make related purchases. This possibility does not exist in all retail settings. If a jewelry retailer promotes a line of diamonds at a 10 percent markup, it will probably sell a large quantity of diamonds; but it will not be very likely to sell other items to the bargain-hunting purchaser of diamonds. On the other hand, the supermarket pricing milk and eggs at low markups will likely sell other items, since many grocery purchases are made on impulse. There, the more traffic in the store the greater sales will be.

A second key to successful leadership pricing is the lead item's appeal to a large proportion of the potential clientele. It must be an item that most of the clientele are in the market for or will be in the market for shortly. A supermarket using pickled pigs' feet as a lead item would meet with dismal results since most people are not regularly in the market for pickled pigs' feet.

Third, the lead item must be visible enough to potential customers to appear as a bargain. Thus, the potential customers should have a general idea of the regular price of the item or else they will have little basis on which to judge if it is a bargain. Also, the lead item will need to be advertised so that potential customers will be aware of the low price. To be highly effective, leadership pricing cannot involve only instore promotion. Since the goal is to build store traffic, out-of-store promotion is necessary. That will typically consist of advertising in the mass media.

Finally, the potential savings must be sufficiently large to attract customers to the store. As we know, travel costs are a significant factor in determining if a consumer will visit a store. To increase the number of people willing to visit the store, prices need to be cut sufficiently to offset the travel costs that are restraining customers from visiting the store.

If the retailer follows the preceding suggestions, it is likely to use leadership pricing successfully. However, leadership pricing is not without its drawbacks. Of primary concern to the retail manager should be the effect of aggressive leadership pricing on channel relations. Manufacturers and, to a lesser extent, wholesalers will often put a lot of effort into developing brand or product quality image. They may invest millions of dollars in developing the brand image. If a retailer prices the product at rock bottom, the manufacturers' marketing efforts have been diluted. Manufacturers become especially concerned, because once their product is used as a lead item by a single retailer, the practice will spread within that city or trade area very rapidly, since competing retailers will desire to maintain their market share. The net result is that relations between manufacturers, wholesalers, and retailers become strained, and less channel cooperation is likely.

Another problem with leadership pricing is ethical and legal. Retailers will sometimes use it to bring customers into the store and then use salespeople to soft-pedal the lead item and try to switch the customer to a higher-priced item. This technique, also called "bait-and-switch" advertising, was discusssd in Chapter 8. This technique not only has serious legal ramifications but is also unethical. A second legal problem with leadership pricing is that it might violate certain state "below-cost selling" acts if the markups are too low. We also discussed this potential legal problem in Chapter 8.

Off-Even Pricing   A casual perusal of retail advertisements in newspapers will reveal that many retailers price items either slightly below an even dollar figure ($4.97 versus $5.00) or just below an even denomination ($495 versus $500). If you were to query retailers about the rationale behind these off-even prices they would suggest that they create significantly higher sales. Supposedly the consumer more readily perceives these off-even prices and also tends to associate the price with a substantially lower price. That is, the $495 seems more like $400 than like $500, and the $4.97 seems more like $4.00 than $5.00. Whether this is indeed true is debatable. In fact, the empirical research is inconclusive.[7] Nonetheless, the use of this pricing technique by retailers will result in markup percentage that may slightly deviate from those the store might otherwise use. For example, a furniture retailer might buy a sofa at $254 and might typically have a markup of 50 percent on such items—which would imply a price of $508. But if the retailer believes in off-even pricing, it might price the item at $497, which would yield a markup of 48.9 percent.

Markup Determinants   In planning initial markups, it is useful to know some of the determinants of the magnitude of markups. These are summarized below.

1. As goods are sold through more retail outlets, the markup percentage decreases. On the other hand, being sold through few retail outlets means a greater markup percentage.
2. The higher the handling and storage costs of the goods the higher the markup should be.
3. The higher the alteration and workroom costs attributable to the goods, the higher the markup should be.
4. The greater the risk of a price reduction due to the seasonality of the goods, the greater the magnitude of the markup percentage early in the season.
5. The lower the demand elasticity of price for the goods, the greater the markup percentage.

Although these determinants can be identified, there are others that are unique to each line of trade and are only learned by in-depth experience in the respective lines, such as how much to mark up produce in a supermarket at different seasons.

7. Zarrel V. Lambert, "Perceived Prices as Related to Odd and Even Price Endings," *Journal of Retailing* 51(Fall 1975): 13–21, 78.

MARKDOWN MANAGEMENT

During our discussion of markups we pointed out that the initial markup on an item is seldom equal to the maintained markup. This is due to three kinds of reductions: markdowns, shortages, and employee and customer discounts. Our discussion will focus primarily on markdowns since they explain most of the differences between initial and maintained markups.

For effective retail price management, markdowns should be planned. In principle, they need to be planned because pricing is not a science with high degrees of precision but an art form with considerable room for error. If the retailer knew everything it needed to know about demand and supply factors then it could use the science of economics to establish a price that would maximize profits and ensure the sale of all the merchandise. Unfortunately, it does not possess perfect information about supply and demand factors. As a result, the pricing decision is subject to considerable error, which makes it necessary to markdown merchandise. Three basic errors can occur: (1) buying errors, (2) pricing errors, and (3) promotion errors.

Buying Errors   Errors in buying occur on the supply side of the pricing question. They result as the retailer buys the wrong merchandise, or the right merchandise in too large a quantity. The merchandise purchased could have been in the wrong styles, sizes, colors, patterns, or price range. Too large a quantity could have been purchased because demand was overestimated or a recession was not

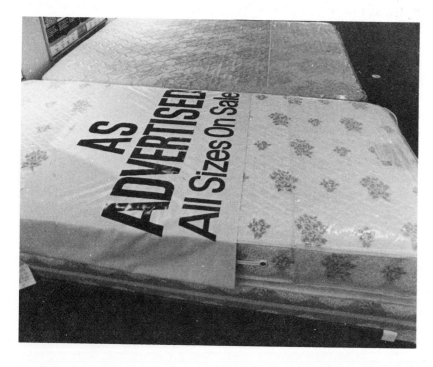

Markdowns can be used to improve stockturns. (Photo courtesy of Sears.)

foreseen. Whatever the cause of the buying error, the net result is a need to cut price to move the merchandise. Often price cuts are below the actual cost of the merchandise to the retailer.

Thus, buying errors can be quite costly. As a consequence, you might expect that the retail manager would wish to minimize buying errors. However, this is not the case. The retailer could minimize buying errors by being extremely conservative. It could buy only what it knew the customer wanted and what it could be certain of selling. Then buying errors would be minimized, but at the expense of lost profit opportunities on some riskier types of purchase decisions. Recall that when we reviewed the determinants of markups we mentioned that the riskier the potential price reduction the higher the markup percentage. This is simply another way of recognizing that taking a gamble on some purchases that represent buying errors can be profitable if initial markups are high.

Pricing Errors   Errors in pricing merchandise can be another cause of markdowns. They occur when the price of the item is too high to move at the speed and in the quantity desired. The goods may have been bought in the right styles, at the right time, and in the right quantities, but the price on the item may simply be too high. This would create purchase resistance on the part of the typical customer.

An overly high price is often relative to the pricing behavior of competitors. Perhaps in principle, the price would have been optimum, but if competitors price the same item substantially lower, then the original retailer's price becomes too high.

Promotion Errors   Finally, it is often the case that the right goods were purchased in the right quantities and were priced correctly but the merchandise fails to move as planned. In this situation, there is most often a promotion error. The consumer has not been properly informed or prompted to purchase the merchandise. The advertising, personal selling, sales promotion activities, or in-store displays were too weak or sporadic to elicit a strong response from potential customers.

Markdown Policy   Retailers will find it advantageous to develop a **markdown timing policy.** In almost all situations, retailers will find it necessary to take markdowns; but the crucial decisions become when and how quickly to take them. In principle, there are two extremes to a markdown timing policy—early and late.

Early Markdown Policy   Most retailers who concentrate on high inventory turnover pursue an early markdown policy. Markdowns taken early speed the movement of merchandise and also generally enable the retailer to take less of a markdown per unit to dispose of the goods. This will allow the dollars obtained from selling the merchandise to be used to help finance more salable goods. At the same time, the customer seems to benefit, since markdowns are offered quickly on goods that some consumers still think of as fashionable. Another advantage of the early markdown policy is that it allows the retailer to replenish lower-priced lines from the higher ones that have been marked down. For instance, many womenswear retailers will regularly take slow-moving dresses from higher-priced lines and move them down to the moderate- or lower-priced lines. In effect, this represents a markdown, even though it is not recognizable by the consumer.

Late Markdown Policy   Allowing goods to have a long trial period before a markdown is taken is called a late markdown policy. This policy avoids disrupting the sale of regular merchandise by too frequently marking goods down. As a consequence, customers will learn to look forward to a semiannual or annual clearance, in which all or most merchandise is marked down. Thus, the bargain hunters or low-end customers will be attracted only at infrequent intervals.

Markdown and GMROI   The profit effect of varying markdown policies on merchandise can be analyzed in relation to the gross margin return on inventory (GMROI) model that was introduced in Chapter 13. The GMROI model, as you might recall, suggests that inventory investments be gauged in terms of the multiplicative effect of gross margin percentage and inventory turnover. The important thing to recognize is that the quicker merchandise is marked down, the more rapidly inventory will turn over, but at the expense of lower gross margins. On the other hand, if markdowns are postponed then gross margins will remain high but inventory turnover will be low.

Let us assume that the retailer purchases $40,000 in merchandise and expects to be able to sell the merchandise in twelve weeks without using any markdowns, at a retail value of $50,000. The average investment in inventory annually is:

$$\text{Average inventory investment} = \left(\frac{\text{Beginning inventory} + \text{Ending inventory}}{2} \right) \left(\frac{\text{Stockturn in weeks}}{52 \text{ weeks}} \right)$$

$$= \left(\frac{40{,}000 + 0}{2} \right) \left(\frac{12}{52} \right)$$

$$= \$4615$$

Annual inventory turnover would be sales divided by average inventory investment annually ($50,000 ÷ $4615), or 10.83 times. Given a gross margin of 20 percent, one would obtain a GMROI of $2.17 or (20% × 10.83). Now let us assume that instead of not marking down the merchandise, it is marked down by $3,000 after three weeks and liquidated in another three weeks. Consequently, average inventory investment annually would be:

$$\left(\frac{40{,}000 + 0}{2} \right) \left(\frac{6}{52} \right) = \$2308$$

Inventory turnover would be (47,000 ÷ 2308), or 20.36 times. The gross margin would be (7,000 ÷ 47,000), or 14.89 percent. GMROI would thus be (14.89% × 20.36), or $3.03. From this analysis you should conclude that the markdown of $3,000 was profitable, since it bolstered GMROI from $2.17 to $3.03.

Amount of Markdown An issue related to the timing of markdowns is their magnitude. If the retailer waits to use a markdown at the last moment, then the markdown should probably be large enough to move the remaining merchandise. This, however, is not the case with an early markdown. Then, the markdown only needs to be large enough to give sales a stimulant. Once sales are stimulated, the retailer can watch merchandise movement; when it slows, the retailer can give the merchandise another stimulant by again marking it down. Which is the more profitable strategy depends on the GMROI effect.

PRICE EXPERIMENTS

It has been noted that one of the major causes of markdowns is errors in pricing. Pricing errors are common because the retailer, in reality, has little knowledge of consumer demand factors. However, knowledge can be improved through conducting **price experiments.** A retailer conducts a price experiment when it systematically varies the price of an item while trying to control for extraneous factors and then observes the resulting change in quantity demanded.

The initial step is to develop an experimental design. A popular and easy-to-use experimental design in applied marketing research is the before-after with control group design.[8] With this design, the retailer needs at least two stores that have similar operations and trade areas. Both stores receive a before-and-after measure, but only one store receives the experimental variable—the price change. The store not receiving the experimental variable is the control store.

In Exhibit 16.5 an example is presented. The sales volume at both stores for the week of July 2–7 was measured (the before measure) and equated to an index of 100.0. Next, the price on a merchandise line was cut 15 percent in Store *A* and held at the same level at Store *B*. An after measure on each store reflected the unit volume of sales in terms of an index number corresponding to the before measure. Store *A* experienced a sales increase of 40.0 percent after the price cut. However, Store *B*, which had no price cut, experienced a sales increase of 22.0 percent over the same time period. Obviously, other factors besides the price cut caused sales to rise in Store *B*, and it is assumed that these other factors were also operating for Store *A*. Consequently, the net effect of the price reduction can be estimated as (140.0 − 122.0).

	STORE	UNIT SALES BEFORE (JULY 2–7)	15% PRICE REDUCTION (JULY 8)	UNIT SALES AFTER (JULY 8–14)
EXHIBIT 16.5 **Before-After with Control Price Experiment**	A	100.0[a]	yes	140.0
	B	100.0	no	122.0

[a]The before unit sales are standardized to a base of 100.0, which can be read as 100.0 percent; the after measure is an index number corresponding to the before measure—140.0 means 140 percent of the base.

8. Gilbert A. Churchill, Jr., *Marketing Research: Methodological Foundations* (Hinsdale, Ill.: Dryden Press, 1979), pp. 84–86.

With most retail price experiments it is wise to have after measures at several points in time, because the increase in quantity demanded due to a price cut could be due to **stocking-up behavior**: the consumer may simply be purchasing for future consumption. This is true of many grocery products when a lower price will not induce people to eat more, although it could induce them to purchase more. In Exhibit 16.6 we show what could happen in the same before-after pricing experiment with several after measures. The data in this exhibit reveal that although unit sales immediately increased in the test store for the week following the price reduction, in subsequent weeks sales were actually below those in the control store. Even more startling was the fact that the average sales index for the three weeks (July 8–28) was 119.0 for the store receiving the price reduction and 118.3 for the control store. Obviously, the price reduction only had a short-run effect on quantity demanded. Over the long run, it had no noticeable effect.

			UNIT SALES AFTER			
EXHIBIT 16.6 **Before-After with Control Time Series Price Experiment**	*STORE*	*UNIT SALES BEFORE (JULY 2–7)*	*15% PRICE REDUCTION (JULY 8)*	*July 8–14*	*July 15–21*	*July 22–28*	*Average (July 8–28)*
	A	100.0	yes	140.0	114.0	103.0	119.0
	B	100.0	no	122.0	118.0	115.0	118.3

Retail price experiments have become easier to conduct with the advent of the universal product code and electronic cash registers. These machines allow the retailer to keep close tabs on product movement (even by hour of day and day of week), which can easily be correlated with price changes or changes in promotional activity.

SUMMARY

Price decisions are among the most frequent a retailer must make. It is, therefore, prudent to understand pricing concepts and techniques. Price decisions cannot be made independently; they interact with the merchandise, location, promotion, credit, customer service, and store image decisions.

Retail decision makers should be demand-oriented when establishing prices. For this, a useful frame of reference is the three-dimensional demand model. This model suggests that the retailer pay particular attention to several important demand variables: population density, consumer travel costs, and the maximum demand price. Demand elasticity is product-specific and refers to the change in quantity demanded that is due to a change in a demand determinant. Demand determinants may be environmental, household, or managerial.

Retailers should also be supply-oriented when setting prices. They should know both their fixed and variable cost curves and recognize their need for profit. The profit needed can be viewed as a cost of the use of the retailer's capital and payment for taking risks.

A useful frame of reference for supply-oriented pricing is the markup equation, which simply states that, per unit, the retail selling price is equal to the dollar cost plus the dollar markup. Since the initial price may not be attractive enough to sell all of the merchandise, the initial markup may need to be reduced. When we talk of actual selling prices versus initial prices, we are discussing the difference between an initial and a maintained markup.

Initial markups should be planned. The retailer should establish a storewide price policy—at the market, above the market, or below the market. Next, the initial storewide markup percentage can be determined by using operating expenses, net profit, alteration costs, cash discounts, markdowns, stock shortages, employee and customer discounts, and sales. The retailer must recognize that not all items can be priced by mechanically applying this markup percentage. Some lines will need to be priced to yield a considerably higher markup and others, a substantially lower markup. Some concepts that help explain varied markup are price lining, leadership pricing, and odd-even pricing.

The initial markup is seldom equal to the maintained markup because of three kinds of reductions: markdowns, shortages, and employee and customer discounts. Because the retailer does not possess perfect information about supply and demand, markdowns are inevitable. Markdowns are usually due to errors in buying, pricing, or promotion. Since markdowns are inevitable, the retailer needs to establish a markdown policy. Early markdown speeds the movement of merchandise and also allows the retailer to take less of a markdown per unit to dispose of the merchandise. Late markdown avoids disrupting the sale of regular merchandise by too frequent markdowns. The best policy from a profit perspective depends on how it influences GMROI.

Increasingly, it has become possible for retailers to improve their pricing decisions by conducting price experiments. A price experiment consists of systematically varying the price of an item while trying to control for extraneous factors and then observing the resultant change in quantity demanded. The technology of the universal product code and electronic point-of-sale terminals have made price experiments more easy to conduct in an actual retail setting.

QUESTIONS

1. What is the relationship between a household's travel cost and a retailer's pricing decisions?

2. Explain how markdowns can be profitable.

3. What effect should fixed costs have on retail price decisions?

4. Do a retailer's promotion and credit policies influence its pricing decisions?

5. Why may an initial markup be equal to the maintained markup? Might an initial markup be less than the maintained markup? Give an example to illustrate your answer.

6. Would it be easier for a mail-order retailer or a department store retailer to conduct a price experiment? Explain by developing an example.

7. In a practical sense, how should retailers establish price levels?

8. Explain the difference between initial and maintained markups.

PROBLEMS AND EXERCISES

1. Compute the markup on cost and on retail for an item that is priced at $19.95 and costs $11.20.

2. If an individual would be willing to pay $28 for an item and a local retailer has it priced at $26, but the consumer must travel seventeen miles across town to purchase the item, should the individual purchase the item? Assume the travel costs for the individual are $0.18 per mile.

3. If the demand elasticity of price for an item is 1.8, the item is currently priced at $14, and the retailer slashes price by 10 percent, what will be the effect on dollar sales? Assume that currently 100 units a month are being sold.

4. An item has a markup on cost of 53 percent; what is its markup on retail?

5. Assume that a retailer plans to achieve a net sales of $1.5 million and expects operating expenses to be $375,000. The net profit goal is $100,000. Planned reductions include $88,000 for markdowns, $38,000 for merchandise shortages, and $14,000 for employee and customer discounts. Cash discounts from suppliers are expected to be $30,000. At what percentage should initial markups be planned?

6. Visit a general merchandise retailer. Look at their men's suits or women's dresses to assess the price lines being used. Evaluate the price lines.

7. Carefully read through your local newspaper and try to locate any retail price advertisements that appear to be deceptive or misleading.

8. An appliance retailer purchases $48,000 in color televisions and expects to be able to dispose of all of them in sixteen weeks at an average gross margin of 31 percent. However, the retailer feels that it could sell all the sets in six weeks if prices were slashed 12 percent to yield an average gross margin of 19 percent. Which alternative should be pursued?

SUGGESTED READINGS

Jolson, Marvin A. "A Diagrammatic Model for Merchandising Calculations." *Journal of Retailing* 51(Summer 1975): 3–9, 92.

McNair, Malcolm and Eleanor G. May. "Pricing for Profit: A Revolutionary Approach to Retail Accounting." *Harvard Business Review* 35(May–June 1957): 105–122.

Parsons, Leonard J. and W. Bailey Price. "Adaptive Pricing by a Retailer." *Journal of Marketing Research* 9(May 1972): 127–33.

Whalen, Bernard F. "Strategic Mix of Odd, Even Prices Can Lead to Increased Retail Profits." *Marketing News* (March 7, 1980): 24.

17

Overview *This is the first of two chapters that focus on the retail promotion decision. Promotion is the major generator of demand in retailing. In this chapter we will discuss advertising, sales promotion, and publicity. All of our discussion is managerial, and is directed at showing you not how to design effective promotions, but how to manage promotion resources.*

Retail Promotion: Advertising, Sales Promotion, Publicity

ALL RETAILERS could generate some sales without spending any dollars on promotion. Sales could come from households close to the retailer who frequent it because of its location. This is especially the case for retailers selling convenience goods. Or, sales could be derived from passers-by that might occasionally visit the store for an impulse purchase. Promotional expenditures are not a prerequisite to generating sales. Rather, they are a means of generating sales above those which could be obtained merely from location and traffic flow.

THE RETAIL PROMOTION MIX

Retailers need to manage at least four basic promotion components: advertising, sales promotions, publicity, and personal selling. Collectively, these components comprise the retailer's promotion mix. Each component is defined below and will be discussed from a managerial perspective in this and the following chapter.

1. **Advertising** is "any paid form of nonpersonal presentation and promotion of ideas, goods, and services by an identified sponsor."[1] Common retail advertising vehicles are newspapers, radio, television, and printed circulars.
2. **Sales promotions** are those "marketing activities, other than personal selling, advertising, and publicity that stimulate consumer purchasing and dealer effectiveness, such as display, shows and exhibitions, demonstrations."[2] The most popular sales promotion tools in retailing are point-of-purchase displays and consumer premiums such as free gifts, trading stamps, and games.
3. **Publicity** is any "nonpersonal stimulation of demand for a product, service or business unit by planting commercially significant news about it in a published medium or obtaining favorable presentation of it upon radio, television or stage that is not paid for by the sponsor."[3] Popular examples are Macy's Thanksgiving Day Parade and 7-11's sponsorship of the Jerry Lewis Telethon.
4. **Personal selling** is an "oral presentation in a conversation with one or more prospective purchasers for the purpose of making a sale."[4] Many retail employees are involved in personal selling.

All four components of the retailer's promotion mix need to be managed in a systems perspective. That is, they need to be mixed together to achieve the retailer's promotion objectives. Each must reinforce the others. If the ad-

---

1. Reprinted with permission from Ralph S. Alexander, et al., *Marketing Definitions: A Glossary of Marketing Terms* (Chicago: American Marketing Association, 1960), p. 9, published by the American Marketing Association.

2. Alexander, et al., *Marketing Definitions*, p. 20. Reprinted with permission of the American Marketing Association.

3. Alexander, et al., *Marketing Definitions*, p. 19. Reprinted with permission of the American Marketing Association.

4. Alexander, et al., *Marketing Definitions*, p. 20. Reprinted with permission of the American Marketing Association.

vertising conveys quality and status, so must the personal selling, publicity, and sales promotion. Otherwise, the consumer will receive conflicting or inconsistent messages about the retailer, which will result in confusion and loss of patronage.

INTEGRATED EFFORT

The management of promotional efforts in retailing must fit into the retailer's overall plan. Promotion decisions relate to and must be integrated with other decision areas such as location, merchandise, credit, cash, building and fixtures, price, and customer service. Let us explore this important point in slightly more detail with the following examples.

1. A consumer will travel only a maximum distance to visit a retail store, and thus a retailer's location will help determine whom to promote to. Basically, the most effective promotion dollars are those directed toward households in the retailer's trade area.
2. Retailers need high levels of store traffic to keep their merchandise rapidly turning over. Promotion helps build traffic.
3. A typical retailer's credit customers are more store-loyal and purchase in larger quantities; and thus they are an excellent target for increased promotional efforts.
4. A retailer confronted with a temporary cash flow problem can use promotion to increase short-run cash flow by having a special event of anywhere from a couple of hours ("Midnight Madness") to a week or more ("Summer Bargain Days").
5. A retailer's promotional strategy must be reinforced by its building and fixture decisions. Promotional creativity and style should coincide with building and fixture creativity and style. If the ads are exciting and appealing to a particular target market, so should be the building and fixtures.
6. A retailer will seldom push product features, because manufacturers typically do this. Consequently, retailers will often feature price in their advertising. Obviously, therefore, price management and advertising management should be highly interrelated by the retail decision maker.
7. Promotion provides customers with more information, which will help them make better purchase decisions, because risk is reduced. Promotion, therefore, can actually be viewed as a major component of customer service (see Chapter 19).

The retailer that systematically integrates its promotional programs with other retail decision areas will be better able to achieve high performance results.

PROMOTION AND THE MARKETING CHANNEL

The retailer is not the only marketing channel member that uses promotion. Suppliers (wholesalers and manufacturers) also invest in promotion for many of the same reasons retailers do—to move merchandise more quickly, speed up cash flow, better serve customers, and so on. However, the promotional activities of the retailer's channel partners may not be in harmony with the retailer's promotion objectives.

For example, automobile manufacturers in any given model year will want to sell as many units as possible, because they have an extremely high investment in fixed costs. Therefore, as unit volume increases, the average cost per automobile drops rapidly. Consequently, the manufacturer will want to produce and sell as many cars as possible in each model year. On the other hand, the automobile dealer faces a relatively constant cost per automobile. The dealer wants to sell as many cars as possible without drastically cutting the retail price. But manufacturers who want to sell a large number of cars will put pressure on retail dealers to promote price heavily. In many cases, it would be more profitable for the dealer to sell substantially fewer cars at a higher price per unit. However, this would cut into the profits the manufacturer could achieve by producing more cars. Basically, the dealer and manufacturer can get into serious disagreements over promotional programs because they have incompatible goals.

As we discussed in Chapter 4, perceptual incongruity can also be a source of supplier-retailer conflict. Let us illustrate this with our automobile example, and relate it to the promotion area. Assume that the general rate of real economic growth has slowed considerably and that industry auto sales are off 21 percent from last year. The manufacturer believes that the recession will be short lived and therefore does not want to offer any price rebates or special promotions from the factory. However, the automobile dealers believe that the recession will be fairly prolonged, and they therefore feel that advertising by the manufacturer should be hyped and that special allowances should be given for increased local advertising. They would also like to see the manufacturer tie in this increased advertising program with a $300 rebate from the factory. Because the manufacturer and dealer have different beliefs about the future, there could be serious conflicts between them.

LAW, ETHICS, AND PROMOTION

In Chapter 8 we discussed the regulation of promotion; and a review of this material might be helpful to you. The retail manager should become familiar with the legal constraints on promotion in retailing. At the same time, a strong ethical philosophy (what is right and wrong practice in retail promotion) should be developed by the retail manager early in his or her career. Promotion decisions in retailing are probably the most ethically tainted ones that will be encountered. A few examples may show you some of the legal or ethical issues that can develop.

One area involves deceiving the consumer. This can be done in several ways, but two common methods are to advertise sale prices that are not actually special prices, and to claim in the advertising that items are being marked down more than they actually are. Regarding the first practice, Exhibit 17.1 deals with a retail appliance chain and its practice of continually advertising the same portable color television to be on sale.

Deception occurs because the typical consumer tends to look at an advertisement on the day it is considering buying a color television set. Thus, the consumer is likely to believe that there is a significant saving to be made by buying during the 'sale.' In reality, the set frequently sells at the advertised price or an even lower one.[5]

Unfortunately, this practice occurs all too often in retailing.

EXHIBIT 17.1 **Appliance Chain's Advertised TV Set Prices**	*DATE (1973)*	*PRICE*	*TYPE OF SALE (HEADLINE)*
	May 23	$229.00	Stock Reduction Sale, Thursday and Friday, 10–9:30
	May 25	229.88[a]	Memorial Day Sale, Saturday, 10–9:30; Sunday, 11–5
	June 1	229.88	June Jubilee, Saturday, 10–9:30; Sunday, 11–5
	June 5	228.00[b]	6-Hour Spectacular, Wednesday only, 3–9 P.M.
	June 8	229.88	Super Saturday, Saturday, 10–9:30; Sunday, 11–5
	June 19	236.00[c]	Dollar Day, Wednesday only, 10–9:30
	June 27	237.00	Portable TV, two big days to save
	July 3	229.88[d]	6 Hours only, July 4th, 10–4

Special designations:
[a]Sale price
[b]Color TV specials
[c]Dollar day price
[d]6-hour sale

Source: Reprinted with permission from James R. Krum and Stephen K. Keiser, 'Regulation of Retail Newspaper Advertising," *Journal of Marketing* 40(July 1976): 32, published by the American Marketing Association.

Regarding the second practice, consider a discount drug chain that heavily advertised numerous items to be on sale. In the advertisements the "regular" price of the item was compared to the "sale" price and the consumer was led to believe that the sale price was approximately 50 percent less than the regular price. Deception occurred because the regular price "was not the usual price of the item prior to the sale, the actual savings were less than the comparison advertising implied, a clear case of deception."[6] Exhibit 17.2 presents data that help to illustrate this case. The ceiling price was the highest permissible price that could be charged during the time under investigation because of a federal price freeze that was in effect. Given this price freeze, the statement of the "regular" price was obviously inaccurate. This provided a unique opportunity to determine the actual selling prices on advertised items and thus develop the comparative data in Exhibit 17.2. This example is not unusual; too many retailers advertise price markdowns that distort the true potential savings to the consumer.

5. James R. Krum and Stephen K. Keiser, "Regulation of Retail Newspaper Advertising," *Journal of Marketing* 40 (July 1976): 32.
6. Krum and Keiser, "Regulation of Newspaper Advertising," p. 32.

EXHIBIT 17.2
Price Comparisons for a Discount Drug Chain

PRODUCT	PRICES		
	Ceiling	Regular[a]	Sale[a]
Binaca Mouthwash, 15 oz.	$1.17	$1.50	$ .89
Scope Mouthwash, 24 oz.	1.43	2.05	.99
Coppertone Suntan Lotion, 6 oz.	1.89	2.39	1.59
Johnson's Baby Oil, 10 oz.	1.19	1.39	.79
Bromo Seltzer, 9 oz.	1.77	2.29	1.19
White Rain Hair Spray, 13 oz.	1.09	1.49	.79
Off Insect Repellent, 7 oz.	.97	1.19	.77
Micrin Mouthwash, 18 oz.	1.17	1.59	.69
Body All Deodorant, 8 oz.	1.57	1.90	.99

[a]As advertised June 14, 21, or 28, 1973

Source: Reprinted with permission from James R. Krum and Stephen K. Keiser, "Regulation of Retail Newspaper Advertising," *Journal of Marketing* 40(July 1976): 32, published by the American Marketing Association.

PROMOTION AND CREATIVITY

Promotional programs and decisions by the retailer cannot totally be determined by analytical and scientific methods. On the contrary, promotion offers the opportunity for highly creative thought. In fact, by using creativity you can make the promotion mix differentiate your store from competitors. Usually, however, where the retailer has the greatest opportunity for being creative, it dodges that opportunity.

One needs only to read the daily newspapers from several large metropolitan areas to quickly notice that retailers have a terrible habit of copying each other. Within the same city and across cities in the United States, most retailer advertising looks the same. In addition, retailers heavily copy the items to promote. When one department store has a sale on fashion designer jeans, the other department stores in town follow suit. One appliance retailer has a sale on color TVs, so other stores in town do likewise. Imitation also applies to other facets of the promotional mix. One bookstore will have a noted author visit the store to sign books, so other bookstores in town will have authors visit (probably different authors). One shopping center will have an arts and crafts show in its mall, so other shopping malls have shows.

The root of this problem is that retailers do not take the time to think. Creativity does not come from harried executives trying to meet deadlines. If we decide on Tuesday afternoon that we want to move more merchandise this weekend and thus need to get an advertisement to the newspaper by noon on Wednesday, we cannot expect that ad to be creative. Creativity requires time to think without worrying about other problems. This may sound idealistic, and retailers may argue that the pressures and fast pace of retailing do not allow for the luxury of time to think and be creative. But if retailers want a good return on their promotional expenditures, then each promotional event must be different and creative; it must attract traffic to the store and must be talked about by the consuming public.

PROMOTION OBJECTIVES

To efficiently manage the promotion mix, the retail manager must first establish promotion objectives. These should be the natural outgrowth of the retailer's strategic and administrative plans. As such, all promotion objectives should ultimately improve the retailer's financial performance, since this is what strategic and administrative plans are set up to accomplish.

In Exhibit 17.3 we attempt to show how promotion objectives should relate to financial performance objectives. As this exhibit shows, promotion objectives can be established to help improve both long and short-run financial performance.

EXHIBIT 17.3
**Possible
Promotion
Objectives
in Retailing**

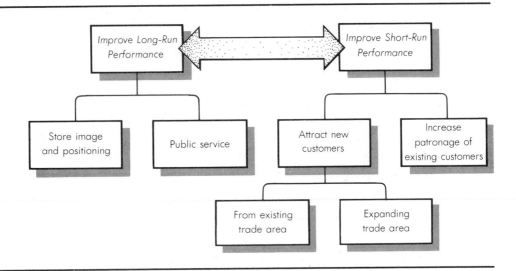

Long-Run Objectives   The retailer can establish two major types of promotion objectives to improve long-run financial performance: store image and positioning objectives, and public service objectives.

Store Image and Positioning   The first type of objective is intended to reinforce in the consumer's mind the store image and position the retailer wants to convey. For example, when the consumer thinks of ABC Appliance Store, the retailer may want him or her to perceive an elegantly designed store featuring nationally branded appliances backed by an excellent service and repair program and friendly and helpful store employees. Promotion directed at fulfilling this objective will have its major effect on improving the retailer's long-run financial performance. However, as you might expect, this type of promotion will occasionally help sales in the short run.

Public Service Promotion   The second type of objective is directed at getting the consumer to perceive the retailer as a good citizen in the community. Retailers may sponsor public service advertisements to honor local athletes and scholars. For example, several retailers in Madison, Wisconsin, placed ads to honor the four athletes from Madison who won medals in the 1980 Winter Olympics. Other retailers have placed ads in honor of Nobel Prize winners from their community. Still others place ads that feature helpful consumer buying tips or promote public causes such as conservation of natural resources.

Short-Run Objectives   In the short run, the retailer can establish two major promotional objectives to help improve financial performance: increase patronage of existing customers, and attract new customers.

Increased Patronage from Existing Customers   Increased patronage is probably one of the most common promotion objectives found in retailing. Simply stated, promotion expenditures should be directed at current customers in order to encourage them to make more of their purchases at the retailer. In other words, it attempts to make present customers more store loyal. For example, if the typical household of four spends $2,800 a year on food purchases at grocery stores and if, currently, Supermarket *A*'s average customer (that represents a family of four) is spending 37 percent of its food dollar at Supermarket *A*, then its yearly expenditures at supermarket *A* are $1,036. If, with a good promotional program, the retailer can increase the 37 percent to 43 percent, then average expenditures per household at Supermarket *A* will rise from $1,036 to $1,204, for an increase of $168 per year. If the supermarket was serving an equivalent of 2,100 four-person households, then the net increase in the retailer's annual sales would be 2,100 × 168, or $352,800.

Attraction of New Customers   A second major short-run promotion objective may be to increase the number of customers that can be attracted to the store. One approach is to try to attract new customers from the retailer's existing trade area. There are always some households within the existing trade area that, for a variety of reasons, do not patronize the retailer. Perhaps they do their shopping at a retailer close to their place of employment or perhaps they simply do not think that the retailer's store is attractive—maybe they once had a bad experience while shopping there and vowed never to return. A second approach is to attempt to expand the trade area and therefore attract customers from outside the existing trade area.

Interdependence   Exhibit 17.3 shows that although promotion objectives can be established to improve either long- or short-run financial performance, programs designed to achieve either objective will actually benefit the other as well. This is shown in Exhibit 17.3 by the dashed line connecting the short- and long-run objectives. What is done promotionally to build long-run financial performance will begin to have an effect almost immediately, but also will have a cumulative effect over time. Similarly, what is done to promote short-run financial performance will carry over to affect the long-run future of the retailer.

RETAIL ADVERTISING MANAGEMENT

The discussion to follow will develop in some detail a perspective for managing the advertising component of the retailer's promotional mix. Throughout the discussion, you should remember that advertising decisions should be integrated with other promotional decisions.

Types of Retail Advertising   Retail advertisements can be classified in several ways, but the most popular system categorizes retail advertisements into institutional and promotional ads. Institutional advertisements are most beneficial in increasing long-run retailer performance. **Institutional ads** attempt to sell the store rather than the merchandise in it, attempting to build the store image and create a unique position for the retailer in the consumer's mind. On the other hand, **promotional advertisements** attempt to bolster short-run performance by advertising product features or price as a selling point.

Although dividing retail advertising into institutional and promotional ads is useful and intuitively appealing, it can be somewhat artificial. All good retail advertisers have come to learn that all advertising should have institutional overtones. Most retail advertisers would agree with the statement, "Any ad for merchandise that does not place the store in a favorable image is a mistake."

In Exhibit 17.4 we present a case study of a new retail advertising concept called lifestyle advertising. As you can learn from the case study, lifestyle advertising is both institutional and promotional.

EXHIBIT 17.4
Lifestyle Advertising

Lifestyle advertising is an attempt by retailers to promote the store as reinforcing or fulfilling certain consumer lifestyles. For example, in the late 1970s Saks Fifth Avenue's lifestyle advertising theme was, "We are all the things you are at Saks Fifth Avenue."

A notable example of lifestyle advertising involves Aspen Leaf. Aspen Leaf is a nine-unit Denver-based sporting goods chain with stores ranging from 16,000 to 20,000 square feet. The chain's advertising theme is "This is your life; you'll find it at Aspen Leaf." This simple theme has improved the store's image, traffic, and sales.

Regarding Aspen Leaf, *Chain Store Age Executive* has stated, "While more than half the chain's television ads are still price-item spots, there's a growing emphasis on lifestyle ads, which blend elements of both price-item and institutional ads. The effect is to turn a two-dimensional ad featuring product and price into a spot with a third dimension—how the product fits into the shopper's way of life."*

*"Retailer Turns over New Leaf" *Chain Store Age Executive* 56(March 1980): 14.

Sponsorship   At the start of this chapter, we defined advertising as a paid form of nonpersonal presentation. The actual sponsor of the advertising can be the retailer, supplier, or several retailers. Most retail advertising is paid for solely by the retailer. If suppliers pick up part or all of the cost of the advertising, it is called **vertical cooperative advertising.** If several retailers share the cost of advertising, it is called **horizontal cooperative advertising.** Let us elaborate on each of these.

Vertical Cooperative Advertising   The first form of retail advertising allows the retailer and other channel members to share the advertising burden. For example, the manufacturer may pay up to 40 percent of the cost of the retailer's advertising of the manufacturer's products up to a ceiling of 4 percent of annual purchases by the retailer from the manufacturer. If the retailer spent $10,000 on advertising the manufacturer's products, then it could be reimbursed 40 percent of this amount, or $4,000, as long as the retailer purchased at least $100,000 over the last year from the manufacturer.

The responsibilities of each party in a vertical cooperative advertising arrangement are typically specified by means of a contract. In Exhibit 17.5, a typical contract is provided. As you will notice, the supplier has a good degree of control over the general content of the advertising, considerably constraining the distinctiveness of the retailer's advertising. To illustrate, consider the relatively high possibility that in a large city (over 250,000 in population), two or more retailers in the same area of the city would cooperate with the same manufacturer on a particular merchandise line. In this situation their advertisements will appear very similar to the consumer. This will result in the retailers directly competing against each other.

There is a strong temptation among retailers to view vertical coop advertising money as free. The retailer must remember that even if the supplier is putting up 50 percent of the money, it must put up the other 50 percent. Another way to look at it is that since the supplier exercises considerable control over the content of the advertising, the retailer is actually paying 50 percent of the supplier's cost of advertising rather than vice versa.

In principle, you must ask yourself if you can get a better return on your money with horizontal coop dollars or by total sponsorship of the advertising. A detailed example may be helpful. Assume you are considering the possibility of advertising two alternative merchandise lines. You have $5,000 to spend on advertising either line *A* or line *B*. With line *A*, you have been offered a coop deal from a supplier, which roughly translates into the supplier paying 50 percent of the cost of the advertising. This would allow you to purchase $10,000 of advertising for a $5,000 investment. No coop deal is being offered by the supplier of line *B*, but line *B* is an increasingly popular line among consumers, and you believe it could benefit substantially from $5,000 in advertising. What should you do?

The answer to the preceding question will depend on two major factors. First, how much will the sales of line *A* increase with $10,000 in advertising versus how much will the sales of line *B* increase with the $5,000 in advertising that can be spent on it? Second, what is the gross margin percentage for each line? Generally, any given merchandise line will be a more attractive candidate for increased advertising as its sales are more responsive to increased advertising expenditures and its gross margin percentage is higher. For the situation at hand let us examine some specific figures. Line *A* has a 50 percent gross margin and line *B* has a 60 percent gross margin. Currently, line *A* has sales of $80,000, and it is expected that a $10,000 advertising program will push sales up to $110,000. At the present time, line *B* has sales of $18,000 and it is expected that a $5,000 advertising program will increase the sales volume to $60,000. In Exhibit 17.6 we show the preceding sales response functions for lines *A* and *B*.

EXHIBIT 17.5
**Example of
Vertical
Cooperative
Advertising
Contract**

MICROCOOK
Cook Electronics, Inc.
1331 Queen Street
The Cook Building
Queensboro, AZ 86201

Cook Electronics, Inc.
Thomas C. Cook, President
Roy P. Cook,
    Vice President

COOPERATIVE ADVERTISING CONTRACT

The dealer _____ has read the terms of this contract and wishes to enter into a cooperative advertising agreement with MICROCOOK, a division of Cook Electronics, Inc.

TERMS OF CONTRACT

1. MICROCOOK will allow to an authorized dealer, 5% of the dealer's gross purchases of microwave ovens (based on distributor costs) to be used for the cooperative advertising of MICROCOOK microwave ovens.
2. Coop funds apply only to nationally recognized local media and will be paid at the standard rate for local advertisers.
3. The coop fund is not to be used for production costs. It applies only to payment of media space, radio time costs, or special promotional material.
4. Cooperative advertising funds are figured by computing the 5% of the dealer's MICRO-COOK purchases for a 6-month period and applying it to 50% of the cost of the dealer's advertising of MICROCOOK microwave ovens. Cooperative funds not used during each 6-month term will expire.
5. Only MICROCOOK microwave ovens are eligible for coop funds and the dealer must show adequate stock and prominent in-store display of MICROCOOK products.
6. The MICROCOOK trademark must be prominently displayed in all advertisements.
7. The dealer shall not use MICROCOOK microwave ovens in any advertisements in which a competing microwave oven appears.
8. Dealers will be supplied with newspaper advertisements of MICROCOOK microwave ovens by Cook Electronics, Inc. The copy and layout of any ads other than those supplied by MICROCOOK or Cook Electronics must be cleared before use.
9. To receive credit the following must be sent to the Advertising Manager, MICROCOOK:
    a. a completed copy of form #A-216 "Cooperative Advertising Claim"
    b. a full-page tearsheet of all printed advertisements
    c. a verified copy sheet of all radio or TV advertisements
    d. a receipted copy of the media invoice
    e. the dealer's invoice claiming 50% credit of the total cost of the MICROCOOK advertising.
10. All claims will be checked against purchases and media advertising dates.

_____   _____
          dealer   MICROCOOK

_____   _____
          date   date

Mail to: Advertising Manager, MICROCOOK, Cook Electronics, Inc., 1331 Queen Street, The Cook Building, Queensboro, AZ 86201

EXHIBIT 17.6
**Sales Response
Curves for
Two Lines**

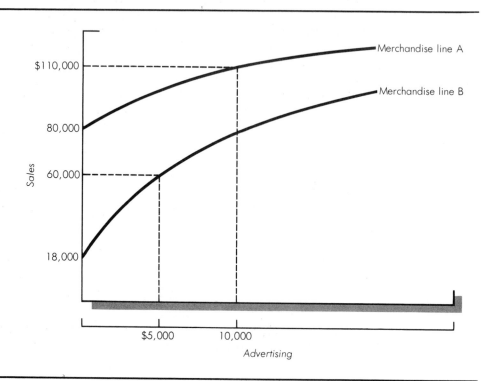

Notice that merchandise line B, although its current sales are relatively low, is very responsive to advertising expenditures in relation to the responsiveness of merchandise line A. Below we present the numerical analysis that will help you determine which line to advertise.

	LINE A		LINE B	
	Before	*After*	*Before*	*After*
Sales	$80,000	$110,000	$18,000	$60,000
Cost of merchandise	40,000	55,000	7,200	24,000
Gross profit	40,000	55,000	10,800	36,000
Advertising	0	5,000[a]	0	5,000
Contribution profit	$40,000	$50,000	$10,800	$31,000

[a]Actually, $10,000 was spent, but the net cost to retailer was $5,000 since supplier paid the other $5,000.

The numerical analysis suggests that it would be more profitable for you to pass up the coop deal on line A and spend $5,000 on advertising line B.

Horizontal Cooperative Advertising   With horizontal cooperative advertising, two or more retailers band together to share the cost of advertising. Significantly, this tends to give small retailers more bargaining power in purchasing advertising. Also, if properly conducted, it can create substantially more store traffic. For example, retailers in shopping malls will often jointly sponsor multiple-page spreads in newspapers promoting special sales events such as "George Washington's Birthday Sale Days" or "Moonlight Madness" sales. These events are good traffic generators. They pull significantly more people to the shopping center than any individual merchant's advertising could expect to, and thus all retailers benefit from the increased traffic in the shopping center or district.

Advertising Objectives The advertising objectives should flow from the retailer's promotion objectives, but should be more specific because advertising itself is a specific element of the promotion mix. When we discussed promotion objectives, we did not specify how the elements of the promotion mix should be used to achieve the overall promotion objectives. The advertising objectives will suggest how advertising will help the retailer achieve its overall promotional objectives.

Not a Panacea Before we explore the specific advertising objectives the retailer might develop, we need to stress that advertising is not a panacea. It will not cure all the retailer's financial performance problems. Many retailers improperly believe that heavy doses of advertising can cure their minor as well as major problems. Advertising, regardless of its quality, can simply not do the following:

1. Advertising cannot sell merchandise that people do not want to buy.
2. Advertising cannot sell merchandise in profitable quantities without the backing of every other division of the store (credit department, janitorial services, and so on).
3. Advertising cannot succeed to the fullest extent unless it is used continuously.[7]

What Advertising Can Accomplish Although advertising is not a panacea, it can be powerful if properly used. All retail advertising will be either institutional or promotional, but this refers to its purpose and not to its more specific objectives. The objectives advertising can accomplish are many and varied. Examples include the following:

- Increase traffic during slow periods
- Move old merchandise at the end of a selling season
- Explain store policies
- Attract newcomers in the community to the store
- Strengthen the store's image or reputation
- Identify the store with nationally advertised brands
- Reposition the image of the store in the minds of consumers

7. C. M. Edwards, Jr., and R. A. Brown, *Retail Advertising and Sales Promotion*, 3rd ed. (Englewood Cliffs, N.J.: Prentice-Hall, 1954), p. 14.

These possible objectives suggest advertising's power when properly managed. To illustrate this power, the case study in Exhibit 17.7 deals with how advertising was used to reposition a store in the minds of consumers.

The development of advertising objectives should be the first priority in establishing an effective retail advertising program.

Setting a Budget   A well-designed retail advertising program requires capital that could have been spent on other areas (more consumer credit, more merchandise, higher wages for employees). The retailer hopes that the dollars spent on advertising will bring back many more dollars, which can be used to finance other areas of the retail enterprise. The decision on how much to spend on advertising in any given budget period (typically three to twelve months) can be made with one of the three following methods: the affordable method; the percentage-of-sales method, or the task and objective method.

Affordable Method   Many small retailers allocate the funds to advertising that they can afford in any given budget period. They view advertising as a residual. Given their expected sales volume, operating expenses, and desired profit, they back into what they can afford to spend on advertising. The logic of this approach suggests that advertising does not stimulate sales or profit, but rather is supported by sales and profit. However, in all fairness, we should mention that many small retailers have little choice but to use this approach. A small retailer cannot go to the bank and borrow $100,000 to spend on advertising. If the advertising isn't successful and if the retailer has little collateral, the bank will most likely have no choice but to write off the loan. This is not to suggest that banks will not lend to small retailers—they will, but they will tend to loan

---

EXHIBIT 17.7
Store
Repositioning

Creative advertising and analytical research can be used to reposition a store in the minds of consumers. For example, Hoeppner Advertising of Sioux City, Iowa, and Grapentine & Co. of Nevada, Iowa, have successfully repositioned a retail chain patronized mostly by farmers into one capable of attracting both farmers and urban residents.

The farm supply store they repositioned carried products similar to those found in Target and K-mart. However, consumer research indicated that they were perceived as high-priced farm supply stores, with little or nothing to offer the urban housewife. Rather than compete head-on with the K-marts and Targets, the store was positioned as a specialty discount department store that would stock a broader and deeper line of home improvement, hardware, and selected household items than that carried by the competition. TV ads were created to reposition the chain as the specialty discount department store that offered real value.

Regarding the success of the program, Hoeppner has stated that the "chain has not only increased traffic and sales among urban dwellers, but profits are at record levels while maintaining less than a 3% advertising cost in relation to total sales." Importantly, the chain has also increased its market share in the farm communities.

Source: Based on data from "Farmer Stores Repositioned to Attract Urban Consumers," *Marketing News,* March 21, 1980, p. 12.

funds only for tangible property (inventory, fixtures, equipment) and not for intangibles such as advertising. This is unfortunate, since the small retailer might benefit more from advertising than from more inventory or equipment. Thus, we see that although the affordable method may not be ideal in terms of advertising theory, it is certainly defensible given the capital constraints that confront the small retailer.

Percentage of Sales In the **percentage-of-sales method** of budgeting for advertising, the retailer targets a specific percentage of forecasted sales to be used for advertising. Where does the percentage to spend come from? First, it could come from the traditional percentage of sales the retailer has spent on advertising. For example, historically, a retailer may have fallen into the habit of spending X percent of sales on advertising. If it experienced good results with this advertising budget, there would be little incentive for deviating from it. Second, the percentage could be obtained from a retail trade association's operating results study. For instance, Exhibit 17.8 shows the average percentage of sales that different types of retailers spend on advertising (see page 528).

Advertising budgets based on the percentage-of-sales method do not require great analytical skills and can be developed quickly. As you might expect, however, this method has several limitations, noted by William Haight:[8]

1. It puts the cart before the horse. It bases advertising on sales, ignoring the fact that sales derive (in part at least) from advertising.

2. It looks back rather than forward. It assumes that the percentage appropriate a year or two ago is appropriate for a future budgeting period.

3. If an "average" industry ratio of advertising to sales is used, it may be inappropriate for a particular store. An average is simply the product one obtains by adding a long list of widely disparate figures, then dividing the sum by the number of figures on the list. Many profitable stores may have a substantially higher or appreciably lower ratio. Industry averages also include (and tend to be reduced by) stores which do no advertising, some of which may be about to fail for lack of customers or in the process of being bought out by more aggressive competitors.

4. An undue fascination with averages or with past ratios may cause a small independent store to give up one of its main advantages over the larger chain-store competitors and the big discount houses: flexibility in adjusting to rapid changes in local market conditions.

5. The percentage-of-sales method fails to recognize rising advertising costs; using the same ratio of advertising to sales as in a prior year may actually result in a store's doing less advertising than was really intended.

6. If the ad budget is based on a sales forecast that is too optimistic, the store may end up overspending early in the year and face a drought of funds for important promotions during the peak end-of-year season.

Task and Objective Method With both of the preceding budgeting methods, advertising seemed to follow sales results. With the **task and objective method,**

8. From *Retail Advertising: Management and Technique* by William Haight. Copyright © 1976 by Silver Burdett Company. Reprinted by permission of Scott, Foresman and Company, pp. 116–17.

EXHIBIT 17.8
**Advertising
as a Percentage
of Sales
for Five
Retail Lines**

LINE OF TRADE	ADVERTISING AS A PERCENTAGE OF SALES
Hardware stores (1977)	1.9%
Floorcovering retailers (1978)	3.2
Drugstores (1977)	1.2
Discount department stores (1977)	2.5
Department stores (1978)	2.4

Sources: 1978 Management Report: Hardware Store Financial Operating Results (Indianapolis, Indiana: National Retail Hardware Association, 1978), p. 8; *1979 Management Report: 1978 Operating Results Study Floorcovering Retailers* (Norman, Okla.: The Retail Floorcovering Institute and Distribution Research Program, The University of Oklahoma, 1979), p. 20; *Lilly Digest 1978: A Survey of Community Pharmacy Operations for 1977* (Indianapolis: Eli Lilly and Company, 1978), p. 7; *Operating Results of Self-Service Discount Department Stores 1977–78* (Ithaca, N.Y.: Cornell University 1978), p. 32; *Financial and Operating Results of Department and Specialty Stores of 1978* (New York: National Retail Merchants Association, 1979), p. 15.

the logic is properly reversed; advertising leads to sales or some other measure of financial performance. Basically, the retailer establishes its advertising objectives and then determines the advertising tasks that need to be performed to help achieve those objectives. Associated with each task is an estimate of the cost of performing the task. When all of these costs are summed, the retailer has its advertising budget. In short, this method begins with the retailer's advertising objectives and then determines what it will cost to achieve those objectives.

Exhibit 17.9 gives an example of the task and objective method. Notice that the retailer has five major advertising objectives and a total of eleven tasks to perform to accomplish these objectives. The total cost of performing these tasks is $99,020. The task and objective method of developing the advertising budget is the best of the three methods from a theoretical and managerial control perspective.

Allocation of Advertising Dollars   Regardless of the method by which the retailer determines its budget, it will subsequently need to decide how to allocate its advertising dollars. It will probably not be profitable to heavily advertise all merchandise lines or departments. Even if it were, most retail advertising budgets would not be large enough to do so. Thus, in either case, some conscious decision on where to spend advertising dollars is necessary.

Deciding on what lines or departments to spend advertising dollars is not easy. Advertising theory would suggest that the retailer's limited advertising funds be allocated to products or departments so as to maximize the retailer's overall profitability. In practice, due to uncertainty and inadequate information, such a theoretical allocation rule would be difficult to implement. Rather, the retailer must settle for an allocation that is approximately correct.

It is important for you to become familiar with the factors that indicate a

EXHIBIT 17.9	OBJECTIVE AND TASK	ESTIMATED COST
The Task and Objective Method of Advertising Budget Development		
	Objective 1: Increase traffic during dull periods.	
	Task A: 15 full-page newspaper advertisements to be spread over these dates: February 2–16; June 8–23; October 4–18	$22,500
	Task B: 240, 30-second radio spots split on two stations and spread over these dates: February 2–16; June 8–23; October 4–18	4,320
	Objective 2: Attract new customers from newcomers to the community.	
	Task A: 2,000 direct-mail letters greeting new residents to the community	1,000
	Task B: 2,000 direct-mail letters inviting new arrivals in the community to stop in to visit the store and fill out a credit application	1,000
	Task C: yellow-page advertising	1,900
	Objective 3: Build store's reputation.	
	Task A: weekly 15-second institutional ads on the 10 P.M. television news every Saturday and Sunday	20,800
	Task B: one half-page newspaper ad per month in the home living section of the local newspaper	9,500
	Objective 4: Increase shopper traffic in shopping center.	
	Task A: cooperate with other retailers in the shopping center in sponsoring transit advertising on buses and cabs	3,000
	Task B: participate in "Midnight Madness Sale" with other retailers in the shopping center by taking out 2 full-page newspaper ads—one in mid-March and the other in mid-July	3,000
	Objective 5: Clear out end-of-month, slow-moving merchandise.	
	Task A: run a full-page newspaper ad on the last Thursday of every month	18,000
	Task B: run 3, 30-second television spots on the last Thursday of every month	14,000
	Total advertising budget	$99,020

merchandise line or department that is a candidate for a high advertising allocation. They are summarized in Exhibit 17.10.

Gross Margin Percentage Merchandise lines or departments that have a high gross margin percentage are potentially more able to benefit or produce profit from high levels of advertising. If a merchandise line has a gross margin of 20 percent, then to pay for each dollar of advertising at least five dollars in merchandise needs to be sold. If the merchandise line has a gross margin of 50 percent, then only two dollars in sales have to be created for each dollar of advertising.

Advertising Elasticity of Demand The product's advertising elasticity of demand is the percentage of change in unit sales as a result of a percentage change in advertising. For example, an advertising elasticity of demand of 3.8 suggests that as advertising is increased by 1 percent, unit sales will rise by 3.8 percent. When demand is more elastic, demand is more expandable, and therefore the product is a better candidate for a high advertising expenditure.

EXHIBIT 17.10 **Factors in Allocating Advertising Dollars**	HIGH ADVERTISING ALLOCATION	LOW ADVERTISING ALLOCATION
	High gross margin percentage	Low gross margin percentage
	High advertising elasticity of demand	Low advertising elasticity of demand
	Dominant or potentially dominant market share in department or merchandise line	Low market share and limited potential for being dominant market share department or line
	Good backup resources (space, inventory, accounts receivable, people)	Poor backup resources (space, inventory, accounts receivable, people)
	Willingness to allocate enough to achieve "critical mass"	Unwillingness to allocate enough to achieve "critical mass"

Market Share Dominance   Retailers have found through experience and limited empirical research that there is a close correlation between market share by merchandise classification and profit.[9] Similarly, retailers with large market shares enjoy an unusually large consumer franchise that can be protected only with high levels of advertising. Thus, retailers with dominant-market-share merchandise lines or departments should allocate a disproportionate share of advertising to them. The same also applies to lines or departments that are growing rapidly and have the potential of being dominant in terms of market share.

Backup Resources   A merchandise line or department should not receive a heavy dose of advertising unless it is supported sufficiently by other resources. Adequate inventory needs to be in stock to handle sales generated from the advertising. Similarly, there needs to be sufficient space to display the goods and employees to serve the customers when they visit the store. If the type of merchandise that is being advertised is often sold on credit, then the retailer should have adequate funds to finance the consumer credit or some method by which to get the needed funds quickly.

Critical Mass   The retailer needs to have sufficient funds to allocate to a department or merchandise line so that the advertising funds can really make a difference in the line's or department's performance. The question is not whether a line should receive a high proportion of a retailer's advertising budget, but whether that high proportion is sufficiently high in absolute dollars to make things happen. Otherwise, the dollars are better spent on another line or department. The alternative may not require as much in absolute advertising dollars to make things happen.

9. Bert C. McCammon, Jr., et al., "The New Parameters of Retail Competition: The Intensified Struggle for Market Share," in Ronald W. Stampfl and Elizabeth Hirschman, *Competitive Structure in Retail Markets: The Department Store Perspective* (Chicago: American Marketing Association, 1980), pp. 108–18.

Media Alternatives The retailer has many media alternatives to select from. Each medium has strengths and weaknesses that you should acquaint yourself with. Let us briefly review these.

Newspaper Advertising The most frequently used advertising medium in retailing is the newspaper. First, most newspapers are local—that is, they circulate among a well-defined community. This is advantageous since most retailers appeal to a local market or a trade area within a local market. Second, a low technical skill level is required to create advertisements for newspapers, helpful because the majority of retailers are small and relatively unsophisticated in the design and creation of ads. Third, newspaper ads take only a short time between copy deadline and when the ad will appear. Since most retailers do a poor job at planning their advertising program over a prolonged period and since they tend to use advertising to respond to crises (poor cash flow, slackening of sales, need to move old merchandise), the short lead time for placing newspaper ads is a significant advantage.

Retail newspaper advertising also has its disadvantages. Here are four major ones: (1) the life of any single issue of a newspaper is short—it is read and subsequently discarded; (2) the typical person spends relatively little time with each issue, and the time spent is spread over many items in the newspaper; (3) newspapers have poor reproduction quality, which leads to ads with little appeal; and (4) if the retailer has a small target market, much of its advertising money will be wasted, since newspapers tend to have a broad appeal.

Radio Advertising Many retailers like radio because it can be used to target messages at select groups. In most communities there are five to ten or more radio stations, each of which tends to appeal to a different demographic group. Radio is also good for developing distinctive and appealing messages through the use of proper variations in volume and types of sounds. In short, there is a lot of flexibility. Also, many radio audiences develop strong affection and trust for their favorite radio announcers. When these announcers endorse the retailer, the audience is impressed.

Radio advertising also has its drawbacks. It is frequently listened to during work hours and tends, over time, to become part of the background environment. After a time, active listeners become passive listeners as the blare of the radio blends into what they are doing. Radio also is increasingly suffering from too many ads. People listen to radio for the music or programming and not for the ads. They get disturbed when ads are too frequent and thus selectively block them from their perceptual processes. When people do perceive the ad, their memory of it is rather short, and unfortunately once they forget the ad, they can't go back in time and relisten to it. Another disadvantage is that since radio is nonvisual, it is impossible to effectively demonstrate or show the merchandise that is being advertised. And, finally, radio signals tend to cover an area much larger than a retailer's trade area. Therefore, a good portion of the retailer's advertising dollars may be wasted.

Television Advertising Most retailers shy away from television advertising. For a small retailer, a half-dozen well-designed television ads may use up the total ad budget. In addition, for the small or even intermediate size retailer, a television ad would reach well beyond its trade area. A final disadvantage of television advertising is that competition is high for the viewer's attention. During advertising periods, the viewer may take a break and leave the room or may be exposed to several ads, one right after another—often advertising different brands of the same product or different retailers in the same line of trade.

In spite of the preceding drawbacks, television advertising can be a powerful tool for generating higher sales. The American public spends more time relaxing in front of the television than in any other recreational activity. Television has broad coverage; over 95 percent of homes in the United States have at least one television set. Many of these sets are color and offer the retailer a vehicle in which both sight and sound can be used to create a significant perceptual and cognitive effect on the consumer.

Recently, the widespread development of cable TV has made television more attractive to local retailers. Local cable operators have been selling retailers advertising on channels reserved for local programming. The cost of advertising on such programs is quite competitive with that of newspaper advertising.

Magazine Advertising Relatively few local retailers advertise in magazines, unless the magazine has only a local circulation. Nationally based retailers such as Sears or Penney's will allocate some of their advertising budget to magazines. Typically, the retail ads that these retailers place in magazines are institutional.

Magazine advertising can be quite effective. In relation to newspapers, the other major print medium, magazines perform well on several dimensions. They have a better reproduction quality than newspapers; they have a longer life than newspapers per issue; and consumers spend more time with each issue of their magazine than their newspaper. An added benefit is that featured articles in the magazine can put people in the mood for a particular product class. For example, a feature article on home remodeling in *Better Homes and Gardens* can put people in a frame of mind to consider purchasing wallpaper, carpeting, tile, draperies, paint, and other home improvement items.

Direct-Mail Advertising With direct-mail advertising, the retailer can precisely target its message at a particular group as long as a good mailing list of the target population is available. Also, the message can be personalized as much as desired, which can be quite effective for very high priced luxury and status-oriented retailers.

On the negative side, direct-mail advertising is relatively expensive per contact or message delivered. Also, the ability to reach the target market depends totally on the quality of the mailing list. If the list is not kept current then advertising dollars will be wasted. A related problem is the incidence of unopened or unexamined mail, especially when it is addressed to "occupant" or is mailed using third-class postage.

Shopping-guide advertising tends to be promotional, emphasizing special prices, but this piece is also institutional, reinforcing the store's image of convenience. (Ad courtesy of Safeway Stores, Inc.)

Miscellaneous Media The retailer can advertise using media other than those previously identified: yellow pages; outdoor advertising; transit advertising (on buses, cabs, subways); and shopping guides (newspaper-like printed material, but with no news). Each of these is usually best used to reinforce the other media and should not be relied on exclusively unless the retailer's advertising budget is minimal. Outdoor, transit, and yellow-page advertising tends to be institutional, wheras shopping-guide advertising tends to be promotional.

Media Selection To select the best media, the retailer needs to know the strengths and weaknesses of each medium—which we have just reviewed—and needs to determine the coverage, reach, and frequency of each medium that is being considered.

Coverage refers to the theoretical percentage of a retailer's target market that can be reached by a medium—not to the percentage actually reached. For example, if a newspaper is circulated to 70 percent of the 20,000 households in a retailer's trade area (i.e., target market) then the theoretical coverage is 14,000 households.

Reach, on the other hand, refers to the actual coverage of an advertising medium. If, on any given day, only 90 percent of those households which receive a newspaper have time to read it then the reach of the newspaper is 0.90 × 0.70 × 20,000, or 12,600 households. Another useful term is **cumulative reach,** which is the actual coverage that is accumulated over time. Using the newspaper example, if 90 percent of the households read the paper on the day they receive it, 8 percent read it on the second day after receiving it, and another 1 percent on the third day after receipt, then the cumulative reach is 0.99 × 0.70 × 20,000, or 13,860.

Frequency is the average number of times each person who is reached is exposed to an advertisement during a given time period. If the newspaper advertisement that we have been using as an example is run for five days straight and if the average person sees three of the ads, then the frequency is three.

Differing media can be evaluated by combining knowledge on the cost of ads in a medium and the medium's reach and cumulative reach. The most commonly used method for doing this is the **cost per thousand method (CPM).** The most appropriate way to compute the CPM is to take the cost for an ad or series of ads in a medium and divide by the reach or cumulative reach. If the newspaper ad we were discussing previously cost $500 and the cumulative reach was 13,860, then the cost per thousand reached by the ad is $36.08. The newspaper may have actually reached 48,200 households in the community, but if only 13,860 were reached in the retailer's trade area, then that is the relevant statistic.

The CPM is good for comparing similar-size advertisements in the same media type—for example, two local newspapers. But, when comparing different media (TV versus newspapers) the CPM can be misleading. A medium such as television may cost more on a CPM criterion, but if it has a significantly greater impact, it may be the better buy. **Impact** refers to how strong an impression an advertisement will make and how well it will ultimately lead to a purchase.

The retailer can use several other methods to select media besides the cost per thousand method. Many advertising agencies use computerized models to aid in selecting media. However, they are too complex to review properly in this text.[10]

Timing of Advertising   When should a retailer time its advertisements to be received by the consumer? What time of day, day of week, week of month, and month of year should the ads appear? No uniform answer to these questions is available for all lines of retail trade. Rather, the following conventional wisdom should be considered.

1. Ads should appear on, or slightly precede, the days when customers are most likely to purchase. If most people shop for groceries on Thursday through Saturday then grocery store ads might appear on Wednesday and Thursday.
2. Advertising should be concentrated around the times when people receive their payroll checks. If they get paid at the end of each month, then advertising should be concentrated at that point.
3. If the retailer has limited advertising funds, it should concentrate its advertising during periods of highest seasonal demand. For example, a lawn

---

10. A good discussion of these models is available in David A. Aaker and John G. Myers, *Advertising Management* (Englewood Cliffs, N.J.: Prentice-Hall, 1975), pp. 469–94.

and garden retailer would concentrate its advertising in the spring and early summer months and perhaps early fall.

4. The retailer should try to minimize advertising during periods of bad weather, since poor weather keeps people indoors and few sales will bring them outdoors. For this reason, some retailers subscribe to weather forecasting services.[11]

5. The retailer should time its ads to appear during the time of day or day of week when the best reach will be obtained.

6. The higher the degree of habitual purchasing of a product class, the more the advertising should precede the purchase time.[12]

7. The greater the carryover effect (i.e., the ad is remembered and influences sales in the future), the more the timing of the advertising should precede the purchase time.[13]

As we mentioned earlier in the chapter, many retailers use advertising to react to crises, and of course if this is the situation, the timing of ads is not planned in advance. This is unfortunate and a source of much inefficiency in retail advertising.

Advertising Results   Will the advertising produce results? It depends on how well designed the ads are and how well the previously mentioned advertising decisions were made. A consistent record of good retail advertising decision making can be made only if the retailer effectively plans its advertising program.

Some retailers will try systematically to assess the effectiveness and efficiency of their advertising.[14] **Advertising effectiveness** refers to the extent to which the advertising has produced the result desired (i.e., helped to achieve the advertising objective). **Advertising efficiency** is concerned with whether the advertising result was achieved with the minimum effort.

If effectiveness or efficiency is assessed in some systematic fashion, then typically certain quantitative or statistical tools are used. Some tools are multiple regression, experimental design, and computer simulation. These are beyond the scope of this text. It should be mentioned, however, that recent developments in electronic point-of-sale terminals and universal product codes have significantly increased the retailer's ability to obtain valid and timely data to put into mathematical models.[15]

The effectiveness or efficiency of a retailer's advertising can be assessed on a subjective basis. Simply ask yourself: Are you satisfied with the results produced? Do you believe you got those results at the least cost?

11. "Can You Plan for Rain?" *Chain Store Age—General Merchandise Edition* (March 1974): 24.

12. This principle is discussed in more detail in Lawrence Jacobs, *Advertising and Promotion for Retailing: Text and Cases* (Glenview, Ill: Scott, Foresman, 1972), p. 92.

13. Jacobs, *Advertising and Promotion*, p. 92.

14. Marcel Marantz, "Evaluating Department Store Advertising," *Journal of Advertising Research* 7 (March 1967): 16–21.

15. "Scanning Data . . . the Real World Applications," *The Nielsen Researcher* no. 4 (1978): 2–8; "Scanning Data Can Measure Long-Run Promotion Response," *Marketing News*, January 11, 1980, p. 11.

Most, but not all, ineffective advertising is due to six errors:

1. The retailer may be bombarding the consumer with so many messages and sales that any single message or sale tends to be discounted. A retailer that has a major sale every week will tend to wear out its appeal.
2. The advertising may not be creative or appealing. It may be just more "me too" advertising in which the retailer does not effectively differentiate itself from the competition.
3. The advertisement may not give the customer all the information he or she needs. The store hours or address may be absent because the retailer assumes that everyone already knows this information. Or, information may be lacking on sizes, styles, colors, and other product attributes.
4. The advertising dollars may have been spread too thinly over too many departments or merchandise lines.
5. There may have been poor internal communication between salesclerks, cashiers, stockboys, and management. For example, customers may come to see the advertised item, but salesclerks may not know the item is on sale or where to find it, and cashiers may not know the sale price.
6. The advertisement may not have been directed at the proper target market.

Inefficiency in advertising can also be traced to major decision errors, four of which are most common:

1. The retailer didn't consider all media options. A better buy was available, but the retailer didn't take the time to find out about it.
2. The retailer made too many last-minute changes in the advertising copy, increasing the cost of the ad.
3. The retailer took coop dollars just because they were free and therefore thought to represent a good deal.
4. The retailer used a medium that reached too many people not in the target market. Thus, too much money was spent on advertising to people who were not potential customers.

SALES PROMOTION MANAGEMENT

At the outset of this chapter, sales promotions were defined as "those marketing activities, other than personal selling, advertising, and publicity that stimulate consumer purchasing and dealer effectiveness, such as display, shows and exhibitions, demonstrations. . . ."[16] In retailing, the most popular sales promotions are displays, consumer premiums such as gifts or trading stamps, games of chance, and product demonstrations.

Role of Sales Promotions Sales promotion tools are excellent demand generators. Many can be used on relatively short notice and can help the retailer achieve its overall promotion goals. Furthermore, sales promotions can be significant in helping the retailer differentiate itself from competitors. A noted authority has suggested,

16. Alexander, et al., *Marketing Definitions*, p. 20.

It takes more than merchandise to make a store take wing and rise above others, and some of that buoyancy is the excitement of in-store happenings. Chop them out, chop the stuff that makes them happen, and you've chopped visibility. You've chopped some of the very things that lift one store above and beyond all others.[17]

In the retailer's overall promotion mix, the role of sales promotion is quite large and often represents a larger expenditure than advertising. Many retailers do not recognize this because of their poor recordkeeping systems. They know the cost of advertising because most of that is paid to parties outside the firm. However, the cost of sales promotion includes the cost of building end-of-aisle displays, giving product demonstrations, increasing energy consumption, etc. Basically, the cost of sales promotions often includes many in-store expenses that the retailer does not trace to promotion activities. If these costs were properly traced, many retailers would discover that sales promotion represents a sizable expenditure. Therefore, promotions warrant more attention by retail decision makers than is typically given.

The role of sales promotion in the retail organization should be consistent and reinforce the retailer's overall promotion objectives. Most sales promotions are not institutional although they should have institutional overtones; they are promotional—as their name implies. They also tend to be directed at improving the retailer's short-run performance. As we saw in Exhibit 17.3, short-run performance can be improved by increasing the patronage of existing customers or by attracting new ones—either from within the existing trade area or from an expanded trade area. The retailer should attempt to develop sales promotion objectives that relate to the preceding promotion objectives. With well-designed sales promotion, all of the preceding objectives can be achieved. In fact, it has been empirically demonstrated that sales promotion can expand a retailer's trade area by a substantial amount—at least temporarily.[18]

Sales Promotion Tools   We will discuss the more frequently used sales promotion tools, including displays, consumer premiums, games, and product demonstrations.

Store Displays   Store displays are of two major types—window and interior. Window displays have actually declined in importance since the early 1960s. In fact, in many new suburban stores, there is very little, if any, window display space. In regional shopping malls, the outside perimeter typically has no windows. All windows are on the inside, but even then each store has a very small storefront and window displays are kept to a minimum. In downtown department stores, window displays are still dominant. In downtown shopping, there is considerable foot traffic as people walk from store to store. This sidewalk traffic can be intercepted with good window displays that urge people to stop and enter the store.

Interior displays are much more widespread in contemporary retailing.

17. M. Seklemian, *Sek Says* (New York: Retail Reporting Bureau, 1979), p. 71.

18. Arno K. Kleimenhagen, Donald G. Leeseberg, and Bernard A. Eilers, "Consumer Response to Special Promotions of Regional Shopping Centers," *Journal of Retailing* 48(Spring 1972): 2–29, 95.

Most are point-of-purchase merchandise displays, which have been shown to be significant demand generators.[19] Technically, interior displays also include store signs and banners—which can also, if properly designed, help generate demand. Regardless of their type, interior displays can generate demand, because many shoppers buy some of their purchases on impulse.[20] In some lines of retailing, such as groceries, up to half of purchase decisions may be made after entering the store. Thus, interior displays can be significant aids in helping the consumer to make purchase decisions. In fact, good signing and display can be a service to the customer.

As a potential retail manager, you should appreciate the potential return achievable from well-designed displays. You should also know that most of your advertising budget may be wasted if the displays don't reinforce the advertising to help close the sale. Advertising may bring people to the store, but displays are needed to prompt the people to make a purchase decision.

Although space does not allow us to instruct you on how to design good displays, you can benefit from knowing the characteristics of good display:

1. The display is *distinctive and dramatic*. . . . Attention and interest are aroused by the dramatic interplay of such forces as color, lines, props, and accessories, lighting arrangement, and motion.

2. It is *pleasing and appropriate*. . . . Harmony is one keynote. All the elements must be in agreement so that the effect produced is one of unity.

3. It is *simple*. Simplicity means that the display message can be quickly received and understood.

4. It generally has a dominant *theme*. The display problem is simplified when merchandise is featured alone and without any special theme, but attention and interest pulling power are enhanced when a central theme is used. In many merchandise lines, for example, events commonly selected for such purposes are Easter, Mother's Day, and Saint Valentine's Day.

5. It emphasizes the *merchandise in use*. Arrangements, pictures, mannequins, and demonstrations that show or suggest the goods in use add greatly to the effectiveness of displays and also afford an opportunity to show and promote the sale of related items and accessories. When practical, the utilization of motion or movement can add much to the realism and appeal of the display.

6. The display is *clean and neat in appearance*. It should not be necessary to mention cleanliness, yet the matter frequently is overlooked or neglected. Nothing detracts so promptly and completely from the value of the display as dirty windows, dusty floors and backgrounds, soiled merchandise, or shabby-looking props and fixtures.[21]

Consumer Premiums Premiums typically involve a tie-in arrangement: the customer gets a free gift or a discount on a gift if he or she purchases a particular product or quantity of merchandise. For example, a grocery retailer may

19. Michel Chevalier, "Increase in Sales Due to In-Store Display," *Journal of Marketing Research* 12(November 1975): 426–31.

20. David T. Kollat and Ronald P. Willett, "Customer Impulse Purchasing Behavior," *Journal of Marketing Research* 4(February 1967): 21–31.

21. William R. Davidson and Alton F. Doody, *Retailing Management*, 3rd ed. (New York: Ronald Press, 1966), pp. 658–59.

offer a four-piece table setting at $1.99 each time the consumer accumulates $20 in purchases. Or an appliance retailer might offer a free portable twelve-inch television with each complete stereo system purchased.

One can give single- or multiple-transaction premiums. With the **single-transaction premium,** the consumer will receive or qualify for the premium through a single transaction (e.g., the free TV example). With the **multiple-transaction premium,** the consumer will receive or may qualify for the premium through one or more transactions (the tableware example could qualify since it may take the customer several purchases or visits to the store to accumulate $20 in purchases).

The most popular multiple-transaction consumer premium is the trading stamp. **Trading stamps** are given to the customer in proportion to purchases made. For example, often the consumer receives ten stamps for each dollar in purchases. These stamps can be accumulated and traded for merchandise—usually durable goods—at a redemption center. The value of the merchandise received by the customer with his or her trading stamps is typically more than the cost of the stamps to the retailer. Thus, if the retailer were to give a cash discount to the customer equal to the cost of the stamps, the customer would receive less value.

Most trading stamps are offered by food retailers. They enjoyed widespread popularity from the mid 1950s through the mid 1960s. However, since that time, their popularity has declined,[22] basically, for two reasons. First, widespread use of trading-stamp programs by food retailers tended to neutralize their effect. When all or most food retailers in a given metropolitan area were offering trading stamps, they no longer became a tool to help the retailer differentiate its offering. In fact, by not offering them when all other retailers were, a retailer could promote its store as a low-price, no-gimmick place to shop. Second, shopper interest in trading stamps gradually declined. The appeal wore off, but some consumers felt compelled to collect the stamps if retailers offered them, because otherwise they would be throwing money away.[23] Thus, consumers weren't collecting because they wanted the stamps, but because they realized they paid for the stamps in higher food prices. They were actually collecting stamps to get back part of the high prices they were paying.

To use trading stamps effectively as a consumer premium, Duncan and Hollander find that the retailer should meet the following four criteria:[24]

1. Sufficient excess capacity to permit absorbing a 10–20% increase in sales without an appreciable change in total overhead costs

2. A location in reasonably close proximity to a group of stores in various fields who do not provide harmful competition but who do use the same accumulation by consumers

3. A willingness to promote the stamps, i.e. a willingness to encourage customers to take them, save them, and redeem them

22. Fred C. Allvine, "The Future for Trading Stamps and Games," *Journal of Marketing* 33(January 1969): 45–52.

23. Allvine, "Future for Trading Stamps and Games."

24. Delbert J. Duncan and Stanley C. Hollander, *Modern Retailing Management*, 9th ed. (Homewood, Ill.: Richard D. Irwin, © 1977), pp. 486–87. Reprinted with permission.

4. The ability to meet competitors in terms of convenience of location, prices, selection and quality of merchandise, courteous and friendly service, cleanliness of housekeeping, and type and quality of services

Strict adherence to these criteria implies that trading stamps will not be the most effective consumer premium for the majority of retailers. However, trading stamp programs continue to produce good results for select retailers if they meet the preceding criteria.

Games of Chance   Games give the customer a chance of winning a gift. The major difference between games and premiums is the fact that with a consumer premium, everyone who meets the requirement gets a free gift or a reduced-price gift, whereas with games only a few patrons receive a gift. The gifts can be large (a free automobile, television, or vacation) or small (a free bath towel or record album). Naturally, the larger the gift, the less likely a customer is to win. At the same time, the large gifts elicit the most excitement and fanfare. A delicate balance between these factors needs to be achieved. The retailer wants to create excitement but also wants to have enough winners to provide incentive for the customer to try to win.

Most games are relatively short-run in their appeal and thus are best used for building short-run market share. In the long run, if games are continually used and are successful, competitors will act to offset the retailer's advantage with games of their own. Another problem that dilutes the effectiveness of games is the antilottery laws in most states. Because of these laws, most retailers will have to offer anyone over the age of eighteen a chance to win regardless of whether they make a purchase at the store or not.

Product Demonstrations   Some retailers will use in-store demonstrations to help generate demand for a product. Many times, in-store demonstrations are paid for, in part or whole, by suppliers.

In food stores, product demonstrations may take the form of free taste samples, which may cause consumers to decide to purchase the item. In apparel stores, the product demonstration may consist of a fashion show. And in appliance stores, the product demonstration may consist of a person demonstrating how to prepare foods with a microwave oven. Whatever the case, the product demonstration is designed to encourage impulse purchasing.

Evaluating Sales Promotions   Since sales promotions are intended to help generate short-run increases in performance, they should be evaluated in terms of their sales- and profit-generating capability. As with advertising, sales promotions can also be evaluated with sophisticated mathematical models. However, the development and use of such models is usually not cost effective.

A simpler approach is to monitor weekly unit volume before the sales promotion and compare it to weekly unit volume during and after the promotion. The before measure provides the retailer with a benchmark that can be compared to results during the sales promotion. But this comparison should be adjusted by the information provided in the after measure, since the sales promotion may have borrowed sales from future time periods.

Consider a grocery store retailer that featured Tide detergent in an end-of-aisle display for two weeks. Before the display, typical weekly movement of Tide was 8 cases. During the display, movement accelerated to 13.2 cases per week. But for the four weeks after the sales promotion, movement was 4.8, 5.3, 6.7, and 7.1 cases per week. In the fifth and subsequent weeks, movement returned to 8 cases per week. Thus, the net impact of the sales promotion was to move an additional 2.3 cases over the two-week display period over what would normally have been moved.[25] Most of the increase in sales during the two-week display period was due to customers buying for future needs. This helps to illustrate a general point about sales promotions: for staple and necessity items, sales promotions will generally encourage people to stock up, but seldom will it encourage them to consume more. Thus, the value of sales promotions for these goods rests on their ability to expand the retailer's trade area and capture customers that would have purchased these items elsewhere. Selling more to existing customers at the expense of their buying less in the future will not economically justify the promotion.

PUBLICITY MANAGEMENT

Publicity was defined at the outset of this chapter as any "nonpersonal stimulation of demand for a product, service or business unit by planting commercially significant news about it in a published medium or obtaining favorable presentation of it upon radio, television, or stage that is not paid for by the sponsor."[26] In part, this definition is misleading. Although the retailer does not directly pay for publicity, it can be very expensive to have a good publicity department that plants the commercially significant news in the appropriate places. It may be even more expensive to create the news that is worth reporting. For example, J. L. Hudson's Thanksgiving Day Parade in Detroit and McDonald's muscular dystrophy contribution represent significant dollar expenditures. They create favorable publicity, but they are expensive. Whether the money could be better spent in other ways is debatable.

We will not pursue a detailed discussion of publicity management, since most retail enterprises do not formally have a publicity department or even a person in charge of publicity. Rather, let us mention that publicity (as was the case with other forms of promotion) has its strengths and weaknesses. Perhaps the major advantages are that it is objective and credible and appeals to a mass audience. The major disadvantages are that publicity is difficult to control and time. Publicity-related events are hard to plan and if they are to be planned, the cost can become exorbitant.

If publicity is formally managed in the retail enterprise, it should be integrated with other elements of the promotion mix. In addition, all publicity should reinforce the store's image.

25. The 2.3 cases are obtained by the following computation: movement during promotion period minus normal movement during promotion period if there had been no promotion minus sales borrowed from future periods; numerically, $(13.2 \times 2) - (8 \times 2) - (8 - 4.8) - (8 - 5.3) - (8 - 6.7) - (8 - 7.1) = 2.3$.

26. Alexander, et al., *Marketing Definitions*, p. 19.

SUMMARY

Retail promotion is comprised of advertising, sales promotions, publicity, and personal selling. All four components must be integrated. In addition, the promotion mix must be integrated with other retail decision areas such as location, merchandise, credit, cash, building and fixtures, price, and customer service. Using its strategic and administrative plans as a backdrop, the retailer should establish promotion objectives that are either directly or indirectly related to improving financial performance.

Retail advertisements can be institutional—attempting to sell the store—or promotional—attempting to bolster short-run performance by advertising product features or price. Nonetheless, all good retail advertising should have institutional overtones. Any ad that does not give the store a favorable image is a mistake.

In budgeting advertising funds, retailers tend to use the affordable method, the percentage-of-sales method, or the task and objective method. Once the budget is established, it should be allocated in such a way that it maximizes the retailer's overall profitability. In determining allocations, retailers can choose from a variety of media alternatives, primarily newspapers, radio, television, magazines, and direct mail. Each medium has its own advantages and disadvantages. To choose among the media, the retailer should know their strengths and weaknesses, coverage and reach, and the cost of an ad. After the retailer selects a medium, it must decide when its ads should appear.

The ability of advertisements to produce results depends on how well the retailer plans its advertising program. Advertising results can be assessed in terms of efficiency and effectiveness. Effectiveness is the extent to which advertising has produced the result desired. Efficiency is concerned with whether the result was achieved with minimum effort.

Sales promotion is a second component of the retail promotion mix. The most popular forms are displays, consumer premiums, games of chance, and product demonstrations. They can be used to help the retailer bolster its short-run performance. As with advertising, the retailer should evaluate the effectiveness and efficiency of sales promotions.

Publicity is a third component of the retail promotion mix. Although the retailer may not directly pay for publicity, the indirect cost can be quite significant. Most retail enterprises do not have formal publicity departments or directors, but some of the more progressive retailers do. The major advantage of publicity is that it is objective, credible, and appeals to a mass audience. The major disadvantage is that publicity is difficult to control and schedule.

QUESTIONS

1. What is the relationship between retail promotion decisions and the marketing channel?

2. Is advertising by retailers any different from advertising by manufacturers?

3. Should all retailers advertise? Explain.

4. What are the two major types of retail advertising? When should each be used?

5. Is publicity free? Explain. Why is it hard to plan and control publicity?

6. How should a retailer decide whether to offer trading stamps?

7. What are the major strengths of advertising in each of the following media: newspaper, radio, television, magazine, direct mail.

8. How should advertising and sales promotions be evaluated?

9. How should the retailer decide to allocate its advertising budget to different merchandise lines?

PROBLEMS AND EXERCISES

1. You have been invited by the local retail merchants association to make a speech on the design of retail displays. Prepare an outline for this speech.

2. Develop a sales promotion program for a hardware store that desires to increase its business during the summer and winter seasons.

3. Select two local jewelers and obtain copies of their local newspaper advertising over the last several months. Are the images projected by the advertisements different? Visit the two jewelers and assess whether the exterior and interior of the store and the store personnel reinforce the image presented in the advertising.

4. Interview the sales manager of a local radio station about the benefits of radio advertising to retailers.

5. A retailer is offered a coop advertising deal from a major supplier. The supplier will pay 60 percent of the retailer's advertising expense as long as the advertising uniquely features the supplier's product line. The retailer is considering spending $8,000 on advertising the supplier's line, since the supplier will pick up $4,800 of it. The product line has a gross margin of 64 percent, and the retailer expects the advertising to increase sales by 30 percent. Current sales are $100,000. Should the retailer do it?

SUGGESTED READINGS

Albaum, Gerald, Roger Best, and Del Hawkins. "Retailing Strategy for Custom Growth and New Customer Attraction." *Journal of Business Research* 8(March 1980): 7–19.

Bellenger, Danny N. and Jack R. Pingry. "Direct-Mail Advertising for Retail Stores." *Journal of Advertising Research* 17(June 1977): 35–39.

Berger, Paul D. "Vertical Cooperative Advertising Ventures." *Journal of Marketing Research* 9(August 1972): 309–12.

Curhan, Ronald C. "Shelf Space Allocation and Profit Maximization in Mass Retailing." *Journal of Marketing* 37(July 1973): 54–60.

Krugman, Herbert E. "Why Three Exposures May Be Enough." *Journal of Advertising Research* 12(December 1972): 11–15.

Lavidge, Robert and Gary A. Steiner. "A Model for Predictive Measurements of Advertising Effectiveness." *Journal of Marketing* 25(October 1961): 59–62.

Strang, Roger A. "Sales Promotion—Fast Growth, Faulty Management." *Harvard Business Review* 54(July–August 1976): 115–24.

Whitney, John O. "Better Results from Retail Advertising." *Harvard Business Review* 48(May–June 1970): 111–20.

18

Overview *In this chapter we will discuss the personal selling decisions in retail enterprises. Specifically, we will discuss from a managerial perspective the compensation of salespeople; the selection, training, determination of number, and scheduling of salespeople; and the evaluation of salespeople.*

Retail Promotion: Personal Selling

FROM EXPERIENCE AND OBSERVATION, we can probably all recall situations when retail salespersons have been a major factor in our purchase decisions. For example, when the retail salesperson is busy helping someone else, rude, or not helpful, we will often walk out of the store empty-handed. When the salesperson is available, friendly, and helpful, we, as customers, will often be influenced to enter into a transaction with the retailer. The management of the retail sales force plays a crucial role in demand generation for retail enterprises.

TYPES OF RETAIL SALESPEOPLE

In many retail settings, the employees that are called salespeople are simply order takers. For example, consider the role of a salesperson in a typical discount department store such as a K-mart. The employee might show the customer where the merchandise is located in the store or may go to the storeroom to get an item that is not on the shelf, but seldom, if ever, does he or she attempt to sell the merchandise. That these employees should be called *salespeople* is debatable. Perhaps they should be referred to as *retail clerks*. Nonetheless, one must recognize that these order takers can influence demand. If you are in a store such as K-mart and cannot find a retail clerk to assist you when you need help, you may get frustrated and leave the store without making a purchase.

Retailers selling specialty products should have informed salespeople. (Photo courtesy of Scotty's, Inc.)

Retail employees that are most appropriately labeled **salespeople** should be order getters as well as order takers. Order getters are involved in conversation with prospective purchasers for the purpose of making a sale. They will inform, guide, and persuade the customer in order to culminate a transaction either immediately or in the future.

The emphasis the retailer places on its employees being order takers depends on the line of retail trade and the retailer's strategy. Lines that concentrate on the sale of shopping goods (e.g., automobile dealers, furniture retailers, and appliance retailers) will want their salespeople to be both order getters and takers. In lines of retail trade where convenience goods are predominantly sold (gasoline service stations and grocery retailers) the role of the salesperson (or what many may call the retail clerk) will be to take orders. In terms of strategic orientation, it is generally true that retailers with high margins and high levels of customer service will place more emphasis on order getting. Those with low margins and a low customer service policy will tend to emphasize order taking.

Clearly, however, regardless of the line of retail trade or the retailer's strategic thrust, all retail enterprises must carefully evaluate the role of the salesperson in helping to generate demand.

COMPENSATION

A Performance Imperative   In most lines of retail trade the productivity of retail salespeople has been stagnant or slightly declining since the early 1970s. Retailers appear to have been caught in a vicious circle in which the relatively low wages they offer salespeople has attracted low-quality employees, which tends to perpetuate the low wage cycle.

Let us elaborate on this point further. Retail salespeople are not motivated by low wages and thus quickly lose morale. Consequently, many of them become disgruntled, and employee turnover rises and productivity falls. The decline in productivity and the prospect for continued high turnover prompts retailers to keep wages low. In short, retailers have created a self-fulfilling prophecy.[1] It is not surprising, therefore, that in some retail stores the sales force you see today is totally different from the one you would have seen last year or the one you will probably see next year.

The profit impact of increased salesforce productivity in retailing is dramatic. As we mentioned in earlier chapters, retailers operate very close to their break-even point due to the relatively high costs of opening the store doors each morning. Therefore, a 10 to 15 percent increase in salesforce productivity would, in most part, directly translate into a proportional improvement in store profits. Consequently, retail managers should accept a major performance imperative to increase salesforce productivity in the future.

1. Bert C. McCammon, Jr., and William L. Hammer, "A Frame of Reference for Improving Productivity in Distribution," *Atlanta Economic Review* 59(September–October 1974): 9–13.

To program operations to increase salesforce performance over forthcoming budget periods, a retailer needs to develop frames of reference for the following decision areas: compensation, selection, training, size, scheduling, and evaluation.

If you wish to develop a highly productive retail sales force you must first decide on a compensation program. It will be essential in attracting, motivating, and retaining that sales force. The retailer should develop a profitable compensation program, and the most profitable compensation program is not always the least expensive one. Consider a shoe retailer paying its salespeople a straight salary of $220 per week in comparison to one paying its salespeople $180 weekly salary plus a 3.5 percent commission on all sales, with the net result that the average salesperson earns $295 per week. If the sales force of the second shoe retailer is able to generate substantially higher sales than the sales force of the first, the second retailer will be more profitable—even though its salesforce compensation costs are considerably higher in absolute dollars.

This illustration is intended to demonstrate that in establishing retail salesforce compensation, the name of the game is not cost control but profit control. Any retailer can control its salesforce compensation costs simply by refusing to pay higher wages or by reducing the number of salespeople. It is more difficult to determine the compensation program that will maximize its profit potential.

Compensation Programs   Retail salesforce compensation programs can be conveniently broken into three major types: (1) straight salary, (2) straight commission, and (3) salary plus commission, each with advantages and disadvantages.

Straight Salary   In the straight salary program, the salesperson receives a fixed salary per time period (usually per week) regardless of the level of sales generated or orders taken. However, over time, if the salesperson does not help generate sales or take enough orders, he or she will likely be fired for not performing adequately. Similarly, over time, if the salesperson helps to generate more than a proportionate share of sales or fills more than a proportionate number of orders, the retailer will be unable to retain the employee without a raise.

Most small retailers use this compensation method, because they typically assign nonselling duties to their salespeople. Therefore, if the employees were paid on a commission basis they would spend little if any time on their nonselling duties, and the retail organization would suffer. Also, many promotional and price-oriented chain stores whose salespeople are merely order takers will use the straight salary method because the salesperson is not much of a causal factor in generating many additional sales.

The salesperson may view this plan as attractive because it offers income security or as unappealing because it gives little incentive for extraordinary effort and performance. Thus, for the method to be effective it must be combined with a periodic evaluation so that superior salespeople can be identified and singled out for higher salaries.

Straight Commission Income of some salespeople is limited to a percentage commission on each sale they generate. The commission could be the same percentage on all merchandise or it could vary depending on the profitability of the item. Retail salespeople working on a straight commission typically receive commissions of 2 percent to 8 percent.

The straight commission plan provides substantial incentive for retail salespeople to generate sales. However, when the general business climate is poor, retail salespeople may not be able to generate enough volume to meet their fixed payment obligations (mortgage payment, auto payment, food expenses). Because of that problem, most retailers slightly modify the straight commission plan to allow the salesperson to draw wages against future commissions up to some specified amount per week. For instance, the employee may be able to draw $200 per week, which will be paid back with future commissions.

A major problem with the straight commission plan is that it may provide the retail salesperson with too much incentive to sell. He or she may begin to use pressure tactics to close sales, hurting the retailer's image and long-run sales performance. Similarly, the employee may not be willing to perform other duties such as helping customers with returned merchandise or helping to set up displays, because after all, compensation is paid to sell and not to handle customer complaints or displays.

Salary Plus Commission Sometimes the salesperson is paid a fixed salary per time period plus a percentage commission on all sales or on all sales over an established quota. The fixed salary is lower than that of the salesperson working on a straight salary plan, but the commission structure gives one the potential to earn more than the person on the straight salary plan. In fact, most salespeople on the salary plus commission program earn more than their counterparts on a straight salary program.

This plan gives the employees a stable base income—and thus incentive to perform nonselling tasks—but it also encourages and rewards superior effort. Therefore, it represents a good compromise between the straight salary and the straight commission programs.

Any quotas in the commission portion of the plan must be properly established. Developing the quota-based commission plan involves four steps:

1. Determining the weekly (or monthly) quota for the department or unit. This is usually based on past sales, with adjustment for changed conditions and for seasonal fluctuations. If $1,500 has been the average weekly sales in the past, this figure may be used as the quota. To be a sales stimulus, the quota should remain within the reach of practically all the salespeople. Yet it cannot be too low or everyone will reach it without much effort.

2. Establishing the basic salary. This salary is usually determined on the basis of the past wage-cost ratio adjusted in the light of competitive practices. If this ratio has been about 7 percent, the basic salary might be established at 7 percent of the quota; that is, $105 on a $1,500 quota.

3. Setting the commission rate for sales in excess of the quota. In practice this commission is usually set considerably below the store's average wage cost.

Frequently, the commission is set at about 2 percent. In some cases the bonus is a specific dollar amount, rather than a percentage of sales in excess of the quota.

4. Deciding whether each period involves a "fresh start" (noncumulative plans) or whether salespeople who fail to make their quota in one period have to fill the deficiency before becoming eligible for a bonus in the next period (cumulative plans). Most plans today are noncumulative.[2]

Supplemental Benefits   Retail salespeople, in addition to receiving regular wages (salary, commission, or both) also can receive three types of supplementary benefits: employee discounts, insurance and retirement benefits, and PMs.

Employee Discounts   Almost all retailers offer their salespeople discounts on merchandise they purchase for themselves or for their immediate family. About the only line of trade where the discounts are not offered is grocery retailing. This is because grocery retailers operate on relatively thin gross margins. In other lines of retail trade the discounts range from 10 to 20 percent

Insurance and Retirement Benefits   Traditionally, retail salespeople have not been provided with any insurance or retirement benefits. In most situations this is still the case. But a few retailers are providing their salespeople with either free or low-cost group health and life insurance. Still others are making profit sharing, stock ownership, and retirement programs available to long-tenure salespeople.

PM   A final type of supplementary benefit is the PM, standing for "push money," "prize money," or "premium merchandise"; in the retail trades it is called "spiffing."[3] The PM is paid to the salesperson in addition to a base salary and regular commissions. It is said to encourage additional selling effort placed behind particular items or merchandise lines.

PMs can be either retailer or supplier sponsored. A retailer may give a PM in order to get salespeople to sell old or slow-moving merchandise. The salesperson who sells the most may win a free trip to Hawaii or some other prize. Or possibly everyone who sells an established quantity of merchandise may get a prize or premium. On the other hand, the supplier tends to offer PMs to retail salespeople for selling the top-of-the line or most profitable items in the supplier's product mix. These supplier-offered PMs are common in the appliance, furniture, jewelry, and floorcovering industries.

Often there may be a conflict between the supplier and retailer over the offering of PMs. This conflict arises because the supplier may be offering the retailer's salespeople an incentive to push an item or merchandise line that may not be the most profitable line for the retailer, although it may be highly profitable to the supplier.

2. Delbert J. Duncan and Stanley C. Hollander, *Modern Retailing Management*, 9th ed. (Homewood, Ill.: Richard D. Irwin, © 1977) 235–36. Reprinted with permission.

3. Dale Varble and L. E. Bergerson, "The Use and Facets of PM's—A Survey of Retailers," *Journal of Retailing* 48(Winter 1972–73): 40–47.

SALESPERSON SELECTION

Selecting retail salespeople should involve more than casually accepting anyone who walks into the store seeking gainful employment. In fact, the casualness with which many retailers have selected people to fill sales positions is one cause of poor productivity.

Criteria

To select salespeople properly, the retailer must decide what its criteria will be. What is expected from retail salespeople? Is the retailer looking for a work force that has low turnover, low absenteeism, the ability to generate a high volume of sales, or some combination? Unless you know what you are looking for in salespeople you will be certain not to acquire a sales force that possesses the proper qualities.

Predictors

Once the criteria have been determined, you must identify the potential predictors (which will help to predict the criteria). The most common predictors used in selecting retail salespeople are demography; personality; knowledge, intelligence, and education; and prior work experience.

Demography Depending on the specific line of retail trade, demographic variables can be important in identifying good retail salespeople.[4] For example, a record and stereo store appealing to teens will probably benefit from retail salespeople under thirty years of age. A high-fashion women's apparel store appealing to eighteen- to thirty-year-old, career-oriented, and upwardly mobile females would probably not desire forty-five-year-old salespeople from lower social class backgrounds. And a motorcycle shop would probably not want sixty-year-old ladies selling motorcycles. Obviously, there are exceptions to each of the preceding rules, but the essential point is that retailers can use demographic variables to help screen applicants for sales positions.

Personality A person's personality can reflect on his or her potential as a retail salesperson. The retailer would most likely prefer salespeople that are friendly, confident, stable, and empathetic. These personality traits can be identified either through a personal interview with the applicant or by paper-and-pencil personality inventories. In most lines of retail trade the personal interview will be sufficient.

Knowledge, Intelligence, Education Many products that retailers sell are technically complex. Consider for example minicomputers, solid-state televisions, microwave ovens, 35 mm cameras, and ten-speed bicycles. Salespeople

---

4. For a good discussion of how demographic data can be systematically used to select retail salespeople, see J. N. Mosel and R. R. Wade, "A Weighted Application Blank for Reduction of Turnover in Department Store Salesclerks," *Personnel Psychology* 4(1951): 177–84; and Robert F. Hartley, "The Weighted Application Blank Can Improve Retail Employee Selection," *Journal of Retailing* 46(Spring 1970): 32–40.

with knowledge of these products will be better able to sell them. Similarly, to be able to respond to customer inquiries in a logical fashion, retail employees will need to possess some level of education and intelligence.

Experience One of the most reliable predictors of success as a salesperson is prior work experience, especially selling experience. If an applicant has performed well in prior jobs, there is a good chance that he or she will perform well in the future. The correlation, however, is not perfect. Also, many applicants for retail selling jobs will be young and have no prior work experience of any magnitude. These applicants are better assessed on their personal character and apparent ambition, drive, and work ethic.

SALESPERSON TRAINING

After salespeople are selected, they should be exposed to some form of training.[5] This is true even if they have selling experience, since each retailer will have its own store policies that new employees will need to learn. Furthermore, the retailer may believe that inexperienced salespeople should become familiar with and knowledgeable about the retailer's merchandise, the different customer types they may have to deal with, and the selling strategies for different customer choice criteria.

5. Irving Burstiner, "Current Personnel Practices in Department Stores," *Journal of Retailing* 51(Winter 1975–76): 3–14, 86; and "Retailers Discover an Old Tool: Sales Training," *Business Week*, December 22, 1980, pp. 51–52.

Successful retailers recognize the need to train the sales force to become friendlier, more informed, and more efficient. (Photo courtesy of K-mart Corporation.)

Store Policies   The retail salesperson many times will be the spokesperson for the retailer. In most situations, the interface between the customer and retailer takes place through the salesperson. It is thus important for the salesperson to become familiar with the store policies, especially those which may involve the customer directly. Some of these policies would relate to merchandise returns and adjustments, shoplifting, credit terms, layaway, delivery, and price negotiating. In addition, the retail salesperson should become knowledgeable about work hours, rest periods, lunch and dinner breaks, commission and quota plans, nonselling duties, and standards of periodic job evaluation. It might also be useful to inform sales employees about criteria used for promotion and advancement within the retail enterprise.

Merchandise   If the merchandise includes shopping goods, the retailer will want to train its salespeople to be familiar with the strengths and weaknesses of the merchandise. This will allow salespeople to assist customers in shopping for the best goods to meet their needs. It also suggests that the salesperson become knowledgeable of the competitor's merchandise offerings and their strengths and weaknesses.

Increasingly, retail salespeople need to be familiar with the warranty terms on merchandise the retailer handles and also the serviceability of the merchandise. This implies that the salesperson know something about the reputation of each manufacturer the retailer represents.

Customer Types   Retail salespeople can be taught how to identify and respond to certain customer types. The twelve basic customer types are described in Exhibit 18.1. By knowing how to handle each of these customers the salesperson can generate added sales.

Customer Choice Criteria   The retail salesperson should also learn how to identify the customer's choice criteria and how to respond to them.[6] There are four choice criteria situations: (1) the customer has no active product choice criteria; (2) the customer has product choice criteria but they are inadequate or vague; (3) the customer has product choice criteria but they are in conflict; and (4) the customer has product choice criteria that are explicit and well defined. For each situation there is an appropriate selling strategy that the salesperson should learn.

No Active Product Choice Criteria   The best sales strategy when there are no criteria is to educate the customer on the best choice criteria and possibly how to weigh them. For example, a prospective customer enters an automobile dealership to purchase a used automobile but does not know what criteria to use to select the best car. The car salesperson may present convincing arguments on why the customer should consider four criteria in the following order of

6. Much of the following is based on John O'Shaughnessy, "Selling as an Interpersonal Influence Process," *Journal of Retailing* 47(Winter 1971–72): 32–46.

EXHIBIT 18.1   **How Salespeople Should Handle the Twelve Types of Customer**

	CUSTOMER			SALESPERSON
Basic Types	Basic Characteristic	Secondary Characteristics	Other Characteristics	What to Say or Do
Arguer	Takes issue with each statement of salesperson	Disbelieves claims, tries to catch salesperson in error	Cautious Slow to decide	Demonstrate Show product knowledge Use "yes, but . . ."
Chip on shoulder	Definitely in a bad mood	Indignation Angry at slight provocation	Acts as if being deliberately baited	Avoid argument Stick to basic facts Show good assortment
Decisive	Knows what is wanted	Customer confident his choice is right	Not interested in another opinion— respects salesperson's brevity	Win sale—not argument Sell self Tactfully inject opinion
Doubting Thomas	Doesn't trust sales talk	Hates to be managed	Arrives at decision cautiously	Back up merchandise statements by manufacturer's tags, labels Demonstrate merchandise Let customer handle merchandise
Fact-finder	Interested in factual information— detailed	Alert to salesperson's errors in description	Looks for actual tags and labels	Emphasize label and manufacturers' facts Volunteer care information
Hesitant	Ill at ease—sensitive	Shopping at unaccustomed price range	Unsure of own judgment	Make customer comfortable Use friendliness and respect
Impulsive	Quick to decide or select	Impatience	Liable to break off sale abruptly	Close rapidly Avoid oversell, overtalk Note key points
Indecisive	Little ability to make own decision	Anxious—fearful of making a mistake	Wants salesperson's aid in decision—wants advisor—wants to do "right thing"	Emphasize merits of product and service, "zeroing" in on customer-expressed need and doubts
Look around	The "shopper"— getting ideas— what's new	Doesn't want salesperson hovering about	"Handles" a lot of goods	Watch for "buying" signals Be courteous and enthusiastic Emphasize store service
Procrastinator	I'll wait 'til tomorrow	Lacks confidence in own judgment	Insecure	Reinforce customer's judgments
Silent	Not talking—but thinking!	Appears indifferent but truly listening	Appears nonchalant	Ask direct questions— straightforward approach Watch for "buying" signals
Think it over	Refers to need to consult someone else	Looking for another advisor	Not sure of own uncertainty	Get agreement on small points "Draw out" opinions Use points agreed upon for close

Source: From *Learning Experiences in Retailing* by C. Winston Borgen, p. 293. Copyright ©1976 Goodyear Publishing Company. Reprinted by permission.

importance: warranty, fuel economy, price, and comfort. Once the salesperson and customer agree on this list, they can work together at finding the used car on the dealer's lot that best fits the criteria.

Inadequate or Vague Choice Criteria   When the criteria are vague, the range of products that will satisfy them is often wide. Perhaps the easiest thing for the salesperson to do would be to try to show that a particular product fits a customer's choice criteria. Since the choice criteria are vague this would not be difficult and little actual selling would be involved. But since the criteria are vague, the customer may have trouble believing that the product the salesperson selected is the best one to meet his or her needs. The customer may therefore choose to shop around at other stores.

If the salesclerk is interested in repeat business and customer goodwill and has a wide range of products to sell, a preferable strategy would be to help the customer define his or her problem in order to arrive at a set of choice criteria. The customer and salesclerk would work together in defining the criteria of a good product and then select the product that best fits the criteria.

Choice Criteria in Conflict   Prospective customers with choice criteria that are in conflict frequently have trouble making purchase decisions. There are two basic ways in which choice criteria can be in conflict. First, the customer may want a product to possess two or more attributes that are mutually exclusive. For example, a person purchasing a ten-speed bicycle may wish it to be of high quality and low price. This person will quickly find that these two attributes do not exist in common. The best strategy in this situation is for the salesperson to play down one of the attributes and play up the other. A second way the choice criteria could be in conflict is when a single attribute possesses both positive and negative aspects. Consider a person thinking of purchasing a high performance automobile. High performance automobiles have both positive aspects (status, speed, and pleasure fulfillment) and negative aspects (high insurance and low mileage per gallon). For this type of conflict, the best selling strategy is to enhance the positive aspects and depreciate the negative aspects.

Explicit Choice Criteria   When the customer has well-defined, explicit choice criteria, the best selling strategy is for the salesperson to illustrate how a specific product fits the criteria. ''The salesclerk guides the customer into agreeing that each attribute of his product matches the attributes on the customer's specification. If, at the end of the sales talk, the customer does not agree to the salesclerk's proposition, he appears to be denying what he has previously admitted.''[7]

NUMBER OF SALESPEOPLE

The number of salespeople you will need to staff a store depends on customer traffic and the level of customer service you want to provide. The greater the level of store traffic and the more that traffic fluctuates by time of day, week,

7. O'Shaughnessy, ''Interpersonal Influence Process,'' p. 41.

and season, the larger the sales staff you will require. At the same time, the more you wish to minimize the amount of time a prospective customer has to wait for sales assistance, the larger sales staff you will need. To a considerable extent, this latter decision on customer service will depend on competitive practice. If competitors offer high levels of customer service, you have less flexibility in doing otherwise.

Waiting-Line Theory   In Exhibit 18.2 we view the optimal sales force size decision as a problem in waiting-line theory.[8] When customers arrive at the store they can enter three possible states. They can immediately be assisted by a salesperson, they can search for what they want unassisted, or they can wait for service. Let us examine how in each of these states a customer would progress to finally exiting the store.

Assisted Search   When a person enters a store and is immediately greeted by a salesperson one of two things can happen. The person may accept the offer of assistance and allow the salesclerk to do his or her job. Once the salesclerk has assisted the customer, the customer will leave the store either with or with-

EXHIBIT 18.2   **Customer Service Outcomes**

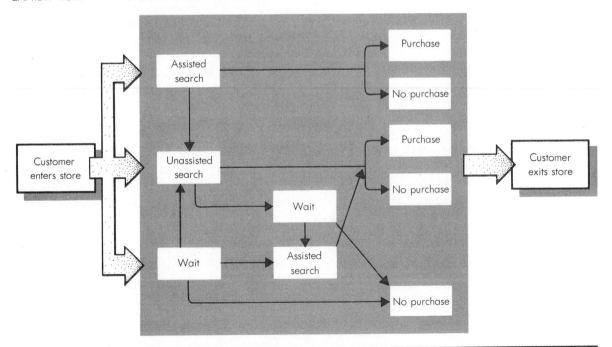

8. Two excellent articles in this regard are Robert J. Paul, "The Retail Store as a Waiting Line Model," *Journal of Retailing* 48(Summer 1972): 3–13; and R. Dale Von Riesen, "Toward Staffing Optimality in Retail Selling," *Journal of Retailing* 49(Winter 1973–74): 37–47.

out having made a purchase. Or, the person may tell the salesclerk that no assistance is wanted. In this case, the person enters the unassisted search state (see Exhibit 18.2).

Unassisted Search   If the customer enters the store and immediately begins an unaided search for merchandise, or if the customer was first offered assistance but refused it, or if the customer was waiting for service but got frustrated and decided to search without help, then the customer is in an unassisted search state. What happens to the customer in this state? The shopper may find what is wanted, pay for the item, and exit the store. Or, the shopper may not find what is wanted and leave in disgust. Or, after unassisted search, the shopper may decide that help is needed and wait for service. While waiting, the shopper may renege and exit the store. Or, after waiting, the shopper may be assisted by a salesclerk and ultimately exit the store either with or without making a purchase.

Waiting   The final possible state is waiting. Here, on entering the store, the customer immediately decides that assistance is wanted but, since it is not available, waits. The wait should be short and the customer quickly assisted by a salesclerk. After being assisted, the customer will exit the store either with or without a purchase.

If the customer waits too long for assistance, he or she may renege and exit the store empty-handed. Another possibility that could come from a long wait is that the customers may decide to hunt the merchandise themselves and will go through the unassisted search process.

Staffing

The optimum number of salesclerks is a direct outgrowth of the waiting-line model in Exhibit 18.2. More salesclerks (given a certain level of customer traffic) can help more people immediately if they desire assistance. People will then spend less time waiting. The impact on revenue generation would be positive because as waiting time decreases and sales assistance increases, the probability of the customer finding what is wanted also increases and thus retail sales increase. Also, as waiting time declines, customers are less likely to exit the store in frustration. Finally, cutting down on waiting time removes congestion; as waiting time increases, the store becomes more congested, which can create an unpleasant atmosphere and damage business.[9]

The staffing problem basically involves comparing the marginal cost of increasing the number of salesclerks and the marginal revenue attained through increased customer service in terms of shorter waiting lines and less in-store congestion. Robert Paul summarizes this notion quite succinctly when he says that the retailer

> wants waiting lines short enough to minimize customer ill will (maximize customer satisfaction), while realizing that he cannot afford to provide enough service

9. Gilbert D. Harrell, Michael D. Hutt, and James C. Anderson, "Path Analysis of Buyer Behavior Under Conditions of Crowding," *Journal of Marketing Research* 17(February 1980): 45–51.

facilities to be certain that no waiting line will ever exist. Essentially the manager balances the increased cost of additional service personnel against his estimate of the cost of customer ill will, which increases as the average length of the waiting line increases.[10]

In Exhibit 18.3, we diagram the optimal staffing decision in terms of a pair of cost curves: the opportunity cost of lost sales as the customer has to wait too long for assistance, and the payroll cost of the additional salesclerks needed to reduce waiting time. As is evident in Exhibit 18.3, the two curves move in opposite directions. When more salespeople are added, the payroll costs rise but the cost of lost sales declines. By summing the two cost curves, one can obtain the relevant total cost curve. The minimum of this total cost curve will represent the optimal size sales force.

SCHEDULING

Knowing the optimal size sales force does the retailer little good if it badly allocates the sales force to different times of the day, days of the week, and even months of the year (i.e., when vacations should be taken). This allocation is called the salesforce scheduling decision.

Scheduling would be simple if customers were to arrive at the store evenly throughout the day, week, or month. Operating under this ideal situation, the retail manager would simply divide its salesclerks evenly over time. Unfortunately, the customer does not behave in such a predictable and orderly fashion.

EXHIBIT 18.3
**Optimal
Salesforce Size**

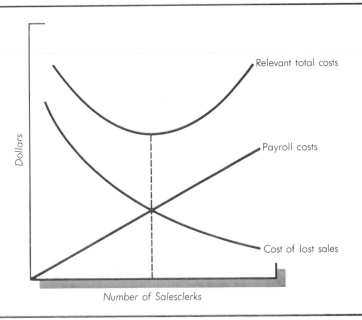

10. Paul, "Waiting Line Model," p. 7.

For example, a disproportionate number of people shop downtown department stores from 11 A.M. to 2 P.M., which coincides with the lunch hours of downtown offices. Furniture retailers will do a brisker business in the evenings and weekends when both husband and wife can shop together; the same is true of automobile dealerships. Toy stores will do 40 percent of their business in November through December. Garden and lawn supply stores will have their peak selling season in the spring and early fall. In short, demand is time dependent. And this time dependency is the major factor the retailer needs to consider in scheduling its salesclerks.

The Ideal Schedule   Strictly from the retailer's and customer's perspective, and ignoring what salesclerks might desire, the ideal schedule would be to match consumer shopping patterns precisely with salesclerks scheduling patterns. Let us consider a suburban, full-service department store. When the retailer opens its doors at 9:30 A.M. there are always six to ten shoppers waiting to enter the doors. Traffic through the doors is relatively low, but at about 10:30 A.M. it starts to build rapidly and stays high until about 1:00 P.M., when it begins to drop substantially. From 2:00 P.M., until 5:00 P.M. there are relatively few customers in the store. At about 5:30 P.M. store traffic once again starts to build and reaches a peak at about 7:30 P.M., when it begins to taper off and then declines to the point at which the manager must personally escort a few stragglers out of the store when it closes at 9:30 P.M.. Ideally, the retailer would employ salespeople in one-hour (or even smaller) increments and schedule in direct proportion to the preceding customer traffic flow. Very few salespeople would be on hand at 9:30 A.M., but from 10:30 A.M. to 1:00 P.M. more salespeople would arrive to assist customers. From 2:00 to 5:00 P.M. most salespeople would leave the store and be off the payroll, because customer traffic is sparse. Then at about 5:30 P.M. the retailer would schedule more salespeople to work as the evening flow of customers increases. At about 7:30 P.M. the retailer would start to send salespeople home so that by 9:30 P.M., when the doors are closed, there would not only be few customers on hand, but also few salesclerks.

As you might well expect, this ideal scheduling plan minimizes payroll costs while achieving high levels of customer service, but no retailer could get employees to agree to such a schedule. Most salesclerks will simply refuse to come in for an hour or two and then be off the payroll for several hours only to return to work later in the day for another few hours. Retail wages are simply not attractive enough to allow the retailer to demand such a burdensome schedule.

Realistic Scheduling   Although the ideal scheduling pattern is not achievable in practice, you can develop a realistic scheduling pattern that will both control costs and facilitate salesforce productivity. To accomplish this, you must determine the preferences and desires of the salesclerks, and you must establish tasks other than selling that the salesclerks can perform when customer traffic is low.

Preferences of Salesclerks   Salesclerks will not allow their work hours to be totally manipulated by the store manager merely for store efficiency. However, the salesclerks will vary in their working hour prefernces, and you should capitalize on these preferences. Some clerks may want to work only four-hour days; others may only want to work on weekdays; some may prefer evenings; others may want to be at home at 3 P.M. to take care of schoolchildren; still others may want to work only four days but would be willing to work ten- to twelve-hour days on weekends if they can get three days off per week. The starting point then is to analyze your clerks' preferences.

In practically all situations, the preferences of the salesclerks will not perfectly coincide with the retailer's staffing requirements. You then have two options, which can be separately or jointly pursued. One is to develop some priority system in which the longer the tenure of the employee, the greater the employee's flexibility in working a preferred time schedule. Another is slowly to replace clerks that quit or are fired with those who express a desire or willingness to work a specified schedule. For example, if you find that the store is under-staffed on weekends and evenings and none of the existing clerks prefer those hours, then new salesclerks should be screened to make sure that they would be willing to have or actually prefer weekend or evening hours.

Nonselling Duties Since you will be unable to schedule the salesclerks to match customer traffic patterns precisely, there will be times when the store is over- or under-staffed. When it is over-staffed the salesclerks will be idle. Idle salesclerks are a problem in several ways. They tend to leave the sales floor more often for breaks and wandering around the store and, therefore, are not available when an unexpected increase in traffic occurs during a normally slow period. When idle, they are also more likely to steal or conspire with other employees to steal. Also, it creates a poor impression when a customer enters a store and notices several employees standing idly around with nothing to do but talk with each other or read a book, magazine, or newspaper. Idle employees tend to lose morale quickly. Finally, they represent wasted payroll dollars.

To minimize the extent to which salesclerks are idle during periods of slow customer traffic, they should be assigned nonselling duties. Such duties can include straightening and rearranging, replenishing, pricing and unpacking merchandise, handling returns, taking inventory, and helping to build merchandise displays.

EVALUATING SALESPEOPLE

The retailer should develop a systematic method for evaluating both individual salespeople and the total sales staff. Rather than subjectively evaluating performance, the manager should develop standards for its sales staff. The tools for developing scientific performance standards are available and can be readily applied in a retail setting.[11]

11. Robert J. Paul and Robert W. Bell, "Quantitative Determination of Manpower Requirements in Variable Activities," *Journal of Retailing* 43(Summer 1967): 21–27, 67.

Performance Standards   Several standards can be developed to measure a salesperson's performance. Some of them apply only to individual effort, whereas others assess both individual and total salesforce effort.

Conversion Rate   The conversion rate is computed by dividing the total number of customers who walk out of the store with a purchase by the total number of customers who entered the store. This measure reflects the percentage of shoppers who were converted into customers and the overall salesforce performance.

A poor conversion rate can be caused by a variety of factors. Perhaps there were not enough clerks on hand when customers needed them. This could have resulted in a high degree of unassisted search and long customer waiting times, with many customers exiting the store without making a purchase. Or the number of salesclerks could have been adequate to handle the flow of customers but the salesclerks may not have done a good selling job. A poor selling job could have been caused by a variety of factors, such as poor qualifications of the clerk, giving inadequate product information to the customer, disagreeing or arguing too strongly with the customer, demonstrating the product poorly, having an unfriendly attitude, or giving up too early. Also, a low conversion rate may have been due to factors beyond the salesperson's control, such as inadequate merchandise levels. The important point is that when a substandard conversion rate exists, the retailer should try to identify the causes and work to remedy the situation.

Sales per Hour   Perhaps the most common measure of a salesperson's or sales force's performance is sales per hour, which is computed by taking total dollar sales over a particular time frame and dividing by total salesperson or salesforce hours. With a well-designed record keeping system, a retailer can compute this simple measure for each salesperson, any group of salespeople, or the entire sales force.

When employing this measure, remember that standards should be specific to the group or person being evaluated for a particular time period. For example, in a department store the sales per hour of selling effort cannot be expected to be the same for the toy department as for the jewelry department. Nor could one expect the same sales per hour during July and December, because of the heavy Christmas demand for toys and jewelry.

Use of Time   Standards can be developed for how salespeople should spend their time. A salesperson's time can be spent in four ways:

1. **Selling time** is any time spent in assisting customers with their needs. This would be time spent talking, demonstrating, writing sales receipts, or assisting the customer in other potentially revenue-generating ways.
2. **Nonselling time** is any time spent on the nonselling tasks previously mentioned.
3. **Idle time** is time the salesperson is on the salesfloor but is not involved in any productive work.

4. **Absent time** occurs when the salesperson is not on the salesfloor. He or she may be at lunch, in the employee lounge, in another part of the store, or in some other inappropriate place.

The retailer may develop standards for each of these types of time. For example, the standard time allocation may suggest that salespeople spend 60 percent of their time selling, 28 percent of their time on nonselling activities, 5 percent idle, and 7 percent absent. Any deviation from these standards should be investigated and corrective measures should be taken if necessary.

Data Requirements To establish proper standards of performance the retailer needs data. What are good standards for the conversion rate? sales per hour? time allocation? Only data will help answer these questions. The data can come from retail trade associations, consulting firms, or the retailer's own experience.

Once the retailer obtains the data on which to base standards, it must collect additional data continually or at least periodically on actual performance. The actual conversion rate, sales per hour, and time allocation must be contrasted to their respective standards. If the actual data differ significantly from the standard, an investigation of the cause is warranted. Both favorable and unfavorable variances should be investigated, because you may learn just as much from unusually good performance as from unusually poor performance.

SUMMARY

The purpose of this chapter was to illustrate the role of the retail salesperson in demand generation. We saw that regardless of whether salesclerks were primarily order getters or order takers they played a paramount role in demand generation. However, the role played by the order getter was obviously more important in this regard.

The productivity of retail salesclerks has been stagnant since the early 1970s. This problem was traced to low wages, poor morale, high turnover, and a general inability of retailers to properly manage their salespeople. To improve salesforce productivity we suggested that retailers give more careful consideration to compensation programs; to the selection, training, and scheduling of salespeople; to determining salesforce size; and to evaluating salespeople.

QUESTIONS

1. What type of compensation program would you develop for salespeople in an auto dealership? a discount department store? Explain.

2. What should retail salespeople know about consumer behavior?

3. A major retail discount department store chain has analyzed the annual sales per salesperson in twenty of its stores located in different cities across the United States. On a storewide basis, the sales per salesperson range from a low of $91,000 to a high of $134,000. Develop a list of factors that might help to explain this wide variation.

4. Is it possible to increase expenditures on salespeople as a percentage of sales and increase the overall profitability of the firm?

5. How can salesforce productivity be increased?

6. What is the relationship between a retailer's advertising and personal selling efforts?

7. Avon Products (a major nonstore retailer) experiences substantial variations in sales per door-to-door representative. What may be some of the causes for this high variation?

8. Can retailers increase the productivity of their salespeople if they pay them higher wages? Explain your answer.

9. What should retail salespeople know about customer choice criteria?

10. What are the factors that influence the number of salespeople a retailer should hire?

PROBLEMS AND EXERCISES

1. Develop a list of predictor variables you would use to screen applicants for a sales position in (a) a jewelry department in a high-prestige department store, (b) a used-car dealership, (c) a health club, (d) an antique shop.

2. Visit several local TV and appliance retailers to find out as much technical information as you can about color televisions. Did the salespeople you talked to vary substantially in their knowledge? Which salespeople were you most impressed with? Why?

3. Visit a car dealership (for either new or used cars) to shop for a car. Tell the salesperson that you are not sure what you want in a car (be very vague about your preferences). How does the salesperson help you narrow down your choice? Does the salesperson attempt to use any high-pressure selling techniques?

4. A shoe store has weekly fixed costs of $3,500. Average weekly sales are 510 pairs of shoes at an average price of $20. The average cost is $10 per pair. Currently, five sales-clerks are employed at $230 per week. The store manager is considering changing to a weekly salary of $190 and a 3 percent commission on all sales. How much will sales productivity (weekly sales per employee) need to increase to justify this change?

SUGGESTED READINGS

Churchill, Gilbert A., Robert H. Collins, and William A. Strang. "Should Retail Sales-persons Be Similar to Their Customers?" *Journal of Retailing* 51(Fall 1975): 29–42, 79.

Crissy, W. J. E., William H. Cunningham, and Isabella C. M. Cunningham. *Selling: The Personal Force in Marketing* (New York: Wiley, 1977).

French, Cecil L. "Correlates of Success in Retail Selling." *American Journal of Sociology* 66(September 1960): 128–34.

Furash, Richard. "Salesforce Schedules Simplified," *Stores* 57(June 1975): 5.

Pennington, Allan L. "Customer-Salesman Bargaining Behavior in Retail Transactions." *Journal of Marketing Research* 5(August 1968): 255–62.

Woodside, Arch G. and J. Taylor Sims. "Retail Sales Transactions and Customer 'Purchase Pal' Effects on Buying Behavior." *Journal of Retailing* 52(Fall 1976): 57–64, 95.

19

Overview *The purpose of this chapter is to demonstrate the key role that customer service can play in generating demand. We will discuss common customer services as well as the determination of an optimal customer service level. We will also highlight some of the key management problems that confront service retailers.*

Customer Service Planning and Management

RETAILING is a service-oriented business. Patrons of retail establishments not only seek to purchase tangible products but also expect and demand customer services. Therefore, customer services will help to determine the demand a retailer can generate.

To establish a basis for the following discussion a definition of customer service, as it relates to retailing, is in order. **Customer service** consists of all those activities performed by the retailer which influence (1) the ease with which a potential customer can shop or learn about the store's offering, (2) the ease with which a transaction can be completed once the customer attempts to make a purchase, and (3) the customer's satisfaction with the merchandise after the transaction. These three elements of the definition of customer service are the pretransaction, transaction, and posttransaction components of customer service.[1]

Retailers should design their customer service program around pretransaction, transaction, and posttransaction elements in order to obtain a competitive advantage. In today's world of mass distribution, almost all retailers have access to the same merchandise and, therefore, a retailer can seldom differentiate itself from others solely on the basis of merchandise stocked. It can, however, as we will shortly see, obtain a high degree of differentiation through its customer service program. Customer service in retailing can be a significant dimension on which to build a strong and unique competitive strategy.

DEMAND GENERATION

Serving the customer before, during, and after the transaction can help to create new customers and strengthen the loyalty of present customers. If customer service before the transaction is poor, the probability of a transaction occurring will decline. If customer service is poor at the transaction stage, the customer may back out of the transaction. And, if customer service is poor after the transaction, the probability of a repeat purchase at the same store will decline. All of the preceding propositions suggest that the level of customer service will influence demand.

Transient Customers The customer who visits a store and finds service below expectations will become a **transient customer.** This transient customer will seek to find a store with the level of customer service it feels is appropriate. At any given moment, for all lines of retail trade, there are a good number of transient customers. The retailer with a superior customer service program will have a significant advantage in intercepting these transients and converting them into loyal customers. Thus, customer service can play a significant role in building a retailer's sales volume.

1. This perspective is offered in Bernard J. LaLonde and Paul H. Zinszer, *Customer Service: Meaning and Measurement* (Chicago: National Council of Physical Distribution Management, 1976).

Research Studies   Let us review two research studies that will illustrate the role of customer service in generating demand. The first study deals with grocery retailing and the second with department store retailing.

The first research study was conducted in 1973 by Progressive Grocer and the Home Testing Institute.[2] In this study consumers were asked to attach weights to thirty-seven store characteristics. Eleven of these characteristics were found to be crucial in determining store-switching behavior. In other words, when a customer's present store didn't score well on them, the consumer tended to switch grocery stores. Of these eleven characteristics, seven were directly related to customer service: (1) open late hours, (2) new items that I see advertised are available, (3) good assortment of nonfood merchandise, (4) check-cashing service, (5) short wait for checkout, (6) good parking facilities, and (7) don't run short of items on special. We clearly see that in grocery retailing, good customer service is a crucial variable in attracting and retaining customers. In other words, customer service is a demand generator.

The second research study was conducted in 1980 by R. H. Braskin Associates, a market research firm, for ten major retailers in New York (including Macy's, Saks, and Gimbel's).[3] The study examined consumer attitudes and perceptions about department store shopping. Results of the research indicated that shoppers have ten common complaints about department store shopping:[4]

1. "Every time you want to try on a new item, you have to get dressed and leave the fitting room."
2. "The department store sells clothes too far in advance, such as selling winter clothes at the end of summer."
3. "When they have a big sale, they don't have enough help and you have to wait too long."
4. "If I need a different size while I'm in the fitting room, there are no salespeople to get it for me."
5. "You're not allowed to bring enough garments into the fitting room."
6. "Department stores have less and less people to serve me."
7. "The lines to pay at department stores are too long for me to shop during lunch hour."
8. "There's no way of telling which size will best fit me without trying the garment on."
9. "You have to go from place to place all over the store to get a refund or exchange."
10. "When they have a clothing sale, they don't have enough stock in the most popular items."

2. Robert F. Dietrich, "37 Things You Can Do to Keep Your Customers—Or Lose Them," *Progressive Grocer* (June 1973): 59–64.

3. "10 Commandmants Aid Department Stores," *Chain Store Age Executive* (September 1980): 10.

4. "10 Commandments Aid Department Stores," © *Chain Store Age Executive* (September 1980): 10. Lebhar-Friedman, Inc., 425 Park Ave., N.Y., N.Y. 10022. Used by permission.

These findings suggest that department stores can gain a major competitive advantage by upgrading their customer service levels, especially in fitting rooms.

Although the two preceding research studies have dealt specifically with grocery retailing and department store retailing, the conclusion drawn from them—that good customer service generates demand and builds customer loyalty—is true of all lines of retail trade and is accepted by managers in all lines of retail trade.

CUSTOMER SERVICE AS INTEGRATIVE

A customer service philosophy should be integrated into all aspects of retail management. It is not an area unto itself but involves the management of all aspects of the retail enterprise to serve the customer.

Merchandise Management One of the most significant ways a retailer can serve a customer is by having the merchandise on hand that the customer wants. There are few things more disturbing to a consumer than to make a trip to a store for a specific item only to discover that the item is out of stock. Basically, the better the merchandise manager is at allocating inventory in proportion to customer demand patterns, the better the customer will be served.

Credit Management The management of credit should also be integrated into the customer service program. Credit is a significant aid in helping the customer purchase merchandise. It helps to generate and facilitate transactions. The retailer's credit policies will influence the customer's perception of how well he or she is being serviced.

Building and Fixtures Management Management decisions regarding building and fixtures can have a significant effect on how well the customer can be served. For example, consider the following building and fixture dimensions and how they might influence customer service:

- Heating and cooling levels
- Availability of parking space
- Ease of finding merchandise
- Layout and arrangement of fixtures
- Placement of restrooms and lounge areas
- Location of check cashing, complaint, returns, desks, etc.
- Level of lighting
- Width and length of aisles

This list is not comprehensive; it is intended merely to provide evidence for the proposition that customer service considerations need to be taken into account in building and fixture decisions.

Promotion Management   Promotion provides customers with information that can help them make purchase decisions. Therefore, you should be concerned with whether the promotion programs you develop help the consumer. Consider the following questions, which will help you assess if your promotion is serving the customer:

1. Is the advertising informative and helpful?
2. Does the advertising provide all the relevant information the customer needs?
3. Are the salespeople helpful and informative?
4. Are the salespeople friendly and courteous?
5. Are the salespeople easy to find when needed?
6. Are sufficient quantities available on sales promotion items?

This list is also not comprehensive but intended only to show that customer service programs need to be considered in designing promotional programs.

Price Management   Price management will also influence how well the customer is served. Are prices clearly marked and visible? Is unit pricing available? Is pricing fair, honest, and not misleading? Are customers told the true price of credit? These questions suggest that the pricing decision should not be made in isolation from the retailer's customer service program.

A Recap   Integration, therefore, should be a key managerial orientation when retailers develop their customer service programs. Without a doubt, much of what has already been discussed in this book somehow, either directly or indirectly, relates to one of the three broad categories of customer service: pretransaction, transaction, and posttransaction. By devoting a separate chapter to customer service, we hope to reinforce the notion that customer service is a key demand generator and a dimension on which retailers can build a strong competitive advantage.

COMMON CUSTOMER SERVICES

Much of the discussion on merchandise, credit, fixed assets, pricing, and promotion in previous chapters had implications for serving the customer. However, many of the more popular types of customer services have not been mentioned or have received sparse coverage. Let us review some of them.

Pretransaction Services   The most common pretransaction services are convenient hours, information aids, and food service. Each of these makes it easier for the potential customer to shop or to learn of the store's offering.

Convenient Hours   The more convenient the operating hours of the store are to the customer, the easier it is for the customer to visit the store. Convenient operating hours is one of the most basic but essential services that you should provide to your customers.

The operating hours you establish will often depend on competition. If your main competitor is willing to stay open until 9 P.M. six nights per week to serve customers, it would probably not be wise to close every night at 5 P.M. The exception would be if not enough revenue were generated for you to stay open six nights per week.

Customer service programs, as all retail management decisions, should be assessed on the profit impact of the program. To do so, you need to assess your target market and its shopping habits to estimate how your customers would respond to a change in store operating hours. The target market may flock to an all-night drug store but stay away from a dress shop opening at 8 A.M. The retailer must ascertain what the customers want and weigh those wants against the costs of providing them and the additional revenues that would be generated.

Information Aids   As we already mentioned, the retailer's promotional efforts help to inform the customer. Also, many retailers offer customers other information aids that help them enter into intelligent transactions. For example, some retailers regularly offer use counseling lessons that instruct the consumer in how to use, operate, or care for a product. Not surprisingly, many retailers that offer these lessons can increase their market shares because many customers are afraid to buy a new item (such as a microwave, videotape machine, home computer, or electric wok) without first knowing how to use it. If the retailer offers classes or specific instruction on the use of a product, the customer will be less resistant to trying and ultimately purchasing the product. For many items that are technologically sophisticated or represent significant departures from traditional ways of doing something, the customer will tend to buy from the retailer who teaches.

Some retailers will also offer booklets that provide useful consumer information. In this regard, Sears' *How To Choose and Use Retail Credit* has been very popular among consumers and educators. Other consumer information booklets published by Sears include *Floor Coverings: Their Selection and Care; Kitchen Planning Basics; How to Select Furniture; How to Select Hand and Power Tools;* and *Fabric Care Manual.* Consumer information booklets can be important sources of pretransaction information to the consumer. Retailers that provide such booklets are not only serving potential and existing customers, but also building goodwill.

Food Service   Because of rising energy prices, consumers are making fewer but larger and longer shopping trips. When they decide to go shopping it often is an all-day event. These long trips create a need within the consumer for convenient and easy-to-consume food. Many retailers are cashing in on this consumer need by providing restaurants within their stores; by providing this service, they allow customers to eat without leaving the store in which they are shopping. In Exhibit 19.1 you will find a case study that highlights the rising importance of food service in retailing.

EXHIBIT 19.1
**The Rising
Importance
of Food Service**

In today's environment a shopping trip is increasingly involving eating out. With many households facing a scarcity of time, the combining of shopping and dining becomes more logical. In fact, in the late 1970s over 25 percent of food was eaten away from home.

For many years the very finest department stores have provided food service. As far back as 1874 Bon Marche in Paris offered in-store food service. But today a host of other retailers are capitalizing on the strong demand for food away from home. These retailers include supermarkets, discount department stores, specialty stores, convenience stores, and so on.

There are many variations on the type of food service being offered by retailers. Listed below is a rundown of the kinds of food service being offered.*

- Haute cuisine   Formal decor, maximum staffing, elaborate menu. Linen, china, silver, crystal.
- Traditional table service   Toned-down Haute Cuisine, complete but not posh. Decor harmonized with balance of store.
- Coffee shop   Informal, usually cheerful decor. Tables and counter. Stable menu beamed for steady "regulars." Long hours.
- Cafeteria   Lean, clean decor. Menu mainly basics topped with daily "surprises." Engineered for fast transit.
- Speak-up self-service   Fast-turn tables and take-out. May be "cute-sy" but must be quick, clean.
- Buffet smorgasbord   All you can eat of a wide variety of salads, meats, vegetables, desserts, etc. Risky, without tight portion control.
- Fast food   In-store knock-offs of McDonald, Treacher, and such. Food ready-prepared but assembled to order. Low prices.
- Snack bar   Set up wherever niche of 100 or more trafficked feet show up. Highly disliked by adjacent merchandise departments. (Debris, greasy hands, light fingers.) Highly profitable per se.
- Specialty boutique   Often ethnic—Chinese, Italian, Mexican, Scandinavian, Soul. Narrow menu, nice profit.
- Scatter system   A cluster of specialty booths that can include pizzas, submarines, hamburgers, hot dogs, fruits, and yogurts. Dense seating, stand-up counters, take-out.
- Vending   Adequate in budget atmosphere if faithfully serviced. Items from candy-bar "desserts" to radar-heated soups, sandwiches. Often supplementary to snack bar.

*All definitions (except buffet smorgasbord) from Lewis A. Spalding, "Where and What Your Customers Eat!" Reprinted with permission from *Stores* magazine 62(May 1980), p. 55. © National Retail Merchants Association, copyright 1980.

If properly managed, food service can be directly profitable to the retailer. Regardless of its impact on sales of other products, the provision of food service itself can be profitable. Some retailers, however, will design their food service to break even by offering the customer good food at a low price. This actually helps to bring more traffic into the store, which can stimulate sales.

Transaction Services   The most important transaction services are credit, layaway, wrapping and packaging, check cashing, personal shopping, and merchandise availability. These services help to facilitate transactions once customers have made a purchase decision.

Credit   One of the most popular transaction-related services offered by retailers is consumer credit. As discussed in Chapter 14, credit can be a very expensive customer service, but if handled correctly, it can increase profits substantially.

Offering credit in one or more forms can be of great service to the customer because it enables shopping without the need to carry large sums of money. In addition, it allows the customer to buy now and pay later. Credit can be a benefit to the retailer also: it increases sales by increasing impulse buying. Of course, credit can decrease profits if the credit policy is too lenient.

Layaway   When a layaway service is offered to the customer, the customer can place a deposit (usually 20 percent) on an item, and in return the retailer will hold the item for the customer. The customer will make periodic payments on the item and, when it is paid for in full, can take it home. In a sense, a layaway sale is similar to an installment credit sale; however, the retailer retains physical possession of the item until it is completely paid for.

Wrapping and Packaging   Customers are typically better served if their purchase is properly wrapped or packaged. The service may be as simple as putting the purchase into a paper bag or as complex as packaging crystal glassware in a special shatterproof box to prevent breakage.

The retailer must match its wrapping service to the type of merchandise it carries and its store image. A discount grocer or hardware store does quite well by simply putting the merchandise into a paper sack. Specialty clothing stores often have dress and suit boxes that are easy to carry home. Some more upscale retailers are now even putting the purchased merchandise in decorated shopping bags or prewrapped gift boxes. This reduces considerably the number of packages that must be gift wrapped.

Many larger department stores and most gift shops offer a gift wrapping service. Usually there is a fee for gift wrapping, but many stores also offer a courtesy wrap, which consists of a gift box and ribbon, or a store paper that identifies the place of purchase. This type of wrap is not only a goodwill gesture, but a form of advertising.

Check Cashing   Most retailers offer some form of check-cashing service. The most basic type of check-cashing service consists of allowing qualified customers to cash a check for the amount of purchase. A **qualified customer** is one who has applied to and been accepted by the retailer for check-cashing privileges. Often these customers are provided with an identification card that entitles them to pay for merchandise with a personal check. More liberal check-cashing services allow qualified customers to cash checks for amounts in excess of the purchase price, usually not for more than $50. At the extreme in check cashing service, are a few retailers who will cash checks in excess of the purchase price if the consumer presents sufficient identification at the time of transaction.

Also worth noting is the practice of some retailers in providing payroll check cashing services, in which retailers cash payroll checks from recognized local employers. This develops goodwill and usually results in some increase in sales, since many customers feel guilty asking a retailer to cash their payroll checks without purchasing anything. Retailers who do a significant amount of payroll check cashing will need to plan to have ample cash on hand to coincide with payroll dates of local employers.

Personal Shopping   Personal shopping is the activity of assembling for a customer an assortment of goods that the customer has ordered. This can be as varied a service as picking out clothing, filling a telephone order, assembling a supply of groceries and sending them to the customer's home, or selecting a wedding gift. Personal shopping services are usually found in stores with a higher price image and affluent customers.

Merchandise Availability   Merchandise availability as a service simply relates to whether the customers can find the items they are looking for in the store. Two causes exist for the customer being unable to find an item: the item can be out of stock,[5] or the customer cannot locate it. The retailer can minimize out-of-stock conditions by good merchandise management, although some out-of-stocks are inevitable. It can increase the customer's ability to locate an item in the store by having good in-store signing, layout, and displays, and helpful and informative employees.

Merchandise availability is an element of customer service that many retailers take for granted, but they shouldn't. When customers do not find items they are looking for in a store—regardless of the cause—they will be slow in forgetting their bad experiences.

Posttransaction Services   Posttransaction services consist of activities performed by the retailer that influence the customer's satisfaction with the merchandise after the transaction. The major and most frequently encountered posttransaction services are complaint handling, handling merchandise returns, merchandise repair, and servicing and delivery.

Complaint Handling   A retailer's proper handling of customer complaints can mean the difference between surviving or faltering. Dealing with customers is a tricky business because it involves employees who make human errors dealing with customers who make human errors. In essence, this doubles the chance of misunderstanding and mistakes between the two parties. Unfortunately, these mistakes and misunderstandings often lead to a poor image of the retailer. It is, therefore, essential that the retailer try to solve customer complaints. If the retailer solves the customer's problem then the customer is being served.

5. For a discussion of how retail stockouts can be modeled, see C. K. Walter and John R. Grabner, "Stockout Cost Models: Empirical Tests in a Retail Situation," *Journal of Marketing* 39(July 1975): 56–68.

There are several ways of handling and solving customer complaints. For a large retailer, the central complaint department is most efficient. Here, all customer complaints are heard by a staff that is especially trained for this task. This method leaves the sales force free to do its job and allows the customer to deal with someone who has the authority to act on most complaints. For a small retailer, however, this system is usually not necessary; the owner, store manager, or department head can handle the few complaints the average small retailer would get. (If there are more than a few complaints, the retailer should attempt to find out why and make the necessary corrections.)

Another way of handling customer complaints is to have the salespeople in each department hear them. This is often unsatisfactory, because the individual salespeople often do not have the authority to settle the problems. As a consequence, they often end up having to call in someone else to take care of the problem and usually the customer must repeat the problem once again. A second drawback of this system is the fact that a salesperson who is listening to a past customer complaining cannot serve present customers who, incidentally, are overhearing complaints. Whether consciously or subconsciously, these complaints register in the minds of the customers and help create a negative attitude toward the retailer.

Regardless of the complaint-handling system, you need to remember three things when handling complaints. The customer deserves courteous treatment, fair settlement, and prompt action.

Merchandise Returns   The handling of merchandise returns is an important customer service, making the difference between making a profit and losing money. The return policy can range from no returns, no exchanges to the customer is always right. As a retailer, you need to decide if you want either of these extreme policies or a more moderate one. Few services build customer goodwill as quickly as a fair return policy. On the other hand, the return service is probably the most widely used and abused service by American consumers.

In Exhibit 19.2 we identify the key cost elements of a return. Because of its size, some merchandise has to be picked up by a delivery service when it is returned, which can become costly. Also, the amount of time spent by the recordkeeping people is increased because records must be made on every item that is returned, and often earlier records on the item must be changed. In addition, there is a restocking cost, especially if all price and code tags have been removed.

Depending on the item returned, there can be a substantial loss due to the time the item was out of stock. Beach or patio furniture, for example, wouldn't sell as well in the winter, and a returned snow shovel would be in low demand in the summer. Because of this delay, returned merchandise is often stored until the proper season or sold at a reduced price. Reducing the price is also common practice if the merchandise has been used. There is also an opportunity cost—the foregone interest or return on investment dollars. This money is tied up in merchandise that is in the possession of the customer but hasn't been paid for and will be returned.

To best serve customers, the retailer should plan to conduct business in

EXHIBIT 19.2
**Cost Elements
of a Return**

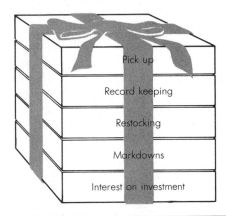

Pick up

Record keeping

Restocking

Markdowns

Interest on investment

such a way that customers will need to return less merchandise. This implies training delivery people so they will not damage merchandise in transit, and salespeople so they will avoid pushing unsuitable merchandise on the customer.

Servicing and Repair Any new product with more than one moving mechanical part is a candidate for future servicing or repair. In fact, even items without moving parts such as clothing, coffee tables, and paintings are candidates for repair. Retailers who offer merchandise servicing and repair to their customers tend to generate a higher sales volume. And, if the work they perform is good,

Many customers expect servicing and repairs from retailers selling major appliances. (Photo courtesy of Sears.)

they also can generate repeat business. For example, if the service department of a TV and appliance store has a reputation for doing good work at fair prices, customers will not only purchase a TV at the store but will also tend to purchase radios, stereos, washers, or whatever else is sold.

Retailers who might receive substantial benefit from offering repair and servicing of merchandise are TV and appliance stores, jewelry stores, bicycle stores, auto dealers, clothing stores, lawnmower and small engine shops, and furniture stores.

Repair and servicing is perhaps one of the most difficult customer services to manage. While good repair and servicing can stimulate additional sales, the converse is also true. Simply stated, when customers get substandard repair and service work, they do not return to the same retailer for future purchases of merchandise. Also these disgruntled customers will tell their friends, relatives, and acquaintances of the retailer's poor work.

Retailers who perform service and repair work will find it advantageous to behave ethically and in good conduct. The National Business Council for Customer Affairs has recommended a Code of Responsible Practices that retailers should openly embrace. The key components of this code are:

1. Customers should be offered an estimate of cost in advance of services to be rendered.

2. Customers should be promptly notified if service appointments cannot be kept.

3. Only repairs authorized in writing by the customer should be performed, except where other arrangements have been made to the customer's satisfaction.

4. A written itemized invoice for all parts, labor and any other charges should be given to the customer on completion of the work.

5. All repair services should be guaranteed for a reasonable length of time.

6. Appropriate records of services performed and materials used should be maintained by the service company for at least one year.

7. Service technicians should not be paid according to the size of the customer's repair bill.

8. The service dealer should maintain insurance coverage adequate to protect the customer's property while it is in his or her custody.

9. Service dealers should cooperate with consumer protection agencies at all levels of government to ensure satisfactory resolution of customer complaints.

10. Customers should be treated courteously at all times, and all complaints should be given full and fair consideration.[6]

Delivery   Delivery of merchandise to the customer's home can be a very expensive service, especially because of the rising cost of energy. Nonetheless, the benefits derived from providing delivery may be worth the expense if the store, merchandise, and customer characteristics warrant it.

The retailer can offer free delivery (which is actually absorbed in slightly higher prices) or it can charge the customer a small fee to help offset the cost.

---

6. National Business Council for Consumer Affairs, Sub-Council on Performance and Service, *Product Performance and Servicing* (Washington, D.C.: U.S. Government Printing Office, 1973), pp. 39–40.

There are three types of delivery service: the store-owned system; the co-op system; and the independent contractor system.

The **store-owned system** consists of a store employee delivering merchandise in a store-owned vehicle. It could involve a sole proprietor using a car, or a fleet of drivers in store-owned trucks. Advantages of this system include control over employees, tailored delivery routes for individual customer purchases, and advertising created by displaying the store's logo on the vehicle. The main disadvantage of the store-owned system is its relatively high cost.

With the **co-op system,** several retailers jointly own and operate the delivery service. This system offers significant economies of scale because the number of deliveries in a geographic area can be increased and, therefore, the cost per unit of delivery can be significantly decreased. In Exhibit 19.3, we show how goods to be delivered to each retailer's customers are consolidated by the delivery company and subsequently grouped into delivery areas or zones to be delivered on certain days or at certain times. One of the major disadvantages of this system is fitting customers into a delivery timetable that is convenient to them. A purchase to be delivered to Area Z in Exhibit 19.3 may be inconvenient if the customer is not available on Tuesday afternoons to receive the delivery. A second problem with the system is a lack of control over the delivery employees, because the delivery personnel are no longer store employees.

A third delivery alternative is the use of an **independent contractor.** A good example of this system is United Parcel Service. Charges for this service

EXHIBIT 19.3
Co-op Delivery System

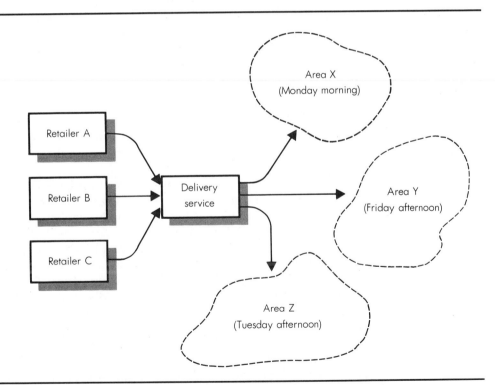

may be made on a per parcel rate, which may be based on size or weight of the package; a flat rate charge per week; or a combination of both. The main advantage of this system is that the retailer doesn't incur the expense of owning and operating the delivery service while still being able to reap the benefits of consumer approval for offering delivery service. The main drawback is the lack of control over the quality of delivery service, and the inability to customize delivery to fit customer wants.

DETERMINING CUSTOMER SERVICE LEVELS

It is not easy to determine the optimal number and level of customer services to offer. Theoretically, however, one could argue that a retailer should add customer services until the incremental revenue that is generated by higher service levels is equal to the incremental cost of providing those services. In short, this argues for the retailer to establish the level of customer services that maximizes retailer profitability. Of course, the effect on long-run profits should be the overriding concern because, in the short run, profits can usually be increased by cutting back on costly customer services.

Difficulty is also encountered in deciding what specific customer services to offer in order to increase sales volume. As illustrated in Exhibit 19.4, there are six pointers that help to determine the customer services to offer: the store characteristics, the services offered by the competition, the type of merchandise handled, the price image of the store, the income of the target market, and the cost of providing the service. It is the retailer's job to study these six areas to arrive at the service mix that will increase long-run profits by keeping present customers, enticing new customers, and projecting the right type of store image. Above all else, you must remember to be realistic and not to expect to be capable of satisfying the wants and needs of all customers. No strategy could be less profitable.

Store Characteristics   Store characteristics include store location, store size, and store type. It is especially important to look at these three store characteristics when considering adding a service.

Services offered in the downtown area of a large city would probably be different from those offered by a similar store in a rural shopping center. For example, a drugstore in the downtown area might offer free delivery of prescriptions as a service to its clientele. This service would be of great benefit to city dwellers without cars and business people who don't want to spend time waiting at the drugstore for a prescription. This same service in a rural community shopping center would not be as important. Rural residents usually drive to most stores they visit, travel greater distances, and take many multiple-purpose trips. Therefore, the rural druggist might get a better return on investment by offering such services as check cashing, credit, and plenty of free parking rather than free delivery of prescriptions.

The size and type of store also help determine which services to offer. A major department store would offer a different assortment of services than a

EXHIBIT 19.4
**Pointers for
Determining
Customer
Service Mix**

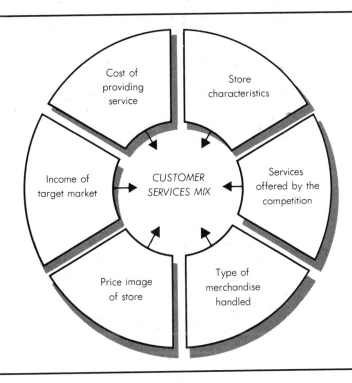

grocery or hardware store. There would also be a difference between a large and a small store of the same type. The customer would expect more services from a large retailer, and probably fewer but more personalized services from the small retailer.

Competition   The services offered by competitors will have a significant effect on the level and variety of customer services offered. You must also offer these services or suitable substitutes, or you must offer lower prices.

Suppose, for example, that there are three clothing stores of the same general type, price range, and quality within a given area. Store *A* and Store *B* offer free gift wrapping, standard alterations, bank card credit, and a liberal return policy. Store *C*, on the other hand, offers only store credit and has an exchange only return policy. Customers who are shopping for gifts generally frequent stores *A* and *B* over *C* because they feel confident that whatever they purchase will ultimately be just right. It can even be gift wrapped there at the store. If the gift isn't suitable, the receiver can have it altered to fit, exchange it, or even get a cash refund. In this situation, Store *C* can do two things to compete: It can either add services or lower prices.

Type of Merchandise   The merchandise lines carried can be an indication of the types of services to offer. The principle reason is that certain merchandise lines benefit from complementary services: bicycles and free assembly; major appliances and set up and delivery; men's suits and alterations; and sewing machines and free instruction.

Price Image

Generally, customers will expect more services from a store with a high price image than from a discount retailer. When a customer perceives a store as having high prices, it also sees the store as possessing an air of luxury. Therefore, the services rendered by this store should also carry the image of luxury or status. Some of the typical high price image services are elegant food service, personal shopping, a home design studio, free gift wrapping, free delivery, and free alterations. For example, see Exhibit 19.5, which profiles some services offered by Marshall Field's in Chicago.

	CUSTOMER SERVICE	DESCRIPTION
EXHIBIT 19.5 **Selected Customer Services of Marshall Fields'**	Silver repair and replating	Restoration and repair of silver dinnerware and other prized possessions by skilled craftsmen.
	Monogramming	A personalized monogram can be placed on everything from shirts to linens in a variety of tasteful designs.
	Dry cleaning	Dry cleaning services for fine apparel and draperies by experts. Pickup or delivery is available.
	Fur protection	Storage of your furs in temperature controlled vaults. Also insurance protection on furs all year long whether they are in storage or being worn.
	Clothing restyling	Expert seamstresses can restyle hats and remodel dresses to give them new appeal or an up-dated look.
	Clothing repair	Repair of fine suits, leather, and other fine wearing apparel is provided on garments regardless of where they were purchased.
	Custom framing	Skilled craftsmen can custom frame your treasures, such as a beloved photograph or a favored lithograph.
	Engraving	Machine and hand engraving services are available, which allow the customer to personalize a piece of jewelry or family heirloom.
	Watch repair	Expert watchmakers provide a complete repair service on all jeweled watches, whether they be standard, automatic, calendar, or pocket styles. Antique watches are also repaired.
	Custom finishing of stitchery work	The customers can bring in their needlepoint and crewel creations and have them transformed by skilled craftsmen into pillows, bell pulls, upholstered chairs, and stools.

On the other end of the scale, discount stores needn't offer luxury services, because customers who shop there are seeking low prices and not fancy customer services. A discount retailer or one with a low price image might offer such basic services as free parking, layaway, bank card credit and convenient store hours.

Target Market Income   The higher the income of the target market, the higher the maximal demand prices that consumers will pay. The higher the prices consumers will pay, the more services the retailer can profitably provide. Some customers may expect more services than they are able to afford, but the retailer must avoid the strong temptation of providing costly services to such consumers. In the long run, the retailer will have to raise prices to pay for the services and then it will quickly lose its share of low-income customers.

Young mothers, for example, usually have low discretionary income. If the retailer's target market is these young families, it needs to gear the customer service program to their purchasing power level. Although these young mothers may want free delivery, gift wrapping, elegant food service, and many other services, the retailer will need to raise prices to provide them. And, by raising prices, it will lose a portion of the target market.

Cost of Services   It is imperative that you know the cost of a service so that you will have an idea of how much in additional sales would need to be generated to pay for the service. For example, if a customer service were expected to increase costs by $20,000 per year and the store operated on a gross margin of 25 percent, then you would have to expect that the service would stimulate sales by at least ($20,000 ÷ 0.25) or $80,000. In this sense, customer services are evaluated in a manner similar to promotional expenditures. The key criterion becomes the financial effect of adding or deleting a customer service.

GEOGRAPHICALLY DISPERSED RETAILERS

Chain stores or department store organizations operating in several different geographic areas need to be especially careful in designing the correct mix of customer services. Many geographically diversified retail organizations try to standardize their operations in an attempt to achieve better control and scale economies. Unfortunately, if they try to standardize customer services, they end up not being responsive to local needs. The best posture appears to consist of offering a core of services at all locations and allowing store or regional managers to tailor other services to the needs of their trade areas.

A retail organization that operates in many geographic areas and has successfully managed its customer service mix is Federated Department Stores. At Federated, each store knows how best to serve the customers and its community. All twenty divisions have certain common customer service strategies, including consumer advisory councils; seminars on credit systems, buyer booklets, brochures, and applications in several languages; in-store warranties; automatic adjustments and refunds; employee training on consumer rights; and comprehensive product safety programs.[7]

In addition, each Federated division develops its own programs. Some of these programs are on page 580.[8]

Some of these programs are on page 580.[8]

7. "What Changing Consumer Attitudes Mean and How to Cope," *Stores* (February 1977): 38.
8. "What Changing Consumer Attitudes Mean and How to Cope." Reprinted with permission from *Stores* magazine (February 1977): 38. © National Retail Merchants Association, 1977.

- Rike's, Dayton: A consumer ombudsman to elicit consumer likes and dislikes about Rike's; seminars on cost adjustments and consumer rights.
- Burdine's, Miami: Special on-location grooming sessions for senior citizens, the retarded, and the young.
- Foley's, Houston: Appeal to Mexican-Americans through Spanish-language signs, sales notices, and applications.
- Shillito's, Cincinnati: Consumer groups in product areas to advise buyers on what people want in fashion, according to personal tastes and needs.
- Ralph's Supermarkets, Los Angeles: Consumer groups from individual stores to inform the store on the cultural tastes of the community; a nutritional education program headed by a full-time economist.
- Lazarus, Columbus: Private appliance labels on how better to use small appliances to conserve energy.

SERVICE RETAILING

Many retailers are uniquely in the business of selling services. Common examples include barber and beauty shops, health spas, auto repair shops, movie theaters, and amusement parks. When retailers sell services more than tangible products, the management of customer service becomes more important. This is because there is simply more service to manage. You will find it helpful to recognize some of the problems in managing a service-oriented retail enterprise.

Goods Versus Services   What is the distinction between a *good* and a *service*? Sasser, Olsen, and Wyckoff say,

> A **good** is a tangible physical object or product that can be created and transferred; it has an existence over time and thus can be created and used later. A **service** is intangible and perishable. It is an occurrence or process that is created and used simultaneously or nearly simultaneously. While the consumer cannot retain the actual service after it is produced, the effect of the service can be retained.[9]

We thus see that a key distinction is whether the item the retailer sells is tangible and can be inventoried or intangible and not capable of storage. Careful reflection, however, should lead you to conclude that almost all retailers provide both services and goods. For example, the convenience food store selling a quart of milk is selling more than milk (a tangible item) but also place and time utility (intangible attributes). In other words, besides purchasing the milk, the customer is also paying for the convenience of having the milk at the time and place desired. On the other hand, the beautician who does a hairstyling is also selling goods, since he or she must use materials such as hair spray, shampoo, and water.

We therefore must conclude that all retailing involves services; but of course, the degree of service orientation can vary considerably. For instance, in

9. W. Earl Sasser, R. Paul Olsen, and D. Daryl Wyckoff, *Management of Service Operations: Text, Cases and Readings* (Boston: Allyn and Bacon 1978), p. 8.

a self-service grocery store almost all the purchase price goes for goods, whereas in a motel almost all the price of a room goes for services.

Management Problems For retailers that sell almost totally services (motel, movie theater, barber shop, and so on), four major management problems must be addressed: competitive differentiation, inventory, demand forecasting, and creation of tangibleness.

Competitive Differentiation Services, unlike tangible products, are easy to replicate. In a service there seldom can be any hidden technology, and obtaining a patent on a service is impossible. Consequently, services have short life cycles. For instance, if TWA comes up with a new service such as seat assignments for the entire portion of your air trip, United Airlines can quickly follow suit. If Avis develops a quick check-in procedure for returning your rental car to an airport, Hertz can quickly copy it.

The preceding suggests that service retailers must constantly modify their services in order to continue to differentiate themselves from competitors.

Inventory Because services cannot be inventoried, it is very difficult to meet fluctuations in consumer demand. If an airline seat or a classroom seat is not occupied, the potential revenue from that seat at that time is lost forever. "In essence, the service manager is without an important 'shock absorber' available to most of his counterparts in the manufacturing sector to absorb fluctuations in demand."[10]

Forecasting Demand Since services cannot be inventoried, it is crucial that the demand for them be accurately forecast. If demand is accurately forecast then the proper number of service employees can be on hand to fill demand. On the other hand, if too many employees are on hand to service demand, employee productivity will fall; if there are too few, customers will leave dissatisfied. Try to apply this logic to how many hair stylists there should be at the place where you have your hair done.

Forecasting of demand is also crucial for determining the quantity of other service resources to have available. For example, the forecast of demand will determine how large an airplane to schedule for a particular flight, or how large a classroom to schedule for a public lecture. See if you can think of other examples.

Creation of Tangibleness Since services are intangible, it is difficult for the consumer to compare the services of competing service retailers. How do you compare a Ford you rent from Avis to one you rented from Hertz?

To help consumers compare competitive service offerings, service retailers attempt to make their service offerings tangible by packaging them.[11] Airlines,

10. Sasser, Olsen, and Wyckoff, *Management of Service Operations*, p. 16.
11. G. Lynn Shostock, "Breaking Free from Product Marketing," *Journal of Marketing* 41(April 1977): 73–80.

for instance, will paint their airplanes with distinguishable colors, upholster their seats in leather, or outfit their cabin attendants in attractive attire. Beauty and barber shops will carefully arrange the shop decor to be attractive, will pipe in music to relax you, or will give you free hair grooming samples or booklets. In short, by creating a tangible aspect of their service offering, they can more easily position themselves in the minds of consumers.

SUMMARY

The purpose of this chapter was to demonstrate that customer service is a key revenue-generating variable in retail decision making. To properly manage the customer service decision area, the retailer needs to integrate customer service with merchandise management, credit management, building and fixtures management, price management, and promotion management. Only an integrated customer service program will allow the retailer to achieve maximum profits.

It was not our goal to provide a comprehensive list of all customer services found in all types of retail establishments. Rather, we classified customer services into pretransaction, transaction, and posttransaction services. Pretransaction services make it easier for a potential customer to shop at a store or learn about its offering. Common examples are convenient hours, informational aids, and food service. Transaction-related services make it easier for the customer to complete a transaction. Popular transaction-related services are consumer credit, wrapping and packaging, check cashing, personal shopping, and merchandise availability. Posttransaction services influence the customer's satisfaction with the merchandise after the transaction. The most frequently encountered are handling of complaints, merchandise returns, servicing and repairing, and delivery.

The optimal customer service mix for any retailer should be evaluated on a long-run profit perspective, because in the short run, retailers can always increase bottom-line performance by reducing services. In the long run, however, this strategy could be unprofitable if a significant number of customers switch their shopping patronage to another retailer that offers a more satisfactory service mix. Conventional wisdom suggests that in establishing the mix of customer services the retailer should consider six factors: store characteristics, competition, type of merchandise, price image, target market income, and cost of the service.

Retail enterprises that operate stores in geographically dispersed areas should avoid the temptation of standardizing customer services at all their stores. Each geographic area will have customers with somewhat different needs and wants, and thus some flexibility has to be designed into customer service programs to allow the tailoring of the customer service mix to each area.

In this chapter we also discussed some of the management problems that retailers of services confront. The major management problems of service retailers are competitively differentiating their services, inability to inventory services, forecasting demand in order to schedule service resources, and creating tangibleness of services.

QUESTIONS

1. Explain the role of customer service in generating demand for a retail establishment such as a supermarket.

2. Retailers with high levels of customer service operate on higher gross margins than retailers with low gross margins. Agree or disagree and defend your point of view.

3. Could a retailer segment its market according to consumer preferences for customer service?

4. How is a retailer's customer service policy related to other retail management decisions?

5. How should a retailer determine its optimal customer service level?

6. Identify some of the major management problems that service retailers face.

PROBLEMS AND EXERCISES

1. Assume you are the vice president of marketing for Hertz. Design a program to make your rent-a-car services competitively unique.

2. Visit a local furniture retailer and discuss with the general manager how their delivery service has changed as a result of the rapid inflation in energy prices.

3. Interview ten to twenty of your acquaintances of various backgrounds and ages about the maximum length of time they would wait in line to check out and pay for groceries in a supermarket. Try to explain the variance in responses. That is, why are some people willing to wait longer than others? What does this suggest in terms of retail strategy?

SUGGESTED READINGS

Bessom, Richard M. and Donald W. Jackson, Jr. "Service Retailing: A Strategic Marketing Approach." *Journal of Retailing* 51 (Summer 1975): 75–84.

George, William R. "The Retailing of Services—A Challenging Future." *Journal of Retailing* 53 (Fall 1977): 85–98.

Morey, Richard C. "Measuring the Impact of Service Level on Retail Sales." *Journal of Retailing* 56(Summer 1980): 81–90.

Zinszer, Paul H. and Jack A. Lesser. "An Empirical Evaluation of the Role of Stock-Out on Shopper Patronage Processes." In Richard P. Bagozzi et al. (eds.) *Marketing in the 80s: Changes and Challenges* (Chicago: American Marketing Association, 1980), pp. 221–24.

Case

Virginia Newell Lusch

Zig Zag

BACKGROUND

IN MAY of 1980, two friends who had met in college, Tina Rhodes and Art Ramirez, decided to become partners in a retail venture. The retail enterprise they jointly envisioned would be a specialty store of modest size, but they hoped of sufficient magnitude to provide them with a reasonable income while allowing them both to pursue careers they felt would be fulfilling. Tina had just completed her undergraduate degree in art with an emphasis in fashion design. She believed that the retail venture would be a good vehicle for using her creative talents. Art had just finished a two-year junior college program in business administration. He was eager to try the skills he had acquired in college in the real world and envisioned the retail enterprise in which he and Tina planned to be partners as a good vehicle for applying his analytical training.

The store would be located in a coastal city in Texas of approximately 300,000 in population. It would cater to the young adult (eighteen to twenty-six) of moderate income. The merchandise mix would feature unisex clothing (custom T-shirts, Mexican and other imported clothing) and also custom-made beach wear. In addition to the clothing, the store would carry unique accessories for both male and female customers, handmade jewelry, candles, and gift items. The store would bear the name Zig Zag.

Several months later, on a sultry Friday morning, Zig Zag was opened. But before the opening day, Tina and Art had done considerable planning and preparation. After conceptualizing the store, they had to go through all the legal paperwork in establishing the partnership; find a location; obtain financing; buy merchandise; develop advertising messages; and much more. They quickly found out that the planning and preparation was more time-consuming

Note: Reprinted with permission of the author. This case was prepared as a basis for class discussion rather than to illustrate appropriate or inappropriate handling of retail situations.

and complex than they had initially contemplated. Nonetheless, the big day finally arrived and they held their Grand Opening on August 1 and 2, 1980.

The building they had chosen was located, according to Art's calculations, in an excellent spot to attract its target customers. The store was in a neighborhood shopping center composed of specialty shops, a nationally affiliated supermarket, and a movie theater. The center was adjacent to one of the main highways leading out of the city and in the direction of one of the busiest beaches in the metropolitan area. The building was only five years old, in excellent condition, and the right size for Zig Zag (2,400 square feet). It had previously been used by a real estate firm, which had recently moved its office to a more central location. The store was located near the end of the strip of shops, between a shoe store and Marcelle's—an exclusive dress shop.

During the planning and preparation stages, Art had handled most of the financial and marketing problems while Tina concentrated on the store decor and layout. Her artwork decorated the walls and store front. Exhibit 1 shows

EXHIBIT 1   **Storefront of Zig Zag**

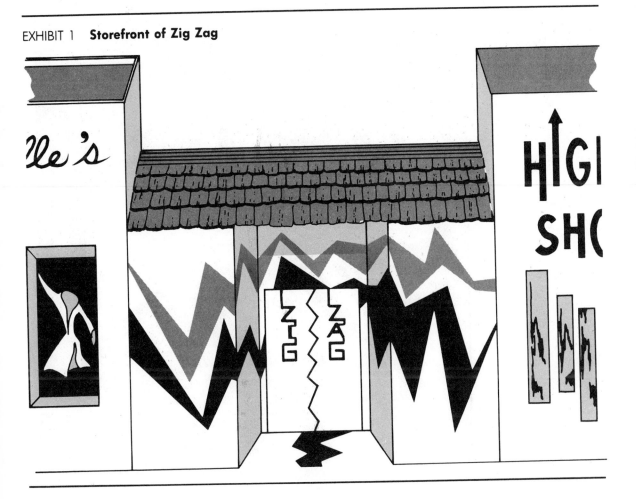

the storefront Tina designed and Exhibit 2 illustrates the layout she developed for Zig Zag.

CURRENT SITUATION

A month after the opening, Art announced that sales had not been quite as good as they had anticipated (see Exhibit 3). Ironically, however, the number of people who had come into the store had been greater than expected. Art attributed the low sales to the fact that school had recently started and that a significant proportion of their target group had less discretionary income to spend for a couple of months. "Things will pick up," he assured Tina.

EXHIBIT 2
Interior Layout of Zig Zag

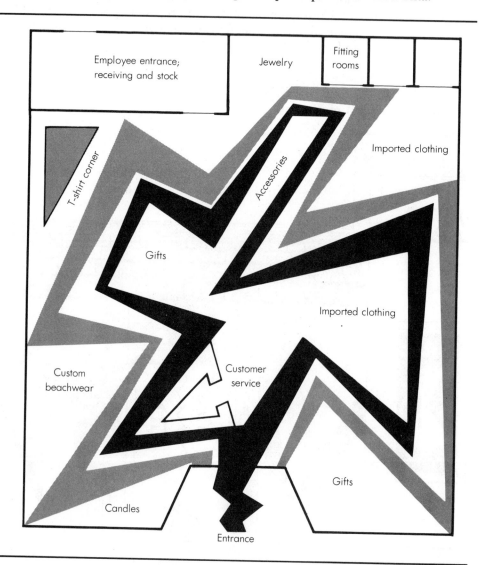

EXHIBIT 3 Zig Zag Daily Sales Volume (first two months of operation)	8/1	$248.16	8/17	Closed (Sunday)	9/1	$ 29.21	9/16	$58.41
	8/2	311.37	8/18	$61.38	9/2	41.73	9/17	71.29
	8/3	Closed (Sunday)	8/19	60.41	9/3	48.48	9/18	98.81
	8/4	54.18	8/20	88.39	9/4	99.77	9/19	134.47
	8/5	84.13	8/21	96.38	9/5	151.47	9/20	149.35
	8/6	98.46	8/22	136.31	9/6	147.28	9/21	Closed (Sunday)
	8/7	164.72	8/23	178.74	9/7	Closed (Sunday)	9/22	40.55
	8/8	168.98	8/24	Closed (Sunday)	9/8	49.43	9/23	51.79
	8/9	189.47	8/25	73.18	9/9	57.30	9/24	98.71
	8/10	Closed (Sunday)	8/26	84.71	9/10	62.28	9/25	224.49
	8/11	59.79	8/27	109.41	9/11	89.99	9/26	288.37
	8/12	87.41	8/28	279.34	9/12	119.30	9/27	290.41
	8/13	94.70	8/29	271.87	9/13	149.47	9/28	Closed (Sunday)
	8/14	161.37	8/30	346.38	9/14	Closed (Sunday)	9/29	58.71
	8/15	198.32	8/31	Closed (Sunday)	9/15	41.32	9/30	92.91
	8/16	182.44						

Another month went by, and the traffic began to drop off. Sales were down, but something more astounding was happening. Merchandise was missing. Tina first noticed this one afternoon after four teenage girls left the store after trying on some new embroidered tops. When Tina went back to clear the dressing room for the day, she discovered several empty hangers. Discouraged by this, she went into the storage room to unpack some more of the tops. On entering, she spied an old purse stuffed under some shelves. When she bent to pull it out she knocked several boxes of T-shirts off the shelves. "This really isn't my day!" she muttered. Picking up the boxes she noticed how light in weight they were. Opening them, she found them empty. At this moment the bells on the entrance jangled, indicating a customer. She left the storeroom and reentered the sales area.

Two middle-age women had just entered and were looking at the gifts. Tina wished that Art would return from the bank so that she could show him what she had discovered in the storeroom, but putting on a happy face she approached the two women. "May I help you?" she asked smiling.

One of the women turned to her and answered, "No, I don't think you have anything here that we want. We were at Marcelle's next door and thought your store looked interesting. We have appointments at the Beauty Salon across the street every week, and usually come over here to do a little shopping while waiting for the bus. This is a cute place, but we have to go now. Goodbye."

Several days later, Art was beginning to close for the night when a couple in their late teens entered.

"Hi, said Art, "Can I do something for you?"

"Yes," said the girl. "My boyfriend wants to buy me a custom bikini for my birthday. I heard that you have them here."

"Right over here," Art indicated. "Pick out the style and size from the samples hanging on the rack, then choose the fabric. The prices are on the tags. Let me know if I can help you. The fitting rooms are in the back. Just follow the Zig Zag Rainbow carpet. Closing time is in fifteen minutes, but if you need a little extra time it's OK."

Art went back to straightening the imported tops and jeans when he overheard the two young people as they made their way to the fitting rooms.

"Wow!" exclaimed the boy, "I see what Sheila meant when she said that this place was weird. This follow the Zig Zag Rainbow sounds like something out of the *Wizard of Oz*. Who does this turkey think he is anyway? I think I would like you in style *D* made out of that blue flowered Hawaiian stuff. What do you think?"

The girl replied, "That would be super. It would be the prettiest suit at the beach, but did you see the price?"

"Don't worry about that. Mr. Zig Zag Rainbow must be loaded. All of the people in this shopping center are rich. He doesn't need our money."

"Excuse me, sir," the boy called, "My girlfriend likes one of the suits. Can you help her decide on the fabric?"

Putting the overheard conversation out of his mind, Art replied, "Sure. Let's go back to the beach-wear area and I'll show you some samples."

Together they went back to the beach-wear area where Art unfolded the five fabric samples she indicated and laid them on the counter. Among them was the blue flowered Hawaiian material they had discussed earlier.

"We like this one," stated the boy, indicating a multicolored stripe cotton, "but don't you have it in any other color combinations?"

"I don't think so," Art replied "but here's a print that's nice for that suit."

"No, we like the stripes. Is this all of your sample stock?"

"Well, no. Actually, I just received a shipment this afternoon that isn't unpacked yet. If you can come back tomorrow I'll show it to you. I'm certain there are several striped pieces in the order."

"We can't do that! This place is ten miles from her house and I have to work tomorrow. Anyway, today's her birthday, and I'd really like to do it now. Couldn't you check and see if the stripes are there? We can wait."

"OK," said Art, "I'll be right back."

"We'll just look around while you look."

Art went back to the store room and opened the box from the fabric mill. He was right. There were several different striped samples. When he returned to the sales area, the couple was looking at the T-shirts.

"Here are the samples," Art called as he went back to the beachwear area.

"We're coming," laughed the girl, "along the Zig Zag Rainbow."

The couple ordered a suit made out of a multishade green fabric and left fifteen minutes past closing time.

Art was tired, but at least, he thought to himself, he had closed a sale for his extra effort. As he refolded the fabrics he had shown them, he noticed that the blue Hawaiian print was missing, and as he found out later, so was the style *D*, size 9 sample suit, several T-shirts, a hand-hammered copper chain, and a belt. He felt sick. Looking at the order form for the custom suit, he realized that the address given was for the public library.

After only two months of operation, Art and Tina had realized that Zig Zag had a real problem. The location was good, but the store just wasn't drawing the right customers. There were more middle-age women who shopped in the other center shops or frequented the beauty salon coming in but rarely purchasing anything. There were also numerous young teens who came in packs from the school nearby. Some of them made purchases, and most seemed really turned on to the store atmosphere.

Art decided something had to be done. He spent that entire weekend taking a physical inventory to identify all thefts and preparing a profit and loss statement for the first two months of operation (see Exhibit 4) and a balance sheet as of September 30, 1980 (see Exhibit 5). In addition, he spent considerable time developing some merchandise operating statistics for the seven major merchandise lines Zig Zag handled (see Exhibit 6).

After the long weekend with the books and paperwork, Art informed Tina that they were losing almost as much money as they were taking in. Somewhat depressed, he bluntly told Tina they could probably get out of their six-month lease, close the doors, and take their losses. Alternatively, he mentioned, they could try to hold things together for a couple more months while rapidly making some changes to try to improve sales and profits.

EXHIBIT 4
Zig Zag
Profit and Loss
Statement
(8/1/80–
9/30/80)

Sales		$6635
Less: Cost of goods sold		3666
Gross profit		$2969
Less: Operating expenses		
Rent	$2400	
Advertising	600	
Wages	2000	
Theft and pilferage	749	
Utilities	343	
Insurance	200	
Phone	96	
Interest	884	
Miscellaneous	371	
Total operating expenses		7643
Profit or (loss)		$(4674)

EXHIBIT 5
Zig Zag
Balance Sheet
(9/30/80)

ASSETS		LIABILITIES AND NET WORTH	
Current assets		Current liabilities	
Cash	$ 483	Accounts payable	$ 3,443
Inventory	22,292	Note payable	30,000
Total	$22,775	Total	$33,443
Fixed assets		Long-term liabilities	0
Equipment and fixtures	$ 9,400	Net worth	$ 1,107
Leasehold improvements	2,375		
Total	$11,775	Total liabilities and net worth	$34,550
Total assets	$34,550		

**EXHIBIT 6
Zig Zag
Operating
Statistics
(first two
months of
operation)**

MERCHANDISE LINE	SQUARE FEET[a]	DOLLAR SALES	AVERAGE INVENTORY (AT COST)	GROSS MARGIN PERCENT[b]
Candles	150	876	$1,732	45.3
Custom beach wear	170	375	692	47.1
T-shirts	222	1,291	1,608	31.3
Gifts	388	429	9,240	39.2
Jewelry	137	1,647	4,659	43.7
Accessories	93	1,408	3,043	29.4
Imported clothing	400	609	3,038	34.0

[a]Total square feet was 2,400; that not devoted to merchandise lines was for aisles, checkout, fitting rooms, and the stockroom.

[b]Gross margin percent equals sales minus cost of goods divided by sales.

QUESTIONS

1. What do you see as the major problems that have afflicted Zig Zag?

2. What steps should Art and Tina take to correct their problems? Should they close the doors and quit?

3. Draw a new layout pattern that would increase efficiency and security while promoting the proper atmosphere.

Case

Robert F. Lusch
University of Oklahoma

B. G. Morgan's

IN MIDYEAR 1979 Mr. Vance Womack, the buyer for the menswear department at B. G. Morgan's, requested permission from the general merchandise manager to change the present pricing policy on men's suits. Mr. Womack felt that a change in pricing was necessary due to increased local competition in this merchandise category.

BACKGROUND

B. G. Morgan's is a locally owned and operated full-line department store in a midwestern city of approximately 250,000 inhabitants. The store was founded by Billy George Morgan in 1902. The store remains in its original downtown location and is still primarily owned and operated by the Morgan family. Tom Morgan, the grandson of B. G. Morgan, is the current president and chief executive officer. In 1978 annual sales approached $12 million. The company has consistently shown a profit every year since 1902 except 1932, 1933, and 1957.

Since 1974 competition has intensified in B. G. Morgan's trade area, which happens to be the entire SMSA. Sears remodeled their downtown store and opened another store in a regional shopping mall on the outskirts of the city. In addition K-mart has built three new stores since 1974. Specialty store competition has also intensified, especially in women's and menswear. B. G. Morgan's has always been one of the most fashionable places for upper-middle- and upper-class residents to purchase their clothing. In many situations several generations of families have purchased their clothes at B. G. Morgan's.

In the area of menswear, one competitor that has grown to be a dominant market leader is Franklin's. Franklin's is a locally owned company that was founded in 1959. The store sells only menswear and womenswear in about a

Note: This case was prepared as a basis for class discussion rather than to illustrate appropriate or inappropriate handling of retail situations.

65/35 mix. Franklin's first store was located downtown, directly across the street from B. G. Morgan's. Today they have a total of five stores, and in 1978 their sales were $5.3 million. In 1970 their sales were $1.8 million. Franklin's sells moderate to good quality clothing at a relatively low markup. They are very promotional and price-oriented and concentrate on high inventory turnover. Recently they have introduced a line of high-grade men's suits priced at $249, which most local retailers (including B. G. Morgan's) sell in the $300 to $350 price range. This line has been heavily promoted in the local newspaper.

CURRENT SITUATION

Vance Womack is concerned about the sales performance of the men's suit lines at B. G. Morgan's. In 1970 Morgan's sold 1,445 suits, but in 1975 that number had dropped to 1,208, and in 1978 suit sales were only 940. 1979 results even look less promising.

On July 24, 1979, Vance wrote a memo to John Stern, the general merchandise manager, about this slackening of demand.

Memorandum

TO: Mr. Stern, General Merchandise Manager
FROM: Mr. Womack, Buyer, Menswear

It is time we came up with a strategy to combat our declining sales of men's suits. The inroads that Franklin's and other specialty stores are making into our market share is increasingly becoming a problem. We continue to hold on to our loyal patrons but the transient bargain seeking shopper is being intercepted by competition. Furthermore the problem is not one of poor buying. We have as good a selection and assortment of suits as anyone in town. And in addition our sales assistance and alteration department are superior. In short, I believe we are simply not price competitive. Given the level of competition, our present prices are simply too high.

In response to this memo, Mr. Stern immediately phoned Vance and told him that he concurred with his observation. John instructed Vance to put together relevant merchandising statistics for men's suits for the first six months of 1979 and also to develop pro-forma merchandising statistics based on his proposed price changes. These statistics are provided in Exhibits 1 and 2.

After Vance had started to compile these statistics he realized that B. G. Morgan's did not have the selection he initially thought they had, especially in the moderate- to lower-priced range. In fact they currently had no suits priced under $189. As a result two lower priced lines were added—one at $129 and another at $98, and in addition the $189 priced line was reduced to $169. Neither of these lines was expected to be best sellers, but Vance thought they might help to generate more traffic in the menswear department.

An increased level of advertising was also suggested by Vance. Currently advertising of men's suits had been averaging 1.9 percent of net sales. Vance proposed this be increased to 3.8 percent of net sales. Most of the advertising would be directed at the $298 and $398 lines and the $98 and $129 lines. Some consideration was given to putting the $98 line in a new bargain basement department of the store, but Vance felt this would defeat the purpose of generating more traffic in the upstairs menswear department.

EXHIBIT 1 **Merchandising Statistics for Men's Suits (1/1/79–6/30/79)**

PRICE LINE	COST RANGE (billed cost)	AVERAGE MARKON[a]	AVERAGE UNIT STOCK	UNIT SALES	WORKROOM COST PER UNIT	CASH DISCOUNTS (as percentage of billed cost)	RETAIL REDUCTIONS (as percentage of original retail)[b]
$419	$200–240	$213	60	50	$21	2%	8.1%
329	160–199	155	90	108	18	2	9.8
259	125–159	118	120	154	13	2	18.1
189	90–124	80	70	47	12	2	19.4

[a] Average markon represents original markup over original billed cost.
[b] Retail reductions include markdowns, employee discounts, and shortages as a percent of original retail.

EXHIBIT 2 **Projected Annual Performance on Men's Suits**

PRICE LINE	COST RANGE (billed cost)	AVERAGE MARKON[a]	PLANNED UNIT STOCK	PLANNED UNIT SALES	PLANNED WORKROOM COST PER UNIT	CASH DISCOUNTS (as percentage of billed costs)	PLANNED REDUCTIONS (as percentage of original retail)[b]
$398	$200–240	$192	78	140	$20	2%	3.1%
298	160–199	124	96	312	16	2	6.2
219	125–159	78	128	420	12	2	10.4
169	90–124	60	96	164	11	2	9.8
129	74– 89	48	96	140	9	2	6.1
98	54– 73	37	78	116	9	2	5.1

[a] Average markon represents original markup over original billed cost.
[b] Retail reductions include markdowns, employee discounts, and shortage as a percent of original retail.

QUESTIONS FOR DISCUSSION

1. Why did B. G. Morgan's wait so long to respond to its declining sales volume in men's suits?

2. Will the price cuts be profitable?

3. How will competition react to the price cuts?

4. What are the pros and cons of advertising both high- and low-priced men's suits?

5. What are the pros and cons of starting a bargain basement department?

Case

Robert F. Lusch
University of Oklahoma

Hoffman's Furniture

HOFFMAN'S FURNITURE is located in a city of roughly 200,000 in the Southwestern United States. The company is owned and operated by Tom Hayes, who acquired the company in 1975 from Benny Hoffman. Over the last five years Tom has experienced good success in owning and operating Hoffman's. In 1979 sales were $997,000, which produced a profit (after taxes) of $26,500. The profit was after Tom had paid himself a $36,000 salary for managing the store. Tom, with the help of seven full-time and three part-time employees, operates all aspects of the firm. Sales volume since 1975 has grown at an annual rate of 12.1 percent. Unfortunately, however, first quarter 1980 results were not as encouraging. Sales were off 2.1 percent from the corresponding 1979 quarter, and profits were a mere 0.6 percent of sales.

BACKGROUND

Since Tom acquired Hoffman's in 1975 he has worked at positioning the firm as a promotionally oriented home furnishings retailer with a liberal credit policy and a broad assortment of merchandise. Approximately 7 percent of sales are spent on advertising, which is considerably above the industry average for home furnishing retailers. In addition, 70 percent of all sales are made on credit. The installment credit plan that Tom designed requires that the customer put at least 10 percent down on an item and that the balance be paid off in six, nine, or twelve equal monthly installments. The interest charge is 1.5 percent per month on the unpaid balance. In every year since 1975 Hoffman's

Note: This case was prepared as a basis for class discussion rather than to illustrate appropriate or inappropriate handling of retail situations. Names and data are disguised. Special thanks are given to facts: Marketing and Economic Research Corporation, United Founders Tower, Oklahoma City, Oklahoma 73112.

has made money on their credit operation. That is, interest income has more than offset the cost of capital, bad debts, and expenses of administering the credit program.

Tom believes that Hoffman's risks in selling on credit are relatively low because of the financial stability of Hoffman's target market. Hoffman's typical customers are aged twenty-five to forty-four; have at least some college; have a household size of three or four members; live in their own house versus an apartment; are self-employed, a professional, or a manager; and have an annual income of over $15,000. The quality of this target market has resulted in bad debt expense typically being only 1.4 percent of sales.

CURRENT SITUATION

In early 1980 the economy began to slow down. Most households had overspent for Christmas. Furthermore, because inflation in 1979 had accelerated to a 13 percent rate, real incomes had actually declined in many cases. At the same time interest rates began to climb. Hoffman's itself was facing a 15 percent cost of capital from its local bank just to finance inventory during the slowdown. Tom believed that if Hoffman's could move inventory at a more rapid rate, even if it did so by selling the merchandise on credit, it would be better off.

Many consumers were becoming increasingly pessimistic about the short- and long-run outlook for the economy because of rising unemployment, rising interest rates, and rapid inflation. In early 1980 the rise in the consumer price index was approaching 20 percent annually. In contrast, however, Tom felt the time was never better for households to purchase major appliances and home furnishings. Manufacturers and retailers were cutting prices to move inventory, and retail credit in terms of its cost to the consumer could not go beyond its present level of 18 percent annually because of state usury laws. Also consumers could be almost certain that prices of furniture and appliances would be significantly higher in the future.

Tom believed that this consumer resistance could be overcome with a strong thirty-day promotional program. It was felt that up to $10,000 could be committed to this promotional campaign with the goal of moving $150,000 (at retail) of excess and old inventory. Part of the promotional campaign would consist of direct-mail advertising to all past charge customers over the last twenty-four months. This would comprise about 1,600 households. The second part of the promotional campaign would consist of heavy radio advertising for thirty consecutive days. Radio was selected because it offered the best potential for communicating with a specific target market. To assist in selecting the best station on which to advertise, Tom ordered the most recent copy of the Radio Audience Profile (RAP) from facts: Marketing and Economic Research Corporation in Oklahoma City. Selected data from this RAP report are presented in Exhibits 1 and 2. All of the radio stations had special package buys. Typically these special buys consisted of from 180 to 360 spots over a thirty-day period at a substantial discount over the single-spot price. Relevant data on these special buys is provided in Exhibit 3.

Tom was not sure which items he should try to promote most heavily. He had even considered not promoting any specific merchandise lines but rather to merely advertise storewide savings. Tom requested that his controller prepare merchandise statistics for 1979 so that he could better decide which merchandise lines might warrant special attention. These statistics are displayed in Exhibit 4.

EXHIBIT 1   **Listening Profile of Seven Radio Stations in Metropolitan Area (First Quarter 1980)**

| | AGE | | EDUCATION | | FAMILY SIZE | | | RESIDENCE | OCCUPATION | INCOME |
| | | | | | | | | | | |
STATION	25–34	35–44	Some College	College Graduate	2	3	4	Single Family	Professional, Managerial, or Self-Employed	Over $15,000
KEGN-AM	32.2%	17.9%	35.7%	14.3%	14.3%	32.1%	17.9%	78.6%	28.6%	43.1%
KEGN-FM	35.8	14.8	37.5	22.5	34.6	19.8	21.0	71.6	35.8	52.0
KFDE-AM	7.8	22.1	11.8	11.8	35.1	15.6	11.7	76.6	32.9	44.1
KFDE-FM	19.6	21.5	25.5	15.7	27.5	23.5	9.8	78.4	33.4	44.8
KBDI-FM	15.6	18.8	27.0	33.3	34.9	17.5	17.5	88.9	36.5	53.3
KOKE-AM	30.7	21.8	30.7	28.7	31.0	25.0	19.0	87.1	44.5	51.6
KBCT-AM	25.0	3.6	38.1	8.3	31.0	23.8	15.5	68.7	33.5	43.2

EXHIBIT 2   **Anticipated Purchasers in Seven Radio Station Audiences in Metropolitan Area[a] (First Quarter 1980)**

ITEM	KEGN-AM	KEGN-FM	KFDE-AM	KFDE-FM	KBDI-FM	KOKE-AM	KBCT-AM
Mattress or box springs	700	700	3,300	500	1,700	1,900	2,100
Major household appliance	1,400	4,000	2,400	2,900	1,400	3,100	5,700
Antiques	1,200	1,400	1,700	1,900	2,100	3,800	3,600
Furniture	1,400	5,700	2,400	2,100	3,100	7,400	6,900
Carpeting	1,700	3,300	2,100	1,900	1,900	3,800	4,800
Draperies or other interior decorating items	1,900	5,500	3,600	3,600	4,000	6,900	6,700
Major home remodeling	500	1,900	1,700	1,900	2,400	3,300	1,700
Television	700	2,600	1,700	1,900	1,900	1,900	3,800
Radio or stereo	3,100	6,700	1,000	2,600	700	5,500	8,600
Buying a house	1,700	4,000	2,100	2,100	1,200	3,800	6,400

[a]Responses in the categories above indicate that one or more persons in the respondent's household is considering purchasing or spending money on an item in the indicated category within the next three months. The numbers reported are projected households in the survey area (rounded to the nearest hundred) anticipating a purchase. All station names are disguised.

EXHIBIT 3 **Radio Station Rates for 30-Second Spots**

STATION	PROGRAM FORMAT	SINGLE 30-SECOND SPOT	180/30/30 BUY[a]	240/30/30 BUY	360/30/30 BUY	720/30/30 BUY
KEGN-AM	Contemporary	$ 6	$ 972	$1,152	$1,512	$2,592
KEGN-FM	Contemporary	9	1,539	1,836	2,592	4,860
KFDE-AM	Modern country	9	n/a	1,944	2,592	4,536
KFDE-FM	Progressive country	8	n/a	1,824	2,448	4,320
KBDI-FM	Beautiful music	7	1,197	1,512	2,142	3,780
KOKE-AM	Middle-of-the-road	9	n/a	1,836	2,430	3,888
KBCT-AM	Album-oriented rock	10	n/a	1,920	2,340	3,600

[a]A 180/30/30 buy consists of 180, 30-second spots broadcast over 30 days; other combinations are similar.

EXHIBIT 4
Hoffman's Merchandise Statistics (1979)

MERCHANDISE LINE	NET SALES TO TOTAL SALES	INVENTORY TURNOVER[a]	GROSS MARGIN	PERCENTAGE OF PURCHASES ON INSTALLMENT CREDIT
Living room furniture	32.4%	3.4x	42.8%	83.1%
Dining room furniture	8.7	1.6	40.7	78.0
Bedroom furniture	11.3	2.0	41.3	76.4
Bedding	9.1	3.7	43.4	10.8
Kitchen furniture	3.1	2.5	47.1	70.4
Floor coverings	6.1	2.9	34.6	65.8
Draperies and curtains	2.5	3.1	39.1	48.1
Radio and stereo	3.0	2.2	37.0	87.2
Television	5.6	2.6	24.2	83.4
Washers, dryers, irons	4.8	2.5	32.0	67.1
Lamps and shades	2.1	1.1	48.1	21.4
Refrigerators	2.9	3.1	29.1	79.4
Stoves and ranges	4.9	3.0	33.7	80.7
All other	3.5	1.8	36.7	58.1

[a] Sales divided by inventory at cost.

QUESTIONS FOR DISCUSSION

1. Does it make sense for Hoffman's to try to shift some of its inventory investment into accounts receivable?

2. Should Hoffman's use radio as the major media vehicle for their special thirty-day promotional campaign?

3. What would be Hoffman's best radio buy?

4. What should Hoffman's try to communicate through their thirty-day promotional program?

Case

Jack A. Lesser
Miami University

Ramco Retailers

JOHN MYERS, head buyer for Ramco Retailers, was preparing to meet with store managers assembled across the country to lead a seminar entitled, "Stock-Out: More Than Just an Ordering Problem." Ramco Retailers was a national discounter which had been experiencing serious erosion of profits from its increasing costs of doing business in the 1970s. Myers was sure that increasing costs were due in part to excess inventories at the store level.

Ramco was a chain of small variety stores, called Ramond's, until the 1960s. Ramond's hired away a former executive of K-mart, who, immediately after assuming the presidency, changed the name of the company and circulated a master plan to make it another K-mart. He immediately increased the number of product lines which Ramco carried to make each store a one-stop shopping center. Also central to his strategy was a policy to never be undersold, and to never be out-of-stock of advertised sale items. The president left Ramco a couple of years later, and although no formal corporate policy remained in effect for pricing and stockout, a large number of store managers continued to support the philosophy he instilled in them.

BACKGROUND

Responsibility for buying was almost entirely at the store level. It was a decision of department managers of each store. Store managers usually exerted their influence in two ways. First, on a daily basis, they would walk through the store, and if a stockout was noticed, or if they received a complaint from a customer, they would confront the department manager about it. Secondly, store managers received a bimonthly product-line inventory report which listed

Note: Reprinted with permission of the author. This case was prepared as a basis for class discussion rather than to illustrate appropriate or inappropriate handling of retail situations.

on an item basis purchases made and aggregate sales of each department. Store averages of purchases and sales were also included in the reports, and store managers sometimes looked for deviations in the averages in order to determine when to tell department managers to curtail their buying.

Largely though, stockout management was synonymous with complaint management. Department managers were fairly autonomous to order as much as they wanted and about the only time that anyone interfered was when a complaint was received. Customer complaints were growing increasingly common, and department managers were visibly defensive about this trend. When stockouts did occur, department managers would usually fill their displays with other merchandise so that the stockout would not be noticed.

CURRENT SITUATION

Because of increasing complaints, Ramco hired a marketing research firm to conduct a study on customer perceptions. A sample of 7,189 customers was interviewed when leaving one of nine representative Ramco stores. Customers were asked what sale and nonsale purchases they had planned to make before entering the store, and then were to indicate which purchases were actually made. If a planned purchase was not made, customers were to explain why they decided not to make a purchase. Forty-eight percent of all reasons were because the item sought was out of stock. Shoppers who failed to make a planned purchase because the item was stocked out represented 9.7 percent of the entire sample. Of these respondents, 8.7 percent of the sample, or 629 individuals, faced stockouts for nonsale items while 1.0 percent, or 74 individuals, found stockouts for sale purchases. The research showed that stockout was equally an important purchasing determinant to those who experienced stockouts as compared to those who did not.

Customers were also asked to rate the store they were shopping in on a 0 to 10 scale for a number of characteristics. In Exhibit 1 we show how customers who experienced a stockout on sale and nonsale items lowered their ratings on 20 different store characteristics.

On average, $7.94 was spent by customers who did not experience a stockout and $6.89 for the shopper's who did experience a stockout. The drop in $1.05 was not as large as anticipated and suggested that a large proportion of customers experiencing stockouts were willing to substitute purchases instead of shopping elsewhere, or postpone purchases.

However, the likelihood that customers were dissatisfied with the visit increased markedly when a stockout was experienced. Only 2.7 percent of all customers not experiencing a stockout were dissatisfied with the store visit, while 17.9 percent of the customers experiencing a stockout on a nonsale item and 28.9 percent of the customers experiencing a stockout on a sale item were dissatisfied.

Furthermore, substantial drops were registered in practically all of the twenty perceptions for customers experiencing a stockout in a nonsale item. The decline went beyond merchandise selection perceptions and extended to

EXHIBIT 1	STORE CHARACTERISTIC	CUSTOMERS EXPERIENCING STOCKOUT ON SALE ITEM	CUSTOMERS EXPERIENCING STOCKOUT ON NONSALE ITEM
Decline in Customer Ratings of Store Characteristics	Low everyday price	None	Large[b]
	Sale prices	None	Large
	Friendly employees	None	Large
	Knowledgeable employees	Small[a]	Large
	Fully-stocked shelves	Large	Large
	Enough employees	None	Large
	Variety of merchandise	None	Large
	Attractive decor	None	Large
	Ease of finding items	None	Large
	Ease of charging merchandise	None	Large
	Speedy checkout	Small	Large
	Quality of merchandise	None	Large
	Easy to walk through store	None	Small
	Cleanliness	None	Large
	Convenient location	Small	Large
	Variety of merchandise	None	Large
	Convenience to other stores	Small	Large
	Fairness of adjustments	None	Small
	Easy to return merchandise	None	Small
	Fashionable clothing	None	Large

[a]Small represents a drop of .3 or less on a 10 point scale.
[b]Large represents a drop of greater than .6 on a 10-point scale.

most of the store characteristics. Customers experiencing a stockout on a sale item were not as unanimous in their changes of perceptions. Exhibit 1 indicates that only one of the twenty perception ratings declined very much for these customers. These customers appeared to be much less likely to blame Ramco for a stockout.

Customers were also asked to evaluate, on a 0 to 10 scale, the likelihood that they would make a purchase from each of the twenty-eight product categories listed in Exhibit 2. Analysis of the data in Exhibit 2 suggested two basic conclusions: declines in the likelihood of future purchases depended on the specific product category being stocked out; and, as with store perceptions, customers experiencing a stockout on a sale item underwent smaller declines than did customers experiencing a stockout in a nonsale item.

Generally speaking, clothing articles, electronics, and hobby supplies were most sensitive to stockouts. Small appliances, domestic goods, gift items, and unfinished furniture were relatively resistant to stockout. Candy, infant's clothing, electronics, health and beauty aids, house plants, and stationery were much less sensitive to sale stockouts than they were to nonsale stockouts.

Myers did not know what to make of this data. On one hand, it showed that customers who experienced stockout perceived Ramco less favorably and

EXHIBIT 2 **Decline in Likelihood of Future Purchases** PRODUCT CATEGORY	CUSTOMERS EXPERIENCING STOCKOUT ON SALE ITEM	CUSTOMERS EXPERIENCING STOCKOUT ON NONSALE ITEM
Small appliances (toasters, mixers, blenders)	None	None
Automotive supplies	Small[a]	Small
Candy	Small	Large[c]
Boy's clothing	Moderate[b]	Large
Girl's clothing	Moderate	Moderate
Infant's clothing	None	Large
Men's clothing	None	Moderate
Women's hosiery	Large	Large
Women's fashion accessories (handbags, scarfs, gloves)	Small	None
Costume jewelry	Small	Large
Women's clothing	Moderate	Large
Domestic goods (sheets, pillow cases, curtains, drapes)	Small	None
Decorative and gift items (knickknacks, pictures, plaques)	None	None
Electronics (TV, radios, stereos, tape players, CB radios)	None	Large
Fabrics and sewing notions	Moderate	Large
Footwear	Small	Large
Unfinished furniture	None	None
Hardware, plumbing, and paint supplies	None	None
Health and beauty aids	None	Moderate
Kitchen accessories (pots, utensils, serving pieces)	None	Small
Lawn, garden supplies, and equipment	None	Small
Pets and pet supplies	None	Small
House plants, planters, and potting soil	None	Moderate
Records and tapes	Moderate	Large
Sporting goods and accessories	Small	None
Stationery, office supplies, greeting cards, photo and picture frames	None	Large
Craft and hobby supplies	Small	Large
Toys	Small	None

[a]Small represents a drop of .3 or less on a 10-point scale.
[b]Moderate represents a drop of from .3 to .6 on a 10-point scale.
[c]Large represents a drop of greater than .6 on a 10-point scale.

might be less likely to make purchases from Ramco in the future. However, sales declines from the 9.7 percent of customers who experienced a stockout were not very large for that given visit, and the customers who experienced stockouts on sale items were not affected much at all.

About the only thing he was sure he was going to say was, "You guys better shape up and cut down our wasted inventory or we'll make the ordering decisions at headquarters."

QUESTIONS FOR DISCUSSION

1. Who was responsible for the excess inventories? Why?

2. How did complaint management contribute to the inventory problem? What roles did the current corporate stockout policy and bimonthly inventory reports play?

3. What were the implications of the differences between customers experiencing stockouts in sale and nonsale items?

4. What dangers, beyond the $1.05 loss in customer expenditures, might be encountered when a customer is prevented from making a purchase because of a stockout?

Glossary

accounts receivable turnover. Annual credit sales divided by average annual investment in accounts receivable. The higher the turnover of accounts receivable, the quicker customers pay their bills.

acid-test ratio. A measure of liquidity, the ratio of cash (and equivalents) to current liabilities. Analysts say that cash should be about 15 to 20 percent of current liabilities.

administrative fit. Occurs when the retailer acquires the proper mix and quantity of resources (financial, human, and location) to implement and carry out its strategy and thus maximize its performance potential.

administrative planning. Planning for the acquisition of resources that will be necessary to successfully carry out the retailer's strategy.

advertising. The presentation of information about a retailer or its goods or services in one of the media.

advertising efficiency. The extent to which advertising has produced the desired result at the least cost.

asset turnover. Annual net sales divided by total assets. This is a basic measure of how productively the retailer is using its capital to generate sales.

atmosphere. The image a store projects as the result of its layout and fixtures. The main determinants of atmosphere are the type and density of employees, merchandise, fixtures, sound, and odor and visual factors.

bait-and-switch advertising. Advertising merchandise at unusually attractive prices and, once the consumer is baited to come into the store, trying to persuade the customer that the low-priced model is not a good buy because of poor quality and durability. The goal is to try to sell a high-priced, nonadvertised model.

basic stock method. A method of dollar merchandise planning having as its foundation a baseline or fixed level of dollar inventory investment regardless of expected sales volume. On top of this foundation is a variable element that increases or decreases at the first of each month in the same dollar amount as sales are expected to increase or decrease.

beginning-of-the-month stock-to-sales ratio. A ratio telling the retailer how much dollar stock to have on hand at the beginning of the month to support that month's dollar sales. A ratio of 7.2, for example, means that dollar stocks at the beginning of the month should be 7.2 times as great as expected sales for that month.

boutique layout. A variation on the free flow layout that creates mini-stores within a larger store. Each mini-store is aimed at a specific target group and is often a grouping of merchandise from a single designer or company.

brainstorming. In this technique of creative thinking, participants freely toss out ideas, which are recorded but not discussed by the group as they are suggested. The purpose is to obtain the greatest number of ideas possible, even wild ones, for the greater the number of ideas, the greater the chance of obtaining one or more that is innovative.

break-even point. The point at which the retailer's total sales equal total costs or expenses. The point at which neither a profit or loss is made: sales below break-even mean a loss; sales above mean a profit.

cash budget. A cash control technique that shows the timing of the retailer's cash disbursements and receipts and how they affect the retailer's cash balance.

census of retail trade. A comprehensive survey of all retail establishments in the United States conducted every five years in the years ending in 2 and 7 by the U.S. Department of Commerce.

central business district (CBD). The geographic point where most cities originated and grew up. Also typically the point at which all public transportation systems converge.

central place theory. A location theory developed by Walter Christaller in 1933. A central place is a center of commerce composed of a cluster of retail institutions—typically what today is called a village, town, or city. According to the theory, central places are established in a geographic space so as to minimize aggregate travel costs for the consumer.

chain-store retailer. As defined by the Department of Commerce and the Bureau of the Census, any retailer with eleven or more units.

closure. The process of bringing customers in the store to the point where the evidence before them conclusively suggests that the product or service being offered should be bought. Not the same as outcome, which is purchasing or not purchasing.

conflict. An inevitable occurrence between retailers and suppliers because of their interdependence. Conflict is any action by the supplier or retailer that is inconsistent with the goals of the other.

consignment sales. Sales in which the supplier, typically a manufacturer or wholesaler, retains title to the goods while the retailer has physical possession and attempts to sell the goods. Typically when the goods are sold they are paid for.

contingency funds. Funds that a new retailer should set aside for unforeseen emergencies. Contingency funds of 15 to 20 percent of the total capital requirements to start the venture are recommended.

contingency strategy. A strategy the firm has ready in case the most likely configuration of environmental factors does not occur, and the core strategy becomes obsolete.

contribution profit. Net sales less cost of goods sold and any expenses that can be directly traced to the goods sold.

conventional marketing channel. A marketing system in which each member is loosely aligned with the others and is mainly oriented toward the next institution in the channel.

conversion rate. The percentage of shoppers who were converted into customers. The measure is computed by dividing the number of customers who walk out of the store with a purchase by the number of customers who entered the store.

cost-based markup percentage. The retail selling price of the item minus the cost of the item divided by the cost of the item. More rarely used than the *retail-based markup.*

coverage. The theoretical maximum percentage of a retailer's target market that can be reached by an advertising medium.

credit. See *installment credit, open-charge credit,* and *revolving credit.*

credit scoring. An objective technique for determining whether to grant credit. Points are awarded to the applicant according to demographic characteristics that indicate the degree of credit risk—for instance, more points are awarded for owning a home than for renting. The credit decision is based on the total score.

cross-market opportunity analysis. A step in retail location analysis in which the retailer looks across several or many markets (communities) for the most attractive one before focusing on a precise location for a new store.

current ratio. The ratio of current assets to current liabilities, a basic measure of a retailer's solvency. Analysts suggest retailers should have a current ratio of 2.0 times.

customer service. All those activities performed by the retailer that influence (a) the ease with which a potential customer can shop or learn about the store's offerings, (b) the ease with which a transaction can be completed once the customer attempts to make a purchase, and (c) the customer's satisfaction with the merchandise after the transaction.

debt capital.   Capital provided by anyone other than the owners of the firm. Common sources are bond financing, supplier financing, bank and financial institution financing, and government financing.

Delphi technique.   A method used in futures research to attain a consensus of opinion from a group of experts without having the experts confront each other, but still allowing them to know the opinions of the others involved.

demand density.   The extent to which the potential demand for the retailer's goods and services is concentrated in certain census tracts or parts of the community.

demand elasticity.   The percentage change in quantity demanded that is due to a percentage change in a demand determinant such as price or advertising.

depreciation tax shelter.   Depreciation can be a source of recurring capital because it is a noncash expense and can therefore allow the retail enterprise to cut its tax bill. The depreciation tax shelter is equal to the depreciation expense multiplied by the tax rate.

dissonance.   Doubt that occurs in the consumer's mind when he or she becomes aware that unchosen products, brands, or stores have desirable attributes or that chosen products, brands, or stores have undesirable attributes.

divertive competition.   Occurs when a retailer intercepts or diverts customers from competing retailers. For example, supermarkets, when they sell oil, divert customers from service stations and auto supply stores.

dollar merchandise control.   The procedures used to ensure that the buyer does not make commitments for merchandise that would exceed the dollar merchandise plan. The major control technique used is open-to-buy.

dollar merchandise planning.   Planning the total dollars to have invested in inventory, usually done by month or season.

dual distribution.   Occurs when a manufacturer sells to independent retailers and also through its own retail outlets.

earnings per share.   Total earnings available to common stockholders divided by shares of common stock outstanding. It shows the profit that each share of common stock has earned.

equity capital.   Capital provided by owners of the firm, including paid-in capital and retained earnings.

exclusive dealing.   See *one-way exclusive dealing* and *two-way exclusive dealing*.

external forces.   Uncontrollable elements outside the retail firm that influence or impact on its performance. The external forces can be categorized as the behavior of consumers, the behavior of competitors, the behavior of channel members, the legal system, the state of technology, and the socioeconomic environment.

factoring. A retailer selling its accounts receivable to a third party (usually a bank) at a discount.

FIFO. The first-in, first-out method of valuing inventory. With FIFO, the goods purchased first are assumed to be the items sold first. Compare *LIFO*.

financial leverage. Dividing the retailer's total assets by net worth to show the extent to which the retailer is using debt in its total capital structure. A leverage ratio around 2.0 times is generally considered comfortable for a retailer.

fixed costs. The costs in a particular time period that the retailer will incur regardless of the quantity of goods or services sold.

formal organizational structure. The way employees in an organization should behave in terms of lines of authority and responsibility. Contrast with *informal organizational structure*.

franchising. A vertical marketing system in which one firm (the franchisor) licenses a way of conducting business to a number of outlets (franchisees), who market a product or service using the franchisor's trade names, trademarks, servicemarks, know-how, and methods of doing business.

free flow layout. A store layout in which the fixtures and merchandise are grouped into patterns or left free standing, thereby creating an unstructured traffic pattern.

free-standing retailer. Location of a retail establishment outside the central business district but not in a shopping center. Usually located along major traffic arteries.

frequency The average number of times each person who is reached by an advertising medium is exposed to a particular advertisement during a given time period.

full-line forcing. Occurs when a manufacturer forces a retailer to buy its entire line of products in order to get the better-established lines the retailer desires.

futures research. Research analyzing the future environments the firm might confront.

grid layout. A store layout in which all the counters and fixtures are at right angles to each other, thereby forming a maze.

gross margin return on inventory (GMROI). The ratio of gross profit to average inventory investment at cost. When the gross margin percentage is multiplied by stockturn (net sales divided by average inventory at cost), the result is GMROI.

gross profit.   Net sales less cost of goods sold.

high performance results.   A retailer achieves high performance results when it achieves financial performance in the upper 25 percent of retailers in terms of profitability, liquidity, and sales growth.

horizontal cooperative advertising.   An arrangement in which two or more retailers join together to share the cost of advertising.

horizontal price fixing.   An illegal arrangement by which competing retailers establish a fixed price at which to sell their merchandise.

human resource audit.   A careful examination, by top management or an outside consultant, of the strengths and weaknesses of all employees.

informal organizational structure.   How the employees in an organization actually do behave in terms of lines of authority and responsibility. Contrast with *formal organizational structure.*

initial markup percentage.   The initial asking price of the item minus its cost, divided by the initial asking price of the item. Not the same as *maintained markup percentage.*

installment credit.   Usually granted the customer for a single purchase. Payment is over a fixed period of time, generally monthly, and a finance charge is typical.

institutional advertising.   Retail advertising that attempts to sell the store rather than the merchandise in it by emphasizing the store image and creating a unique position for the retailer in the consumer's mind.

interorganizational management.   The management of relationships between organizational entities, such as the relations between retailers and their suppliers.

intertype competition.   Competition between different types of retail outlets selling the same lines of merchandise in the same trade area, such as both drugstores and supermarkets selling health and beauty aids.

intratype competition.   The most common type of competition, occurring when any two or more retailers of the same type compete with each other for the same households, such as one hardware store competing with another.

law of retail gravitation.   See *retail gravity theory.*

layaway.   A customer service in which the customer places a deposit on an item, which the retailer holds for the customer. The customer makes periodic payments on the item and, when it is completely paid for, can take it home.

layout.   The arrangement of selling and nonselling space, aisles, fixtures, displays, and equipment in the proper relationship to each other and to the fixed elements of the building. See *boutique layout, free flow layout,* and *grid layout.*

leadership pricing. Establishing a price on an item at a markup significantly lower than the demand for that item warrants. The goal of leadership pricing is to build store traffic and thus help generate sales of related items.

leasehold improvements. Any permanent fixtures which a retailer must add to a space that is leased and which must remain with the building when the lease ends. Examples may include lighting fixtures, carpeting, or partitions.

lifestyles. The patterns in which people live and spend time and money. Lifestyles are typically defined in terms of a person's activities, interests, and opinions.

LIFO. The last-in, first-out method of valuing inventory. With LIFO, the most recently purchased goods are assumed to be the items sold first. Useful in inflationary times as a technique for reducing taxes. Compare *FIFO.*

liquidity. The retailer's ability to meet its current payment obligations, measured by the *acid-test ratio, current ratio,* and *quick ratio.*

maintained markup percentage. The actual selling price of the item minus its cost divided by the actual selling price of the item. Contrast with *initial markup percentage.*

markdown. Reductions in the price of an item to stimulate sales. Markdowns are necessary because of buying errors, pricing errors, or promotion errors.

marketing channel. The set of institutions that are necessary and incidental in moving goods from points of production to points of consumption.

marketing functions. The eight marketing functions are buying, selling, storing, transporting, sorting, financing, information, and risk taking. These functions must be performed in getting goods to consumers, but marketing systems vary in who performs them.

marketing institutions. These institutions can be meaningfully broken into two categories. The primary marketing institutions take title to goods; the facilitating institutions do not actually take title but facilitate the marketing process by specializing in the performance of certain functions.

market intensification. A retail strategy in which expansion is restricted to a limited number of core markets rather than expanding erratically into geographically distant markets.

market saturation. The extent to which a particular market area, typically a town or city, is overpopulated with retailers in a particular line of trade.

market segmentation. Breaking a heterogeneous market into more homogeneous groups.

merchandise breadth.   The number of product lines found in the merchandise mix.

merchandise depth.   The average number of items within each line of the merchandise mix.

merchandise line.   A group of products that are closely related because they are intended for the same end use (all televisions); are sold to the same customer group (junior miss sportswear); or fall within a given price range (budget sportswear).

merchandise management.   The analysis, planning, acquisition, and control of inventory investments in a retail enterprise.

merchandise mix.   The merchandise lines carried by a retailer as a whole or within a unit, such as a department, of a large retailer.

merchandise variety.   The interrelatedness of the product lines represented in the merchandise mix.

mobility.   In retail location theory, the ease with which people can travel. People who are mobile are willing to travel greater distances to shop; therefore, there will be fewer, but larger stores in a community.

model stock plan.   The precise items and their respective quantities that should be on hand for each merchandise line.

nonstore retailing.   A retail strategy in which selling takes place outside a store, either by mail, phone, or home computer, or in the home of the customer or a third party.

off-even pricing.   Pricing items slightly below an even dollar figure ($4.97 rather than $5.00) or just below an even denomination ($499, not $500).

100 percent location.   The location that is the best possible site for a retailer within an area. Generally, the location with the greatest amount of the kind of traffic desired. A 100 percent location for one type of retailer may not be for another type of retailer.

one-way exclusive dealing.   A supplier agreeing to give a retailer the exclusive right to merchandise the supplier's product in a particular trade area without the retailer agreeing to do anything, in particular, for the supplier. A legal arrangement; contrast with *two-way exclusive dealing.*

open-charge credit.   Credit in which a credit limit is established for each customer, who is allowed to purchase on credit up to this limit in any given month. At the close of the month or other thirty-day period, the customer is billed and is expected to pay the bill in full.

open-to-buy.   The dollar amount that a buyer can currently expend on merchandise without exceeding the planned dollar stocks. Open-to-buy is equal to (1) end-of-month planned retail stock, (2) plus planned sales for the month, (3) minus stock on hand at retail, (4) equals planned purchases at retail, (5) minus commitments at retail for current delivery. Note that open-to-buy is computed at retail prices.

operating profit. A measure of the performance of a merchandise line, defined as net sales less cost of goods sold, direct expenses, and a share of all indirect expenses incurred by the retailer.

operations fit. Occurs when the retailer effectively uses the resources at its disposal.

operations planning. Planning the efficient use of available resources in order to manage the day-to-day operations of the firm successfully.

overstored markets. Markets in which the number of stores per thousand households in a community is so high that expected average returns on retail investment fall below the level needed to make investment in a retail enterprise attractive.

ownership groups. Retail enterprises that have purchased previously independent retailers and in some cases other retail chains. The ownership group allows individual stores to maintain their image and management and merchandising programs, except for the centralizing of some staff functions. Examples include Federated Department Stores and Allied Stores Corporation.

palming off. Representing merchandise as being made by a firm other than the true manufacturer; an illegal practice.

patent. The government's granting of a 17-year monopoly for the marketing of a product or process.

percentage variation method. A method of dollar merchandise planning postulating that the percentage fluctuations in monthly stock from average stock should be half as great as the percentage fluctuations in monthly sales from average sales.

periodic unit control system. An inventory control system in which the items in stock are counted at regularly scheduled intervals, such as the end of the month.

perpetual unit control system. An inventory control system in which inventory records are constantly updated as items are sold and purchased. Inventory is not physically counted; rather, invoices and other accounting records are used to keep track of inventory on paper.

personal selling. An oral presentation by a salesperson to one or more prospective purchasers for the purpose of inducing them to make a purchase.

planning. Deciding in the present what to do in the future. The future can be any upcoming time; tomorrow, next month, next year, or even five, ten, or one hundred years from today.

planning personalities. The way a retailer views the future and the need to plan. The four types are the discounter, who has little faith in planning; the extrapolator, who views the future as an extrapolation of the past; the goal setter, who aims to achieve a goal; and the cyberneticist, who is oriented to all departments and functions within the firm and to all external forces the retailer faces.

PM. This stands for "push money," "prize money," or "premium merchandise." In retailing it is also sometimes called "spiffing." The PM is paid to the salesperson in addition to a base salary and regular commissions to encourage additional selling effort behind particular items or merchandise lines. PMs can be either retailer or supplier sponsored.

population density. The number of persons per square mile or the number of households per square mile in a community.

power of supplier. The ability of the supplier to control the decision variables of the retailer. The more dependent the retailer is on the supplier, the more power the supplier has.

price discrimination. Occurs when two retailers or other business firms buy identical merchandise from the same supplier but pay different prices. Not necessarily illegal.

price experiment. A research method in which a retailer systematically varies the price of an item while trying to control for extraneous factors and then observes the resulting change in quantity demanded.

price line. A specific price within a price zone at which a representative stock is carried.

price zone. A range of prices for a particular merchandise line that appeal to customers in a certain demographic group.

principle of compatibility. As formulated by Richard Nelson, "two compatible businesses located in close proximity will show an increase in business volume directly proportionate to the incidence of total customer interchange between them, inversely proportionate to the ratio of the business volume of the larger store to that of the smaller store, and directly proportionate to the sum of the ratios of purposeful purchasing to total purchasing in each of the two stores."

problem identification subsystem. The part of the retail information system that scans trends in the behavior of consumers, channels, and competitors; monitors the legal, socioeconomic, and technological environments; and monitors asset, revenue, and expense trends.

problem recognition. The stage of retail patronage behavior in which the consumer's ideal state of affairs departs sufficiently from the actual state of affairs so as to place the consumer in a state of unrest. Shopping behavior can be triggered by the recognition of four needs: (1) buying, (2) gather information, (3) socializing, (4) other personal needs such as the need to feel power by having others wait on you.

problem solution subsystem.   The part of the retail information system that is used to obtain information on recurring or nonrecurring problems in the retail enterprise. The problems could either be strategic, administrative, or operations.

profit margin.   The ratio of net profit (after taxes) to net sales, showing how much profit a retailer makes on each dollar of sales after all expenses and taxes have been met.

programmed merchandising agreements.   A joint venture in which a retailer and a supplier develop a comprehensive plan to market the supplier's product line. These plans usually last six months, but some last longer.

promotional advertisements.   Advertising that attempts to bolster the retailer's short-run performance by advertising product features or price as a selling point.

publicity.   Inducing demand for a product, service, or business by planting favorable news about it or by obtaining favorable presentation of it in the media.

purchase probability.   How likely a consumer is to purchase a particular product within a given time, usually from three to six months.

quick ratio.   The ratio of current assets less inventory to current liabilities. Analysts suggest a quick ratio of about 1.0 times.

reach.   The percentage of a retailer's target market that is exposed to a particular advertising medium.

resale price maintenance.   See *vertical price fixing*.

retail-based markup percentage.   The retail selling price of the item minus the cost of the item divided by the retail selling price. More commonly used than *cost-based markup*.

retail diversification.   A retail strategy in which a retailer operates multiple businesses marketing different merchandise mixes or aimed at different market segments.

retailer owned cooperatives.   Wholesale organizations organized and owned by retailers that offer scale economies and service to member retailers, allowing them to compete with larger chain-buying organizations.

retail gravity theory.   Based on William Reilly's law of retail gravitation, which mimics the gravitational law of physics by replacing mass with the population of a community (distance remains distance). The law suggests that the larger a community is, the more it attracts customers from surrounding smaller communities, but the farther away the surrounding communities are, the less it attracts customers from them.

retail information system.   A blueprint for the continual and periodic systematic collection, analysis, and reporting of relevant data about any past, present, or future developments that could or already have influenced the retailer's performance.

retailing. Any firm that sells merchandise or provides services to the final consumer is performing the retailing function. In terms of goods, retailing is the final move in the progression of merchandise from producer to consumer.

retractive advertising. Occurs when the Federal Trade Commission requires a retailer who has made false or deceptive statements in advertising, to run a new advertisement in which the former statements are contradicted and the truth stated.

return on assets. The ratio of net profit (after taxes) to total assets, which shows the return on all assets employed in the retail enterprise regardless of who financed them.

return on equity. See *return on net worth.*

return on net worth. Net profit (after taxes) divided by net worth, which shows the return on the capital that the owners or stockholders have invested in the retail enterprise.

return on sales. See *profit margin.*

revolving credit. A credit system in which customers are given a credit limit that cannot be exceeded by credit purchases. The customer is billed regularly (usually monthly), but has to pay only a minimum payment rather than the entire balance.

sales promotions. Any activity other than personal selling, advertising, or publicity that stimulates purchases. The most common types are point-of-purchase displays and consumer premiums.

selling space productivity. A measure of how efficiently the retailer is using its space. A measure of output to input; the input is square feet of selling space, but the output can be either net sales, gross profit, contribution profit, or operating profit.

semifixed costs. Costs that are constant over a range of sales volume, but past a crucial point increase to a higher plateau, where they again remain constant.

servicemark. Any word, symbol, or design, or a combination of these used to identify a service, such as a car wash.

shopping center. A cluster of stores, ranging in size from the neighborhood center (50,000 square feet), through the community center (150,000 square feet) and regional center (400,000 square feet), to the super-regional center (over 1 million square feet).

space allocation. The decision the retailer must make in regard to how much space to allocate to different departments or merchandise lines and to selling and nonselling space. Because space is a scarce resource, this decision is critical in determining the retailer's financial performance.

spiffing. See PM.

standard layout. A simple arrangement of entrance, counter, checkout area, and exit used mainly for businesses whose major concern is moving customers in and out rapidly.

standard metropolitan statistical area (SMSA). A territorial unit used by the Census Bureau that includes cities and their suburbs that total more than 50,000 people.

statement of mission. The retailer's overall justification for existing, which should be stated generically so as to be applicable over long periods of time.

statement of objectives. The retailer's specific goals, which can be financial (profitability, productivity, market position), societal, and personal.

stockturn. A concept that tries to capture how long inventory is on hand before it is sold. Items with a high stockturn are on hand a short time; those with a low stockturn are on hand longer. Sometimes referred to as inventory or merchandise turnover.

store attributes. The evaluative criteria consumers use to evaluate stores. Attributes can be both objective and subjective. The most frequently used attributes are price, merchandise, physical characteristics, sales promotions, advertising, convenience, services, and store personnel.

store image. The personality the store projects to the consumer through its design features, employees, merchandising strategy, etc. The image of the store is conveyed through the functional characteristics of the store as well as through their psychological properties.

store positioning. A retail strategy in which the retailer identifies a well-defined market segment according to demographic or lifestyle variables and then appeals to this segment with a clearly differentiated approach involving all dimensions of the retail store.

strategic fit. Occurs when the retailer achieves the best match between its mission and objectives and the opportunities it perceives in the external environment.

strategic planning. Matching the retailer's mission and goals with available opportunities in the retailer's environment.

strategic profit model. A measure of a retailer's profit performance obtained by multiplying the retailer's profit margin by its rate of asset turnover to arrive at return on assets. The return on assets is then multiplied by the retailer's financial leverage to yield its return on net worth.

supermarket retailing. A retail strategy involving five basic principles directed at improving retail productivity and reducing the cost of distribution: (1) self-service and self-selection displays, (2) centralization of customer services, usually at the checkout counter, (3) large-scale, low-cost physical facilities, (4) a strong price emphasis, and (5) a broad assortment and wide variety of merchandise to facilitate multiple-item purchases.

supply density. The extent to which retailers are concentrated in particular census tracts or geographic areas.

task analysis. A method of human resource planning involving identifying all of the tasks the retailer needs to perform and breaking those tasks into jobs.

territorial restrictions. Attempts by a supplier, usually a manufacturer, to limit the geographical area in which a retailer may resell its merchandise.

three-dimensional demand function. The relationship of price, distance, and demand. For retailers, quantity demanded by a household is inversely related to prices charged and distance to the store.

trademark. Any word, symbol, or design, or a combination of these used to identify a product, such as a refrigerator.

trading area. The region within which a store's customers reside. A trading area is a series of demand gradients or zones in which, as distance from the retailer increases, the probability of the store being patronized decreases.

transportation costs. The costs of a consumer traveling to a store, including actual cost (the dollar cost for transportation), opportunity cost (lost time to do something other than shop), and psychic cost (psychological effect of traveling to the store and back).

two-way exclusive dealing. A potentially illegal arrangement in which a supplier offers a retailer the exclusive distribution in a given trade area of a merchandise line or product only if, in return, the retailer agrees to do something for the supplier—usually not handle competing brands. See *one-way exclusive dealing*.

tying arrangement. Occurs when a seller with a strong product or service forces a buyer (the retailer) to buy a weak product or service as a condition for buying the strong one. Not necessarily illegal.

understored markets. Markets in which the number of stores per thousand households in a community is low enough that expected average returns on retail investment are higher than the level needed to keep the capital invested in retailing.

unit stock planning. Planning how the dollars invested in inventory will be spent on different items of inventory. In most part it involves planning the assortment of items that will comprise the merchandise mix.

universal product code. Twelve vertical bars placed on the package of all grocery products (except produce and meats) to identify each product. The bars are then read by optical scanning machines at the checkout counter to compute the customer's bill automatically.

variable costs. Costs that increase proportionately with increases in the retailer's sales volume.

vertical cooperative advertising. An arrangement in which a retailer and other channel members (typically the manufacturer) share the cost of advertising. The responsibilities of each party in such an arrangement are specified in a contract.

vertical marketing systems. Centralized, highly managed marketing systems. Corporate systems are either manufacturers integrating forward to reach consumers or retailers integrating backwards. Contractual systems include *wholesaler-sponsored voluntary groups, retailer owned cooperatives,* and *franchises* (see entries). Administered systems are similar to conventional marketing channels but with one member leading the other members of the channel.

vertical price fixing. Illegal arrangements in which members of a marketing channel agree to fix the resale price of an item. Sometimes referred to as resale price maintenance.

warranty. Express warranties are explicit verbal or written agreements between retailers and consumers covering from one to all attributes of purchased merchandise. Implied warranties of merchantability are made by every retailer selling goods—the selling of merchandise implies that it is fit for the ordinary purpose for which such goods are used. Implied warranties of fitness for a particular purpose arise when a customer relies on the retailer to assist him or her or to select the right goods to serve a particular purpose.

weeks' supply method. A method of dollar stock planning in which stocks are set equal to the demand for a predetermined number of weeks.

wholesaler-sponsored voluntary groups. Marketing systems in which wholesalers offer a coordinated merchandising and buying program to independent retailers in the same line of trade in return for the retailers agreeing to concentrate their purchases with the wholesaler.

within-market opportunity analysis. A step in retail location analysis consisting of evaluating the density of demand and supply within each market (a census tract or other meaningful geographic area) and identifying the most attractive sites available for new stores within each market.

zoning. Actions by governmental units (usually municipal) to restrict the uses to which land can be put. Zoning regulations may prevent retailers from locating in certain areas of a community.

Author Index

Subject Index